second edition

managerial process and organizational behavior

second edition

managerial process and organizational behavior

ALAN C. FILLEY
Department of Management
University of Wisconsin, Madison

ROBERT J. HOUSE
Shell Professor of Organization Behavior
Faculty of Management Studies
University of Toronto

STEVEN KERR
College of Administrative Science
The Ohio State University

scott, foresman and company

Glenview, Illinois
Dallas, Texas • Oakland, N.J.
Palo Alto, Cal. • Tucker, Ga.
Brighton, England

Library of Congress Cataloging in Publication Data

Filley, Alan C
Managerial process and organizational behavior.

Includes bibliographies and indexes.
1. Industrial management. I. House, Robert J., joint author. II. Kerr, Steven, 1941- joint author. III. Title.
HD31.F513 1976 658.4 75-25716
ISBN 0-673-07857-4

The authors gratefully acknowledge permission to reprint quotes and illustrative materials from the following sources:

Chapter 2: p. 27—From *Organizations*, by J. G. March and H. A. Simon (John Wiley & Sons, 1958). Reprinted by permission. p. 29—From "Administrative Behavior: A Study of Decision-Making Processes," in *Administrative Organization*, by Herbert A. Simon. **Chapter 3:** pp. 49, 50—From "Managerial Problems and the Experimental Method," by L. L. Cummings and D. L. Harnett, *Business Horizons*, 1968. Reprinted by permission. **Chapter 4:** p. 60—From *The Management Process: Theory, Research, and Practice* by John B. Miner. Copyright © 1973, The Macmillan Company. **Chapter 5:** pp. 74, 76, 84—From *Personality: A Behavioral Analysis* by Robert W. Lundin. Copyright, Robert W. Lundin, 1969. The Macmillan Company, p. 72—Ross Macdonald. *The Goodbye Look* (New York: Alfred A. Knopf, Inc., 1969). pp. 75-76—From "Animal Clinical Psychology: A Modest Proposal," by D. S. Tuber et al., *American Psychologist*. Copyright 1974 by the American Psychological Association. Reprinted by permission. **Chapter 6:** p. 94—From *The Management Process: Theory, Research, and Practice* by John B. Miner. Copyright © 1973, The Macmillan Company. p. 97—C. Barnard. *The Functions of the Executive*. Boston: Harvard University Press, 1938. pp. 98-99, 100, 103-104—From "The Locus and Basis of Influence on Organizational Decisions," by M. Patchen, *Organizational Behavior and Human Performance*, 11, 1974. Reprinted by permission of Academic Press and the author. **Chapter 7:** p. 107—From *Winnie the Pooh* by A. A. Milne. Copyright 1926 by E. P. Dutton & Co.; renewal, 1954 by A. A. Milne. Reprinted by permission of the publisher, E. P. Dutton & Co., Inc., and Associated Book Publishers, Inc. pp. 110-11—From "Administrative Behavior: A Study of Decision-Making Processes," in *Administrative Organization* by Herbert A. Simon (Macmillan: 1957). Copyright, 1945, 1947, 1957 by Herbert A. Simon. p. 115—Adapted from "A Model of Trust Investment Behavior," by G. P. E. Clarkson, in *A Behavioral Theory of the Firm*, ed. by R. M. Cyert and J. G. March (Prentice-Hall, Inc., 1963). Reprinted by permission. p. 121—From *Organizations in Action* by James D. Thompson (McGraw-Hill Book Company, 1967). Reprinted by permission. **Chapter 8:** p. 135—From "Committees on Trial," by Rollie Tillman, Jr. *Harvard Business Review*, 38, pp. 6-8+. Reprinted by permission. pp. 145-46, 154—From *Handbook of Small Group Research* by A. Paul Hare, Copyright © 1962 by The Free Press. p. 147—P. E. Slater. "Contrasting Correlates of Group Size." *Sociometry*, 21 (1958). p. 150—From *Interaction Process Analysis* by R. F. Bales (Addison-Wesley Publishing Co., 1951). Reprinted by permission of the author. p. 151—From *The Managerial Grid* by Robert R. Blake and Jane Srygley Mouton (Houston: Gulf Publishing Company, Copyright © 1964, p. 10). Reprinted by permission of the publisher and authors. **Chapter 9:** p. 176—From "Methods of Resolving Superior-Subordinate Conflict: The Constructive Use of Subordinate Differences and Disagreements," by R. W. Burke, *Organizational Behavior and Human Performance*, 5, 1970. Reprinted by permission of Academic Press and the author. **Chapter 10:** p. 183—Text from *Peanuts* by Charles M. Schultz; © 1958 by United Feature Syndicate, Inc. p. 184—From "Maslow Reconsidered: A Review of Research on the Need Hierarchy Theory," by

M. Wahba and L. Bridwell, from *Organizational Behavior and Human Performance,* 13 (3), 1975. Reprinted by permission. p. 199—From "Herzberg's Dual Factor Theory of Job Satisfaction and Motivation," by R. J. House and L. A. Wigdor, *Personnel Psychology,* 20, 1967. Reprinted by permission. **Chapter 11:** p. 215—From "A Leader Behavior Description for Industry," by E. A. Fleishman, in *Leader Behavior: Its Description and Measurement,* by R. M. Stogdill and A. E. Coons. Bureau of Business Research, The Ohio State University, 1957. Reprinted by permission. p. 232—From *The American Soldier: Adjustment During Army Life,* Volume 1 of *Studies in Social Psychology in World War II,* ed. by S. A. Stouffer et al. (Table 12, p. 408.) Copyright © 1949 by Princeton University Press. Reprinted by permission. **Chapter 12:** p. 240—From "Major Barbara" by George Bernard Shaw, from *Selected Plays of Bernard Shaw.* Reprinted by permission of The Society of Authors on behalf of the Bernard Shaw Estate. pp. 244-45—From "A Theory of Leadership Effectiveness," by Fred E. Fiedler. Copyright 1967 by McGraw-Hill Book Company. Used with permission of McGraw-Hill Book Company. pp. 248-51—From *Leadership and Decision-Making* by Victor H. Vroom and Philip W. Yetton, by permission of the University of Pittsburgh Press. Copyright © 1973 by the University of Pittsburgh Press. p. 252-53, 257—From "Path-Goal Theory of Leadership," by R. J. House and T. R. Mitchell, from *Contemporary Business.* Reprinted with permission of the *Journal of Contemporary Business.* Copyright 1974. **Chapter 13:** pp. 274-76—T. Burns and G. Stalker. *The Management of Innovation.* London: Tavistock Publications, Ltd., 1961. p. 282—From "Bureaucratic Elements in Organizations," S. H. Udy, Jr., *American Sociological Review,* 23, 1959. Reprinted by permission of the American Sociological Association and the author. **Chapter 14:** pp. 304-5—C. Barnard. *The Functions of the Executive.* Boston: Harvard University Press, 1938. p. 306—From *Administrative Behavior: A Study of Decision-Making Processes in Administrative Organization* by Herbert A. Simon. Copyright, 1945, 1947, 1957 by Herbert A. Simon. The Macmillan Company. p. 332—From "Some Problems in Organization and Administration," by W. Bennis from *Administrative Science Quarterly,* 4, 1959, pp. 285-87. Reprinted by permission of *Hospital Administration.* **Chapter 15:** p. 345—From "An Interdisciplinary Analysis of Job Enlargement: Technology, Costs, and Behavioral Implications," by E. H. Conant and M. D. Kilbridge. *Industrial and Labor Relations Review,* 18, 1965, pp. 377-95. p. 348-49—From *The Man on the Assembly Line,* by C. R. Walker and R. H. Guest. Copyright © 1952 by the President and Fellows of Harvard College. Reprinted by permission of Harvard University Press. p. 352—M. D. Kilbridge. "Turnover, Absence and Transfer Rates as Indicators of Employee Dissatisfaction with Repetitive Work." *Industrial and Labor Relations Review,* 15, 1961. p. 353—P. Hall and H. W. Locke. *Incentives and Contentment.* London: Pitman (1938). **Chapter 16:** p. 360—From "I Ching: Taoist Book of Days, Calendar-Diary," by Khigh Alx Dhiegh. New York: Ballantine, 1975. Reprinted by permission of Shambala Publications, Inc. p. 363—From *Program and Project Management in a Matrix Organization: A Case Study,* by A. Delbecq and A. C. Filley. Bureau of Business Research and Service, University of Wisconsin, 1974. **Chapter 17:** p. 380—From P. Drucker, *The Practice of Management.* Harper & Row Publishers, Inc., 1954. **Chapter 18:** p. 411—H. Koontz and C. O'Donnell. *Principles of Management,* 5th edition. McGraw-Hill, 1972. **Chapter 19:** p. 461—Reprinted from "Control Theory in Brazilian Organizations," by G. F. Farris and D. A. Butterfield, *Administrative Science Quarterly,* 17 (1972), pp. 574-85, by permission of the publisher. **Chapter 20:** p. 469, 472—From *The Management Process: Theory, Research, and Practice* by John B. Miner. Copyright ©1973 by The Macmillan Company. p. 471—From "Overcoming Resistance to Change," by L. Coch and J. R. P. French. *Human Relations,* 1 (1948), pp. 512-32. p. 476—From "Management Development as a Process of Influence," by Edgar H. Schien, *Industrial Management Review,* 2 (1961). pp. 480-82—From "Influence and Organizational Change," by Gene W. Dalton from *Modern Organizational Theory,* by Anant R. Negandhi (ed.), pp. 343-72. Kent, Ohio: Kent State University Press. **Chapter 21:** p. 504—From *The Managerial Grid* by Robert R. Blake and Jane Srygley Mouton (Houston: Gulf Publishing Company, Copyright © 1964, p. 10). Reprinted by permission of the publisher and authors. p. 507—From *Organizations: Structure, Processes, Behavior,* by J. L. Gibson, J. M. Ivancevich, and J. H. Donnelly, Jr. (Business Publications, Inc., 1973, p. 80). Original source: *Human Organizations* by R. Likert (McGraw-Hill Book Company, 1967). Reprinted by permission. **Chapter 22:** p. 527—From *Modern Organization Theory* by M. Haire (John Wiley & Sons, Inc., 1959). Reprinted by permission.

Preface

This book is an introduction to the current state of management study and practice. It shows how behavioral science and quantitative methods contribute to increased understanding of the discipline, and it further shows how the appropriate, selective use of prescriptions emerges from research concerning the managerial process and organizational behavior.

We have concerned ourselves with management as a general process, to be applied in many different organizations, rather than with business management alone. Thus the material presented here should be useful in basic management courses in other fields as well.

The text material is divided into four parts. *Part 1: Introductory Concepts* includes a description of the evolution of management theory, a discussion of the importance and relevance of theoretical knowledge, and a description of the scientific process by which such knowledge has been developed. *Part 2: Behavior in Organizations* is concerned with several psychological and sociological processes that are relevant to the practice of management. *Part 3: Organizational Structure and Design* deals with both the design of and management practices in complex organizations. Here we are primarily concerned with how objectives are established, policies defined, and work divided; we also discuss some of the unique problems faced by managers whose subordinates are professionals. *Part 4: Organizational Dynamics* focuses on the dynamic aspects of organizations as they change and are changed over time.

In this second edition, we have retained the "theory-proposition-evidence" format for many of the chapters. Where there are integrated theories of the phenomenon in question, we present those theories, followed by a statement of key propositions derived from them. We then review the empirical evidence related to each proposition.

We have made a greater effort in this edition to draw explicit conclusions regarding the degree to which the propositions are or are not supported. This constitutes an important change from the first edition. While we have not oversimplified the evidence, or forced conclusions where they are not justified, we have stated at the end of each chapter to what extent the propositions are valid, invalid, or qualified as a result of the evidence reviewed in the chapter.

We have attempted in this book to bring together and make operational some of the relevant findings from research in the fields of sociology, psychology, political science, and economics, as well as that of business management itself. In this we are simply attempting to demonstrate that if scholars address themselves to *problems* rather than to the boundaries of traditional disciplines, they will find a wealth of information at their disposal.

There are doubtless other topics which others would include in a management text which are not in this book. We can only say that in choosing its content we have been guided by our own areas of competence and interest, as well as the experiences we and others have had in using this book as a college textbook. We hope we have avoided the fallacy that if something is mentioned in a book it has therefore been analyzed. We treat only what we feel we know and understand. Each of us has contributed equally, and we feel that the collaborative process has added insight to and broadened the perspective of this book.

We should like to express our gratitude to all who have helped us prepare the book. Many users of the first edition and other reviewers have generously given their time to reviewing our manuscript. W. Edward Bell, Lee Danielson, Jon English, William Litzinger, Karl Magnusen, Newton Margulies, Robert Piersol, Norm Stander, Marc Wallace, Richard Whiting, and Bruce Wonder are among those who helped. We thank them. Thanks should also go to Anne Harlan, Elaine Kerr, Tom Mawhinney, Richard Pegg, and Ted Wiese for their assistance on the manuscript, and to Robert Johnson of Scott, Foresman for his editorial assistance.

Alan C. Filley
Robert J. House
Steven Kerr

Contents

Part 1

Introductory Concepts

The first section is designed to orient the reader by placing current material into a historical perspective and by describing the characteristics and practical value of theory and research.

Chapter 1 describes the history and evolution of management thought, beginning at the turn of the century with classical thought and continuing to the contemporary use of behavioral and operations research.

Chapter 2 discusses the nature of theory—how it is constructed, the tests of good theory, and how it is applied.

Chapter 3 deals with the processes of scientific inquiry and the criteria used in evaluating empirical research. This material, as well as that contained in the first two chapters, will be useful in understanding the theories presented later in the text and in interpreting the research which we shall be reporting.

Chapter **1**

The Evolution of Management Theory

No point of view, once expressed, ever seems wholly to die. . . .
Our ears are full of the whisperings of dead men.

ALEXANDER GRAY
The Development of Economic Doctrine

The purpose of this chapter is to briefly sketch the major schools of management thought. These are classical theory, neoclassical theory, behavioral science, and operations research. Many of the topics outlined here will be discussed in more detail elsewhere in the text.

Classical management theory may be said to have had its origins thousands of years ago. Its popularity as a formal area of study, however, dates from around the turn of the century, while the majority of modern organizational theories have been formulated within the last twenty-five years. In fact, the development of these theories has been so recent, rapid, and dynamic that, while each has profoundly affected managerial practice and decision making, neither has yet evolved into a single, unified body of theory.

Classical Management Theory

As is true of most fields of study, management contains a body of classical theory which provides a conceptual framework and a body of terminology for its students, researchers, and practitioners. Where a system of thought is developed deductively,[1] as was true to a great extent with classical management theory, there is an ever present danger that the theory may be judged to be valid merely because of its internal logical consistency and theoretical elegance, rather than because it is consistent with the real world and can predict phenomena in it. On the other hand, a deductive system of thought can be a useful device for classifying knowledge.

To best understand classical and related theory as it exists today, we can benefit from a historical perspective. At least three areas in the historical

[1] Deductive theories begin with broad theoretical propositions, or statements, from which specific, testable hypotheses are developed; see Chapter 2 for a full discussion.

development of classical management thought can be identified. These are: (1) classical scientific management, beginning about 1910; (2) bureaucratic theory, which began at approximately the same time; and (3) classical administrative theory, beginning around 1930. It should be emphasized that the dates associated with each of these refer to the approximate time of widespread attention and acceptance. The origins of these theories and their underlying concepts can be traced to much earlier times.[2]

Scientific Management

The first of the classical phases to be discussed, scientific management, is closely identified historically with the work of Frederick Taylor and his associates. Taylor (1856–1915) was an engineer by training. He rose from laborer to chief engineer at the Midvale Steel Works, later worked for the Bethlehem Steel Works, and also served extensively as a business consultant. His views were first published in 1895. His classic pig-iron experiments at Bethlehem Steel were conducted in 1899 and written up for the first time in 1901. Expansions of his views and elaborations of his experiments were published in 1903 and 1911 (with, apparently, considerable embellishment—see Wrege and Perroni, 1974, for a thorough account).

Scientific management was based upon four main principles:

1. The development of an ideal or best method. This included an analysis of each job to determine the "one best way" of doing it; the primary means of analysis was time and motion study.
2. The selection and development of workers. This involved selecting the right person for a particular job and training that person in the proper method.
3. The combination of the best method and selected and trained workers. Taylor believed that this would cause a mental revolution on the part of management. The key to overcoming workers' resistance to the new methods was the utilization of an incentive system, whereby each worker was paid according to the number of units produced. It was therefore possible for workers under the scientific management system to substantially increase their earnings.

---

[2] In fact, the origins of present theory are quite ancient. For example, the exception principle and the notion of a limited span of supervision are discussed in the Bible by Jethro, the father-in-law of Moses (Exodus 18:17–26). Decentralization was valued and practiced by the Egyptians in 2600 B.C. and production control and wage incentives by Nebuchadnezzar in 600 B.C. Motion study was practiced by Cyrus in 400 B.C. and the principle of specialization enunciated by Plato some fifty years later. The medieval and renaissance arts of government closely resemble the management of large modern corporations (Jay, 1968). Adam Smith (1796) described specialization of labor and the "one best way," Charles Babbage (1832) anticipated many of the characteristics of scientific management, and Robert Owen (1813) previewed the human relations movement. For an interesting capsule look at many early contributions see George, 1972, pp. vii–xiii.

4. The close cooperation of managers and workers. This principle involved primarily a division of labor, with managers assigned responsibility for the planning and "preparation" of work.

Enjoying wide popularity today, scientific management was not accepted without a storm of criticism. Friedmann (1955) has summarized some of the reactions of the time:

> In the Navy arsenals where Scientific Management was applied, an inquiry had to be organized and resulted in a severe appraisal by Rear-Admiral Edwards. In private industry the trade unions of the American Federation of Labor, a moderate and prudent organization, nevertheless showed their hostility which resulted in the Hoxie investigation of 1915. Organized by the House of Representatives, the investigation . . . ended in "a major condemnation of the Taylor system. . . ." In particular, the Hoxie report cast doubt on the scientific value of time-study and drew attention to the psychological, moral, and social disadvantages of selection by output and of the degradation of skilled labor (pp. 40–41).

Other than Taylor, the major contributors to scientific management theory were H. L. Gantt (1916), Harrington Emerson (1912), and Frank and Lillian Gilbreth (see F. Gilbreth, 1912).

An example of the application of scientific management is provided by Taylor's description (1911) of an improved method of bricklaying devised by Frank Gilbreth, a contemporary of Taylor's who developed many of Taylor's suggestions. During a bricklaying apprenticeship, Gilbreth became puzzled by the many ways that experienced bricklayers performed their jobs. Since bricklaying is one of the oldest crafts, dating back before Biblical times, one would suppose that trial and error would have produced the best possible method. To Gilbreth, however, this was obviously not the case.

Studying the various methods used, Gilbreth selected the most suitable and developed his own system, specifying standard processes and materials and describing the positioning of the bricklayers and their tools. He also designed a scaffolding which could hold the bricklayer at one level, the bricks at a second, and the mortar at a third. The materials and the bricklayers were thus always in proper position to the structure being built. Gilbreth specialized the work by having a laborer carry the bricks to the bricklayers and place them with the best edge up; formerly, bricklayers had obtained their own bricks, inspecting each one to find the best side before laying it. Gilbreth also developed a standard formula for the mortar to insure that it would always have the same consistency.

According to Taylor, Gilbreth's efforts resulted in a reduction of the movements of the bricklayer from 18 to 5 and an increase in output from

120 to 250 bricks per hour. In just a few weeks, Gilbreth had been able to accomplish through a scientific approach to the problem what bricklayers had not achieved despite more than two thousand years of experience.

This example shows the potential benefits of studying the job and standardizing the best procedure. It also illustrates the division of labor that Taylor stressed between the person doing the job and the planner. We shall return to this issue in Chapter 19, when we discuss the nature and purpose of planning.

Bureaucratic Theory

This concept is closely identified historically with the work of Max Weber (1864–1920). Educated in Germany in law, economics, and legal history, he visited the United States during the latter half of 1904 to view at first hand the role of bureaucracy in a democratic state. Upon his return to Germany, however, and for many years thereafter, he was evidently in no hurry to publish his ideas; in fact, many of his most important theories and concepts, including those pertaining to bureaucracy, were not published until years after his death.

In the sense that Weber used the term, "bureaucracy" referred to "certain characteristics of organizational design. Weber viewed bureaucracy as the most efficient form, that which could be used most effectively for complex organizations—business, government, military, for example—arising out of the needs of modern society" (Kast and Rosenzweig, 1974, p. 62).

Among the characteristics of organizational design that Weber saw as typifying the bureaucratic organization were the following:

1. A continuous organization of official functions bound by *rules.* These rules are supposed to serve as the bases for organizational behavior by managers and workers alike, and can therefore contribute to predictability and standardization among individuals, over time, and across different situations.
2. Specific *areas of competence,* determined by the division of labor and accompanied by the provision of adequate authority for carrying out the functions of the specific areas. The different areas of competence within an organization are usually distinguished by titles (quality control engineer, defensive tackle, nurse); they are supposed to provide the advantages of specialization and they also contribute to predictability and standardization.
3. Utilization of the principle of *hierarchy,* whereby each office is placed under the supervision and control of another, higher office. As a result:

> Plans can be drawn up by elements near the top of the organization and passed down the chain of command for action. The performance of the lower units can be monitored and controlled so that they function according to plan. In the same way, problems

that occur during the task effort of lower units can be passed up the chain of command until they reach a level with the proper amount of knowledge and authority to solve the problem or make the decision (Bobbitt et al., 1974, p. 43).

4. Promotion into the administrative ranks of only those individuals who have *demonstrated technical competence;* this should assure the rational administration of rules, since only those individuals who have received *expert training* will be placed in supervisory positions.
5. Administrative acts, decisions, and rules to be *recorded in writing,* to provide permanent files. Written records of actions taken and decisions made are supposed to further increase predictability and standardization, by providing the organization with a memory so that recurring problems in the future can be solved in a manner consistent with past solutions (Weber, 1947).

One of the most fundamental underpinnings of Weber's bureaucratic theory is the notion of "*bureaucratic*" or "*rational-legal*" authority, that is, authority that is accepted by subordinates because the exerciser of that authority occupies a certain position within the hierarchy. A description of bureaucratic authority and some alternatives to bureaucratic authority is contained in Chapter 6.

Administrative Organization

Unlike scientific management, which focused upon production, administrative organizational theory was concerned with the entire organization. It sought to suggest ideal designs for organizational structure along the lines of hierarchical level, spans of supervision, departmentation, line and staff, and the like. It also classified management activities into those of planning, organizing, and controlling—a classification system still commonly used in the management literature.

In general, the classical writers viewed the organization as a giant machine. Discovery of the universal laws governing the machine was considered to constitute permanent and unchanging knowledge of its operation. These universal laws were set forth as *principles.*

A major figure during this phase was Henri Fayol, a French industrialist, who wrote his most important work in 1916 although it was not translated and made available in America until 1930. Other contributors to classical administrative organizational theory included J. D. Mooney and A. C. Reiley (1931), L. Urwick (1933), Gulick (see Gulick and Urwick, 1937), Mary Parker Follett (1942), and R. C. Davis (1951). Max Weber's work on bureaucracy, discussed earlier, bears remarkable similarity to this body of theory—remarkable because while his theories were published in German in 1921, they were apparently unknown to these theorists in the 1930s.

Administrative organizational theory can be illustrated by the work of R. C. Davis (1951). By integrating the work of many earlier management writers as well as adding to the resulting system, Davis provided a comprehensive and internally consistent theory. He viewed the organization as an abstract legal entity, formed and directed by a rational system of rules and authority. The enterprise had as its primary service objective the provision of salable value to consumers, and justified its existence and contributed to its members' needs by meeting that objective. Attainment of the objective also enabled the organization to reward contributors (management, workers, suppliers, stockholders) for their services, and was aided by attainment of the secondary objectives of economy and efficiency.

Davis saw the work of the administrator as consisting of planning, organizing, and controlling. Planning effort was described primarily in terms of decision making, goal setting, policy development, and proper allocation of work activities (called functions) to organizational units. Planning thus led to organizing, since the allocation of functions involved the identification and proper arrangement of units (e.g., positions, departments, divisions).

Concepts of authority, responsibility, and accountability were used to relate organizational units; in this sense *authority* referred to the right to command or advise assigned to any job, *responsibility* to the work duties assigned to that job, and *accountability* to the obligation of reporting to a unit of higher position on the exercise of authority and responsibility.

Administrative theory identified various bases (such as product, customer, and geographical area) for creating organizational units to divide the organization horizontally into segments (called *departmentation*). The horizontal grouping of the reporting relationships of individuals—the number of persons who do or should report to a person at a higher level—is discussed by Davis under the topic heading of *span of control,* and is examined in this text in Chapter 18.

Levels of authority are created by a vertical division of the organization, with the origin of the formal authority flow at the top of the structure. The grouping of functions into departments and the setting of objectives for organizational units provided a basis for Davis' distinction between line and staff, discussed in this text in Chapter 17.

R. C. Davis also provided an early, insightful analysis of control activities. Some he saw as occurring *before* action began, while others took place during or after action. This important, unconventional distinction has only recently been made explicit in modern theory. In enumerating the various control functions, Davis was able to draw conclusions about which could be assigned to someone other than the immediate supervisor of a work process and which could not.

Davis' analysis of the topics mentioned above is much more extensive than is apparent from this brief summary, which is intended only to identify some of the major topics and concepts that formed the foundation of classical administrative organizational theory.

Limitations of Classical Theory

Later chapters of this text will expand upon many of the topics mentioned in classical theories of scientific management, bureaucratic theory, and administrative organizational theory. This section will deal with some of the limitations and shortcomings of these theories, as well as criticisms of those tests and studies which sought to examine these theories.

It has been argued that the classical theories suffered more from what they failed to say than from what they actually did say. Their major limitations are now believed to be numerous, but include the following:

—Classical theories are time-bound. Their assumptions about people's emphasis upon financial motives were probably more appropriate in the early years of the twentieth century than they are today. Then, many workers were probably concerned with satisfying the most basic, physiological needs. Today, minimum wage legislation, unemployment insurance, and welfare systems have combined to provide most workers with security about these basic needs, and other wants and needs have taken on greater concern.

—Classical theories are deterministic; they suggest that the satisfactory performance of principle A, B, etc., is necessary and sufficient for group success and organizational effectiveness. Classical theories fail to deal with mutual dependency among variables, and often their prescriptions are not really necessary. For example, observing the classical prescription "one boss for every employee" may reduce the likelihood of role conflict and ambiguity in many instances; however, there are methods whereby employees can report to several bosses in a functional manner, and there are situations where such a system is probably desirable.

—Classical theories fail to consider many dimensions of managerial and organizational behavior. For example, they do not adequately deal with problems of leadership, choice, motivation, power, group drive and cohesiveness, and informal relations.

—Classical theories do not often make their assumptions explicit. The often incomplete or erroneous assumptions *implicit* in classical management theories, as identified by Massie (1965, p. 405), include the following:

1. The efficiency of any undertaking can be measured solely in terms of productivity. *Efficiency* in this sense can be defined as the economic use of resources, without consideration of human factors.
2. Human beings always act rationally, and management therefore need only be concerned with the formal and official activities of individuals and groups of individuals who are logically pursuing organizational goals.
3. It is possible to predict and establish clear-cut patterns of future activities and relationships among activities. Groups and sequences of tasks can be outlined in advance of execution. Coordination will not be achieved unless planned and directed from above, however, and organizational members will be unable to work out the relationships between their positions without detailed guidance from their supervisors.

4. Human beings prefer the security of a clearly delineated task to the freedom of determining their own approach to problems; they prefer to be directed. Unless clear direction is provided, and clear limits to jobs defined and enforced, members will become confused and will trespass upon the domain of others.
5. Group activities can be viewed on an objective and impersonal basis, without concern for personal problems and characteristics.
6. Workers are motivated almost solely by economic needs and wants; incentives should therefore be monetary.
7. People do not like to work, and close supervision and accountability must therefore be emphasized. Management must lead people fairly and firmly in ways that are not part of their inherent nature.
8. Authority has its source at the top of the hierarchy; lower-level members can only obtain authority as it is delegated downward.
9. Because simpler tasks are easier to master, productivity can be increased by concentrating on a narrow scope of activity.
10. Managerial functions in varied types of activities have universal characteristics and can be performed in a given manner regardless of the environment, and without concern for the qualities of the personnel involved.

Reliance upon these assumptions by classical theorists was unfortunate; logical consistency seems to have often been confused with reality. Today, as we shall see, behavioral research has provided us with much evidence from the real world that casts doubt upon the validity of many of the implicit assumptions listed above. This evidence has enabled us to qualify and complete the assumptions of classical theory. For example, we now believe that measures of organizational efficiency should not ignore the maintenance activities which hold a social group together; these activities have been found to be governed by emotional needs as well as by rational processes. We also now recognize that the classical theorists paid inadequate attention to the desires of many individuals to act responsibly, and to the negative effects of excessive supervision and control. It has been found that many people do like to work and will contribute to organizational goals without being coerced.

Human Relations Theory

As indicated earlier, the human element was either oversimplified or ignored by classical writers. It is not surprising, then, that a school of thought emerged which sought to supplement and challenge classical theories. This school of thought, "human relations" theory, may be termed *neoclassical* rather than modern because it follows the theoretical form of classical theory and emphasizes the human dimension of management as a counterpoint against the impersonality of classical theory.

Human relations theory might also be seen as part of an evolving discipline of industrial relations. It supplemented the initial wave of enthusiasm for personnel management which occurred after World War I, as well as the emphasis on labor relations which developed in the middle 1930s. Personnel management became popular in the 1920s largely through the widespread use of testing for selection in the military in World War I, plus the paternalistic attitude of employers during the prosperity of that period. Labor relations became a subject worthy of serious attention by students of management following the development of industrial union organizations and the organization of the CIO, aided also by the stipulation in the Wagner Act of 1935 that management had to recognize unions and bargain with them in good faith.

The major thrust of human relations theory was that:

> The dominant focus of organization was transformed from a rational model, free from the friction of man's emotions, to a model which appears to be less determined and unfathomable. That is, the new look in organizational theory took cognizance of the unanticipated consequences of organizations: workers' feelings, beliefs, perceptions, ideas, and sentiments—exactly those elements of passion Weber believed escaped calculation. Administrators began to take seriously—in part through the seminal work of several social scientists—not only their formal organizational chart, but workers' feelings about the structure and hierarchy. This model of organization . . . took as its major assumption that man could be motivated to work more productively on the basis of fulfilling certain social psychological needs. This "new look" of organizations was no less rational than the earlier machine model, except that man's motivation was a trickier and more elusive concept than the machine (Bennis, 1959).

If one particular event can be said to serve as a precursor of an entire movement, the human relations approach was born when Elton Mayo and others from Harvard University were invited to participate in research at the Hawthorne Plant of the Western Electric Company. The program, begun as the result of a grant made by the Rockefeller Foundation to study group attitudes and behaviors, took place from 1927 to 1932; the best-known publication resulting from the program is the classic *Management and the Worker* (Roethlisberger and Dickson, 1939).

The Hawthorne Studies

The researchers at Hawthorne began by studying the effects of various human engineering variables (lighting, heat, fatigue, physical layout) upon productivity. From a scientific management standpoint, these effects could be expected to be significant. Mayo's notion, however, was that social and emotional factors would prove to be far more important.

Illumination Experiments. The first of the Hawthorne experiments, which took place even before the entry of Mayo's team, was an evaluation of the effects of illumination upon the efficiency of industrial workers. A sample of workers was divided into two groups: (1) a test group, which was exposed to different intensities of light, and (2) a control group, who worked under constant lighting intensity. It was found that, as illumination was increased in the test group, *both* groups increased production. Furthermore, when intensity for the test group was *decreased,* output in both groups continued to increase. Not until the intensity of illumination had been reduced to the equivalent of ordinary moonlight was there any appreciable decline in output.

Relay Assembly Test Room Experiment. Five assemblers and one layout operator volunteered to work under controlled conditions in a separate area of the plant. Various changes (in temperature, humidity, refreshments) were introduced, with little resultant effect on productivity. However, the shortening of the work day or work week increased output, suggesting to the researchers that fatigue might be a major inhibitor of productivity. When the original conditions of work were restored, though, output reached a new high for every operator, despite the fact that the *rate* of output per operator decreased.

A second relay assembly experiment was undertaken in which a group of female workers was placed at one end of the large relay assembly department. This time each of the five experienced operators received a special *group* incentive as their wage payment. Output again increased, by a group average of 12.6 percent.

The illumination and relay assembly experiments thus determined that there was no simple and direct relationship between improvements in material conditions, work methods, etc., and productivity; similarly, individual wage incentives and relief from fatigue and monotony had little or no effect. These findings were in sharp contrast to the prescriptions and principles of scientific management, and suggested that social factors were more important determinants of productivity than physiological factors.

The Interview Program. The Hawthorne researchers pondered the results—or lack of results—of their attempts to relate physical conditions to output, and concluded that human factors apparently were more important than technical factors in determining productivity and reactions to change. Attitudes and perceptions about change, it seemed, were more important than the change itself.

To gain more information about attitudes and sentiments, the researchers embarked upon an extensive program of interviews, involving more than 20,000 workers. In the process, they developed and refined a new interview method, called the nondirective technique. The rationale behind this approach was explained by Roethlisberger (1941, p. 92) as follows:

> . . . What people say is necessarily an important part of the data from which I have to make a diagnosis. Therefore, my first object is to get people to talk freely and frankly about matters which are important to them. . . . In the interview I use a number of simple rules or ideas; I listen, I do not interrupt. I do not give advice. I avoid leading

questions. I refrain from making moral judgments about the opinions expressed. I do not express my own opinions, beliefs, or sentiments. I avoid argument at all costs.

Out of these interviews came the first important insights into the observation that the group as a whole largely determined the output of its individual members by enforcing an informal standard of a "fair day's work."

Bank Wiring Observation Room Experiment. To test the hypothesis that the group would seek a "fair" rate for each individual rather than a maximum earning for all based on the speed of the faster workers, another experiment was conducted. This experiment was concerned with the effect of a group piecework incentive pay plan on the output of a work group in a bank wiring room. The room contained fourteen wiremen, soldermen, and inspectors.

Classical theorists would have predicted that the groups would seek to increase total output. However, the researchers discovered that output is actually a form of social behavior; to be accepted, workers had to act in accordance with the standards of the group. Workers were afraid to underproduce, but also to overproduce (since "rate busters" were as likely to incur group disapproval as were "chiselers"). Thus it was concluded that the social standards set by the group corresponded neither with dexterity nor with intelligence, and that wage incentives were less important in determining individual output than was social acceptance.

The Resulting Theory

The human relations theory which evolved from this study has as a central notion the importance of attitudes and sentiments in determining the results of changes in a job situation. The classical theorists had claimed, in effect, that a physical change directed toward greater efficiency would almost automatically bring about the desired result. That is:

change ⟶ response

As a result of the Hawthorne studies it was concluded that workers reacted to change in terms of the meaning change had for them, namely:

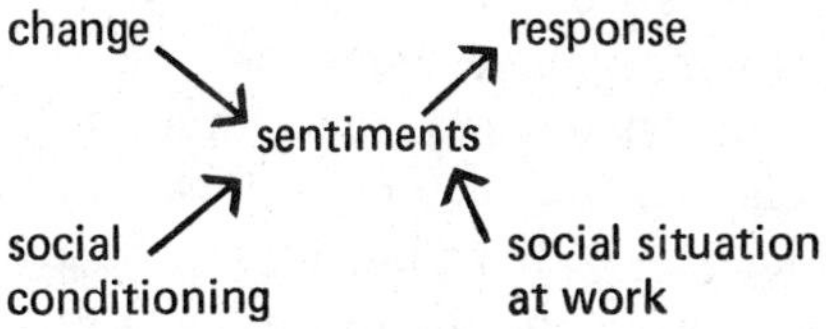

The meaning workers assigned to any change depended upon their *social conditioning* (values, hopes, fears, etc., derived from their family and group connections outside the work environment) and upon their *social situation at work,* in which group pressures determined attitudes and sentiments. It was found that work groups develop a social organization and achieve social stability, in which member roles and status are for the most part clearly understood. Any change which seems likely to threaten this stability will usually be feared and resisted, and these reactions will tend to offset any increase in output expected from the change.

Similar reasoning on a larger scale was found to apply to the organization as a whole. The formal, official patterns of behavior specified in the rules and policies of the firm are designed to achieve maximum efficiency (e.g., cut costs, increase output, improve quality, reduce waste, improve technology). Yet factors that foster efficiency sometimes oppose other factors that contribute to employee happiness, collaboration, and morale. The findings from the Hawthorne studies suggest the wisdom of pursuing a balanced approach, rather than seeking exclusively to maximize either efficiency or morale.

Limitations and Importance

By today's standards of research methodology, the Hawthorne studies suffered from a great many inadequacies and shortcomings. For example, the researcher observers continually "meddled" with their own experiments, intervening where no intervention had been planned to comfort and reassure subjects and to alter and even cancel experiments which the employees found distasteful. The researchers also asked for subject opinions while other subjects were present, and often told the workers what the desired outcomes were. Furthermore, the participation permitted by management was only to include areas "where the stake was large for workers and small for management, and where mutuality of interest was most pronounced" (Krupp, 1961, p. 31).

Notwithstanding these and other difficulties, the Hawthorne studies represent a benchmark in studies of human behavior. Whether or not they *should* have been accepted at face value, they *were* accepted, and generated tremendous interest in the human problems of the workplace, which in turn contributed substantially to the development of human relations theory and practice.

> As a result of Mayo's work, the industrial woods abound today with behavioral scientists, personnel counselors, industrial chaplains, sensitivity trainers, group dynamicists, sociogram analysts, nondirective interviewers, role-playing instructors, critical incident teachers, and industrial psychologists—each trying to satisfy management's demand for the creation of a work situation conducive to a maximum long-run productivity (George, 1972, p. 137).

Human relations theory began in the 1930s and became a fad after

World War II, when industrial training programs in human relations were commonplace. Many of these programs were conducted with the faulty premise that a happy group is necessarily a productive one. It was not until later research showed that such training programs often had no effect at all on productivity that human relations materials began to be used more intelligently. Recent research has contributed to an understanding of the limiting factors necessary if human relations training is to have a positive effect on output.

The Influence of Barnard

Chester Barnard's classic work *The Functions of the Executive* (1938) became a starting point for many modern theories of organization and management. Barnard's ideas were enumerated and expanded upon by Herbert Simon (*Administrative Behavior,* 1947). Barnard's primary contribution lay "in his logical analysis of organization structure and his application of sociological concepts to management. Some scholars do not include Barnard in the behavioral school, but in a new school evolving around his social system concept. This concept is, of course, closely related to the human behavior approach. . . ." (George, 1972, p. 153).

A more extensive discussion of many of Barnard and Simon's ideas as they relate to individual decision making will be presented in Chapter 7. Among their other major contributions, however, are the following:

1. Barnard saw the organization as "a system of consciously coordinated activities or forces of two or more persons," rather than merely as an abstract legal entity.
2. The survival of any organization depends upon both its *effectiveness* (in attaining the overall cooperative goal) and its *efficiency* (its satisfaction of participant motives).
3. Efficiency depends upon *organizational equilibrium,* the balance between *inducements* offered by the organization and *contributions* offered by the individual.
4. Formal organizations arise from *informal organizations,* and formal organizations in turn create and require informal organizations. As compared to earlier classical views that the informal organization was dysfunctional to the formal organization and that capable management could prevent its development, Barnard emphasized that the informal organization serves to (a) aid communication, (b) maintain cohesiveness within the formal organization, and (c) strengthen individual feelings of integrity, self-respect, and independent choice. Later, Simon (1947) defined the informal organization as "interpersonal relations in the organization that affect decisions within it but either are omitted from the formal scheme or are not consistent with that scheme" (p. 148).
5. The decision as to whether or not an order has authority does *not* reside

with those who give the orders (i.e., persons "in authority," the assumption made by the classical theorists) but rather "rests with the acceptance or consent of individuals" who receive the order. A given order may or may not therefore have authority for subordinates, depending in large part upon the subordinate's *zone of indifference*, which will be discussed more extensively in Chapter 6.

Barnard's concepts and theoretical formulations have become major points of departure from classical theory for modern writers. Consciously or unconsciously, many present-day authors have expanded upon Barnard's notions of the relationship between the individual and the organization, the limits on decision making, the acceptance of authority, and many others.

Behavioral Science Research

Although the term "behavioral science" as applied to management had been used earlier, it came into popular use about 1951 as a shorthand description for a Ford Foundation program on individual behavior and human relations (Berelson, 1963). Further popularization of the approach occurred with the establishment in 1952 of the Foundation for Research on Human Behavior, whose goals were to promote support of behavioral research in business, government, and other organizations.

The behavioral science approach to the study of management may be broadly described as the study of observable and verifiable human behavior in organizations. Making use of scientific procedures, it focuses on the issue of human behavior and draws from all pertinent literature, particularly in psychology, sociology, and anthropology. From a behavioral science standpoint:

> . . . the task of administration is to choose those arrangements, broadly speaking, that are most likely to evoke a system of cooperative relationship among the people who are to achieve the mission of the organization. In contrast to other approaches, the behavioral view centers more on the people, their interactions and cooperation. It emphasizes . . . the development of insight and understanding based on empirical investigation. It challenges administrators and students to understand non-rational as well as rational, and informal as well as formal, aspects of organizational behavior (Gordon, 1963, p. 295).

Behavioral science has unquestionably added much to earlier management theory, and has provided a means for empirically testing earlier theory. In some cases the body of theory which preceded the behavioral science approach has stood the test well, while in others it has been modified or abandoned. This text will be concerned with both the additions to early management theory from the behavioral sciences and the appraisal of early theory through comparisons with recent research.

As it has evolved since the early 1950s, behavioral science research can be classified in terms of three levels of analysis. The first of these relates to the behavior of the *individual* in an organization. Here research may be concerned with such topics as personality, change, motivation, attitudes, and leadership style. The second level has to do with the behavior of the *group*. Much of this research has been performed upon small experimental groups in a laboratory setting. Studies of group behavior have dealt with such topics as norms, interaction patterns, conflict, emergent leadership, and problem solving.

The third level of behavioral science research deals with the *complex organization* as an institutional whole. Here the total organization is examined in relation to other total organizations—as in systems of organizational classification—or the design of the total system and its effects on behavior are studied. Much of the work in this area has sprung from tests of Max Weber's theory of bureaucracy (1947).

These three levels of individual, group, and total organizational behavior, once pursued with little overlap or coordination by psychologists, social psychologists, and sociologists respectively, have now become problem centers for management writers and researchers who take a behavioral science approach. As a result, much of the provincialism that existed in management research and education before 1950 has disappeared. For example, it was once the practice to have separate bodies of literature for business administration, public administration, hospital administration, and so on. Now, with the realization that individual and organizational behavior within all institutions has much in common, management and the behavioral sciences are drawing from essentially the same body of literature. This has encouraged attention to the problems of management by people from many academic disciplines and has brought to specialists, academicians, and practicing managers alike a better understanding of their roles, while helping to remove the erroneous connotation of "theory versus practice."

Since this text emphasizes behavioral science theory and research, we shall not now go beyond the identification of the behavioral approach presented above. Later chapters will deal with the wealth of information now available in this area.

Operations Research

The operations research approach to the study of management focuses upon the making of decisions. Its name comes from the fact that organizations and their components carry on goal-oriented activities, which can be called "operations." The systematic study of decisions concerning what operations should be undertaken and how they should be undertaken can be called "research." While behavioral scientists also conduct research about organizational operations, they tend to be concerned primarily with *describing* the nature of various operations and with how organizational decisions are *actually* made. Operations researchers, on the other hand, seek to *prescribe* the nature of operations and are concerned with how decisions *ought* to be made, that is, with determining the best solution, decision, or procedure.

The operations researcher is not ordinarily able to use experimental methods. The operations which are the focus of study are frequently impossible to manipulate and control for experimental purposes; in fact, they may not even exist at the time a decision is desired. Thus operations researchers are forced to build a mathematical model of the problem under investigation, which can then be manipulated. The model contains, first, an equation which includes a measure of organizational effectiveness as a dependent variable, and measures of the resources which management can manipulate as independent variables. This equation, called the *objective function,* reflects at least to some degree an organizational objective.

The other part of the model consists of statements (usually mathematical) which limit the permissible values of the variables. These statements are called *constraints.* An optimum solution to any problem consists of a set of values for the independent variables which maximize (or minimize) the value of the objective function, while still satisfying all problem constraints.

Like behavioral science research, operations research is problem-centered. However, whereas behavioral science draws primarily from psychology, sociology, and anthropology, operations research utilizes theories and studies from mathematics, statistics, and economics. Although operations researchers deal with problems in which people often play important roles, they are mostly interested "in those properties of an operation which would not change if we were to replace persons and/or equipment by others. The psychological aspects of interest . . . are not those of individuals but those common to any group carrying out that operation" (Morse, 1961).

Operations research was born during World War II, when British scientists from many specialized fields were combined into a team to determine ways that radar systems could be made more effective. The techniques associated with operations research became popular in American industry in the early 1950s.

Closely related to operations research is a methodology called "systems analysis." The relation of the two has been described as follows:

> Systems analysis is derived from operations research, which came into use during World War II when some scientists discovered that they could use simple quantitative analysis to get the most out of existing military equipment. A reasonably clear objective was given, and ways to cut the cost of achieving it could be developed, using essentially statistical models. Operations research today is largely identified with specific techniques: linear programming; Monte Carlo (randomizing) methods; gaming and game theory. While there is no hard and fast division between operations research and systems analysis, a rough

> separation may perhaps be made. The less that is known about objectives, the more conflict, the larger the number of elements to be considered, the more uncertain the environment, the more likely it is that the work will be called a systems analysis. In systems analysis there is more judgment and intuition and less reliance on quantitative methods than in operations research (Wildavsky, 1966, p. 298).

While this text will focus primarily on behavioral and classical approaches to management, we shall discuss some of the elements of operations research in the chapters dealing with planning and decision making.

Modern Versus Classical Theories

The marked change in management theory from a static, abstract, discipline-oriented focus to a dynamic, empirical, problem-centered focus has created conflict among people working in the field. Too many modern writers are quick to minimize developments in management and organization theory generated over the last twenty years. Similarly, many classical writers even today persist in ignoring the rich body of research and theory in the behavioral sciences. It is our intent to demonstrate in this text that the two bodies of literature are not fundamentally opposed; instead, there is much to be learned from both.

References

Babbage, C. 1832. *On the economy of machinery and manufactures.* C. Knight.

Barnard, C. 1938. *The functions of the executive.* Harvard University Press.

Bennis, W. G. 1959. Some problems in organization and administration. *Hospital Administration.*

Berelson, B. 1963. *The behavioral sciences today.* Basic Books.

Bobbitt, H. R. Jr.; Breinholt, R. H.; Doktor, R. H.; and McNaul, J. P. 1974. *Organizational behavior: Understanding and prediction.* Prentice-Hall.

Davis, R. C. 1951. *The fundamentals of top management.* Harper & Row.

Emerson, H. 1912. *The twelve principles of efficiency.* Engineering Magazine Co.

Fayol, H. 1930. *Industrial and general administration* (1916). Pitman.

Follett, M. P. 1942. *Dynamic administration: The collected papers of Mary Parker Follett,* ed. by H. Metcalf and L. Urwick. Harper.

Friedmann, G. 1955. *Industrial society.* Free Press.

Gantt, H. L. 1916. *Organizing for work.* Harcourt, Brace and World.

George, C. S. Jr. 1972. *The history of management thought,* 2nd ed. Prentice-Hall.

Gilbreth, F. B. 1912. *Primer of scientific management.* Harper.

Gordon, P. J. 1963. Transcend the current debate on administrative theory. *Academy of Management Journal* 6: 290-302.

Gray, A. 1931. *The development of economic doctrine.* Longman's, Green.

Gulick, L., and Urwick, L., eds. 1937. *Papers on the science of administration.* Columbia University Press.

Jay, A. 1968. *Management and Machiavelli.* Holt, Rinehart and Winston.

Kast, F. E., and Rosenzweig, J. E. 1974. *Organization and management: A systems approach,* 2nd ed. McGraw-Hill.

Krupp, S. 1961. *Pattern in organizational analysis: A critical examination.* Holt, Rinehart and Winston.

Massie, J. L. 1965. Management theory. In *Handbook of organizations,* ed. by J. G. March. Rand-McNally.

Mooney, J. D., and Reiley, A. C. 1931. *Onward industry!* Harper.

Morse, P. M. 1961. Operations research is also research. In *Progress in operations research,* vol. 1, ed. by R. L. Ackoff. Wiley.

Owen, R. 1948. *A new view of society* (1813). Free Press.

Roethlisberger, F. J. 1941. *Management and morale.* Harvard University Press.

———., and Dickson, W. J. 1939. *Management and the worker.* Harvard University Press.

Simon, H. A. 1947. *Administrative behavior* (2nd ed., 1957). Macmillan.

Smith, A. 1937. *An inquiry into the nature and causes of the wealth of nations* (1776), ed. by E. Cannan. Modern Library.

Taylor, F. W. 1895. A piece rate system. Paper delivered to the American Society of Mechanical Engineers.

———. 1901. Shop management. Paper delivered to the American Society of Mechanical Engineers. (Cited in Wrege and Perroni, 1974.)

———. 1903. Paper delivered to the American Society of Mechanical Engineers.

———. 1911. *The principles of scientific management.* Harper.

Urwick, L. 1933. *Management of tomorrow.* Nisbet.

Weber, M. 1947. *Theory of social and economic organization* (1921), tr. and ed. by A. M. Henderson and T. Parsons. Oxford University Press.

Wildavsky, A. 1966. The political economy of efficiency: Cost-benefit analysis, systems analysis, and program budgeting. *Public Administration Review* 26: 292-310.

Wrege, C. D., and Perroni, A. G. 1974. Taylor's pig-tale: A historical analysis of Frederick W. Taylor's pig-iron experiments. *Academy of Management Journal* 17: 6–27.

Chapter **2**

Theory and Practice of Management

There is nothing so practical as a good theory.

KURT LEWIN

In Chapter 1, we introduced several lines of theoretical thought concerning management practices and organizational behavior. Subsequent chapters will introduce theories which purport to explain important phenomena that occur within organizations, including theories of leadership, motivation, organization design, organization growth, decision making, and management development.

In several chapters more than one theory is presented, each of which offers different explanations for a given phenomenon. For example, Chapter 12 presents three theories of leadership. Each attempts to explain how the behavior of leaders affects the performance and satisfaction of their followers.

How can the "best" theory—the one that provides the most complete, accurate, and useful explanation of leadership—be determined? In order to answer this question, it is first necessary to understand the nature of theory. Following that, we will briefly discuss the implications and importance of theory for practicing managers.

The Nature of Theory

Students and practitioners of management are occasionally reluctant to describe the frame of reference they use for thinking and making decisions as a theory. This reluctance stems from the feeling that theory is somehow apart from the real world; as we will see, however, theory is the basis for practice and application. The real world, with all of its complexities, must be ordered in a systematic fashion before we can hope to act in it or upon it. Theoretical formulation is the ordering process.

Viewed in this way, theory is a *goal* that is valued in its own right; theories integrate and order empirical findings. They are an efficient and economical means for abstracting, codifying, summarizing, integrating, and storing information. As we will see in Chapter 3, theory is also a tool, in that it directs empirical investigation.

Theories consist of concepts, propositions, and laws. *Concepts* are class names that may refer to objects, properties of objects, events, or properties of events. *Propositions* are provisional statements of relationships between those objects and events. Researchers frequently derive hypotheses from propositions; hypotheses are specific statements of what the researcher expects to find as a result of empirical investigation. *Laws* are hypotheses that have been supported by a vast amount of research. The term law usually refers to a regular, predictable relationship between variables (concepts). To some, it also refers to a strongly established theoretical or abstract principle.

In any discussion of theory, it is important to keep in mind that scientists accept explanations and appraise findings with an attitude of skepticism. The scientific approach is characterized by caution, tentativeness, and a healthy respect for possible error. Indeed, even long-standing laws can be rejected or qualified if additional data are found that appear to contradict them.

Criteria of Acceptability for Theory

A sound theory should first have *internal consistency;* that is, its propositions should be free from contradiction. Internal contradiction, or lack of logical consistency, confuses rather than clarifies the significance of variables and leads to contradictory conclusions and predictions. Logical consistency allows theorists to state a chain of "if-then" propositions and to test them indirectly by experimenting with a small number of critical variables.

Second, a theory should have external consistency; that is, it should be consistent with observations and measures of real life. This criterion of theory is usually called the *test of empirical reference.*

Third, it must be possible to test the predictions of the theory. If a theory is not stated so that its predictions can be verified, it may carry unintended bias or error. A theory is said to be *operational* when its formulation permits evaluation of its major premises or predictions.

Fourth, a theory should have the characteristic of *generality,* in order to provide a wide range of application and an extension of the field of knowledge. That is, a theory should be capable of explaining more than isolated, specific incidents. It must posit a set of relationships within a well-defined class of events, and these relationships must explain the events that fall within the defined class. For example, Dollard et al. (1939) advanced a theory that all aggressive acts are stimulated by a frustrated feeling on the part of the aggressor. This theory applies to fights between children, acts of war between nations, and conflict between departments within a business firm. Thus, this theory provides a general explanation for a specific class of events—aggressive acts.

Finally, a practical theory should have the attribute of *scientific parsi-*

mony. If two theories both accurately predict the outcome of events and are equally supported by evidence, the less complex of the theories—that is, the one involving fewer hypotheses—should be selected.

Descriptive Dimensions of Theory

It is useful to describe theory in terms of the following six dimensions, which serve much the same purpose in describing theories as the characteristics of height, weight, sex, or intelligence serve to describe individuals.

Method of Development. Theories rest on two basic types of development: the flow of logic from abstraction to data (deduction) or from data to abstraction (induction).

Theories that are developed deductively begin with a statement that expresses a relationship between two or more variables; these assumed relationships provide the basis for deducing relationships between observable events. The statements are made in law-like form such as "if A, then B follows," or "there is a positive correlation between A and B," or "the existence of A is a necessary condition for the prediction of C; the existence of A and B together constitute both the necessary and sufficient conditions for the prediction of C."

An example of a deductive theory is given by House (1971). House began with several assumptions concerning employee perceptions, task demands, and motivation; these assumptions were suggested by prior research. He assumed, first, that when subordinates perceive that their efforts lead to effective performance and personal rewards, they will be more motivated to work harder than when they perceive that their efforts will not lead to effective and rewarding performance. Second, he assumed that when task demands are unclear to subordinates they will have unclear perceptions of the relationship between effort and rewards, and thus will not expect their efforts to lead to effective performance or to be rewarded.

House then deduced a series of law-like statements (propositions) concerning the relationships between the original variables and leader behavior. The intent of this set of statements was to explain how various kinds of leader behavior affect the expectations of subordinates, and thus their motivation, under varied task conditions. In terms of role-clarifying behavior by leaders,[1] for example, House deduced that when task demands are unclear to subordinates, leader behavior that clarifies subordinates' perceptions of task demands will result in increased motivation.

From this illustration we can see that House began with two assumed, law-like statements. The first assumption was that expectations determine, to a significant extent, subordinate motivation. Secondly, he assumed that

[1] Similar deductions were drawn concerning other kinds of leader behavior (participative leadership, authoritarian leadership, close supervision, hierarchical influence) as they interact with various task characteristics (task frustration, stress, satisfaction, and ambiguity). For a thorough description see House (1971) and House and Mitchell (1974).

clarity of task demands affects expectations. He then deduced a specific condition (unclear tasks) under which a certain kind of leader behavior (role clarifying behavior) would affect subordinate expectations. Thus he began with two assumed, "law-like" statements and deduced a third statement from them, namely that "leader behavior that leads to clarification of subordinate perceptions concerning task demands will result in increased motivation." This third statement is both logically linked to the initial propositions and testable through empirical observation.

The validity of deductive theory rests on two major criteria: the internal consistency of the assumed relationships and the degree to which conclusions deduced from the relationships are shown to hold in subsequent research. If part of the theory is shown to be inconsistent, for example, conclusions that *rest on the inconsistency* will be in error. The fact that a theory contains inconsistent propositions does not, in itself, render the theory useless; contradictory propositions may stand until it is possible to substitute more consistent propositions for them. But inconsistencies do indicate significant gaps in knowledge (Cyert and March, 1963) and signal the need for caution in using the theory in practice.

Deductive theory, as we have seen, emphasizes the flow of logic from the general to the specific. It is generally stated in the form of basic principles or propositions. It can also be stated in some symbolic or schematic representation of reality and, hence, lends itself well to mathematical formulation and manipulation.

In contrast to deductive development, a theory is developed inductively when it is formulated primarily from observations of empirical events. Induction is the process of inferring a set of theoretical propositions from empirical observation rather than deducing empirically-testable hypotheses from theoretical propositions. Induction is the reverse of deduction.

An example of an inductively-derived theory is also provided by House (1967). House reviewed the sociological, psychological, business, anthropological, and political science literature concerning socialization and development of managerial talent. The survey yielded a set of findings that appear to be acceptable empirical generalizations:

1. Managers who possess favorable attitudes about formal methods of education will gain more from formal developmental efforts than those who have unfavorable attitudes.
2. Managers' attitudes toward formal developmental methods will be largely a reflection of their supervisors' attitudes and behavior.
3. Attempts to improve managerial performance that conflict with existing policies and procedures will be less successful than attempts that do not conflict with existing policies and procedures.
4. Attempts to change behavior in a direction that is contrary to the values and attitudes of the members of the organization will be less successful than attempts to change behavior compatible with member values and attitudes.

5. Attitude change resulting from development is positively related to the participant's initial satisfaction with the organization.

After these empirical generalizations were extracted, an attempt was made to find the common threads that ran through them: What do successful development programs have in common that is absent from unsuccessful programs? If favorable initial attitudes are associated with successful development, attitudes must be a partial determinant of management development success. If the attitudes of a supervisor influence the participant's attitude toward development, the supervisor's attitude must account for some of the effects of development efforts. If the attitudes of the supervisor and the participant are influenced by policies and procedures of the organization, then these, too, must account for some of the effects of development.

These inferences and the earlier empirical findings led to the following proposition: *The consequences of management development depend on the degree to which social influences in the manager's work environment are viewed by the manager as motivations to learn, and the degree to which they reinforce learned behavior during and after the development effort.* From this theoretical proposition, several specific hypotheses can be derived. For example: When group solidarity is strong, the attitudes of one's associates have great influence on the developmental outcome. When individuals attempt to change behavior, they require support and assistance from their peers and supervisors, as well as from formal policies and procedures. When the participants have this support they are more likely to gain from development than when they do not. These hypotheses can then be subjected to further empirical investigation.

Purpose. The second dimension of a theory is its purpose, which may be either prescriptive or descriptive. It is prescriptive if it prescribes what should take place. For example: "Everyone in an organization should understand the responsibility and authority of their jobs." Prescriptive theory is also called normative theory.

Descriptive theory, also called positive theory, tells or explains what is rather than what should be. Some theorists feel strongly that a scientist must not judge, but rather must only describe.[2] Others feel that scholars must be prescriptive if they are to share the fruits of their insight and competence with others.

Scope. A theory may be either microcosmic or macrocosmic. Microcosmic theory typically starts with a small unit of analysis (e.g., single person, small group, or foreman with subordinates) and builds from these parts into a theory of the whole. Following the turn of the century, for example, Frederick Taylor and his associates concerned themselves primarily with the way in which a production foreman could elicit the greatest econ-

---

[2] For example, see Simon (1957). It is our opinion that the danger is not so much prescription as it is prescription without sufficient basis. The theorist can prescribe so long as the prescription is based on sound logical or empirical proof. Otherwise, the practitioner has less accurate knowledge of the basis on which to make decisions.

omy and effectiveness of operation from subordinates. The principles and techniques developed were then applied to other departments, on the assumption that the entire organization would benefit.

Macrocosmic theory, on the other hand, typically starts with the entire environment of the phenomenon in question, then moves to smaller units within it. For example, some macrocosmic theories discuss and analyze the objectives and functions of an organization, then move to an analysis of the goals of divisions and subdivisions, and on down to the individual organization member.

A preference for a microcosmic or macrocosmic approach can influence a management researcher's conclusions. In the former case, the firm is seen as a collection of individuals or small groups, and often the total enterprise is assumed to be nothing more than a collection of these units. In the latter case, the firm is viewed as an entity and smaller parts, such as departments, are assumed to be merely segments of the whole.

Orientation. A theory may be discipline-oriented or problem-oriented. Discipline-oriented theory is originated and promulgated by "experts" who claim a specific area of knowledge as their own. Thus we may find theories of hospital administration, business management, or public administration, and experts in each of these disciplines.

In contrast, problem-oriented theory focuses on the question at hand, drawing knowledge or substance from any appropriate source. A manager faced with the problem of determining the proper number and location of company warehouses will probably draw knowledge from such disciplines as accounting, law, marketing, business management, and economics. Similarly, in recent years, the problem of organizational and group behavior has become the concern of researchers who draw their information from a number of disciplines in the social sciences and the study of "organization theory" has emerged.

Mutual Dependence of Parts. Another dimension of theory focuses on the extent to which the various parts of the theory are interrelated. At one extreme is static theory, which in one sense may be distinguished by certain timeless rules that are felt to be fixed and unchanging, and in another sense expressed through simple relationships between factors of the theory. Static theories usually suggest that A causes B; that is, that factor A is both necessary and sufficient for result B. For example, the assertion from classical management theory that "an organization should meet its service objective to its customers" is based on the rationale that providing the customer with the goods or services desired is necessary to justify the economic existence of the organization, to guarantee its survival, and to make the organization profitable.

Most organizational behavior is not so simply explained, however. Factor A may be a necessary condition for result B to take place, but often it is by no means the only necessary condition. It is true, for example, that an organization must provide the customer with at least a minimum level of salable value in order to succeed, but it must also provide value sufficient to attract a market segment rather than a single person, and it must do so at costs low enough to permit a profit. Moreover, if the firm can limit the supply of the item through market control, satisfaction of customer needs is in part manipulated by the supplier. The static formulation of "service leading to success" may be suitable for some theoretical purposes, but it is obviously oversimplified.

Dynamic theory is different from static theory in that more complex relationships and more interdependencies are contained in its explanations. Single factors are seldom related in any simple cause-and-effect relationship; they usually tend to be mutually dependent. Consider, for example, a worker's willingness or lack of willingness to participate in the organization and meet its goals. One might state simply that a happy employee will participate and be productive. In contrast, one might consider participation and production to be determined by a balance of forces; such a theory of adaptive behavior is illustrated in Figure 2–1.

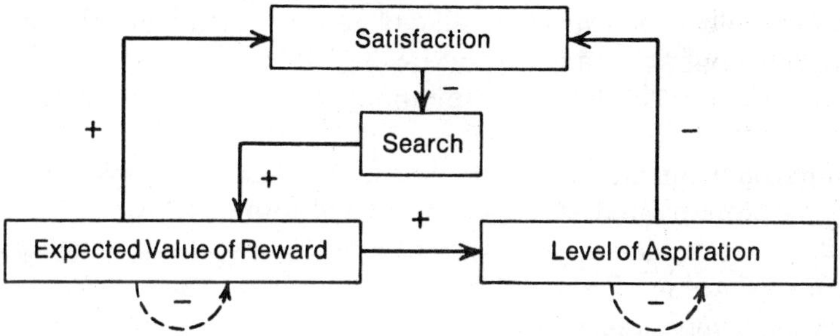

Figure 2–1. Dynamic Theory of Adaptive Employee Behavior.

The dynamic theory of March and Simon suggests that the lower the satisfaction of workers, the greater their search for alternative sources of satisfaction—which may include leaving the organization, staying and producing, or staying and not producing. Search behavior is stimulated by the expected value of rewards: the greater the expected value of reward, the greater the search, and the higher the levels of satisfaction and aspiration. But increasing aspiration levels also decrease satisfaction. Thus, a worker's decision to participate and the particular level at which the worker will perform are determined by a balance of both positive and negative forces. It may be seen from this example that dynamic theory expresses the decision to participate less simply but perhaps more realistically than does static theory.

Exposition. Finally, a theory may be expressed verbally or quantitatively. Verbal presentation permits an expression of differences among kinds of variables and the relationships among the variables, but it does not permit the precise expression of differences in degree. For precise expression of degree it is essential to use some common index, such as percentages or weights, which must necessarily be reduced to a numbering system and therefore requires quantification. Such theory relies heavily on mathematical presentation; quantification permits precision and specificity through the use of mathematical symbols.

Some theories consist of several constructs, each of which bears a relationship to one or more other constructs. For example, the March and Simon theory diagrammed in Figure 2–1 includes seven relationships among the variables. For a theory as complex as this, it is helpful to use a mathematical representation of the set of relationships. March and Simon have stated their theory in the form of propositions and have translated the propositions to mathematical exposition as follows:

1. The lower the *satisfaction* (3.34) of the organism, the more *search* for alternative programs (3.35) it will undertake [3.35:3.34].

2. The more search, the higher the *expected value of reward* (3.36) [3.36:3.35].

3. The higher the expected value of reward, the higher the *satisfaction* [3.34:3:36].

4. The higher the expected value of reward, the higher the *level of aspiration* (3:37) of the organism [3.37:3.36].

5. The higher the level of aspiration, the lower the satisfaction [3.34: 3.37].

March and Simon state that with a few additional assumptions their theory can be translated into a mathematical form:

Let S = satisfaction, A = level of aspiration, L = search rate, and R = expected value of reward. The following equations correspond to the set of verbal propositions:

$$(1) \qquad \frac{dA}{dt} = \alpha(R - A + a), \qquad \text{where } a > 0, \alpha > 0.$$

This interprets proposition 4 and adds to it an assertion about the dynamic process that leads to equilibrium. Since a is positive, at equilibrium the aspiration level will exceed the reward.

$$(2) \qquad S = R - A.$$

This interprets propositions 3 and 5.

$$(3) \qquad L = \beta(\bar{S} - S), \qquad \text{where } \bar{S} > 0, \beta > 0.$$

This interprets proposition 1. It also postulates a "desired" level of satisfaction, $\bar{S}$, at which search for increased satisfaction would cease.

$$(4) \qquad \frac{dR}{dt} = \gamma(L - b - cR), \qquad \text{where } \gamma > 0, b \geqq 0, c > 0.$$

This interprets proposition 2. It postulates that a certain amount of search, $(b + cR)$, is required just to maintain the current level, R, of reward.

From this example we can see that mathematical representation of a theory forces the theorist to be extremely clear in defining constructs and their relationships. Further mathematical representation helps the theorist expose and clarify implicit assumptions. Such a representation also permits one to derive new conclusions that would not be apparent from the verbal propositions alone. Finally, mathematical representation permits the manipulation and analysis of several variables simultaneously.

The Use of Theory in Practice

Theory provides managers with a description of their environment. It also serves to broaden their range of knowledge, for by deriving predictions from theory in the form of hypotheses, they are able to relate specific facts to broader explanations. They use theory to guide their search for variables relating to practical problems and in their efforts to deduce optimum solutions. Whereas the scientist attempts to describe and predict behavior without attempting to guide it, practitioners attempt to predict and control behavior along lines that are judged to be desirable.

From theory, practitioners derive guides that are useful for analysis of problems, prediction of events, and control of variables. In a very real sense, knowledge of theory makes practitioners better able to solve problems that arise in their own particular environments.

But how are practitioners to judge "good" theory from "bad" theory? [3] What should they consider in developing or selecting a valid and useful theory to help explain their organizational environments and solve the problems that confront them?

Requirements for Practical Application of Theory

Bennis, Benne, and Chin (1962) advanced a set of criteria for valid practical application of social science theory; such theory should:

1. Take into consideration the behavior of persons operating within specific institutional environments.

---

[3] "It is sometimes thought that, since the words 'good' and 'bad' often occur in sentences written by students of administration, the science of administration contains an essential ethical element. If this were true, a science of administration would be impossible, for it is impossible to choose, on an empirical basis, between ethical alternatives. Fortunately it is not true. The terms 'good' and 'bad' when they occur in a study on administration are seldom employed in a purely ethical sense. Procedures are termed 'good' when they are conducive to the attainment of specified objectives, 'bad' when they are not conducive to such attainment. That they are, or are not, so conducive is purely a matter of fact, and it is this factual element that makes up the real substance of an administrative science" (Simon, 1957, p. 249).

2. Account for interrelated levels (self, role, group, and large organization) within the social change context.
3. Include variables the practitioner can understand, manipulate, and evaluate.
4. Select from among variables those most appropriate to a specific local situation in terms of its values, ethics, and morality.
5. Accept the premise that groups and organizations as units are as amenable to empirical and analytical treatment as is the individual.
6. Take into account "external" social processes of change as well as interpersonal aspects of the collaborative process.

Conclusion

In this chapter we discussed the nature of theory and the application of theory to practice. An understanding of these two subjects will help the reader critically evaluate the theories presented in the remainder of this book. Furthermore, and more importantly, such an understanding will help in the evaluation of new theories as they appear in the management and organization behavior literature.

Since the scientific study of management and organization behavior is relatively new, it is highly probable that many of the existing theories will be modified or replaced as a result of future research. If this is true, the "consumers" or appliers of new theories will need to critically evaluate them in order to decide which are most applicable and practical. An understanding of the content of this chapter should help in such decisions.

References

Bennis, W. G.; Benne, K. D.; and Chin, R. 1962. *The planning of change: Readings in the applied behavioral sciences.* Holt, Rinehart and Winston.

Cyert, R. M., and March, J. G. 1963. *A behavioral theory of the firm.* Prentice-Hall.

Dollard, J. L.; Doob, W.; Miller, N. E.; Mowrer, O. H.; and Sears, R. R. 1939. *Frustration and aggression.* Yale University Press.

House, R. J. 1967. *Management development: Design, implementation, and evaluation.* Bureau of Research Relations, University of Michigan.

———. 1971. A path-goal theory of leader effectiveness. *Administrative Science Quarterly* 16: 321–28.

———., and Mitchell, T. R. 1974. Path-goal theory of leadership. *Journal of Contemporary Business.*

March, J. G., and Simon, H. A. 1958. *Organizations.* Wiley.

Simon, H. A. 1957. *Administrative behavior,* 2nd ed. Macmillan.

Chapter **3**

Scientific Investigation in Management

In the discovery of secret things and in the investigation of hidden causes, stronger reasons are obtained from sure experiments and demonstrated arguments than from probable conjectures and the opinions of philosophical speculators of the common sort.

WILLIAM GILBERT (1600)

As we saw in the previous chapter, theory is a goal that is valued in its own right because it orders and integrates our knowledge of the real world. Theory is also a tool that directs empirical investigation, which in turn either validates or invalidates hypotheses. Indeed, according to scientific convention, hypotheses are meaningless if their validity cannot be proven by public demonstration.

Two of the criteria of acceptability of theory, discussed in Chapter 2, deal directly with this issue. These are the need for a theory to be testable and the requirement of external consistency. Scientific convention requires that methods employed to test hypotheses meet highly rigorous standards which have been followed since Descartes introduced the scientific method in the seventeenth century. As will be seen, some of these methods apply to natural settings (as in the application of physics to predict the movement of the planets) while others apply to settings constructed by the scientist for the specific purpose of conducting research (as in the use of a wind tunnel to test aerodynamic hypotheses).

The specific methodologies that can be used to test theories of organizational behavior and management practices will be discussed in this chapter. Two general categories of research methods that we will discuss are research by analogy and empirical research.

Just as scientists often develop new theories by drawing analogies from observable phenomena, reasoning by analogy also permits researchers to infer the validity of propositions from empirical tests of analogous propositions. This process of conducting research by analogy is described in the first part of this chapter.

Certain "rules of evidence" have been established to guide tests of theories and for the conduct of scientific inquiry. These "rules" require that researchers make their empirical data available to others. That is, they require public demonstration of the researcher's methodology and findings. These rules thus make it possible for others to assess the quality of data used to support or reject a theory. Stated another way, the requirement of public demonstration permits others to assess the degree to which a theory has met the criterion of external consistency. These rules of evidence will be discussed next.

Finally, we will describe the methods of empirical research that are most commonly used in reference to management and organizational behavior. As we also explained in reference to the nature of theory, an understanding of the nature of scientific investigation will be useful in critically evaluating the theories and research presented in subsequent chapters. This understanding will also be helpful in assessing the validity of new theories as they appear in the management and organizational behavior literature.

Research by Analogy

Much of today's management theory has been developed from the practical experience of managers or on the basis of uncontrolled observation. Such experience and observation have provided the theorist with significant and useful information for the development of prescriptions, guides, or principles of action. However, actual tests of such principles (which might be more accurately termed *hypotheses*) are still rare. This condition is not surprising, since the dynamics of industrial and organizational life make research in the real-life situation difficult and expensive. Yet the student of management need not be limited to observing principles *in actual practice* before their validity can be assessed. As a starting point it might be profitable to turn to other academic disciplines for previously conducted studies of analogous hypotheses or propositions, from which valid inferences might be drawn.

Our point can be illustrated by using the principle of unity of command as an example. The principle states that "no individual should receive orders or directions from more than one person." The rationale is that if a person receives orders, evaluations, and commands from more than one source in the organization, there is a strong likelihood that such orders will conflict (Gulick, 1937). Such conflict will make the recipient uncertain as to which orders carry the highest priority and feelings of frustration and tension may develop, and decision making may therefore be delayed. This conflict will also cause dissatisfaction and undesirable managerial performance.

Since the principle of unity of command is based upon the expectation of conflict, we might expect to draw useful inferences from psychology about individual conflict arising from incompatible role demands imposed on a person as an employee, parent, or citizen. For example, research on the behavior of children responding to conflicting family-church value systems might provide useful data from which inferences about the validity of the principle of unity of command can be drawn. Such inferences constitute an *implicit* test of the principle in question. Such implicit testing facilitates the researcher's work by providing direction by suggesting variables that must be considered in research designed to *explicitly* test hypotheses in actual situations relevant to the researcher's area of interest.

By recognizing the possibility of drawing valid inferences from situations *other than* those directly concerned with managerial or organizational behavior, the student of management can draw on a large body of potential information. Many analogous studies drawn from the behavioral sciences have been conducted within highly rigorous research designs. By analyzing such studies with a view toward identifying critical variables, the student might *discover* as well as *test* pertinent classifications, essential factors, or significant relationships that might otherwise be overlooked. Two examples will illustrate the significance of this point:

Stogdill (1959) was able to identify and explain factors that accounted for and reconciled apparently inconsistent findings concerning the relation between productivity and member satisfaction. Some studies revealed a direct relationship between productivity and satisfaction; others indicated just the opposite. To account for this, Stogdill analyzed studies from such diverse fields as political science, military strategy, biology, learning theory, mathematical group theory, sociology, and social, abnormal, and personality psychology.

Etzioni (1961), in an analysis of similarly diverse studies, arrived at a system of classifying authority according to the nature of an organization. The system allowed the theoretical explanation and prediction of the effects of punitive, remunerative, and normative rewards.

But further testing is warranted only when a review of the analogous research suggests all of the following conditions:

1. The available analogous empirical studies suggest the presence of a definite pattern of relationships.
2. The relationships established have logical consistency.
3. The relationships suggested are not contradicted or opened to serious question by other empirical studies.

It is important to note, however, that inferential research should not draw on studies of nonanalogous situations. To prevent this, the researcher must determine that the essential properties of the phenomenon under investigation are included in the research from which inferences are drawn. For example, psychological research on small children might be analogous to the problems of unity of command *if* the variables closely approximate the variables of authority and reward as used in managerial environments. Experiments concerned with the behavior of rats when subjected first to a reward for a response and then to punishment for the same response might yield fruitful information concerning the physiological effects of frustration. "But instinctually based ant societies, for example, do not yield particularly valuable information for understanding rationally conceived human organizations. . . . For systems to be analogous, *they must exhibit inherent structural similarities or implicitly identical operational* principles" (Scott, 1962, p. 151).

In the latter parts of this book, many of the well-established prescriptions of management will be subjected to implicit testing by use of inferences based on analogous research from many of the social sciences. Explicit tests of management theory will also be reviewed when available.

We have stressed the need for the student of management to be aware of the relation between theoretical and empirical endeavors, to consider available analogous research findings, and to give consideration to such findings even if they may be a product of inquiry into fields only indirectly related to the problems of management. The student who subscribes to this argument still needs a set of criteria to direct the selection or rejection of research findings. To minimize the probability of drawing invalid inferences, it is necessary to establish some guides for applying and evaluating the various research methods most commonly used in the study of management.

To provide guides for evaluation, we will first discuss the general requirements for objectivity in scientific research. These criteria help us determine the degree to which a particular research method is scientifically rigorous in its design. We will then describe each of the commonly used research methods in some detail, stating the specific kinds of questions to which each method is best applied. And we will classify these research methods according to their level of scientific rigor.

Evaluating Empirical Research

According to scientific convention, as stated earlier, the appraisal and acceptance of empirical findings must be made cautiously, tentatively, and with a healthy respect for probable error. This convention of skepticism stimulates the careful evaluation of evidence and leads the evaluator as well as the experimenter to seek methods of verifying hypotheses. Accordingly, all reports of scientific research must include sufficient information and description to permit readers and future investigators to comprehend fully the methodology used, and to allow replication of the research for purposes of public demonstration.

The requirement of public demonstration ensures a corrective method to compensate for unintended bias or error: It is intended to prevent the construction of theories and the formulation of general laws on the basis of inadequately tested hypotheses. The requirement of demonstration is satisfied when the research design includes (1) a priori *hypotheses;* (2) a priori *criteria that can be used to measure the acceptability of those hypotheses;* (3) *isolation and control of the variables under investigation;* and (4) *methods of measuring and verifying the variables in the investigation.*

Stating a Priori Hypotheses and Criteria

If both the hypotheses and the criteria for the acceptance of the hypotheses are stated in advance, the need to make assumptions and to exercise judgment in accepting or rejecting hypotheses on the basis of research findings is significantly reduced. An example will help clarify this point. A golfer declares that he will drive a golf ball approximately 270 yards, and that the ball will land within 25 feet of the green. If he makes good his prediction, most people will be more inclined to bet on his ability to repeat the demonstration than if he had not predicted the accomplishment of the same feat. By the technique of prediction, a golfer is better able to convince onlookers that his accomplishment was not a result of mere luck but rather a result of his control of the ball. If the golfer were merely to declare, "I am going to hit a long ball that will fall near the green," observers would not be able to compare the results of the demonstration with the prediction as precisely as if he had specified the length of his drive and the distance the ball would fall from the green.

The use of a predictive hypothesis and a criterion of measurement provides both "researcher" and witnesses with a basis of evaluation which is not subject to interpretation, judgment, or opinion. Under this arrangement, assumptions are stated explicitly in advance (e.g., definition of key terms such as the green, 270 yards, etc.), and acceptance or rejection of the hypothesis is based on a comparison of findings with the *a priori* criteria. If both the hypothesis and the criteria are stated unambiguously in advance, and if no judgment is necessary to make the findings comparable to the criteria (if the comparison of prediction with accomplishment is based on unambiguous measurements), the comparison process becomes highly objective. The provision of *a priori* hypotheses and criteria thus serves to concentrate the exercise of subjective analysis in the predictive phases of the research, rather than in the assessment of the validity of the findings.

Isolating and Controlling Variables

Although there are many ways in which variables may be isolated and controlled, the process can be illustrated by referring to two important strategies commonly used by researchers. The first is the method of concomitant variation, or correlation; the second is the method of difference. Both methods were described as early as 1851 by John Stuart Mill.

Concomitant variation is the relationship between a series of paired numerical values. Concomitant variation measures the degree of association between values. For example, Figure 3–1 shows a hypothetical relationship between age and level of productivity for ten workers. As the age of the workers increases, their level of productivity decreases. If the two variables change in opposite directions, as in our example, the relationship is negative. If the variables change in the same direction (e.g., increase follows increase, decrease follows decrease) the relationship is positive.

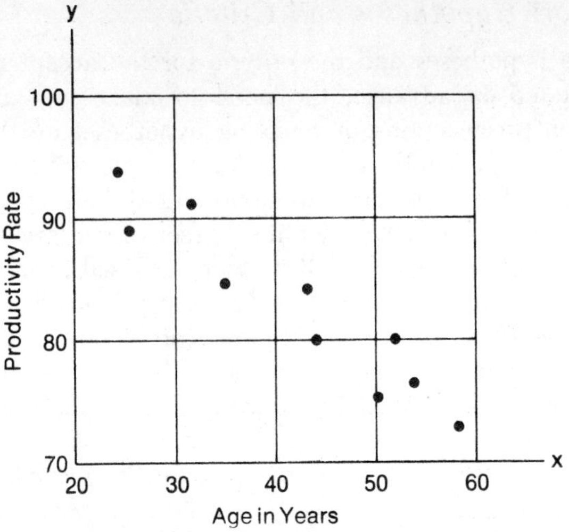

Figure 3-1. Correlation or Method of Concomitant Variation.

Concomitant variation does not demonstrate a cause-and-effect relationship—even though one may exist—because both variables might be the effects of a third variable, which causes both to vary in some related manner.

The *method of difference* is expressed in basic experimental design. Unlike concomitant variation, which involves the conceptual manipulation of variables, experiment uses physical manipulation or control of variables. The logic of experimentation, illustrated in Figure 3–2, is quite simple. Two groups are matched by random assignment of subjects, or by equivalence of known characteristics. Measures of variables (called *dependent* variables) are made in both of the groups under investigation. One group is then subjected to *experimental intervention,* such as a change in physical arrangement, information about member roles, or a change in leadership style. The effect of the experimental variable, also called the *independent* variable, is subsequently measured by reviewing the dependent variables in both the manipulated (experimental) group and the group not manipulated (the control group). The difference between the two groups after the experiment, less any difference that may have existed before, is considered to be the effect of the experimental variable. Thus, the method of difference is the closest that researchers can come to demonstrating cause and effect.

The use of control groups in experimentation is particularly important in social science research, because it ensures that change in an experimental group before and after experimental manipulation is in fact due to that manipulation, rather than to the passage of time or to some uncontrolled change (see Berelson and Steiner, 1964, pp. 18–25). The basic experimental

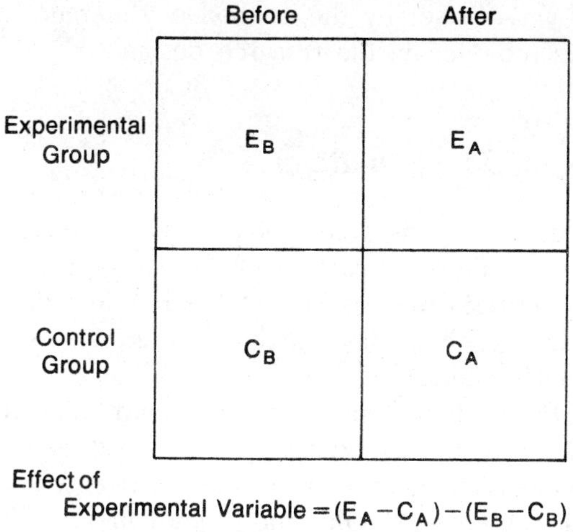

Figure 3-2. The Basic Experimental Design.

design may be used with individuals or with groups, and may be applied in both the laboratory or in a real job setting (field experimentation).

Measuring and Verifying Variables

The requirement of measurement suggests the need for an unambiguous expression of findings. The use of numerical indices and classifications, based on explicitly stated assumptions, permits an evaluation of research results in degree as well as in kind. Thus findings can be stated precisely and different studies can be compared.

The essential characteristics of scientific verification are prediction and observation. As Greenwood (1962) states:

> The canons of science require that, after the theory has been formulated, it must be subjected to empirical validation. This consists of making an extrapolation from the theory in the form of a prediction and testing by observation its correctness. Predictability is the scientist's criterion of validity. If our theoretical formulations of what causes suicides, snow storms, droughts, crime waves and economic depressions are correct, we should be able to predict where and when instances of these phenomena will occur, and the number of correct predictions should deviate decidedly from chance (p. 78).

When research is directed by *a priori* hypotheses derived from theory, and when the variables can be isolated, measured, and verified by the method of concomitant variation or by the method of difference, a basis for valid generalization is provided in the research design.

Three Levels of Research Rigor

The most commonly used methods of managerial research represent three levels of scientific rigor, each of which can be judged by the number of the foregoing criteria used as part of the research design. To illustrate, we will show how each method might be used to test the management principle of span of control.

According to classical theory, there is an optimum number of people that one manager can supervise directly: Between three and eight managers should report to another manager and between twenty and thirty operative (nonmanagerial) employees should report to any first-level supervisor (Fayol, 1930, p. 70). Most classical theorists qualify their recommended spans with the statement that the ideal number may actually be outside recommended limits, depending upon the particular circumstances of the situation.

For purposes of empirical evaluation, we might hypothesize that (1) there is an optimum span of supervision for each situation, and (2) optimum spans will be found to be from three to eight or twenty to thirty, as appropriate. We will illustrate each method of research by describing some actual and other hypothetical studies.

First Level of Rigor

Research methods of the first (or lowest) level of rigor treat the variables under analysis in a qualitative and narrative manner, and provide a minimum of classification or enumeration of variables. These methods are useful for suggesting critical variables, as well as hypotheses to be tested by more rigorous methods. First-level methods include authoritative opinion, single-case study, and narrative history.

Authoritative Opinion. Authoritative opinion means descriptive writing based on the observations of experienced practitioners, or persons who have had direct contact with the environment they seek to describe and explain. Many of the early writings in management fall into this category. Most frequently, such writings and opinions are based on a retrospective analysis of personal experience over a considerable period of the writer's career. Such opinions are frequently insightful, and suggest managerial practices that the writer believes will lead to success. Frequently the practices recommended are those to which the writer attributes his personal success as a manager, or the success of persons he has observed over time. Examples of writers who have advanced authoritative opinions concerning span of control are Henri Fayol (1930) and R. C. Davis (1951). Both of these writers asserted that a manager's span of control should be between three and eight.

Authoritative opinion is limited by the fact that the observations are not experimentally controlled and are subject to interpretation and selectivity. Not only are the reported events based on casual observation but they are also recorded a considerable length of time after their occurrence. Consequently, the objectivity of the reporting is subject to distortion because the reported events may be a reflection of the "eye of the beholder," and also because it is difficult to recall precisely and report accurately events that happened at an earlier time.

A Single Case. The study of a single case is defined by Argyle (1957) as "an investigation of an individual or group in which the variables which are measured and whose empirical relation is explored are characteristics of the individual or group and not of a sub-unit of it" (p. 40).

To apply this to our example of span of control, Dale (1952) found that well over thirty subordinates report to the Chief of Staff of the United States Army, the Chief of the Air Force, and other highranking military men.

> General Eisenhower told the author [Dale] in an interview that in World War II he had at one time 150 battalion commanders reporting to him, and that through his personal, though brief, contact with them he was able to influence the men to such an extent that a superb supply job was performed.

The chief limitations of single-case study are the following. (1) Since no attempt is made to control environment, only rarely does one find two cases that can be meaningfully compared in terms of essential characteristics. (2) Since the data are usually collected without rigorous classification or control of variables, case studies can rarely be repeated or their findings verified. (3) Since the data are seldom collected to test an *a priori* hypothesis, the significance of the findings is left to the subjective interpretation of the researcher. (4) Because they are narrative, case studies usually require a great deal of time and space for findings to be reported, and the significance of those findings is limited to a particular set of circumstances whose recurrence is usually unpredictable and speculative. (5) Case study offers a narrow and limited base for generalization.

Narrative History. A narrative history contains a retrospective analysis of events that have been reported or that have taken place in the past. Here the researcher is usually concerned with such questions as: What gave rise to certain events? What were the cause-and-effect relationships? What might have happened if certain other events had or had not also occurred? From historical study the student can gain perspective on current events in the light of earlier experiences of a similar nature. Some authors advance explanations for the events and changes they record.

Historical study may reveal explanations for events that occurred under conditions so well-defined that there is little historical contradiction. For example, there is little question that there was a Civil War in the United

States, and that it occurred in the nineteenth century. Yet there is considerable controversy over the causes of the Civil War. One would be hard-pressed to find a method for determining objectively just what these causes were, since the data were recorded so long ago, in fragmentary fashion, and for many different purposes. Historical study also provides a tentative basis for generalizations about large-scale developments, such as the growth of major institutions or movements.

Consider the following application to our example: If we were to examine the payroll records, organizational charts, and managerial titles of a firm from 1900 to 1950, we would be able to assess the approximate width of the official managerial spans of control at different points in time and for each level in the organization. By examining budget records and policy records, we might even be able to relate spans of control to the degree of budget decentralization. We might arrive at conclusions concerning *major* changes in budget and decentralization policies, and such findings could serve as hypotheses for future research.

Historical study is limited chiefly by the fact that the events or conditions being studied usually have taken place before the time of the study. Therefore, in using these data, the researcher must of necessity exercise opinion, interpretation, and judgment both about the validity of the data and about the proper classification of the information in his analysis. The only way to check the validity of information on past events is by comparing it with other information recorded at the same time but usually for other purposes; therefore, conclusions drawn on the basis of historical studies must be limited to major or extreme incidents and their effects, or else they must be stated as tentative hypotheses. And conclusions so stated depend heavily upon the conditional statements and assumptions used in the analysis.

Scientific convention requires researchers to qualify conclusions by describing their sources of information and by explicitly citing and explaining any inferences they make. Since most historical studies are based on information drawn from several sources, and inferences are usually necessary to reconcile or adjust records originally collected for other purposes, a complete report usually requires lengthy narrative.

Second Level of Rigor

The methods of second-level rigor include survey research, longitudinal or time series analysis, and uncontrolled experimentation.

Survey Research. Survey methods may be subdivided into polling surveys and analytical surveys. Polling surveys, or polls, are used to investigate current practices and events. They are concerned with the distribution of responses on any one item: How many firms have formalized planning procedures? What proportion of organizations employ personnel specialists? Analytical surveys take the data produced by a polling survey and subject them to statistical analysis of relationships among variables.

Polls are used to collect data to identify and establish the degree to which certain elements are present, or certain practices are current at a given point in time. In management, polls are used primarily to determine the prevalence of certain practices or trends, and to compare one's own managerial practice with that of competitors, other practicing managers, or with earlier practices. Polls shed some light on the emergence of trends, the importance of existing resources and practices, and the relationships among these variables. Polls also provide valuable data for future comparisons.

Examples of polls concerned with span of control have been provided by Healey (1956) and Dale (1952). Healey submitted a questionnaire to chief executives and requested information concerning their managerial practices. Of the chief executives who answered the questionnaire, 94 percent reported that they had a span of fewer than nine subordinates; 76.3 percent reported spans of control from three to eight. Dale reported a survey of 100 large companies known to have "good organizational practices." He found that the *median* number of subordinates supervised by the president was between eight and nine. But ". . . several of these instances revealed well over thirty subordinates and several score of committees reporting to the president!"

The chief advantage of polling surveys is that they can be replicated at different times and in different geographical areas, so that their data can be compared and contrasted with other survey data. But they are primarily limited to simply a description of the current state of practice. For example, the surveys taken by Healey and Dale revealed that managers tend to exercise spans of control slightly greater than that prescribed by traditional theory. However, this finding does not tell us whether the existing managerial practice is desirable, and whether it permits effective management. Answering such questions requires the more complex method of analytical survey.

When a researcher is aware of factors that might account for survey findings, an hypothesis can be stated relating the survey data to those factors. Such an hypothesis can then be tested by analytical survey methods. As we have said, analytical surveys take the data collected by a polling survey and subject them to further statistical analysis. In such analysis, distinctions are made among data groups, and comparisons and tests are applied to determine their inherent differences, similarities, or relations. When found, these relations provide a basis for describing the phenomena studied, as well as a basis for hypotheses of cause-and-effect relations.

There are two important limitations of the analytical survey method of research. First, establishing statistically significant relations between data does not demonstrate *how* the variables are related. Statistical tests can only discover degrees of correlation greater than that which can be ascribed to chance. When significant statistical relationships are identified, it is necessary to determine which variables are causes and which are effects, and whether variables are effects of a common cause or if they are interdependent.

Second, analytical surveys do not indicate whether relationships will hold true under different conditions, because the data are a reflection of a particular relationship observed at a single point in time, as in a photograph. For example, if a survey reveals that spans of control within the range of three to eight are associated more with effective managers than with ineffective managers, we only know that the data describe sample distributions at the time the data were collected. If a change in the environment takes place, it would be necessary to conduct another survey to find out if the relation between span of control and managerial effectiveness continues to hold. From the statistical relations disclosed in such studies, we cannot predict that the same relation will hold in the future without specifying the condition that the circumstances be the same.

Longitudinal or Time Series Analysis. Longitudinal or time series analysis involves continuous or intermittent observations made over time, recording data to describe changes that take place within a given environment. Such data are usually classified, and observations may be controlled in order to test hypotheses.

For example, observations might be made of major organizational changes taking place over a period of six to eighteen months. Researchers would record events that appear related to the process of organizational change. They might even pay special attention to certain classifications of changes, such as reductions or extensions of managerial spans of control. When they observe such reductions or extensions, they might interview participants to determine their reaction to the change, review minutes of meetings in which the change is discussed, and observe the effects of change on the social environment of the department or organization.

If the findings reported from this method are based on the investigators' controlled observations, and the variables are isolated, longitudinal findings can be compared with findings from other studies, and can therefore be subjected to public demonstration.

Longitudinal studies are limited chiefly by the fact that the variables are not within the control of investigators. Frequently, observed variables may be influenced by other unknown variables. Even when the investigators are aware of extraneous variables at work, they may not be able to measure their influence. As in an analytical survey, it cannot be determined whether correlative relationships are cause-effect relations or relations to an unidentified third variable.

Uncontrolled Experimentation. Uncontrolled experimentation consists of the collection of data at a point in time, and the comparison of these data with subsequently collected data. Thus, the first measurement is used as a bench mark or standard against which change is measured. Between the two measurements, an experimental variable is inserted. In terms of our example, behavioral observations may be made when a manager has a span of control of three and again at a later time when the span has broadened to nine. The assumption is made that any significant difference in observed behavior is due to the introduction of a new variable—a change in the manager's span of control. Where all of the variables that could account for a change in data are both known and observed, and where no such variables change—except for the introduction of an experimental variable—there is a basis for inferring a cause-effect relation between measured data and the experimental variable.

Since only in rare cases are all crucial variables known and sufficiently understood, the use of before-and-after measurements of experimental data is confined to a very limited set of circumstances; otherwise, researchers have no basis for valid conclusions.

Third Level of Rigor

The third level of research rigor consists of those methods (usually laboratory experimentation, experimental simulation, and controlled field experimentation) that attempt not only to manipulate variables to verify cause-effect relations, but also to isolate critical relations and variables. Controlled experimentation is an especially desirable method of research (1) when research questions concern hypotheses of an "if-then," stimulus-response, or cause-effect character, rather than hypotheses which seek to describe a phenomenon, or (2) when the primary purpose of the investigation is to construct or verify a theory.

Laboratory Experimentation.[1] A *laboratory* is any setting that allows investigators to control closely the conditions under which observations can be made. In a laboratory experiment, the conditions under which an event occurs are manipulated so that the effects of the experimental variables and the antecedent conditions can be contrasted. The intention is to isolate theoretically relevant variables, and to measure the response of dependent variables when either independent or intervening variables are manipulated.

Laboratory experiments attempt to study generic processes in their most fundamental form. To accomplish this purpose, experimenters create a situation in which only the essential aspects of a phenomenon being studied are present. The degree to which determining factors exist in the situation are then varied.

Perhaps the most classic example of an experiment is Galileo's use of the inclined plane. Here Galileo was interested in studying the effect of friction and weight on the speed of a falling body. By the use of the inclined plane he could vary the amount of friction and thus discover the laws governing the relationships between friction, gravity, and weight of the falling body. Note that no attempt was made to simulate a "real life" experience such as the descent of an elevator or of an airplane. Yet the information obtained from such experiments makes it possible to calculate the effect of such factors as the speed of the airplane when beginning its approach, the gradient of approach, and the effect of wind resistance on speed.

---

[1] This discussion is based on the concepts and argument presented by Zelditch and Hopkins (1961).

In the same manner social scientists can conduct laboratory experiments on behavioral properties that are presumably fundamental to all organizational (and other) settings. Examples of such fundamental properties that have been studied in laboratory experiments are patterns of communication networks, development of group norms, determinants of group cohesiveness, causes and consequences of interpersonal attraction, and pressures for conformity in informal groups.

Laboratory experimentation is useful when the conditions required to test an hypothesis are not readily obtained in existing natural situations, and when the variables to be tested can be simulated or replicated under laboratory conditions. It is usually concerned with the manipulation and measurement of a small number of variables which are hypothesized as being of crucial theoretical importance.

As an example of the laboratory experiment, the performance and attitudes of two equivalent groups simulating supervisors with broad spans of control might be compared to determine the effect on work performance and attitudes, if any, of the similarity or difference of functions performed. Theory would suggest that broad spans of control are effective when employees are performing similar functions, but ineffective when employees are performing different functions. The design can be summarized as follows:

1. Select two equivalent groups by random assignment or assignment on the basis of criteria of equivalency. Theory would suggest that for many tasks a span of 30 subordinates under one manager would be a broad span; this span would be used here.
2. Define the dependent variable(s) and establish how each would be measured. For example, a rating scale might be used to measure attitude toward the task, and the number of problems solved or products manufactured might be the measure of performance.
3. Give both the experimental group and the control group a task in which the members of each group of employees perform similar functions.
4. Take a "before" measure of attitudes and performance.
5. Define the experimental variable to make clear what conditions of task complexity are to be imposed on the experimental group. In this case the complexity of the task would be changed in one group and remain the same in the other group.
6. Take "after" measures of attitudes and performance in both groups.

The major assumption involved in drawing conclusions from laboratory experimentation on management problems concerns the relevance of laboratory events to the actual operation of organizations. "Events in laboratory groups and events in actual operations, like events in any two different social settings, can be related to one another only if both are relevant to the same set of propositions in a theory" (Zelditch and Hopkins, 1961, p. 468). Thus, to be meaningful, a laboratory test of propositions must contain the same *essential* properties as a real-world situation, and it must be possible to replicate the essential characteristics under question in the laboratory simulations.

Experimental Simulations. Experimental simulations refer to investigations that attempt to study continuous organizational processes rather than the effect of separate interventions or discrete changes made by experimenters. In experimental situations an attempt is made to create a relatively realistic representation of an ongoing organization. Observations are made of the continuous behavior of people participating in the simulation. J. E. McGrath (1964) points out three aspects of the simulation that distinguish it from the laboratory experiment:

> First, the stimulus situation within which the individual is operating is more or less continuous in an experimental situation, in contrast to the laboratory experiment which usually consists of a series of discrete trials. Secondly, as a part of the continuous nature of experimental simulations, participants' responses at any particular point in time partly determine (along with the "rules of the game") the stimulus situation in which they will be operating at subsequent points in time. Finally, experimental simulations differ from laboratory studies in that they attempt to simulate or model properties of "real-life" organizations, which is the key defining property of this class of methods in the schema (p. 537).

An example of a successful laboratory simulation for research purposes is the study by Chapman et al. (1959).[2] These authors had set up a series of simulations of air defense direction centers. Using elaborate staging apparatus, as well as electronic computers, they succeeded in simulating the environment of an air defense direction center. Air Force people who had previous experience in real centers were used as the subjects.

The physical environment of an air defense direction center was simulated by making a close functional approximation to the tools of the real center. The physical layout, the communication net, the central displays, and the general atmosphere of one particular center were copied as literally as possible. The cultural environment was simulated by using Air Force personnel. The task environment consisted largely of several series of tracks appearing on eight radar scopes. The hardware itself functioned sufficiently like a radar scope to cause the Air Force personnel to respond to these artificial presentations in the same way that they responded to the real thing. Elaborate procedures were developed for gathering data on the participants' behavior while the experiments were in progress. These included the use of tape recorders, photographs, and observers activating a specially coded keyboard for punching cards.

Each of the four man-machine simulations was successful in developing task-oriented organizations that behaved like living organisms. The people in each experiment learned both to improve their own individual perfor-

---

[2] This example is discussed in Cohen, K. J., and Cyert, R. M. "Simulation of Organizational Behavior," in *Handbook of Organizations,* edited by J. G. March, Rand-McNally, 1965.

mance and, more importantly, to improve their organizational structure and procedures so that over time there was a marked increase in the operating effectiveness of each group.

The use of the simulated experiment permitted the researchers to determine that operational flexibility is the most important characteristic for this type of organization. This finding is in contrast to the more traditional theory of management which prescribes standardized procedures and processes and a rigid organizational structure that constrains the reporting relationships among people to the chain of command.

Controlled Field Experimentation. Controlled field experimentation is a method also intended to control or hold constant all variables except the experimental variable, and to measure the effect of the experimental variable by use of before-and-after measurement—all in a natural setting, however, rather than in a laboratory.

For example, a controlled field experiment might be employed to determine the effect of increased span of control on group performance. As in the case of the laboratory experiment, the control group consists of a sample sufficiently similar to the experimental group to allow comparisons between the two, but it is not subjected to the experimental variable. Differences in performance are measured to determine the effect of changing the span of control of the experimental group. For example, if the spans of control are increased in one department (the experimental group) and not in a similar department, and if there is no change in the personnel or the operation of either department, any change in the team performance of the experimental department can be attributed to the increase in the spans of control.

Here the assumption is made that no variable other than the experimental variable (increased span) affects either group alone, and that any other variable (such as changes in top management or consumer demand) that affected one group also affected the other in the same way and to the same degree.

These assumptions can be tested by repeating the experiment, using the control group of the first experiment as the experimental group of the second. If the same results occur in the second experiment as in the first, the researcher can place greater reliance on the experimental findings.

A less frequently used control of field experimentation involves data classification and statistical comparisons, within the experimental sample. For instance, assume that all the managers of a firm were instructed in a training program that the most effective span of control is between three and eight—but that there are circumstances which justify the violation of the three-to-eight prescription, one being when a manager makes use of one or more staff assistants to aid in maintaining a span of control of nine or more.

Observations could be made to test the hypothesis that, after training, wide spans will be reduced *or* more use will be made of staff assistants. If the hypothesis is confirmed, the changes *might* be attributable to the training program. However, greater certainty could be attained by testing the further hypothesis that those who add staff assistants will retain their span of control, and those who do not add staff assistants will reduce their span of control. Confirming the second hypothesis would be additional evidence for concluding that the changes resulted from the training, because the changes are of the nature that would be expected from such training and are in keeping with the prescriptions of the training.

Advantages and Disadvantages of Experiments and Simulations. The major advantage of laboratory experiments and simulations concerns the ability of investigators to control the environment in which the observed behavior takes place and thus to be more certain about the factors that determine the kind of behavior that does take place. Using these methods investigators can vary the conditions of the experiment, by changing the experimental instructions to the subjects, the physical environment, the group composition, or other aspects of the experiment that are believed to be relevant to the research question. Since the experimental situation is designed specifically for research purposes experimenters can determine the kinds of information to be obtained and the particular points in time during or after the experiment when such information is to be gathered. Further, experimenters can choose whether to use questionnaires, observations, or measurements of productivity as the methods of data collection. Thus, laboratory studies of the sort described above permit the situation to be controlled and the data to be collected specifically for the purpose of the researchers.

The major disadvantage of such experimentation concerns the external validity and generality of the findings, that is, whether or not they can be generalized to other situations. It frequently occurs that experimenters unwittingly induce the subjects, through subtle cues, to behave in certain ways (see the discussion of the Hawthorne study in Chapter 1). For example, subjects frequently try to determine the intent of the experiment. If they are in sympathy with the objectives of the experimenters they may attempt to validate the experiment by behaving in a way consistent with the research hypothesis. If they are antagonistic to the experimenters or to their objectives, they may intentionally behave in a manner contrary to the research hypothesis. Under such conditions, the subjects are responding to cues other than those that are consciously built into the experimental design. Since replications of the same experiment may result in similar findings because of similar experimental cues, these findings cannot be generalized beyond the experimental setting. Thus, under such conditions the experiment may appear to have a high degree of control of extraneous variables and accurate measurement while in actual fact subtle variables unknown to the experimenters have crept into the experiment and destroyed the validity of its results.

These subtle cues to experimental subjects are referred to as "demand characteristics" of the experiment; that is, the characteristics of the experiment are said to demand certain kinds of behavior of the subjects. To control for this possibility, an attempt should be made to determine whether demand characteristics indeed are operating in an experiment. The one method that is frequently used is to interview experimental subjects upon completion of the experiment to determine whether they have been responding to the experimental variables rather than attempting to behave in a manner consistent with the research hypothesis. Another method for control of demand characteristics is to describe the experiment to a group of naive subjects (subjects not involved in the original experiment) and ask them if they can determine the purpose of the research. If they are not able to do so the researcher has more confidence that experimental subjects would not be able to do so either. Several other methods of controlling for demand characteristics are available. The important point to be noted here is that each experimental study may be potentially invalid because of such demand characteristics and that it is the responsibility of the investigators to provide some checks on the effects of such characteristics.

Controlled Experimentation and Management Theory

Many managers and students of management have questioned the relevance and the reliability of controlled experimentation in the study of management. In order to critically evaluate the research reviewed in this book, both the advantages and the limitations of this method as it applies to management theory and practice must be understood. Cummings and Harnett (1968) discuss this issue at some length. They argue that experimentation is a better basis for the development of theory and for managerial decision making than either intuitive opinion or case study, because:

> First, experimentation allows the researcher to maintain *control* over the variables involved in his model of a problem. In contrast to observational methods, the goal of experimentation is to manipulate (vary) the variables assumed to be critical or most important and to control (hold constant) all other variables known or thought to influence the phenomenon in question. Holding certain variables constant helps clarify the nature of the relationships being examined and also facilitates concise interpretation of the resulting data.
>
> Second, experimentation as a method of knowledge generation forces the business researcher to design studies so that he will know precisely under what conditions his knowledge has been acquired. This explicitness in design produces knowledge about the variables studied that has high *generality*. One argument cited by those questioning the utility of the experimental method for the study of managerial problems is that the method yields results that cannot be generalized beyond the conditions surrounding the specific study in question. Therefore, goes the argument, since potential and present managers need to operate under a variety of different conditions, we should generate "practical" knowl-

edge through intuitive methods and case studies. On the contrary, these methods normally tell the decision maker very little concerning the conditions under which the information to which he is exposed has been produced. Actually, he is justified in generalizing such information only to very similar conditions. These may, indeed, be difficult to locate.

Experimentation, on the other hand, allows the decision maker, in cooperation with the researcher, to design studies aimed at a basic understanding of the processes and behavior underlying managerial problems. Generalization, even to apparently dissimilar conditions, thereby becomes less risky to the manager for two reasons: (1) he has available for consideration the exact conditions under which the information was generated, and (2) the resulting knowledge concerns basic processes and underlying causes rather than merely manifest symptoms. Certainly not all "real-world" decision-making situations can be replicated in the laboratory; neither can the student nor the practitioner of administration have the opportunity to experience all cases. So there appears to be a significant range of managerial problems within which experimental methods of study are both more reliable (in the sense of control and explicitness of design) and practical (in the sense of generality of basic processes and causal relationships) (pp. 41–48).

Cummings and Harnett argue that not only is an experimental method superior to other methods, but that it can be used under conditions where other methods cannot be used and therefore has greater flexibility. Specifically, they argue that nonmanagers can be used as substitutes for managers under conditions designed to simulate the essential properties of a management problem. They support this position by citing two studies using college students as experimental subjects. The findings of one study were replicated using managers as subjects, and the findings of the second study were replicated using marketing professors and government employees as subjects.

The major limitation concerning the relevance of experimental findings to "real-world" situations involves the question of whether the properties of the problem under examination can be simulated in an experimental setting. On this point, Cummings and Harnett quote K. E. Weick (1965):

. . . even though a (real world) problem is reformulated and transposed, it will retain its relevance to natural organizations if the experimental situation retains some properties of the setting, task and participation associated with natural organizations. . . . Because laboratory experimentation is much more flexible than most persons realize, the laboratory can be adapted to exceedingly complex and ambiguous problems. At the same time, many organizational problems are encumbered with extraneous and superfluous details. These details can be removed with little effect on generality. It is this continual balance

> between altering the method and losing control and altering the problem and losing validity that accounts for much of the drama of organizational experimentation.

They also quote V. H. Vroom's conclusion from his extensive review (1968) of industrial-social psychology literature:

> The basic assumption underlying laboratory experimentation on any system . . . is that complex phenomena may be explained by reducing them to their basic and most elementary forms and by studying these forms under highly controlled conditions. The experiments cited in this (review) illustrate that systems having some of the properties of organizations can be created in the laboratory and that behavior of these systems varies in a predictable and reliable manner with experimental conditions (p. 44).

Thus, when evaluating reports of laboratory or field experimentation, the reader must ask whether or not the conditions under which the experiment was conducted are analogous to the theoretical issue under consideration. (Other considerations such as the appropriateness of the measurement and statistics employed are the same for all research methods.)

The major limitations of experimental method are those of time, practicality, and the ethics involved in subjecting humans to experimental treatment. Obviously, the introduction of variables that would disturb or harm the individuals involved would be considered unethical and therefore not amenable to experimental manipulation.

Levels of Rigor Versus Quality

There is a danger that we might undervalue the importance of the techniques in the first two levels of research rigor. The direction of search is a prerequisite for correlational and experimental designs which isolate and verify meaningful variables and findings. The generation of hypotheses to be tested and the construction of theory are aided substantially by a qualitative and sometimes even an intuitive understanding of the variables to be investigated. Such understanding can come about only through extensive observation of real-life situations and by extensive reading of the works of others who have described their experiences in observing the same variables. If observation were to be conducted only under controlled conditions, the chances are that many unexpected subtleties would be missed, or that controls would prevent the occurrence of important events. Consequently, for an experiment to be meaningfully designed, it must ordinarily rest on previous descriptive research methods, such as case history, which do not attempt to arrive at valid generalizations, but which do attempt to specify areas of search and hypotheses for testing.

However, once a hypothesis has stood the test of the methods included in our first and second levels of research rigor, it is still necessary to apply experimental testing under controlled conditions; as Seashore (1962) says:

> A single well-designed experiment can, in principle, produce information of such unequivocal nature that it outweighs any number of case studies or demonstrations. . . . An example of the failure of nonexperimental method comes to mind. Marriott's review of the research on the efficacy of incentive payment plans in raising individual and organizational work performance produced the startling conclusions that, in spite of many hundreds of "successful" introductions of incentive pay plans, one cannot know whether the reported effects are produced by the pay plans or by other concomitant factors. There have been a total of three experiments on the matter, but all were done about thirty years ago and all involved numbers of less than 10 individuals. The amount of useful information from this vast amount of work is remarkably small (p. 2).

It is also important to point out that the levels of research rigor do not imply that the higher the level, the greater the quality of the research. A highly controlled experiment may be of very low quality if the measurement instruments, the variables studied, or the sample are poorly selected. The quality of a particular investigation depends on such considerations as the nature of the data, the care taken by the researchers in collecting and analyzing it, the degree to which they adhere to *a priori* criteria, the soundness of the criteria, and the clearness of their hypotheses.

Several studies reporting similar findings are obviously better than one study, and very rarely, if ever, can a single research study offer a general conclusion, that is, a law or principle, regardless of objectivity or rigor of design.

References

Argyle, M. 1957. *The scientific study of social behavior.* Methuen.

Berelson, B., and Steiner, G. 1964. *Human behavior: An inventory of scientific findings.* Harcourt Brace.

Chapman, R. L.; Kennedy, J. L.; Newell, A.; and Beil, W. C. 1959. The systems research laboratory's Air Defense experiments. *Management Science* 5:3, 250–69.

Cohen, K. J., and Cyert, R. M. 1965. Simulation of organizational behavior. In *Handbook of organizations,* ed. by J. G. March. Rand-McNally.

Cummings, L. L., and Harnett, D. L. 1968. Managerial problems and the experimental method. *Business Horizons* 11: 41–48.

Dale, E. 1952. *Planning and developing the company organization structure.* Research Report No. 20, American Management Association.

Davis, R. C. 1951. *The fundamentals of top management.* Harper & Row.

Etzioni, A. 1961. *A comparative analysis of complex organizations.* Free Press.

Fayol, H. 1930. *Industrial and general administration* (1916). International Management Institute.

Greenwood, E. 1962. The practice of science and the science of practice. In *The planning of change: Readings in the applied behavioral sciences,* ed. by W. G. Bennis, K. D. Benne, and R. Chin. Holt, Rinehart and Winston.

Gulick, L. 1937. Notes on the theory of organization. In *Papers in the science of administration,* ed. by L. Gulick and L. Urwick. Institute of Public Administration.

Healey, J. H. 1956. *Executive coordination and control.* Monograph No. 78, Bureau of Business Research, The Ohio State University.

McGrath, J. E. 1964. Toward a 'theory of method' for research on organizations. In *New perspectives in organization research,* ed. by W. W. Cooper, H. J. Leavitt, and M. W. Shelly II. Wiley.

Scott, W. G. 1962. *Human relations and management: A behavioral science approach.* Irwin.

Seashore, S. E. 1962. Field experiments on complex organizations. Paper presented at the AFOSR Research Conference on Organization Behavior, Athens, Georgia.

Stogdill, R. M. 1959. *Individual behavior and group achievement.* Oxford University Press.

Vroom, V. H. 1968. Industrial social psychology. In *Handbook of social psychology,* vol. 11, 2nd ed., ed. by G. Lindzey and E. Aronson. Addison-Wesley.

Weick, K. E. 1965. Laboratory experimentation with organizations. In *Handbook of organizations,* ed. by J. G. March. Rand-McNally.

Zelditch, M. J. Jr., and Hopkins, T. K. 1961. Laboratory experiments with organizations. In *Complex organizations: A sociological reader,* ed. by A. Etzioni. Holt, Rinehart and Winston.

Part **2**

Behavior in Organizations

This part of the book concerns psychological and sociological principles and problems relevant to the management of organizations. Since organizations are made up of individuals, who work together in groups, we have drawn upon the literature of individual psychology, social psychology, and sociology for these chapters.

Chapters 4 and 5 are short chapters that describe aspects of perception and learning that are particularly important for understanding individual behavior in organizations. Since the "real world" is essentially the world as each individual perceives it, an understanding of the perceptual process and of factors which impinge on our perceptions is useful in understanding human behavior. Chapter 5 deals with behavioral descriptions and cognitive theories of learning and their practical applications in the organizational setting.

Chapter 6, also a brief chapter, describes how power, authority, and influence relationships are reflected in both the design of organizations and in the ways people relate to each other within (and despite) those designs.

Chapter 7, the first chapter in the theory-proposition-evidence format described earlier, focuses on Herbert A. Simon's administrative theory of individual decision making. Drawing upon some of the concepts discussed earlier, it deals with the limitations upon man's ability to "rationally" make decisions.

Chapter 8 deals with formal groups in organizations—committees, boards, commissions, and the like—and draws heavily for its discussion upon the extensive literature on small group process and characteristics. The reader will learn what kinds of group processes are most appropriate for different kinds of objectives.

Problem solving and a related issue, conflict resolution, are the subjects of Chapter 9. Particular emphasis is placed upon conditions which tend to elicit conflict behavior and upon the processes which may be used to provide a problem solving mode of behavior or a conflictive mode of behavior. The discussion includes an exposition of the integrative method of problem solving.

Individual motivation, the focus of Chapter 10, is one of the most crucial problems facing today's managers; it is also one of the most difficult and least understood aspects of individual behavior. Six prominent theories of motivation are described within the framework of two basic managerial questions: What motivates people to join an organization and to remain within it? What conditions motivate employees to produce at the rate desired by the organization? Each theory is then subjected to empirical evaluation.

This section closes with two chapters on the subject of leadership. Chapter 11 considers trait and behavioral approaches which, while tending to oversimplify factors which determine leader effectiveness, nevertheless do lay important groundwork for more current approaches to the study of leadership. Chapter 12 continues with a description of three important situational theories of leadership. These theories describe the interactions between leaders, followers, and the environment which affect leader success.

An understanding of the phenomena treated in this part will provide insights into the psychological and sociological processes that occur within organizations, and which help or hinder organizations in reaching their objectives.

Chapter **4**

Perception

Poor Man:	*Lord, is it true that to you a thousand years is like a minute?*
Lord:	*Yes, that's true.*
Poor Man:	*And is it also true that to you a thousand dollars is like a cent?*
Lord:	*Yes, that's so.*
Poor Man:	*Then, Lord, could you give me a thousand dollars?*
Lord:	*Yes, in a minute.*

Among the most important activities required of individuals in organizations are choosing among alternatives, making decisions, and solving problems. To do these things it is necessary for us to process information on an almost continuous basis; in theory, we are supposed to process this information "rationally," focusing attention on "the facts" of the matter and permitting "emotional biases" and "perceptual distortions" to intrude to a minimal degree. However, the research literature provides ample evidence that few if any of us are capable of processing information in this manner. Instead, we often perceive and process information which is, from an objective standpoint, useless to the decision-making process, while at the same time we often fail to perceive data which could be very important. In addition, information which is perceived is often, however unintentionally, distorted and biased.

Anyone who has ever studied or been involved in police work knows that the cliché "seeing is believing" is a gross oversimplification, and that "eyewitnesses" frequently disagree with one another and are seldom correct about even the most basic and fundamental characteristics of what they have seen. Numerous experiments have produced similar lack of agreement with respect to subjects' senses of hearing, taste, and touch.

If our impressions of reality are only loosely derived from "objective reality" itself, fortunately it is also true that such impressions are *not* merely the result of processing information in a random and chaotic way. On the contrary, there *is* both system and order in the way people perceive other people, objects, and events, and it is therefore possible to understand and to predict why and how people perceive things as they do.

The purpose of this chapter is to examine the perceptual process from the perspective of the perceiver and also to consider various situational effects upon what is perceived. An understanding of factors that affect perception will provide many insights into the decision-making and information-processing activities of organizational members.

Components of Perception

In its most basic form,

> The perceptual system acts like a computer, taking in multiple sources of information, selecting, integrating, abstracting, comparing, testing, sorting, outputting, and then repeating all these again and again. Each perceptual act is a construction or creation of reality based on all of the relevant past and current information available to the organism. Far from being a direct experience of "things as they are," perception is thus a *mediated* process of organized conclusion drawing about the "real" world of time, space, objects, and events, based on much more than simply the stimulus input (Zimbardo and Ruch, 1975, p. 238).

Because it is probably true that no two individuals have available the same sensory cues and the same experience, it may safely be said that no two people perceive the world in quite the same way. Individual differences may arise from several sources:

> Some of these differences are due to differences in the brains or minds of the observers, some to differences in their sense-organs, some to differences in physical situation: these kinds may be called respectively psychological, physiological, and physical. A remark made in a language we know will be heard, whereas an equally loud remark in an unknown language may pass entirely unnoticed. . . . Such differences are psychological. The differences between a long-sighted and a short-sighted man . . . are physiological. . . . Physical differences between two observers will be preserved when the observers are replaced by cameras or recording machines. . . . If two men both listen to a third man speaking, and one of them is nearer to the speaker than the other is, the nearer one will hear louder and slightly earlier sounds than are heard by the other (Russell, 1962, pp. 16–17).

There are several components of the perceptual process. The first of these, usually referred to as *selection* or *screening*, concerns the actual sensing of a stimulus by an individual. Numerous sensations are constantly competing to be sensed by each person's sensory system, while only a comparative few can succeed in gaining awareness. Our sense organs are said to have *absolute thresholds of activation*, and stimuli whose strength does not reach or exceed these thresholds will not be perceived.

Just as there are important differences in perceptual processes between individuals, there are also differences which affect the *same* individual at different times. A clock's ticking, for example, may be so loud as to be distracting to one individual, yet it may not be heard by another individual in the same room. After a while, however, the first person may suddenly stop "hearing" the clock entirely. This phenomenon, known as *sensory adaptation,* usually leads to reduced sensitivity to stimuli after continued exposure (Bobbitt et al., 1974).

However, while the first person begins to screen out ticking noises which are distracting, the second individual, who did not even hear the clock at first, may now hear it growing louder and louder until it is all but impossible to concentrate on anything else. This might be likely to happen if, for example, the individual were waiting anxiously for a phone call, or for a child to return home from a late date. It therefore seems safe to say that, while stimuli whose energy levels are inadequate to reach a sensory organ's threshold will never be perceived, stronger stimuli *may or may not* be perceived, depending partly upon factors unrelated to the strength of the stimuli.

A second component of the perceptual process is *interpretation,* whereby information which is sensed is *organized* by an individual in order to derive some meaning from it. Interpretation is based on many things, including the past experiences and value systems of the perceiving individual (Kast and Rosenzweig, 1974), as well as the individual's motivation, personality, and learning (Luthans, 1973). These and other factors which influence interpretation will be discussed more fully later on.

An integral part of the interpretation process is categorization.

> We stimulate an organism with some appropriate input and he responds by referring the input to some class of things or events. . . . On the basis of some defining or criterial attributes in the input, what are usually called cues . . . there is a selective placing of the input in one category of identity rather than another. The category need not be elaborate: "a sound," "a touch," "a pain," are also examples of categorized inputs. The use of cues in inferring the categorial identity of a perceived object . . . is as much a feature of perception as the sensory stuff from which percepts are made (Bruner, 1967, p. 29).

The central function of the categorization process is to reduce initially complex information into simpler categories (Scott and Mitchell, 1972).

A third major component of perception is the individual's *reaction* or *response,* which is "the behavioral interpretation of perception. A response, either overt or covert, is necessary if perception is to be considered a behavioral event" (Luthans, 1973, p. 338). In the absence of any response by the perceiving individual, the question of whether stimuli were actually perceived or not is probably of only academic interest.

To this point, we have described perception as an extremely *selective* process in which a limited amount of incoming information is selected to be processed, is interpreted, and is acted upon—simply because we cannot assimilate all of the stimuli which simultaneously clamor for our attention. As will be seen in the next section, even if we could we often prefer to ignore certain inputs which would be threatening to our self-concepts or to our cherished beliefs.

Characteristics of the Perceiver Which Influence Perception

There are a number of factors which affect the way incoming stimuli are perceived; many of these relate to the perceiver and affect the extent to which certain kinds of categorizing responses will sometimes be available and other times unavailable. The most important factors relevant to the perceiver include defense mechanisms, such as projection, stereotyping, displacement, and selective perception; the Gestalt principles of closure, constancy, and expectancy; attitudes, needs, and values; and halo effects.

Defense Mechanisms

A variety of techniques are utilized by most people to help them adjust to ego-involving frustrations and to maintain a flattering self-concept. These techniques, called defense mechanisms, are pertinent to our discussion because they affect the perceptual process by protecting people from being deluged by incoming information, particularly information which might threaten them and cause a lowering of self-esteem. These defenses tend to act as buffers between ourselves and "objective reality," keeping us from perceiving things which would upset us. Some of the more important defense mechanisms, and their effects upon the perceiver, are as follows:

Projection. This is a method of relieving feelings of guilt and failure by attributing (projecting) one's own forbidden and socially unacceptable unconscious wishes, thoughts, and motives to someone else. Huse and Bowditch (1973) illustrate the applicability of this technique to many labor-management relationships, where each side attributes its own suspicion, malice, and distrust to those on the other side.

In a classic test of this defense mechanism, Murray (1933) had one group of children play a game of "Murder" while a comparison group did not. Those who had played the game, and who had for the most part become quite aroused and involved in it, subsequently perceived significantly greater tendencies toward violence and malice in some photographs of people than did those who had not played the game. The photographs viewed by both groups were the same; the differences in perceptions were apparently the result of projection.

In another study of the effects of projection upon perception, Sears (1936) found that individuals who were high in traits such as stinginess and disorderliness were much more likely to describe others as being high in the same traits than were individuals who did not possess these characteristics.

Stereotyping. This term refers to an overgeneralization that groups different individuals into a single category on the basis of presumed similarities among them. The most common occasion for the use of stereotypes is when the perceiver knows only the overall category of which the person being perceived is a member (Luthans, 1973). The problem with stereotyping is that

> When we discover that a person is a union leader, a student activist, or a social scientist, our frame of reference for these types of roles immediately calls up an entire network of expectations that may be automatically applied as representing characteristics of the person. . . . We may even go to the extreme of ignoring or distorting information about the person which does not fit into our personal frame of reference. . . . We mentally force the individual into one of our categories because of our mind's inability to handle an infinite number of images. As a result, we may miss much of who the person is. . . . (Hellriegel and Slocum, 1974, p. 281.)

In a study of the effects of stereotyping upon perception, Haire and Grunes (1950) induced conflict between the stereotype often associated with the descriptive phrase "works in a factory" and the positive adjective "intelligent." They found that, while some subjects were able to alter their stereotype so as to include the "fact" that the factory worker was in fact intelligent, many others distorted the facts so as to force them to fit their stereotype, or denied that the factory worker was intelligent. For these subjects stereotyping acted as a perceptual defense, permitting them to retain their prior belief in the unintelligence of factory workers by failing to perceive the fact that the intelligent workers being described were factory workers, or that the factory workers being described were intelligent.

Displacement. This is a process whereby emotions such as anger, fear, or hostility are rechannelled (displaced) from the original target person or group toward another person or group who is viewed as more vulnerable and less formidable and, therefore, a safer target. Supervisors who have just been disciplined by their bosses may "take it out on" their own subordinates, or may kick their dogs upon returning home. Torgersen and Weinstock (1972) suggest that this defense mechanism is often responsible for feelings of prejudice and discrimination toward minority groups.

Selective Perception. This mechanism, briefly mentioned earlier, is obviously an important part of any discussion of psychological defense mechanisms. Its use as a perceptual defense technique can be illustrated in any number of ways. For example, it has been found by many marketing researchers that purchasers of a product will notice and pay attention to advertisements for that product to a far greater degree than they did prior to purchase; the more expensive the purchase, the more extreme is this tendency. The apparent reason for this is that the purchase, particularly of a major commodity, evokes doubts and second thoughts, creating in the purchaser a need for reassurance which the advertisements provide.

Another illustration results from a study by Dearborn and Simon (1958), who presented corporation executives with a case study and found that almost all of them perceived the problem in terms related to their particular specialty. For example, public relations managers defined the basic problem as one of human relations, while those in the marketing department perceived that the primary concern was in the area of sales.

In another study, Haire (1955) presented business executives and labor leaders with photographs of two men. Half the subjects in each group were told that the first man was a labor official and the second man was a plant manager. The other half of both groups were given the same photographs, but with the descriptions reversed. Haire found that, *no matter which photo was alleged to be the labor official*, labor leaders described the man in very flattering terms, while being far less charitable concerning the man they believed to be the plant manager. The executives, of course, reversed this pattern.

A final illustration is offered by Miner (1973, pp. 401–2):

> A number of studies have been conducted in which laboratory groups have been set in competition with each other on various problem-solving tasks. One finding of these studies is that groups consistently evaluate their own solutions as better and their groups as more effective than others. . . . This result closely parallels the N.I.H. (not invented here) factor long noted in research and development laboratories. . . . N.I.H. refers to the frequent tendency for scientists to view ideas developed outside the organization as inferior, research conducted in other departments as inferior to that in one's own, and others as less competent and creative researchers than oneself.

Principles of Gestalt Psychology

Certain basic principles of perception have emerged from the phenomenological or Gestalt school of psychology. These differ from the processes discussed above in that they are not necessarily aimed at defending the individual from painful and threatening stimuli, although they may serve this function. Whether or not they protect the individual, they influence the way incoming information is interpreted and may cause distortions and inaccuracies in perception. Three principles which relate to the perceiver will be discussed below; two others will be introduced in the discussion pertaining to characteristics of the perceived.

Closure. As a result of the tendency in people to seek "the full picture" of a situation, people often perceive far more than actually exists. Thus the perceiver may fit together very incomplete information to form a whole. The information which is not available from the incoming stimuli is made up and merged with the available information in ways that "make sense," at least to the perceiver, without threatening or disrupting any cherished attitudes, values, or beliefs.

Constancy. This process enables individuals to perceive the world as essentially stable in certain ways, even though the stimuli actually received are constantly fluctuating. For example, "When Jimmy stands but five feet from us and George is fifteen feet from us, then our sense, because of the nature of the physical stimuli, and the angle of view, tell us that Jimmy is larger than George. . . . But we know George to be the adult. . . . Thus we perceive Jimmy to be smaller" (Bobbitt et al., 1974, p. 88).

Expectancy. The concept of expectancy has become one of the most important in all organizational behavior literature, and plays an important part in the dominant motivation and leadership theories in vogue today. In connection with the present discussion, Goethe once observed that "we see only what we know," an allusion to the fact that most individuals tend to perceive what they *expect* to perceive. People carry with them a perceptual *set,* an internal predisposition or readiness to respond to incoming stimuli. A large part of this set is determined by the extent to which the stimuli are familiar. A tremendous amount of research has shown that familiar stimuli are perceived more readily than those which are unfamiliar or which were unexpected. For example, one investigation found that when words were flashed briefly upon a screen, frequently used words were recognized much sooner and more easily than words used infrequently (Scott and Mitchell, 1972). This study has been repeated many times in slightly different ways, with consistent results.

As mentioned, the research literature relating to expectancy is enormous; only two classic studies will be described here. In the first of these, Bruner and Postman (1949) presented subjects with a deck of playing cards whose colorings were the opposite of normal decks; that is, spades and clubs were red, while hearts and diamonds were black. When viewed for only a brief interval, the deck was perceived to be normal; it required a relatively long exposure before many subjects were able to see the cards as they actually were, rather than as they were expected to be.

In the second study Kelley (1950) found that when students were issued biographies of a substitute teacher—biographies which were identical except that half described him as "warm" and half as "cold"—substantial differences resulted both in their subsequent evaluation of him and in their interaction patterns with him. Those who expected the substitute to be warm actually perceived him to be so, and rated him more favorably and interacted with him more as a result.

Advertisers often attempt to employ the expectancy process to their own advantage, as in this description by Ruch (1967, pp. 312–13):

> . . . Advertisers try to build up an expectation of desirable qualities in their products. . . . Cigarette manufacturers make distinctive

> claims for the taste, aroma, and soothing qualities of their particular brand, and habitual smokers profess to have deep-seated preferences for one kind of cigarette over another. Yet "blindfold tests" . . . have shown that relatively few smokers can accurately identify different brands when they cannot see the label (Husband and Godfrey, 1934). The same thing is apparently true of different brands of cola (Pronko and Herman, 1950).

In summary, stimuli which are different in some respect from what was expected will often not be perceived at all or, if perceived, will tend to be interpreted in such a way that they will seem consonant with what was expected.

Attitudes, Needs, and Values

In addition to perceiving what they expect to perceive, people also have a tendency to perceive what they *want* to perceive. For example, it has been shown that objects toward which the perceiver feels positively are recognized far more quickly than objects which evoke neutral or negative feelings (Scott and Mitchell, 1972). Emotionally disturbing or threatening stimuli, on the other hand, not only require a longer time period to be recognized, but also tend to be "so misperceived as radically to alter their form or meaning, and to arouse their characteristic emotional reactions even before they are recognized" (Shull, Delbecq, and Cummings, 1970, p. 47).

In an important early study which showed the influence of the perceiver's needs upon perceptions, Bruner and Goodman (1947) presented ten- and eleven-year-old children with lights whose beams could be adjusted to form circles of different diameters; the children were asked to adjust the size of the beams to represent coins of different sizes, from a penny to a half dollar. In one series children worked from memory, and in another with real coins present. Meanwhile, a control group was following identical procedures with medium-gray cardboard disks which were identical in size to the coins.

In general, they found that the sizes of the more valuable coins were overestimated, while less valuable coins were underestimated. No significant distortions were observed for children working with the cardboard disks. Furthermore, children from a slum area overestimated the size of the coins considerably more than children from prosperous families.

To investigate the possibility that factors other than needs and values were responsible for the Bruner and Goodman findings, Ashley, Harper, and Runyon (1951) hypnotized subjects and then gave them "autobiographies" which included details of their wealth or poverty. It was found that when subjects believed they were wealthy, they set their light circles significantly smaller than they had prior to being hypnotized; when told they were poor, the settings were much larger. Furthermore, even their postures were observed to change, from a careful erect stance when they were "poor" to casual indifference when they were "wealthy."

Other studies (reported by Zimbardo and Ruch, 1975, p. 267) have provided very interesting and consistent evidence for this same point:

> By using a measure of content analysis of children's drawings at different times of the year, investigators have discovered that Santa Claus drawings made before Christmas were bigger than those after the holiday. This was not a general euphoria effect but a "Santa-specific" one since only drawings of Santa got bigger as his coming approached (Solley and Haigh, 1957; Sechrest and Wallace, 1964). In another carefully controlled study, the avoidance motive of fear seems to be implicated in the finding that the average size of drawings of witches *decreased* at Halloween (Craddick, 1967).

These findings suggest that as the need subjects feel for objects increases, the value they place on the objects increases—and the distortion of perceptions connected with the objects increases, as well.

Researchers have also discovered that the more interested a perceiver was in some topic, the quicker the perceiver was able to recognize words related to that topic (Postman, Bruner, and McGinnies, 1948); that experimental subjects who were deliberately frustrated in their attempts at goal attainment perceived pictures of money more often and overestimated the size of money more than subjects who were not frustrated (Knott, 1971); and that subjects who had gone increasingly long periods without food began to perceive more and more associations connected with food (Levine, Chein, and Murphy, 1942). We also know from Ruch (1967, p. 323) that

> Time spent in monotonous work is usually overestimated. Time spent in interesting work is usually underestimated. . . . Judgement of time is related to feelings of success or failure. Subjects who are experiencing failure judge a given interval as longer than do subjects who are experiencing success (Harton, 1939). A given interval of time is also estimated as longer by subjects trying to get through a task in order to reach a desired goal than by subjects working without such motivation.

In addition to the effect of needs and expectancies on perception, it is also important to realize that they interrelate with one another. In this connection, Bruner (1958, p. 94) points out that:

> When we are hungry we tend to be alerted to signs of restaurants. . . . Our "restaurant" category has become highly "available." But we look for and expect restaurants at the street level and not in the sky or atop trees. It is this balancing of need-induced alertness and

event-matching expectancy that makes it possible for perception to act in the service of needs and interests and, at the same time, with due regard for reality.

The implications of attitudes, needs, and values for the study of organizational behavior are enormous and cannot be adequately discussed within the space of this chapter. Rather, as was the case with expectancy, the effects and implications of these factors will be discussed in future chapters as they relate to the setting of objectives, decision making, conflict resolution, motivation, etc. It is probably worth reiterating here, though, that since it is probably true that no two individuals have identical sets of needs and values, the important influence of needs and values on the perceptual process underscores our conclusion that each person perceives a unique, tailor-made "reality." This point is especially worth keeping in mind in future chapters, since it will help explain the developing trends in organizational literature toward situational approaches and away from "one best way" notions.

Halo Effects

It has been observed in a large number of research settings that data which, from a strictly "objective" point of view, should not even be processed is often weighted very highly by the perceiving individual. For example, it has been demonstrated that people whose photographs show them smiling are usually judged to be more honest than those whose photos show them not smiling (Zalkind and Costello, 1969). It has also been found that negative information (about a job applicant, for example) tends to be weighted disproportionately high in comparison with positive information (e.g. Hollman, 1972), and that information which comes from respected, trusted, or favored sources also receives exceedingly high weight in people's perceptions.

Halo effects are those processes whereby perceivers permit knowledge of a single trait or characteristic of a person to shape their impressions of all other attributes of that person. Alternatively, perceivers may have no specific information at all about an individual but only a general impression, which then serves as the basis for forming opinions about specific characteristics of the individual. A halo effect can exist with respect to either positive or negative opinions, but in either case it "serves as a screen keeping the perceiver from actually seeing the trait he is judging" (Zalkind and Costello, 1969, p. 209).

One situation in which halo effects are common is the employee evaluation; here the concern is that the supervisor may allow one job-related characteristic (or, worse yet, one personal characteristic which is not even job-related) to shape the rating of all other characteristics of the subordinate being rated. Zalkind and Costello (1969) describe an Army study in which those officers who were well liked were judged to be more intelligent than those who were disliked, despite the similar average intelligence test scores of each of the two groups.

In another study of halo effects, Asch (1946) presented subjects with identical personality descriptions of two individuals, except that one trait was described differently. He found that this single trait largely overshadowed all of the others, such that subjects perceived very different attributes in the two individuals described.

There is some limited evidence that halo effects tend to be most severe when the characteristics being evaluated are associated with morality or immorality, when the evaluator has little knowledge or experience in the areas under evaluation (Bruner and Taguiri, 1954), and when the evaluation is of someone well known to the evaluator (Symonds, 1925).

Characteristics of the Situation Which Influence Perception

Influence of What Is Perceived

Considerable research has been concerned with how various characteristics of what is perceived, whether object, event, or person, affect people's perceptions. As was mentioned earlier, complete information about what is perceived is never available, and so the perceiver must improvise to fill in the gaps. Toward this end substitutes for full information—cues, tests, hints, expressive gestures, status symbols (Goffman, 1959)—are employed as predictive devices, to permit the perceiver to know in advance what is likely to happen. In practice, of course, the perceiver is unlikely to "know" what will happen, because the improvisation of facts is subject to all of the biases and distortions discussed above.

As was also mentioned earlier, certain incoming stimuli may be overrelied upon and weighted disproportionately high, due to characteristics of the perceiver. This may be particularly true when another individual is the object of perception. For example, in various cultures a person's race, religion, or occupation may be important characteristics that determine others' perceptions of the individual (Triandis and Triandis, 1965). Thibaut and Riecken (1955) found that an individual's status can be an important determinant; other studies have shown that age, sex, skin color, and apparent mood and manner can also substantially affect a person's overall impressions of another person.

The order in which information is received has been found by many researchers to be critically important to the overall perception. There are a number of cases where information perceived first tends to be assigned the greatest weight; this has been labeled as a *primacy effect.* At other times a *recency effect* may result in dominance by the data received last.

Two principles of Gestalt psychology are pertinent to the topic. These are discussed here because, unlike the three Gestalt principles mentioned earlier, they are defined specifically in terms of characteristics of what is perceived. The first of these is *proximity,* whereby stimuli which are close together in space or time tend to become associated with one another such that they are perceived as belonging together. In fact, perception of any one of several closely grouped stimuli may act as a cue upon the perceiver, such that a single stimulus may evoke an image of all of them.

Just as there is a tendency to see closely grouped objects as belonging together, there is a likelihood that stimuli which are alike will be perceived as being part of a common group. Luthans (1973) illustrates this tendency by pointing out that minority group members who are alike in religion, race, or skin color may be perceived (say, by management) as comprising a single unit, with similar goals, complaints, etc. Female employees may also be perceived as being part of a common group, and individual differences among them virtually ignored. This Gestalt principle, called *similarity,* may affect perceptions both of objects and of individuals.

With regard to perceiving an object, Luthans (1973) has summarized some of the experimental results concerning the effects on perception of intensity, size, contrast, repetition, motion, novelty, and familiarity of a stimulus:

> The intensity principle of attention states that the more intense the external stimulus, the more likely it will be perceived. . . . The larger the object, the more likely it will be perceived. . . . External stimuli which stand out against the background or which are not what the person is accustomed to perceiving will receive his attention. . . . A repeated external stimulus is more attention-getting than a single one. . . . A person will pay more attention to moving objects in his field of vision than he will to stationary objects. . . . Either a novel or familiar external situation can serve as an attention-getter. New objects or events in a familiar setting or familiar objects or events in a new setting will draw the attention of the perceiver (pp. 339–42).

The reader can probably think of many applications of these principles to such organizationally-relevant problems as advertising, job design, and training.

Influence of the Situational Context

The context of a stimulus or the situation in which it is perceived is an important determinant of how the stimulus will be interpreted. Of course, the situational context does not always serve as an aid to accuracy; it can be beneficial on the one hand, or so misleading as to increase distortion on the other.

One process that is critical for integrating a stimulus and its surroundings is related to the principle of *embeddedness.* Ambiguous words, for example, take on specific meanings when placed in sentences which give them contexts. A physical object may appear to have different properties in different surroundings. Regarding social perception, "it is the surrounding situation which makes it possible to determine the motivations and intentions that lie behind a specific overt behavior" (Heider, 1967, p. 316).

One extremely important situational factor involves the concept of *role.* Role refers simply to the parts played by individuals, whether in organizations or in society. All organizations and societies establish social rules, called *norms,* which define expected behavior for role incumbents. Norms tell us what role incumbents must, can, and cannot do in certain situations. Based upon what we have seen earlier about expectations, it is easy to understand how a person's expectations regarding roles and norms can affect perception.

But roles and norms also affect the perceiver; while not necessarily legally punishable, nonconformity to norms is almost always punished by the group. Such punishment most often takes the form of loss of prestige, friendship, and cooperation. While these are not necessarily severe punishment when coming from irrelevant outsiders, when the *reference group*—that group of people with which a person relates or identifies (Litterer, 1973)—threatens loss of friendship, it can be a strong pressure for conformity. Thus, as Litterer states, reference groups are "one of the key influences in forming attitudes, absorbing values, and obtaining interpretation—in short, in forming perceptions. . . ." (p. 107).

The literature pertaining to the importance of group influence in determining perceptions is voluminous; it is obviously impossible to provide a comprehensive review here. Later chapters will deal with roles, norms, and reference groups as they relate to an individual's perceptions of others in conflict and problem-solving situations and to individual perceptions of organizational rewards, task-difficulty, and organizational change. A few of the classic experiments relating to these topics will be reviewed here, however.

In one experiment Asch (1951) asked each of eight group members to publicly announce their judgment concerning which of three lines a fourth line was most equal to in size. Unbeknownst to the eighth member in each group, all other members had met previously with the experimenter and had agreed to incorrectly "judge" the sets of lines. The experiment's object was to investigate the effects of this situation upon the eighth person's perceptions.

In general, Asch found a definite movement away from the objectively obvious choices toward the incorrect choices voiced by the majority in the group. However, despite the felt pressure to conform, the majority of estimates (typically about two-thirds) made by the eighth member of each group were correct. As might be expected, individual differences among subjects were extreme. In follow-up interviews Asch found that most of those individuals who went along with the majority experienced *distortion of judgment,* whereby they decided that their perceptions (which were in fact correct) must be incorrect. A few individuals suffered *distortion of per-*

ception under the stress of group pressure; they actually "saw" the majority's choice as correct.

Subsequent experiments involving *two* naive subjects within each group of eight revealed that subjects experienced significantly less pressure to go along with the majority, now that the majority was not a unanimous one. However, incorrect judgments by naive subjects were still more prevalent than in control groups where the majority's judgments were correct.

In a related experiment, Bovard (1951) found that individual perceptions of objective stimuli by members of a unit which was "group-centered"—that is, which encouraged group discussion and participation—shifted much more in the direction of the group's consensual norms than did individual perceptions among members of a comparatively autocratic, "leader-centered" unit. Other researchers have also discovered that the friendliness of climate and presence or absence of opportunities for interaction have an important influence upon perceptions. It is known, for example, that when people are given an opportunity to interact in what is defined as a friendly situation, they have a tendency to see other people as similar to themselves. If, therefore, situations can be created which are cooperative rather than competitive, the likelihood that people will perceive others as similar to themselves will increase (Zalkind and Costello, 1969). This is important, since there are data indicating that people are attracted to those they perceive as similar to themselves (Scott and Mitchell, 1972).

Overall, this sketchy view of some research pertinent to the question of group influences upon perception reveals a great many individual and situational differences, but it also shows a strong constant trend across the various experiments for perceptions to be substantially affected by norms, reference groups, and other facets of the situational context within which perceptions occur.

Conclusions

We stated at the outset of this chapter that most human beings experience a variety of difficulties in attempting to "objectively" process incoming stimuli, and that biases and distortions in perceptions typically ensue. We added, however, that these biases and distortions are for the most part systematic, so it is possible both to explain and to predict human perceptions. Unfortunately, to do so we must know a good deal more than simply the objective "facts" pertinent to the person, object, or event.

The reader may have noticed that the space allocated in this chapter to characteristics of the perceiver far exceeded that spent on attributes of the person or object perceived. While perhaps an uncomfortable reminder, such treatment is consistent with claims voiced elsewhere that, for example, the hire-no hire decision may be better predicted from knowledge of the interviewer than of the person being interviewed, or that information about jury members is more useful in forecasting a verdict than is testimony from the trial itself.

We have discussed a wide variety of influences upon the perceiver and characteristics of the perceived and of the situation which are important in shaping and maintaining perceptions. Perhaps most important of all of these are two forces which act upon the perceiver—expectancies and needs. This may be why social scientists, apparently without due concern for the "real" situation, so often express interest in the expectations and aspirations of their clients and their subjects. This is certainly the reason why later chapters in this book will show continued concern for these concepts. Value/expectancy theory, for example, is one of the important motivation theories discussed in Chapter 10, and the influences of expectations and aspirations upon responsiveness to change are shown in Chapter 20 to be considerable.

The summary point to be made in the present chapter is that, by focusing attention on individual expectations and aspirations, and also by considering the stimuli themselves and the situational context within which they are perceived, we shall be better able to understand the complexities and intricacies of human perception.

References

Asch, S. E. 1946. Forming impressions of personalities. *Journal of Abnormal and Social Psychology* 41: 258–90.

———. 1951. Effects of group pressure upon the modification and distortion of judgments. In *Groups, leadership, and men,* ed. by H. Guetzkow. Carnegie Press.

Ashley, W. R.; Harper, R. S.; and Runyon, D. L. 1951. The perceived size of coins in normal and hypnotically induced economic states. *American Journal of Psychology* 64: 564–72.

Bobbitt, H. R. Jr.; Breinholt, R. H.; Doktor, R. H.; and McNaul, J. P. 1974. *Organizational behavior: Understanding and prediction.* Prentice-Hall.

Bovard, E. W., Jr., 1951. Group structure and decision. *Journal of Abnormal and Social Psychology* 46: 398–405.

Bruner, J. S. 1958. Social psychology and perception. In *Readings in social psychology,* ed. by E. E. Maccoby, T. M. Newcomb, and E. L. Hartley. Holt, Rinehart and Winston.

———. 1967. On perceptual readiness. In *Current perspectives in social psychology,* ed. by E. P. Hollander and R. G. Hunt. Oxford University Press.

———., and Goodman, C. 1947. Value and need as organizing factors in perception. *Journal of Abnormal and Social Psychology* 42: 33–44.

———., and Postman, L. 1949. On the perception of incongruity: A paradigm. *Journal of Personality* 18: 206–223.

———., and Taguiri, A. 1954. The perception of people. In *Handbook of social psychology,* ed. by G. Lindzey. Addison-Wesley.

Craddick, R. A. 1967. Size of witch drawings as a function of time before, on, and after Halloween. *American Psychologist* 17: 307.

Dearborn, D. C., and Simon, H. A. 1958. Selective perception: A note on departmental identification of executives. *Sociometry* 21: 142.

Goffman, E. 1959. *The presentation of self in everyday life*. Doubleday-Anchor.

Haire, M. 1955. Role perceptions in labor-management relations: An experimental approach. *Industrial and Labor Relations Review* 8: 204–16.

———., and Grunes, W. F. 1950. Perceptual defenses: Processes protecting an organized perception of another personality. *Human Relations* 3: 403–12.

Harton, J. J. 1939. An investigation of the influence of success and failure on the estimation of time. *Journal of General Psychology* 21: 51–62.

Heider, F. 1967. Perceiving the other person. In *Current perspectives in social psychology*, ed. by E. P. Hollander and R. G. Hunt. Oxford University Press.

Hellriegel, D., and Slocum, J. W., Jr. 1974. *Management: A contingency approach*. Addison-Wesley.

Hollman, T. D. 1972. Employment interviewer's errors in processing positive and negative information. *Journal of Applied Psychology* 56: 130–34.

Husband, R. W., and Godfrey, J. 1934. An experimental study of cigarette identification. *Journal of Applied Psychology* 18: 220–23.

Huse, E. F., and Bowditch, J. L. 1973. *Behavior in organizations: A systems approach to managing*. Addison-Wesley.

Kast, F. E., and Rosenzweig, J. E. 1974. *Organization and management: A systems approach*, 2nd ed. McGraw-Hill.

Kelley, H. H. 1950. The warm-cold variable in first impressions by people. *Journal of Personality* 18: 431–39.

Knott, P. D. 1971. Effects of frustration and magnitude of reward in selective attention, size estimation, and verbal evaluation. *Journal of Personality* 39: 378–90.

Levine, R.; Chein, I.; and Murphy, G. 1942. The relation of the intensity of a need to the amount of perceptual distortion: A preliminary report. *Journal of Psychology* 13: 283–93.

Litterer, J. A. 1973. *The analysis of organizations*. Wiley.

Luthans, F. 1973. *Organizational behavior*. McGraw-Hill.

Miner, J. B. 1973. *The management process: Theory, research, and practice*. Macmillan.

Murray, H. A. 1933. The effect of fear upon estimates of the maliciousness of other personalities. *Journal of Social Psychology* 4: 310–29.

Postman, L.; Bruner, J.; and McGinnies, E. 1948. Personal values as selective factors in perception. *Journal of Abnormal and Social Psychology* 43: 142–54.

Pronko, N. H., and Herman, D. T. 1950. Identification of cola beverages: IV. Postscript. *Journal of Applied Psychology* 34: 68–69.

Ruch, F. L. 1967. *Psychology and life*, 7th ed. Scott, Foresman.

Russell, B. 1962. *The ABC of relativity*. New American Library.

Scott, W. G., and Mitchell, T. R. 1972. *Organization theory: A structural and behavioral analysis*. Irwin.

Sears, R. R. 1936. Experimental studies of perception, I. Attribution of traits. *Journal of Social Psychology* 7: 151–63.

Sechrest, L. B., and Wallace, J. 1964. Figure drawing and naturally occurring events: Elimination of the expansive euphoria hypothesis. *Journal of Educational Psychology* 55: 42–44.

Shull, F. A., Jr.; Delbecq, A. L.; and Cummings, L. L. 1970. *Organizational decision making.* McGraw-Hill.

Solley, C. M., and Haigh, G. A. 1957. A note to Santa Claus. *Topical Research Papers, The Menninger Foundation* 18: 4–5.

Symonds, P. M. 1925. Notes on rating. *Journal of Applied Psychology* 7: 188–95.

Thibaut, J. W., and Riecken, H. W. 1955. Some determinants and consequences of the perception of social causality. *Journal of Personality* 24: 113–33.

Torgerson, P. E., and Weinstock, I. T. 1972. *Management: An integrated approach.* Prentice-Hall.

Triandis, H. C., and Triandis, L. M. 1965. Some studies of social distance. In *Current perspectives in social psychology,* ed. by I. Steiner and M. Fishbein. Holt, Rinehart and Winston.

Zalkind, S. S., and Costello, T. W. 1969. Perception: Some recent research and implications for administration. In *Readings in organizational behavior and human performance,* ed. by L. L. Cummings and W. E. Scott. Irwin.

Zimbardo, P. G., and Ruch, F. L. 1975. *Psychology and life,* 9th ed. Scott, Foresman.

Chapter 5
Learning

Miss Trutwell: "Don't fatherize, please, Mr. Archer."
Archer: "Why not? I don't believe people know everything at birth and forget it as they get older."

ROSS MACDONALD
The Goodbye Look

Learning is usually defined to be a relatively permanent change in behavior which occurs as a result of practice. Kimble (1969, p. 94) points out that (1) by restricting learning to relatively permanent changes, modifications of behavior that are due to motivational factors, sensory adaptation, and fatigue are excluded, and (2) the emphasis upon practice is designed to rule out behavioral changes resulting from maturation or from physiological variables. However, we should not think of practice as requiring a "complete rehearsal of the response ultimately to be performed. Otherwise it would be impossible to learn anything from maps, demonstrations, books, or lectures" (Kimble, p. 96).

This definition points out a major barrier to understanding and studying learning:

> It is impossible to observe directly the process that we call learning. The fact that learning has occurred can only be inferred from a comparison of an individual's behavior prior to and subsequent to experiences of specific kinds. This is not to say that there has been no "learning" if there is no overt behavioral change, but this cannot be *known* unless there *is* a behavioral change (McCormick and Tiffin, 1974, p. 224).

Because of this difficulty, some students of learning believe we can only provide *descriptions* of learning (which do not refer to or depend upon unobservables) rather than theories of learning (which do). As B. F. Skinner (1950, p. 193) writes, a theory is "any explanation of an observed fact which appeals to events taking place somewhere else, at some other level of observation, described in different terms, and measured, if at all, in different dimensions." Theories of learning, then, as we will see later in this chapter, ascribe learning to events (expectations, cortical activity, etc.) within the individual, or to some combination of events within the environment and the individual.

After discussing some of the more important descriptions and theories of learning, their importance and implications for the practice of management will be reviewed.

Descriptions of Learning

Descriptions of learning typically explain behavior changes in terms of environmental *stimuli* and specific acts of behavior called *responses.* Some relationships involve antecedent stimuli and subsequent responses, and are termed S-R descriptions; others deal with coinciding stimuli and responses, where behavior changes are ascribed to the contiguity of S and R. Many students of learning believe that what is "learned" in such cases are the connections between various stimuli and accompanying responses. From this viewpoint, responses which have occurred frequently and recently will have a tendency to recur if the same stimulus is again encountered; the concept of reinforcement is not crucial to this explanation.

Other behavioralists, however, view reinforcers as an essential component of the learning process. To them "the point is that practice *alone* does not produce learning, but only fatigue or extinction" (Kimble, 1969, p. 95; these terms will be defined shortly). They would redefine learning to be a relatively permanent change in behavior which occurs as a result of *reinforced* practice.

Classical and Operant Conditioning Descriptions

There are two fundamental forms of learning that are known as conditioning. The first, *classical conditioning,* was discovered in a series of experiments by the Russian physiologist Pavlov. Pavlov blew meat powder into a dog's mouth and recorded the animal's salivary response. At first the dog would salivate only when the food was placed in his mouth. After several trials, however, the animal began to salivate at the sight of the food, even before it was placed in his mouth. After more trials the dog began to salivate at the sight of the food dish, and after still more trials at the sound of his trainer's approaching footsteps. Furthermore, after many trials during which a bell was rung immediately before the food was placed in the dog's mouth, the ringing of the bell produced the salivary response *even when no food was present.* Pavlov called the food in the dog's mouth an *unconditioned stimulus,* which produced the *unconditioned response* of salivation. The bell, then, by virtue of its connection with the unconditioned stimulus, became a *conditioned stimulus,* which caused the *conditioned response* of salivating when the bell was rung, in the absence of food (Zimbardo and Ruch, 1975).

Most forms of learning are more complicated than classical conditioning. While classical conditioning depends upon *prior* stimulation, *instrumental* or *operant conditioning* features a delay in presenting the unconditioned stimulus until the subject makes the desired response. The unconditioned stimulus is, then, the reinforcer which affects the rate of subsequent responses. In simple terms, "if the outcome is pleasing to the individual, the probability of his repeating the response is apt to be increased. If the consequence is displeasing to the individual, the probability of his repeating the response is apt to be decreased. The process of inducing such change (usually an increase) in the response rate, is called operant conditioning" (Nord, 1969). The task which confronts those who would attempt operant conditioning is therefore "to manipulate carefully various environmental dimensions and examine their differential effects on individual behavior" (Jablonsky and DeVries, 1972, p. 341).

Some differences between classical (respondent) and instrumental (operant) conditioning are described by Lundin (1961, p. 60):

> Respondent conditioning involves a response elicited by a given stimulus. In this sense, it is "pulled out." In operant conditioning, we do not know the original stimulus that causes the response. Once it occurs, however, we are in a position to bring the response under control. We "set the occasion" for the response. . . . In respondent, the response is strengthened by pairing the reinforcer with a given neutral stimulus. In operant conditioning, the reinforcement is contingent upon the response.

The concept of reinforcement, referred to by Lundin above, is worth closer examination. A *reinforcer* is said to be any object or event which succeeds in increasing or maintaining the strength of a response (Bass and Vaughan, 1966). A distinction between classical (sometimes called Pavlovian) reinforcement and instrumental (operant) reinforcement is offered by Skinner (1963, p. 210):

> Pavlov himself called all events which strengthened behavior "reinforcement" and all the resulting changes "conditioning." In the Pavlovian experiment, however, a reinforcer is paired with a *stimulus;* whereas in operant behavior it is contingent upon a *response*. . . . In operant conditioning we "strengthen" an operant in the sense of making a response more probable or in actual fact more frequent. In Pavlovian or "respondent" conditioning we simply increase the magnitude of the response elicited by the conditioned stimulus and shorten the time which elapses between stimulus and response.

A classic experiment on reinforcement was conducted by E. L. Thorndike, who placed a hungry cat in a box from which he could escape by pressing a lever, and who was rewarded with food when he did escape. Numerous repetitions of the experiment resulted in shorter and shorter time periods being necessary for the animal to escape. Although Thorndike contended that trial-and-error learning rather than thought processes were involved, the cat "solved its problem as well as if it were a 'reasoning' human being, though perhaps not so speedily" (Skinner, 1963, p. 207).

Thorndike concluded that the cat's behavior (pressing the lever) was "stamped in" by the activities (door-opening, food-obtaining) which followed, and proposed what he called the *Law of Effect:*

> Of several responses made to the same situation, those which are accompanied or closely followed by satisfaction to the animal will, other things being equal, be more firmly connected with the situation (Thorndike, 1911, p. 244).

In a similar vein, Thorndike pointed out that responses which are followed closely by discomfort will be less likely to recur.

Although rewards are often reinforcers, as used in the classical and instrumental conditioning literature the terms are not synonymous. A reinforcer is defined in terms of its effects upon a response, and not with regard to its pleasantness or aversiveness to the individual. Specifically, people are rewarded, but only responses are reinforced. One might presume that an individual has been reinforced because an apparently pleasant stimulus has been given either prior to or as a consequence of a certain response. However, unless a change in the relationship between S and R results, that is, unless subsequent presentation of the stimulus elicits the response or unless the rate of response increases, no reinforcement can be said to have occurred.

Two interesting examples which illustrate some of the concepts we have been discussing are presented below; both of these involve *counterconditioning,* which is especially useful in ridding the subject of some undesirable response.

> Higgins is an affable four-year-old Old English Sheep Dog of Goliath proportions whose tranquil demeanor was breached only by an intense fear of thunderstorms. At the first indication of an impending storm, Higgins would begin an accelerating pattern of aimless pacing, profuse salivation, and marked panting which was rapidly climaxed by the hurling of his 110-pound body against any obstacle in a futile attempt to escape. A variety of confinement procedures and tranquilizers had been tried without success. . . . The crisis that threatened the relationship between Higgins and his petite owner occurred when they were forced to share the owner's foreign sportscar during a thunderstorm. . . .
>
> Having satisfied ourselves that a stereophonic reproduction of a thunderstorm would elicit the fear—Higgins actually overwhelmed the three people in the room with him—the stimulus situation was presented in graded steps. . . . Beginning at an intensity that did not evoke the fear, Higgins was brought under command to lie down, and the subsequent

> occurrence of thunder was paired with a food reward of chocolate bars. As long as Higgins remained calm . . . the intensity of the recreated, artificial storm was gradually increased. . . . Over the course of the first five conditioning sessions we had progressed from a thunder intensity level of a meager 35 decibels to that of a resounding 75 decibels when a typical summer thunderstorm intervened to test our efforts. Happily, the owner reported that Higgins initially exhibited only a mild version of the original fear response, that he was easily brought under control, and that she was able to successfully practice the training as we had done in the laboratory (Tuber, Hothersall, and Voith, 1974, pp. 762–63).

> One of the "cures" for drinking involves this process. A person has previously acquired the drinking habit. He is then presented with his beloved beverage (conditioned stimulus) along with some substance called an *emetic* (unconditioned stimulus) which has the properties of causing nausea. The vomiting response (unconditioned response) is unlearned and is naturally called out by the noxious substance. Through pairing of the nauseating substance with the liquor, eventually the liquor takes on the function of eliciting nausea (conditioned response) (Lundin, 1961, p. 53).

As is true of counterconditioning, instrumental conditioning (control of operant responding) can also be useful in the modification of behavior, particularly in the case of human behavior, which is predominantly of the operant type. The following is an interesting example of instrumental (operant) conditioning:

> The purpose of this research was to determine the effect of a verbal reinforcement introduced immediately following a plural noun response on the frequency of plural noun responses.
>
> . . . in the case of the experimental group, immediately after each plural noun response the verbal reinforcement, "Mmm-hmmm," was introduced by the experimenter. No reinforcement was introduced for the control group.
>
> . . . it was found that the experimental group gave a significantly larger number of plural nouns than the control group. None of the experimental subjects was able to verbalize any change in his behavior (Greenspoon, 1966, p. 460).

A characteristic often encountered in conditioning is called *generalization.* This occurs when the subject perceives some new stimulus to be very similar to one which has previously produced some response. The subject "generalizes" from the old to the new stimulus, to the extent that the new stimulus elicits the same response that was elicited by the old one. Thus a person may be thrown by a large, untrained horse while learning to ride, and subsequently be frightened at the sight of all horses, however small and tame. *Discrimination,* the opposite process, may serve to combat generalization, as when the person begins to recognize that only from untrained horses are falls probable, and only from large ones are falls likely to hurt. In the absence of discrimination "we would constantly be calling people by the wrong names, eating improper kinds of food, and generally making a variety of inappropriate responses" (Lundin, 1961, p. 103).

Another characteristic pertinent to conditioning is *extinction,* which relates to the fact that if the conditioned response stops being reinforced, eventually the subject stops making that response. Pavlov showed, for example, that it was possible to eliminate an already-formed conditioned response (salivating when the bell was rung) by repeatedly presenting the conditioned stimulus (the bell) without the unconditioned stimulus (the food). While this is an example of classical extinction, the concept is equally relevant to instrumental conditioning, as is evident from Skinner's remark (1963, p. 212) that "if we lose a fountain pen, we reach less and less often into the pocket which formerly held it. If we get no answer to telephone calls, we eventually stop telephoning. If our piano goes out of tune, we gradually play it less and less. If our radio becomes noisy or if programs become worse, we stop listening."

The subject's behavior during the extinction period depends upon the nature of the conditioning which precedes it. If relatively few responses had been reinforced prior to extinction, extinction will normally occur quickly. On the other hand, a long history of prior reinforcement will usually succeed in delaying extinction for some time. As Skinner (1963, p. 213) points out, "we must know the history of reinforcement. For example, though we have been reinforced by an excellent meal in a new restaurant, a bad meal may reduce our patronage to zero; but if we have found excellent food in a restaurant for many years, several poor meals must be eaten there, other things being equal, before we lose the inclination to patronize it again."

Important research conducted by Skinner, among others, has shown that other things besides the number of previous reinforcements influence the speed of extinction. Behaviors acquired under *partial reinforcement,* for example, where reinforcement only occasionally follows the response, tend to continue for longer periods of time once positive reinforcement is stopped than do behaviors acquired under *continuous reinforcement,* where reinforcement is given on each conditioning trial. This is true for both instrumental and classical conditioning, and:

> . . . is especially likely when the extinction period involves not only extinction of the learned response but acquisition of a new one to replace it. Subjects required to reverse a habit—responding positively to black and negatively to white, for example, instead of the other way around, as previously—are able to do so more quickly if the original habit was learned with continuous reinforcement than if it was learned with intermittent reinforcement. . . . (Ruch, 1967, p. 189).

Differences in extinction patterns may also be attributable to whether the reinforcement schedule is *fixed-interval* (where the reinforcement is presented for the first response occurring after a specified time period) or *variable-interval* (where the interval is randomly varied around some given time value), *fixed-ratio* (where reinforcement is given after a certain number of responses) or *variable-ratio* (where the number of responses required for a reinforcement varies around some average ratio). Some of the consequences of the reinforcement schedule chosen for extinction are presented by Lundin (1961, pp. 81–93):

—Under fixed-interval reinforcement, the extinction follows a smoother and regular rate of responding compared to that found during extinction in regular reinforcement; the behavior tends to be more resistant to extinction.
—Under variable-interval reinforcement, extinction characteristics are similar to those under fixed-interval extinction. In the early stages of extinction the behavior will be maintained at approximately the same rate as occurred during conditioning. Extinction is generally slow to take place.
—Under fixed-ratio reinforcement, extinction is characterized by a continuation of the response rate at a high level, followed by a rather abrupt stopping of behavior. As compared to fixed-interval extinction, fixed-ratio extinction is sudden and rather complete.
—Under variable-ratio reinforcement, extinction behavior is similar to that found under fixed-ratio. Sustained runs of responses will be interrupted by pauses, which become longer as extinction becomes more complete.

It should be clear that the timing and type of reinforcement schedule employed can have important effects for the behavior of individuals within organizations. Some of the implications of utilizing one reinforcement schedule as opposed to another will be considered later in this chapter.

Extinction should not be confused with *forgetting*, although the apparent results of the two processes may be the same. Extinction concerns the weakening of behavior as a result of stopping reinforcement while, so far as we know, forgetting concerns a loss of conditioning due to the passage of time. However, this is not to imply that forgetting is simply a passive process; rather, we may say that conditioning is subject to the *law of interference*, whereby conditioned responses may be weakened or inhibited by new learning which interferes with them (Dethier and Stellar, 1964, p. 85). This interference is often referred to as *retroactive inhibition*.

If we use the term retroactive inhibition to refer to instances when new learning interferes with prior learning, it is also true that sometimes prior learning interferes with an individual's ability to learn new materals. This phenomenon is called *proactive inhibition*, and can be illustrated by the following problem:

> You have just purchased a car, and wish to test it on a hill which is exactly one mile up and one mile down. You would like to average 60 miles per hour for the two mile trip but, due to the steepness of the hill, can only average 30 for the first mile. How fast will you have to come down the hill so as to average 60 for the two miles?

Most people reason that, since they've already done one mile at 30 mph, and since they must do the two mile trip at 60, they must do the second mile at 90 mph. After all, $30 + 90 = 120$, and $120 \div 2 = 60$, right? Haven't you done many problems like that in high school?

Well, you probably have *not* done many problems like that at all and, for that matter, 90 is not the correct answer. The correct way to attack the problem is to ask yourself: "How many minutes have I to do the two miles, so as to average 60 mph?" Clearly, the answer to that is two minutes, since two miles in two minutes equals 60 miles in 60 minutes. But you've already used up your two minutes just getting up the hill! Therefore, there is *no* speed for the second mile which will achieve your goal. (Incidentally, one mile at 30 mph and one at 90 mph yields an average of only 45 mph.)

If you tried to answer this problem by employing a $30 + 90 = 120$, $120 \div 2 = 60$ formula, and if you are *still* convinced that the book must be wrong (since, damn it, $30 + 90 = 120$ and $120 \div 2 = 60$), then you are probably the victim of proactive inhibition because, had you not learned to solve somewhat similar problems in a certain way, you would have been more likely to attack the problem correctly.

As was the case with extinction, the rate and extent of forgetting is influenced by a number of factors. Some of these are described by Ruch (1967, pp. 211–14 and 248–52):

- –The level of retention for "meaningful" material is higher than for material which is not meaningful, such as nonsense syllables.
- –In general motor learning, such as ball playing or roller skating, is more permanent than verbal learning.
- –Determination to recall material is often a significant factor in an individual's success at remembering.
- –Length of time to learn is another important factor, for both nonsense syllables and motor learning. Fast learners show more reminiscence over periods of a few days to a few weeks, but slow learners remember more than fast learners over periods of a few months.
- –Forgetting is much quicker and easier for materials which were originally learned only partially or incompletely.
- –Meaningful organization of the learned material decreases forgetting.
- –The more agreement there is between the material that is learned and the individual's own attitudes and beliefs, the longer and more clearly it will be remembered.

Extinction should also not be confused with *punishment*, a term which often is defined in very ambiguous ways. Azrin and Holz (1966, p. 381) consider punishment to be "*a consequence of behavior that reduces the future probability of that behavior.* Stated more fully, *punishment is a reduction of the future probability of a specific response as a result of the immediate delivery of a stimulus;* the entire process is designated as *punishment.*"

Although extinction and punishment both concern reducing the probability of a response, punishment generates more potential by-products than does extinction, and has more negative consequences. Nord (1969) discusses some of these:

> First, the probability of the response may be reduced only when the threat of punishment is perceived to exist. Thus, when the punishing agent is away, the undesired response may occur at its initial rate. Secondly, punishment only serves to reduce the probability of the one response. This outcome does not necessarily produce the desired response. . . . A third effect, is that the punishment may interfere with the response being made under desired circumstances. . . . There are some other important by-products of punishment. Punishment may result in a person making responses which are incompatible with the punished response. Psychological tension, often manifested in emotional behavior such as fear or anxiety, is often the result. Secondly, punishment may lead to avoidance and dislike of the punishing agent. . . . Finally, punishment may generate counter-aggression.

All of us are familiar with instances where behavior *increased* rather than decreased in rate, even though it was followed consistently by what certainly seemed to be unpleasant consequences. What explanation is there for a child who is administered an aversive stimulus as a consequence for using obscene language, and who uses such language to an even greater extent after being "punished" (Costello and Zalkind, 1963, p. 215)? The answer may be that the child is actually being reinforced by the parental attention which accompanies the attempted punishment. The problem faced by the child's parents in such a case is not unlike that found in many industrial contexts, where a would-be punishment of a worker by a supervisor is followed by the reinforcing attention of the punished individual's fellow workers (Jablonsky and DeVries, 1972). In such cases ignoring rather than seeking to punish the child's language (or the worker's behavior) might be a more effective solution, in that the result could well be extinction.

According to Walters and Cheyne (1969, p. 228), punishment is most likely to be effective in the following circumstances:

- When a physical punishment occurs very early in the response sequence.
- When the physical punishment is intense.
- When a warm relationship between the punisher and the one being

punished has previously been established.

—When physical and verbal punishment are combined and administered early in the response sequence, and when the physical punishment is relatively intense.

—When verbal punishment and very weak physical punishment are combined and administered late in the response sequence.

Cognitive Theories

While the stimulus-response descriptions reviewed above provide clear, precise answers to questions involving basic learning occurrences, critics have long maintained that learning is often much more complex than such descriptions seem to recognize. Cognitive theorists believe that learning is a process which involves the individual's total personality.

> For example, they note that learning may occur simply by thinking about a problem. . . . They reject the theory that learning occurs by the building up, bit by bit, of established S-R connections. They look at the phenomen of insight, long-coming or instantaneous. To them, "the whole is more than the sum of the parts" (Margulies and Raia, 1972, p. 87).

To cognitive theorists, "the significant process in learning is the acquisition of *information* (including abstract concepts and generalizations) rather than of specific *responses*" (Zimbardo and Ruch, 1975, p. 110).

One of the most important cognitive theorists was E. C. Tolman who, although less concerned than some with conscious perceptual experiences, believed that overall patterns and relationships were vitally important to learning. To Tolman, learning involved changes in *cognition* as a result of individual experiences. These cognitions were thought to stem from individual perceptions of the environment.

Tolman's view of the learning process is described by Zimbardo and Ruch (1975, p. 110) as follows:

> . . . organisms learn to expect an environment organized in meaningful patterns. They learn that some stimuli are signs that certain events will follow or are usually associated with other stimuli; thus stimuli not only function as response elicitors but also supply information, as cues or signs. These signs are part of a whole pattern that includes memories from past experiences as well as data from current perceptions. Thus learned behavior is not merely the automatic, blind emission of responses that have been associated with particular stimuli and reward patterns in the past. Rather, learned behavior always involves implicit and explicit goals and also hypotheses and expectations about how to achieve them. Thus learning is purposive and rationally directed.

In sum, cognitive learning theories may be said to place far greater emphasis than stimulus-response descriptions upon purposiveness and upon analytical and perceptual processes such as reasoning and problem solving. This emphasis upon purposiveness, goals, and expectations will be shown in Chapter 10 to be the basis for one of the most important theories of motivation, value/expectancy theory.

Determinants of Learning

A number of factors are influential in determining the extent to which learning will normally occur. Some of these include: motivation to learn, knowledge of results, existence of prior learning, the form in which material to be learned is presented, and type of practice periods provided.

Motivation to Learn. Considerable research shows that people's determination to learn is an important factor in the degree to which learning actually takes place. It may therefore be said that the most favorable time to teach another person something is when some need exists to know the new material; Watson (1972, p. 239) observes in this connection that "much that is now taught children might be more effective if taught to responsible adults."

It is obvious, with reference to what was said earlier, that the kind and amount of rewards and punishments available to the teacher for use on the student will, through their effect on the learner's motivation to learn, influence the rate at which learning will occur.

Knowledge of Results. There is also a great deal of evidence that learning is enhanced by provision of feedback about the learner's performance. Summaries of the research which has been conducted in this area have been prepared by Mosel (1958), Ammons (1956), Annett (1968), Welford (1968), and others. From these summaries, the following general conclusions about the consequences of providing or failing to provide knowledge of results can be stated:

—Although there are occasions when merely being exposed to or becoming familiar with the learning situation and materials will result in learning, in general learning cannot take place without knowledge of results. It has been suggested by Sir Frederick Bartlett that "it is not practice but practice *the results of which are known* that makes perfect." Knowledge of results almost always increases both the speed of learning and the total amount learned.

—If justified, negative as well as positive feedback will benefit learning; generally speaking, however, positive feedback will be more effective.

—Knowledge of results should be presented the learner in as specific a form as possible. The more specific the feedback, the greater will be both the speed of learning and total amount learned. Needless to say, feedback should be pertinent to the task at hand.

—Rather than consisting merely of broad measures of achievement or of a general reminder of the goal, the information fed back should make the learner aware of the gap between what was intended and what was achieved.

In sum, knowledge of results aids the learning process by serving as a correction device, furnishing individuals with the *ability* to improve, and also serving as a powerful positive reinforcer, which increases motivation and thus affects the individual's *willingness* to learn. The consequences of increasing the learner's motivation have already been discussed above.

Prior Learning. We have already considered the case of proactive inhibition, whereby past learning interferes with an individual's ability to learn new materials. More commonly, however, prior learning has been found to facilitate new learning, particularly when "the prior task and the present task have some similar stimulus-response combinations" (Ruch, 1967, p. 227). This is most likely to occur when the prior learning involves the same task as must be performed in the future.

Whole vs. Part Learning. A great deal of research has been conducted into the question of whether material to be learned should be offered to the learner in its entirety, or divided into parts. Reviews of this literature by Costello and Zalkind (1963), Welford (1968), Blum and Naylor (1968), and McCormick and Tiffin (1974) have led to the following general conclusions:

—Where rote learning is involved, short tasks are easier to master than long ones; it is therefore more efficient to do rote learning in parts rather than all at once.
—Where the division into parts of materials to be learned will interfere with its meaningfulness, whole learning will usually prove superior to learning by parts.
—Where the task to be learned is a closely coordinated one, such as aiming a rifle, it is better to learn the entire task at once. However, when task components must be performed in a certain order, but each is independent of the others, learning by parts is often advantageous.
—Where the task to be learned is complex, whole learning is normally more efficient than learning by parts, provided that the task components are highly dependent on one another. When task components are not highly interdependent, but the task is still complex, learning by parts is often more efficient.

As Costello and Zalkind (1963, p. 225) have stated, in most circumstances "a flexible method, combining the advantages of whole or part learning seems best. Begin with an overview of the whole problem or material, discover the difficult parts and practice them, then integrate them into the whole process as a final step."

Distribution of Practice. Reviews by Costello and Zalkind (1963), Bass and Vaughan (1966), and Welford (1968) have drawn a number of conclusions concerning the relative advantages of massed as opposed to distributed learning sessions. Some of these conclusions are:

–*Distributed* practice (that is, relatively short learning periods, with time between each period) has been found to be more of a facilitator of learning motor skills than learning verbal or other complex material.
–Distributed practice is well suited to relatively less meaningful material, to voluminous material, and to difficult material.
–*Massed* practice (that is, long concentrated or continuous learning periods) is often preferred by older people.
–Where insights are necessary for the completion of a task an initial long period of massed practice, followed by several shorter, distributed sessions, is often most effective.

As with the other general conclusions presented in this chapter, the reader must remember that they are not intended to apply to every individual or to every learning setting. With regard to distribution of practice, for example, Welford (1968, p. 293) reminds us that:

> It will depend very much on what is done during the times between practice periods. If they are spent in rehearsal of the material these times effectively form a part of the total practice time and learning will benefit accordingly, unless the task is fatiguing in which case the continued practice may depress subsequent performance. . . . If on the other hand times between practice periods are spent on another task, learning or later recall of the first task may be impaired. . . .

Organizational Applications and Implications

Primary and Conditional Reinforcers. Lundin (1961, pp. 64, 127) distinguishes between these in the following manner:

> Reinforcers such as food, water, or sexual contact are designated as primary because they have *biological importance*. . . . A neutral stimulus, through repeated associations with one that is primarily reinforcing, can acquire a reinforcing function by itself. Such stimuli we call *conditioned* or *secondary* reinforcers. . . . Once established, these stimuli also possess the capacity to increase and maintain behavior in a manner like those of the primary reinforcers. However, unlike the primary reinforcers, which continue to operate as long as the organism is appropriately deprived, the conditioned reinforcing function *may* extinguish after a time if it is not further reinforced by association with the primary stimulus.

Most organizations are unable to make much use of primary reinforcers, and so are almost totally reliant upon conditional reinforcers. A great many conditional reinforcers are normally available within the organizational context; Skinner (1953) suggests the following are of particular importance:

1. Attention. Often a supervisor can provide reinforcement simply by paying attention to a subordinate.
2. Appreciation and approval. This kind of attention, when awarded by a supervisor to a subordinate, can be particularly reinforcing. Of course, there is no requirement that employees of different ranks be involved; as with attention, these can be given by the work group to any of its members.
3. Affection. Skinner states that the expression of affection tends to be a stronger reinforcer, because its linkage to a primary reinforcer is most clear.
4. Submission of others. For people who have strong needs to dominate others, submission behaviors by others are extremely reinforcing, as evidenced by the fact that "giving in to the bully's demands serves to increase the probability of his bullying again" (Lundin, 1961, p. 141).
5. Tokens. Money is probably the most important "token," and the clearest example of a conditional reinforcer.

Using Money as a Conditional Reinforcer. A wide variety of compensation programs are currently used by organizations, and these may be expected to have differential effects upon what behaviors are reinforced and how strongly. As should be evident from the earlier discussion of reinforcement alternatives available (partial vs. continuous, ratio vs. interval, variable vs. fixed, etc.), the timing, amount, and contingencies under which financial (as well as nonfinancial) payments are made will be critical determinants of which behaviors will and will not occur.

One obvious choice to be made concerns whether compensation ought to be for "performance," however defined, or whether it should be determined exclusively by factors unrelated to performance, such as the task performed and length of service. Many organizations have programs which are consistent with each of these extremes, and there are of course many alternatives in between. From what has already been mentioned in this chapter, however, we would be safe in concluding that linking pay to outcomes other than performance will serve to diminish its usefulness as a conditional reinforcer of performance-related activities.

Once it is decided that compensation will be used to reinforce performance, other choices have to be made. One of these concerns whether an individual incentive program, a group program, or some combination of both should be employed. Rosen (1973, pp. 32–33) points out for example that:

> Profit-sharing plans, like Christmas turkey bonuses, are designed to produce a payoff for *everyone* in an organization—there are no losers.

> . . . A number of organizations that have used one or another type of profit-sharing plan with great anticipation abandoned it after a few years. . . . For one thing, it often is difficult for the employee to see *the link between his behavior and his reward* from such plans. Thus, while the behavior-incentive link is relatively easy for the employee to see under individual incentive plans and only somewhat more difficult to see under group piecework plans, the link is quite obscure in overall organization profit-sharing plans. . . . Most employees are well aware that overall organization profits are dependent upon many factors in addition to their on-the-job behavior.

Rosen goes on to mention that when the organization is a large one an overall profit-sharing plan is least likely to be effective, and Lawler (1971, p. 173) explains that this is so simply because "the larger the organization, the less influence any one individual has over companywide results, and the less an individual feels that his pay is related to performance. Thus, where individual-based pay plans are not possible . . . it may in fact be better to have no incentive pay plan at all."

Nord (1969) offers the argument, however, that when tasks to be performed are interdependent, reinforcement must be contingent upon group rather than individual responses. Furthermore, he points out that the work group sometimes makes "social rewards" dependent upon restriction of output, in which case individual incentive programs that ignore the influence of group norms are likely to fail.

Another choice concerns whether to employ a continuous reinforcement plan or one which reinforces according to some partial formula. Interestingly, this is an area where stimulus-response descriptions and those depending upon cognitions suggest different approaches. From a cognitive standpoint, it would be logical to conclude that a continuous reinforcement schedule (where, say, each successful performance activity is followed by a reinforcer) would most clearly establish the linkage between performance and reward. However, we have already noted that from an instrumental or operant viewpoint a number of advantages are associated with partial, as opposed to continuous, reinforcement.

An experiment bearing on this question was conducted by Yukl, Wexley, and Seymore (1972), in which the authors simulated a job situation in a laboratory and compared the effects of a 25¢ incentive with a continuous reinforcement schedule against a 50¢ incentive with a 50 percent variable ratio schedule, and found the variable ratio schedule to be significantly more efficient, even though the economic value of the two plans was identical.

Immediate vs. Delayed Reinforcement. Making the choice between compensation plans offering immediate reinforcement and those featuring delayed reinforcement ought to be easy, since the research reviewed earlier in this chapter suggests that an immediate reinforcement system is clearly superior. Yet many organizations employ systems in which "long delays often intervene between the occurrence of the desired behavior and its intended consequences" (Bandura, 1969, p. 229). One example of such a system is given by Jablonsky and Devries (1972, p. 344):

> . . . A new teacher in a large secondary school may perform initially at a high level, trying to impress his principal. His superiors may attempt to reward him for this extra effort by raising his salary. However, the request may not be approved until months later. By this time the teacher's high level of motivation has likely been extinguished, and when the salary increase finally occurs, the teacher is, in effect, being reinforced for mediocre performance.

Concern for the immediacy of reinforcement is also related to the pessimism expressed by Rosen (1973, p. 33) toward profit-sharing plans, where "the long time lag makes it difficult for the employee to develop any feeling of making progress toward a goal," and to the respect that Nord (1969) has for social as opposed to economic rewards, on the ground that rewards and punishments from one's peers are likely to be administered immediately and frequently following some response.

Increasing Participation Through Reinforcement. A number of studies show that participation by individuals is to a large extent a function of the reinforcement received. In one experiment Cieutat (1959) provided positive reinforcement to subjects in the form of attention and occasional nods of the head, and negative reinforcement in the form of inattention. It was found that the amount that individuals spoke was directly related to the amount of attention or inattention received.

In another experiment Oakes, Droge, and August (1960) provided positive reinforcement in the form of a light which indicated that subjects had made an "insightful" comment; other subjects were given negative reinforcement via the same light, which they were told signified a statement lacking insight. Results were consistent with those of Cieutat, as well as with later studies (e.g., Hastorf, 1965). These experiments counter the argument that participation is almost exclusively determined by personality characteristics; while individual differences have been found to be important, reinforcement has also been found to play an important part.

One Company's Experience

An attempt to incorporate much of the knowledge detailed in this chapter into a program of "positive reinforcement" is currently being made by the Emery Air Freight Corporation. The company defines positive reinforcement to be "a carefully controlled system of rewards. . . . This means devising ways of letting an individual employee regularly learn how well he is meeting specific company goals, and rewarding performance improvement—chiefly through frequent praise and recognition" (*Business Week,* 1971).

The essence of the Emery Corporation program can be stated as follows:

> In bestowing praise and recognition, Emery follows Skinner pretty closely. There is the same emphasis on reinforcing specific behavior; the same insistence that the behavior be reinforced as soon as possible after it has taken place; the same assertion that you reinforce frequently in the beginning to shape desired behavior, but that as time goes on, maintaining the desired behavior requires progressively less frequent and unpredictable reinforcement (anonymous, in Tosi and Hamner, 1974, p. 115).

In the early stages supervisors are urged to supply praise and recognition at least twice a week, and to continue this until desired behaviors have been established. The heart of the system, though, is the virtually continuous self-feedback which every employee receives.

> Emery, in each area where it has utilized positive reinforcement, has required each employee to keep a record himself of what he or she has accomplished each and every day. In customer service, for example, each representative ticked off daily on a sheet how long it had taken to reply to each call. It took no special skill to compare this with the standard of 90 minutes (anonymous, in Tosi and Hamner, 1974, p. 116).

At Emery money is *not* used as a positive reinforcer, in part because management believes that praise, recognition, and feedback are adequate to do the job.

Some Criticisms and Limitations

While not addressing themselves specifically to the Emery Corporation program, theorists such as Argyris (1971), Whyte (1972), Hamner (1974), and Schneier (1974) have suggested that there are a number of potential obstacles which may limit the effective use of the instrumental (operant) approach in organizational reward systems. For example:

—It may be that some who use operant approaches, by assuming that external rewards are critical to employee motivation, oversimplistically ignore the fact that intrinsic qualities of the job itself can also provide reinforcement.

—It is a further oversimplification to assume that all reinforcers can be consistently administered within the organization's formal reward system. In many cases conflicting norms and attitudes among various individuals and work groups will create a situation where a particular response is simultaneously rewarded and punished by different people within the organization.

—It is also incorrect to assume that the recipient of a reward will accurately perceive the reinforcement, or that the reward will be interpreted precisely as the reinforcer intends. The value to be placed on the reward, the reinforcement schedule employed, etc., will all depend upon the perceptions of the recipient, making an orderly and systematic organizational reinforcement program quite difficult.

These potential errors of interpretation should be carefully considered before any attempt is made to apply the operant approach to behavioral change within any organization. Such concerns notwithstanding, today there is an increasing interest by organizations in the kind of "positive reinforcement" program in use at Emery Corporation and elsewhere. Speaking very generally, Hamner (1974) summarizes the steps necessary to develop such a program:

1) The selection of reinforcers sufficiently powerful and durable to maintain responsiveness while the desired behavior patterns are being established.
2) The designing of contingencies in such a way that the reinforcing events become contingent on desired behaviors.
3) The designing of contingencies such that reliable procedures for inducing the desired responses are established. If this is not done, the reinforcer will have few chances to influence the desired behaviors.

An interesting consequence of employing a positive reinforcement system, assuming that one can really be employed successfully, is that "as for responsibility and goodness—as commonly defined—no one . . . would want or need them. They refer to a man's behaving well despite the absence of positive reinforcement that is obviously sufficient to explain it. Where such reinforcement exists, 'no one needs goodness'" (Swanson, 1972, p. 704).

On the other hand, it is important to recognize that positive reinforcement, like any other behavior modification approach, has its limits. As has been wryly observed by Seligman and Hager (1972, p. 59): "You can lead a horse to water but no amount or manner of conditioning will teach it to talk."

References

Ammons, R. B. 1956. Effects of knowledge of performance: A survey and tentative theoretical formulation. *Journal of General Psychology* 54: 279–99.

Annett, J. 1968. The role of knowledge of results in learning: A survey. Cited in *Industrial psychology* (pp. 242–43), ed. by M. L. Blum and J. C. Naylor. Harper & Row.

Anonymous. 1974. In *Organizational behavior and management: A contingency approach,* ed. by H. L. Tosi and W. C. Hamner. St. Clair Press.

Argyris, C. 1971. Beyond freedom and dignity by B. F. Skinner, a review essay. *Harvard Educational Review* 41: 550–67.

Azrin, N. H., and Holz, W. C. 1966. Punishment. In *Operant behavior: Areas of research and application,* ed. by W. K. Honig. Appleton-Century-Crofts.

Bandura, A. 1969. *Principles of behavior modification.* Holt, Rinehart and Winston.

Bass, B. M., and Vaughan, J. A. 1966. *Training in industry: The management of learning.* Wadsworth.

Blum, M. L., and Naylor, J. C. 1968. *Industrial psychology.* Harper & Row.

Business Week. 1971. New tool: 'Reinforcement' for good work. Dec. 18, 1971: 76–77.

Cieutat, V. J. 1959. Surreptitious modification of verbal behavior during class discussion. *Psychological Report* 5: 648.

Costello, T. W., and Zalkind, S. S., eds. 1963. *Psychology in administration: A research orientation.* Prentice-Hall, Inc.

Dethier, V. G., and Stellar, E. 1964. *Animal behavior.* Prentice-Hall, Inc.

Greenspoon, J. 1966. The effect of a verbal stimulus as a reinforcement. In *The experimental analysis of behavior,* ed. by T. Verhave. Appleton-Century-Crofts.

Hamner, W. C. 1974. Reinforcement theory and contingency management in organizational settings. In *Organizational behavior and management: A contingency approach,* ed. by H. L. Tosi and W. C. Hamner. St. Clair Press.

Hastorf, A. H. 1965. The 'reinforcement' of individual actions in a group situation. In *Research in behavior modification,* ed. by L. Krasner and L. P. Ullman. Holt, Rinehart and Winston.

Jablonsky, S. F., and DeVries, D. L. 1972. Operant conditioning principles extrapolated to the theory of management. *Organizational Behavior and Human Performance* 7: 340–58.

Kimble, G. A. 1969. The definition of learning. In *Readings in organizational behavior and human performance,* ed. by L. L. Cummings and W. E. Scott, Jr. Irwin.

Lawler, E. E., Jr. 1971. *Pay and organizational effectiveness.* McGraw-Hill.

Lundin, R. W. 1961. *Personality: An experimental approach.* Macmillan.

Margulies, N., and Raia, A. P. 1972. *Organizational development: Values, process, and technology.* McGraw-Hill.

McCormick, E. J., and Tiffin, J. 1974. *Industrial psychology,* 6th ed. Prentice-Hall.

Mosel, J. N. 1958. How to feed back performance results to trainees. *Journal of the American Society of Training Directors* 12: 37–46.

Nord, W. R. 1969. Beyond the teaching machine: The neglected area of operant conditioning in the theory and practice of management. *Organizational Behavior and Human Performance* 4: 375–401.

Oakes, W. F.; Droge, A. E.; and August, B. 1960. Reinforcement effects on participation in group discussion. *Psychological Report* 7: 503–514.

Rosen, N. 1973. *Supervision: A behavioral view.* Grid.

Ruch, F. L. 1967. *Psychology and life,* 7th ed. Scott, Foresman.

Schneier, C. E. 1974. Behavior modification in management: A review and critique. *Academy of Management Journal* 17: 528–48.

Seligman, M. E. P., and Hager, J. L. 1972. Biological boundaries of learning. *Psychology Today* 6: 59.

Skinner, B. F. 1950. Are theories of learning necessary? *Psychological Review* 57: 193–216.

———. 1953. *Science and human behavior*. Macmillan.

———. 1963. Operant behavior. In *Psychology in administration: A research orientation*, ed. by T. W. Costello and S. S. Zalkind. Prentice-Hall, Inc.

Swanson, G. E. 1972. Review symposium: Beyond freedom and dignity. *American Journal of Sociology* 78: 702–5.

Thorndike, E. L. 1911. *Animal intelligence: Experimental studies*. Macmillan.

Tuber, D. S.; Hothersall, D.; and Voith, V. L. 1974. Animal clinical psychology: A modest proposal. *American Psychologist* 29: 762–66.

Walters, R. H., and Cheyne, J. A. 1969. Some parameters influencing the effects of punishment on social behavior. In *Readings in organizational behavior and human performance,* ed. by L. L. Cummings and W. E. Scott, Jr. Irwin.

Watson, G. 1972. What do we know about learning? In *Contemporary readings in organizational behavior,* ed. by F. Luthans. McGraw-Hill.

Welford, A. T. 1968. *Fundamentals of skill*. Methuen.

Whyte, W. F. 1972. Skinnerian theory in organizations. *Psychology Today* 5: 66 and 68+.

Yukl, G.; Wexley, K. N.; and Seymore, J. D. 1972. Effectiveness of pay incentives under variable ratio and continuous reinforcement schedules. *Journal of Applied Psychology* 56: 19–23.

Zimbardo, P. G., and Ruch, F. L. 1975. *Psychology and life,* 9th ed. Scott, Foresman.

Chapter **6**

Power, Authority, and Influence

"When a Warrant Officer flies a plane [Vossler explained] *his copilot may be a Lieutenant and his navigator a Captain—but they both have to obey the orders of the pilot." "But that's terrific!" Kamnitzer exclaimed with a genuine enthusiasm. "Performance before rank and ability before authority! Why don't we hear more of it?"*

H. H. KIRST
What Became of Gunner Asch

Power, authority, and influence are three of the most fundamental concepts required to understand the nature and functioning of complex organizations. They help explain both what relationships *ought* to exist between individuals (at least in the minds of those who design an organizational structure) and what actually *is*. This ought-is distinction can be seen at both the macrocosmic and microcosmic levels; our discussion of power, authority, and influence will focus on both points of view.

Before going any further, however, we should first define our terms, for while they are in many ways complementary and are sometimes used interchangeably, there are important distinctions between them.

Power refers to the ability of an individual or a group to get some other individual or group to change in some manner. If A can cause B to do something that B otherwise would not have done, then A may be said to have power over B. In its purest form, a power relationship exists when A gets B to do something against B's will through manipulation of rewards (Schein, 1965). The nature of the rewards which are manipulated serves as the basis for a classification of types of power advanced by Etzioni (1961, pp. 5–6):

> *Coercive* power rests on the application, or the threat of application, of physical sanctions such as infliction of pain, deformity, or death; generation of frustration through restriction of movement; or controlling through force the satisfaction of needs such as those for food, sex, comfort, and the like.
>
> *Renumerative* power is based on control over material resources and

> rewards through allocation of salaries and wages, commissions and contributions, "fringe benefits," services and commodities.
>
> *Normative* power rests on the allocation and manipulation of symbolic rewards and deprivations through employment of leaders, manipulation of mass media, allocation of esteem and prestige symbols, administration of ritual, and influence over the distribution of "acceptance" and "positive response." (A more eloquent name for this power would be persuasive, or manipulative, or suggestive power.) . . . There are two kinds of normative power. One is based on the manipulation of esteem, prestige, and ritualistic symbols (such as a flag or a benediction); the other, on allocation and manipulation of acceptance and positive response (Parsons, 1951, p. 108).

If power is the ability to act, *authority* is the right to act. It is legitimate power, vested in a particular person or position and accepted as appropriate and recognized as legitimate not only by the power-wielder but also by those over whom it is wielded (Katz and Kahn, 1966). If A can cause B to do something that B otherwise would not have done, *and* if B recognizes that A has the *right* to so affect B's behavior, then A may be said to have authority over B.

How is power legitimated and thereby transformed into authority? According to Weber (1947), three legitimating devices exist:

(1) Power that is accepted because it is inherent, preordained, and long-standing becomes traditional authority. Kings, for example, may rule by virtue of traditional authority.

(2) Power that is accepted because of rules and regulations becomes bureaucratic or rational-legal authority. In this case, authority resides in a position rather than in its occupant; it therefore remains when individuals leave the position. Presidents (of corporations, of the United States) rule by virtue of bureaucratic authority.[1]

(3) Power that derives from personal qualities becomes charismatic authority. In the extreme, charismatic leaders are viewed by those who follow them "as possessed by and transmitting an uncanny and compelling force" (McIntosh, 1970, p. 902). Jesus Christ and Martin Luther King are examples of charismatic leaders; neither occupied a formal position, yet both caused millions to do things they otherwise would not have done.

Influence, defined narrowly, refers to the capacity of A to get B to do something B would otherwise not have done *without* resorting to the manipulation of rewards and punishments (Presthus, 1962, p. 138). Viewed more broadly:

---

[1] Some authors describe bureaucratic authority as stemming from the technical expertise and knowledge of the office-holder. In fact, Weber thought of bureaucratic authority as legitimated both by technical expertise and by the office itself; since promotions into authority-wielding positions were to be made only after demonstration of technical competence (see Chapter 1), further clarification and distinction between these two forms of legitimation seemed to Weber to be unnecessary.

> It refers to any behavior on the part of one individual which alters the behavior, attitudes, feelings, and so on, of another. Thus advertising is as much an influence process as is a directive from a management superior. One person may influence another by virtue of control over sanctions, by persuasion, by playing upon attitudes held toward him, by exercising control over significant aspects of the other person's environment, or as a consequence of an exchange agreement which provides for influence as one part of the bargain . . . (Miner, 1973, pp. 298–99).

Thus we can say that whenever a power relationship exists, an influence relationship is also present; whenever an authority relationship exists, both power and influence are present; influence, however, may be present where neither power nor authority exist.

This discussion indicates that power, authority, and influence have two distinct yet complementary aspects; the first involves planned or spontaneous superordinate-subordinate relationships, while the second involves influence-submission relationships among individuals. Both of these aspects have important implications for topics to be dealt with in later chapters (including leadership, command, and control) and are apparent at both macrocosmic and microcosmic levels of analysis.

The Macrocosmic View

Organizational charts, policy manuals, job descriptions, and the like express the formal power and authority relationships that *ought to be* in complex organizations. Indeed, the formal organization is created by the disposition of power and authority and the resulting differences in functions. Stogdill (1959) describes such organizations as based upon a system of positions (hierarchical), as impersonal, and as unaffected by the entrance and departure of individuals to and from the system. Through the design of formal organizations, the interactions and relationships among organizational units and position incumbents are prescribed; through rules and procedures, minimum standards of behavior are established. A more complete discussion of the properties of formal organizations will be presented later in this text; what concerns us here is that in the classical view, authority flows from the top to the bottom of the structure of formal organizations. Koontz and O'Donnell (1972, pp. 57–58) explain:

> Until recent years, it rarely occurred to writers on management that there could be any argument about the source of a manager's authority. One had only to trace authority delegations upward from any managerial position. Thus, the supervisor of cash control obtained his authority from the assistant treasurer, who obtained his from the treasurer, who in turn got his from the president of the company, whose authority was delegated by the board of directors, who obtained

> theirs from the stockholders, who held theirs by virtue of the institution of private property as modified by incorporation and other laws. Thus, in a business firm, the ultimate source of authority lies principally in the institution of private property. . . .

This view may be labeled the "economic" concept of authority, since it is based upon the idea that rights and authority reside in and derive from the ownership of private property. This view may also be termed "executive" authority, since it views authority as being vested in the chief executives of an organization—the president, top executive staff, and board of directors. Marcson, (1960, pp. 121–22) explains that "within prescribed limits, responsibility, along with the corresponding authority, may be delegated from the chief to his subordinates." However, as he points out, the "ultimate control over top policy and over the limits within which subordinates can make decisions rests with the top executive and, in the final analysis, with the chief executive." There are no organizational means for executives to draw on their subordinates' advice and participation.

In addition to their formal design characteristics, organizations also contain various informal alignments which reflect the sentiments and expectations of members concerning "proper" and "acceptable" behavior. These sentiments and expectations are frequently enforced by group norms or by informal (i.e., not formally authorized) control of privileges and resources. In this way, power and authority explain the relationships that exist between people, and thus help describe what *is*. These complex systems of informal relations constitute informal networks of power and influence, an *informal organization* (defined in Chapter 1). For example, an office group may formally consist of an office manager and ten subordinates; informally, one of the ten subordinates may be a leader whose influence is accepted by the group, and who represents the consensus of group member values and sentiments in influencing the office manager.

As opposed to executive authority, Marcson (1960, p. 130) states that "colleague" authority:

> . . . emphasizes a relationship of association, alliance, and working together, while at the same time accepting whatever inequality in status that may be present. These inequalities are subordinate to the association of colleagues for work purposes, but the controls of authority and the decision-making mechanisms remain in force. . . . Authority in the final analysis rests in the group rather than in the individual.

The Microcosmic View

As on the macrocosmic level, the ought-is distinction can also be seen on the microcosmic level. The manner in which manager A is supposed to relate to employee B is usually prescribed, at least in part, in terms of power and authority. At the same time, the manner in which manager A actually affects the perceptions, attitudes, and behavior of employee B can also be described and understood in such terms.

At this level, the economic concept of authority takes the form of rights of command which one person or office has over another. It is assumed that each position in the organization carries with it explicit authority (through job description) or implicit authority (through tradition). Degrees of formal authority range from the right to make independent decisions, to make decisions after considering advice from others, to make decisions so long as others concur, to the right to advise and recommend. (The relationship between decision and advisory authority is examined in greater detail in Chapter 17.)

The concept of economic or executive authority can be quite useful in reflecting the relationships which "should" exist; the fact that managerial influence often goes beyond that stated in the organizing plans, and that subordinates often choose to ignore authoritative directions, does not negate its presence or its usefulness in providing a guide to action. Yet, we are forced to ask why such authority is sometimes ignored, that is, why economic and executive authority does not always explain what "really" happens in an organization.

Because the classical view of economic authority assumes that an order, once given, will be acted upon, it fails to consider the willingness of subordinates to accept the order. For example, Bierstedt (1954, p. 71) stated:

> The fiat of the leader lacks legitimacy. One may follow or not and no sanction except possibly the informal sanction of being regarded as odd by other followers is applied to those who abstain. The situation is different with respect to authority. A leader can only request, an authority can require. The person subjected to an order by "competent authority" has no alternative but to obey. The examination must be taken at the appointed time, taxes must be paid, the draft induction notice must be observed. Obedience to an authoritative command is not a matter of a subordinate's arbitrary decision.

This position ignores the fact that examinations are often postponed due to non-attendance, taxes are often not paid, and draft induction notices have in recent years often gone unobserved. To better understand the relationship between authority and actual behavior we need a somewhat different concept of authority, in which it is viewed not in terms of the right to command but in terms of one individual's willingness to accept direction from another. We shall call this notion the "political" concept of authority, since it depends upon the consent of the governed.

This concept of authority has been set forth most completely by Barnard (1938) and Simon (1947). Barnard claimed that:

> Authority is the character of a communication (order) in a formal

> organization by virtue of which it is accepted by a contributor to or "member" of the organization as governing the action he contributes; that is, as governing or determining what he does or is not to do so far as the organization is concerned . . . under this definition the decision as to whether an order has authority or not lies with the persons to whom it is addressed, and does not reside in "persons of authority" or those who issue those orders (p. 163).

The area in which a subordinate is willing to accept direction from a supervisor was called by Barnard the "zone of indifference," and by Simon the "zone of acceptance." Barnard's description of this term is as follows:

> If all the orders for actions reasonably practicable be arranged in the order of their acceptability to the person affected, it may be conceived that there are a number which are clearly unacceptable, that is, which certainly will not be obeyed; there is another group somewhat more or less on the neutral line, that is, either barely acceptable or barely unacceptable; and a third group unquestionably acceptable. This last group lies within the "zone of indifference." The person affected will accept orders lying within this zone and is relatively indifferent as to what the order is so far as the question of authority is concerned (1938, pp. 168–69).

Under the economic concept of authority, two foremen with the same job descriptions would be considered to have the same authority; however, the political authority granted to each, as a result of the zone of indifference, might be quite different.

Bases of Power

It should not be supposed from the above discussion that individuals within organizations restrict their power-granting to a single formal supervisor. Power relations in organizations form complex networks in which a member may display a willingness to be influenced by another member. This will depend upon (1) the nature of the issue, (2) the availability of one or more persons whose status determines their right to make authoritative decisions or initiate actions, and (3) the base of power to which the member is willing to respond.

Many attempts have been made to identify the bases upon which one individual might influence another. Such sources of power as confidence and social approval (Simon, 1957), rapport (Presthus, 1960), persuasion (Gilman, 1962), control of information and personal affection (Cartwright, 1965), and prestige and power by numbers (Bierstedt, 1950) have all been proposed.

Probably the best known and most widely used list of bases of power is the one proposed by French and Raven (1959), in which they described five bases "which are especially common and important." In a sense, this list may be considered to be an elaboration of Etzioni's classification (1961) of types of power, discussed earlier. In particular, the first two items in each classification appear nearly identical.

(1) *Reward power* is defined simply as power whose basis is the ability to reward. The example presented by French and Raven is that of adding a piece-work incentive plan in a factory to increase production.

(2) *Coercive power* is similar to reward power except that, rather than adding attractive consequences and removing unattractive ones, the subordinate is threatened with the addition of unattractive ones.

Possible confusion between reward power and coercive power arises when we pose such questions as: "Is the withholding of a reward equivalent to a punishment?" This question was considered in detail in the chapter on learning, but for our purposes now it is sufficient to note that French and Raven believe the distinction to be important, and that to combine the two power bases into a single category (say, called "sanctions") would constitute an oversimplification. They point out that reward power may over a period of time produce an independent system, whereas the effects of coercive power will continue to be dependent. Furthermore, reward power tends to increase the attraction of the subordinate toward the wielder of power. Coercive power decreases attraction, often resulting in negative feelings that tend to spread to other aspects of the subordinate's situation. The subordinate may finally react by leaving the situation altogether.

(3) *Legitimate power* stems from internalized values within the subordinate which dictate that the power-wielder has a right to influence him. As described by French and Raven, such power becomes "authority" for the subordinate as it is legitimated by one of the methods we have talked about earlier in this chapter.

(4) *Referent power* comes about through the identification of the subordinate with the power-wielder. By identification is meant the acceptance of influence by an individual "because he wants to establish or maintain a satisfying self-defining relationship to another person or group" (Kelman, 1958, p. 52). An explanation of the process and consequences of identification is contained in Chapter 17.

(5) *Expert power* is a function of the amount of knowledge or perception which the subordinate attributes to the power-wielder within a given area, usually compared to the subordinate's own knowledge. French and Raven present as examples accepting an attorney's advice and following street directions given by a stranger.

Patchen (1974, p. 196) has suggested that the French and Raven classification is limited because the various bases of power are not defined in a conceptually parallel way. He points out that:

> . . . Reward power and coercive power are defined in terms of *resources* available to the influencer. . . . Referent power is described not in terms of the resources of the influencer but in terms of the

> *characteristics and motivations* of the target. Similarly, legitimate power is defined in terms of the target person's characteristics and motivations. . . . Finally, "expert power" is discussed in terms which appear that it in part depends on certain characteristics of the influencer (e.g., his credibility) and in part on certain resources he possesses (e.g., facts).

Patchen's own attempt to distinguish between characteristics of the power-wielder and those of the target of influence is illustrated in Table 6–1.

Two Studies

Further insight into the sources and bases of power is provided in a study by Filley and Grimes (1967) conducted in a non-profit organization. In the organization, 44 full-time professional employees reported to a single director and associate director. While all employees worked independently, they performed similar functions and common task groups did exist. Thirty-six of the organization members were interviewed about eight hypothetical incidents which might require them to seek a decision from the director or associate director. Respondents were asked who they *should* go to for a decision, who they would *like* to go to, and who they would *in fact* go to, and why. Answers to the "why" questions were classified according to the bases of power the organization members responded to:

(1) *Formal authority.* This refers to actual or perceived legitimacy, a general job title, or general decision-making rights. Included were references to the general authority of the respondents or of a superior, the need for approval from a higher authority, the general decision rights of an authority, or accepted group leader status. In this class were placed such broad statements about authority as "he's the boss" or "he makes the decisions for the organization," rather than specific statements about power and authority.

(2) *Responsibility and function.* This class refers to situations where a matter or activity was identified as legitimate with an emphasis upon "responsibility" for an activity. If individuals were designated as responsible for making a particular *type* of decision or because of their functions, the response was included in this class. Also included were broad statements which did not identify specific areas of responsibility, although they often emphasized performance of a specific function or responsibility for a specific type of decision. These responses included three types of emphasis. The first was upon responsibility itself ("that's his responsibility"), the second was upon a type of decision ("he makes that kind of decision"), and the third was upon the function of the level and usually concerned resolution of disputes ("disagreements between sections have to be resolved at his level").

These first two power bases clearly contain elements of bureaucratic authority and executive authority, described earlier.

TABLE 6–1. A Framework for Analyzing Social Influence, With Some Examples (Patchen, 1974).

Person exerting influence			Target(s) of influence			
Characteristics	Resources	Decision role with respect to target	Characteristics	Needs	Decision role with respect to influencer	Effect of influencer on target
Expertise; special training, special experience, etc.	Knowledge about how to reach certain goals	Investigates, makes tests, gives information to others	Unexpert	Wants to find best ways to reach goals	Reviews information presented by experts	Sees new options; sees new favorable or unfavorable consequences following various actions
Occupies important position in hierarchy	Control over material rewards (money, promotion, etc.)	Makes request, coupled with promise of reward for compliance	Occupies less important position in hierarchy	Wants rewards controlled by influencer	Decides whether to accede to request of others	Compliance seen as means to reward
Occupies important position in hierarchy	Control over material penalties (fines, demotions, etc.)	Gives orders, coupled with threats of punishment for noncompliance	Occupies less important position in hierarchy	Wants to avoid punishment but maintain self-esteem	Decides whether to accede to order	Compliance seen as way of avoiding penalty but may be seen as blow to self-esteem
Strong; successful; has attractive qualities	Approval	States own opinions, preferences	Less strong, less successful	Wishes to be similar to, approved by, influencer	Hears opinions, preferences of influencer	Seeks compliance as way of being similar to, approved by, influencer
Occupies legitimate position of authority; secured position by legitimate methods	Symbols of legitimacy; label of others' action as right or wrong	Announces decision; asks for support	Occupies position of subordination; accepts legitimacy of others' position	Wishes to fulfill moral obligations	Gets request from authority	Sees conformity to requested action as morally correct
Is affected by certain decisions (by virtue of work neecs, responsibilities, etc.)	Own cooperation (may also have some resources listed in other rows)	Vigorously makes preference known to others	Peers or final decision-making authority	Want high level of cooperation from influencer	Decide whether to accept recommendation	Sees accepting recommendation as leading to future cooperation by influencer

(3) *Manipulation.* This class refers to situations where individuals were selected because it was felt they would do something to meet the respondents' wishes. These individuals were chosen by the respondents because they could "get the job done." It is quite possible, of course, that choices falling into this class presupposed legitimacy or control of resources by the decision makers chosen.

(4) *Default or avoidance.* Statements indicating that a decision maker was chosen because the more appropriate or desired source was unavailable were placed in this category, as were remarks that the respondents merely wished to rid themselves of the problem and there was "no one else to go to."

(5) *Autonomy.* This class contains statements indicating that respondents felt that they did not have to see anyone else, that it was their decision to make—notwithstanding the fact that the problem posed situations where the respondents would normally be expected to seek official approval or resolution.

(6) *Expertise.* In this class are statements suggesting that the individuals who were sought for a decision were closer to or had better knowledge of the situation or had some special ability which was relevant. (Statements indicating that the knowledge sought could be obtained from several sources, i.e., "general information-seeking," were placed in the next category; this category is therefore quite consistent with French and Raven's "expert power" base.)

(7) *Control of resources.* This class includes statements about control of money, general information, procedures, or other resources. Statements in this category were primarily of two types. The first, general information-seeking, referred to cases where the decision makers were sought not so much because they were the only ones who had information or technical expertise, but because they "would know what to do" about a situation. The second, control over money, reflects the fact that individuals who control monetary resources in an organization clearly have a strong basis for power over others.

(8) *Bureaucratic rules.* In this class are statements referring to policy, regulations, channels, and levels, which emphasized response to an impersonal rule or regulation perceived by the respondent. Statements such as "that is policy" and "that is the rule" were common. Such statements typically reflected the role of rules as standardized means for dealing with recurring incidents.

(9) *Traditional rules.* This class contains statements referring to custom and seniority. References to length of service were included here inasmuch as seniority was not included in the formal rule system.

(10) *Collegial.* This class contains statements referring to respondents' preferences for consultation with their peer groups or for participation in general. Also included were statements indicating that respondents sought the decision makers because of courtesy, or to give information because of the decision maker's "right to know." Statements here either emphasized

some kind of group action or decision or stressed the importance of giving information to others; this category is therefore representative of "colleague authority," discussed earlier in this chapter.

(11) *Friendship.* Statements placed in this class largely reflect French and Raven's "referent power" in that they describe affection, friendship, and goodwill toward the decision makers, who were selected because of the respondents' personal relationship with the decision makers.

(12) *Equity.* This class contains statements describing the selection of decision makers on the basis of their use of merit and fairness in dealing with a problem. Apparently not only was the presence of power important, but fairness in the use of power as well.

Two limitations of this study discussed by Murray (1967) are worth mentioning. First, power is operationally defined in the Filley and Grimes study as the extent to which one person sees another as being able to solve a problem. As Murray points out, it is possible that the decision maker is perceived simply as having power over the problem, not over the respondent himself. Second, the study does not distinguish between the reward-controller and the strategy used by the respondents to get what they want from the reward-controller. It is possible, for example, that the decision maker is selected only because of the decision maker's influence over the real power source in the organization. These limitations do not, however, negate the usefulness of the study, which represents an empirically derived statement of organizational bases of power.

Another investigation into the sources and bases of power was conducted by Patchen (1974), who examined 33 specific purchasing decisions in 11 firms. In each organization, a person knowledgeable about the purchasing function was interviewed about a nonrepetitive purchase made in the firm, typically one where a product was bought for the first time or where it had been purchased only infrequently. For each decision, this knowledgeable person was asked to supply the names and titles of others who were involved in the purchase.

A total of 180 interviews were conducted concerning the 33 cases; these interviews were with those designated originally as being involved in the purchase and with others whose importance to the decision-making process was revealed during the initial interviews. Individuals involved in the decision were asked (1) who brought the problem to their attention and with whom they discussed the problem; (2) their role in the decision; (3) who was involved during each stage of the decision; (4) what differences of opinion existed within the firm; (5) how such differences were resolved; and (6) whom they judged to have had the greatest influence on the decision, and why.

One of the most striking findings in this study was the lack of agreement among people interviewed as to who had had the most influence in making the decision. Patchen suggests that only in a few cases was there a single, prime decision maker; his data show that most often the decision was made through a process of accommodation and consensus, and that meetings, problem-solving, and "getting additional information" were much more frequently used to resolve conflicts than were decisions made by persons with higher authority.

A variety of answers were obtained in response to the question, "Why did the person named as most influential in the decision have so much influence?" The majority of the responses concerned characteristics of the influential individual. The characteristics most frequently mentioned related to the extent to which the person would be affected by the decision.

> Sometimes the explanation for influence was a general statement that someone would be affected. For example, in a company which makes musical instruments, the choice of a tractor truck was said by one informant to have been influenced most by the traffic supervisor. "He lives with the situation so he must have the choice," he said. Closely related is the somewhat more specific assertion that a certain person was influential in the decision concerning a purchase because the product would be used by him or by his department. . . . In addition to being affected by virtue of having to use the product, a man may be affected in other ways by the decision. A variety of responsibilities, the meeting of which might be affected by the decision, were mentioned as reasons for great influence (Patchen, 1974, pp. 209–11).

The characteristics mentioned next most frequently had to do with the expertise of the individual with influence; this expertise sometimes took the form of specific information, sometimes a more general kind of knowledge. Formal responsibility of the influential individual to play a key role was also mentioned as a frequent basis for power, as was the fact that the individual had formal, legitimate authority.

While many responses referred to individual *characteristics*, as indicated above, other respondents suggested that the *activities* of certain persons were the reason for their influence. The two most commonly mentioned activities were "prodding others to act" (that is, bringing the need for the new product to others' attention) and those connected with information-gathering and technical matters.

Patchen concluded by examining his data with particular reference to the French and Raven classification of power, described earlier in this chapter:

> . . . The data indicate first that coercive power and reward power are noticeable chiefly by their absence. Influence was never attributed to the characteristics of control over material sanctions, nor to activities involving use of such sanctions (e.g. threat, promise, punishment, reward). It is possible that some respondents were reluctant to talk about such modes of influence. It may be, too, that the possible use of sanctions lurks behind other characteristics or activities which were sometimes mentioned. . . . Also apparently rare in these situations was

> referent power. . . . Influence did appear to be due often to expert power. A man's expertise was frequently mentioned as the reason he was influential in a decision. . . . A second basis of power which was present was legitimate power. The responsibilities, duties, or formal authority which a man had, the characteristics of someone with legitimate power, were given with some frequency as reasons for influence (pp. 216–17).

Conclusions

Both the economic and the political concepts of authority contribute to an understanding of individual and group relations in organizations. For example, formal leaders may expand their subordinates' zones of indifference through the exercise of various bases of power, and a great deal of managerial activity may be interpreted in these terms. Such diverse activities as indoctrination programs, pep talks, threats, and the adoption by management of a "human relations" attitude can be viewed as attempts to expand one or another of the power bases (referent, coercive, etc.) and, if successful, to widen subordinates' zones of indifference.

The various concepts of authority, and the viewpoint expressed in this chapter that *influence* may exist even in cases where power and authority do not, help us understand the effect that informal leaders may have over other organizational members, even in the absence of "legitimacy."

Consideration of the different bases of power also permits a fuller understanding of the possible conditions of conflict between line managers with legitimate authority and staff personnel who lack formal authority but who can be very influential because of expertise, control over resources, or ability to manipulate the system.

It should be apparent from the discussion in this chapter that formal authority alone is a far from adequate explanation for the presence of power, authority, and influence in organizations. Furthermore, it is clear that the political concept of authority, whereby the leader rules with the consent of the governed, is an important extension of the classical economic concept. However, notice should be taken of arguments such as that of Presthus (1962, pp. 137, 145). In light of the hierarchical and status differences between power wielders and subordinates, Presthus warns that the notion of subordinate "acceptance" of authority must be taken with a grain of salt:

> To say that authority is defined by "acceptance" suggests that the individual has a real choice between acceptance and refusal, that authority is an "either-or" proposition. But this assumes too great a degree of free will and too simple a social situation. . . . The individual is trained from birth onward to defer to authority. He develops a generalized deference to the authority of parenthood, experience, knowledge, status, and so forth. . . . So many degrees of compliance exist,

ranging from enthusiasm to resignation, that explicit rejection becomes a crude and unlikely alternative, particularly among highly socialized individuals. . . . The resulting pattern of "anticipated reactions" is the main basis upon which organizations function. An obvious (although rather extreme) example is the effect of rank insignia in the military. The mere sight of a high-ranking officer, identifiable at twenty paces, evokes a whole battery of conditioned responses from his subordinates.

References

Barnard, C. 1938. *The functions of the executive.* Harvard University Press.

Bierstedt, R. 1950. An analysis of social power. *American Sociological Review* 15: 730.

———. 1954. The problem of authority. In *Freedom and control in modern society,* ed. by M. Berger, T. Abel, and C. Page. Van Nostrand.

Cartwright, D. 1965. Influence, leadership, control. In *Handbook of organizations,* ed. by J. G. March. Rand-McNally.

Etzioni, A. 1961. *A comparative analysis of complex organizations.* Free Press.

Filley, A., and Grimes, A. 1967. The bases of power in decision processes. *Proceedings of the Annual Meeting of the Academy of Management,* pp. 133–60.

French, J. R. P., and Raven, B. 1959. The bases of social power. In *Studies in social power,* ed. by D. Cartwright. University of Michigan.

Gilman, G. 1962. An inquiry into the nature and use of authority. In *Organization theory in industrial practice,* ed. by M. Haire. Wiley.

Katz, D., and Kahn, R. L. 1966. *The social psychology of organizations.* Wiley.

Kelman, H. C. 1958. Compliance, identification, and internalization: Three processes of attitude change. *Conflict Resolution* 2: 51–60.

Koontz, H., and O'Donnell, C. 1972. *Principles of management: An analysis of managerial functions,* 5th ed. McGraw-Hill.

Marcson, S. 1960. *The scientist in American industry.* Princeton University Press.

McIntosh, D. 1970. Weber and Freud: On the nature and sources of authority. *American Sociological Review* 35: 901–11.

Miner, J. B. 1973. *The management process: Theory, research, and practice.* Macmillan.

Murray, V. 1967. Comments on paper by Filley and Grimes. *Proceedings of the Annual Meeting of the Academy of Management,* 161–63.

Parsons, T. 1951. *The social system.* Free Press.

Patchen, M. 1974. The locus and basis of influence on organizational decisions. *Organizational Behavior and Human Performance* 11: 195–221.

Presthus, R. V. 1960. Authority in organizations. *Public Administration Review* 20: 86–91.

———. 1962. *The organizational society.* Knopf.

Schein, E. H. 1965. *Organizational psychology.* Prentice-Hall.

Simon, H. A. 1947. *Administrative behavior* (2nd ed. 1957). Macmillan.

———. 1957. Authority. In *Research in industrial human relations*, ed. by C. M. Arensberg, et al. Harper & Row.

Stogdill, R. M. 1959. *Individual behavior and group achievement.* Oxford University Press.

Weber, M. 1947. *The theory of social and economic organization* (1921), tr. and ed. by A. M. Henderson and T. Parsons. Free Press.

Chapter **7**

Individual Decision Making

Here is Edward Bear, coming downstairs now, bump, bump, bump on the back of his head. It is, as far as he knows, the only way of coming downstairs, but sometimes he feels that there really is another way, if only he could stop bumping for a moment and think of it. And then he feels that perhaps there isn't. Anyhow. . . .

A. A. MILNE
Winnie the Pooh

A significant portion of a manager's time is devoted to making decisions. In fact, most planning and organizing activities require the making of key decisions regarding strategy and allocation of resources, and most control activities depend upon decisions concerning corrective actions once plans no longer seem practical. Psychologists, economists, political scientists, statisticians, organization theorists, and management scientists have all taken an interest in the thought processes which lead to effective decision making. As a result, a large amount of information has been produced concerning how individuals actually make decisions.

This chapter will be concerned with decision making from the standpoint of administrative as opposed to classical theory. First, however, we shall examine the implications of the differences between these two approaches; we will then describe Simon's "administrative individual" theory in greater detail and consider the research evidence pertinent to some of the most important questions about individual decision making.

Decision Making: Goals and Processes

The classical theory of decision making assumed that decisions are directed toward a single, unchanging goal and that rational decisions could be reached to meet that goal. To a great extent, these assumptions were derived from the theory of the "economic" individual. Economic individuals are assumed to know all alternatives available in a given situation and the consequences of each. It is further assumed that they behave rationally, that is, they are *able* to order their preferences according to their own hierarchies of values, and they always seek to *maximize* some desired value.

The assumption that economic individuals maximize derives from the philosophies of Jeremy Bentham and John Stuart Mill, who proposed that the prime goal of human behavior is to seek pleasure and avoid pain. Any object or action can thus be evaluated according to the ratio of its pleasure-giving utility to its pain-giving utility; human behavior is assumed to be guided by a calculation of the course of action which will yield maximum pleasure and minimum pain. Thus, economic individuals will always seek to maximize utility.

Classical theory has, however, come under serious criticism from modern management theorists and behavioral scientists. They criticize classical theory for assuming that once an imbalance has been resolved by an appropriate decision the matter is settled once and for all. They agree that the more organizational members are united and guided by common, stable, and well-defined goals, the more likely it is that the organization will be effective and its members satisfied; however, modern theorists argue that goal stability and consensus can never be fully realized, due to both environmental changes and individual differences.

As a result of a great deal of research, we now believe that decisions are aimed at a sequential rather than a simultaneous resolution of conflict. Each decision must "strike a balance among so many conflicting values, objectives, and criteria that it will always be suboptimal from any single viewpoint. Every decision or choice affecting the whole enterprise has negative consequences for some of the parts" (Katz, 1970, p. 13). Thus, each resolution of conflict creates other conflict, as do developments in the environment over which decision makers have little or no control. In effect, decision makers must precariously make their way through an unending series of imbalances toward a constantly redefined goal. The result is continuous rejection, clarification, redefinition, and alteration of goals.

Hirschman and Lindblom (1962) believe that such sporadic and erratic decision making may in the long run produce better results than decisions aimed at stable and clearly defined goals, most of which are only vaguely understood anyway. In their view, progress may actually be impeded by the kind of centralized and rational decision making prescribed by classical theory. They favor instead a view that has been termed by Cyert and March (1963) a "quasi-resolution" of conflict and believe this to be characteristic of most organizational decision making.

To illustrate what has been said so far, consider a university. As opposed to the classical notion of a single goal toward which all organizational members will strive (in this case, probably advancement of knowledge), the faculty, staff, and students probably have, among others, the following goals:

Faculty: time away from campus (for research, tennis lessons, or whatever);
Staff: running the university at low cost, to avoid having to go before wealthy alumni, state legislators, or whomever to beg for additional funds;

Students: small classes, courses taught by faculty rather than graduate students, and classes that remain open rather than being closed because too many students have enrolled.

Even with these greatly simplified sets of goals, there can be no single decision which will succeed in resolving all imbalances (unless we were to assume that resources are unlimited, which would be unrealistic). What occurs in the absence of a "win-win-win" solution is a "win-win-lose" one (see Chapter 9), with the weakest party in all probability being the loser. The first-stage solution to this dilemma in many universities was therefore to simultaneously provide faculty with their goal (time off) and staff with theirs (running at low cost). This was accomplished, of course, by having large courses, using graduate students liberally as teachers, and closing courses when necessary to preserve this situation, even at the cost of delaying some students' graduation.

This solution is said to be only a "quasi-resolution" of conflict, however, because over time the power dynamics change, making redefinitions and clarifications necessary. In this case several forces, including parental complaints and student riots, combined to make a new solution necessary. As a result, many universities today make great efforts to keep class size down and courses open, and there have also been movements in many places to "get the faculty back in the classroom." In some cases this has resulted, at least temporarily, in an imbalance relating to faculty goals of time off. In others (perhaps where faculty were more marketable or better organized) faculty goals were met, but staff members were forced to search for additional funds so more faculty could be hired.

The quasi-resolution model is based upon circularity; that is, there is no ideal end-goal toward which decisions should be rationally directed; rather, there is a continual evolution. Since the future is unknown, uncertain, and too complex for human beings to grasp, decisions will probably be better if they ignore some aspects of a problem and deal primarily with the more tangible and predictable aspects of it. In time, a creative synthesis may be possible.

From this viewpoint decision making is seen to be remedial, serial, and fragmented, featuring both intentional and unintentional neglect of some of its consequences. Human behavior is viewed as an ongoing series of testing and feedback processes through which we determine our interests and effectiveness.

Cyert, Simon, and Trow (1956) illustrate how the actual phases of a decision-making process differ from the traditional rational choice mechanisms, and how some aspects of traditional theory may fail to adequately explain what actually happens. The decision process they observed took place in a medium-sized corporation; it dealt with the feasibility of using electronic data-processing equipment.

The search for potential courses of action constituted a large part of the decision process. For example, the individual assigned to study the question began by talking to representatives of computer manufacturers, reading the literature pertinent to the subject, and interviewing consultants. He then had to decide what consultants to hire as advisors, and what studies it would be necessary to conduct. After deciding that several information-gathering studies should be made, he was faced with procedural decisions and with gaining the cooperation of those who would supply the information.

The consultants' recommendation that a centralized system be introduced drew criticism, and additional experts and computer company representatives were asked to evaluate the consultants' report. This led to the need to consider and decide upon a partially electronic system, and to other considerations as well.

In this illustration the original alternatives were to install or not to install an electronic system, in contrast to the more common and difficult decision among several alternatives. Even so, the nature of the decision made it necessary to engage in information-gathering activities which yielded a number of alternatives at each step. Few if any of the decisions could be based on a single criterion, and consequently comparisons had to be made between alternatives which were not directly comparable.

The authors of this case suggest that search processes and information-gathering strategies are critically important elements which must be incorporated into any theory of decision making if it is to be considered adequate.

Simon's Administrative Theory of Decision Making

The central focus of this chapter is the "administrative" theory of decision making, first advanced by Herbert A. Simon in 1947. This theory differs from earlier classical theory in both its assumptions and its predictions.

Simon criticized the economic individual theory on the grounds that its assumptions are invalid in real situations and that the question of values in decision making must be decided by the decision maker, not by the theoretician. He suggested that management authors concentrate upon what *is*, rather than what they believed *ought to be*. The result of this change in emphasis was administrative man theory.

Simon saw two important differences between the artificial "economic" individual and his true-to-life decision-making "administrative" individual.

First, he rejected the notion that people can be fully informed about anything, arguing that since consequences always lie in the future, it is impossible for any person to know all potential alternatives and to anticipate all potential results. In actual practice only a few alternatives can be known, and future values can only be anticipated as projections of the imagination. Because of this physical limitation upon the administrator's ability, Simon advanced the principle of *bounded rationality:*

> When the limits to rationality are viewed from the individual's

> standpoint, they fall into three categories: he is limited by his unconscious skills, habits, and reflexes; he is limited by his values and conceptions of purpose, which may diverge from the organizational goals; he is limited by the extent of his knowledge and information. The individual can be rational in terms of the organization's goals only to the extent that he is *able* to pursue a particular course of action, he has a correct conception of the *goal* of the action, and he is correctly *informed* about the conditions surrounding his action. Within the boundaries laid down by these factors his choices are rational-goal oriented (1957, p. 241).

According to the administrative theory of decision making, "choice is always exercised with respect to a limited, approximate, simplified 'model' of the real situation" (March and Simon, 1958, p. 139). In place of the concept of "objective rationality," Simon offered the concept of "subjective rationality," which depends on the individual's personal values and unique modes of perceiving, learning, and thinking. Whereas objective rationality is *in fact* the correct behavior for maximizing given values in a given situation, subjective rationality maximizes attainment relative to the actual knowledge of the individual (Simon, 1957, p. 76). Accordingly, people would be considered subjectively rational if they attempted to maximize an end even if the attempt failed, or even if the end was inappropriate. Rationality, then, can only be defined in terms of the decision maker's own frame of reference.

Second, according to Simon, the administrative individual *satisfices* rather than optimizes when making most decisions. "Satisficing" means that when individuals are confronted with a situation where a decision must be made, they begin by searching for possible alternatives and for information concerning the consequences of each alternative. This search continues only until an alternative is found that meets a subjective *minimum standard* with respect to the things being sought. In other words, rather than continuing the search until an optimum alternative is located, individuals discontinue their search as soon as one is found which is satisfactory. The economic individual's goal of searching the haystack for the sharpest needle is replaced by the more modest objective of finding one sharp enough to sew with (March and Simon, 1958, p. 141).

There are several reasons why the decision maker has a strong tendency to satisfice. First, a decision must often be made on the basis of more than a single value; second, the decision maker's value system is most likely subjective and implicit rather than objective and explicit; third, the decision maker is inevitably unable to perform the mental calculations necessary to compare a great many values and to assign them proper weights. Thus the substitution of satisficing for optimizing greatly reduces the demands upon the decision maker. Of course, when simultaneously confronted with several alternatives, a decision maker may be able to compare their relative values and choose the best one. In other circumstances, however, where all available alternatives cannot be known, the decision maker will tend to continue to search only until a "good enough" solution is found, and then stop searching.

Simon also introduced another important concept related to search behavior—the modifying influence of the searcher's aspiration level. Borrowing from previous empirical research conducted by Lewin (1948), Simon asserted that the criteria for a satisfactory alternative will be determined by the level of aspiration of the decision maker, which is itself determined largely by prior successes and failures. Simon asserted that this aspiration level is dynamic, changing over time in response to subsequent experiences. Therefore, if the search for a satisfactory alternative proves unsuccessful, decision makers will eventually reduce their level of aspiration. Conversely, the discovery of satisfactory alternatives will tend to elevate the aspiration level.

Propositions

The literature pertaining to individual decision making is truly voluminous, and we could not hope to deal with even a major part of it within the space of a single chapter. The following four propositions, therefore, although proposed by Simon as being central to his administrative theory, are by no means intended to be a fully comprehensive statement of decision-making theory.

1. Choice is always made with respect to a simplified model of the real situation.
2. Decisions are made within the unique frame of reference or "psychological set" of the decision maker. This frame of reference is the decision maker's *subjective rationality.* The elements of a situation are therefore not "given" objective facts, but are themselves outcomes.
3. Search behavior is concerned only with the discovery of *satisfactory* alternatives; only in exceptional cases is it concerned with the discovery of *optimum* alternatives.
4. Continued failure to achieve a minimum standard of satisfaction results in the successive lowering of the standard until an acceptable compromise is reached; conversely, easy success tends to raise minimum standards.

Empirical Evidence

Our assessment of the administrative theory of decision making will consist of two parts: First, a review of two explicit tests of the entire model; second, a review of laboratory studies which constitute inferential tests of the validity of individual propositions.

Tests of the Model

Cyert and March (1963) attempted to develop a computer model to simulate the processes involved in price and output decisions in a large retail department store. After considering about a dozen departments within the store, they chose one to be the subject of intensive investigation. This department made relatively independent price and output decisions for the purpose of meeting a sales objective and realizing a specified average mark-up on goods sold. For both price and output it was assumed that future estimates served as goals against which departmental activities would be compared, and that once these levels were achieved standard rules would be used to make mark-up and reorder decisions. When the estimates were not achieved, search would be stimulated and decision rules revised, based on the first acceptable alternative presented to the decision maker. Finally, it was assumed that sales goals and mark-up goals would be gradually adjusted, based on success or failure in meeting initial goal estimates. By studying the actual behavior of decision makers the researchers inferred the rules governing sales and mark-up decisions and the constraints within which the decision maker worked.

Predictions of the sales estimates, advance orders and reorders, and mark-up decisions were then derived from the model. New data, which were not used to develop the model, were then used to test the model. Compared to actual sales estimates, the model's predicted sales estimates turned out to be accurate within 5 percent *in each of four separate instances.*

Predictions concerning advance orders were more difficult to test, because the firm did not keep records of such orders for any length of time. The model's predictions could be compared with actual figures for four instances, however, and the comparisons yielded the following results:

Season	*Predicted Advance Orders*	*Actual Advance Orders*
1	18,050	16,453
2	26,550	24,278
3	36,200	35,922
4	43,000	35,648

More complete data were available to test the model's prediction of price determination. Of 197 predicted prices, 188 (95 percent) were correct to the penny. Of 58 predictions concerning sales prices, 56 (96 percent) were also perfect. Of 159 prices of selected marked-down items, 140 (88 percent) were correct.

Another test of the model was made by Clarkson (1963), which also resulted in generally accurate predictions of individual decisions. Clarkson constructed a model of the trust investment process used by trust officers in a bank. To construct the model, Clarkson studied the trust departments of several banks, interviewed department officers, and observed behavior at meetings where past and future decisions were reviewed. Attention was then focused upon one investment officer, who was chiefly responsible for all decisions concerning portfolio choices. The histories of several accounts were examined and models were constructed to reflect what seemed to be invariant decision processes, that is, processes which seemed not to vary among accounts.

To aid in developing hypotheses, and to discover how prior decisions had been made, the trust officer was asked to permit a transcript to be made of what he said as he thought through the decision process; he was also asked to read articles from financial reports and journals to which he subscribed and to comment upon their ideas, forecasts, and facts.

On the basis of these techniques a model was constructed to consider the problem of investing the funds of new accounts in common stocks. The unique frame of reference of the decision maker was governed by standardized rules of thumb. Search behavior consisted of examining company, industry, and market data of companies whose stock might be purchased, and satisficing criteria were established in the form of standard operating procedures and rules of thumb. Provision for changes in goals, based on success or failure, was also built into the model.

In order to test the model's ability to reproduce the actual behavior of the trust investor—to simulate the trust investment process—the model was required to select portfolios for a specific set of actual accounts. The four accounts chosen had been handled by the trust officer, but they had not been used to develop the model. The model's selections, along with the actual selections made by the trust officer, are shown in Table 7–1.

The reader will probably agree that the similarity of the two lists is striking. Incidentally, as a further test of the model the portfolios it selected were compared with portfolio selections made by random, naive models; it was found that Clarkson's trust investment model selected a greater proportion of correct securities than did any of the random models.

To obtain further confirmation, the processes by which the model generated the portfolios were compared to the recorded decision processes of the trust investor. Clarkson concluded that "although it is not possible to state that all the decision processes were unequivocally confirmed, the evidence strongly supports the hypothesis" (p. 266).

Some disagreement exists as to whether these results by Cyert and March and Clarkson "prove" that individuals really do employ satisficing, bounded rationality, etc., when making decisions. It has been suggested by analogy that if a computer can make music that sounds like Beethoven, does this mean that Beethoven used the same principles of composition as the computer? Clearly such results cannot "prove" that people are inherently "administrative" rather than "economic"; however, these results are nonetheless important because they show that use of administrative theory criteria improves our ability to predict individual decision making.

We now turn to inferential tests of the individual propositions of Simon's administrative theory of decision making.

TABLE 7-1: Comparison of Actual with Trust Investment Model Selections.

1. Growth Account. Funds available for investment: $22,000.

The program selected	The trust officer selected
60 General American Transportation	30 Corning Glass
50 Dow Chemical	50 Dow Chemical
10 IBM	10 IBM
60 Merck and Company	50 Merck and Company
45 Owens Corning Fiberglas	45 Owens Corning Fiberglas

2. Income and Growth Account. Funds available for investment: $37,500.

The program selected	The trust officer selected
100 American Can	100 American Can
100 Continental Insurance	100 Continental Insurance
100 Equitable Gas	100 Equitable Gas
100 Duquesne Light	100 General Public Utilities
100 Libbey Owens Ford	100 Libbey Owens Ford
100 International Harvester	50 National Lead
100 Philadelphia Electric	100 Philadelphia Electric
100 Phillips Petroleum	100 Phillips Petroleum
100 Socony Mobil	100 Socony Mobil

3. Income and Growth Account. Funds available for investment: $31,000.

The program selected	The trust officer selected
100 American Can	100 American Can
100 Continental Insurance	100 Continental Insurance
100 Duquesne Light	100 Duquesne Light
100 Equitable Gas	100 Equitable Gas
100 Pennsylvania Power and Light	100 General Public Utilities
100 International Harvester	100 International Harvester
100 Libbey Owens Ford	100 Libbey Owens Ford
100 Socony Mobil	100 Socony Mobil

4. Income Account. Funds available for investment: $28,000.

The program selected	The trust officer selected
100 American Can	100 American Can
100 Continental Insurance	100 Continental Insurance
100 Duquesne Light	100 Duquesne Light
100 Equitable Gas	100 Equitable Gas
100 Pennsylvania Power and Light	100 General Public Utilities
100 International Harvester	100 International Harvester
100 Phillips Petroleum	100 Phillips Petroleum

Source: Clarkson (1963).

Proposition 1

Choice is always made with respect to a simplified model of the real situation.

There has not been much empirical research relating directly to the process people use in analyzing and dealing with complex problems; however, several studies of stereotype formation are relevant to this proposition.

As we saw in Chapter 4, stereotyping is a perceptual defense mechanism which enables individuals to deal with complex stimuli simply. Stereotypes may stem from past experiences, but they are also likely to derive from tradition, school books, and mass media. R. W. Kinghorn (1966) investigated the occupational stereotypes held by personnel managers to determine the extent to which selection of employees is based on preconceived ideas about the characteristics of those in various occupations rather than on the actual qualities of individual applicants. He mailed questionnaires to members of the American Society of Personnel Administrators, located in four midwestern states.

Twelve percent of the respondents did not attempt to answer the questionnaire, claiming that they had no preconceived notions about the characteristics of people in different occupations. Another 12 percent did not believe it possible to associate physical characteristics (e.g., plain looking, wears glasses) with occupations, but did not reject the idea of stereotyped personality characteristics. Only 8.4 percent indicated that stereotyping could be unwise, and the remainder (67.6 percent) apparently considered it a normal and justifiable procedure.

Kinghorn concluded that personnel managers do hold occupational stereotypes which vary considerably in strength. Some occupations were described quickly and easily in very few words, signifying a strong stereotype, while others required a greater range of characteristics to describe them. Kinghorn also found that familiarity with an occupation, measured by whether a personnel manager hires for that occupation, produced no significant difference in stereotypes. This suggests that exposure to or contact with members of a given occupational group will not necessarily change the individual's stereotype of that group.

In addition to describing his own research, Kinghorn (1966) cited a study conducted by Bendig and Hountras (1958) in which college students compared research scientists, engineers, lawyers, and businessmen. Stereotypes were shown to exist for all four occupations. For example, the scientist was thought to lack social grace, but to have greater intellectual skills than the engineer. Kinghorn also cited an experiment by Stagner (1950) in which "anti-labor" students were found to be much more likely than "pro-labor" students to characterize factory workers as "ignorant," "lazy," and "troublesome." Similar results have been described in Chapter 4 of this text.

Much of the evidence which will be considered in our evaluations of Propositions 2 and 3 is also pertinent here. For example, considerable research has shown that people have neither the wits nor the inclination to deal with complex facts and alternatives in search activities. However, there seems to be considerable variety in the extent to which individuals are able and willing to do so. One key variable that has been identified is *cognitive complexity,* which refers to:

> . . . the amount of information a decision-maker can use during any operation, and considers his capacity to integrate a large number of factors and to be open to changes in inputs which indicate more effective modes of procedures. Integration and flexibility of cognitive elements (e.g., concepts, perceptual dimensions) will allow greater use of internal and external information. . . . In the areas of information processing and information search, several researchers have found that groups with more complex member cognitive systems tend to rely on more complex sources of information and spend more time processing such information. Moreover, "complex" decision-makers engaged more often in information search strategies. This information suggests that structurally complex individuals can handle larger amounts of information. . . . (Kerr et al., 1975, p. 183–84)

The concept of cognitive complexity has been found to be linked with such personality characteristics as dogmatism (Long and Ziller, 1965) and tolerance for ambiguity (Dermer, 1973). Much remains to be learned in this area, however, and Dermer (1973, p. 517) cautions that the research to date contains many apparent inconsistencies; he also warns that "the relationship between conceptual abstractness and the amount of information preferred is not independent of the characteristics of the information involved or of the context in which it is to be used."

Proposition 2

Decisions are made within the unique frame of reference or "psychological set" of the decision maker. This frame of reference is the decision maker's subjective rationality. The elements of a situation are therefore not "given" objective facts, but are themselves outcomes.

The general validity of this proposition is widely established in the psychological literature, and some of its aspects and implications have already been examined in Chapter 4. We shall limit ourselves here to a description of research sufficient to illustrate the proposition's validity and its relevance to the management process.

As we have seen, even when individuals believe that they are perceiving facts and making decisions solely on the basis of explicit and relevant cues, they are inevitably responding as well to less obvious and less objective cues which are inherent in the situation. Additional evidence of subjective criteria usage can be found in a wide variety of laboratory experiments concerned with decision making. For example, individuals in rather simple problem-solving situations have repeatedly been found to make choices consistently better than would be expected by chance.

However, subjects tend to become more conservative in their strategies —even though such conservatism is inconsistent with the objective requirements—as the complexity of the decisions to be made increases (Myers and Sadler, 1960). Furthermore, subjects operating under such conditions typically fail to use information that would help them avoid errors, preferring to rely on their own subjective criteria instead (Morin, 1960). Indeed, individuals often cease to seek additional information even when such information could greatly increase the quality of their decisions and could be acquired at low or reasonable cost (Pitz, Reinhold, and Geller, 1969).

Another example of conservatism by laboratory subjects, as compared to the choices which would be made by a truly rational or "statistical" person, is given by Peterson and Beach (1967, p. 32):

> Imagine yourself in the following experiment. Two urns are filled with a large number of poker chips. The first urn contains 70% red chips and 30% blue. The second contains 70% blue chips and 30% red. The experimenter flips a fair coin to select one of the two urns. . . . He then draws a succession of chips from the selected urn. Suppose that the sample contains eight red and four blue chips. What is your revised probability that the selected urn is the predominantly red one? . . . If your probability for the red urn is about .75, your revision agrees with that given by most subjects. However, that revised estimate is very *conservative* when compared to the statistical man's revised probability of .97.

The frame of reference or subjective rationality of the decision maker reveals itself in other ways besides through tendencies toward conservatism. For example, subjective rather than objective rationality is often used in assigning weights to information obtained. As was mentioned in Chapter 4, information received early in the search process may be highly valued, sometimes to the extent that data received later on is virtually ignored; this is called a *primacy effect*. At other times, irrationally greater attention is paid to data received near the end; this has been labeled a *recency effect*. A dramatic and even frightening example of such order effects is presented by Audley (1971, pp. 62–63):

> If one dramatizes the legal evidence from a court case and presents it in different orders, then these orders will influence the opinion that is formed about the guilt of the defendant. In our undergraduate laboratory classes my colleague, Dr. Legge, and I have composed in this way two particular orders of presentation of the testimony from a celebrated American bigamy case. . . . We have always found consistent differences in the average beliefs in guilt resulting from the two orders when these are compared at the end of the evidence. Even more startling is the difference in the number of people actually considering the

> defendant guilty. . . . Summarising the experimental results over four years' work we find that of fifty-six jurors receiving one order of evidence only three plump for 'guilty', for the other order eighteen out of fifty-six jurors regard the defendant as guilty. There is only one possibility in ten thousand that this difference could be due to chance. . . . Of course, this is only an approximation, perhaps even a caricature of the law. But who knows without experiment what some aspects of the law may be a caricature of?

A number of studies (e.g., Coombs and Pruitt, 1960; Coombs and Bowen, 1971) have shown that choices among alternative gambles are only partially based upon attempts to maximize returns, being affected also by such things as skewness and dispersion of possible outcomes (Payne, 1973). In a review of the role of personality traits in subjective probability, Brichacek (1970) describes studies which show that such things as aggression, dominance, autonomy, intelligence, and fear of failure are sometimes associated with the kinds of gambles individuals prefer and with variations in the degree of risk-taking individuals exhibit.

In a more recent review of the research literature, Kerr et al. (1975) present examples of some effects of subjective rationality upon decision making:

> —People generally tend to overestimate the likelihood of events occurring which have low probabilities, while underestimating likelihoods of occurrence for events with high probabilities.
>
> —People tend to exhibit the "gambler's fallacy," predicting that an event will occur in the near future merely because it has failed to occur in a while.
>
> —People tend to overestimate true probabilities of favorable events, while understating those which are unfavorable (p. 173).

Concerning Proposition 2, the evidence rather convincingly demonstrates that individuals apply subjective rationality in decision-making situations and that, as the complexity or difficulty of a problem increases, the use of subjective rationality causes greater and greater departures from objective rationality. Furthermore, data attesting to the effects on decision making of individual differences—such as personality characteristics, expectations, risk-preferences, perceptions, and motivations—further support the proposition that decisions are made with respect to the unique frame of reference of the decision maker.

Proposition 3

Search behavior is concerned only with the discovery of satisfactory alternatives; only in exceptional cases is it concerned with the discovery of optimum alternatives.

This proposition is relatively imprecise in that it fails to specify the conditions under which search behavior will be initiated and terminated and the conditions under which a final choice will be made. It also leaves unresolved the question of what is meant by "satisfactory." For example, it has been argued that satisficing behavior is not very unlike maximizing behavior if it is kept in mind that additional information is always costly, both in time and money (Zeckhauser and Schaefer, 1968). Therefore the decision maker who selects the first acceptable alternative may be thinking "there may be a better one, but it will not be so much better as to make up for the cost of additional search" (Perrow, 1972, p. 149). This attempt at reconciling economic man and administrative man has been criticized, however:

> March and Simon illustrate their satisficing model with the example of looking for a needle in a haystack—you do not search for the sharpest needle, only one sharp enough to sew with. But the example is not apt; no economist (who is supposed to deal only with completely rational man) would argue that you search for the sharpest needle. The real reason why the Simon formulation is so useful is that the costs of search are usually unknown to the individual. He does not know if there is a sharper needle or how long it would take to find it. Therefore, he cannot take into account the cost of search in many cases (Perrow, 1972, p. 149).

Proposition 3 is also imprecise in that it fails to consider the environment in which the decision must be made. Under conditions of *certainty* it may be possible to seek optimum alternatives; even then, however, so many possibilities typically exist that bounded rationality results. Under conditions of *risk,* where the outcomes in any given case are not known in advance, but where knowledge exists of all possible outcomes and the probabilities connected with each can be ascertained, it is still possible that optimum alternatives may be sought. However, under conditions of *uncertainty,* where the full range of outcomes and their associated probabilities are unknown, search is much more likely to be for "satisfactory" alternatives. A fuller description of certainty, risk, and uncertainty is contained in the chapter on planning and control.

Many writers argue that nearly all decisions must be made in an atmosphere of uncertainty; a good description of decision making under such conditions is offered by Newman (1971, p. 4):

> It is uncertainty rather than risk with which the marketing executive must contend as he makes decisions relative to products, packages, promotional efforts, prices, channels of distribution, and the like. Working in a continually changing environment, he typically is confronted with unique situations. . . . He may find it difficult to identify courses of action that deserve serious consideration. Even if the alternatives are seen clearly, their outcomes are likely to be obscure. . . . He frequently

has little information on which to base predictions of how the various factors will affect the outcome of a given program of action at the time it is undertaken.

Another way of looking at the question of uncertainty is offered by Thompson (1967), whose *basic variables of decision* are illustrated in Figure 7–1. Thompson believed that all decision issues involved the major dimensions of (1) beliefs about cause/effect relations, and (2) preferences regarding possible outcomes.

		Preferences regarding possible outcomes	
		Certainty	Uncertainty
Beliefs about cause/effect relations	Certainty		
	Uncertainty		

Figure 7–1. Types of Decision Issues. (Thompson, 1967).

Depending upon which quadrant in Figure 7–1 the decision maker was, specific strategies were called for:

> Where there is certainty regarding both causation and outcome preferences, we will speak of a *computational strategy* for decision making. Although it might seem that no decision is required under such circumstances, if data are voluminous or formulas are intricate, the solution is not obvious. . . . Where outcome preferences are clear but cause/effect relationships are uncertain, we will refer to the *judgmental strategy* for decision making. Where the situation is reversed and there is certainty regarding cause/effect but uncertainty regarding outcome preferences, the issue can be regarded as calling for a *compromise strategy* for decision making. Finally, where there is uncertainty on both dimensions, we will speak of the *inspirational strategy* for decision making, if indeed any decision is forthcoming (Thompson, 1967, pp. 134–35).

Thompson's humorous title for the last quadrant indicates that in this area optimum strategies of any kind are clearly impossible, and that the decision maker would do well to pray for guidance, if not for outright delivery from the situation. The first quadrant, of course, is where optimum alternative-search is possible although, as Thompson, Starr (1971, pp. 148–49) and others have cautioned, such search will still not be easy.

The studies of Soelberg (1966) are very relevant to Proposition 3. Soelberg conducted highly detailed interviews with graduate students who were making postgraduate job decisions. Approximately 100 lengthy interviews with 20 different students were conducted over three- to five-month periods; it was found that the decision-making processes of many students were not only inconsistent with classical theory, but with administrative theory as well. Specifically, Soelberg's decision makers typically continued their search even after finding an acceptable alternative. For the most part, by the time the decision maker was ready to accept a job, at least one other job had been offered.

Soelberg conducted a second study, collecting data from 32 advanced-degree graduates, each of whom answered eight biweekly questionnaires during his job-decision period. The results were strikingly similar to his earlier findings. Eighty–seven percent of his sample members terminated their job search ten or more days before they reported having made their decision. Seventy–four percent reported having one or more acceptable alternatives two weeks or more before terminating their search (Soelberg, 1967).

At the time of search termination the decision makers were uncertain about their eventual choices. The probabilities of choice they assigned to the alternatives they were ultimately to select were: "preferred candidate," 29 percent; "second alternative," 24 percent; and "all other alternatives," 47 percent.

From these data Soelberg concluded that search is a parallel process; that is, several potentially acceptable alternatives are considered at one time. Alternatives which clearly fall short are rejected immediately, but all others are put on "active roster," with little or no systematic comparison until the decision maker is ready to make a final choice. This is directly relevant to Proposition 3 in that Soelberg's decision makers continued to search for new alternatives even after discovering a satisfactory one. Soelberg's explanation of his findings, incidentally, is that the decision maker *had* in fact selected one of the first acceptable alternatives, but found the making of the final decision to be a highly involved, emotionally painful process. At the time of the final decision the decision maker was forced to systematically compare incomparable alternatives and to reject satisfactory (and even, in some ways, superior) alternatives.

Soelberg hypothesized, therefore, that the final decision process is one of *decision confirmation*. The decision maker will not enter into this period until one of the alternatives discovered thus far can be identified as an *implicit favorite*. In other words, decision making during the confirmation phase is an exercise in prejudice—in rationalization rather than in rationality. The decision maker ensures during the confirmation phase that the implicit favorite will indeed turn out to be the "right" choice.

The process of decision confirmation can be briefly summarized as follows: the criteria used by the decision maker to identify a favorite alternative are very few, typically involving no more than one or two primary goal attributes. Comparison among alternatives is quickly reduced to a pro-

and-con argument between two and only two alternatives. The objective of this comparison is to bring his perception of the facts and his evaluation of goal attributes into line with his predisposition toward the implicit favorite. The decision is finally made when a decision rule has been established which satisfactorily explains the dominance of the choice candidate.

Soelberg's hypothesis provided the key to surprisingly accurate predictions. In a second study, the researchers were able to accurately predict *87 percent* of the career job choices two to eight weeks before the decision makers would admit that they had made a decision.

The literature pertaining to human limitations (reviewed in Chapter 4 and in the evaluations of Propositions 1 and 2 in this chapter) suggests that even if most individuals were *motivated* to seek optimum alternatives, their inherent *inability* to behave in accord with rational principles would force them to settle for choices considerably short of optimal. In addition to the less-than-totally-rational behavior already cited (satisficing, stereotyping, primacy and recency effects, rationalization, etc.), Slovic and Lichtenstein (1971) have described several other examples of inherent limitations that affect search behavior:

Extremity of Information. Many studies have found that the weight assigned by an individual to information is strongly influenced by the most extreme item. For example, Himmelfarb (1970) found that neutral information was undervalued in comparison with more polarized information, and Manis, Gleason, and Dawes (1966) found that two negative pieces of information, which were of unequal intensity, generated a much more extreme judgment than would result from averaging the two (cited in Slovic and Lichtenstein, 1971, p. 690).

Inter-Item Consistency. Information whose "surprise value" is great tends to be undervalued or discounted altogether. For example, Anderson and Jacobson (1965) found that a value (e.g., the word "gloomy") which was seen as inconsistent with other values (e.g., the words "honest" and "considerate") was typically given less weight by subjects (cited in Slovic and Lichtenstein, p. 691).

Misaggregation. Many subjects have great difficulty in combining different pieces of information to generate a single response. One illustration of this tendency comes from Phillips (1966), whose subjects misperceived the impact of each bit of data as it was received, and then were inconsistent in their misperceptions when faced with a subsequent aggregation task (cited in Slovic and Lichtenstein, p. 697).

Law of Small Numbers. Even sophisticated decision-makers make incorrect judgments about the amount of error inherent in and the unreliability of small samples of data. Notwithstanding the fundamental truth that a sample's representativeness decreases as the size of the sample decreases, most decision makers act as though small samples are highly representative of the total population (Slovic and Lichtenstein, 1972).

Correlation and Causality. Correlation between two variables means that knowledge of the value of one will enable prediction of the value of the other. Slovic and Lichtenstein (1972) point out that many individuals fall victim to "illusory correlations," where prior belief that a relationship exists leads the decision maker to perceive one even though none does exist. Decision makers also tend to forget that a correlation may indicate unidirectional causality, mutual causality, or merely that a third force is affecting the two variables.

The preceding discussion has centered around evidence obtained from laboratory subjects, but some data from real organizations further supports the position that, whether because of inability or unwillingness to maximize, search behavior is usually concerned with satisfactory rather than optimum alternatives. After reviewing several studies pertinent to search behavior, Stagner (1969, p. 2) concluded that research "has had the effect of further shaking confidence in the relevance of the classical assumptions."

Stagner came to the more specific conclusion, based on the same review, that "with respect to profit maximization as a goal, the empirical data also lead to rejection of the assumption" (p. 2). His own study, based on responses from 217 executives from 109 firms, supported this conclusion. Among the relevant findings were that only "rough estimates" were made of anticipated costs and profits which might result from a decision; that company "image" often outweighed cost factors; and that considerable weight was attached to company traditions.

Another study relevant to the question of whether firms actually employ rigorous, high-powered analytical techniques—which theoretically can provide optimum solutions—was conducted by Reeser (1971), whose sample consisted of project managers in the aerospace industry. Reeser points out that one would logically expect this industry to be sophisticated in this particular area, since its decision makers are almost all engineers who possess mathematical backgrounds and who have been trained in the scientific method. Furthermore, the environment requires frequent decision making and accuracy is critical. It is also true that the industry's ultimate customer is the Department of Defense, whose favorable views toward objective decision making are a matter of public record.

The project managers were asked to indicate the three guides they felt were most important to decisions they had initiated. It was suggested that they consider both quantitative guides such as PERT and linear programming, and qualitative guides such as judgment and experience. Reeser found that:

> . . . Even with this research sample of twenty subjects specifically trained to approach problem solutions objectively, and a sample drawn from an industry in which quantitative methods have been stressed for the past fifteen years, subjective bases for decision making were mentioned over three times as frequently as sophisticated methods of analysis. . . . It is interesting to note that nine of the twenty research

subjects did not mention a single sophisticated analytical method as being valuable to them for making any of their important decisions (p. 68).

The evidence reviewed here clearly suggests that search behavior is typically concerned with the discovery of satisfactory rather than optimum alternatives; in fact, there is little evidence supporting the idea that people are interested in or able to pursue optimum alternatives even in conditions which approximate certainty or risk, let alone under conditions of uncertainty.

Proposition 4

Continued failure to achieve a minimum standard of satisfaction results in the successive lowering of the standard until an acceptable compromise is reached; conversely, easy success tends to raise minimum standards.

The classic research done on levels of aspiration (Lewin et al., 1944) indicates that anticipated performance will vary directly with immediate experience of the problem. When a problem is easily solved the subject will typically anticipate better performance on the next trial; if the subject fails, the estimate of future success is lowered.

Several more recent laboratory experiments have explored this phenomenon. The following examples illustrate the consistency of findings, even when different experimental methods were employed:

–Zander, Natsoulas, and Thomas (1960) and Zander and Medow (1963) undertook studies of levels of aspiration which involved individual participation in group projects. Among the sample of 225 high-school boys, both teams and single subjects raised their levels of aspiration after exceeding a previous standard, and lowered aspiration levels following failure.

–DeSoto, Coleman, and Putnam (1960) asked 96 college students to predict their success or failure on a word association test. It was found that prior experiences of success led them to make more accurate predictions about the likelihood of future successes. This study is only relevant to the proposition under investigation, however, if prediction levels can be considered to be analogous to aspiration levels.

–Myers and Fort (1963) analyzed sequential gambling bets and found that choices on any single bet were largely a function of the immediately preceding pattern of events; a win inspired anticipation of another win, while a loss reduced the anticipation of a subsequent win.

–Zander and Ulberg (1971) gave ballots to 96 high school students, on which they were asked to indicate the scores they expected their teams to achieve on the next trial. The teams consisted of four students each; their task was to rapidly and correctly count holes in punch cards. The highest and lowest estimates within each group were discarded, and the remaining two were averaged and reported to the group as the group's aspiration level.

It was found that aspiration levels rose both in successful and unsuccessful groups; however, the average rise in the aspiration level of successful groups (4.44) considerably exceeded that of unsuccessful groups (1.43).

–Cummings, Schwab, and Rosen (1971) gave performance feedback (either accurate and complete, accurate but incomplete, or erroneously low) to 60 undergraduate students who had performed a simple addition task, and then asked them to indicate their expected performance in a second work period. It was found that "previous performance on the task affects goal levels, the greater the performance, the higher the subsequent goal" (p. 529).

–Ilgen and Hamstra (1972) asked 150 undergraduate psychology students a series of questions and gave performance feedback which was erroneous, but which was apparently believed by the subjects. Following this feedback, subjects were asked to forecast their performance on the next series of questions. It was found that "after five trials, the performance level which subjects expected to obtain on Trial 6 was influenced strongly by the earlier performance feedback. The means for nine of the fifteen groups were within plus or minus five percentiles of the performance reported to the group" (p. 363).

The consistency of these findings should not lead the reader to assume that individual and task differences are not important. In fact, a number of factors influence the extent to which the effects observed in these experiments will occur. For example, Ilgen (1971) found that the level at which subjects initially expected to perform was an important determinant of their reactions to actual performance. Subjects who expected low performance, and who were led to believe that they had performed above or below expectations, were less satisfied than were those who expected average performance and were told that they had performed above or below expectations.

It is also possible that the impact of *many* previous failures upon future standards is different from that of only one or two. Streufert and Streufert (1970) have reported such a finding, as have Forward and Zander (1971, p. 185) who noted that ". . . repeated group failure arouses strong dispositions among members to avoid the negative consequences of failure. . . . Excessively high goal-setting may be seen as a means of avoiding the negative consequences of failure by making the goal irrelevant as a criterion. . . ." Such a tendency by group members would constitute a direct contradiction of Proposition 4; however, Forward and Zander (1971, p. 189) point out that "one avoidance strategy is to select goals for the group which are not challenging and which cannot be used as clear criteria for group achievement."

Further complexities are introduced by the fact that:

> . . . Members often raise the aspiration level after a success more than they lower it after a failure. As a result, the mean level of aspiration tends to be higher after a success than after a failure; yet, the

> discrepancy between the last level of performance and the future level of aspiration . . . tends to be larger after a failure than after a success (Zander and Ulberg, 1971, p. 363).

Ilgen and Hamstra (1972, p. 364) suggest as a possible reason for this that "subjects simply may have been unwilling to accept the fact that they would perform as poorly on the next trial as they did on the last."

Subject to the limitations suggested by the research described above, Proposition 4 seems to adequately deal with the behavior of persons who are subjected to continuing tests of their problem-solving ability or of their estimates of future success or failure. A weakness of aspiration level as a predictive formulation, however, is that it is not dynamic. While it does consider that certain personality need states operate on fluctuations in aspiration, it does not consider a subject's estimate of future conditions that might alter the outcome of events. Indeed, most level-of-aspiration studies are designed to measure the effect of past experience alone and new information is withheld from subjects. Aspiration-level theory does not therefore adequately consider the possibility of rational planning based on cognitive anticipation of future events, assessment of the probability of their occurrence, and desirability of their consequences. The aspiration-level proposition treats behavior as a function only of reactions to past events; the prediction of future happenings is based on very recent experiences and on unconscious needs.

Aspiration level is, however, but one theoretical framework by which behavior responses can be analyzed and predicted. Some theorists have attempted to consider anticipatory behavior as well as behavior based on past experience to allow for a more complete and dynamic framework from which they could devise experiments and tests. One example is the theory of probabilistic functionalism proposed by Brunswik (1955 a, b). According to this theory, individuals subjectively evaluate the probable occurrence of events by associating patterns of actions, sequences, or events learned from past experience with patterns discerned in the present situation. Individuals continuously search for confirmation or disproof of their evaluations and modify their anticipations as new information is acquired and as success or failure is experienced.

According to Brunswik, many peripheral elements within the individual's awareness can act as stimuli for a given sequence of behavior. Brunswik illustrates this point by considering the case of a baseball player stimulated to act by a high fly ball. The ball represents the initial focal variable, but between the arching of the ball and the catch, a variety of stray causes and effects intervene; most of these—for instance, the velocity of the wind, the proximity of other players, and the nearness of the fence—operate at an unconscious yet quite active level. The player's responses must be timed so the ball will be intercepted when it comes into range, yet all of the hazards of outfield play must be avoided.

This model could also be applied to a decision maker faced with having to adjust the cost-income balance of a firm. The initial focal variable might be an accountant's announcement that the firm is losing money. Between receipt of this information and successful resolution of the problem lie a variety of responses. First, possible means of increasing revenues and reducing costs may be scanned and economies that can be introduced into various departments in the company might be considered. Then decisions will be made and mandates issued—perhaps to the production department to lower output, to the sales department to raise prices, or to other areas to reduce their work forces.

Because no market is static, the manager may be faced with the same decision sequence six months later. Forms of feedback, such as weekly sales reports and monthly accounting statements, will be in operation. The manager will make predictions based on past performance, but other variables will also be considered. The manager will be called upon to anticipate the most likely of a wide variety of possible future events, and to alter plans and activities accordingly. Much of the manager's behavior will operate at an unconscious level and will be affected by personal needs and desires. However, as experience is gained in evaluating the unique variables in an enterprise, the manager will typically become more proficient in the art of prediction.

The Brunswik model features continual scanning of an existing situation, and anticipation of future states based on expected changes is built into the model. Decision makers are guided not only by past experience—as in aspiration-level theory—but also by anticipation and unfolding experience. Behavior can therefore be continuously altered as events occur.

Both aspiration-level theory and Brunswik's probabilistic functionalism will normally generate very similar predictions in a given circumstance. Although the findings reviewed above concerning level of aspiration for the most part support Proposition 4, they tell only part of the story for research findings indicate the importance of anticipation and the impact of events other than past experience on levels of aspiration (other relevant findings will be reviewed in Chapter 19).

Summary

Proposition 1: Choice is always made with respect to a simplified model of the real situation. *Confirmed by what evidence is available. However, considerable differences among individuals exist, depending upon personality (e.g., cognitive complexity) and other factors.*

Proposition 2: Decisions are made within the unique frame of reference or "psychological set" of the decision maker. *Strongly confirmed.*

Proposition 3: Search behavior is concerned only with the discovery of satisfactory alternatives; only in exceptional cases is it concerned with the discovery of optimal alternatives. *Generally confirmed.*

Proposition 4: Continued failure to achieve a minimum standard of satisfaction results in the successive lowering of the standard until an acceptable compromise is reached; conversely, easy success tends to raise minimum standards. *Generally confirmed. However, a variety of exceptions and limiting factors exist which make the proposition untrue with respect to certain individuals and situations.*

Conclusions

Whether or not the administrative theory or Soelberg's confirmation theory of individual decision making is totally valid, each has important implications for understanding the process and the effects of managing. For one thing, the propositions reviewed here help explain the nature and functioning of organizations. They aid in explaining why, despite the existence of a large body of "reasonable" and "obvious" principles and prescriptions, we constantly see violations of the most fundamental guides to managing. If criteria for optimum solutions to complex problems are virtually impossible to establish, and if the confirmation process is characteristic of most decision making, then it is easy to understand how organizations can have so many contradictory policies, procedures, and decision rules. If search is continued primarily to confirm an early acceptable alternative rather than to seek additional solutions, it is likely that search will be discontinued before contradictions between short-term satisfactory solutions and previous policies are discovered.

If human rationality is truly bounded by our physiology and by our social environment, it is natural that different people within the same organization will view the same situation differently and will therefore arrive at contradictory conclusions from the "same" evidence. However, as was stated in reference to individual differences in perception (Chapter 4), this does *not* mean that individual decision making is a random, chaotic, and inevitably unpredictable phenomenon. On the contrary, much of the research reviewed in this chapter establishes that there is both system and order in the way most people make decisions, and that specific predictions about decision making are therefore possible. The accuracy of those predictions depends in part upon acceptance of modern theories of decision making, however, and requires a reconsideration of classical theories of organization and of the boundaries and limits within which organizations can be expected to act rationally.

References

Anderson, N. H., and Jacobson, A. 1965. Effect of stimulus inconsistency and discounting instructions in personality impression formulation. *Journal of Personality and Social Psychology* 2: 531–39.

Audley, R. J. 1971. What makes up a mind? In *Decisions, organizations and society*, ed. by F. G. Castles, D. J. Murray, and D. C. Potter. Penguin Books.

Bendig, A. W., and Hountras, T. 1958. College student stereotypes of the personality traits of research scientists. *Journal of Educational Psychology* 49: 309–14.

Brichacek, V. 1970. Use of subjective probability in decision making. In subjective probability, ed. by G. de Zeeuw; Vlek, C. A. J.; and Wagenaar, W. A. *Acta psychologica* 34: 241–53.

Brunswik, E. 1955a. Representative design and probabilistic theory in a functional psychology. *Psychological Review* 62: 193–217.

———. 1955b. In defense of probabilistic functionalism: A reply. *Psychological Review* 62: 236–42.

Clarkson, G. E. 1963. A model of trust investment behavior. In *A behavioral theory of the firm,* ed. by R. M. Cyert and J. G. March. Prentice-Hall.

Coombs, C. H., and Bowen, J. N. 1971. A test of VE-theories of risk and the effect of the central limit theorem. *Acta Psychologia* 35: 15–28.

———., and Pruitt, D. G. 1960. Components of risk in decision making: Probability and variance preferences. *Journal of Experimental Psychology* 60: 265–77.

Cummings, L. L.; Schwab, D. P.; and Rosen, M. 1971. Performance and knowledge of results as determinants of goal setting. *Journal of Applied Psychology* 55: 526–30.

Cyert, R. M., and March, J. G. 1963. *A behavioral theory of the firm.* Prentice-Hall.

———.; Simon, H. A.; and Trow, D. B. 1956. Observation of a business decision. *Journal of Business* 24: 237–48.

Dermer, J. D. 1973. Cognitive characteristics and the perceived importance of information. *The Accounting Review* 48: 511–19.

DeSoto, C. B.; Coleman, E. B., and Putnam, P. L. 1960. Predictions of sequences of successes and failures. *Journal of Experimental Psychology* 59: 41–6.

Forward, J., and Zander, A. 1971. Choice of unattainable group goals and effects on performance. *Organizational Behavior and Human Performance* 6: 184–99.

Himmelfarb, S. 1970. The impact of neutral information about a person. Unpublished paper.

Hirschman, A. O., and Lindblom, C. D. 1962. Economic development, research and development, policy making: Some converging theories. *Behavioral Science* 7: 211–22.

Ilgen, D. R. 1971. Satisfaction with performance as a function of the initial level of expected performance and the deviation from expectation. *Organizational Behavior and Human Performance* 6: 345–61.

———., and Hamstra, B. W. 1972. Performance satisfaction as a function of the difference between expected and reported performance at five levels of performance. *Organizational Behavior and Human Performance* 7: 359–70.

Katz, R. L. 1970. *Management of the total enterprise.* Prentice-Hall.

Kerr, S.; Klimoski, R. J.; Tolliver, J.; and Von Glinow, M. 1975. Human information processing and problem solving. In *Managerial accounting: The behavioral foundations,* ed. by J. L. Livingstone. Grid Publishing Co.

Kinghorn, R. W. 1966. Occupational stereotypes held by operating personnel managers. M. S. thesis, University of Wisconsin.

Lewin, K. 1948. *Resolving social conflicts.* Harper.

———.; Dembo, T.; Festinger, L.; and Sears, R. 1944. Levels of aspiration. In *Personality and the behavior disorders,* ed. by J. McVey. Ronald Press.

Long, B. H., and Ziller, R. C. 1965. Dogmatism and predecisional information search. *Journal of Applied Psychology* 49: 376–78.

Manis, M.; Gleason, T. C.; and Dawes, R. M. 1966. The evaluation of complex social stimuli. *Journal of Personality and Social Psychology* 4: 404–19.

March, J. G., and Simon, H. A. 1958. *Organizations.* Wiley.

Morin, R. E. 1960. Strategies in games with saddle-points. *Psychology Report* 7: 479–85.

Myers, J. L., and Fort, J. G. 1963. A sequential analysis of gambling behavior. *Journal of General Psychology* 69: 299–309.

———, and Sadler, E. 1960. Effects of range of payoffs as a variable in risk-taking. *Journal of Experimental Psychology* 60: 306–9.

Newman, J. W. 1971. *Management applications of decision theory.* Harper & Row.

Payne, J. W. 1973. Alternate approaches to decision making under risk. *Psychological Bulletin* 80: 439–53.

Perrow, C. 1972. *Complex organizations: A critical essay.* Scott, Foresman.

Peterson, C. R., and Beach, L. R. 1967. Man as an intuitive statistician. *Psychological Bulletin* 68: 29–46.

Phillips, L. D. 1966. Some components of probabilistic inference. Technical Report No. 1, Human Performance Center, University of Michigan.

Pitz, G. F.; Reinhold, H.; and Geller, E. S. 1969. Strategies of information seeking in deferred decision making. *Organizational Behavior and Human Performance* 4: 1–19.

Reeser, C. 1971. The use of sophisticated analytical methods for decision making in the aerospace industry. *MSU Business Topics* 19: 63–9.

Simon, H. A. 1947. *Administrative behavior* (2nd ed., 1957). Macmillan.

Slovic, P., and Lichtenstein, S. 1971. Comparison of Bayesian and regression approaches to the study of information processing in judgment. *Organizational Behavior and Human Performance* 6: 649–744.

———., and ———. 1972. From Shakespeare to Simon: Speculations—and some evidence—about man's ability to process information. Paper #86, Oregon Research Institute, University of Oregon.

Soelberg, P. 1966. Unprogrammed decision. *Papers and Proceedings,* 26th Annual Meeting, Academy of Management, 1966, 3–16.

———. 1967. Unprogrammed decision making. *Industrial Management Review* 8: 19–29.

Stagner, R. 1950. Stereotypes of workers and executives among college men. *Journal of Abnormal and Social Psychology* 45: 743–48.

———. 1969. Corporate decision making: An empirical study. *Journal of Applied Psychology* 53: 1–13.

Starr, M. K. 1971. *Management: A modern approach.* Harcourt Brace Jovanovich.

Streufert, S., and Streufert, S. C. 1970. Effects of failure in a complex decision-making task on perceptions of cost, profit and certainty. *Organizational Behavior and Human Performance* 5: 15–32.

Thompson, J. D. 1967. *Organizations in action.* McGraw-Hill.

Zander, A., and Medow, H. 1963. Individual and group levels of aspiration. *Human Relations* 16: 89–105.

———.; Natsoulas, T.; and Thomas, E. J. 1960. Personal goals and the group goals for the member. *Human Relations* 13: 333–44.

———., and Ulberg, C. 1971. The group level of aspiration and external social pressures. *Organizational Behavior and Human Performance* 6: 362–78.

Zeckhauser, R., and Schaefer, E. 1968. Public policy and normative economic theory. In *The study of policy formation,* ed. by R. A. Bauer and K. J. Gergen. Free Press.

Chapter **8**

Formal Groups

When many are got together, you can be guided by him whose counsel is wisest. . . . If a man is alone he is less full of resource, and his wit is weaker.

HOMER
The Iliad

In this chapter we turn to an investigation of formal groups that are found in complex organizations; these formal groups are commonly identified as committees, boards, commissions, and the like. Although mentioned in classical texts on management and organizations, consideration of such groups has been largely omitted from any systematic theory of management, perhaps because they violate the authoritarian principles of formal hierarchy. Yet such groups seem to be a fact of organizational life; the question seems to be less whether to use them than how to use them most effectively.

We will be aided in our consideration of this subject by the extensive research literature on small group behavior. Experimental groups are analogous to different forms of formal group operation. While experimental groups are not exactly like formal groups in formal organizations, there are nevertheless close parallels with respect to such issues as leadership, characteristics of membership, group process, and size.

Definitions of Formal Groups

In the discussion which follows, we shall use the term "formal group" to mean an organizational unit which is formally designated as a group rather than in terms of positions arranged in hierarchical fashion. Perhaps the most common type is the committee. Classical writers (Allen, 1955) suggest that a committee is a special type of meeting, characterized by a limited membership, a specific task or goal, a designated leader, and an explicit or implicit plan of action. It is also extra-organizational in structure: It serves as a self-contained staff group within the larger organization, providing assistance to the organization rather than service to clients. It is not typically placed in a supervisory position with respect to others.

The presence of formal committees is directly related to organization size. For example, in a survey of 1200 *Harvard Business Review* subscribers, Tillman (1960) found that 94 percent of the firms with more than 10,000 employees reported having formal committees, compared to only 64 percent of the firms with fewer than 250 employees. A survey of organization practices in 620 manufacturing firms (Healey, 1955) showed a similar positive relationship between committee use and plant size. The Healey study also indicated a positive relationship between committee use and spans of supervision. These results are consistent with the definition of the committee as a self-contained staff group since the presence of staff is related to spans of control (see Chapter 18).

Unlike formal committees, boards and commissions (such as corporate boards of directors or public utility commissions) are identified as formal supervisory bodies within a formal organization structure. Such groups are legitimated by the legal system in which the organization resides. For example, all corporations must have a board of directors to represent the interests of their stockholders, though they may not utilize the board according to its full potential.

Formal Group Functions

Since formal groups, like formal organizations, tend to emerge even if they are not intentionally planned, it seems logical that there are certain functions which are performed better or which can only be performed in formal groups. These functions may be summarized as: (1) the generation or recall of ideas; (2) judgment or evaluation; (3) leader influence; and (4) information dissemination or exchange.

The specific functions that committees perform in business have been identified as (1) exchanging views and information; (2) recommending action; (3) generating ideas; and (4) making policy decisions (*Management Review*, 1957). The first of these may be most common. After observing 25 conferences (which were also referred to as committees) in government agencies, service organizations, and manufacturing firms, Kriesberg (1950) concluded that most were concerned either with communicating information or with aiding the executive decision process. When asked why they called conferences, executives replied that they used them to "sell" ideas, rather than for group decision making itself. So long as the executive does not engage in covert manipulation of the group, this activity is probably quite legitimate since it allows committee members to influence and to some extent participate in executive decision making.

Unquestionably, some committees also make specific operating decisions which commit individuals and organizational units to certain prescribed goals. Such is often the province of general management committees, typically composed of top-level line and staff executives. These committees are known by various names: The Ford Motor Company and General Motors have policy committees, Continental Oil and Sun Chemical have management committees, American Airlines has a senior officers' council, and American Cyanamid Corporation has a general staff (Nicholson, 1963). The popularity of the general management committee is suggested by Table 8–1, which shows the results of Tillman's *Harvard Business Review* survey (1960). His survey may have biased the response in favor of top-level executives, thus reducing the degree of functional committee participation reported, but it is clear that the management committee is a widely used organizational device.

TABLE 8–1. Committees: What Varieties Are There and How Do They Differ?

Type of Committee	Per Cent of Total Executive Committeemen Who Serve on Each Type of Committee	Average Number of Members per Committee	Average Number of Meetings per Year
General Management	77.4%	8.6	27
Finance and Control	37.7	6.7	23
Marketing	23.9	7.4	24
Production	25.2	8.9	28
Labor and Personnel	39.4	7.1	14
Research and Development, and New Products	14.9	8.2	18
Public Relations	5.5	7.4	9
Others	21.1	8.3	14

Tillman (1960).

When company presidents sit as members of management committees, the committees' decisions often have immediate authority for action. When the committees deliberate without the chief executives, decisions are more often only recommendations which may or may not be accepted. By sitting with the committees, presidents give tacit approval to committee decisions—decisions which the presidents are likely to influence strongly, since they are considered to be responsible for the actions of committees upon which they serve. Single accountability is therefore retained.

Group Process

The following discussion may be summarized at the outset with a simple statement: Idea-getting is an individual process which is facilitated by the presence of others; idea-evaluation is generally better when performed by groups. Now let us see what this means in more detail. As we indicated earlier, one function of a group is idea generation. This occurs when, for example, one wants to develop a list of possible solutions to a problem. In such cases, the critical group process requirement is to have every member develop ideas at the same time, duplicating effort (see

Table 8–2). Where group members can be present, the most appropriate method seems to be the nominal group process, whereby group members list their ideas silently in the presence of each other (Delbecq, Van de Ven, and Gustafson, 1975). For the idea-generation function, leader control concerns itself with the process of group activity, not with the content itself.

TABLE 8–2. Formal Group Functions and Process Requirements.

Function	Leader Control	Type of Group Process	Critical Process Requirement
Idea Generation	Process	Nominal	Duplicate Effort
Judgment and Evaluation	Process	Interaction	Exchange and Verify Facts; Check Logic
Leader Influence	Process and Content	Two Way Communication	Leader Response to Need
Information Dissemination or Exchange	Process and Content	One or Two Way Communication	Message Clarity

Another function of formal groups is making decisions through judgment or evaluation. Here the critical process requirement is the exchange of facts and logic, unencumbered by status, power, or other conditions which might cause unequal participation by the group members. The group process is balanced discussion by members of the group. Leader control is limited to process control, since the group as a unit will generally do as well as or better than the best individual decision maker in the group (Shaw, 1971).

The third formal group function is leader influence of the group. This occurs when the leader wants to persuade the group in some way, *not* when the group need is for the most accurate judgment or for maximum idea getting. Leader influence requires that the leader enhance or create expectations of enhancement of member needs through the accomplishment of some event or activity desired by the leader. The group process here involves finding out the needs of group members and linking those with the expectations of the leader. The process is one of bargaining with each group member or with a representative of the group rather than giving a pep talk. The leader in such cases will control not only the process but also the content of the discussion.

Finally, the fourth formal group function is information dissemination or exchange. In this case the critical process requirement is one of message clarity. In some cases the group process involves one-way communication from the message sender to the others in the group; the leader is therefore controlling both the process and the content of the group activity. In others, the group members exchange information, and the leader controls process and relevance.

It should be apparent at this point that it is impossible to answer the question "How should I run a committee?" without first asking "What do you hope the committee to accomplish?" Process requirements, leadership roles, and other characteristics of groups will vary according to the functions to be performed.

Group Authority

There are several types of authority commonly vested in formal groups. Some formal groups have the right to make decisions over a wide range of issues and to expect compliance with their directives. The management committee discussed earlier often displays such broad, directive authority.

Other groups may have more limited functional authority, either legislative or judicial. The first concerns the policy-making aspects of group work. A marketing committee, for example, establishes rules regarding channels of distribution, product quality, product mix, or make-buy strategies, which limit the action of organization units affected by these policies. Judicial functional authority deals with the interpretation of policies which have already been prescribed. A management bonus committee, for example, decides on the distribution of executive bonuses according to criteria defined by the committee itself (under its legislative functional authority) or prescribed by top management.

Finally, a formal group may have advisory authority, where group decisions regarding operating problems or policies must be approved by top management, or a group may have no authority, functioning merely as an educative or communicative tool of management.

The exact distribution of these types of authority among business and nonbusiness committees is not presently known, but the relative importance of committee authority in industry is suggested by a survey of 79 top-level business executives regarding committee use in their firms (*Management Review*, 1957). Respondents were asked to state whether an individual, the board of directors, or a committee was responsible for decisions in eight major areas. Results showed that individuals most often made decisions concerning pricing policy, advertising and promotion plans, production volume, personnel policy, and the employment of executives. Boards made key decisions in the areas of long-range planning and major capital investment. Committees made decisions most often only in the area of new product adoption. On the other hand, 27 respondents (or about 34 percent) reported that most non-board decisions were made by committees. Whether these committee decisions were only advisory or carried the weight of functional authority is not specified, but the degree of committee influence is apparent.

Where experience with a formal group is unsatisfactory, the trouble usually lies either in faulty organization or in using a group for purposes better suited to individual action. In connection with organization, we shall examine size, leadership, membership, and the location of the group in the complex organization of which it is a part.

Formal Group Size

The classical literature has generally suggested that formal groups should be relatively small. R. C. Davis (1951) endorses three to nine; Keith Davis (1957) advises that five is the preferred number. Implicit in such discussions is the fact that such small groups are preferred where the task of the formal group requires relatively equal participation and influence by the group members who must interact in the task and are generally involved in making a judgmental decision. Where the task involves idea getting, then very large groups may be used. Since idea getting is an individual process the main requirement is getting ideas from a lot of individuals at the same time. Further, where the group task is one of communicating information from a central source to a group then group size is limited only by the capacity to communicate. Since formal groups like committees and boards are often engaged in discussion and judgment, we would expect such groups to be relatively small.

Surveys of actual practice seldom miss the prescriptions by much. In the 1658 business committees recorded in the *Harvard Business Review* survey (Tillman, 1960) the average membership was eight. (More detailed size characteristics, according to type of committee activity, are shown in Table 8-1.) When asked for their preference, the 79 percent who answered Tillman's survey suggested ideal committee sizes that averaged 4.6 members. Similarly, Kriesberg (1950) reports that, for the 75 organizations analyzed, there were typically five or six conferees in the meetings studied.

A survey of 514 manufacturing and 341 nonmanufacturing corporations indicated that manufacturing boards varied in size from 3 to 28 directors with a median size of 11 (Bacon, 1973). There is a direct, positive relationship between corporate size and the size of the board, with companies having assets of less than ten million averaging 6 board members and those with a billion or more having 15 members. Among the nonmanufacturing boards the size varied from 5 to 36 with a median of 13.

It appears that when business or government formal groups become large, they deal with the consequent problems of balanced influence and discussion by using subcommittees and executive committees. The larger groups seem to be more collections of subgroups than truly integrated operating units, and the judgments or analyses are probably provided by the smaller groups.

Formal Group Leadership

Most people probably serve on some type of board, committee, or commission in the process of participating in church, school, political, or social organizations, and while in that capacity have observed the effect that the leader has on the group. When, for example, the leader starts a meeting by saying, "Well, we all know each other here, so we'll dispense with any formality," the group usually flounders until someone else takes a directive role.

In order to meet its objectives, formal groups need someone who can control the process of the meeting if not its actual content. As will be discussed later the leader will require some degree of skill in both the exercise of social facilitation and of task accomplishment.

Surveys of executive opinion support the impression that the chairman has a big effect on successful committee operation. As Tillman (1960) stated: "The greater majority [of the suggestions from survey respondents] lead to this conclusion: the problem is not so much committees in management as it is the management of committees" (p. 162). The following comment by a partner in a large management consulting firm is typical:

> Properly used, committees can be most helpful to a company. Most of the criticism I have run into, while probably justified, deals with the way in which committees are run (or committee meetings are run) and not with the principle of working with committees (p. 168).

The problem is not necessarily that the chairman is too passive in his role. Indeed, the chronic problem in Congress has been the domination of committee processes by the chairman. This results from the way in which the chairman is typically selected: By tradition, the chairman is the member of the majority party who has the longest uninterrupted service on the committee. The dangers in such domination have been described (Udall, 1957) as follows:

> If there is a piece of legislation that he does not like, he kills it by declining to schedule a hearing on it. He usually appoints no standing subcommittees and he arranges the special subcommittees in such a way that his personal preferences are taken into account. Often there is no regular agenda at the meetings of his committee—when and if it meets. They proceed with an atmosphere of apathy, with junior members, especially, feeling frustrated and left out, like first graders at a seventh grade party (p. 17).

We shall gain a fuller understanding of the necessity for proper formal group leadership when we investigate the experimental literature on group processes. As might be supposed, the role of the chairman depends to a great extent on the needs of the group membership and the task involved.

Formal Group Membership

Membership and performance in formal groups requires different skills than membership and performance in a hierarchical arrangement of positions. The superordinate and subordinate roles and the atmosphere of bargaining common to the formal organization structure are not the same behaviors which are likely to be found in successful formal groups (Filley, 1975). In addition, participation in formal groups may require social skills which are less practiced as well. For example, the Institute for Social Research (*Nation's Business*, 1958) reported that thing-minded production people are less outgoing in their relationships than people-minded salesmen and, hence, have more difficulty in formal group participation.

In general, we may say that formal group members should be both functionally and personally qualified for the task. Functionally, they should represent a special point of view or possess certain technical knowledge necessary for achieving group goals. Personally, members should have analytical and social skills. They should be able to communicate, to relate to others, and to analyze and solve problems. In addition, since group members may represent other groups or departments outside the formal work group, they should be able to represent those outside interests adequately.

If group roles and composition are important to group success, then how do members get into formal work groups in the first place? We find five general types of group attachment:

1. appointment
2. selection by group members
3. election by nongroup members
4. volunteers
5. predetermined by office or job contract

Surprisingly, neither research nor authoritative opinion indicates the effects of these forms of attachment on the group attitudes or behavior. Observation would suggest, however, that the basis for group membership has important consequences on the integration and productivity of the group. We can gain some insight into the probable results of different forms of membership by considering why people want to join groups.

In general, we may say that the attractiveness of formal group membership is a function of the needs of the individual and the properties of the group (Cartwright and Zander, 1962; Litterer, 1973). In some ways the group can serve as a means for achieving personal goals beyond the immediate aims of the group itself; in other ways, participation in the group meets individual needs directly.

Whether participation in the group is a means or an end, it can potentially serve needs classified as either task or social (see Figure 8–1). Given this cross-classification, we may distinguish four general attractions the group may hold for the member: First, the group may serve as a means for accomplishing external social needs. For example, membership on a management committee may enhance an individual's social status in other groups. Second, it may serve as an end in itself, by accomplishing social needs. Thus, a member may find participation with others in a project group to be socially satisfying. Third, it may serve as a means for accomplishing external task needs. For example, participation on a planning committee may enable the member to gain desired resources for the department which the member represents. Finally, participation may be an end in itself, by providing the member with rewards for task needs. Such is the case, for example, when a member exerts task leadership in the group toward the solution of a problem in which the member is interested.

	Social Needs	*Task Needs*
Committee as Means	(1) Status of Membership	(3) Control of Environment Better Wages
Committee as End	(2) Social Participation	(4) Leadership Control Problem Solving

Figure 8-1. Reasons Why Group Is Attractive to Members.

The source of attraction to the group has been shown to affect group behavior in at least three of these four situations. In an experimental study of two-person groups working on a photo-interpretation problem, Back (1951) created cohesive and noncohesive groups using three bases of cohesion: personal attraction for other group members (type 2), prestige of membership (type 1), and task accomplishment (type 4). Members of groups constructed on the basis of personal attraction engaged in long, pleasant conversations, and were highly influenced by the opinions of the others. Those oriented toward prestige acted cautiously, engaged in fairly short discussions, and were careful not to antagonize each other and thereby lose status. Finally, groups based on task accomplishment completed their task quickly and efficiently, keeping their discussion relevant to the work at hand. In all three types there was more mutual influence among members than in groups of low cohesiveness. Unfortunately, the study provides no measure of the quality or quantity of task accomplishment among the different groups.

We have seen that successful group operation apparently depends upon the participation of individuals who are functionally and personally qualified to make a contribution, and that the combination of individual talents and unit representation may also affect performance. The type of membership recruitment and the reasons for attraction are also important factors, as is the degree to which the group operates as a cohesive unit. One would expect, then, that cohesive groups cooperate, and cooperative groups are productive.

Formal Groups in the Organization Structure

Another consideration regarding formal groups involves their proper placement in the structure. We shall consider both the committee and the noncommittee forms of formal groups in this regard.

Committees. Committees are best placed in an organization as a self-contained staff group with no supervisory responsibility. That is, they should have no subordinate organization reporting to them. Like most staffs, they either report to the person they serve (personal staff) or to the executive at the next higher level above that which they serve (organizational staff). Supervision by a group creates conditions which are problems in the case of committees but turn out to be functional in the case of commissions and boards. That is, supervision by a committee: (1) leads to dual authority; (2) causes decisions to be made slowly; (3) delays decision making, since such groups don't meet continuously; (4) leaves much discretion up to the people reporting to the committee since it cannot continuously monitor their work.

Boards and Commissions. Boards and commissions, in contrast with committees, serve as superordinates to individuals. They have direct authority over the work of others. While the guidelines for group process are similar for all formal groups, the placement is different. The factors which limited the effective use of committees in a supervisory role appear to be advantageous for the board or commission in an executive role.

This form of formal group generally represents the interests of parties external to the organization. The board of directors, for example, represents and protects the interests of the stockholders. The government commission represents the public interest. Since groups are effective as judges but cannot meet continuously to supervise the work of others, one would expect the board or commission to be involved in making judgments, including evaluation of performance by key administrators, and at the same time by its nature to provide individuals subordinate to it with considerable freedom. Thus, for example, the corporate board cannot direct the affairs of the corporate president. It can merely appoint officers, establish policy, and review progress.

In the DuPont Company this structure has been carried one step further (Mylander, 1955). An executive committee composed of a nominal president and nine vice-presidents serves as a multiple executive with respect to the general managers in the various company divisions. This formal group also serves as an executive committee of the DuPont board of directors. DuPont operations are federally decentralized below the executive committee level into ten manufacturing divisions, each headed by a general manager. The general managers function like company presidents, with full authority to run their businesses as they please—so long as they observe overall company policy and earn a satisfactory return on investment. The executive committee tells the general managers: You are the bosses, we are the philosophers.

Formal Group Time and Cost

A frequently voiced objection to formal group activity is its use of time and, since time costs money, the consequent expense of meetings. The *Harvard Business Review* survey (Tillman, 1960) suggested, however, that executives object less to scheduled committee activity than to the time actually spent in such meetings. The survey reported that respondents who felt the time spent in committee meetings to be too short averaged two and three-quarter hours per week in such meetings. Those who found the time spent to be adequate averaged three hours per week, and those who felt the time spent to be excessive averaged four and a half hours per week.

Executives in the survey also reported spending an average of nine and a half hours per week in informal conferences and consultation, though they did not object to this use of time. The exact nature of this consultation is unclear—it may include contacts with single individuals—but it does indicate the amount of interaction which takes place in business organizations.

The Kriesberg survey of conference practices in 75 organizations (1950) reported that executives averaged ten hours per week in apparently formal group meetings of some type. Both studies reported more meetings at higher organizational levels, and Kriesberg observed that men in staff positions spent more time in committee meetings, since they more often dealt with problems which crossed lines of authority.

Given the fact that executives do spend a great deal of time in meetings, does this mean that such time is costly and wasteful? Probably not. For one thing, although they are staff units, committees meet intermittently. An ad hoc committee can be easily terminated, but staff must be employed full time or else discharged. Assuming that the work in question can be done either by regular staff employees or by a staff committee, the committee probably allows greater flexibility.

Considered in terms of time use, formal groups also fare rather well. For example, an executive who meets with four others for one hour uses five man-hours; a one-hour meeting with each person individually uses eight man-hours. Thus, in the group situation the executive saves three hours. The difference is further highlighted if we attach cost figures to the alternatives. Assuming that the executive earns $20,000 per year and the subordinates $15,000, the total cost of the individual meetings would be

$84.10; the group meeting would cost $45.66, or 54.3 percent of the cost of individual meetings. The group meeting could be almost twice as long as the individual meetings and still cost the same. It can be similarly demonstrated that (1) as the size of the committee increases, the cost advantage increases; and (2) as the difference between the salary of the executive and the mean earnings of committee members increases, the cost advantage also increases. In terms of the total salary expense to the company, the executive expense is the same either way.

Once again we see that the problem is not so much how to eliminate committees and other formal groups as how to use them properly. A number of suggestions have been offered for efficient operation:

1. State formal group objectives, functions, and authority in a description.
2. Locate the group properly in the organization structure, stating the person to whom it is accountable.
3. Place limits on formal group size.
4. Specify means of selecting the chairman and the source of membership.
5. Schedule meetings on the same day every week or every month.
6. Plan and distribute agenda and supporting material before the meeting.
7. Assemble technical data before the meeting.
8. Use subcommittees and an executive committee where appropriate.
9. Record and send minutes to members.
10. Appoint a permanent secretary to whom communications may be addressed.
11. Specify procedure for decision making.
12. State ending time at the outset.
13. Start the meeting on time.

Propositions

Three areas which seem to be vital in formal group use are size, leadership, and the composition and activity of membership. Thus we shall evaluate the following propositions:

1. The ideal formal group size is five members.
2. Efficient and effective formal group operation requires a leader who is directive and task-oriented.
3. Integrated, cooperative group membership is more effective in meeting goals than nonintegrated, competitive membership.

Empirical Evidence

Proposition 1

The ideal formal group size is five members.

The scientific basis for this proposition, if there is any, may be explored by examining the literature of small-group research.[1] The extent to which a number is "ideal" may be measured by both internal and external criteria. Internally, size may affect socio-emotional relations among group members and, thus, the extent to which the group operates as an integrated whole rather than as fragmented subunits. Other internal criteria are the extent to which decision quality and the time required to reach decisions are affected by size.

External criteria of group effectiveness include the extent to which size affects the task contribution of the group to the larger organization, and the extent to which the group contributes to the maintenance or integration of the larger system. Since small experimental groups are examined almost entirely from the standpoint of internal criteria, our discussion and evaluation will, of necessity, ignore important external factors.

Group size is a seductive problem; like age, sex, and "level of education," it is an independent variable that can be easily measured. With respect to the number five itself, we might suspect that a self-fulfilling prophecy is at work, were it not for the fact that natural groups often vary widely in size, depending upon such things as culture, age, duration and intimacy of contact, and spatial constraints (see Hare, 1962).

Variables that are related to group size seem to include individual capacity to attend to differing numbers of objects; the impact of group size on interpersonal relations, communication, and problem-solving functions; and the feelings that group members have about proper group size (the effects of these variables are of course interrelated).

Individual Attention. Each member in a group will attend both to the group as a whole and to each individual as a member of the group. There seem to be limits on a person's ability to perform these processes—limits which vary with the size of the group and the time available. For example, summarizing a study by Taves (1941), Hare (1962) reports that "experiments on estimating the number of dots in a visual field with very short-time exposures indicate individual subjects can report the exact number up to and including seven with great confidence and practically no error, but above that number, confidence and accuracy drop" (p. 227).

When two observers (Bass and Norton, 1951) assessed leadership characteristics in problem-solving groups of college students, the raters were found to reach maximum agreement in groups of 6, rather than in groups of 2, 4, 8, or 12. Apparently leadership is less easily distinguished in smaller groups, and attention is restricted in the larger ones.

The apparent limits on ability to attend both to the group and to the individuals within it have led Hare (1962) to conclude:

> The coincidence of these findings suggests that the ability of the observing individual to perceive, keep track of, and judge each member separately in a social interaction situation may not extend much beyond the size of six or seven. If this is true, one would expect members of

[1] For additional material on group size as it relates to work groups, see Chapter 18.

> groups larger than that size to tend to think of other members in terms of subgroups, or "classes" of some kind, and to deal with members of subgroups other than their own by more stereotyped methods of response (p. 228).

Interpersonal Relations and Communication. Given a meeting lasting a fixed amount of time, the opportunity for each individual to communicate is reduced—and the type of communication becomes different among group members—as group size increases. Bales (1951) has shown that, in groups ranging from 3 to 8 members, the proportion of infrequent contributors increases at a greater rate than that theoretically predicted from decreased opportunity to communicate. Similarly, as reported by Stephen and Mishler (1952), size is correlated positively in groups of 4 to 12 to the difference between participation initiated by the most active member and participation initiated by the next most active member.

Increasing group size also seems to limit the extent to which individuals want to communicate. For example, Gibb (1951) studied idea productivity in 48 groups in eight size categories from 1 to 96. His results indicated that, as group size increases, a steadily increasing proportion of group members report feelings of threat and less willingness to initiate contributions. Similarly, Slater's study (1958) of 24 groups of 2 to 7 men, each working on a human-relations problem, indicated that members of the larger groups felt the meetings to be disorderly and time-consuming, and complained that the other members of the group became too pushy, aggressive, and competitive.

Thus an increase in group size seems to distort the pattern of communication and create stress in some group members, but a decrease in group size also has dysfunctional effects. In the study by Slater (1958), check-list responses by members rating smaller groups of two, three, or four were complimentary; yet observer impressions were that such small groups engaged in superficial discussion and avoided controversial subjects. Inferences from post hoc analysis suggested that small-group members are too tense, passive, tactful, and constrained to work together in a satisfying manner. They are afraid of alienating the others. Similar results are reported in other studies, regarding the inhibitions created by small group size (Thomas and Fink, 1963), particularly in groups of two (Bales and Borgatta, 1955).

Groups of three have the problem of an overpowerful majority, since two members can form a coalition against the unsupported third member. Four-member groups provide mutual support when two members oppose the other two, but such groups have higher rates of disagreement and antagonism than odd-numbered groups (Bales and Borgatta, 1955).

The data reported above are not altogether consistent regarding the reasons for dysfunctional consequences of small groups. The "trying-too-hard-for-agreement" finding of the Slater study seems at odds with the conflict situations found by Bales and Borgatta, yet both studies agree that for some reason tension is present.

Although it is always dangerous to generalize about "ideal" numbers (or types, for that matter), there does appear to be logical and empirical support for five members as a suitable group size where balanced interaction is desired. In the Slater study, for example, none of the subjects felt that a group of five was too small or too large to carry out the assigned task, though they objected to the other sizes (two, three, four, six, and seven). Slater (1958) concluded:

> Size five emerged clearly . . . as the size group which from the subjects' viewpoint was most effective in dealing with an intellectual task involving the collection and exchange of information about a situation, the coordination, analysis, and evaluation of this information, and a group decision regarding the appropriate administrative action to be taken in the situation. . . .
>
> These findings suggest that maximal group satisfaction is achieved when the group is large enough so that the members feel able to express positive and negative feelings freely, and to make aggressive efforts toward problem solving even at the risk of antagonizing each other, yet small enough so that some regard will be shown for the feelings and needs of others; large enough so that the loss of a member could be tolerated, but small enough so that such a loss could not be altogether ignored (pp. 137–38).

Viewed from the standpoint of committee members' ability to attend to both the group and its members, or from the standpoint of balanced interpersonal needs, it seems safe to suggest that the number five has normative value in planning group operations. When considered from the standpoint of tasks which do not require balanced interaction, however, the appropriate group size may be much larger.

Proposition 2

Efficient and effective formal group operation requires a leader who is directive and task-oriented.

We will confine our discussion here to leader roles and functions, using three approaches. First, we will discuss the nature of task leadership in the group and the apparent reasons for this role. Then we will view more specifically the different roles that the leader or leaders of the group may play. Finally, we will consider the extent to which these more specific roles may be combined in a single individual. (The subject of leadership within the regular organizational hierarchy is discussed in Chapters 11 and 12.)

Task Leadership. Studies of leadership in task-oriented decision-making groups show a functional need for—and a member preference for—directive influence by the chairman. The nature of this direction is illustrated in a study by Schlesinger, Jackson, and Butman (1960). The problem was to examine the influence process among leaders and members of small problem-solving groups. The designated leaders varied on the rated degree of control exerted. As part of an initial investigation, 106 members of 23 interdepartmental middle-management committees described, on a 16 item questionnaire, the amount of control and regulation each member exercised when in the role of chairman. On the basis of questionnaire responses, each person was characterized as a high-control or a low-control chairman, according to their scores in relation to the median. The questionnaire data also showed that individuals seen as high in control were rated as more skillful chairmen—and even as contributing more to committee proceedings in their regular membership role.

Each group was then given a simulated but realistic problem, lasting one and a half hours, under controlled conditions and in the presence of three observers. The chairman was designated by the research investigator, supposedly on a chance basis. Interactions were recorded and three degrees of control were distinguished: direction, suggestion, and request. The results showed that, as a percentage of the acts of the chairmen themselves, the three degrees of control were fairly evenly distributed and did not differ significantly between high- and low-control chairmen. When chairman behavior was compared with group acts in the various categories, however, high-control chairmen performed many more acts of control than low-control chairmen.

The foregoing study suggests that leadership derives from group acceptance, rather than from the unique acts of the chairman. "When the participants do not perceive the designated leader as satisfactorily performing the controlling functions, the participants increase their own attempts to influence their fellow members" (Schlesinger, Jackson, and Butman, 1960, p. 363). The acceptance of leaders was based upon task (good ideas) and chairmanship skills, and had little to do with their personal popularity as group members.

The importance of chairman control in group action has been demonstrated in several other studies (Berkowitz, 1953; Fouriezos, Hutt, and Guetzkow, 1950; Shelley, 1960). In his study of 72 management conferences, for example, Berkowitz found that a high degree of "leadership sharing" was related inversely to participant satisfaction and group work output. The norms of these groups supported a "take-charge" chairman. When the chairman failed to meet these expectations, he was rejected, and both group satisfaction and group output suffered.

These studies do not necessarily suggest that members of formal groups less concerned with task goals also prefer a directive chairman. Where the groups are composed of more socially oriented members, the preference for leader control may be less strong (Anderson, 1959).

Leadership Roles. A second approach to understanding the leadership of formal groups is to investigate leadership roles in small groups. Here we return to the distinction between task and social needs raised earlier in this chapter.

Pervading the research literature is a basic distinction between group activities directed to one or the other of these two types of needs, and a parallel distinction regarding leaders who meet such needs. The two roles are defined by Benne and Sheats (1948) as (1) task roles, and (2) group-building and maintenance roles. The former are related to the direct accomplishment of group purpose, such as seeking information, initiating, evaluating, and seeking or giving opinion. The group-building and maintenance roles are concerned with group integration and solidarity through encouraging, harmonizing, compromising, and reducing conflict. Benne and Sheats also identify a third set of roles, which they define as "individual roles." These involve primarily dysfunctional acts, such as aggression, domination, and seeking recognition.

Similarly, Bales (1951) and his associates distinguished two main classes of group behavior, instrumental (or task) and social-emotional (or expressive). The various kinds of behavior associated with each class are shown in Figure 8–2. In defining leadership roles associated with these categories, Bales found that two types frequently emerged. The instrumental leader was the person with the "best ideas," while the expressive leader was the "best liked." These roles were sometimes played by different individuals in the group.

A parallel classification and more rigorously derived distinction is found in studies published by the Personnel Research Board of The Ohio State University (Stogdill and Coons, 1957). Basing their work on factor analysis of descriptions of managerial behavior, the Ohio State researchers found two independent factors that appeared repeatedly in different types of organizations. The first, "consideration," measures the leader's warmth and friendliness toward group members, concern with group welfare, respect for member integrity, willingness to accept new ideas, and the like. The second factor, "initiating structure," describes the leader's willingness to be specific on work assignments and to emphasize deadlines, evaluate work quality, and establish a structural environment. These factors have been reported to be both negatively (Fleishman, 1957) and positively (Halpin, 1954) correlated.

Finally, we may note a role classification which has less empirical reference, but which has become widely used in management training circles. Blake and Mouton (1964) devised a two-dimensional scheme for describing managerial style, using questionnaire responses. One dimension was "concern with people," the other "concern with task" (see Figure 8–3). Training programs aim at an "ideal" (9,9) pattern, indicating concern for both task and people. The model implies that other combinations are less desirable.[2]

This same two-way classification, with the occasional addition of other types, is described in an *a priori* or *a posteriori* fashion by many other writers (Schutz, 1958; Zaleznik and Moment, 1964; Slater, 1955). It is clear

[2] See Chapter 21 for a discussion of the Blake and Mouton model as an organizational development technique.

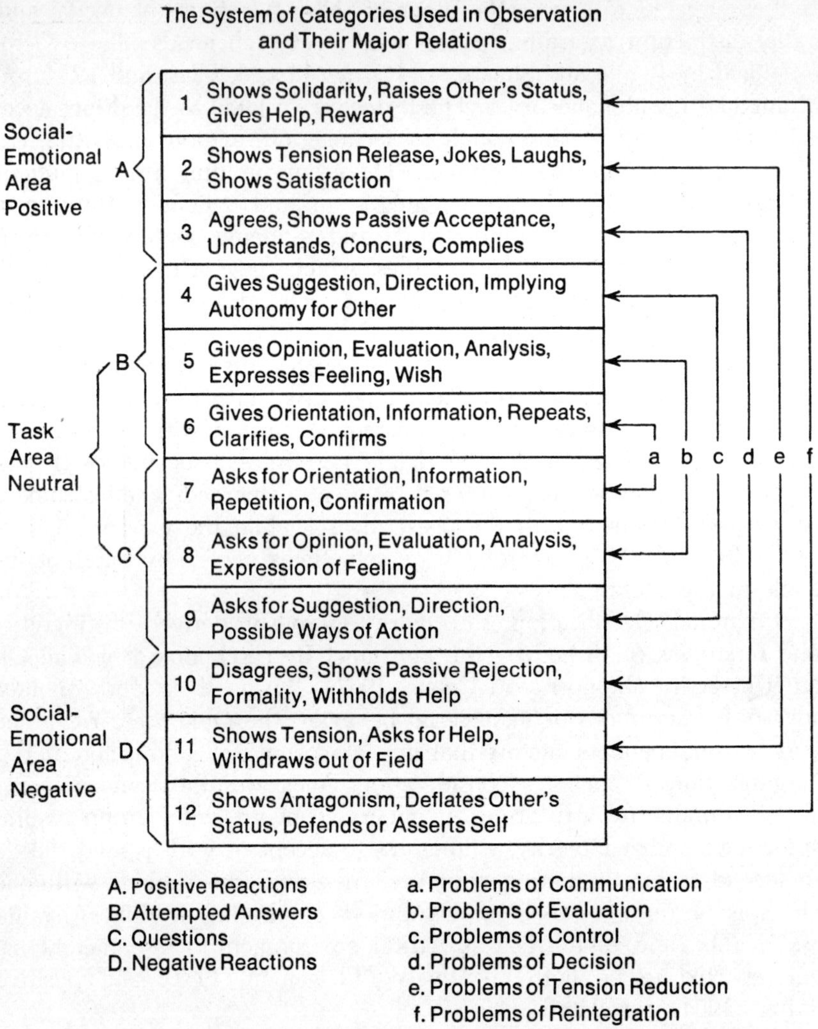

Figure 8-2. Classification of Group Behavior.

from these studies that such roles are played in varying degrees by all members of the group, with role division based on needs for specialization and complementarity. Exact interpretation is further clouded by the fact that many studies of these types of roles are concerned with emergent leadership in initially leaderless groups. Nevertheless, it appears that the task leader becomes a dominant force in the group, e.g., the "chairman," and only when the formal chairman abdicates role responsibility in some way does the dominant role of task leader shift to someone else in the

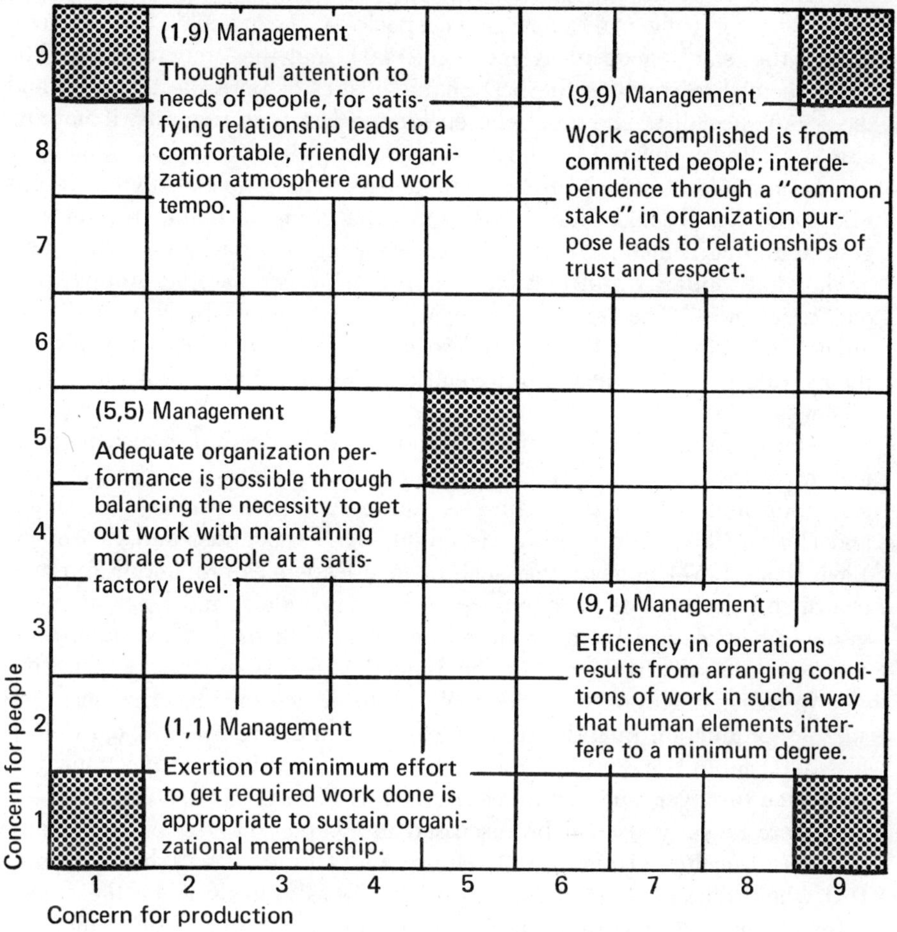

Source: Blake and Mouton, 1964, p. 10.

Figure 8-3. Dimensions of Managerial Style.

group. This interpretation is consistent with our theoretical discussion of chairman control.

Combined Roles. With so much emphasis placed on the difference between task and maintenance roles in the group, we may well ask whether or not these roles can or should be combined in a single leader. The prototypes of the formal leader and the informal leader inherited from classical management theory tend toward the conclusion that a combination is somehow undesirable or even impossible. Research literature also occasionally supports this point of view (Bales, 1951; Slater, 1955).

In contrast, there is much to be said for a combination of roles For example, Zaleznik and Moment (1964) describe four role types perceived by participants in small groups. These were the "technical specialist" (good ideas, but not congenial), the "social specialist" (congenial, but no good ideas), the "star" (good ideas and congenial), and the "underchosen." The "star" seemed to combine the best characteristics of both the technical and the social specialist. The label chosen for the last type suggests, if nothing else, the value associated by the researchers with the role type.

In a similar fashion, "great men" assigned to problem-solving groups (Borgatta, Couch, and Bales, 1954) gave the groups a higher rate of suggestion and agreement, a lower rate of "showing tension," and higher rates of showing solidarity and tension release than in comparable groups without "great men." The "great men" were selected on the basis of high task ability, individual assertiveness, and social acceptability. They also retained their ratings as "great men" throughout a series of different problem-solving sessions.

The question of combining task and social leadership is also partially answered by results of studies using the Ohio State measures of consideration and initiating structure. A number of such studies (Fleishman and Harris, 1962; Halpin, 1957; Hemphill, 1957; Oaklander and Fleishman, 1964; Rush, 1957) indicate that such diverse leaders as production foremen, chairmen of college departments, aircraft commanders, and hospital supervisors—when viewed by their subordinates as high on both structure and consideration—are likely (1) to be judged effective by their supervisors; (2) to manage groups with desirable performance on objective measures such as production quantity and scrap rates; and (3) to have more satisfied and stable organizations, as measured by satisfaction questionnaires, employee turnover, and grievance frequency.

More recently, as will be discussed in Chapter 11, research by House and his associates (House, 1971; House and Dessler, 1974) has suggested that where the task is relatively unstructured, as is likely to be the case in formal groups, leader initiating structure should improve performance and satisfaction in the group. On the other hand, since the tasks of formal groups are non-routine and often intrinsically satisfying, considerate behavior by the leader would have only moderate effect on attitudes or performance except where it facilitates group interaction or reduces stress (House, Filley, and Kerr, 1971). It should be noted as well that when leaders are perceived as high in consideration, they can exercise relatively high levels of initiating structure without reducing member satisfaction (Yukl, 1971). Thus, once again we are led to the conclusion that task leadership is important in determining formal group leader effectiveness.

The only divergent evidence for this proposition might be the work of Fiedler (1967, 1974). His model of contingency leadership (see Chapter 12) contains two cells which are directly related to formal groups. Cell IV in the model is based upon studies of boards of directors with low task structure, low leader position power, and good leader-member relations after the task is completed. In such cases Fiedler reports a positive relationship between LPC scores (differentiating between the most and least preferred co-workers) and group performance. In Cell VIII of the model, also based on studies of boards of directors, task structure and leader position power are low, but leader-member relations are poor. In this cell the leader LPC scores were negatively related to performance. This means that a relationship-oriented leader would be best for Cell IV. However, Fiedler also offers some evidence which suggests that where conditions are favorable, high LPC leaders will display task-oriented behavior. Cell VIII in the model is consistent with other leadership studies indicating the importance of task-oriented leadership in formal groups.

In general, it appears that the proposition regarding task-oriented leadership in formal groups is supported. It appears that the leader clarifies ambiguity inherent in formal group tasks and therefore increases both satisfaction with the leader and group performance. Acceptance of task-oriented leadership may be moderated by social or considerate behavior, however.

Proposition 3

Integrated, cooperative membership is more effective in meeting formal group goals than nonintegrated, competitive membership.

In order to evaluate Proposition 3, we must consider two related problems: (1) the effects of member cooperation or competition on group effectiveness; and (2) the effects of homogeneous or heterogeneous membership on formal group effectiveness.

Cooperation and Competition. A number of studies (see Hare, 1962) have contrasted the impact of competition and cooperation on group satisfaction and productivity. In some cases, when the group is established it is given a cooperative or competitive "treatment" by direction or incentive. In others, cooperation and competition are inferred from measures of groups in which members are operating primarily for personal interest, in contrast with groups in which members are more concerned with group needs. These studies show fairly consistently that "group members who have been motivated to cooperate show more positive responses to each other, are more favorable in their perceptions, are more involved in the task, and have greater satisfaction with the task" (Hare, 1962, p. 254).

Perhaps the best-known study regarding the effects of cooperation and competition was conducted by Deutsch (1962), using ten experimental groups of five college students each. Each group met for one three-hour period each week for six weeks, working on puzzles and on human relations problems. Subjects completed one weekly and one post-experimental questionnaire. Observers also recorded interactions, and completed overall rating scales at the end of each problem. In some groups, a cooperative atmosphere was established by instructing the members that the group as a whole would be evaluated in comparison with four other similar groups, and that each person's course grade would depend upon the performance of the group itself. In other groups, a competitive relationship was established by telling members that their grades depended upon their contributions to the group solution of problems. The results, as summarized by Hare (1962), were that:

> . . . compared with the competitively organized groups, the cooperative groups had the following characteristics:
>
> 1. Stronger individual motivation to complete the group task and stronger feelings of obligation toward other members.
> 2. Greater division of labor both in content and frequency of interaction among members and greater coordination of effort.
> 3. More effective inter-member communication. More ideas were verbalized, members were more attentive to one another, and more accepting of and affected by each other's ideas. Members also rated themselves as having fewer difficulties in communicating and understanding others.
> 4. More friendliness was expressed in the discussion and members rated themselves higher on strength of desire to win the respect of one another. Members were also more satisfied with the group and its products.
> 5. More group productivity. Puzzles were solved faster and the recommendations produced for the human-relations problems were longer and qualitatively better. However, there were no significant differences in the average individual productivity as a result of the two types of group experience nor were there any clear differences in the amounts of individual learning which occurred during the discussions (p. 263).

Similar evidence was found in a study of 72 decision-making conferences by Fouriezos, Hutt, and Guetzkow (1950). Based on observer ratings of self-oriented need behavior, correlational evidence showed that such self-centered behavior was positively related to participant ratings of high group conflict, and negatively related to participant satisfaction, group solidarity, and task productivity.

Finally, studies of group cohesiveness (reviewed in Lott and Lott, 1965; and Shaw, 1971) often use group attractiveness or cooperation as a proxy for cohesiveness. Such studies (Goodacre, 1951; Hemphill and Sechrest, 1952; Strupp and Hausman, 1953) generally show a positive relationship between group performance and cohesiveness. It should be noted, however, that these are studies of work groups rather than the formal groups as described here. Seashore's research (1954) suggested that in industrial groups, cohesiveness was related to high or low productivity, depending upon the objectives of the group itself. Thus, cohesive groups are more likely to conform to group standards, although the standards of the group may be for high or low performance as defined by those external to the group. In other words, a highly cohesive, cooperative group might choose to produce at a consistently low level, using its resources for social rather than task performance objectives.

In addition, studies of cohesiveness also show a positive relationship between that variable and member satisfaction with the group (Van Zelst, 1952; Marquis, Guetzkow, and Heynes, 1951; Gross, 1954).

In general, the findings of the foregoing and other studies (Stendler, Damlin, and Haines, 1951; Mintz, 1951; Grossack, 1954; Gottheil, 1955; Harnack, 1955; Zander and Wolfe, 1964) suggest that groups whose members are more cooperative are more satisfied and productive in meeting their own goals than groups whose members compete or otherwise seek personal needs.

Homogeneity and Heterogeneity. A second way to determine the degree of integration in a formal group is to determine the relative homogeneity or heterogeneity of group members. Homogeneous groups are identified as having members who are relatively similar on the basis of personality, value orientation, attitudes to supervision, sex, status level, income level, or other measures of diversity or similarity. Similarity or difference may also be induced by creating varying expectations regarding potential contributions by group members.

As will be seen, some homogeneous groups prove to be productive while others are unproductive when compared with heterogeneous groups. The answer to this paradox may be related to the different definitions used for group composition in the studies, but it appears that the interpersonal requirements involved in group tasks may offer a better explanation (Collins and Guetzkow, 1964).

In some studies, homogeneity clearly leads to more effective group performance. The work of Schutz (1955; 1958) is illustrative. In his earlier writing, Schutz distinguished between two types of interpersonal relationships: power orientation and personal orientation. The first emphasizes authority symbols. The power-orientation person follows rules and adjusts to external systems of authority. People with personal orientations emphasize interpersonal considerations.

Using attitude scales, Schutz established four groups whose members were compatible in high need for personal relations with others, four whose members were compatible in low personal orientation, and four containing subgroups differing in these needs. Each of the groups met 12 times for a period of six weeks and participated in a series of different tasks.

The results showed that all the compatible groups were significantly more productive than the groups consisting of incompatible subgroups. There was no significant difference between the productivity of the two types of compatible groups (personal and counter-personal). As might be expected, the difference in productivity between compatible and incompatible groups was greatest for tasks which required the most interaction and agreement under conditions of pressure.

A similar positive relationship between homogeneity and productivity was reported for groups in which compatibility was established on the basis of prejudice or degree of conservatism (Altman and McGinnies, 1960; Haythorn et al., 1956); managerial personality traits (Ghiselli and Lodahl, 1958); congeniality induced by directions from the researcher (Exline, 1957); and status congruence (Adams, 1953). In the Adams study, technical performance first increased, then decreased, as status congruence became greater, but group social performance increased continuously with greater homogeneity.

More recently, Brief, Delbecq, and Filley (1974) reported that adoption groups in city government were more likely to approve proposals for change or innovation when they were less differentiated by income or education. Similarly, Friedlander (1966) reported that group members who were homogeneous in attained education perceived their group as a more effective team, meetings as more valuable, and their leader as more approachable.

The positive relationship between homogeneity and productivity does not always hold, however. In some studies, heterogeneous groups were more productive than homogeneous ones. For example, Hoffman (1959) selected heterogeneous and homogeneous groups, based on personality profiles, and had them work on two different types of problems. The first required consideration of a wide range of alternatives of a rather specific nature. The second problem primarily required group consensus and had no objectively "good" solution. On the former task, heterogeneous groups produced significantly superior solutions. The difference between group types was not significant on the second type of problem. Ziller (1955) also found heterogeneity to be positively correlated with the ability of Air Force crews to judge the number of dots on a card.

Homogeneous and heterogeneous group performance in groups with from two to five members has been compared with individual performance (Goldman, Dietz, and McGlynn, 1968). Performance was measured by problem-solving accomplishment. Results showed more difference between group and individual performance in larger than in smaller groups. In four and five person groups, heterogeneous groups did better than their controls. In homogeneous two and five person groups, individual controls performed better than the group. It seems that heterogeneous groups perform better where diversity of opinion, knowledge, or background is important in performance (Ziller and Exline, 1958; Hoffman, 1959; Triandis, Mikesell, and Ewen, 1962).

Thus, where the task is to agree or to perform prescribed duties with a minimum of interpersonal difficulty, homogeneity is favored. If the purpose is to increase the creative and problem-solving potential of the group, heterogeneous groups appear to be more effective.

In sum, when considered from the standpoint of cooperation versus competition, cooperative groups generally display better performance and attitudes than competitive groups. When considered from the standpoint of group composition however, a clear conclusion is not possible. Increasing heterogeneity will have (Collins and Guetzkow, 1964) at least two effects on group behavior: (1) increase the difficulty of building interpersonal relations, and (2) increase the problem-solving potential of the group. The latter occurs since it is more likely that errors will be eliminated, more alternatives will be generated, and issues will be viewed critically. This dilemma between task effectiveness versus interpersonal effectiveness would be resolved if it was possible to develop heterogeneous, cohesive groups. There is evidence that such may be accomplished (Lott and Lott, 1965; Bennis and Shepard, 1955).

Summary

Proposition 1: The ideal formal group size is five members. *Unsupported (depends on task and performance criteria).*

Proposition 2: Efficient and effective formal group operation requires a leader who is directive and task-oriented. *Generally supported.*

Proposition 3: Integrated, cooperative membership is more effective in meeting formal group goals than nonintegrated, competitive membership. *Supported in terms of cooperation (neither supported nor rejected in terms of homogeneity of membership).*

Discussion and Application

Formal groups are generally developed to deal with judgement, idea generation, influence, or information dissemination and exchange. Where judgment and problem solving are the purpose and where balanced interaction between members is desired, then a small group of five members is probably desirable. However, where one wants to elicit ideas or information from others the ideal group size might be quite large. Thus, Proposition One is supported only on the basis of desirable interaction patterns, not on some universal criterion.

Since formal groups lack the task structure endemic to arrangements of individual positions in an organization or to structured work flows, it is logical that they require someone to facilitate the accomplishment of task goals. There is much evidence to suggest that the leader in such groups should be directive, instrumental, and task-oriented. Such behavior is likely to be associated with both effective performance and satisfaction. It is likely, however, that such relationships are mediated by social leadership as well.

Finally, the achievement of cooperative relations in the group is clearly warranted. While cooperation may be achieved through homogeneity of membership, to do so is to lose resources gained through diversity. Perhaps the best strategy for groups involved in tasks which involve judgement and creativity is to develop cohesive, heterogeneous groups through conscious efforts at team building.

References

Adams, S. 1953. Status congruency as a variable in small group performance. *Social Forces* 32: 16–22.

Allen, L. A. 1955. Making better use of committees. *Management Record* 17.

Altman, I., and McGinnies, E. 1960. Interpersonal perception and communication in discussion groups of varied attitudinal composition. *Journal of Abnormal and Social Psychology* 60: 390–5.

Anderson, R. C. 1959. Learning in discussions: A resume of the authoritarian-democratic studies. *Harvard Educational Review* 29: 201–14.

Back, K. 1951. Influence through social communication. *Journal of Abnormal and Social Psychology* 46: 9–23.

Bacon, J. 1973. *Corporate directorship practices: Membership and committees of the board.* The Conference Board.

Bales, R. F. 1951. *Interaction process analysis.* Addison-Wesley.

———. 1954. In conference. *Harvard Business Review* 32: 44–50.

———., and Borgatta, E. F. 1955. Size of group as a factor in the interaction profile. In *Small groups: Studies in social interaction,* ed. by A. P. Hare, E. F. Borgatta, and R. F. Bales. Knopf.

Bass, B. M., and Norton, F. M. 1951. Group size and leaderless discussions. *Journal of Applied Psychology* 35: 397–400.

Benne, K. D., and Sheats, H. A. 1948. Functional roles of group members. *Journal of Social Issues* 4: 42–7.

Bennis, W. G., and Shepard, H. A. 1955. A theory of group development. *Human Relations* 9: 415–37.

Berkowitz, L. 1953. Sharing leadership in small decision-making groups. *Journal of Abnormal and Social Psychology* 48: 231–8.

Blake, R. R., and Mouton, J. S. 1964. *The managerial grid.* Gulf.

Borgatta, E. F.; Couch, A. S.; and Bales, R. F. 1954. Some findings relevant to the 'great man' theory of leadership. *American Sociological Review* 19: 755–9.

Brief, A. P.; Delbecq, A.; and Filley, A. C. 1974. An empirical analysis of adaption behavior. Proceedings of the National Meeting, Academy of Management, Seattle, Washington, 1974.

Cartwright, D., and Zander, A. (eds.) 1962. *Group dynamics,* 2nd ed. Harper & Row.

Collins, B. E., and Guetzkow, H. 1964. *A social psychology of group processes for decision making.* Wiley.

Davis, K. 1957. *Human relations in business.* McGraw-Hill.

Davis, R. C. 1951. *Fundamentals of top management.* Harper & Row.

Delbecq, A; Van de Ven, A. H.; and Gustafson, D. H. 1975. *Group techniques for program planning.* Scott, Foresman.

Deutsch, M. 1962. The effects of cooperation and competition upon group process. In *Group dynamics* (2nd ed.), ed. by D. Cartwright and A. Zander. Harper & Row.

Exline, R. V. 1957. Group climate as a factor in the relevance and accuracy of social perception. *Journal of Abnormal and Social Psychology* 55: 382–8.

Fiedler, F. E. 1967. *A theory of leadership effectiveness.* McGraw-Hill.

———., and Chemers, M. M. 1974. *Leadership and effective management.* Scott, Foresman.

Filley, A. C. 1975. *Interpersonal conflict resolution.* Scott, Foresman.

Fleishman, E. A. 1957. Leader behavior description for industry. In *Leader behavior: Its description and measurement*, ed. by R. M. Stodgill and A. E. Coons. Monograph No. 88, Bureau of Business Research, The Ohio State University.

———., and Harris, E. F. 1962. Patterns of leadership behavior related to employee grievances and turnover. *Personnel Psychology* 15: 43–56.

Fouriezos, N. T.; Hutt, M. L.; and Guetzkow, H. 1950. Measurement of self-oriented needs in discussion groups. *Journal of Abnormal and Social Psychology* 45: 682–90.

Friedlander, F. 1966. Performance and interactional dimensions of organizational work groups. *Journal of Applied Psychology* 50: 257–65.

Ghiselli, E. E., and Lodahl, T. M. 1958. Patterns of managerial traits and group effectiveness. *Journal of Abnormal and Social Psychology* 57: 61–6.

Gibb, J. R. 1951. The effects of group size and of threat reduction upon creativity in a problem-solving situation. *American Psychologist* 6: 324.

Goldman, M.; Dietz, D. M.; and McGlynn, A. 1968. Comparison of individual and group performance related to heterogeneous-wrong responses, size, and patterns of interaction. *Psychological Reports* 23: 459–65.

Goodacre, D. M. III. 1951. The use of a sociometric test as a predictor of combat unit effectiveness. *Sociometry* 14: 148–52.

Gottheil, E. 1955. Changes in social perceptions contingent upon competing or cooperating. *Sociometry* 18: 132–7.

Gross, E. 1954. Primary functions of the small work group. *American Journal of Sociology* 60: 24–30.

Grossack, M. M. 1954. Some effects of cooperation and competition upon small group behavior. *Journal of Abnormal and Social Psychology* 49: 341–8.

Halpin, A. W. 1954. The leadership behavior and combat performance of airplane commanders. *Journal of Abnormal and Social Psychology* 49: 19–22.

———. 1957. The observed leader behavior and ideal leader behavior of aircraft commanders and school superintendents. In *Leader behavior: Its description and measurement,* ed. by R. M. Stodgill and A. E. Coons. Monograph No. 88, Bureau of Business Research, The Ohio State University.

Hare, A. P. 1962. *Handbook of small group research.* Free Press.

Harnack, R. V. 1955. An experimental study of the effects of training in the recognition and formulation of goals upon intra-group cooperation. *Speech Monographs* 22: 31–8.

Haythorn, W. A.; Couch, E. H.; Haefner, D.; Langham, P.; and Carter, L. 1956. The behavior of authoritarian and equalitarian personalities in groups. *Human Relations* 9: 57–74.

Healey, J. H. 1955. *Executive coordination and control.* Monograph No. 78, Bureau of Business Research, The Ohio State University.

Hemphill, J. K. 1957. Leader behavior associated with the administrative reputations of college departments. In *Leader behavior: Its description and measurement,* ed. by R. M. Stogdill and A. E. Coons. Monograph No. 88, Bureau of Business Research, The Ohio State University.

———., and Sechrest, L. 1952. A comparison of three criteria of air crew effectiveness in combat over Korea. *American Psychologist* 7: 391.

Hoffman, L. R. 1959. Homogeneity of member personality and its effect on group problem-solving. *Journal of Abnormal and Social Psychology* 58: 27–32.

House, R. J. 1971. A path-goal theory of leader effectiveness. *Administrative Science Quarterly* 16: 321–28.

———., and Dessler, G. 1974. The path-goal theory of leadership, some post hoc and a priori tests. Mimeograph.

———.; Filley, A. C.; and Kerr, S. 1971. Relation of leader consideration and initiating structure to R&D subordinates' satisfaction. *Administrative Science Quarterly* 16: 19–30.

Kriesberg, M. 1950. Executives evaluate administrative conferences. *Advanced Management* 15: 15–7.

Litterer, J. A. 1973. *The analysis of organizations,* rev. ed. Wiley.

Lott, A. J., and Lott, B. E. 1965. Group cohesiveness as interpersonal attraction: A review of relationships with antecedent and consequent variables. *Psychological Bulletin* 64: 259–302.

Management Review. 1957. Committees: Their role in management today. 46: 4–10, 75–8.

Marquis, D. G.; Guetzkow, H.; and Heynes, R. W. 1951. A social psychological study of the decision-making conference. In *Groups, leadership and men,* ed. by H. Guetzkow. Carnegie Press.

Mintz, A. 1951. Non-adaptive group behavior. *Journal of Abnormal and Social Psychology* 46: 150–9.

Mylander, W. 1955. Management by executive committee. *Harvard Business Review* 33: 51–8.

Nation's Business. 1958. Make committee work effective. 46: 62–67.

Nicholson, S. 1963. Mysterious management committee. *Dun's Review and Modern Industry* 81: 57–9, 123–6.

Oaklander, H., and Fleishman, E. A. 1964. Patterns of leadership related to organizational stress in hospital settings. *Administrative Science Quarterly* 8: 520–32.

Rush, C. H. 1957. Leader behavior and group characteristics. In *Leader behavior: Its description and measurement,* ed. by R. M. Stodgill and A. E. Coons. Monograph No. 88, Bureau of Business Research, The Ohio State University.

Schlesinger, L.; Jackson, J. M.; and Butman, J. 1960. Leader-member interaction in management committees. *Journal of Abnormal and Social Psychology* 61: 360–4.

Schutz, W. C. 1955. What makes groups productive? *Human Relations* 8: 429–65.

———. 1958. *FIRO: A three-dimensional theory of interpersonal behavior.* Holt, Rinehart and Winston.

Seashore, S. E. 1954. *Group cohesiveness in the industrial work group.* University of Michigan Press.

Shaw, M. 1971. *Group dynamics.* McGraw-Hill.

Shelley, H. P. 1960. Status consensus, leadership, and satisfaction with the group. *Journal of Social Psychology* 51: 157–64.

Slater, P. E. 1955. Role differentiation in small groups. In *Small groups: Studies in social interaction,* ed. by A. P. Hare, E. F. Borgatta, and R. F. Bales. Knopf.

———. 1958. Contrasting correlates of group size. *Sociometry* 21: 129–39.

Stendler, C., Damlin, D., and Haines, A. 1951. Studies in cooperation and competition: I. The effects of working for group and individual rewards on the social climate of children's groups. *Journal of Genetic Psychology* 79: 173–79.

Stephen, F. F., and Mishler, E. G. 1952. The distribution of participation in small groups: An exponential approximation. *American Sociological Review* 17: 598–608.

Stogdill, R. M., and Coons, A. E. (eds.) 1957. *Leader behavior: Its description and measurement.* Monograph No. 88, Bureau of Business Research, The Ohio State University.

Strupp, H. H., and Hausman, H. J. 1953. Some correlates of group productivity. *American Psychologist* 8: 443–4.

Taves, E. H. 1941. Two mechanisms for the perception of visual numerousness. *Archives of Psychology* 37: 265.

Thomas, E., and Fink, C. 1963. Effects of group size. *Psychological Bulletin* 60: 371–84.

Tillman, R., Jr. 1960. Problems in review: Committees on trial. *Harvard Business Review* 38: 6–8+.

Triandis, H. C.; Mikesell, E. H.; and Ewen, R. B. 1962. *Task set and attitudinal heterogeneity as determinants of dyadic creativity.* Technical Report No. 8, University of Illinois.

Udall, S. L. 1957. Defense of the seniority system. *New York Times Magazine* 17: 64–7.

Van Zelst, R. H. 1952. Sociometrically selected work teams increase production. *Personnel Psychology* 5: 175–86.

Yukl, G. 1971. Toward a behavioral theory of leadership. *Organizational Behavior and Human Performance* 6: 414–40.

Zaleznik, A., and Moment, D. 1964. *The dynamics of interpersonal behavior.* Wiley.

Zander, A., and Wolfe, D. 1964. Administrative awards and coordination among committee members. *Administrative Science Quarterly* 9: 50–69.

Ziller, R. C. 1955. Scales of judgment: A determinant of accuracy of group decisions. *Human Relations* 9: 153–64.

———., and Exline, R. V. 1958. Some consequences of age heterogeneity in decision making groups. *Sociometry* 21: 198–211.

Chapter **9**

Conflict Resolution and Problem Solving

I do not wish to seem over-dramatic, but I can only conclude from the information that is available to me as Secretary-General, that the Members of the United Nations have perhaps ten years left in which to subordinate their ancient quarrels and launch a global partnership to curb the arms race, to improve the human environment, to defuse the population explosion, and to supply the required momentum to development efforts. If such a global partnership is not forged within the next decade, then I very much fear that the problems I have mentioned will have reached such staggering proportions that they will be beyond our capacity to control.

U THANT
(1969)

In this chapter we shall be concerned with two related but different processes: conflict resolution and problem solving. As we shall see, conflict is the exercise of power between two or more parties (individuals or groups); problem solving, on the other hand, is the exercise of fact or logic by parties seeking a high quality, mutually acceptable solution to a problem.

As the term will be used in this discussion, conflict is neither good nor bad; similarly, outcomes of conflict, while predictable, are also neither good nor bad. Left to their own devices, conflict processes will end in the defeat of one party or in the division of resources. We shall show how these conflict processes can be changed into problem solving processes. Additionally, conflict need not develop for problem solving to take place. What we are concerned with here is the process of conflict and the resolution of conflict through problem solving.

Types of Conflict

There are two basic categories of conflict behavior. Some conflicts follow definite rules and are not typically associated with angry feelings, while others involve irrational behavior and the use of violent or disruptive acts. For this reason, we distinguish between conflicts which are competitive and those which are disruptive. In competitive situations, as we define them here, there is ordinarily a victory for one side only at a cost of the other party's total loss, and the way in which the parties relate to each other is governed by a set of rules. The parties strive for goals which are mutually incompatible. The emphasis of each party is upon winning rather than the defeat or reduction of the opponent. The actions of each party are selected using criteria based on the probability of achieving successful outcomes, and the competition terminates when the results are obvious to both sides (Rapoport, 1960).

In disruptive conflict, on the other hand, the parties do not follow a mutually acceptable set of rules and are not primarily concerned with winning. Instead, they are intent upon reducing, defeating, harming, or driving away the opponent. The means used are expedient, and the atmosphere is one of stress, anger, or fear. In extreme cases the parties in disruptive conflict will abandon rational behavior and behave in any manner necessary to defeat the opponent. Unlike competition, where the end of the conflict is apparent to the parties, the end of the disruptive form is not at all clear.

Observation suggests that actual conflicts are distributed somewhere between pure competition and pure disruption. Shifts in position also take place, as when anger arises in a game.

The Conflict Process

The development of conflict and its resolution tend to follow a pattern. As indicated in Figure 9–1, which is based on the work of Pondy (1967), there are at least six steps which may be identified.

Antecedent Conditions. A number of conditions have been shown to be correlated with the degree of conflict (Walton, Dutton, and Cafferty, 1969; Corwin, 1969). They are not necessarily causes of conflict but they seem to be associated with higher rates of conflict and may well predispose a situation in that direction. There seem to be four types of such conditions:

a) unclear roles, in which the expectations of one or both parties regarding their own or the other's behavior are not clear (e.g., a husband and wife who have not agreed upon who will do the dinner dishes may experience conflict over the issue);
b) desire for scarce resources, in which the parties seek to increase or protect their share of a fixed and scarce resource (two neighbors may argue about the boundary of their adjoining property, for example);
c) distancing mechanisms, which serve to separate or define two or more parties (a necessary ingredient for conflict to take place seems to be a we-they distinction: men versus women, old versus young, management versus labor, sales versus manufacturing); and

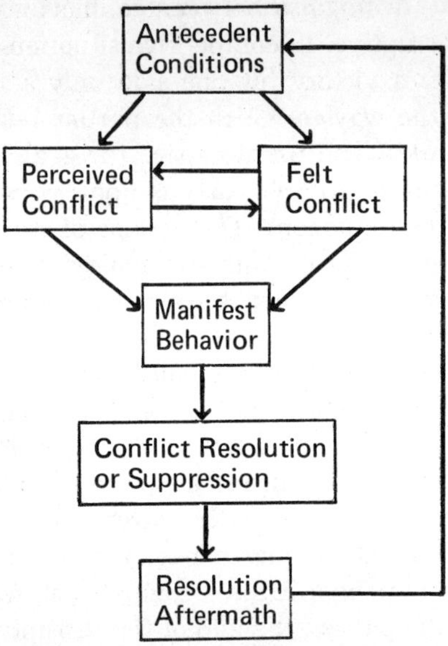

Figure 9-1. The Conflict Process.

d) unifying mechanisms, which highlight differences as greater intimacy or unity is sought (for example, the opportunity for conflict may increase as a couple learns more about each other, or it may increase where consensus is required).

While the above conditions may be present without conflict or absent in conflict, they are frequently associated with the development of conflict behavior.

Perceived Conflict. Another part of the conflict process has to do with how parties perceive the situation or each other. Parties often engage in conflict because they perceive a situation as involving limited alternatives, when in fact such is not the case. For example, when a husband says "Let's go to a movie tonight" and the wife responds "I don't want to go" the situation has been defined as one in which the alternatives are limited to a choice between going and not going.

Conflicts may also be perceived where no antecedent conditions exist. Such may be the case when parties misunderstand each other's positions or when positions taken by the parties are based upon a limited knowledge of facts. (As we will see later in this chapter, dealing with facts and reality, and sharing information, will aid in avoiding or resolving conflict.) Finally, initial perceptions of conflict may trigger avoidance mechanisms and, therefore, not produce conflictive behavior. This occurs when parties choose to attend to issues which are regarded as serious and to avoid conflicts where the possible gain or loss is minimal (Pondy, 1967). It also occurs when parties deal with conflicts having institutionalized mechanisms for their resolution, such as grievance procedures or arbitration, and ignore situations which have no recognized resolution processes.

Felt Conflict. In addition to perception, feelings and attitudes alter the relationship between objective conditions and potentially conflictive outcomes. Where parties value cooperation and believe that success in their relationship depends upon attainment of the needs of both, their behavior is likely to be different than when the parties value competition and believe that one can win only at the other's expense. Similarly, the degree of trust held by the parties about each other can alter behavior in various ways. Trust manifests itself in a willingness to share information and to share influence with others. These examples suggest the role played by feelings in the conflict process.

Manifest Behavior. Eventually "something happens." The game begins, the fight breaks out, the argument starts, the negotiation is begun. It is also possible that the parties will perceive a problem to exist and begin problem solving behavior at this point, without ever having engaged in conflict. If conflict does occur, the parties will engage in activities which in some way interfere with the goal attainment of each other.

Conflict Resolution or Suppression. Conflict resolution or suppression activities are those which are directed at reducing or ending such conflict. In the next section we shall describe a variety of methods which are used to resolve conflicts. Some of these essentially involve the victory of one side and the defeat of the other. Others involve splitting the difference or compromising. Still others involve the use of problem solving. Thus, it may be possible to take a situation in which the parties are engaged in conflict and to resolve the conflict through the use of problem solving. It has been suggested elsewhere (Filley, 1975) that the prevalence of the former methods of domination and compromise over problem solving is probably due to the fact that they are so widely practiced, rather than because they are necessarily better than problem solving.

Resolution Aftermath. The resolution of conflict leaves a legacy which will affect the future relations of the parties and their attitudes about each other. Where one party wins and the other loses, the defeat may lead to antagonistic or self-depreciating feelings on the part of the loser. In a compromise, the parties often believe that they have given more than they have received, exhibit feelings of defeat, and manifest a low level of commitment to agreements (Burke, 1970; Blake, Shepard, and Mouton, 1964). Finally, where conflicts are resolved through problem solving it is likely that trust and commitment are enhanced and that future conflicts will be handled more effectively than when resolutions are not the result of problem solving.

Strategies for Dealing with Conflict

The various methods for dealing with conflict may be grouped according to their likely outcomes. These outcomes may be called win-lose, lose-lose, and win-win.

Win-Lose Methods. Methods that typically result in win-lose outcomes include dominance through power or authority, ignoring attempts at influence, majority rule, and railroading. The use of dominance through power or authority is common. Through it, arbitrary actions are justified by saying, "You must follow my orders because I am your parent (or teacher, or boss) and I know what is good for you." The effect of this exercise of unilateral power is predictable. Losers typically engage in more non-productive behavior than winners; they screen communication to the winners, making it positive; they address more remarks to the winners; they become non-aggressive in their statements; and they fail to identify with the goals of the organization containing them. The creation of losing feelings may actually alter the energy, creativity, and measured intelligence of the losers in a negative direction.

Ignoring or failing to respond to another can result in a win-lose outcome. For example, in a company sales conference if a salesperson says "I think we ought to reorganize the sales territories" and no one responds, the salesperson will probably feel a loss. Failing to deal with employee complaints may have similar effects.

A third win-lose method is majority rule. Majority rule appears to be functional where the group votes together over a period of time and voting factions are not fixed. Thus one person may win on some votes and lose on others. It also works where the voting alternatives are all acceptable to the parties, with some merely preferred more than others (Neill, 1960). It is *not* functional, however, when a group is split into fixed factions and when the result of voting is a disgruntled minority.

Finally, railroading occurs when a minority so intimidates the majority or so embarrasses any attempts at opposition that the majority remains silent. Railroading also occurs when the majority is apathetic and willing to be led without question.

Lose-Lose Methods. These methods are based on the notion that "half a loaf is better than none," or that "something beats nothing all to hell." Typical lose-lose methods are compromise, bribing, resort to arbitration, and resort to rules. In compromise, the parties generally disagree about two solutions and settle for something in between. For example, two people arguing about who will get a telephone directory may settle the issue by tearing the directory in half. Another lose-lose strategy involves side payments or bribes, as when a company overpays people who dislike their work or when a mother promises her daughter a new dress if the daughter will eat spinach even though she dislikes it.

A third lose-lose method is the resort to third parties as arbitrators. While arbitration is sometimes a win-lose method, the third party seems to want an outcome in which each party can get something; therefore, neither party wins all of what they wanted. Finally, lose-lose outcomes frequently occur when parties resort to rules for the solution to a conflict. Like arbitration by a third party, resort to rules may also result in win-lose outcomes. The result of such approaches is illustrated when a driver runs out of gasoline and attempts to purchase some with a check. If the station owner emphasizes that the station has a policy of not taking checks, both parties lose. (The station owner may choose to problem solve, of course, by determining a way to provide the driver with gasoline without running the risk of accepting a bad check.)

Common Characteristics of Win-Lose and Lose-Lose Methods. The methods discussed above have several things in common:

1. There is a clear we-they distinction between the parties.
2. Parties direct their energies toward each other in an atmosphere of victory and defeat.
3. Parties see the issue from their own point of view.
4. The emphasis is on solutions rather than on the attainment of goals, values, or objectives.
5. Conflicts are personalized and judgmental.
6. There is no differentiation of conflict-resolving activities from other group processes, nor is there a planned sequence of those activities.
7. The parties take a short-run view of the issues.

Win-Win Methods. This third set of methods is distinctly different from those discussed above. They are consensus and integrative decision making. Both are referred to as problem solving in this chapter, and both are called win-win methods because they attempt to meet the needs of both parties.

Consensus decisions occur when a group of two or more people, who are dealing with a judgmental issue, reach a decision which is not unacceptable to anyone. Hall (1971) has shown that when certain group process rules are used, the group decision is frequently better than the best individual decision. For this reason, consensus decisions are recommended for the final selection of alternatives in integrative decision making (Filley, 1975), which will be discussed below.

In a popular simulation exercise, groups of people are asked to rank-order a group of items in terms of their desirability for a trip across the moon. Typical process rules that lead to consensus decisions in such cases (Hall, 1971; Hall and Watson, 1971; Guetzkow and Gyr, 1954; Filley, 1975) suggest that participants focus on defeating the problem rather than each other; that they avoid voting, trading, or averaging to make their decisions; that they use facts rather than force to solve problems; that they accept conflict as helpful, providing it does not elicit threat or defensiveness; and that they avoid self-oriented behavior to the exclusion of consideration for other's needs or positions.

The second win-win method is integrative decision making. As will be explained shortly in more detail, integrative methods involve a joint identification of the needs and values of both parties, an exhaustive search for alternatives which might meet these goals, and selection of the best alternative. This process is quite familiar; its relevance is highlighted, however, when one observes that conflicts ordinarily occur because of arguments about two solutions. Integrative methods change such solution-minded situations into problem-oriented situations, and for that reason they are useful when two parties are polarized in their positions.

The differences between win-win methods and those discussed earlier are further highlighted when we consider the individual styles of conflict behavior.

Personal Style in Conflict Behavior

One's individual style in dealing with potentially conflictive situations may be described by considering two dimensions. The first is the extent to which individuals are willing to assert themselves in order to meet their own needs, goals, or values. The second dimension is the extent to which individuals want to meet the needs of the other parties and want to cooperate with those parties. The first dimension is self-oriented, while the second is relationship-oriented. Figure 9–2 illustrates these two dimensions and some of the individual styles of conflict behavior that can result when varying degrees of each dimension are exhibited.

Several writers (e.g. Thomas, 1974; Blake and Mouton, 1970; Hall, 1969; Follett, 1941) have described similar formulations which indicate that, at one extreme, assertive action to seek one's own goals while ignoring the needs of others must surely lead to attempts to defeat the opponent, while, on the other hand, a non-assertive posture with respect to one's own needs and a

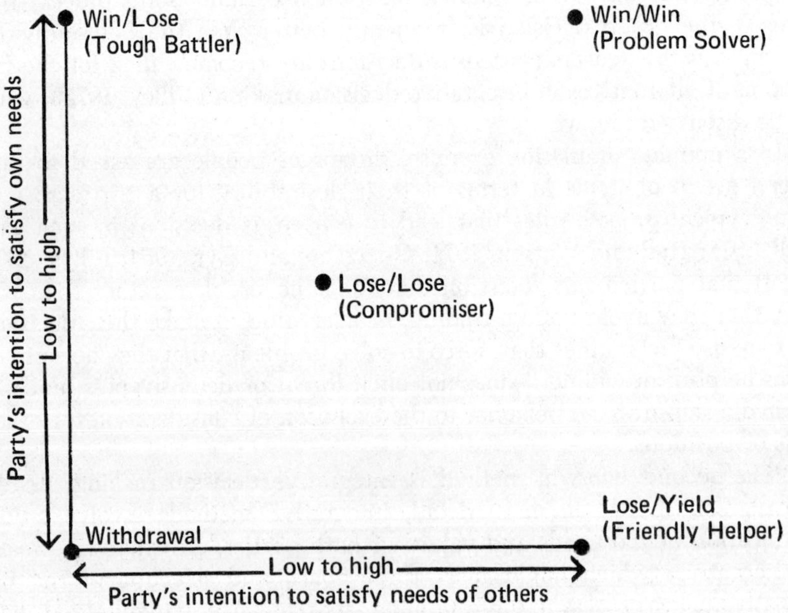

Figure 9–2. Styles of Conflict Resolution.

strong desire to maintain a relationship with another party leads to appeasement or accommodation. In terms of the integrative method of problem solving, then, both parties assert their own goals *and* desire to maintain a cooperative relationship with others by helping them to meet their goals, too.

Personal styles have also been investigated by Cummings and his associates (Cummings et al., 1971, 1972; Harnett et al., 1973). They identify bargaining styles observed in dyadic bargaining situations, which we shall label here as "Tough Battler," "Friendly Helper," and "Problem Solver" (see Figure 9–2). The descriptions of these styles are sufficiently close to those discussed above to permit us to infer what would happen when, for example, a Tough Battler meets a Friendly Helper or a Problem Solver (see Table 9–1). As indicated, Cummings estimates that Battlers frequently find themselves in a stalemate with other Battlers. They often win when engaging a Friendly Helper and win over half the time with a Problem Solver. Friendly Helpers also frequently stalemate with other Friendly Helpers, since each is busy yielding to the other's wishes, and they yield to the needs of Problem Solvers. Finally, two Problem Solvers seem to establish ready agreement since they deal with the facts of the problem at hand. If the bargaining styles are similar to conflict styles, then these estimates suggest that Problem Solvers may have more favorable outcomes than Tough Battlers.

TABLE 9-1. Estimated Outcomes in Dyadic Combinations of Conflict Style in Bargaining. Courtesy, Larry L. Cummings, University of Wisconsin.

	Tough battler	Friendly helper	Problem solver
Tough battler	Stalemate 80%	Battler wins 90%	Battler wins over 50%
Friendly helper	X	Stalemate 80%	Problem solver wins
Problem solver	X	X	Quick agreement

Distributive Versus Integrative Methods

Just as personal style affects the methods individuals will adopt in conflict situations, how a conflictive situation is viewed by the parties also determines whether conflict becomes overt or problem solving begins. If the parties view a situation as one in which one's gain can only come through the other's loss, the situation is viewed from a distributive dimension. If both parties see that they both can gain, it is viewed from an integrative dimension (see Figure 9–3).

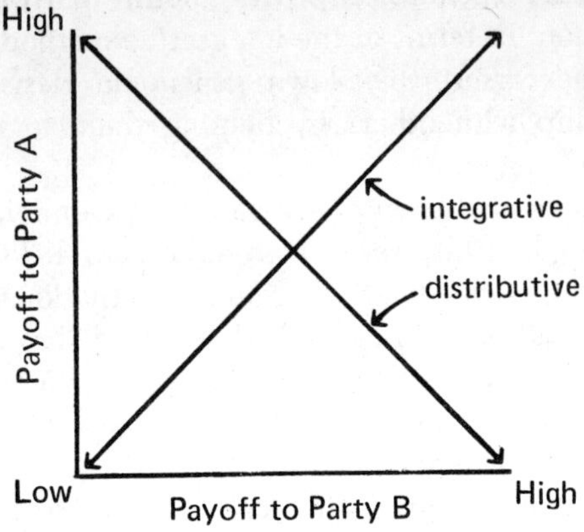

Figure 9-3. Integrative and Distributive Approaches.

According to Thomas (1974, pp. 27, 28):

> The integrative component is, roughly speaking, the total amount of satisfaction for both parties. The distributive component is the proportion of satisfaction going to each party. In other words, the integrative dimension represents the size of the pie available to both parties; the distributive dimension represents the way they divide it up.

The satisfaction Thomas refers to may be feelings about the outcome ("I'm not here to make friends"), or literal distribution of valued resources ("Shall we give the additional money to sales or engineering?").

Often, the view of a problem as distributive or integrative depends more on the perception of a fixed versus an enlargeable "pie," rather than on the literal presence of a fixed "pie." It has been emphasized that people will frequently assume that resources or alternatives are fixed when that is not the case. This generally occurs because of a tendency to focus on solutions rather than to define a problem based on ends, goals, or values.

To illustrate: A young married couple engaged in a conflict about the use of the single air-conditioned room in their apartment. The room also contained a television set. The husband wanted to watch sports events on television at the same hour that the wife wanted to study. This distributive situation was changed to an integrative situation by dropping the argument about two solutions (should husband or wife use the room) and instead defining the problem. The problem statement was to find a way to use the room so that the wife could study without distraction and the husband could hear and see sports events on television. After discussing a variety of alternatives they decided that the husband would watch the television and listen to the games through earphones while the wife would study with her back to the television set.

The Integrative Decision Method of Problem Solving

The integrative decision method of problem solving has been described by Filley (1975). As indicated in Figure 9–4, it contains the following steps.

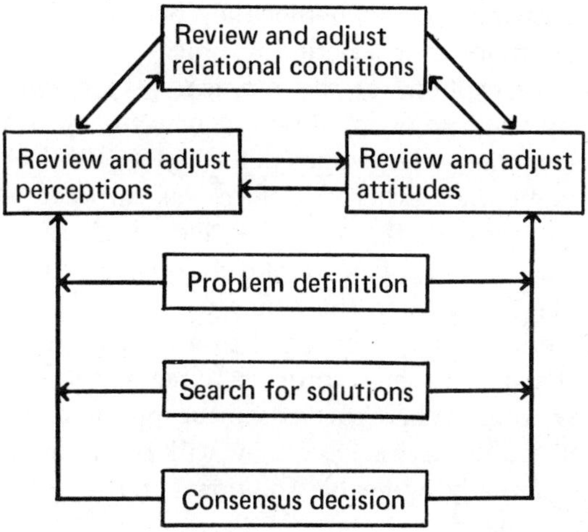

Figure 9–4. The Integrative Decision Making Process.

Review and Adjustment of Relational Conditions

The first step in the integrative process is a review of the actual conditions which exist, both related to the disagreement itself and to the conditions surrounding the disagreement. Perhaps the antecedent conditions which lead to conflict can be adjusted. In addition, it may help to adjust the process of group interaction in a manner that promotes cooperation and reduces the likelihood of conflict:

–Spatial arrangements which provide a clear separation into two sub-groups may be changed to avoid a we-they distinction.
–Large groups with nine or more people often break into sub-groups and make balanced discussion difficult; group size may be adjusted to five or seven people.
–Group leaders who impose their own content may be changed to leaders who control the process of discussion according to problem-solving processes.
–Information which has been hoarded or distorted for the advantage of some group members may be shared with all members.
–Opportunities may be provided to deal with problems as they occur rather than holding them for discussion at a later date.

Review and Adjustment of Perceptions

Another step in the integrative process is that of reality-testing perceptions. Here each party asks "Am I viewing the situation or characteristics of the other party as they actually exist?" In this regard it is helpful to have multiple measures to improve the reliability of the possible judgment. This may be done by asking others whether they perceive the same thing or by observing the conditions over a period of time.

The parties' perceptions of the problem play major roles in shifting from a potentially win-lose or lose-lose outcome to a win-win outcome. For example, in one company a large open office had a tiled floor and a coffee pot was located in one corner; when the office was carpeted with an expensive plush carpet, the president issued a directive which said "No more coffee drinking at the desks." The office employees objected. Both sides perceived the problem to be "Shall there be coffee at the desks or not?" When the solution-minded approach was changed to a statement of the problem the parties agreed that it was "how to drink coffee at the desk while avoiding spills on the new rug." When parties see the problem to be one in which there must be a winner and a loser they will get what they expect; when they see that a mutually agreeable solution is possible they are also likely to get what they expect.

Review and Adjustment of Attitudes

The attitudes and feelings of individuals constitute another screen through which information about conditions or other parties is processed, sometimes distorted, and frequently judged. Insofar as possible, the attitudes and feelings of parties who may engage in integrative processes should be identified before problem definition and later steps take place. Since integrative methods depend upon trust, mutuality of interest, and cooperation, they have little chance of success if the parties are distrustful, hostile, and competitive. If these basic conditions are not present it may be better for parties to use some other conflict resolution method. Changes in attitudes and feelings should occur before problem definition takes place since feelings are taken as given at that point.

Walton and McKersie (1965, pp. 225–49) have suggested tactics for influencing cooperative attitudes on the part of parties. These tactics are based on balance theory (Newcomb, 1953; Heider, 1958), the basis of which is that individuals prefer consistency in their perceptions and beliefs about other persons. That is, if Party A feels that Party B is threatening, but B behaves in a nonthreatening manner, then such inconsistency must be removed in A's mind, perhaps by realizing that B is not threatening after all. Balance theory suggests that:

–Cooperation will be increased when one party shares the likes and dislikes of another.

–Common association between parties through interaction will lead to increased cohesiveness between parties.
–When a party becomes identified with or associated with something which is positively valued by the other party, cooperation will be enhanced.
–Cooperation will be enhanced when one party dissociates from objects or situations which the other party dislikes.
–Cooperation is enhanced when A acknowledges help from B, because B would not help someone whom B disliked.

Problem Definition

For the "I.D.M." method of problem solving to take place, the ends, values, or goals of the parties must be identified. The parties may have different goals but each party must accept the stated goals of the other and not consider the problem solved until the solution is acceptable to both parties. Where there is truly a fixed sum of value which is divided between the two parties, then one party's gain is at a cost to the other party. In such situations the best solution is one which is considered to be fair by both parties. It is likely, however, that the majority of conflicts which are *assumed* to deal with a fixed sum of resources do not.

It may also be demonstrated that most conflicts are arguments about two *solutions.* As suggested earlier, if a husband says to his wife "Let's go to a movie tonight" and she says "I don't want to go," they are disagreeing about two solutions; they are not identifying the goals they seek. Such choice situations may be changed to problem situations by asking each party to identify what they hope to gain with the solution and then combining the needs of both sides. For example, if the husband really wants to see *Gone with the Wind* and the wife wants to avoid going out because she is tired, then an integrative solution might be to go to *Gone with the Wind* the next night.

Alternative Generation

While the parties who have the problem are responsible for defining their needs, *anyone* may have the high quality, highly acceptable integrative solution. For that reason, the emphasis in this step is upon gathering as many solutions as possible without judgment or evaluation. There are many techniques for doing this, including brainstorming, discussion groups, or surveys. Two recently developed techniques, nominal grouping (used when the respondents can be gathered in the same place) and Delphi techniques (when they cannot), are particularly promising.[1]

---

[1] A description of how to perform each method is contained in A. Delbecq, A. Van de Ven, and D. Gustafson, *Group Techniques for Program Planning,* Scott, Foresman (1975).

Evaluation and Consensus Decision

Evaluation of all possible solutions and arrival at an agreement which is acceptable to all of the parties is the final step in the integrative process. Where measures of quality and acceptability are clear and verifiable, the evaluation process entails little more than routine calculation. Yet this frequently is not the case. Many problem solving situations involve both factual, verifiable elements and elements which depend upon judgment and qualitative evaluation. For example, two business partners trying to agree on which of several suppliers to engage for materials used in a production process will find that, in addition to elements of cost and quality, there are such subjective considerations as assurance of delivery dates, personal relations with suppliers, billing arrangements, etc.

Judgments about what criteria to use, about weighting criteria, and about the application of such measures also constitute qualitative elements in the decision process. In such cases, the consensus strategy (discussed earlier) is useful. Consensus decisions will frequently result in better solutions than individual decisions and will result in greater understanding of and commitment to the outcome than will voting methods.

Conflict, Problem Solving, and Organization

As we will see in Chapter 16, there are two fundamental strategies for organization. One is organization by function, where people or machines doing the same type of work are grouped together, e.g., the typing pool, the production division. The other form is organization by goal-oriented unit, such as product divisions, project groups, or geographic divisions. Hunt (1970) observed that the former type of organization is designed for performance and efficiency, the latter for problem solving and creativity. The types of conflict encountered with each type of organization will consequently differ.

Clearly, except for relatively small organizations, there is the greatest conflictive potential in the relationship *between* functional units. Such units are the most differentiated and require the greatest effort to provide integration (Lawrence and Lorsch, 1967). They are formal and non-adaptive (Walker and Lorsch, 1968) and stresses arise between the departments which must rely on each other for performance. It is here that the integrative strategies which have been described are most helpful.

In contrast, the division into autonomous goal-oriented units eliminates the dependency between the units, but because the goal-oriented units tend to be mixtures of specialties working as teams to deal with unique problems or customer needs the stresses are *within* the units. That is, the need to work together and make group decisions is mandated. It is here that the consensual strategies are most useful. Without such consensual integration, goal-oriented units become fragmented among the specialties represented.

Propositions

In discussing problem solving and conflict resolution methods we have assumed that the former is a superior form of conflict management. Since that is a major assumption it is well to evaluate it with available information.

1. Problem-solving methods are positively related to effective conflict management.

In addition, we have suggested that one's personal behavior and personality can affect the outcome of a potentially conflictive situation. We have stressed that the problem solving role is assertive and proactive rather than passive and yielding (as with the pacifist) or dominating and controlling (as with the aggressor).

2. Problem solving is more likely when parties are perceived by each other as having the power to fight but the preference to cooperate.

Empirical Evidence

Proposition 1

Problem-solving methods are positively related to effective conflict management.

Research on organization behavior, on problem solving, and on bargaining behavior provides a basis for inferring the relative effects of the conflict resolution methods described above. Lawrence and Lorsch (1967) examined the use of confrontation (similar to the win-win methods), forcing, and smoothing in six organizations. They concluded that the two highest performing organizations used confrontation to a greater degree than the other four organizations, and that the next two organizations used confrontation more than the two lowest performing organizations.

Burke (1970) reports several studies comparing conflict resolution methods; the first asked 74 managers to describe the way they and their immediate superiors dealt with conflicts between them. Five different methods of resolution—withdrawal, smoothing, compromise, forcing, and confrontation—were identified; these were then compared to dependent variables of "constructive use of disagreement" and to planning and evaluating job performance. Comparing extreme scoring subgroups of constructive use of conflict, the most effective supervisors used the methods in the following order: (1) confrontation, (2) smoothing, (3) compromise, (4) forcing, and (5) withdrawal. The less effective supervisors used instead: (1) confrontation, (2) forcing, (3) withdrawal, (4) smoothing, and (5) compromise. While it is surprising that confrontation is reported most frequently in the less effective group as well, the frequent use of force is not.

The correlation of methods of conflict resolution with constructive use of conflict is shown in Table 9–2. As indicated, withdrawal and forcing were negatively related to good conflict resolution, confrontation and smoothing were positively related to that measure, and compromise was not related.

TABLE 9–2. Pearson Correlation of Methods of Conflict Resolution With Constructive Use of Conflict.

1. Withdrawal	– 19**
2. Smoothing	.20**
3. Compromise	–.08
4. Forcing	–.26*
5. Confrontation	.26*

N = 74 for all correlations.

*Correlation is significantly different from zero at the .05 level of confidence.

**Correlation is significantly different from zero at the .10 level of confidence.

Source: Burke, 1970, p. 400.

When compared with planning measures (such as reliance on planning, superior helpfulness, and joint goal setting) withdrawal was negatively related to six of the seven dependent variables, smoothing and compromise were unrelated, forcing was negatively related, and confrontation was positively related.

In a second study, Burke (1970) obtained 53 descriptions of effective conflict resolution and 53 descriptions of ineffective conflict resolution from 57 respondents. Of these, 58.5 percent of the effective statements were confrontation, and 79.2 percent of the ineffective statements were forcing. In general, the evidence strongly supports the greater effectiveness of win-win methods compared to win-lose methods.

Another body of literature which sheds some light on the relative advantages of the methods has to do with bargaining behavior in dyads. Such simulations generally involve a buyer and a seller, and prices and profits are fixed in a joint payoff table. Unlike consensus and problem solving studies, bargaining studies seek an optimum contract instead of a judgment or ideal ranking. In addition, there is no qualitative shift in the process to a concern with motives or goals. Bargaining studies are useful because they show the relative effects of negotiation versus problem solving and they consider the personality correlates that are associated with different types of bargainers.

In a simulated negotiation involving 92 undergraduates (Lewis and

Pruitt, 1971), participants took a one-sided orientation or a problem-solving orientation. Under the former condition, negotiators were concerned only with their own needs; under the latter, they were concerned with the other's position as well. Also controlled in the study was the aspiration level for payoffs (high versus low aspiration).

Results showed that the total contract size was higher under the problem solving than under the one-sided condition, and greater under a high aspiration than under a low aspiration condition. The relationship between the conditions suggested that "when coupled with a problem solving orientation, high aspirations encourage integrative bargaining and thereby enhance the chances of observing new alternatives that bring high joint payoff" (p. 222).

From the foregoing discussion it would appear that win-win decision strategies are associated with better judgments, favorable organization experience, and more favorable bargains where joint rewards are taken as the criterion.

Proposition 2

Problem solving is more likely when parties are perceived by each other as having the power to fight but the preference to cooperate.

The earlier discussion has suggested that the ideal conflict style is one in which both parties are interested in both their own goals *and* in the goals of others. In other words, neither fighting for a defeat of the opponent nor yielding to the wishes of the opponent is likely to be effective in resolving conflicts. On the face of it this seems reasonable, yet when viewed from the standpoint of popular behavior it seems that people still follow and believe in the other strategies. On the one hand there is the passive or nonresistance form of dealing with conflict. At its best, passive resistance is employed to control a more powerful opponent because one cannot attack a helpless opponent (Haley, 1969). This strategy is also designed to elicit the sympathy and support of observers who see the "bully" picking on the "little guy." Experience tells us that, however inspirational, the peace-loving passive resistor does get mauled enough times to give one pause about the efficacy of the method. There is also supplemental evidence that this will happen (Rapoport and Chammah, 1965).

In contrast, there is still a great deal of popular support for the idea that "might makes right." "In the real world," it is suggested, "nice guys don't win," so one has to be tough and competitive. To the victors go the spoils—wealth, sex objects, power. Perhaps the power-oriented strategy would be effective if the parties involved were independent of each other—neither depending on the other for certain actions. Even the expectation of further interaction is involved, since if one party gains at the expense of another it is probably less likely that the interaction will continue than if both parties gain from their involvement, or, at least, if the issue between them is resolved fairly.

Some insights into the relative advantages of cooperation and competition may be gained from two studies conducted in laboratory settings. In the first (Shure, Meeker, and Hansford, 1965), pairs of bargainers shared the use of a communication device which could be used alternately (cooperation), entirely by one party (dominance), or by neither through mutual interference (standoff). In addition, both parties had the power to force the other out of the device and to prevent their use of it. Finally, both parties had the opportunity to give an electric shock to the other if, for example, they became irritated at the other's continued action of forcing them out of the device.

Each party in the bargaining pairs was programmed by directions and social support to act either as a pacifist or as an aggressor. The typical pacifists would (1) let the other party go first in a series of messages requiring the use of the communication device; (2) claim that alternation was fair and would seek no more time to use the device than was their fair share; (3) place their messages in the device when it was their turn (with the result that their messages were repeatedly forced out of the device by the aggressor); and (4) not make use of any opportunity to shock the aggressor.

Given the compliant behavior of the pacifists, one might expect the aggressors to eventually feel guilty about their exploitation of the other and to adopt a more cooperative approach themselves. However, when 143 aggressor-pacifist pairs interacted for 15 turns, the trend was toward greater domination of the pacifists. Only 18 of the potential aggressors refused to use the shock from the outset. Of the remaining 125 dominators, only 40 adopted a cooperative pattern by the end of the experiment, and 85 continued to dominate and to give electric shocks to the pacifists. In general, the pacifists changed their strategy very little and suffered continued losses to the aggressors.

The pacifist strategy was effective in causing an aggressor to cooperate only if both operators had an opportunity to send each other messages and both used that opportunity. In such cases, the pacifists would emphasize their desire to cooperate, would state their refusal to shock, and would indicate their intention to suffer the shocks if the aggressor continued to act unfairly. After responding to the pacifist, the aggressor would begin to adopt a more cooperative stance. Simply knowing, however, that the pacifist would take a cooperative approach had no effect on the behavior of the aggressor; interaction and communication between the two was required before aggressor behavior changed.

Thus, it would seem that a consistent willingness to cooperate and a refusal to exercise sanctions may simply provide the aggressor with an opportunity to dominate the pacifist with impunity. Pacifist tactics may even invite exploitation and aggression from some who do not start with such intentions!

A second set of experiments sheds further light on this issue (Rapoport,

1966). These experiments involved a series of joint decisions by two people playing a game in which the motives of each party are mixed, that is, there are both reasons to cooperate and reasons to compete. The game is a variety of one known as the Prisoner's Dilemma. For example, a Prisoner's Dilemma could occur in two firms competing for the same market. If each firm has a choice of selling its product at a high or low price, both selling at a high price permits a shared market and large profits. Similarly, both selling at a low price permits sharing. But if one firm sells low while the other sells high, the former gains the market and the latter either goes out of business or attempts to meet the competitor's low price, in which case a price war ensues and both are unable to meet their costs and to make a profit. Assuming that agreement to sell at a high price is not possible, the most favorable outcome is to cooperate and to share the market. In Rapoport's study, the controlled party was directed in one instance to always cooperate, in another instance to always defect, and in a third instance to do what the opponent did on the preceding play. As might be expected, a completely non-cooperative strategy elicited almost no cooperation from the other party. On the other hand, a completely cooperative strategy elicited either complete cooperation or complete exploitation. The greatest amount of cooperation (70 to 80 percent) was elicited by those who gave back what they had received on the preceding play.

Both studies indicate that while cooperation based upon moral values—pacifism, helping, or avoiding the exploitation of others—may occur, the more important ingredient for inducing cooperative behavior is rational self-interest. Having both the power to retaliate and the willingness to use that power may be necessary to impress upon an opponent the cost of competition.

Unfortunately, however, this issue is far from resolved. In some cases the balanced strategy suggested does not elicit cooperation (Wilson, 1969; Komorita, 1972). In other cases, the presence of unilateral power is associated with its use (Deutsch and Krauss, 1962). The cost of not agreeing, the size of demands, the degree of communication between parties, the rates and amounts of concession, and many other variables play a part in determining this question. In general, the presence of personal strength to demonstrate the cost of not agreeing seems warranted, as suggested earlier, but there are inherent dangers to cooperation when strength or power is not balanced between the parties.

Summary

Proposition 1. Problem-solving methods are positively related to effective conflict management. *Supported with limited evidence.*

Proposition 2. Problem solving is more likely when parties are perceived by each other as having the power to fight but the preference to cooperate. *Mixed evidence.*

Discussion

One purpose in this chapter has been to introduce the reader to the qualitative difference that exists between efforts by two parties to split what is considered to be a fixed sum and efforts by two parties to find an answer to a mutual problem which can benefit both. Whether the issue is one of meeting the goals of the organization and its participants (as in most management by objectives programs) or is one of meeting the goals of two people who might otherwise be in conflict, it appears that problem solving is an effective tool in conflict management.

Problem solving depends upon cooperation between the parties. As we have suggested, cooperation is probably more likely where each party believes that the other can fight effectively but chooses to cooperate. It is also more likely where the parties have balanced power since there is evidence that in unbalanced power situations those who have power may use it.

References

Blake, R. R., and Mouton, J. S. 1961. Comprehension of own and outgroup positions under intergroup competition. *Journal of Conflict Resolution* 5: 304–10.

———., and ———. 1970. The fifth achievement. *Journal of Applied Behavioral Science* 6: 413–26.

———., Shepard, H. A., and Mouton, J. S. 1964. *Managing intergroup conflict in industry*. Gulf Publishing Company.

Burke, R. J. 1970. Methods of resolving superior-subordinate conflict: The constructive use of subordinate differences and disagreements. *Organizational Behavior and Human Performance* 5: 393–411.

Corwin, R. G. 1969. Patterns of organizational conflict. *Administrative Science Quarterly* 14: 507–21.

Cummings, L. L., Harnett, D. L., and Schmidt, S. M. 1972. International cross-language factor stability of personality: An analysis of the Shine-Meeker personality/attitude schedule. *The Journal of Psychology* 82: 67–84.

———., ———., and Stevens, O. J. 1971. Risk, fate, conciliation and trust: An international study of attitudinal differences among executives. *Academy of Management Journal* 14: 285–304.

Delbecq, A., Van de Ven, A., and Gustafson, D. 1975. *Group techniques for program planning*. Scott, Foresman.

Deutsch, M., and Krauss, R. M. 1962. Studies of interpersonal bargaining. *The Journal of Conflict Resolution* 6: 52–67.

Filley, A. C. 1975. *Interpersonal conflict resolution*. Scott, Foresman.

Follett, M. P. 1941. *Dynamic administration: The collected papers of Mary Parker Follett*, ed. by H. C. Metcalf and L. Urwick. Harper.

Guetzkow, H., and Gyr, J. 1954. An analysis of conflict in decision-making groups. *Human Relations* 7: 367–81.

Hackman, J. R., and Kaplan, R. E. 1974. Interventions into group process: An approach to improving the effectiveness of groups. *Decision Sciences* 5: 459–80.

Haley, J. 1969. *The power tactics of Jesus Christ and other essays.* Grossman.

Hall, J. 1969. *Conflict management survey.* Teleometrics.

———. 1971. Decisions, decisions, decisions. *Psychology Today* 5: 51–58.

———., and Watson, W. H. 1971. The effects of a normative intervention on group decision making performance. *Human Relations* 23: 299–317.

———, and Williams, M. S. 1966. A comparison of decision-making performances in established and ad hoc groups. *Journal of Personality and Social Psychology* 3: 214–22.

———., and ———. 1970. Group dynamics training and improved decision making. *Journal of Applied Behavioral Sciences* 6: 27–32.

Harnett, D. L., Cummings, L. L., and Hamner, W. C. 1973. Personality, bargaining style, and payoff in bilateral monopoly bargaining among European managers. *Sociometry* 36: 325–45.

Heider, F. 1958. *The psychology of interpersonal relations.* Wiley.

Hunt, R. G. 1970. Technology and organization. *Academy of Management Journal* 13: 235–52.

Komorita, S. S. 1972. Tacit communication and cooperation in a two-person game. In *Contributions to experimental economies* (Vol. III), ed. by H. Sauermann and J. C. B. Mohr. Tubingen.

Lawrence, P. R., and Lorsch, J. W. 1967. *Organization and environment: Managing differentiation and integration.* Division of Research, Graduate School of Business Administration, Harvard University.

Lewis, S. A., and Pruitt, D. G. 1971. Orientation, aspiration level, and communication freedom in integrative bargaining. *Proceedings of the American Psychological Association* 6: 221–22.

Neill, A. S. 1960. *Summerhill: A radical approach to child rearing.* Hart.

Newcomb, T. M. 1953. An approach to the study of communicative acts. *Psychological Review* 60: 393–404.

Pasmore, W. A., Nemiroff, P. M., and Ford, D. L. 1975. The effects of two normative structural interventions on established and ad hoc groups: Implications for the improvement of decision making effectiveness. Paper No. 497, Institute for Research in the Behavioral, Economic and Management Sciences, Purdue University.

Pondy, L. R. 1967. Organizational conflict: Concepts and models. *Administrative Science Quarterly* 12: 296–320.

Rapoport, A. 1960. Experiments in dyadic conflict and cooperation. *Bulletin of the Menninger Clinic* 30: 284–91.

———., and Chammah, A. M. 1965. *Prisoner's dilemma.* University of Michigan.

Shure, G. H., Meeker, R. J., and Hansford, E. A. 1965. The effectiveness of pacifist strategies in bargaining games. *The Journal of Conflict Resolution* 9: 106–17.

Thomas, K. 1974. Conflict and conflict management. Working Paper #74-3, Human Systems Development Study Center, University of California. (To appear as Chapter 21 in *The handbook of industrial and organizational psychology* (Vol. II), ed. by M. D. Dunnette. Rand-McNally. In Press.)

Walker, A. H., and Lorsch, J. W. 1968. Organizational choice: Product vs. function. *Harvard Business Review* 46: 129–38.

Walton, R. E., Dutton, J. M., and Cafferty, T. P. 1969. Organizational context and interdepartmental conflict. *Administrative Science Quarterly* 14: 522–43.

———., and McKersie, R. B. 1965. *A behavioral theory of labor negotiations.* McGraw-Hill.

Wilson, W. 1969. Cooperation and the cooperation of the other player. *Journal of Conflict Resolution* 13: 110–17.

Chapter **10**

Motivation

Snoopy: *Yesterday I was a dog. Today I'm a dog. Tomorrow I'll probably still be a dog. There's just so little hope of advancement.*

CLARK GESNER
You're a Good Man Charlie Brown

Productivity in many jobs depends largely on how much the worker is willing to produce; this is true of most office jobs, and even of many jobs on assembly lines. Moreover, the increasing rate of automation will cause more and more routine jobs to be performed by machines and greater numbers of plant workers will serve in technical capacities, maintaining and repairing automated equipment. There will also be a higher proportion of service workers who will work at processing and transmitting information. Consequently, employees will be permitted greater discretion in allocating their time and effort, and thus will have greater influence on organizational effectiveness. Perhaps even more than at present, one of the major problems that will face future managers will be the motivation of subordinates.

March and Simon (1958) raised two important questions that theories ot motivation must seek to answer:

1. What conditions are required to attract and maintain a work group? That is, what motivates people to join an organization and to remain within it?
2. Under what conditions are employees on the job induced to produce (put forth energy and effort) at the rate demanded by the organization?

Many theories of what motivates individuals to work have been advanced, but only a few have been adequately tested in a variety of situations. Nonetheless, much can be learned from reviewing their historical development and the evidence for and against them. To provide a framework for our review, we will describe six prominent theories which have stimulated considerable research: need theory, human relations theory, two-factor theory, value/expectancy theory, achievement theory, and inequity theory. Our discussion of motivation obviously has far-reaching implications for management and especially for leadership, which will be discussed in the next two chapters.

Need Theory

Originally advanced in 1943 by Abraham Maslow (1943), need theory holds that people are motivated to satisfy a "hierarchy" of needs. It postulates that the satisfaction of earlier, basic physiological needs triggers the emergence of later, more social and psychological needs. Since its initial publication, need theory has become one of the most prominent theories of work motivation in the motivation literature. Many of its concepts have been used to explain and prescribe management practices and organizational design (Davis, 1946; Viteles, 1953; McGregor, 1960; Argyris, 1964; Schein, 1965).

A good description of Maslow's need theory is provided by Wahba and Bridwell (1975):

> Maslow . . . proposed that human needs can be classified into different categories. . . . The hierarchy of needs is as follows (in ascending order of prepotency): the physiological needs, the safety needs, the belongingness or love needs, the esteem needs (self-esteem, recognition and status), and the need for self-actualization. . . .
>
> Maslow utilized the two concepts of deprivation and gratification to provide the dynamic forces that linked needs to behavior. . . . He postulated that deprivation or dissatisfaction of a need of high prepotency will lead to the domination of this need over the organism's personality. . . . Relative gratification of a given need submerges it and "activates" the next higher need in the hierarchy. The activated need then dominates and organizes the individual's personality and capacities, so that instead of the individual being hunger obsessed, he now becomes safety obsessed.
>
> This process of deprivation-domination-gratification-activation continues until the physiological, safety, affiliation, and esteem needs have all been gratified and the self-actualization need has been activated. In a later work (1954), Maslow modified the gratification/activation idea by proposing that in a growth-motivated self-actualizing individual, gratification of the self-actualization needs caused an increase in its importance rather than a decrease. Maslow also acknowledged numerous other exceptions to his theory. Notably, he pointed out that long deprivation of a given need may create a fixation for that need. Also, higher needs may emerge not after gratification, but rather after long deprivation, renunciation or suppression of lower needs. Maslow emphasized again and again that behavior is multi-determined and multi-motivated.

Human Relations Theory

Implicit in the human relations theory of management (see Chapter 1) is the view that motivation depends primarily on the satisfaction of the higher-level needs in Maslow's hierarchy. This view differs from classical theories by its deemphasis of the importance of pay, which it sees as at best able to satisfy only the physiological and (economic) safety needs—and possibly some belongingness and ego needs.

As described by Likert (1961), human relations theory asserts that productive work units are characterized by favorable member attitudes toward all aspects of the job, including other workers, superiors, and the organization. These attitudes are not merely those of easy complacency, but include an identification with the organization and a strong involvement with its goals. As a consequence of these attitudes, dissatisfaction may occur when achievement falls short of set goals.

The managers of productive organizations, according to human relations theory, strive to use all of the factors which yield favorable and cooperative attitudes in such a way that motivational forces are mutually reinforcing. These forces include economic, security, and ego motives, along with curiosity and the desire to be creative. Such managers typically activate these motives by encouraging widespread participation and involvement in decision making.

Two-Factor Theory

The two-factor theory of motivation, first advanced by Herzberg, was inferred from a study of need satisfaction and the reported motivational effects of these satisfactions for 200 engineers and accountants (Herzberg, Mausner, and Snyderman, 1959).

Herzberg and his associates asked subjects to recall a time when they felt exceptionally good about their jobs. The investigators then sought to determine why respondents felt as they did, and whether their feelings of satisfaction had affected their performance, personal relationships, and feelings of well-being. Finally, they attempted to bring out the sequence of events that returned their subjects' attitudes to "normal." In a second set of interviews, the same subjects were asked about instances in which their feelings about their jobs were exceptionally negative and directly related to some happening on the job.

The investigators concluded that high satisfaction is not, in the main, brought about by the absence of factors that cause dissatisfaction, but rather by the presence of certain factors they classified as "satisfiers"—although some factors worked in both directions. Satisfiers were related to the nature of the work itself and to rewards that flow directly from performance of that work. The most important satisfiers foster a sense of personal growth and self-fulfillment: (1) perceived opportunity for achievement on the job; (2) recognition; (3) a sense of performing interesting and important work; (4) responsibility; (5) advancement. The recognition that produces good feelings about the job does not necessarily have to come from supervisors—it may come from peers, customers, or subordinates.

Dissatisfiers were factors associated with the *context* rather than the *content* of the work. The most important were company policies that foster ineffectiveness (inefficiency, waste, duplication) or power struggles within the organization. The second most important dissatisfier was found to be incompetent technical supervision—supervisors who lack knowledge of the job or the ability to schedule work or to coach. Besides company policy and technical supervision, other potent dissatisfiers were interpersonal relations, working conditions, and pay. Lack of recognition and lack of advancement were also found to be able to cause dissatisfaction.

Other interesting findings were:

> —When poor attitudes arise from a short-range event, the feelings are more likely to go away than to linger. This is in contrast to good feelings about jobs which tend to persist, no matter how momentary the events leading to the attitude.
> —Work itself, responsibility, and advancement are much more likely to produce lasting effects than are either recognition or achievement.
> —Since long-range attitude changes are also associated with greater performance effects, the same three factors are also more likely to improve job effectiveness (Herzberg et al., 1959, p. 64).

Satisfier factors were named "motivators," since other findings of the study suggest that they are effective in motivating the individual to superior performance and effort. In a later book, Herzberg (1966) explained why motivators affect motivation in a positive direction:

> When a child learns to ride a bicycle, he is becoming more competent, increasing the repertory of his behavior, expanding his skills—psychologically growing. In the process of the child's learning to master a bicycle, the parents can love him with all the zeal and compassion of the most devoted mother and father. They can safeguard the child from injury by providing the safest and most hygienic area in which to practice; they can offer all kinds of incentives and rewards, and they can provide the most expert instructions. But the child will never, never learn to ride the bicycle—unless he is given a bicycle! The hygiene factors [dissatisfiers] are not a valid contributor to psychological growth. The substance of a task is required to achieve growth goals. Similarly, you cannot love an engineer into creativity, although by this approach you can avoid his dissatisfactions with the way you treat him. Creativity will require a potentially creative task to do (p. 75).

Based on the original study and the above rationale, the major hypotheses of the two-factor theory of motivation are (Herzberg, 1966):

1. The satisfiers—achievement, recognition, work itself, responsibility, and opportunities for advancement—are mainly unipolar; that is, they contribute very little to job dissatisfaction. Conversely, the dissatisfiers—

company policy and administration, supervision, interpersonal relations, working conditions, and salary—are also unipolar; they contribute very little to job satisfaction.

2. Motivation to work results from satisfying the individual's needs for the satisfiers—achievement, recognition, interesting and challenging work, responsibility, and advancement—and not from elimination of the dissatisfiers.

Criticism of the Two-Factor Theory. The two-factor theory of motivation has been criticized from a number of standpoints; perhaps the most important critique has been that of Vroom (1964, 1966). Vroom has pointed out that Herzberg's own earlier review of 15 job-opinion studies (Herzberg et al., 1957), involving more than 28,000 employees, draws conclusions about factors which make workers satisfied or dissatisfied with their jobs which are inconsistent with two-factor theory. Vroom (1964) went on to argue for the importance of further replication studies, but cautioned:

> Even if such research were to perfectly replicate the Herzberg, Mausner, and Snyderman findings on widely different populations, their inference concerning a qualitative difference between satisfiers and dissatisfiers could not be unequivocally accepted. It is still possible that obtained differences between stated sources of satisfaction and dissatisfaction stem from defensive processes within the individual respondent. Persons may be more likely to attribute the causes of satisfaction to their own achievements and accomplishments on the job. On the other hand, they may be more likely to attribute their dissatisfaction, not to personal inadequacies or deficiencies, but to factors in the work environment, i.e., obstacles presented by company policies or supervision (p. 129).

Herzberg (1966) countered with claims that, to the extent that defense mechanisms are at work, their effect would be to

> . . . obscure the motivator-hygiene theory rather than enhance it. The supposition that people would *prefer* to blame hygiene factors rather than motivators for their job unhappiness is naive. . . . The opposite is more often true. Employees who wish to make themselves *look good* are much more prone to say that they are unhappy because they do not have responsibility, are not getting ahead, have uninteresting work . . . than to say that their supervisor is unfriendly, the administration is poor . . . their fellow workers are unsociable, etc. (pp. 130–31).

Some recent research by Kerr, Harlan, and Stogdill (1974) tends to support Herzberg on this point.

Vroom also argued that there is a lack of evidence of any consistent correlation between the recall of satisfying events and actual observations of motivated behaviors:

> Herzberg is losing sight of the distinction. He appears to be arguing that the satisfiers are also motivators, i.e., that those job-content conditions which produce a high level of satisfaction also motivate the person to perform effectively on his job. Consequently, he is exhorting administrators to satisfy workers' needs for self-actualization and growth by making their jobs more challenging and interesting (1966, p. 11).

Additional criticisms, along with a review of studies pertinent to this controversy, will be reviewed later in this chapter.

Value/Expectancy Theory

Originally developed by Lewin (1951) and specifically applied to motivation to work by Vroom (1964), value/expectancy theory is based on the following two premises:

1. People subjectively assign values to the expected outcomes of various courses of action, and therefore have preferences among the expected outcomes.
2. Any explanation of motivated behavior must take into account not only the ends that people hope to accomplish but the extent to which they believe that their own actions contribute to producing the outcomes they prefer.

From these premises, Vroom (1964) advances the following theoretical proposition:

> The force on a person (motive) to perform a given act is based on the weighted value (or utility) of all the possible outcomes of the act multiplied by the perceived usefulness of the given act in the attainment of these outcomes. Whenever an individual chooses between alternatives that involve certain outcomes, it seems clear that his behavior is affected not only by his preferences among outcomes, but also by the degree to which he believes these outcomes to be probable (p. 18).

According to the first premise, an individual's motivation to perform depends partially on the average value of all possible perceived outcomes associated with effective performance. For example, effort may be seen as a means of achieving effective performance. Effective performance in turn is seen as a means to other outcomes, such as an increase in pay, recognition, promotion, or job security.

But motivation to perform depends also on expectations that one can successfully accomplish the task and expectations that performance will result in the desired outcome(s). Accordingly, if people give preference to additional money as a desirable outcome of their behavior on the job, their motivation will depend on the degree to which they believe they can perform effectively *and* the degree to which they believe high productivity is likely to help them financially—either through incentive payments or through promotion to higher-paying jobs. On the other hand, if people at work are seeking other ends, such as satisfaction of their curiosity or task accomplishment, in addition to money, their work performance must permit them to attain these other preferred outcomes.

People may therefore place great value on bringing about a certain outcome, but if they do not believe that anything they do will affect what happens, they will not be moved to act. In the same vein, if they believe their actions can largely determine various outcomes, but if these outcomes are of no interest to them, people will not be moved to act. The more individuals value the result, and the more they anticipate that the result depends upon their own actions, the higher will be their motivation to act.

At least thirty studies testing this theory have been reported since 1964. Since Vroom's work (1964) several elaborations of the theory have been advanced. The most important elaborations include (a) the distinction between intrinsic and extrinsic rewards, and (b) the specification of some of the conditions required for preferences and expectations to affect performance.

Intrinsic vs. Extrinsic Rewards. Originally no distinction was made between *extrinsic* rewards (controlled by others) and *intrinsic* rewards resulting directly from effort and effective performance (usually these take the form of enjoyment with the effort itself or satisfaction with goal attainment). Recently, however, many authors have pointed out that effective performance is itself satisfying to some subjects under some conditions. For example, McClelland and his associates (1951, 1961) have shown that when performance can be readily evaluated as either a success or a failure, the satisfaction that can be potentially associated with a task is a function of both the probability of success and the strength of the individual's need for achievement. The greatest satisfaction with accomplishment would therefore be derived by subjects with high needs for achievement.

Conditions for Preferences and Expectations to Affect Performance. Porter and Lawler (1968) have extended the basic theory by arguing that if individuals perceive a high probability that valued rewards will result from their efforts they will be motivated to put forth such efforts, but that poor performance can still result if (a) necessary abilities are lacking or (b) the individuals' perceptions of what is required for effective performance are erroneous. Thus adequate ability and accurate role perceptions are seen as necessary, though not sufficient, for performance.

Value/expectancy theory recognizes that preferences and expectations differ among individuals, but makes no attempt to describe these differences or to categorize individuals in any way. It is therefore a very general theory dealing with fundamental determinants of motivation; to use it for prediction requires knowledge of the preferences and expectations of the individuals concerned.

Achievement Theory

McClelland (1951, 1961), Atkinson (1958), and their associates have conducted extensive research on the development of a theory to explain *achievement-oriented behavior,* which is defined as behavior directed toward meeting a standard of excellence. Early research disclosed that some individuals are more achievement-oriented than others, that is, have higher needs for achievement. It was also found that some situations arouse more achievement-orientation than others. Achievement theory attempts to explain why such differences exist, the conditions under which achievement-orientation is aroused, and the consequences of such an orientation for effective performance.

Individuals with high needs for achievement tend to be preoccupied by a common pattern of thought when daydreaming, or when planning and doing tasks which require skills and offer opportunities for individual accomplishment. This pattern of thought is characterized by a concern with unique and challenging goals, consideration of personal and environmental barriers to goal accomplishment, development of strategies that will help accomplish such goals, and anticipation of both positive and negative consequences of one's actions with respect to goal accomplishment. Further, such individuals strongly associate their own feelings and self-esteem with actual and anticipated goal accomplishment. Thus, people whose need for achievement is high are likely to frequently engage in daydreaming or meditating about achievement goals; they are also likely to experience and anticipate positive or negative feelings as a result of their anticipated and actual success or failure.

Achievement-oriented individuals also have common patterns of behavior. They tend to assume responsibility for individual achievement, seek challenging tasks, take minimal risks on tasks which serve as stepping stones to future important rewards, take intermediate risks on tasks offering immediate opportunities for achievement, seek information to measure their progress, persist in their pursuit of achievement goals, engage in strategic planning to carry out their goals, and gain more satisfaction from goal accomplishment and more frustration from failure than do nonachievement-oriented individuals.

According to the theory, situations that enable individuals to compete against standards of excellence, require the use of skills rather than luck, present cues which indicate that the task presents a challenge, and permit the individual to evaluate performance in terms of success and failure have been found to arouse tendencies to think and to behave in an achievement-oriented pattern.

To account for these findings, Atkinson (1957) formulated a theory of achievement motivation which includes variables that are related to those discussed earlier in connection with value/expectancy theory. The major proposition of the theory is that the strength of one's tendency to succeed on a task (T_s)

> . . . is a multiplicative function of three variables: motive to achieve success (M_s) which is conceived as a relatively general and stable disposition of personality and measured in terms of need for achievement; and two other variables which represent the effect of the immediate environment—the strength of expectancy (or subjective probability) that performance of a task will be followed by success (P_s), and the relative attractiveness of success of that particular activity, which is called the incentive value of success (I_s). I_s is assumed to be greater the more difficult the task (Atkinson, in Atkinson and Raynor, 1974, p. 14).

This theory was initially used to explain a vast amount of research evidence concerning how individuals behave in situations in which they were given the opportunity to compete with some immediate standard of excellence. The theory is well supported, but it is limited to situations where the individual incentive to achieve is the intrinsic satisfaction of task success, and not extrinsic rewards such as money, promotion, status, or recognition of others.

A recent extension of the theory considers motivation to achieve under conditions in which achievement is both a potential source of satisfaction and also potentially results in extrinsic rewards. Raynor (in Atkinson and Raynor, 1974, pp. 127–29) summarizes this extension of the theory as follows:

> A particular activity is considered the immediate next step in a path. A path consists of a series of steps. Each step represents an activity (task) and its expected outcome(s) or consequence(s). A step is achievement-related if skill activity can result in success or failure. Any achievement-related step may have as expected outcomes one or more extrinsic rewards (positive incentives) or threats (negative incentives). A *consequence* is *called a "goal" when it has positive incentive value.* Steps in the path are identified by their anticipated order of occurrence and by the kind of consequence that is expected. The individual's knowledge of what activities will lead on to what outcomes within a class of incentives determines the length of path.

According to the theory, paths may be either contingent or noncontingent. A path is *noncontingent* if immediate success or failure has no bearing on the opportunity to engage in subsequent activity in the path, and thus success or failure has no influence upon future success or failure.

A path is *contingent* if the individual believes that immediate success is necessary to guarantee the opportunity to strive for some number of future successes, and that immediate failure amounts to future failure through loss of the opportunity to continue on the path. The strength of the expectancy that immediate activity will result in a future success is then assumed to be a multiplicative function of the subjective probabilities associated with each step of the path.

Inequity Theory

Another theory of motivation concerns psychological reactions to feelings of inequity. Here inequity is given a very specific meaning. Inequity is defined as feeling either under- or over-rewarded for one's contribution *relative* to the rewards of others in similar circumstances. Thus, according to inequity theory individuals compare their own situations with others in similar situations, in terms of the contributions each makes and the rewards each derives. It is argued that when an inequitable comparison is perceived, tension is felt. The greater the feeling of inequity the greater the drive to reduce this tension. Individuals respond in various ways in their efforts to reduce tension. For example, they can increase or decrease their efforts to make the contributions and rewards more equitable. With respect to work behavior, it is hypothesized that individuals who feel underpaid, relative to others who make similar contributions, may decrease their efforts (contributions) and individuals who feel overpaid may increase their efforts.

The theory also allows for other methods of reducing inequity. For example, individuals may distort their perceptions of either rewards or contributions by rationalizing that their contributions are really greater (or less) than originally thought. They may also rationalize that the rewards being received are really of more (or less) value than had been expected. One may also leave the situation, by quitting the job or by severing relations with the comparison person. Another alternative is to alter the comparison person's contributions or rewards (by punishing over-production, for example) or to force the comparison person to leave the field.

According to the theory, an individual's choice of methods for reducing inequity are governed by the following propositions:

1. Person will maximize the most-valued outcomes.
2. Person will minimize increasing contributions and rewards that are effortful and costly to change.
3. Person will resist cognitive changes (rationalization) in contributions and rewards that are central to the self-concept and to self esteem.
4. Person will be more resistant to changing cognitions about own rewards and contributions than to changing cognitions about comparison person's rewards and contributions.
5. Leaving the field will be resorted to only when the magnitude of in-

equity experienced is high and other means of reducing it are unavailable. Partial withdrawal, such as absenteeism, will occur more frequently and under conditions of lower inequity. Thus inequity theory, while primarily concerned with causes and consequences of the absence of equity in human relationships, has significant implications for both motivation to work and feelings of satisfaction with work.

Propositions

The six theories described above can be restated in succinct, propositional form, as follows:

Need Theory

a. The higher the deprivation or deficiency of a given need, the higher its importance, strength, or desirability.
b. Gratification of a need at one level in the hierarchy will be positively associated with activation of a need at the next higher level.

Human Relations Theory

a. Lack of satisfaction of a need initially results in increased motivation to satisfy that need; if the individual has the opportunity to satisfy the need, increased motivation will result. If the need cannot be satisfied, frustration and dissatisfaction result.

Two-Factor Theory

a. Motivation to work results from the presence of job satisfiers: recognition, work itself, responsibility, and opportunity for advancement. Conversely, the state of potential dissatisfiers—policy, supervision, interpersonal relations, working conditions, and salary—contributes very little to job satisfaction.
b. Satisfiers increase motivation but dissatisfiers do not decrease motivation.

Value/Expectancy Theory

a. People subjectively assign values to the expected outcomes of various courses of action, and therefore have preferences among expected outcomes.
b. Any explanation of motivated behavior must take into account not only the ends that people hope to accomplish but the extent to which they believe their own actions contribute to producing the outcomes they prefer.

Achievement Theory

a. Individuals whose motivation to achieve is greater than their anxiety over the possibility of failure will become increasingly more motivated to succeed as the length of a contingent path increases, while individuals who are primarily motivated not to engage in immediate activity will become even more inhibited as the length of a contingent path increases.[1]

b. Superiority in performance by the achievement-motivated individual, as compared to the failure-threatened individual, will be greater in contingent than in noncontingent paths of equivalent length, and in the longer of two contingent paths.

c. Individuals whose achievement-motivation exceeds their fear of failure will act to guarantee immediate success in a contingent path in order to ensure the opportunity to strive for success in skill activities in the path.

Inequity Theory

a. Overpaid hourly or salaried subjects will increase their contributions by producing more as a means of reducing inequity.

b. Overpaid piece-rate subjects will produce higher quality and lower quantity than equitably paid subjects.

c. Underpaid hourly or salaried subjects will produce less to achieve a contribution-reward balance.

d. Underpaid piece-rate subjects will produce a large number of low quality output because the production of low quality output permits increasing rewards without substantially increasing contributions.

Empirical Evidence

Need Theory

a. The higher the deprivation or deficiency of a given need, the higher its importance, strength, or desirability.

b. Gratification of a need at one level in the hierarchy will be positively associated with activation of a need at the next higher level.

The scientific status of Maslow's need theory has recently been assessed by Wahba and Bridwell (1975). The authors reviewed 22 studies, from which the validity of the first proposition can be inferred.

From 11 studies which addressed this proposition it was concluded that questionnaire responses did not fall into patterns consistent with the theory. Rather, in some studies there appeared to be two primary clusters of needs: low order (physiological and safety) and high order (ego and

[1] This proposition assumes a constant level of perceived difficulty across steps in the contingent paths.

self-fulfillment). Wahba and Bridwell did find, however, that the strength of the self-fulfillment need was associated with a deprivation of that need in 18 of the 22 studies. This finding is more consistent with Maslow's initial version than his revised one.

None of the four studies reviewed by Wahba and Bridwell which explicitly tested the second proposition found support for it.

Thus, while the Maslow need theory has been generally uncritically accepted in the management and organizational behavior literature, the evidence relevant to it is strongly disconfirming. Wahba and Bridwell point out that these negative results are likely due to the lack of clarity with which the theory was presented, and therefore to difficulties in testing the theory with precision or rigor. Consequently, they state that Maslow's need hierarchy "is almost a nontestable theory" (p. 17). These findings do not rule out the possibility of constructing a valid theory of individual needs, but do require a drastic reformulation of the Maslow theory to explain and reconcile the available evidence.

Human Relations Theory

a. Lack of satisfaction of a need initially results in increased motivation to satisfy that need; if the individual has the opportunity to satisfy the need, increased motivation will result. If the need cannot be satisfied, frustration and dissatisfaction result.

If Maslow's need theory is correct, we should expect a worker to be motivated by the opportunity to achieve satisfaction of needs that are currently unsatisfied; lack of opportunity to satisfy needs should result in poor performance, expressions of dissatisfaction, and acts of hostility toward the organization. Conversely, if human relations theory is correct, we should expect the satisfied worker to be productive, and the dissatisfied worker to be unproductive.

Indices of worker effectiveness include such things as production, turnover and absenteeism, illnesses and accidents, and grievances and complaints. Since individual effort is involved in each of these, we can expect motivation to be an important influence upon them.

Based upon an extensive review of research, Brayfield and Crockett (1955) arrived at two general conclusions: "First, that satisfaction with one's position in a network of relationships need not imply strong motivation for outstanding performance within that system, and, second, that productivity may be only peripherally related to many of the goals toward which the industrial worker is striving." They further argue that: "It is time to question the strategic and ethical merits of selling to industrial concerns an assumed relationship between employe attitudes and employe performance."

In another extensive review of the literature, Herzberg et al. (1957) cite 26 studies which assessed the quantitive relationship between job attitude and productivity. Of these, only 14, or 57 percent, revealed a positive relationship. In the remaining studies, job attitudes and productivity were not related.

Likert (1961) reports research conducted from 1947 through 1961 by the Institute for Social Research at the University of Michigan, which revealed that: "Where productivity of individuals was related to attitude toward the company, a very low positive relationship has usually been observed, but the relationships are so slight as to be negligible."

Vroom (1964) examined 20 studies dealing with the relationship between job satisfaction and job performance. Three studies revealed a negative relationship, the other 17 a positive one. The range of correlations between satisfaction and performance was from −.31 to +.86; however, the median correlation was an unimpressive +.14.

There may be several reasons why a more consistent pattern has not been found. Stogdill (1959) examined the factors statistically identified in ten studies as independent satisfaction measures; he reported, "the differences in the factors found by different investigators are dependent to a considerable degree upon the kinds of items (questions) investigated and also upon differences in the groups studied." More recently, Wanous and Lawler (1972) compared nine operational definitions of job satisfaction, and found that they "do not yield empirically comparable measures of satisfaction" (p. 95). Thus much of the confusion in the literature probably results from the fact that investigators measured a wide variety of satisfactions that were not equally important from group to group, and used instruments which were not equivalent from study to study.

If we reflect on the kinds of conditions necessary for productive work, we see that motivation is only one of them. Thus a second reason for the confusion in the literature probably concerns the effect of situational variables that interact with satisfaction to produce high individual or group performance. Clearly, if we found working conditions, quality of leadership, quality of supplies and equipment, efficiency of scheduling and coordinating procedures, or individual ability to be deficient, we would expect highly motivated behavior to have either little effect on productivity, or possibly cause frustration and thereby interfere with productivity.

The research literature seems to be much more positive and conclusive on the effect of satisfaction on turnover, accidents, and absences. On studies relating attitudes to absenteeism, Herzberg et al. (1957) report 21 of 24 studies that show satisfied workers to be involved in fewer avoidable firings than employees with negative attitudes. In 12 of 13 studies dealing with satisfaction and absenteeism, negative job attitude was found to be positively related to high absenteeism. From these and several other studies, Herzberg concludes that positive job attitudes keep a worker more consistently on the job, reduce the number of accidents, and lower the incidence of psychosomatic illnesses—but that the high producer is not always a "silent partner": Some of the studies show a positive relationship between high productivity and the expression of grievances and complaints. It may be that high producers are more able to view the work situation objectively, or are less fearful of offering suggestions and criticisms. Finally, several extensive reviews of job-satisfaction literature consistently reveal that employee need satisfaction is accompanied by less employee turnover and absenteeism (Clark, 1960–61; Vroom, 1964; Fournet, DiStefano, and Pryer, 1966).

At present, there seems to be general agreement among researchers that the effects of worker satisfaction on motivation and productivity depend largely on situational variables, some of which have yet to be identified by future research.

Two-Factor Theory

a. Motivation to work results from the presence of job satisfiers: recognition, work itself, responsibility, and opportunity for advancement. Conversely, the state of potential dissatisfiers—policy, supervision, interpersonal relations, working conditions, and salary—contributes very little to job satisfaction.

b. Satisfiers increase motivation but dissatisfiers do not decrease motivation.

Herzberg (1966) reports the results of ten studies designed to test the two-factor theory. Within the studies, 17 different populations of employees were interviewed, using the story-telling method. Of 51 significant differences reported for 6 satisfiers, every one was in the predicted direction. For 57 dissatisfiers, 54 were in the predicted direction. In sum, when theoretical predictions were made for each study separately, the predictions were found to be valid in more than 97 percent of the cases.

However, studies based on methods other than story-telling yield widely inconsistent results. Herzberg (1966) reviewed 11 studies based on widely different methods and interpreted the findings of these studies as evidence of the validity of the satisfier-dissatisfier dichotomy. However, Dunnette, Campbell, and Hakel (1967), report a study of their own, and review 10 additional studies, showing that the satisfier-dissatisfier dichotomy does not hold, and that—although in some populations the factors that Herzberg labels "satisfiers" do contribute more to overall job satisfaction than do the dissatisfiers—the effect of the satisfiers is by no means universal and varies widely depending on the specific subjects studied.

The study by Dunnette et al. illustrates both method and results. Respondents were asked to sort 36 statements by description of highly satisfactory or unsatisfactory job situations. Four job dimensions—achievement, responsibility, recognition, and supervisory human relations—were found to be both the most important satisfiers *and* dissatisfiers. For some persons, satisfaction was found to reside in job content; for others in working conditions; for a third group, in a combination of both job content and working conditions. For dissatisfying job situations, the same variety was found. Thus, contrary to the two-factor theory, both satisfying and dissatisfying job situations share many features in common, most of which are common across a broad range of jobs, and individual preferences account for interpretations of specific job situations.

Based on their own study and the additional studies they reviewed, Dunnette, Campbell, and Hakel (1967) conclude that:

> Whatever their various weaknesses, [these] . . . studies . . . certainly [are] characterized by widely differing methodologies. . . . It is noteworthy that the two-factor theory has fared poorly in all of these investigations regardless of the methodology used. It seems that the evidence is now sufficient to lay the two-factor theory to rest. . . . We believe it is important that this be done so that researchers will address themselves to studying the full complexities of human motivation, rather than continuing to allow the direction of motivational research or actual administrative decisions to be dictated by the seductive simplicity of the two-factor theory (p. 173).

It is interesting to note that some of the studies interpreted by Herzberg as support for his theory are the same studies that Dunnette interprets as contrary evidence. It is also interesting that, in a more recent review which included studies not reviewed by Dunnette, Campbell, and Hakel (1967), Soliman (1970) found that in only 3 of 20 studies which employed Herzberg's methodology were Herzberg's results not replicated; however, of more than 20 investigations which used a different method, only 3 supported the theory. In a very real sense, then, the two-factor theory may be said to be "method-bound," in that it is necessary to employ a very specific kind of methodology if results predicted by the theory are to be obtained.

Since many of the studies failing to confirm the two-factor theory used a rating scale rather than the story-telling method employed by Herzberg, the defense offered by Grigaliunas and Herzberg (1971) seems worth considering:

> When faced with an item, subjects seem to have a great deal of difficulty in focusing back to the incident and determining what is important in the incident as opposed to what is important to them generally. The force of social desirability or the pull of their value systems is stronger than the directions. Hence, quite automatically, subjects rate the general importance of an item to them rather than the importance of the items to the incident they have described.

This may or may not be true, but it is well worth remembering Locke's warning that "to claim that one's theory can only be tested using one's own arbitrarily chosen method is to, in effect, assume the validity in advance of that method" (1972).

Herzberg (1966) reports three experimental studies which he interprets as confirming evidence for the second proposition. In one of these, however, extreme differences in the samples being compared (schizophrenic patients vs. nurses) make any conclusions regarding the two-factor theory very speculative. In another, measures of performance and morale are not described, methods of increasing satisfiers are not detailed, and the data are not treated statistically. We shall only be concerned with the third study, therefore, by Graglier and Hamlin (1964), in which a group of college students were assigned a task and the objectives of the task were explained to them, thus clarifying the job context, but they did not perform the task. A second group of students did perform a task and was successful at fulfilling the task requirements. Volunteers were then requested from both groups for future psychological experiments. The second group produced the greatest number of volunteers. Herzberg interprets these results to indicate that the intrinsic aspects of a job (i.e., successful task completion) are more powerful motivators than the extrinsic aspects (i.e., instructions about the job and its purpose).

House and Wigdor (1967) reanalyzed data reported by Herzberg (1966) and also reviewed results of 32 studies published as of 1967; all of these deal with the two-factor theory, and all are based on methods other than Herzberg's story-telling method. From Herzberg's 1966 data, House and Wigdor compiled totals of the number of people mentioning a given factor as a satisfier or dissatisfier. Table 10–1 shows the total number of people who mentioned a given factor (for factors reported in at least 4 studies [2]).

TABLE 10-1. Reanalysis of Satisfier-Dissatisfier Data.

	Reported as	
Factor	Satisfier	Dissatisfier
Achievement	440	122
Recognition	309	110
Work itself	175	75
Responsibility	168	35
Advancement	126	48
Policy and administration	55	337
Supervision	22	182
Working conditions	20	108
Relations with superior	15	59
Relations with peers	9	57

Total number of respondents for each factor: 1220 (House and Wigdor, 1967).

If the factors in Table 10–1 are reranked in order of their reported frequency as dissatisfiers, they become: policy and administration, supervision, achievement, recognition, working conditions, work itself, relations with supervisors, relations with peers, advancement, and responsibility. From this

[2] Restricting the analysis to those factors mentioned more than four times excludes several factors: "opportunity for growth," "interpersonal relations with subordinates," "status," "personal life," "security," and "salary." With the exception of "opportunity for growth," these excluded factors are peripheral to the two-factor theory, and their inclusion would not change the major conclusion suggested by the reanalysis.

it can be seen that lack of achievement was regarded by most respondents as more of a dissatisfier than supervisor relations or working conditions; in fact, achievement can be considered to be the third major dissatisfier. Recognition was also found to be more of a dissatisfier than supervisor relations or working conditions.

Not every factor appeared in every study reported by Herzberg. However, in all the studies each factor had an equal chance of occurring, and the fact that some did not occur was the result of failure of respondents to mention incidents relating to all factors.

Since Herzberg's data do not unequivocally support the satisfier-dissatisfier dichotomy, the second proposition of the two-factor theory, that satisfiers have more motivational force than dissatisfiers, also appears suspect. This is true for two reasons. First, empirical evidence fails to confirm the distinction between satisfiers and dissatisfiers; therefore, attempts to separate the two require an arbitrary definition of the two classifications. Second, unless such an arbitrary separation is employed, the proposition is not testable.

Value/Expectancy Theory

a. People subjectively assign values to the expected outcomes of various courses of action and therefore have preferences among expected outcomes.

b. Any explanation of motivated behavior must take into account not only the ends that people hope to accomplish but the extent to which they believe their own actions contribute to producing the outcomes they prefer.

Value/expectancy theory has become one of the most prominent motivation theories of the 1970s. From 1969 to 1974 alone, more than 32 studies testing various versions of value/expectancy theory have been reported. House, Shapiro, and Wahba (1974) recently reviewed 32 of these studies in order to assess the validity of several of the theory's propositions. While no study has yet tested all relevant variables, some general conclusions can still be drawn with respect to the scientific status of the theory.[3]

1. In general, each variable pertinent to value/expectancy theory has been found to have significant predictive powers in some studies, but not in others.
2. The most consistently positive findings involve the expectancy that performance will result in extrinsic rewards, and that intrinsic satisfaction will result from the work itself. These variables show rather consistent, statistically significant associations (although usually of low or moderate magnitude) with effort and performance.
3. Weighting the expectancy that performance leads to rewards by the value

[3] These conclusions are our own. They are based on our reading of the House, Shapiro, and Wahba paper (1974), but are not necessarily in agreement with the authors of that paper.

placed on extrinsic rewards does not improve power of prediction over that obtained by using the unweighted expectancy that performance leads to rewards.

4. The theory is limited to conditions where subjects have the requisite ability, accurate role perceptions, and accurate perceptions of contingent rewards.
5. The better controlled the study (in longitudinal analyses and laboratory investigations) the more support will generally be shown for the theory. The superiority of such carefully controlled approaches over cross-sectional studies suggests that cross-sectional tests result in underestimates of the theory's predictive validity.

Two studies which illustrate Conclusion 5 will be described here. The first, a longitudinal study by Kopelman and Thompson (1974), reveals both some applications and some limitations of expectancy theory in a natural field setting. The authors administered 339 questionnaires to design and development engineers in three large technology-based firms during 1969. In the three years that followed, those employees who remained with the companies were given questionnaires annually and performance ratings were obtained from their supervisors. By 1973, 210 respondents had participated in the research throughout the four-year period. Measures were also taken of the employees' ability and salary levels and the amount of task difficulty they faced.

Analysis showed that correlations between a motivational measure of expectancy × value and supervisory performance ratings ranged between .45 and .55 among certain sub-groups of the respondents, depending upon their level of pay and type of work. Specifically, the correlation between the motivational index and performance rankings was greatest when a one-year time period was allowed to elapse. This finding suggests that a lag time of approximately one year is required before motivational perceptions have an effect on performance. This finding helps to explain the rather consistently low correlation resulting from cross-sectional research on expectancy theory. Expectations and values with respect to intrinsic factors were found to be significantly more motivational for high-paid than for low-paid individuals. Expectations and values of extrinsic rewards were found to be motivational for both high- and low-paid individuals, and slightly more motivational for low-paid individuals. Expectations and values were most motivational for individuals working on simple tasks who had a high degree of ability relative to the task demands. These findings suggest that the motivational model works best under conditions where individuals have a greater amount of control over their tasks and know exactly what to do in order to perform effectively.

Jorgenson, Dunnette, and Pritchard (1973) report an experimental test of value/expectancy theory under simulated working conditions; 265 male college students were hired to work six consecutive days for four hours each day. The subjects were told that the company that hired them was a newly established firm which mainly contracted for clerical work with companies who did not have the facilities or time to complete their own work. Subjects were told that while the main contract on which they would be working was for clerical work, another contract had been arranged with Science Research Associates to pretest some tests of reactions to routine work. This information was given to the subjects to make the multitude of questionnaires which were part of the experiment seem reasonable, and also to make the job more realistic. After brief instruction, aptitude tests and a one-hour pretest were given to determine the subjects' abilities relative to the task. Half of the subjects were paid on an hourly rate, and half were paid on an incentive basis. Subjects were paid daily to provide feedback about the relationship between performance and pay in the incentive condition. Procedures and pretests were carried out to insure that the amount of incentive was large enough to make it worthwhile to strive for a high level of pay, yet not so large as to make the rates unbelievably high or low.

The following hypotheses were tested.

1a With abilities and role perceptions held constant, individuals under high-incentive pay will have higher expectancy that effort leads to rewards than individuals under low-incentive pay.

1b With the value of pay and all other rewards equal, individuals under the high-incentive pay condition will exert higher effort than individuals under the low-incentive pay condition.

1c With the value of all rewards held constant, individuals under the high-incentive pay condition will have a higher level of job performance than individuals under the low-incentive pay condition.

1d When individuals under high-incentive pay conditions are shifted to low-incentive pay conditions, their expectancy that effort leads to increased pay, and therefore their effort and performance levels, will be lower after the shift than before and will also decrease over time, provided that the values of reward are held constant. When individuals under the low-incentive pay conditions are shifted to the high-incentive pay conditions the opposite effects will occur.

2a With the value of rewards held constant, the higher the expectation that effort leads to rewards, the greater the effort expended by individuals and the greater their job performance.

2b With the expectancy that effort leads to reward held constant, the higher the value of an outcome the greater will be the effort expended by individuals in performing their jobs and the greater their performance.

The results of the experiments showed strong support for all hypotheses except those with respect to effort (2a and 2b). Since the measurement of effort was based on self-ratings reported by the subjects, and since all findings with respect to objectively measured performance are hard to explain without assuming increases in effort, it is likely that the failure to confirm the hypotheses with respect to effort was due to a poor measure of this variable. When an objective substitute for effort, namely performance, is used, it is clear that the study provides strong support for the theory. For example, the performance of subjects while in the high-incentive pay conditions yielded an index of 189, while the performance of subjects in the low-incentive condition yielded an index of 153.65. Thus the high-incentive pay condition resulted in approximately 23 percent higher performance than the low-incentive pay condition. Further, performance was found to correlate consistently and significantly with the expectancy that effort led to rewards, and the value or perceived importance of the rewards.

This study lends strong support to the theory, primarily because of its methodological rigor. The study has the attribute of tight experimental control of variables, while at the same time it is based on data collected in a simulated field setting in which the subjects actually performed a job, for pay, under conditions in which they were not aware of the intent of the experiment. Inferences about causality were tested midway through the experiment by shifting subjects working under each of the two incentive conditions to the opposite condition. This test clearly supported the causality assumptions of the theory. Another strong feature of the study was that it was conducted over a fairly long time period, as compared with most laboratory experiments which are usually limited to a few hours. This longer time period allowed more severe tests of the theory by affording time for short-term behavioral or attitudinal effects to dissipate. It also provided the opportunity to gather a wealth of information about job changes occurring over time.

Achievement Theory

Of the three propositions central to achievement theory, studies pertinent to an evaluation of the first two, restated below, will be reviewed together.

a. Individuals whose motivation to achieve is greater than their anxiety over the possibility of failure will become increasingly more motivated to succeed as the length of a contingent path increases, while individuals who are primarily motivated not to engage in immediate activity will become even more inhibited as the length of a contingent path increases.

b. Superiority in performance by the achievement-motivated individual, as compared to the failure-threatened individual, will be greater in contingent than in noncontingent paths of equivalent length, and in the longer of two contingent paths.

In one kind of study the nature of the path facing individuals was inferred from their ratings of how important it was to "do well" in an immediate activity (an academic course) in terms of some future goals. Individuals who rated "doing well" as high in importance were assumed to face a contingent path relating immediate activity to subsequent achievement; individuals who rated doing well as low in importance were assumed to face a noncontingent path.

Studies by Raynor, Atkinson, and Brown (Chapter 8 in Atkinson and

Raynor, 1974) and one reported by Raynor (Chapter 9 in Atkinson and Raynor, 1974) provide data consistent with predictions that the characteristic motivation and inhibitions of individuals primarily motivated to achieve or avoid goal attainment are accentuated by the presumed contingent path. Specifically, college students classified as being high in the need to achieve and low in test anxiety received higher grades and were relatively more concerned about doing well than were anxious individuals, when the grade was seen as highly related to future goals than when it was not. Four such studies are reported by Raynor (in Atkinson and Raynor, 1974), and all support the above propositions. However, all four are cross-sectional studies in which causation must be inferred from the pattern of relationships among variables.

Raynor (pp. 133–34) also reviews three studies designed to deal more directly with the question of causation; all were supportive of the propositions. In these studies contingent and noncontingent paths four steps long were experimentally introduced. Subjects were told that they could not proceed to the next step without completing the prior step. As predicted, individuals high in achievement-motivation performed significantly better, and individuals high in anxiety significantly worse, in a complex mathematical task when it was the first step in the contingent path than when it was the first step in the noncontingent path. The achievement-oriented group also performed significantly better than the nonachievement-oriented group, within the contingent condition, but this difference was negligible within the noncontingent condition. These findings were replicated in two additional studies of similar design.

The third proposition of achievement theory states:

c. Individuals whose achievement motivation exceeds their fear of failure will act to guarantee immediate success in a contingent path so as to ensure the opportunity to strive for success in skill activities in the path.

Raynor (1972) has conducted a series of seven studies dealing with this hypothesis using experimental games of chance and games of skills with various lengths of contingent and noncontingent paths. The results consistently show that individuals act to guarantee immediate success in a contingent path so as to ensure the opportunity to strive for success in subsequent skill activities in the path, *regardless* of their level of need for achievement or anxiety of failure. Thus, this hypothesis has been shown to be rather consistently disconfirmed in an experimental setting. However, a study by Wish and Hasazi (1972) provides striking confirmation of the predictions by using the actual curricular choices of male college juniors enrolled in a school of management to infer immediate risk-taking in a contingent path. These findings suggest that the experimental induction employed by Raynor may not have been sufficiently strong to motivate the students to continue on the contingent path. That is, the incentive to do well on the contingent path may have been too weak to arouse the motivational components of the theory. Further tests of this hypothesis under more realistic conditions with stronger incentives are thus in order.

Inequity Theory

a. Overpaid hourly or salaried subjects will increase their contributions by producing more as a means of reducing inequity.

b. Overpaid piece-rate subjects will produce higher quality and lower quantity than equitably paid subjects.

c. Underpaid hourly or salaried subjects will produce less to achieve a contribution-reward balance.

d. Underpaid piece-rate subjects will produce a large number of low quality output because production of low quality output permits increasing rewards without substantially increasing contributions.

Inequity theory has been tested in a considerable number of studies since its original publication by Adams (1963). The four propositions relevant to performance motivation and the research on them have been reviewed by Goodman and Friedman (1971). They reviewed four studies that supported the first proposition. In addition, they reviewed several other studies which either failed to support the proposition or resulted in some findings which support and some which reject the proposition. They point out that most of the studies failing to support the proposition had methodological weaknesses. The main criticism against the supporting studies is that, in order to induce subjects to feel they were being paid inequitably, they were told that they were less qualified to perform the work than others but would be paid the same rate. This was an attempt to make subjects feel they were being overpaid. However, the subjects may have actually experienced devalued self-esteem, and may have attempted to minimize the effects of devaluation by comparing overpaid subjects with a control group that was also devalued.

Since subjects in both the overpaid and the control group were both given information that should result in equal devaluation of their self-esteem, no difference should have appeared between these groups if the primary reaction of the individuals was the devaluation of self-esteem. However, the overpaid subjects produced more than the control subjects who were also devalued but who were paid equitably. Thus, while the evidence is somewhat mixed and there are not a large number of studies to support the proposition, those studies that constitute the most adequate tests of the proposition were found to be in support of it.

The second proposition of inequity theory assumes that overpaid subjects will increase their efforts as a means of achieving equity. This increase in effort can lead to a greater quantity or quality. However, increases in quantity can only increase inequity because every unit produced results in further overpayment. Therefore, effort is invested in increased quality rather than quantity. Since increased quality is not rewarded, contributions and rewards per unit achieve a balanced relationship. Goodman and Friedman reviewed ten studies relevant to this proposition. They conclude, "the data from the overpaid piece-rate studies support Adams' hypothesis more consistently than from the hourly studies. . . . overpaid subjects did experience inequity after an initial performance period and differentially emphasized quantity or quality outputs—whichever seemed more successful in resolving inequity" (1971, p. 276). Thus, there is substantial support for this proposition.

Four studies of the third proposition were reviewed by Goodman and Friedman. Two of the studies supported the proposition and two did not. Goodman and Friedman conclude, "there are not enough studies to adequately test the validity of the hourly underpaid hypothesis, but from the few existing studies there appears to be some preliminary support for the hypothesis" (p. 277).

Finally, the fourth proposition was tested in two studies. In both studies inequitably-paid subjects produced a larger number of low quality outputs than equitably-paid subjects. In one of the studies it was demonstrated that the underpaid subjects cognitively devalued their own contributions while at the same time increasing their rewards by producing more low quality products. Subjects therefore brought their contribution-reward ratio into balance by earning more money through piece-rate production, and by rationalizing that they were contributing less.

In conclusion, the limited evidence available from these studies does support the propositions of equity theory and appears relatively free of alternative explanations for the findings.

Summary

Need Theory

a. The higher the deprivation of a given need the higher its importance, strength, or desirability. *Findings are inconclusive with respect to this proposition. Findings with respect to lower order needs (biological and safety needs) support the proposition while findings with respect to higher order needs (affiliation, ego satisfaction, self-actualization) failed to support the proposition.*

b. Gratification of a need at one level in the hierarchy will be positively associated with activation of a need at the next higher level. *Consistently invalidated by available studies.*

Human Relations Theory

a. Lack of satisfaction of a need initially results in increased motivation to satisfy that need; if the individual has the opportunity to satisfy the need, increased motivation will result. If the need cannot be satisfied, frustration and dissatisfaction result. *Findings are inconsistent, most probably due to lack of comparability among measures of need, need satisfaction, and importance of need, and situational variables that have not been identified to date.*

Two-Factor Theory

a. Motivation to work results from the presence of job satisfiers: recognition, work itself, responsibility, and opportunity for advancement. *Consistently supported when the critical incidents-story telling method is employed; consistently not supported when other measures are employed. The general conclusion is that the findings supporting the theory are an artifact of a methodology which is biased in favor of the theory.*

Value/Expectancy Theory

(The two propositions of this theory are summarized here as a single proposition since the studies testing the theory have tested both simultaneously.)

a./b. People subjectively assign values to the expected outcomes of various courses of action, and therefore have preferences among expected outcomes. Any explanation of motivated behavior must take into account not only the ends that people hope to accomplish but the extent to which they believe their own actions contribute to producing outcomes they prefer. *The evidence in support of this theory is mixed. Correlational studies taken at a single point in time provide rather weak, but consistent support for the theory. However, one four-year longitudinal study and two well-designed laboratory simulation studies provide rather strong support for the theory. In general the theory received moderate to strong support in almost all studies.*

Achievement Theory

a. Individuals whose motivation to achieve is greater than their anxiety over the possibility of failure will become increasingly more motivated to succeed as the length of a contingent path increases, while individuals who are primarily motivated not to engage in immediate activity will become more inhibited as the length of a contingent path increases. *Strongly supported by three studies.*

b. Superiority in performance by the achievement-motivated individual, as compared to the failure-threatened individual, will be greater in contingent than in noncontingent paths of equivalent length, and in the longer of two contingent paths. *Strongly supported.*

c. Individuals whose achievement motivation exceeds their fear of failure will act to guarantee immediate success in a contingent path so as to ensure the opportunity to strive for success in skill activities in the path. *Mixed evidence; additional, more realistic studies are required.*

Inequity Theory

a. Overpaid hourly or salaried subjects will increase their contribution by producing more as a means of reducing inequity. *Somewhat mixed findings, with the better controlled studies showing support for this proposition.*

b. Overpaid piece-rate subjects will produce higher quality and lower quantity than equitably paid subjects. *Strongly supported.*

c. Underpaid hourly or salaried subjects will produce less to achieve a contribution-reward balance. *Mixed evidence, with some preliminary support for the proposition.*

d. Underpaid piece-rate subjects will produce a high volume of low quality output because production of low quality output permits increasing rewards without substantially increasing contributions. *Only two studies tested this proposition; both showed support for it.*

Conclusions

Several theories of motivation which have relevance to organizational behavior have been reviewed in this chapter. Three of the most popular of these—need theory, human relations theory, and two-factor theory—have been disconfirmed by a percentage of investigations that is sufficiently large to make them be considered invalid.

Value/expectancy theory, achievement theory, and inequity theory have received adequate support and therefore appear to have relevance for many issues confronting today's managers. Inequity theory suggests that rewards must seem to employees to be fair and makes predictions about how individuals behave when they feel inequitably treated; the theory may thus provide the practicing manager with some useful cues.

Value/expectancy theory and achievement theory both suggest the need for rewards to be tailored to individual values and to be made contingent upon performance. These theories and their supporting evidence suggest that where these guidelines cannot be implemented, individual motivation is likely to be low. When contingent rewards are viewed as equitable, and are highly valued, individual satisfaction should accompany a high state of motivation. Thus effective utilization of inequity, achievement, and value/expectancy theories should result in both effective performance and employee satisfaction, providing other requisites of performance (e.g., ability) are also present.

References

Adams, J. C. 1963. Toward an understanding of inequity. *Journal of Abnormal and Social Psychology* 67: 422–36.

Argyris, C. 1964. *Integrating the individual and the organization.* Wiley.

Atkinson, J. W. 1957. Motivational determinants of risk taking behavior. *Psychological Review* 64: 359–72.

———. 1958. Towards experimental analysis of human motivation in terms of motives, expectancies, and incentives. In *Motives in fantasy, action and society,* ed. by J. W. Atkinson. Von Nostrand.

———., and Raynor, J. O. 1974. *Motivation and achievement.* V. H. Winston and Sons.

Brayfield, A. H., and Crockett, W. H. 1955. Employee attitudes and employee performance. *Psychological Bulletin* 52: 396–687.

Clark, J. V. 1960-61. Motivation in work groups: A tentative view. *Human Organization* 19: 199–208.

Davis, W. A. 1946. The motivation of the underprivileged worker. In *Industry and society,* ed. by W. F. Whyte. McGraw-Hill.

Dunnette, M. D.; Campbell, J. P.; and Hakel, M. D. 1967. Factors contributing to job satisfaction and job dissatisfaction in six occupational groups. *Organizational Behavior and Human Performance* 2: 143–74.

Fournet, F. P.; DiStefano, M. K., Jr.; and Pryer, W. 1966. Job satisfaction: Issues and problems. *Personnel Psychology* 19: 165–83.

Goodman, P. S., and Friedman, A. 1971. An examination of Adams' theory of inequity. *Administrative Science Quarterly* 16: 271–88.

Graglier, A., and Hamlin, R. 1964. Effect of effort and task orientation on activity preference. Paper presented at Eastern Psychological Association Meeting, 1964.

Grigaliunas, B. S., and Herzberg, F. 1971. Relevancy in the test of motivator hygiene theory. *Journal of Applied Psychology* 55: 73–79.

Herzberg, F. 1966. *Work and the nature of man.* World.

———.; Mausner, B.; Peterson, R. O.; and Capwell, O. F. 1957. *Job attitudes: Review of research and opinion.* Psychological Services of Pittsburgh.

———.; ———; and Snyderman, B. 1959. *The motivation to work,* 2nd ed. Wiley.

House, R. J.; Shapiro, H. J.; and Wahba, M. A. 1974. Expectancy theory as a predictor of work behavior and attitude: A reevaluation of empirical evidence. Behavioral Science Supplement, ed. by L. L. Cummings, *Decision Sciences* 5: 481–506.

———., and Wigdor, L. A. 1967. Herzberg's dual-factor theory of job satisfaction and motivation: A review of the evidence and a criticism. *Personnel Psychology* 20: 369–89.

Jorgenson, D. O.; Dunnette, M. D.; and Pritchard, R. D. 1973. Effects of the manipulation of a performance-reward contingency on behavior in a simulated work setting. *Journal of Applied Psychology* 57: 271–80.

Kerr, S.; Harlan, A.; and Stogdill, R. M. 1974. Preference for motivator and hygiene factors in a hypothetical interview situation. *Personnel Psychology* 27: 109–24.

Kopelman, R. E., and Thompson, P. H. 1974. *Factors complicating expectancy theory predictions of work motivation and job performance.* Working paper, Bernard M. Baruch College of the City University of New York.

Lewin, K. 1951. *Field theory and social science.* Harper.

Likert, R. 1961. *New patterns of management.* McGraw-Hill.

Locke, E. A. 1972. 'In defense' of defense mechanisms: Some comments on Bobbitt and Behling. *Journal of Applied Psychology* 56: 297–98.

March, J. G., and Simon, H. A. 1958. *Organizations.* Wiley.

Maslow, A. 1943. A dynamic theory of human motivation. *Psychological Review* 50: 370–73.

———. 1954. *Motivation and personality.* Harper & Row.

McClelland, D. C. 1951. *Personality.* Wm. Sloan.

———. 1961. *The achieving society.* Van Nostrand.

McGregor, D. 1960. *The human side of enterprise.* McGraw-Hill.

Porter, L. W., and Lawler, E. E. 1968. *Managerial attitudes and performance.* Irwin-Dorsey.

Raynor, J. O. 1972. Contingent future orientation as a determinant of immediate risk taking. Unpublished paper, State University of New York at Buffalo.

Schein, E. H. 1965. *Organizational psychology.* Prentice-Hall.

Soliman, H. M. 1970. Motivator-hygiene theory of job attitudes. *Journal of Applied Psychology* 54: 452–61.

Stogdill, R. M. 1959. *Individual behavior and group achievement.* Oxford University Press.

Viteles, M. S. 1953. *Motivation and morale in industry.* Norton.

Vroom, V. H. 1964. *Work and motivation.* Wiley.

———. 1966. Some observations regarding Herzberg's two-factor theory. Paper presented to American Psychological Association, Chicago; Sept. 1-6, 1966.

Wahba, M., and Bridwell, L. 1975. Maslow reconsidered: A review of research on the need hierarchy theory. *Organizational Behavior and Human Performance,* in press.

Wanous, J. P., and Lawler, E. E. 1972. Measurement and meaning of job satisfaction. *Journal of Applied Psychology* 56: 95–105.

Wish, P. A., and Hasazi, J. E. 1972. Motivational determinants of curricular choice behavior in college males. Paper presented at the Eastern Psychological Association, Boston; April, 1972.

Chapter **11**

Leadership: Trait and Behavioral Approaches

Glendower: *I can call spirits from the vasty deep.*
Hotspur: *Why, so can I, or so can any man;*
But will they come when you do call for them?

WILLIAM SHAKESPEARE
Henry IV

One of the most researched and least understood variables of the management process is leadership. Until recently, it was generally assumed that the world was divided into leaders and followers (or subordinates), the leaders being a select few who could drive or inspire others to achieve more than they would ordinarily. We no longer accept this simple, stereotyped view of the leader, but we still have much to learn about the nature of leadership.

To begin with, we must be careful to distinguish between leadership and management. *Management* can be defined as a process, mental and physical, whereby subordinates are brought to execute prescribed formal duties and to accomplish certain given objectives. *Leadership,* in contrast, is a process whereby one person exerts *social influence* over the members of a group. A leader, then, is a person with power over others who exercises this power for the purpose of influencing their behavior (Bennis, 1959).

Leadership involves more than the personal characteristics of the leader. The effectiveness of a group of followers is a matter of interaction between the leader and the group on the one hand, and between individual members of the group on the other. As Cartwright and Zander (1963) point out, "the belief that a high level of group effectiveness can be achieved simply by the provision of 'good leaders,' though still prevalent among many people concerned with the management of groups, now appears naive in the light of research findings."

It is possible to distinguish two kinds of influence that leaders exert on a group. First, the leader's performance determines to some extent the group level of work. However, leaders usually operate in an environment in which their freedom of action is affected by factors over which they have little control. The policies and management philosophy under which they must operate, for example, are determined by top management. (The constraint is no less when, as is frequently the case, the policies and philosophy are implicit rather than precisely expressed; it simply means that the direction managers get from above is less clear and concise.) The technical rules and operating procedures found in most formal organizations are additional constraints. Even the physical and geographical characteristics of the organization are constraining factors; for example, concentration of the members of the organization in a single plant facilitates face-to-face communication; geographic decentralization constrains informal communication, necessitating the use of written communication or such technical methods as teletype, telephone, or telegraph.

Second, leaders exert influence on group stability and member satisfaction. Several studies reviewed in this chapter show that the way in which subordinates regard a leader affects the extent to which they cooperate with each other, their satisfaction with their jobs, and their rates of absenteeism and turnover.

In order to intelligently determine the methods of leadership best suited to their own personalities, knowledge, and experience, to the background and expectations of their subordinates, and to the various situations in which they find themselves, managers should know as much as possible about what has been learned from research on leadership. As Tannenbaum and Schmidt (1958) point out:

> . . . the successful leader is one who is keenly aware of those forces which are most relevant to his behavior at any given time. He accurately understands himself, the individuals and group he is dealing with, and the company and broader social environment in which he operates. . . .
>
> But this sensitivity or understanding is not enough. . . . The successful leader is one who is able to behave appropriately in the light of these perceptions. If direction is in order, he is able to direct; if considerable participative freedom is called for, he is able to provide such freedom (p. 101).

Recent research has brought about much speculation and several theories concerning leadership behavior. Historically there have been three approaches to the study of leadership: the trait approach, the behavioral approach, and the situational approach. While research continues to be carried out in both trait and behavioral leadership areas, the dominant emphasis today is on the development and elaboration of various situational approaches. The underlying assumption of these situational approaches is that, while traits and behaviors of leaders may certainly be important, even crucial to their effectiveness as leaders, there are *no* traits or behaviors which are sufficiently desirable to assure effectiveness *regardless* of the situation, and there are none which are necessarily desirable in *every* situation. Situational theory research is therefore particularly difficult to carry out, since the researcher is still required to obtain data pertaining to traits and behaviors of leaders, and must also gather information about various elements of the situation in which leadership occurs.

This chapter will be concerned with trait and behavioral theories; the next will examine the major situational theories which are important today.

The Trait Approach

Early work in leadership research was directed toward identifying and distinguishing the characteristics, or traits, of leaders, who were defined as any persons holding an office. Many studies were designed to determine the leader's intellectual, social, emotional, physical, and personal makeup in order to discover if there existed any universal traits in effective leaders that would distinguish them from less effective leaders. A *trait* is defined as any distinctive physical or psychological characteristic of the individual to which the individual's behavior can be attributed. Ghiselli (1971) illustrates the concept of a trait:

> Suppose a bus driver frequently collides his bus with other vehicles and pedestrians, starts and stops his bus so quickly that his passengers often fall, and quite commonly closes the door too soon so that not infrequently people are caught in them. We are likely to say that this driver is more accident prone than are his fellows. If a factory worker engaged in a small parts assembly grasps the parts without fumbling, places them together quickly and accurately, he would be described as possessing a high degree of manual dexterity. We note the high productivity of the crew assigned to a foreman, their low incidents of lost time, and their infrequent complaints and grievances. We would probably say this foreman has excellent qualities of leadership (pp. 27–28).

In this example, accident-proneness, manual dexterity, and leadership are considered to be traits of the individual that are inferred from the behavior of the individual. These traits are assumed to explain why the particular behavior of the individual occurs: By assuming a trait of accident-proneness we can account for the behavior of the unsafe driver.

Ghiselli points out that the definition and measurement of human traits is complicated by the fact that we can never observe them directly, but can only note their manifestations. He points out that the traits we developed to explain human behavior are conceptualizations to help us understand human behavior, not "real" entities.

Students of leadership who have been guided by the trait approach believe that there are a finite number of identifiable universal characteristics, or traits, and that these traits differentiate successful from unsuccessful leaders.

The Behavioral Approach

The behavioral approach to the study of leadership holds that leaders may be best characterized by behavior patterns rather than by individual traits. Traits such as intelligence, emotional stability, adaptability, or tolerance of uncertainty cannot be readily observed by others, but behavior patterns can. Thus, the difference in the trait and the behavioral approach is that the trait approach attempts to explain leadership on the basis of what leaders are, while behavioral approaches attempt to explain leadership on the basis of what leaders do.

Substantial research has been based on the assumption that behavior patterns, observable by others, make up a leadership style. The behavioral approach was advanced partially as a result of a new approach to the study of leadership initiated by Kurt Lewin at the Group Dynamics Center at MIT and partially as a result of the human relations research initiated by F. J. Roethlisberger and Elton Mayo at Harvard University in the late 1920s.

Proponents of the behavioral approach have identified four types of leadership: supportive, participative, instrumental, and "great man."

Supportive Leadership

Supportive leaders give consideration to the needs of subordinates; that is, they are concerned with their well-being, status, and comfort. Such leaders seek to create a friendly and pleasant social climate. Supportive leaders assume that subordinates want to do their best, and that they should make it easy for subordinates by supporting their efforts—by helping them rather than commanding them. Supportive leaders seek to gain acceptance from subordinates by treating them with respect and dignity rather than through the use of authority.

Proponents of this style of leadership argue that it is effective because it is more readily accepted by the group than impersonal, strictly task-oriented leadership. They hold that supportive leadership gains the good will and acquiescence of the group members by exhibiting a benevolent and helpful attitude toward them, considering them as individuals with human dignity and individual rights. Accordingly it is argued that members' acceptance of leaders and their methods of operation leads to close cooperation between supervisors and subordinates, an increase in subordinate motivation to work, and a satisfied and productive work group.

Supportive leadership has many proponents because of its moral implications. It rejects the imposition of intellectual authority and the allocation of special privileges on the basis of ownership or appointed position. The recognition of individual rights and dignity are factors that have natural appeal to those accustomed to the tradition of democracy and equality. Several specific behaviors that are characteristic of supportive leaders have been identified by the Ohio State Leadership Group and the University of

Michigan Institute of Social Research. Table 11–1 lists some of these behaviors.

Later in this chapter we shall consider the validity of supportive leadership theory in terms of its effects on productivity and subordinate acceptance and satisfaction.

TABLE 11–1. Typical Behaviors of Supportive Leaders.

Express appreciation when subordinates do a good job.
Do not demand more than subordinates can do.
Help subordinates with their personal problems.
Do not criticize subordinates in front of others.
Stand up for subordinates even though it may be unpopular to do so.
Do not insist things be done their own way.
See that subordinates are rewarded for jobs well done.
Do not reject suggestions for changes.
Try to keep subordinates in good standing with those in higher authority.
Are willing to explain their actions.
Treat all subordinates as their equals.
Are willing to make changes.
Are friendly and can be easily approached.

(Adapted from Table 2 of "A Leader Behavior Description for Industry," by Edwin A. Fleishman, in R. M. Stogdill and A. E. Coons, 1957.)

Participative Leadership

Participative leadership is characterized by the sharing of information, power, and influence between supervisors and subordinates. This kind of leader behavior features the treatment of subordinates as equals, and allowance for subordinates to influence leaders' actions and decisions. Influence sharing is accomplished by participation in both decision making and supervision.

Participative decision making refers to efforts by leaders to ensure that all parties for whom a decision is relevant have an opportunity to influence the final decision. To accomplish this leaders:

—share information with the participants.
—prevent dominant personalities from having disproportionate influence.
—solicit opinions, facts, and feelings from reticent participants.
—assist participants in communicating with one another.
—protect deviant opinions from being rejected prior to fair evaluation.
—minimize blame-oriented statements.
—redirect unfocused discussion back to the problem at hand.
—encourage the generation of alternative solutions.
—delay evaluation of alternatives until all have been presented.
—guide the process of screening alternatives and selecting the solution.

As can be seen, leaders are actively involved in ensuring a participative process. Participative leaders do *not* abdicate the leadership role by becoming a member of the group, except insofar as they contribute substantive (as opposed to process) guidance. Maier's research (1970) on effective group problem solving serves as the basis for this concept of participation. His work demonstrates that the skill requirements described above are trainable.

Participative supervision also encourages suggestions from subordinates and fosters independent thinking and action with respect to such factors as problem analysis, selection of means, and planning and scheduling the work process. As was true of participative decision making, participative supervision is not passive. Participative supervisors may exercise close supervision in providing coaching and feedback to subordinates. They may also exercise (moderate) pressure for goal attainment, and may direct considerable information flow toward subordinates to provide them with adequate communication.

Mitchell (1973) recently described at least four ways in which a participative leadership style can impact upon subordinate attitudes and performance. First, a participative climate should lead to greater clarity of the paths to various goals. Second, it enables subordinates to select goals they value, thus increasing the congruence between individual and organizational goals. Third, participants can increase their control over what happens on the job. If subordinate motivation is higher (as a result of points one and two), then having greater autonomy and the ability to carry out their intentions should lead to increased effort and performance. Finally, when people participate in the decision process they usually become more ego-involved. The decisions made are more their own, and their peers know what is expected, causing social pressures to have a greater impact. Thus motivation to perform will stem from internal and social factors as well as from formal external ones. (As an aside, the reader may note that Mitchell's predictions of the likely consequences of participative leadership follow logically from the postulates of value/expectancy theory, reviewed in the previous chapter.)

Maier (1970) has argued that participation should improve decision making because it is through the participative process that subordinate knowledge and expertise can be brought to bear. That is, participative decision making is an effective means of obtaining relevant subordinate information or expertise, and thus of improving the objective quality of decisions. Further, he argues that when decisions require subordinate acceptance for their implementation, participation will increase such acceptance because subordinates will have had an opportunity to influence the decision-making process, and consequently their feelings are more likely to be expressed and respected. Thus, according to these theoretical perspectives, participation is predicted to increase productivity, quality, emotional orientation of subordinates toward their work setting (the job, the decision makers, and the organization), and subordinate acceptance of decisions.

Instrumental Leadership

Although not denying the importance of the personality characteristics of leaders, classical management theorists explain effective leadership in terms of the ability of leaders to exhibit certain kinds of rational-intellectual (supportive) behavior. They describe effective managers as those who plan, organize, control, and coordinate the activities of subordinates. Taken together, these activities may be described as "instrumental" leadership activities, since they are viewed as functions that leaders perform in order to achieve group accomplishment of organizational objectives.

The importance of instrumental activities is also stressed by sociological theorists (Parsons, 1951), who define instrumental behavior as behavior concerned with obtaining and allocating resources, e.g., labor, materials, equipment, space, and money.

Autocratic and supportive leadership are in direct contrast, but instrumental leaders may adopt either style of behavior. Their real strength lies in their ability to control available resources, to use them in the most effective way.

"Great Man" Leadership

According to the "great man" theory of leadership, the effective operation of any group requires two fundamentally different kinds of leadership behavior. In order for a group to be directed toward attaining its goals, leaders must perform the instrumental activities necessary for planning, organizing, controlling, and coordinating the activities of subordinates. Groups also need leaders who will foster member interaction, and represent and express the group's moral and social values. Thus, in order for groups to function effectively, cooperation is required between two types of leaders—who fill basically different roles and who usually have basically different psychological characteristics. Individuals known to possess both sets of characteristics are rare, and are usually referred to as "great men" (Bales, Borgotta, and Couch, 1954). According to the "great man" theory, anyone exhibiting both instrumental and supportive leadership behavior will be an effective leader in any situation.

Propositions

The remainder of this chapter will review the evidence pertinent to trait and behavioral theories of leadership; this review will be organized around the following propositions, which are central to the various theories:

1. (The Trait Approach) There are a finite number of identifiable characteristics or traits, and these traits differentiate successful from unsuccessful leaders.

2. (Supportive Leadership) Effective leaders are characterized by considerate and supportive behavior toward subordinates.
3. (Participative Leadership) Effective leaders are characterized by the exercise of participative decision making and supervision.
4. (Instrumental Leadership) Effective leaders are characterized by the performance of functions instrumental to the achievement of group goals. These functions consist of planning, organizing, coordinating, directing, and controlling the work of subordinates.
5. ("Great Man" Leadership) Effective leaders are characterized by both supportive and instrumental leadership behavior.

Empirical Evidence

Proposition 1 (The Trait Approach)

There are a finite number of identifiable characteristics or traits, and these traits differentiate successful from unsuccessful leaders.

Many early studies of leaders and organizations indicate that leaders differ significantly from their followers in one or more specific traits. Bird (1940) examined exhaustively the research on leader traits conducted up to 1940, to determine the universality of traits revealed in individual studies. He found that only about 5 percent of the "discovered leadership traits" were common to four or more investigations. Similar results were yielded in a study by Stogdill (1948), which reveals that only the traits of intelligence, scholarship, dependability, responsibility, social participation, and socioeconomic status consistently differentiate between leaders and nonleaders. Two other reviews of the leadership-trait literature concluded that there is no single trait or characteristic which sets off leaders from group members (Jenkins, 1947), and that "numerous studies of the personalities of leaders have failed to find any consistent pattern of traits which characterize leaders" (Gibb, 1954). However, more recent research conducted by Ghiselli (1971) and his associates suggests that intelligence, "supervisory ability," initiative, self-assurance, and individuality are significantly related to both a manager's level and ratings of their performance; this finding was observed in several different organizations.

Intelligence level is an accurate indicator of the probability that someone will achieve success as a manager—until a certain (quite high) intellectual level is reached, above which individuals with higher scores are less likely to be successful managers.

Supervisory ability is defined by Ghiselli as "the effective utilization of whatever supervisory practices are indicated by the particular requirements of the situation." Using opinions and performance ratings to measure this characteristic, Ghiselli found that it related positively and strongly with occupational level. He observed that, of all the traits, "this seems to be of paramount importance. . . . Ability to direct the activities of others, then, is a significant aspect of managerial talent. . . ."

Initiative, according to Ghiselli, consists of two parts. The first is a matter of motivation, and involves the ability to act independently and initiate actions without stimulation and support from others. The second is cognitive, and involves the capacity to see courses of action not readily apparent to others. The measurement Ghiselli used was found to correlate with superiors' ratings of initiative; it was also found to differentiate individuals who say that they want a job in which they can use their initiative from those who disclaim any such desire.

Ghiselli also found initiative to be related to level of occupation. Members of upper management appeared to be particularly outstanding in this trait. He also found initiative to be highly valued at the upper two levels of management, but not at the lower levels of management, or at the nonmanagerial levels.

Self assurance is defined as the extent to which individuals perceive themselves to be effective in dealing with the problems that confront them. Ghiselli found self assurance to be positively related to occupational level. There was a substantial difference between lower and middle management in this respect, and highly placed executives were outstanding in the confidence they had in themselves.

Individuality was measured in Ghiselli's research by the extent to which an individual pattern of traits is unique—that is, the extent to which it is dissimilar from patterns characteristic of many other individuals. Those who displayed the greatest individuality in the way they did their work (although not necessarily in other ways) were also judged to be the best managers.

In summary, the weight of evidence pertinent to the trait approach does not lend strong support to it. Most of the research other than Ghiselli's is negative, and even some of Ghiselli's work, while showing that individual traits are important, does not directly support the proposition. That is, even to the extent that it can be shown that being high in some trait is statistically related to organizational level, or to the value placed on that trait, this is insufficient evidence to claim that *among individuals who are already at that level,* being high in the trait will permit the person to be more successful as a manager.

Proposition 2 (Supportive Leadership)

Effective leaders are characterized by considerate-supportive behavior toward subordinates.

It has been frequently found that, in groups whose leaders are rated as high in supportiveness, subordinate satisfaction is high (Korman, 1966); there is less intragroup stress and more group-member cooperation (Oaklander and Fleishman, 1964); and there are lower turnover and grievance rates (Korman, 1966).

Several surveys using various measures of leader supportiveness reveal that supportive leaders are most often, but not always, viewed by subordinates as desirable leaders. Specifically, supportive leadership has been associated with positive attitudes and satisfaction of subordinates in industrial plants (Comrey, Pfiffner, and High, 1954; Indik, Seashore, and Georgopoulos, 1960; Argyle, Gardner, and Coiffi, 1957); in the military (Moore, 1953; Moore and Smith, 1952; Spector and Suttell, 1960); in forest work (Comrey, Pfiffner, and High, 1954); in school administration (Hemphill, 1950; Seeman, 1960); and in government organizations (Comrey, Pfiffner, and High, 1954).

However, there have also been at least 13 studies that reported little or no association between supportive leadership and some employees' attitudes (see House and Mitchell, 1974, for a review). In all 13 studies those employees for whom satisfaction was unrelated to supportive leadership were working at high level tasks that were *intrinsically* satisfying. It therefore appears that the degree of satisfaction received from sources other than the leader may be an important contingency factor; this point is elaborated upon in the following chapter.

In addition to the attitudes and satisfaction of subordinates, supportive leader behavior has frequently been found to have a positive relationship to departmental and individual productivity (Argyle, Gardner, and Coiffi, 1957; Comrey, Pfiffner, and High, 1954; Blau and Scott, 1962; Katz and Kahn, 1953; Katz, Maccoby, and Morse, 1950; Indik, Seashore, and Georgopoulos, 1960; and Likert, 1961). There are, however, several studies in which supportive leadership had no relationship to performance ratings or productivity of subordinates (Bass, 1957; Halpin, 1954; House, 1971), or to the motivation of subordinates (House and Dessler, 1974; House, Van der Krabben, and Valency, unpublished). All of the studies that revealed no relationship were conducted under conditions where subordinates had considerable freedom from their superiors, where their tasks were intrinsically satisfying, or where effective performance led directly to satisfaction with no dependence upon the leaders for rewards.

The Question of Causality. It has been suggested by several writers that subordinate attitudes and performance are at least as much a *cause* of supportive leader behavior as a *result* of such behavior. According to this argument leaders will behave more considerately toward subordinates who display positive attitudes toward the job and who perform at a high level, than toward negative and poorly performing subordinates. Several laboratory experiments have obtained data which are relevant to this question.

In one of these, Day and Hamblin (1961) systematically subjected small-parts assembly employees to threatening and irritating supervisory and staff treatment and then, on a new job, gave the same workers extraordinary friendliness, help, and praise. Under the considerate and helpful treatment, the employees showed increased production; the difference was greatest during the facilities change-over period. This study suggests that supportive leadership is particularly effective when employees must learn something new or when the task is unfamiliar to them.

In a similar study by Schachter et al. (1961), conducted in a natural work setting in a manufacturing plant, 24 workers were treated with punitive or nonpunitive and close or general supervision. Punitive and close supervision not only reduced output, but also created antagonism toward leaders and co-workers. Also consistent with Day and Hamblin's findings, punitive leadership had the most negative effect when subordinates were engaged in learning new procedures. Similarly, DeCharms and Bridgeman (1961) found that productivity and satisfaction increased when supervisors complied with subordinates' requests, after earlier refusing to comply.

Day (1971) compared the effects of supportive (praising and approving) and nonpunitive leader behavior to nonsupportive and punitive (sarcastic and ego-deflating) behavior. He found that punitive leadership resulted in much more subject anger and aggressiveness than nonpunitive leadership, while supportive leadership caused slightly less aggressiveness than nonsupportive leadership. When leaders were punitive (sarcastic) but at the same time supportive (approving), the negative effects of punitive behavior were vastly reduced. However, subjects' productivity was found to *decrease* in response to leader supportive behavior, and to *increase* in response to punitive leader behavior. These productivity data are consistent with those of Misumi and Toshiaki (1965), who found that leaders who were both directive and supportive had groups higher in productivity than did leaders who were supportive but not directive.

These studies suggest that the effects of supportive leadership upon performance are most positive when subordinates have previously been denied some source of satisfaction. For example, in the experiments by Day and Hamblin (1961), Schachter et al. (1961), and DeCharms and Bridgeman (1961), in which supportiveness (or lack of punitiveness) resulted in increased productivity, subjects were first exposed to threatening, irritating, or frustrating treatment, and then to considerate and helpful treatment. In all three cases, subjects responded favorably. In the studies by Day (1971) and by Misumi and Toshiaki (1965), in which supportive leadership produced negative effects on productivity, subjects had not been previously subjected to nonsatisfying leadership, nor had they been made to feel dissatisfied during the task. Thus it appears that subordinates' immediately previous levels of frustration and dissatisfaction serve to moderate the effects of supportive leadership upon productivity.

We have already mentioned that data from Day and Hamblin (1961) and Schachter et al. (1961) suggest that the effects of considerate, supportive leadership are more critical under conditions where employees are required to learn something new on the job. Thus, to the extent that a relaxed mental state is critical (as would be the case for many kinds of learning to take place), nonsupportive leadership may result in impaired performance by subordinates. Subordinate competence and experience may therefore be thought of as additional factors which moderate the relationship between supportive leadership and performance.

In sum, it is clear from the studies reviewed that supportive leadership is often effective, resulting in improved subordinate attitudes, satisfaction, and performance. Proposition 2 cannot be considered substantiated, however, because many exceptions have been noted. A number of individual, task, and environmental variables have been found to moderate the effects of supportive leadership, and the propositions reviewed in the next chapter, which depend for their conceptual underpinnings upon situational theory, may therefore be said to more accurately reflect the research literature than does Proposition 2.

As a final comment on the question of causality, it should be noted that while the studies reviewed above showed that supportive leader behavior can positively affect subordinate satisfaction and performance, and while more recent longitudinal studies (Greene, 1974) and experimental studies (Dawson, Messe, and Phillips, 1972; Hand and Slocum, 1970) show this also, evidence has also accumulated to the effect that supportive leadership may also be the *result* of subordinate satisfaction and performance (Lowin and Craig, 1968; Greene, 1974; see Kerr and Schriesheim, 1974, for a thorough review). Much remains to be learned about this question, but it is already clear that the traditional assumption that *first* leaders exhibit supportive (or unsupportive) leader behavior and *then* certain subordinate attitudes and behaviors result is an over-simplistic one.

Proposition 3 (Participative Leadership)

Effective leaders are characterized by the exercise of participative decision making and supervision.

Considerable research has been concerned with the effects of participative leadership on subordinate satisfaction, productivity, acceptance of decisions made by superiors, and quality of group decisions, and this research will be the focus of the following section (see also Chapter 20, which examines the effects of participation upon resistance to change).

In his 1966 review of six experimental studies concerned with the effects of participative supervision, Sales concluded that no difference in effectiveness existed between participative and autocratic leadership styles. Since then several additional studies have been reported. We shall attempt to infer from these the conditions under which participative leadership is most likely to be effective.

In general, it may be said that analysis of the evidence in terms of specific outcomes (satisfaction, productivity, etc.), kinds of tasks, and subordinate characteristics (expectations, personality attributes, etc.) is necessary to understand the research and to reconcile apparently conflicting findings. Research evidence and conclusions pertinent to Proposition 3 will be presented in this chapter, and elaboration of those situational variables which moderate relationships between participative leadership and subordinate outcomes will be treated in the next one.

All of the studies reviewed by Sales (1966), along with more recent laboratory experiments concerned with participative leadership effects, are listed in Table 11–2. From the brief summary of results shown in this table, it can be seen that 7 of the 11 studies showed that participative leadership had positive effects upon productivity and 4 had no significant effects. Only 3 of the 11 investigations collected data on subordinate satisfaction and all 3 showed that participative leadership had a positive effect.

Eleven correlational studies of the relationship between participative leadership and subordinate satisfaction or productivity are listed in Table 11–3. The table shows that the relationship is generally positive, as Proposition 3 would predict. In fact, only in the Tosi study (1970) was participative leadership unrelated to productivity, and in this study the measure of productivity consisted of the overall financial performance of the credit office in which the subjects were employed. Since other factors besides employee effort and motivation are doubtless important to financial performance, Tosi's results do not really constitute strong negative evidence.

Finally, 11 field experiments pertinent to our topic are listed in Table 11–4, which, taken together, provide further evidence that participative leadership generally has a positive effect upon both satisfaction and productivity.

There is, however, substantial evidence that participative leadership is

TABLE 11-2. Laboratory Experiments Concerned with the Effects of Participative Leadership on Productivity and Satisfaction.

Experimentors	Effects on:	
	Satisfaction	*Productivity*
McCurdy and Eber (1953)	Not measured	No effect
Shaw (1955)	Positive	No effect
Spector and Suttell (1957)	Not measured	No effect
Tomekovic (1962)	Not measured	Positive
Delbecq (1965)*	Not measured	Positive
Sales (1966)	Not measured	No effect
Shaw and Blum (1966)	Not measured	Positive
Campion (1968)**	Positive	Positive
Cammalleri et al. (1972)	Not measured	Positive
Wexley, Singh, and Yukl (1973)	Positive	Positive
Calvin, Hoffman, and Hardin (1957)**	Not measured	Positive

*Task characteristics moderated effects of participation.

**Individual characteristics moderated effects of participation.

TABLE 11-3. Correlational Studies Concerned with the Relationship Between Participative Leadership and Productivity and Satisfaction.

Experimentors	Relationship to:	
	Satisfaction	*Productivity*
Baumgartel (1956)	Positive	Not measured
Foa (1957)	Positive	Not measured
Argyle, Gardner, and Coiffi (1957)*	Positive	Positive
Vroom (1959)**	Positive	Positive
Likert (1961)	Positive	Not measured
Tosi (1970)	Positive	Zero
Mann and Dent (1954)		Positive
Meltzer (1956)		Positive
Vroom and Mann (1960)	Positive	
Phillipsen (1967; reported in Lammers)*	Positive	Positive
Runyon (1973)**	Positive	Not measured

*Task characteristics moderated effects of participation.

**Subject's characteristics moderated effects of participation.

TABLE 11-4. Field Experiments Concerned with Effects of Participative Leadership on Productivity and Satisfaction.

Experimentors	Effects on:	
	Satisfaction	*Productivity*
Coch and French (1948)	Positive	
Lippitt and White (1958)	Positive	
Solem (1958)	Positive	
Fleishman (1965)	Positive	Positive
Jacobson (1953)*	Positive	
French, Isreal, and As (1960)*	Unclear	Unclear
Lawrence and Smith (1955)		Positive
French (in Likert, 1961)		Positive
French, Kay, and Meyer (1966)		Positive
Morse and Reimer (1956)	Positive	Zero
Tannenbaum and Allport (1958)	Positive	

*Subject's characteristics had moderating effects.

TABLE 11–5. Participative Leadership: Studies Controlling for Task Characteristics.

Investigators	Type of Study	Type of Task	Performance[a]	Attitude[b]
Argyle, Gardner, and Coiffi (1957)	Field Correlational	Machine paced, paid by piece rate-Males	No relationship	No relationship
		Man paced, salary payment-Males	Positive	Positive
Vroom and Mann (1960)	Field Correlational	Independent-non-cooperative tasks		Negative
		Interdependent-cooperative tasks		Positive
Shaw and Blum (1966)	Lab Experiment	Low structure	Positive	
		Medium structure	Positive	
		High structure	Negative	
Phillipsen (reported in Lammers, 1967)	Field Correlational	Low mechanization	Low positive	Low positive
		High mechanization	Higher positive	Higher positive
Delbecq (1965)	Lab Experiment	Routine	Negative	
		Nonroutine	Positive	

[a]Performance based on objective indices of costs or productivity.

[b]Attitudes measured by questionnaire responses.

more appropriate for some tasks than others, and for some people than others. Table 11–5 lists studies in which the effects of participative leadership were analyzed separately for subordinates who performed different kinds of tasks. From this table rather dramatic differences in the effects of participation are evident, depending largely on the nature of the task performed. Theoretical arguments in favor of task as an important situational variable will be advanced in the next chapter, which deals with situational theories, but it is worth mentioning here that Sales (1966) attributed the lack of evidence in favor of participative leadership in the studies he reviewed to the nature of the tasks involved. Sales argued that participative leadership is theoretically expected to be more effective as a result of the greater extent to which it makes productivity a means for need satisfaction. This assumes that participative leadership allows productivity to aid in the satisfaction of ego-esteem and self-actualization needs (see Chapter 10) whereas autocratic leadership serves no such purpose. However, in the experiments Sales reviewed, subordinates were allowed merely to suggest solutions to simple problems, which did not permit much ego-involvement in the task. As a result Sales argued that the tasks failed to meet the conditions under which participation was predicted to affect productivity. He concluded that there was therefore no reason to expect that participative leadership would be particularly effective in the experiments conducted as of that time. Rather than constituting negative evidence against Proposition 3, Sales concluded that the experiments simply failed to provide adequate conditions for a test.

Sales' explanation seems to hold not only for the studies covered in his 1966 review, but for every study listed in Tables 11–2 through 11–5 in which participative leadership was ineffective, since *in each case* subordinate tasks were repetitive and highly routine. Obviously simple, nonambiguous tasks do not lend themselves to participative leadership, for on such tasks there is little to participate about. In fact, it is possible that subordinates on such tasks might see leader efforts at participation as a charade and a sham.

The participation process is also likely to be more satisfying for some people than others, regardless of task. Participation is clearly ego-enhancing and self-actualizing in itself for some people, regardless of whether it is useful for goal-attainment. This would be expected to be the case for people with high needs for independence, who have respect for nonauthoritarian behavior. The weight of evidence supporting this argument is impressive. For example, Delbecq (1965) had leaders explain why they changed from directive to participative leadership. He thus changed the role expectations of the followers, and found more effective performance in the high participative-complex task condition when subordinates had been informed why the leaders changed from directive to participative. Studies by Vroom (1959), Campion (1968), Foa (1957), Tannenbaum and Allport (1958), Bass (1965), and Jacobson (1953) have all shown that participation has its most positive effects on productivity and satisfaction when subordinates are predisposed toward participative leadership. The study by Delbecq (1965) suggests that to some extent such dispositions can be changed by simple instructions and clarifications, when (and probably only when) the task is ambiguous and complex and therefore requires participative leadership. The studies by Campion (1968) and Vroom (1959) suggest that such disposition can be, at least in part, controlled by appropriate selection techniques.

The moderating influence of subordinate personality upon relationships between participative leadership, satisfaction, and performance should not, however, be expected to be strong in all cases. House (1974) has hypothesized that the subordinate's personality will become an important moderator only when the task is unambiguous and not ego-involving. His reasoning is that subordinates who are not predisposed toward participative leadership will find such tasks dissatisfying, whereas subordinates predisposed toward participation will find the task intrinsically satisfying and motivating, due to the opportunities to participate. Supporting evidence in favor of this hypothesis is presented as part of the discussion of the path-goal theory in the next chapter.

There is also evidence that the amount of knowledge possessed by subordinates (Mulder and Wilke, 1970; Cammalleri et al., 1972) and the level of their intelligence (Calvin, Hoffman, and Hardin, 1957) determine the effects of participative leadership. Subordinates with high intelligence contribute more to participative decision-making processes. Further, when subordinates have knowledge of objective facts relevant to the decisions and supervisors do not have such knowledge, participative leadership is more likely to be effective than when the opposite conditions prevail. The studies leading to these generalizations are reported in Table 11–6.

The three studies mentioned above all concern the effect of participative leadership on satisfaction and productivity of subordinates. Productivity was measured in terms of a physical count of the number of units produced, or the number of errors committed. In addition, over 30 laboratory studies have been conducted by N. R. F. Maier and his associates (Maier, 1960; 1970) concerned with the degree to which participative leadership results in effective decision making by leaders and subordinates, as a group. Maier defines decision effectiveness as a function of the degree to which (a) the decision meets the objective economic and physical requirements of the problem (the *quality* criterion); and (b) the decision is acceptable to subordinates (the *acceptance* criterion). Maier argues that some problems demand high quality solutions, some high acceptance, and some both.

Maier and his associates required subjects to role play the part of a person who was in conflict with other group members. In these roles each person possessed critical information for the problem which no other member possessed. Thus the problem could not be solved unless information was pooled and accurately evaluated. As might be expected under these conditions, participation resulted in higher decision quality and acceptance in *all* of the studies. Since the problems Maier's subjects worked on were

TABLE 11-6. Studies Testing the Hypothesis That Subject's Intelligence and Level of Knowledge Moderates the Effects of Participation.

Investigators	Type of Task	Method	Individual Difference Controlled	Effects Without Controlling for Subject's Characteristics	Effects When Controlling for Subject's Characteristics	Direction of Effect of Controlling for Subject's Characteristics
Calvin, Hoffman, and Hardin (1957)	Complex Decision	Lab Experiment	Subordinate Intelligence		Positive[a]	As Predicted
Mulder and Wilke (1970)	Influence over Other in Complex Problem Solving	Lab Experiment	Leader Knowledge	Not Measured	Positive[b]	As Predicted
Cammalleri et al. (1972)	Complex Problem Solving	Lab Experiment	Leader Knowledge	Not Measured	Positive[a]	As Predicted
Kolaja (1965)*	Participative Yugoslav Workers' Council	Field Observation	Desire to Participate and Expertise	Not Measured	Positive	As Predicted
Brockmeyer (1968)*	Participative Yugoslav Workers' Council	Field Observation	Desire to Participate and Expertise	Not measured	Positive	As Predicted

[a]Performance measured in terms of laboratory task completion or accuracy.

[b]Performance measured in terms of amount of attitude change of subjects induced by confederate.

*Cited in Mulder and Wilke, measurement of effectiveness of participation on workers' committees.

complex, his findings are consistent with those summarized in Tables 11–2 through 11–5.

Two caveats are in order. First, it should be noted that Maier (1960) makes the distinction between leadership methods and leadership skills. He argues that the use of the participative method without the necessary skills will not result in more effective supervision or decision making than other methods. Thus, effective use of participation is contingent on the degree to which the user has the skill required. Maier (1949) has shown that most people do not have such skills, but they can be developed by training.

Second, the question of causality, raised during the discussion of supportive leadership, is also appropriate here. It can be argued that first subordinates are effective, and gain the confidence of their supervisors, and *then* are provided opportunities to participate. There is some experimental evidence to support this argument (Lowin and Craig, 1968; Farris and Lim, 1969).

Overall, this chapter's review demonstrates that participative leadership is often effective, as suggested by Proposition 3. The fact that some studies have shown leader behavior to *result from* as well as *cause* subordinate satisfaction and performance does not negate this fact. However, in the strictest sense Proposition 3 cannot be said to be confirmed, because there is ample evidence that the effects of participative leadership are not omnipotent. Rather, for such leadership to be effective leaders must also have the required skills, subordinates must have favorable attitudes toward participation, and the task must be complex, nonroutine, and require either a high quality decision or subordinate acceptance, or both. It therefore seems fair to say that the effects of participative leadership, like supportive leadership, are often positive but situational, and can best be represented by the situational approaches outlined in the next chapter.

Proposition 4 (Instrumental Leadership)

Effective leaders are characterized by the performance of functions instrumental to the achievement of group goals. These functions consist of planning, organizing, coordinating, directing, and controlling the work of subordinates.

The major research contributions in the area of instrumental leadership come from studies conducted by the Ohio State leadership group (Stogdill and Coons, 1957), and by University of Southern California researchers (Comrey, Pfiffner, and High, 1954). As a result of several studies conducted under widely varying conditions, and with such different populations as school administrators, industrial supervisors, air-crew leaders, and naval officers, the Ohio State group developed a 15-item questionnaire factor, entitled "Initiating Structure."

Instrumental leaders who structure work by organizing the use of resources and division of labor may be said to initiate psychological structure for subordinates. Hence, answers to the Ohio State questionnaire may be said to give an indication of the extent to which leaders exercise instrumental leadership. The initiating structure factor measures the degree to which leaders plan and schedule operations, establish standards of job performance and procedures for subordinates, inform them of job requirements, and establish a psychologically structured environment within which they can work. Like supportive and participative leadership, the effects of instrumental leadership are highly mixed and depend on several contingency factors. Kerr et al. (1974) conducted a selective review of the literature on initiating structure and concluded that initiating structure by leaders has its most positive effects when any of the following conditions prevail:

1. There is a high degree of pressure for output due to demands imposed by sources other than the leaders.
2. The task is satisfying to subordinates.
3. The subordinates are dependent on the leaders for information and direction.
4. The subordinates are psychologically predisposed, due to their attitudes, expectations, or personalities, toward being told what to do and how to do it.
5. The subordinates perceive that they have labor mobility, i.e., that there is a demand for their services in organizations other than the one in which they work.

House (1974) also conducted a review of the initiating structure literature and arrived at similar conclusions. In addition to the five factors identified by Kerr et al., House concluded that initiating structure has its most positive effect when:

1. Subordinates' tasks are nonroutine.
2. Subordinates have high occupational-level jobs.
3. Subordinates are under stress due to threat from sources other than the leaders.
4. The number of people working together for the same leader is high (approximately 12 or above).
5. The leader is considerate.

These reviews of the initiating structure literature obviously do not support Proposition 4 as unequivocally true, but rather suggest that it, like the other propositions derived from behavioral leadership theory, portrays an over-simplified picture of reality.

Proposition 5 ("Great Man" Leadership)

Effective leaders are characterized by both supportive and instrumental leadership behavior.

Several studies have been concerned with both the supportive and the instrumental aspects of leader behavior—the two ingredients of the "great man." A major finding of these studies is that supervisors and subordinates view leaders from fundamentally different perspectives and evaluate them in terms of fundamentally different criteria. For example, Moore and Smith (1952) conducted interviews with 301 officers, airmen, and noncommissioned officers, and administered questionnaires to 500 airmen and noncommissioned officers. Characteristics mentioned by airmen and officers describing "good" and "poor" noncommissioned officers revealed that subordinates judged noncommissioned officers to be good leaders if they were considerate; their superiors judged them to be good leaders if they exhibited strongly instrumental behavior. These findings were confirmed in a subsequent factor analysis of 280 ratings of noncommissioned officers in supervisory jobs in which more rigorous statistical tests were used (Moore, 1953). Several other studies yielded essentially the same results; Stouffer et al.'s findings (1949), shown in Table 11–7, are representative of the results generally obtained.

Thus, as Berelson and Steiner (1964) state, "the leader is subject to conflicting demands from above and below. This is a classical situation for foremen and middle managers, chief nurses, committee chairmen, deans, school superintendents, noncommissioned officers and people in similar positions." Supervisors of leaders tend to evaluate highly those leaders who are task-oriented, who exercise close rather than general supervision, and who are decisive (if not autocratic) in their relationships with their subordinates. In contrast, most (but not all) subordinates, at least those accustomed to a democratic social tradition, tend to evaluate highly those leaders who are considerate, who exercise general supervision, and who are permissive or democratic in decision-making processes. As a result of these expectations, leaders are faced with opposing demands. If they exhibit highly structured, task-oriented behavior toward their subordinates, they will be faced with problems of organizational maintenance and morale. Specifically, such behavior often results in high employee turnover, absenteeism, dissatisfaction, and high accident rates. On the other hand, if they fail to exhibit a highly instrumental task-oriented pattern, they run the risk of low effectiveness ratings from supervisors.

Studies using the Ohio State leadership scales suggest that the dilemma may be solved by a combination of high initiating structure and simultaneously high supportiveness as prescribed by "great man" theory.

Fleishman and Harris (1962) found that production supervisors high in initiating structure have higher rates of grievances and employee turnover than supervisors low in initiating structure. However, supervisors high in both consideration and structure incur only slightly undesirable employee reactions. Thus, the researchers concluded that foremen high in consideration could increase structure with very little resulting increase in grievances and no increase in turnover.

Oaklander and Fleishman (1964), using the Ohio State scales, found

TABLE 11-7. Attitudes Toward Noncom Behavior.

	Privates (384)	Noncoms (195)	Officers (31)
Social Relations	*Percent who agree with each statement*		
"A noncom will lose some of the respect of his men if he pals around with them off-duty."	13	16	39
"A noncom should not let the men in his squad forget that he is a noncom, even when off-duty."	39	54	81
Discipline			
"A noncom has to be very strict with his men or else they will take advantage of him."	45	52	68
"A noncom should teach his men to obey all rules and regulations without questioning them."	63	81	90
Work Supervision			
"A noncom should always keep his men busy during duty hours, even if he has to make them do unnecessary work."	16	22	39
"The harder a noncom works his men, the more respect they will have for him."	10	18	42
"On a fatigue detail, a noncom should see that the men under him get the work done, but should not help them do it."	36	37	68

(Stouffer et al., 1949)

that supervisory consideration serves to harmonize working relationships within a group and to minimize intragroup tension, hostility, and nonco-operative relationships among group members. Concurrently, the exercise of initiating structure by the same supervisor serves to prevent tension and conflict between groups.

Cummins (1972) found that initiating structure was most strongly related to performance quality ratings of subordinates when leaders were highly supportive. When leaders were unsupportive, structure was only slightly related to ratings of subordinate performance quality. Similar findings have been reported by Halpin (1954), Halpin and Winer (1957), Beer (1966), Fleishman and Ko (1962), Skinner (1969), Fleishman and Simmons (1970), and Fleishman and Peters (1962). And we have already taken note of Misumi and Toshiaki's finding (1965) that leaders who were both directive and supportive had groups higher in productivity than did supportive but nondirective leaders. On the other hand, House, Filley, and Kerr (1971) tested Proposition 5 on three populations, and found no difference between leader initiating structure and subordinate satisfaction for high- versus low-support leaders.

Almost all research supporting Proposition 5 involved low-skilled workers doing routine, repetitive tasks. In contrast, the populations studied by House, Filley, and Kerr (1971) were highly skilled white collar employees such as engineering technicians, engineers, and scientists. It seems likely that employees doing high-level work are more satisfied with the work itself, and are also more free from leader influence. Consequently, leader initiating structure under such conditions may be less likely viewed as an imposition of unwanted control, and leader consideration and supportiveness may be less likely to moderate relationships between leader structure and subordinate satisfaction and motivation. This point is elaborated upon in the discussion of the path-goal theory in the following chapter.

Overall, the research literature provides support for the claim that subordinates generally prefer that leaders behave in a supportive manner, while the leaders' supervisors prefer that they be high in instrumental leadership. There is also some evidence that a possibly effective reconciliation of these divergent expectations is for leaders to be simultaneously high in *both* supportive and instrumental leadership, that is, to behave in accordance with the "great man" theory of leadership. A real question emerges, however, concerning the likelihood that a particular leader will be able to exhibit both behavioral styles. If we continue to assume that supportive leadership can be measured by the Ohio State "consideration" scale, and instrumental leadership by the "structure" scale, then it is worth noting that:

> . . . Consideration and Structure often fail to be independent, and may in fact be negatively correlated (Lowin, Hrapchak and Kavanagh, 1969; Weissenberg and Kavanagh, 1972; Hammer and Dachler, 1973). This may reflect "realities" of the environment being studied, or may result instead from respondent inability to consider the two dimensions separately. In either case, it is often extremely difficult for a leader to behave in such a way that his subordinates will perceive him to be simultaneously high in both Consideration and Structure (Kerr et al., 1974, p. 63).

Summary

Proposition 1 (The Trait Approach): There are a finite number of identifiable characteristics or traits, and these traits differentiate successful from unsuccessful leaders. *Insufficiently supported.*

Proposition 2 (Supportive Leadership): Effective leaders are characterized by considerate-supportive behavior toward subordinates. *Partially supported; the effects of supportive leadership on performance are most positive when the subordinate has previously been denied some source of satisfaction, or under conditions of frustration or stress.*

Proposition 3 (Participative Leadership): Effective leaders are characterized by the exercise of participative decision making and supervision. *Partially supported; participative leadership has been found to be most effective when task demands are ambiguous to both leaders and followers, when followers have high needs for independence, and when followers have more task-relevant knowledge than leaders.*

Proposition 4 (Instrumental Leadership): Effective leaders are characterized by the performance of functions instrumental to the achievement of group goals. These functions consist of planning, organizing, coordinating, directing, and controlling the work of subordinates. *Partially supported; instrumental leadership has its most positive effects under select conditions (see the review of empirical evidence.)*

Proposition 5 ("Great Man" Leadership): Effective leaders are characterized by both supportive and instrumental leadership behavior. *Partially supported; while leaders characterized by both leadership behaviors have been found to be more effective than others in several studies, there is also evidence that both leader behaviors are not always effective and that their effects vary, depending upon situational factors.*

Conclusion

As our summary of evidence indicates, the trait and behavioral approaches to leadership seem to over-simplify the determinants of successful leadership. While certain traits and behaviors are often associated with effective leadership, *no* trait or behavior has emerged which sufficiently improves subordinate satisfaction or performance *regardless* of the situation. We therefore turn now to an examination of three situational theories which assume that what *is* critical for leader effectiveness is the *fit* between leaders' traits and behaviors, on the one hand, and the situations in which they must lead, on the other.

References

Argyle, M., Gardner, G., and Coiffi, F. 1957. The measurement of supervisory methods. *Human Relations* 10: 295-313.

Bales, R. F., Borgatta, E. F., and Couch, A. S. 1954. Some findings relevant to the great man theory of leadership. *American Sociological Review* 19: 23-40.

Bass, B. M. 1957. Leadership opinions and related characteristics of salesmen and sales managers. In *Leader Behavior: Its description and measurement,* ed. by R. M. Stogdill and A. E. Coons. Monograph No. 88, Bureau of Business Research, Ohio State University.

———. 1965. *Organizational psychology.* Allyn and Bacon.

Baumgartel, H. 1956. Leadership, motivations, and attitudes in research laboratories. *Journal of Social Issues* 12: 24-31.

Beer, M. 1966. *Leadership, employee needs, and motivation.* Monograph No. 129, Bureau of Business Research, Ohio State University.

Bennis, W. G. 1959. Leadership theory and administrative behavior: The problem of authority. *Administrative Science Quarterly* 4: 259-301.

Berelson, B., and Steiner, G. A. 1964. *Human behavior: An inventory of scientific findings.* Harcourt, Brace and World.

Bird, C. 1940. *Social psychology.* Appleton-Century.

Blau, P. M., and Scott, W. R. 1962. *Formal organizations.* Chandler.

Calvin, A. D., Hoffman, F. K., and Hardin, E. E. 1957. The effect of intelligence and social atmosphere on group problem solving behavior. *Journal of Social Psychology* 45: 61-74.

Cammalleri, J. R.; Hendrick, H. W.; Pittman, W. C., Jr.; Blout, H. D.; and Prather, D. C. 1972. *Differential effects of democratic and authoritarian leadership styles on group problem solving and processes.* Research Report 72-1, United States Air Force Academy.

Campion, G. E., Jr. 1968. Effects of managerial style on subordinates' attitudes and performance in a simulated organizational setting. Unpublished Doctoral Dissertation, University of Minnesota.

Cartwright, D., and Zander, A. 1963. *Group dynamics: Research and theory.* Harper & Row.

Coch, L., and French, J. R. 1948. Overcoming resistance to change. *Human Relations* 1: 512-33.

Comrey, A. L., Pfiffner, J., and High, W. S. 1954. *Factors influencing organizational effectiveness.* University of Southern California Bookstore.

Cummins, R. C. 1972. Leader-member relations as a moderator of the effects of leader behavior and attitude. *Personnel Psychology* 25: 655-60.

Dawson, J. A., Messe, L. A., and Phillips, J. L. 1972. Effects of instructor-leader behavior on student performance. *Journal of Applied Psychology* 56: 369-76.

Day, R. C. 1971. Some effects of combining close, punitive, and supportive styles of supervision. *Sociometry* 34: 303-27.

———., and Hamblin, R. L. 1961. *Some effects of close and punitive styles of supervision.* Technical Report, Contract N ONR 816 (11), Washington University.

DeCharms, R., and Bridgeman, W. 1961. *Leadership compliance and group behavior.* Technical Report, Contract N ONR 816 (11), Washington University.

Delbecq, A. L. 1965. Managerial leadership styles in problem solving conferences. *Journal of Academy of Management* 8: 32–44.

Farris, G. F., and Lim, F. G. 1969. Effects of performance on leadership, cohesiveness, influence, satisfaction, and subsequent performance. *Journal of Applied Psychology* 53: 490-99.

Fleishman, E. A. 1965. Attitude versus skill factors in work group productivity. *Personnel Psychology* 18: 253-66.

———., and Harris, E. 1962. Patterns of leadership behavior related to employee grievances and turnover. *Personnel Psychology* 15: 43-56.

———., and Ko, I. 1962. Leadership patterns associated with managerial evaluation of effectiveness. Unpublished Report, Yale University.

———., and Peters, D. R. 1962. Interpersonal values, leadership attitudes, and managerial 'success.' *Personnel Psychology* 15: 127-43.

———., and Simmons, J. 1970. Relationship between leadership patterns and effectiveness ratings among Israeli foremen. *Personnel Psychology* 23: 169-72.

Foa, U. 1957. Relation of worker's expectation to satisfaction with supervisor. *Personnel Psychology* 10: 161-68.

French, J. L. 1961. Cited in R. Likert, *New patterns of management*. McGraw-Hill.

French, J. R., Jr., Isreal, J., and As, D. 1960. An experiment on participation in a Norwegian factory: Interpersonal dimensions of decision making. *Human Relations* 13: 3-19.

———., Kay, E., and Meyer, H. H. 1966. Participation and the appraisal system. *Human Relations* 19: 3-20.

Ghiselli, E. E. 1971. *Exploration in managerial talent*. Goodyear.

Gibb, C. 1954. Leadership. In *Handbook of Social Psychology*, vol. II, ed. by G. Lindzey. Addison-Wesley.

Greene, C. N. 1974. A longitudinal analysis of relationships among leader behavior and subordinate performance and satisfaction. *Academy of Management Proceedings*, 433-40.

Halpin, A. W. 1954. The leadership behavior and combat performance of aircraft commanders. *Journal of Abnormal and Social Psychology* 49: 19–22.

———., and Winer, B. J. 1957. A factorial study of the leader behavior descriptions. In *Leader behavior: Its description and measurement*, ed. by R. M. Stogdill and A. E. Coons. Monograph No. 88, Bureau of Business Research, Ohio State University.

Hammer, T. H., and Dachler, H. P. 1973. *The process of supervision in the context of motivation theory*. Research Report No. 3, Department of Psychology, University of Maryland.

Hand, H. H., and Slocum, J. W., Jr. 1970. Human relations training for middle management: A field experiment. *Academy of Management Journal* 13: 403-10.

Hemphill, J. K. 1950. Relations between the size of the group and the behavior of superior leaders. *Journal of Social Psychology* 32: 11-22.

House, R. J. 1971. A path-goal theory of leader effectiveness. *Administrative Science Quarterly* 16: 321-38.

———. 1974. Leader initiating structure and subordinate performance, satisfaction, and motivation: A review and a theoretical interpretation. Mimeograph.

———., and Dessler, G. 1974. The path-goal theory of leadership: Some post hoc and a priori tests. Mimeograph.

———., Filley, A. C., and Kerr, S. 1971. Relation of leader consideration and initiating structure to R & D subordinates' satisfaction. *Administrative Science Quarterly* 16: 19-30.

———., and Mitchell, T. R. 1974. Path-goal theory of leadership. *Journal of Contemporary Business*. (Also in *Readings in organizational and industrial psychology*, 2nd ed., ed. by G. A. Yukl and K. N. Wexley. Oxford University Press.)

———., Van Der Krabben, and Valency, R. Some tests and extensions of the path-goal theory of leadership. In preparation.

Indik, B. P., Seashore, S. E., and Georgopoulos, B. S. 1960. Relations among criteria of job performance. *Journal of Applied Psychology* 44: 195-202.

Jacobson, J. M. 1953. Analysis of interpersonal relations in a formal organization. Unpublished Ph.D. Dissertation, University of Michigan.

Jenkins, W. O. 1947. A review of leadership studies with particular reference to military problems. *Psychological Bulletin* 44: 54–79.

Katz, D., and Kahn, R. L. 1953. Leadership practices in relation to productivity and morale. In *Group dynamics: Research and theory,* ed. by D. Cartwright and A. Zander. Harper & Row.

———., Maccoby, N., and Morse, N. C. 1950. *Productivity supervision and morale in an office situation (Part I).* Survey Research Center, University of Michigan.

Kerr, S., and Schriesheim, C. 1974. Consideration, initiating structure, and organizational criteria: An update of Korman's 1966 review. *Personnel Psychology* 27: 555-68.

———.; ———.; Murphy, C. J.; and Stogdill, R. M. 1974. Toward a contingency theory of leadership based upon the consideration and initiating structure literature. *Organizational Behavior and Human Performance* 12: 62-82.

Korman, A. K. 1966. Consideration, initiating structure and organizational criteria: A review. *Personnel Psychology* 19: 349-62.

Lawrence, L. C., and Smith, P. C. 1955. Group decision and employee participation. *Journal of Applied Psychology* 39: 334-37.

Likert, R. 1961. *New patterns of management.* McGraw-Hill.

Lippitt, R., and White, R. K. 1958. An experimental study of leadership and group life. In *Readings in social psychology,* 4th ed., ed. by E. E. Maccoby, T. N. Newcomb, and E. L. Hartley. Holt, Rinehart & Winston.

Lowin, A., and Craig, J. R. 1968. The influence of level of performance on managerial style: An experimental object lesson in the ambiguity of correlational data. *Organizational Behavior and Human Performance* 3: 440-58.

———., Hrapchak, W. J., and Kavanagh, M. J. 1969. Consideration and initiating structure: An experimental investigation of leadership traits. *Administrative Science Quarterly* 14: 238-53.

Maier, N. R. F. 1949. Improving supervision through training. In *Psychology of labor-management relations,* ed. by A. Kornhauser. Industrial Relations Research Association.

———. 1970. *Problem solving and creativity in individuals and groups.* Brooks-Cole.

———. 1960. *Problem solving, discussions and conferences: Leadership methods and skills.* McGraw-Hill.

Mann, F. C., and Dent, J. 1954. The supervisor: Member of two organizational families. *Harvard Business Review* 32: 103-12.

McCurdy, H. G., and Eber, H. W. 1953. Democratic versus authoritarian: A further investigation of group problem solving. *Journal of Personality* 22: 258-69.

Meltzer, L. 1956. Scientific productivity in organization settings. *Journal of Social Issues* 12: 32-40.

Misumi, G., and Toshiaki, T. 1965. A study of the effectiveness of supervisory patterns in a Japanese hierarchical organization. *Japanese Psychological Research* 7: 151-62.

Mitchell, T. R. 1973. Motivation and participation: An integration. *Academy of Management Journal* 16: 160-79.

Moore, J. V. 1953. *Factor analytic comparisons of superior and subordinate ratings of some NCO supervisors.* Technical Report, Human Resources Research Center, USAF.

———., and Smith, R. G., Jr. 1952. *Aspects of non-commissioned officer leadership.* Technical Report, Human Resources Research Center, USAF.

Morse, N., and Reimer, E. 1956. The experimental change of a major organizational variable. *Journal of Abnormal and Social Psychology* 52: 120–29.

Mulder, M., and Wilke, H. 1970. Participation and power equalization. *Organizational Behavior and Human Performance* 5: 430-48.

Oaklander, H., and Fleishman, E. A. 1964. Patterns of leadership related to organizational stress in hospital settings. *Administrative Science Quarterly* 9: 520.

Parsons, T. 1951. *The social system.* The Free Press.

Phillipsen. 1967. Cited in Lammers, C. J. Power and participation in decision making in formal organizations. *American Journal of Sociology* 73: 201-16.

Runyon, K. E. 1973. Some interactions between personality variables and management styles. *Journal of Applied Psychology* 57: 288-94.

Sales, S. M. 1966. Supervisory style and productivity: Review and theory. *Personnel Psychology* 19: 275-94.

Schachter, S. L.; Festinger, L.; Willerman, B.; and Hyman, R. 1961. Emotional disruption and industrial productivity. *Journal of Applied Psychology* 45: 201-13.

Seeman, M. 1960. *Social status and leadership: The case of the school executive.* Bureau of Educational Research, Ohio State University.

Shaw, M. E. 1955. A comparison of two types of leadership in various communication nets. *Journal of Abnormal and Social Psychology* 50: 127-34.

———., and Blum, J. M. 1966. Effects of leadership styles upon group performance as a function of task structure. *Journal of Personality and Social Psychology* 3: 238-42.

Skinner, E. W. 1969. Relationships between leadership behavior patterns and organizational situational variables. *Personnel Psychology* 22: 485-94.

Solem, A. R. 1958. An evaluation of two attitudinal approaches to delegation. *Journal of Applied Psychology* 22: 36-39.

Spector, P., and Suttell, B. 1957. *An experimental comparison of the effectiveness of three patterns of leadership behavior.* American Institute for Research. (Cited in Sales, 1966).

Stogdill, R. M. 1948. Personal factors associated with leadership: A survey of the literature. *Journal of Psychology* 25: 35-71.

———., and Coons, A. E. 1957. *Leader behavior: Its description and measurement.* Research Monograph No. 88, Bureau of Business Research, Ohio State University.

Stouffer, S. A.; Jumsdine, A. A.; Jumsdine, M. H.; Williams, R. M., Jr.; Smith, M. B.; Janis, I. L.; Star, S. A.; and Cottell, J. S., Jr. 1949. *The American Soldier.* Princeton University Press.

Tannenbaum A. S., and Allport, F. H. 1958. Personality structure and group structure: An interpretive study of their relationship through an event-structure hypothesis. *Journal of Abnormal and Social Psychology* 53: 272-80.

Tannenbaum, R., and Schmidt, W. H. 1958. How to choose a leadership pattern. *Harvard Business Review* 36: 95–101.

Tomekovic, T. 1962. Level of knowledge of requirements as a motivational factor in the work situation. *Human Relations* 15: 197-216.

Tosi, H. 1970. A re-examination of personality as a determinant of the effects of participation. *Personnel Psychology* 59: 322-27.

Vroom, V. H. 1959. Some personality determinants of the effects of participation. *Journal of Abnormal and Social Psychology* 54: 332-37.

———., and Mann, F. C. 1960. Leader authoritarianism and employee attitudes. *Personnel Psychology* 13: 125-40.

Weissenberg, P., and Kavanagh, M. J. 1972. The independence of initiating structure and consideration: A review of the evidence. *Personnel Psychology* 25: 119-30.

Wexley, K. N., Singh, J. P., and Yukl, J. A. 1973. Subordinate personality as a moderator of the effects of participation in three types of appraisal interviews. *Journal of Applied Psychology* 83: 54-59.

Chapter **12**

Leadership: Situational Approaches

Cusins: *How do you maintain discipline among your men?*
Undershaft: *I don't. They do. . . . every man of them keeps the man just below him in his place. . . . The men snub the boys and order them about; the carmen snub the sweepers; the artisans snub the unskilled laborers; the foremen drive and bully both the laborers and the artisans; the assistant engineers find fault with the foremen; the chief engineers drop on the assistants; the departmental managers worry the chiefs; and the clerks have tall hats and hymnbooks and keep up the social tone by refusing to associate on equal terms with anybody. . . .*

GEORGE BERNARD SHAW
Major Barbara

We saw in the previous chapter that trait and behavioral approaches to leadership over-simplify what actually determines the effectiveness of leader behavior. That is, while certain traits and behaviors are often associated with leader effectiveness, no traits or behaviors are sufficient to improve subordinate satisfaction or performance *regardless of the situation.*

Consequently, since about 1950, researchers have turned their attention to the interaction between leaders and the many variables within their work situations which influence their effectiveness. They have been guided by the situational approach, which views leadership as the exercise of certain kinds of behavior necessary to command the loyalty of followers and to motivate them to accomplish various tasks. Situational leadership research does not seek to identify universal leader characteristics, but is instead directed toward discovering situational variables which cause or permit leader behaviors and characteristics to be effective. Situational theorists would hypothesize, for example, that substantially different characteristics would be effective for combat sergeants and for hospital administrators.

Many theorists have attempted to catalog the situational factors which determine which leader behaviors are appropriate (French, 1949; Cattell, 1951; Davis, 1954; Stogdill, 1959; Bass, 1960; Likert, 1961). According to these theorists, the characteristics required of leaders vary with (1) their personalities; (2) leader and subordinate task requirements; (3) the attitudes, needs, and expectations of subordinates; and (4) the organizational and physical environment. The situational approach, then, is based on a recognition that both the situation and the behavior of leaders must be considered in order to understand the effects of leadership.

A substantial amount of research has been conducted to test various aspects of the situational theory of leadership. Stogdill, Wherry, and Jaynes (1956) conducted a study based on an analysis of organizational charts and manuals; interview responses; estimates of time allocations; relationships between authority, responsibility, and delegation; sociometric responses; and leader-behavior descriptions for 470 officers from 47 different organizations. They tested three fundamental hypotheses of situational theory:

1. Leader behavior is multi-dimensional. These dimensions are finite in number and can be discovered by analysis of leader behavior.
2. The pattern of behavior along different dimensions is in large part determined by the position or job to which a leader is assigned.
3. The pattern of behavior along different dimensions is affected as well by the type of organization to which the jobholder is assigned.

It was discovered that eight types of leader profiles could be differentiated, that each was typical of a different kind of management position, and that most management specialties involved multiple functions. The need for the performance of multiple functions supports hypothesis 1. The presence of recognizable uniformities in the functions of similar specialities in different organizations supports hypothesis 2 as well as hypothesis 1, and the finding that position requirements are partially determined by organizational location and by organizational level of the leader lends support to hypotheses 2 and 3.

Several additional studies have identified unique situational factors on which the effects of different leadership styles are contingent. Unfortunately these studies have centered on widely different variables; therefore, although not contradictory, their findings show little comparability. For example, various styles of leader behavior have been shown to be most effective when associated with such factors as the previous history of the organization, the age of the previous incumbent in the leader's position, and the age and previous experience of the leader (Banaka, 1960); the community in which the organization operates (Seeman, 1960); the particular work requirements of the group (Sterling and Rosenthal, 1950; Lodahl and Porter, 1961); the psychological climate of the group being led (Sterling and Rosenthal, 1950); the kind of job the leader holds (Stogdill, Wherry, and Jaynes, 1956); the size of the group led (Maas, 1950; Hemphill, 1950); the degree to which group-member cooperation is required (Lodahl and Porter, 1961); the cultural expectations of subordinates

(Foa, 1957; French, Israel, and As, 1960; Vroom and Mann 1960); group-member personalities (Gibb, 1954); and the time required and allowed for decision making (Dubno, 1963).

Viewed collectively, these studies offer rather compelling evidence that the situational approach is more realistic than the trait and behavioral approaches reviewed in the last chapter. Even though it is more realistic, however, the situational approach cannot be said to add very much to our knowledge of leadership unless (a) the critical variables of the situation are specified, and (b) the functional relationships between these situational variables and leadership traits and behaviors are also specified. Vroom and Yetton (1973, p. 209) state that it is time for the behavioral sciences to move beyond the generalization that leadership depends upon the situation and to come to grips with the complexities of the phenomenon with which they intend to deal. This chapter will be concerned with three situational theories of leadership which do attempt to deal with these complexities.

These theories are referred to as *contingency theories* because they each include a number of contingency factors. A contingency factor moderates the relationship between two other variables; for example, we might suppose that the amount of intrinsic satisfaction there is in a task would moderate the relationship between leader supportive behavior and subordinate satisfaction with a job. Figure 12–1 illustrates how such a relationship might look. In this illustration it is evident that when tasks are not intrinsically satisfying, subordinates are more satisfied when leaders are supportive. However, when tasks are intrinsically satisfying, there is no apparent

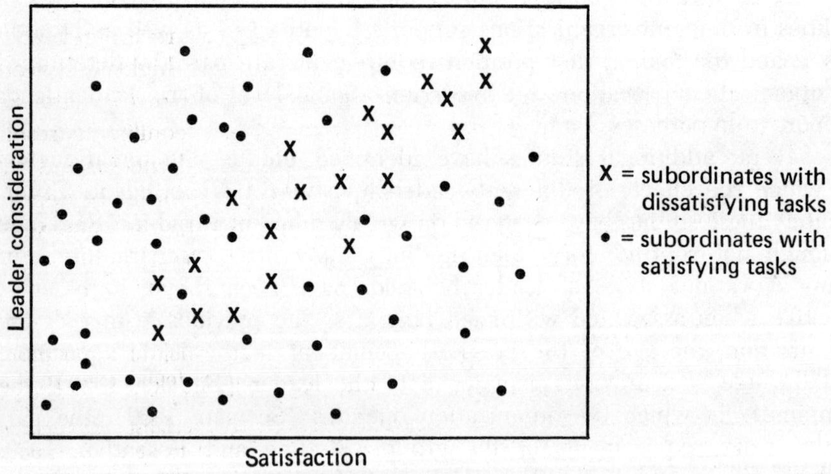

Figure 12–1. Hypothetical Contingency Relationship (Leader Consideration and Subordinate Satisfaction, Moderated by Intrinsic Task Satisfaction).

relationship between leader supportiveness and subordinate satisfaction.[1]

Fiedler's Contingency Model

The first situational theory to be advanced was the "Contingency Model of Leader Effectiveness" developed by Fred E. Fiedler and his associates at the University of Illinois and the University of Washington. In 1951, Fiedler began research on the relationship between organizational performance and leader attitudes. Specifically, he sought to determine whether leaders who are very lenient in evaluating their associates are more or less likely to lead an effective, high-producing group than leaders who are highly demanding or discriminating in evaluating their associates.

To measure discriminating attitudes, two perception factors were developed. One, "Assumed Similarity Between Opposites" (ASO), measures the degree to which leaders perceive their most and least preferred coworkers as very similar. A perception of close similarity between the two suggests that leaders are not discriminating in their preferences about coworkers.

The second factor, "Least Preferred Coworker" (LPC), measures the degree to which leaders see even a poor co-worker in a relatively favorable manner. It is argued by Fiedler and his associates that LPC is therefore a measure of a leader's leniency, or an inverse measure of the degree to which they discriminate when they evaluate others. The researchers found that ASO and LPC scores are highly correlated, and therefore can be used interchangeably.

Fiedler and his associates conducted several studies between 1950 and 1965 to determine how leader scores on the LPC measure are related to group performance. Originally it was hypothesized that high LPC scores would be associated with effective group performance. However, the first several years of research yielded mixed and apparently conflicting results.

To explain their results, Fiedler and his associates hypothesized that the type of leader attitude required for effective group performance depends upon the degree to which the group situation is favorable or unfavorable to the leader. Three situational components were considered:

---

[1] While Figure 12–1 is intended as merely a hypothetical illustration of a contingency relationship, results similar to the data arrayed there have been found in several investigations. For example, Hall and Schnieder (1972) compared the job satisfaction of Catholic priests who held one of three positions: professional specialists, pastors, and assistant pastors. Work satisfaction and job autonomy were found to be highest among the specialists, lowest among the assistant pastors. Leader behavior characterized as highly supportive was found to be unrelated to the satisfaction of the specialists, moderately related to the satisfaction of pastors, and highly related to the satisfaction of assistant pastors. These and similar findings suggest that the more satisfying an individual's task, the less the individual will require or benefit from supportive leadership. See the review of research relevant to supportive leadership in Chapter 11 for further evidence in support of this point.

1. The leader's personal relationship with members of the group.
2. The formal power or authority which the leader's position provides.
3. The degree of structure in the task which the group has been assigned to perform.

Situations high on all three of these components were considered favorable for leaders, because (1) they can usually expect support from group members, (2) they can enforce their will with the legitimate power or legal authority of their positions, and (3) a structured and clearly defined task can be easily delegated, controlled, and evaluated by all members of the organization.

Taking these situational factors into consideration in a reanalysis of the earlier studies, together with data from more recent studies, Fiedler found that a discriminating leader attitude is associated with high group performance when the situation is either highly favorable or unfavorable; when the situation is moderately favorable or moderately unfavorable, a more lenient or permissive and considerate attitude is associated with high group performance. To explain these findings, Fiedler (1967) says that:

> In very favorable conditions, where the leader has power, formal backing, and a relatively well-structured task, the group is ready to be directed on how to go about its task. Under a very unfavorable condition, however, the group will fall apart unless the leader's active intervention and control can keep the members on the job. In moderately unfavorable conditions, the accepted leader faces an ambiguous task, or his relations with group members are tenuous. Under these circumstances, a relationship-oriented, nondirective, permissive attitude may reduce member anxiety or intragroup conflict, and this enables the group to operate more effectively (i.e., the members would not feel threatened by the leader, and considerate, diplomatic leader behavior under these conditions may induce group members to cooperate) (p. 165).

Recognizing that many of the interpretations are still highly speculative, Fiedler advances several hypotheses and strategies for leadership. For example, he states that leaders who have good relationships with group members (are well accepted), and have high position power, might need to be very permissive to work effectively with a group on an ambiguous task: for example, a General working with two enlisted men on a creative task, or a Cardinal with two laymen on a planning committee. The hypothesis is that a large difference in position power would awe low-ranking members and stifle their creativity, unless the leader were permissive and egalitarian in attitude and behavior.

Fiedler further hypothesized that leaders who have moderately poor relations with group members, low position power, and highly structured tasks should also be permissive and accepting, because the most appropriate leader behavior in such a situation is likely to be one of guidance and suggestion rather than attempts to manage and control the group.

Concerning strategies of leadership, Fiedler (1967) says that:

> Inasmuch as LPC or ASO are measures of interpersonal attitudes, a leader can, of course, be trained to modify these attitudes. He will probably be able to do so to the same extent to which he can modify other strongly entrenched attitudes. Changes in perceptions of co-workers seem, therefore, possible, but considerable effort might be required on the part of many individuals to make them.
>
> A more practical alternative would involve the training of leaders in diagnosing their group-task situation and in adopting strategies which capitalize on their particular leadership style. For example, a controlling, managing, and directive (low LPC) leader might find himself faced with a relatively unstructured task . . . he should first attempt to structure and clarify the group's problem in order to move his group to a position in which he could operate more effectively. A high LPC leader with poor group-member relations, an unstructured task, and low position power . . . should first improve his interpersonal relations . . . to move his group so that his leadership attitude would be more appropriate.
>
> A different strategy might be desirable for tasks which increase their structure over time. This is well illustrated by research projects which are tentative and unstructured during the planning phases, but become highly structured and programmed once the design is frozen and the experiment is in progress. It is often quite apparent that the group situation changes in other respects as well. While the leader of the project generally plays a very permissive, democratic role during the initial phase of the project, he tends to become managing and autocratic as the experiment gets under way and the need for strict control increases (pp. 184-85).

Finally, Fiedler speculates about the relationship of a leader's "quasi-therapeutic" attitudes and group performance. He cites several studies suggesting that leaders who are permissive, considerate, and lenient are successful in lessening anxiety under demanding and dangerous conditions, and speculates that perhaps one important situational factor determining appropriate leader attitude is a threatening environment, or stress resulting from the group task. Under such conditions, an attitude of permissiveness and leniency appears to reduce stress and thus increase group effectiveness.

The contingency model is the focus of substantial controversy. Graen et al. (1970) and Ashour (1972), for example, have argued that the data and statistical tests used by Fiedler and his associates are inappropriate and invalid. The major criticism concerning the evidence for the theory is that the sample sizes employed for any given test of the theory were usually small, and the differences obtained were often statistically insignificant. However, a recent well-controlled experimental test (Chemers and Skrzypek, 1972) which suggested relatively strong support for the predictions of the theory used large samples and appropriate statistical tests. The experimental study by Chemers and Skrzypek is especially important in that it constitutes a crucial test of the theory based on predictions of the effects of high and low LPC leaders under all combinations of the three situational factors of the theory.

The theory has also been criticized for not explaining the relative effectiveness of high and low LPC leaders under different situations. Thus, it is argued that the theory is in actuality an empirical generalization, and not an explanation of relationships between leader behavior, situational factors, and group effectiveness. The major problem in this regard is concerned with the measurement of leadership style, that is, LPC. At the present time it is not known which aspects of leader behavior are represented by LPC. Over the course of the research on the contingency model the interpretation of LPC has changed dramatically several times. Thus, while the contingency model has been shown to have predictive validity, and to represent a likely empirical generalization, its usefulness for the practice of management is limited until more is known about the LPC measures.

Vroom and Yetton's Prescriptive Model

A second situational theory of leadership has been advanced by Vroom and Yetton (Chapter 3, 1973). This model is intended to help managers meet the two criteria of effective decision solutions suggested by Maier (1960). That is, the theory is intended to help managers ensure a high quality of solutions to problems they must deal with and also obtain solutions that are acceptable to subordinates, *if* acceptability of solutions is important to effective implementation.[2]

Vroom and Yetton described seven decision-making methods which they believe are likely to have different outcomes under different situations. These methods are presented in Table 12–1. Based on a review of prior literature, in addition to their own theorizing, Vroom and Yetton list eight properties of problems they believe have relevance to the determination of appropriate methods of decision making for specific decisions. Various combinations of the eight properties result in eighteen problem types. Vroom and Yetton state that "the approach taken here is to select the properties of the problem to be solved as the critical situational dimensions

---

[2] The Vroom and Yetton model offers alternative strategies for two additional objectives that managers may wish to pursue: development of subordinates and minimization of man hours in making and implementing objectives. These strategies will not be dealt with here since they are subsidiary to the central thrust of the model.

for determining the appropriate form or amount of participation" (p. 19). The particular problem-attributes which Vroom and Yetton take as their situational dimensions are presented in Table 12–2.

The model specifies eight decision rules which are intended to guide a leader in selecting the most appropriate decision method. The combination of seven decision styles, eight problem attributes, eighteen problem types, and eight decision rules constitute the normative (prescriptive) model. In essence, this is a model designed to help leaders decide how to go about making a decision. That is, it is intended to be a diagnostic tool which leaders can use for choosing the appropriate decision method for a given situation. The model is presented graphically in the form of a decision tree in Figure 12–2. The feasible set of decision-making approaches for each of the eighteen problem types is shown in Table 12–3. It is argued that the approaches within the feasible set all have an equal likelihood of meeting both quality and acceptance requirements of the decision. Once the set of feasible approaches has been identified by analyzing the problem attributes and applying the decision rules, the leader should select the single most suitable approach for the particular situation. Vroom and Yetton state that "when more than one method remains in the feasible set, there are a number of alternative decision rules which might dictate the choice among them" (p. 37). Vroom and Yetton illustrate how additional rules are employed using the number of man hours required to solve the problem as the basis for choice. Other alternative rules for narrowing the choice among the feasible set are alluded to, but are not made explicit.

Vroom and Yetton present a substantial amount of data concerning the decision-making approaches managers report having used under various situations, and the approaches they say they would use for hypothetical problems. These self-reports provide some indication of how well managers are able to diagnose situations in terms of the concepts of the model. These data show

> On both standardized and recalled problems, leaders tend to use participative processes when they lack the necessary information to solve the problem by themselves and when their subordinates have a high probability of possessing that information. This use of participation is a means of protecting the quality of the decision by insuring that the decision making system contains the information needed to generate and evaluate the alternatives. The results from both methods also indicate that acceptance considerations enter into the choice of decision process. Managers tend to employ more participative styles when it is critical for their subordinates to accept the decision in order to get it effectively implemented and when the likelihood of selling an autocratic decision is low (p. 118).

Vroom and Yetton found that in 68.3 percent of the problems the managers' behavior was within the feasible set, that is, did not violate any of

TABLE 12-1. Decision Methods for Group and Individual Problems.

Group Problems	Individual Problems
AI. You solve the problem or make the decision yourself, using information available to you at the time.	AI. You solve the problem or make the decision by yourself, using information available to you at the time.
AII. You obtain the necessary information from your subordinates, then decide the solution to the problem yourself. You may or may not tell your subordinates what the problem is in getting the information from them. The role played by your subordinates in making the decision is clearly one of providing the necessary information to you, rather than generating or evaluating alternative solutions.	AII. You obtain the necessary information from your subordinate, then decide on the solution to the problem yourself. You may or may not tell the subordinate what the problem is in getting the information from him. His role in making the decision is clearly one of providing the necessary information to you, rather than generating or evaluating alternative solutions.
CI. You share the problem with the *relevant subordinates individually,* getting their ideas and suggestions without bringing them together as a group. Then *you* make the decision, which may or may not reflect your subordinates' influence.	CI. You share the problem with your subordinate, getting his ideas and suggestions. Then you make a decision, which may or may not reflect his influence.
CII. You share the problem with your subordinates *as a group,* obtaining their collective ideas and suggestions. Then you make the decision, which may or may not reflect your subordinates' influence.	GI. You share the problem with your subordinate, and together you analyze the problem and arrive at a mutually agreeable solution.
GII. You share the problem with your subordinates as a group. Together you generate and evaluate alternatives and attempt to reach agreement (consensus) on a solution. Your role is much like that of chairman. You do not try to influence the group to adopt "your" solution, and you are willing to accept and implement any solution which has the support of the entire group.	DI. You delegate the problem to your subordinate, providing him with any relevant information that you possess, but giving him responsibility for solving the problem by himself. You may or may not request him to tell you what solution he has reached.

TABLE 12-2. Basic Considerations Underlying the Normative Model: Problem Attributes.

A. If decision were accepted, would it make a difference which course of action were adopted?

B. Do I have sufficient information to make a high quality decision?

C. Do subordinates have sufficient additional information to result in a high quality decision?

D. Do I know exactly what information is needed, who possesses it, and how to collect it?

E. Is acceptance of decision by subordinates critical to effective implementation?

F. If I were to make the decision by myself, is it certain that it would be accepted by my subordinates?

G. Can subordinates by trusted to base solutions on organizational considerations?

H. Is conflict among subordinates likely in preferred solutions?

the rules designed to protect decision quality and acceptance. Further, while there was less than perfect correspondence between the managers' behavior and that of the model, the frequency of agreement was almost double that which would be expected by chance alone.

There were several other findings of interest as well. On both standardized and recalled problems, it was found that the model's normatively prescribed behavior exhibited substantially greater variety in decision processes than did the managers' recalled or hypothetical behavior. Thus the normative model varies the decision process from one problem to another to a greater extent than do managers. This suggests that managers are not likely to describe themselves as being as flexible as the model prescribes. Further, the model makes more extensive use of the two extreme decision processes than do the managers, in that the model is both more autocratic and more participative than the managers described themselves as being.

Self-report data have been shown in prior research to be biased, that is, self-reports tend to disagree with the observations of others (Bass, 1957; Besco and Lawshe, 1959; Campbell, 1956; and Graham and Gleno, 1970). The managers who provided self-reports for Vroom and Yetton did so as part of a management training program. The model presents a theory of rational decision making. It prescribes which behaviors will be effective, thus suggesting what a leader *should do;* the managers, in their self-reports, described what they *actually did* in recalled situations and what they *would do* in hypothetical situations. Given these circumstances, it might be expected that the managers would describe themselves as rational, regardless of how they actually do make decisions. However, Vroom and Yetton cite

A. If decision were accepted, would it make a difference which course of action were adopted?

B. Do I have sufficient information to make a high quality decision?

C. Do subordinates have sufficient additional information to result in high quality decision?

D. Do I know exactly what information is needed, who possesses it, and how to collect it?

E. Is acceptance of decision by subordinates critical to effective implementation?

F. If I were to make the decision by myself, is it certain that it would be accepted by my subordinates?

G. Can subordinates be trusted to base solutions on organizational considerations?

H. Is conflict among subordinates likely in preferred solutions?

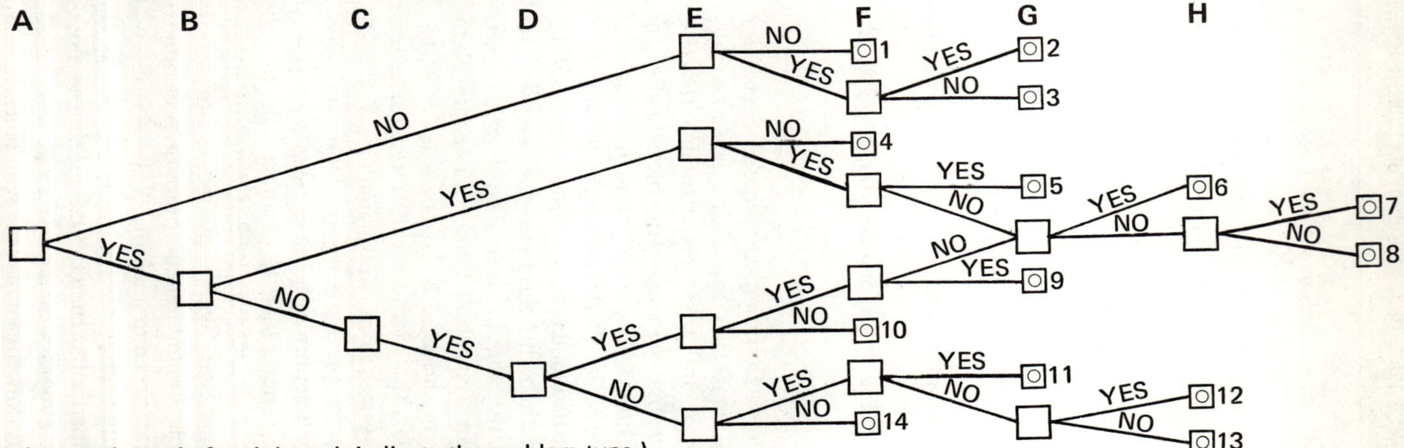

(Numbers at the end of each branch indicate the problem type.)

Source: Vroom and Yetton, 1973.

Figure 12–2. Basic Considerations Underlying the Normative Model: Problem Types.

TABLE 12-3. Basic Considerations Underlying the Normative Model: Problem Types and the Feasible Set of Decision Methods.

Problem Type	Acceptable Methods
1	AI, AII, CI, CII, GII
2	AI, AII, CI, CII, GII
3	GII
4	AI, AII, CI, CII, GII*
5	AI, AII, CI, CII, GII*
6	GII
7	CII
8	CI, CII
9	AII, CI, CII, GII*
10	AII, CI, CII, GII*
11	CII, GII*
12	GII
13	CII
14	CII, GII*

*Within the feasible set only when the answer to *G* is yes.

research by Heller (1971) which indicates there might be some validity to self-report descriptions of decision making.

Even if it is assumed that self-report data are valid indicators of actual behavior, however, they still are not relevant to the validity of the model. In order for agreement between the self-report data and the model to constitute the validity of the model, it would be necessary to study managers who are highly effective in their decision making. There is no evidence that the managers who were studied were selected for their effectiveness. If the managers were representative of a normal population of managers, there would be significant variations in their effectiveness.

An appropriate test of the model, therefore, would be a comparison between the model's prescribed behavior and the observed (as opposed to self-reported) behavior of effective decision makers and between the model and the behavior of ineffective managers. If the model is valid, such a test would reveal that the behavior of effective managers is in substantially higher agreement with the model than the behavior of less effective managers. Vroom and Yetton state that they initially planned to conduct such a test, but that practical difficulties made it impossible.

However, they did compare self-reports of effective and ineffective decision makers with the predictions of the model. Unfortunately, each decision maker reported only one decision and an overwhelmingly high percent of them were rated as effective decisions, thus prohibiting such comparisons. Still, the self-reports were in close agreement with the predictions of the model, and those which violated the rules of the model were rated slightly lower in effectiveness. Thus, this limited evidence is consistent with the model.

The validity of the model remains to be established. Vroom and Yetton recognize this and state that, at present, the validity of the model can only be assessed in terms of its plausibility and logical consistency.

A second criticism of the model relates to its purpose. The model requires the decision maker to choose one of seven kinds of decision-making styles by analyzing a problem in terms of eight attributes and applying eight rules. The resulting choice is between decision-making styles, that is, it requires a decision about how a particular decision is to be made. Application of the model in this way assumes that the choice of decision style can be made deliberately. If this is true it would probably be very time consuming to apply the model to any new decision. Consequently, the more varied the situations in which managers make decisions the more time will be required to decide how decisions are to be made.

While Vroom and Yetton present evidence that training improves managers' abilities to apply the model appropriately to hypothetical case problems, it is possible that managers are not sufficiently rational to apply such a complex decision-making model under pressures of time and stresses of work. Even if such a rational selection of decision-making methods is possible, it is questionable whether managers would or could take the time required to apply the model to normal day-to-day problems. Only additional research can answer whether or not managerial attempts to apply the model will result in more effective decision making.

House's Path-Goal Theory

A third situational theory has been advanced by House (1971) and extended by House and Mitchell (1974). The theory purports to describe how leaders affect the path-goal perceptions (see Chapter 10) and satisfaction of subordinates. Therefore the dependent variables of the theory concern subordinate motivation and satisfaction. The theory is still in a very tentative form. House and Mitchell (1974) state that:

> The initial theoretical work by Evans asserts that leaders will be effective by making rewards available to subordinates and by making these rewards contingent on the subordinate's accomplishment of specific goals. Evans argued that one of the strategic functions of the leader is to clarify for subordinates the kind of behavior that leads to goal accomplishment and valued rewards. This function might be referred to as path clarification. Evans also argued that the leader increases the rewards available to subordinates by being supportive toward subordinates, i.e., by being concerned about their status, welfare and comfort. Leader supportiveness is in itself a reward that the leader has at his or her disposal, and the judicious use of this reward increases the motivation of subordinates.
>
> Evans studied the relationship between the behavior of leaders and the subordinates' expectations that effort leads to rewards and also

studied the resulting impact on ratings of the subordinates' performance. He found that when subordinates viewed leaders as being supportive (considerate of their needs) and when these superiors provided directions and guidance to the subordinates, there was a positive relationship between leader behavior and subordinates' performance ratings. However, leader behavior was only related to subordinates' performance when the leader's behavior also was related to the subordinates' expectations that their effort would result in desired rewards. Thus, Evans' findings suggest that the major impact of a leader on the performance of subordinates is clarifying the path to desired rewards and making such rewards contingent on effective performance.

The initial theory by Evans (1970) has been extended by House (1971) and House and Mitchell (1974) to explain the effects of four specific kinds of leader behavior (supportive leadership, participative leadership, instrumental leadership, and achievement-oriented leadership) under various task conditions. These leader behaviors are hypothesized to have specific effects on (1) the satisfaction of subordinates, (2) their acceptance of the leader, and (3) their expectations that effort will result in effective performance, which will result in personal rewards. The first three kinds of leader behavior—supportive, participative, and instrumental—were discussed in detail in the preceding chapter, but are redefined briefly below.

Supportive leadership refers to behavior which includes giving consideration to the needs of subordinates, displaying concern for their well-being, status, and comfort, and creating a friendly and pleasant climate.

Participative leadership is characterized by the sharing of information, power, and influence between supervisors and subordinates. Participative leaders treat subordinates pretty much as their equals, and allow them to influence their actions and decisions.

Instrumental leadership features the planning, organizing, controlling, and coordinating of subordinate activities by leaders.

Achievement-oriented leadership, which was not considered in the previous chapter, is characterized by leaders who set challenging goals, expect subordinates to perform at their highest level, continuously seek improvement in performance *and* show a high degree of confidence that the subordinates will assume responsibility, put forth effort, and accomplish challenging goals. Thus this kind of leader constantly emphasizes excellence in performance while simultaneously displaying confidence that subordinates will meet high standards of excellence.

The theory, in its initial stage (Evans, 1970), was a tentative explanation of the effects of leader behavior on motivational variables. It was, and remains, incomplete in that it does not explain other kinds of leader behavior and it does not explain the effects of the leader on factors other than subordinate acceptance, satisfaction, and expectations. However, the theory is stated in such a way that additional variables may be included in it as new knowledge is made available.

Briefly, the theory consists of two propositions. The first proposition is that leader behavior is acceptable and satisfying to subordinates to the extent that they see it as either an immediate source of satisfaction or as instrumental to future satisfaction.

The second proposition of the theory is that leader behavior will be motivational (e.g., will increase subordinate effort) to the extent that (1) it makes satisfaction of subordinate needs contingent on effective performance, and (2) it complements the environment of subordinates by providing the coaching, guidance, support, and rewards which are necessary for effective performance and which may otherwise be lacking in subordinates or in their environment.

These two propositions suggest that the leader's strategic functions are to enhance subordinates' motivation to perform, their satisfaction with the job, and their acceptance of the leader. From the research on the value/expectancy theory of motivation (discussed in Chapter 10) it can be inferred that the strategic functions of the leader consist of (1) recognizing and/or arousing subordinates' needs for outcomes over which the leader has some control; (2) increasing personal payoffs to subordinates for goal attainment; (3) making the path to those payoffs easier to travel by coaching and direction; (4) helping subordinates clarify expectancies; (5) reducing frustrating barriers; and (6) increasing opportunities for personal satisfaction, contingent on effective performance.

Stated less formally, the motivational functions of the leader consist of increasing the personal pay-offs to subordinates for work-goal attainment, and making the paths to these pay-offs easier to travel by clarifying paths, reducing road blocks and pitfalls, and increasing opportunities for personal satisfaction en route. Because the motivational functions are stated in terms of paths, needs, and goals, the theory presented here is referred to as the Path-Goal Theory of Leadership.

Contingency Factors

Two classes of situational variables are asserted to be contingency factors; these are (a) personal characteristics of subordinates, and (b) environmental pressures and demands which subordinates must deal with. Other situational factors, not yet identified, may also operate to determine the effects of leader behavior.

As was stated earlier, the first proposition of the theory asserts that leader behavior will be viewed as acceptable by subordinates to the extent that they see it as either an immediate source of satisfaction or as instrumental to future satisfaction. Subordinates' characteristics are hypothesized to partially determine this perception. For example, Runyon (1973) and Mitchell, Smyser, and Weed (1974) show that a subordinate's score on a measure called Locus of Control moderates the relationship between participative leadership style and subordinate satisfaction. The Locus of Control measure reflects the degree to which individuals see the environment as systematically responding to their behavior. People who believe that what happens to them occurs because of their behaviors are called internals. People who believe that what happens to them occurs because of luck or chance are called externals. Runyon (1973) and Mitchell, Smyser, and Weed (1974) found that internals are more satisfied with a participative leadership style while externals are more satisfied with a directive style.

Another characteristic of subordinates hypothesized to moderate the effect of leader behavior is the subordinate's tendency to be authoritarian. Highly authoritarian subordinates are hypothesized to be less receptive to participative leadership and more receptive to directive or even authoritarian leadership.

A third subordinate characteristic which moderates the effects of leader behavior is subordinate perceptions of their own abilities with respect to their assigned tasks. The higher the degree of perceived ability relative to task demands, the less subordinates will view leader directiveness and coaching behavior as acceptable. Where the subordinate's perceived ability is high, such behavior is likely to have little positive effect on subordinate motivation and to be perceived as excessively close control. The acceptability of leader behavior is thus determined in part by the characteristics of subordinates.

The second aspect of the situation, the environment, consists of factors that are not within the control of subordinates but which are important to their need satisfaction or to their ability to perform effectively. The theory asserts that effects of leader behavior on the psychological states of subordinates will be contingent on other aspects of the subordinate's environment which are relevant to motivation. Three broad classifications of contingency factors in the environment are the subordinates' tasks; the formal authority system of the organization; and the primary work group.

Assessment of the environmental conditions makes it possible to predict the kind and amount of influence that specific leader behaviors will have on the motivation of subordinates. Each of the environmental factors mentioned above could act upon subordinates in any of three ways. First, they may serve as stimuli that motivate and direct subordinates to perform necessary task operations. Secondly, they may act to constrain variability in behavior. Constraints may help subordinates by clarifying their expectations that effort leads to rewards, or by preventing subordinates from experiencing conflict and confusion. Constraints may also be counterproductive, to the extent that they restrict initiative or prevent increases in effort from being associated positively with rewards. Thirdly, environmental factors may serve as rewards for achieving desired performance. For example, it is possible for subordinates to receive the necessary cues to do their jobs and the needed rewards for satisfaction from sources other than the leader (e.g., co-workers in the primary work group). The effect of the leader on subordinate motivation, then, is a function of how deficient the environment is with respect to motivational stimuli, constraints, or rewards.

With respect to the environment, the theory asserts that when goals and paths are apparent because of the routine nature of the task, clear group norms, or objective controls of the formal authority systems, attempts by leaders to clarify paths and goals will be redundant and will be seen by subordinates as an imposition of unnecessarily close control. Although such control may increase performance by preventing malingering, it will also result in decreased satisfaction (see Figure 12–3). The theory also asserts that the more dissatisfying the task, the more subordinates will resent leader behavior directed toward increasing productivity or enforcing compliance with organizational rules and procedures.

Finally, the theory states that leader behavior will be motivational to the extent that it helps subordinates cope with environmental uncertainties, threats from others, or sources of frustration. Such leader behavior is predicted to increase subordinate satisfaction with their job context, and to be motivational to the extent that it increases subordinate expectations that their efforts will lead to valued rewards.

These propositions and situational contingencies provide a framework for future research which will hopefully lead to a more fully developed, explicit, and formal theory of leadership. While tentative, they also hopefully provide managers with some insights into the effects of their own leader behavior and that of others. Figure 12–3 provides a summary of the theory.

Relevant Studies

The theory has been tested in a limited number of studies, the results of which have generated considerable support for the theory as well as suggesting areas in which it requires revision. The following is a brief review of these studies.

Supportive Leadership. The theory hypothesizes that supportive leadership will have its most positive effect on satisfaction for subordinates who work on stressful, frustrating, or dissatisfying tasks. This hypothesis has been tested in ten samples of employees (House, 1971; House and Dessler, 1974; Szilagyi and Sims, 1974; Stinson and Johnson, 1974; Schuler, 1973; Downey et al., 1974; Weed, Mitchell, and Smyser, 1974). In only one of these studies was the hypothesis disconfirmed (Szilagyi and Sims, 1974). These findings are consistent with the experimental findings reviewed in the previous chapter which show that supportive leadership has its greatest effect on performance when subordinates are dissatisfied or frustrated.

Despite some inconsistency in research on supportive leadership, the evidence is sufficiently positive to suggest that managers should be alert to the need for supportive leadership under such conditions.

Participative Leadership. In theorizing about the effects of participative leadership, it is necessary to ask about the specific characteristics of subordinates and the specific characteristics of their situation that would cause participative leadership to be viewed as satisfying and instrumental to effective performance.

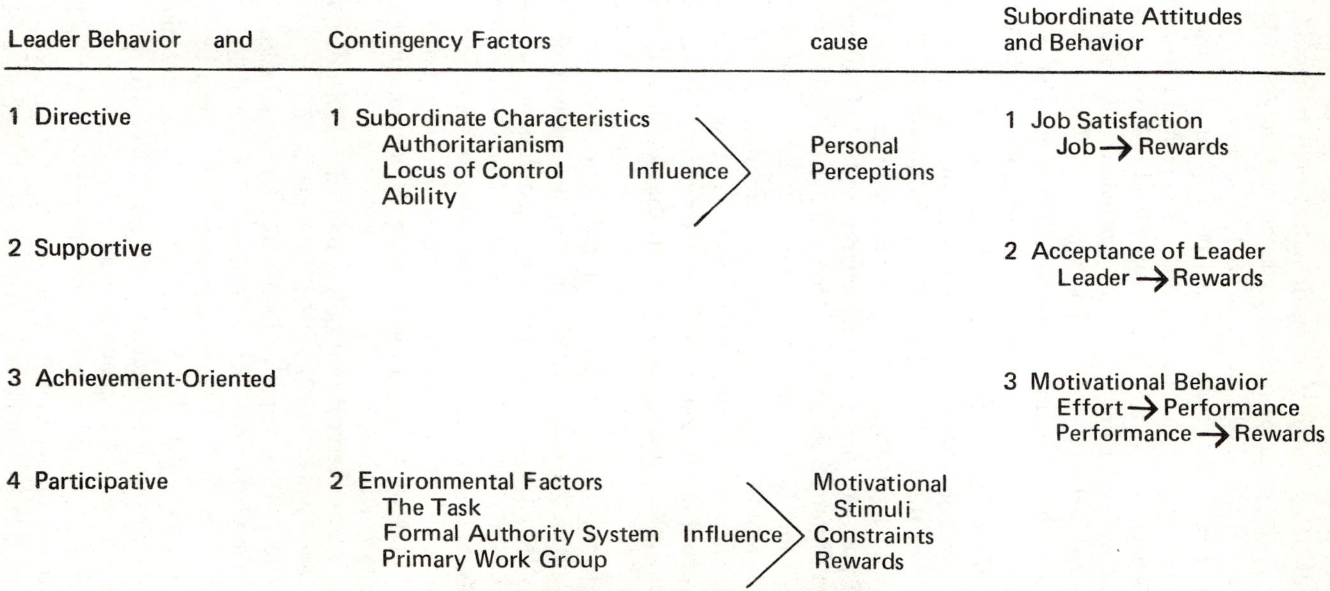

Figure 12–3. Summary of Path-Goal Relationships.

Mitchell's description (1973) of ways in which participative leadership can affect subordinate attitudes and performance, presented in the last chapter, is worth repeating here because his logic is based upon path-goal theory. Mitchell states that first, a participative climate should lead to increased clarity of the paths to various goals. Second, subordinates can select goals they value. Third, they can increase their control over what happens to them on the job. Finally, when people participate they usually become more ego-involved in the resultant decision, their peers have greater knowledge of what is expected, and social pressures tend to have a greater impact. Thus participative leadership can cause increased motivation due to a variety of internal, external, and social factors.

House (1974) has also utilized path-goal theory in an attempt to explain field study data by Tosi (1970) and experimental data by Wexley, Singh, and Yukl (1973) which failed to show that any differences in the effects of participation could be attributed to subordinate characteristics. House argued that the task may have an overriding effect on the relationship between leader participation and subordinate responses, and that individual predispositions or personality characteristics of subordinates may have an effect only under some tasks. He assumed that when task demands are ambiguous subordinates will have a need to reduce the ambiguity and that participative problem solving between subordinates and leaders will result in more effective decisions than when the task demands are clear. He further assumed that when subordinates are ego-involved in a task they will be more likely to want to have a say in the decisions that affect them than when they are not ego-involved. House reasoned that whenever participation is instrumental to reducing ambiguity, or whenever subordinates are ego-involved in the task, participative leadership will be instrumental to both need satisfaction and productivity, regardless of the personality or predispositions of the subordinates. However, when subordinates are not ego-involved in their task and the task demands are clear, participation will have no instrumental or intrinsic value, unless the subordinates are generally predisposed toward having a high degree of independence and respecting nonauthoritarian behavior.

Thus House hypothesized that only when task demands are unambiguous and not ego-involving will subordinate personality or predisposition moderate the effect of participative leadership. On such tasks, subordinates not predisposed toward participative leadership will not find it either instrumentally or intrinsically satisfying. Subordinates who are predisposed toward participation will find it intrinsically satisfying and motivating.

To date, one major investigation (Schuler, 1974) has tested this prediction. Subjects were 354 employees in an industrial manufacturing organization. Personality variables, the amount of participative leadership, task ambiguity, and job satisfaction were assessed. As expected, in nonrepetitive ego-involving tasks, employees (regardless of their personality) were more satisfied under participative leaders than under nonparticipative leaders. In repetitive tasks which were less ego-involving, however, the amount of authoritarianism of subordinates moderated the relationship between leadership style and satisfaction, as predicted. Specifically, low authoritarian subordinates were more satisfied under participative leaders than under nonparticipative leaders. Thus this study, together with the theoretical hypotheses advanced by House, appear to explain why the findings by Tosi (1970) and Wexley, Singh, and Yukl (1973) are at variance with the literature. Further, Schuler's findings provide a guide for anticipating when personality variables will be a determinant of the effects of participative supervision, and when the task will override the moderating affect of the subordinate's personality.

A number of investigations prior to the above formulation supported the idea that participation is motivational (see Tables 11–2 through 11–4 in the preceding chapter). In addition, Mitchell (1973) presents a number of recent studies which support the theory. Further, the findings reviewed above concerning how the relationship between a participative style and subordinate behavior is moderated by both the personality characteristics of subordinates and the situational demands are consistent with the theory.

Instrumental Leadership. Leader directiveness has been found to be positively related to satisfaction and expectancies of subordinates engaged in ambiguous tasks, and to be negatively related to satisfaction and expectancies of subordinates engaged in clear tasks. These findings, consistent with the theory, have been replicated in studies of seven organizations (House, 1971; House and Dessler, 1974; Szilagyi and Sims, 1974; Dermer and Hamilton, 1975; Smetana, 1974); these studies suggest that when task demands are ambiguous, or when organizational procedures, rules, and policies are not clear, a directive leader complements the tasks and the organization by providing necessary guidance and psychological structure for subordinates. However, when task demands are clear to subordinates, leader directiveness acts more as a hindrance.

Other studies have failed to confirm these findings (Weed, Mitchell, and Smyser, 1974; Dermer and Siegel, 1974; Schuler, 1973; Downey, Sheridan, and Slocum, 1974; Stinson and Johnson, 1974). A study by Dessler (1973) suggests a possible resolution of these conflicting findings. He found that for subordinates at the lower organizational levels of a manufacturing firm who were doing routine–repetitive–unambiguous tasks, directive leadership was preferred by closed-minded–dogmatic–authoritarian subordinates and nondirective leadership was preferred by nonauthoritarian–open-minded subordinates. However, for subordinates at higher organizational levels doing nonroutine–ambiguous tasks, directive leadership was preferred by both authoritarian and nonauthoritarian subordinates. Thus, Dessler found that two contingency factors—task ambiguity and degree of subordinate authoritarianism—appear to operate simultaneously. When these factors are measured in combination, the findings are as predicted by the theory. However, when the subordinate's personality is not taken into account, task ambiguity does not always operate as a contingency variable as predicted by the theory. House, Burill, and Dessler (in preparation) recently found a similar interaction between subordinate authoritarianism and task ambiguity in a second manufacturing firm, adding support to Dessler's findings.

Achievement-Oriented Leadership. The theory hypothesizes that achievement-oriented leadership will cause subordinates to strive for higher standards of performance, and to have more confidence in their ability to meet challenging goals. A recent unpublished study by House, Van de Krabben, and Valency provides a partial test of this hypothesis among white collar employees in service organizations. For subordinates performing ambiguous–nonrepetitive tasks, they found a positive relationship between the achievement orientation of the leader and subordinates' expectancy that their efforts will result in effective performance.

Stated less technically, for subordinates performing ambiguous–nonrepetitive tasks, the higher the achievement orientation of the leader, the more subordinates were confident that their efforts would pay off in effective performance. For subordinates performing moderately unambiguous–repetitive tasks there was no significant relationship between achievement-oriented leadership and subordinate expectancies that their effort would lead to effective performance. This finding held in three separate organizations.

Two plausible interpretations may be used to explain these data. First, people who select ambiguous, nonrepetitive tasks may have different personalities from those who select a repetitive job, and may therefore be more responsive to an achievement-oriented leader. A second explanation is that achievement orientation only affects expectancies in ambiguous situations because there is more flexibility and autonomy in such tasks, allowing subordinates a greater opportunity to change in response to leadership style. Neither of the above interpretations has been tested to date.

Theorizing about how leaders affect path-goal perceptions and satisfaction of subordinates under various situational contingencies appears to provide a useful theoretical framework for future research. House and Mitchell (1974) state that since the theory, and the research on it, are relatively new to the literature, ". . . the theory is offered more as a tool for directing research and stimulating insight than as a proven guide for managerial action."

Conclusions

Our review of propositions and theories concerning leader behavior permits several generalizations with respect to the effects and moderators of leader behavior. All three of the current theories of leadership stress the importance of situational moderators of the effects of leader behavior. The Fiedler theory offers substantial promise if the correct interpretation of LPC can be discovered. At present the scientific status of this theory approximates that of an empirical generalization. There appears to be sufficient evidence for the validity of this generalization to warrant additional research to discover an underlying theoretical rationalization for the observed phenomena. Until such research leads to an understanding of what behavior is represented by the LPC response, application of the theory is limited to selection of leaders, using the LPC as a selection criterion, and matching particular leaders to specific situations. A second problem with the theory concerns the static manner in which the moderators are assumed to operate. The theory specifies the match between leaders and situations, but does not specify how the situational moderators will change as the leader asserts influence on the subordinates.

The Vroom and Yetton theory is offered as a prescriptive model to be used to train managers in appropriate decision-making styles. While intuitively appealing, it is sufficiently complex to make it doubtful whether it can be applied by practicing managers under moderately to highly varying task conditions. While there are no obvious logical inconsistencies in the theory, and while the predictions it makes are plausible, there is no empirical evidence on which to judge its validity. The model may represent a valid *description* of the relationships between decision-making approaches, situational variables, and decision quality and acceptance; however, its validity as a prescriptive and predictive tool remains to be established. Consequently, its use as a prescriptive tool is premature. Until validity is established for the descriptive aspects of the model, and until it is shown that managers can be trained to use the model effectively, its usefulness remains in doubt.

The path-goal theory is offered as a guide to future research. Like Fiedler's theory, it suffers from inadequate specification of the effects of leader behavior on the situational moderators. That is, the relationships between leader behavior and subordinate acceptance, and satisfaction and performance, deal with static conditions. The theory does not specify how leader behavior will affect the situational moderators, or how the moderators will stimulate specific kinds of leader behavior. The path-goal theory explains why the effects of leader supportiveness are moderated by task satisfaction, and why the effects of instrumental leadership are moderated by factors identified by Kerr et al. (1974) and House (1974).[3]

Tests of the path-goal theory have been sufficiently promising to warrant continued research, and to suggest that at least some predictions of the theory are supported. However, there is also substantial evidence that more than one moderator and more than one kind of leader behavior interact simultaneously to determine the effects of any given leader behavior. Thus, while it appears that the basic propositions of the theory are supported by research, it also appears that its predictions of the effects of

---

[3] See House (1974) for an explanation of how the theory accounts for the findings of Kerr et al. (1974).

leader behavior would be improved by revising the theory to include more complex interactions of its variables.

In summary, it can be said that much of the confusion in the leadership literature described in the first edition of this book (Filley and House, 1969) has been resolved by subsequent research. Further, not only does the research literature now appear to warrant several meaningful generalizations, but three situational theories are available to guide future research. While these theories all require further testing and development, they also offer promise for substantial gains in our knowledge and understanding of leadership.

References

Ashour, A. S. 1972. The contingency model of leader effectiveness: An evaluation. *Organizational Behavior and Human Performance* 9: 339–55.

Banaka, W. H. 1960. A study of situational factors related to the performance of insurance sales supervisors. *Dissertation Abstracts* 20: 3354-65.

Bass, B. M. 1957. Leadership opinions and related characteristics of salesmen and sales supervisors. In *Leader behavior: Its description and measurement,* ed. by R. M. Stogdill and A. E. Coons. Research Monograph No. 88, Bureau of Business Research, Ohio State University.

———. 1960. *Leadership, psychology and organizational behavior.* Harper & Row.

Besco, R. O., and Lawshe, C. H. 1959. Foreman leadership as perceived by superiors and subordinates. *Personnel Psychology* 12: 573-82.

Campbell, D. C. 1956. *Leadership and its effects on the group.* Monograph No. 83, Bureau of Business Research, Ohio State University.

Cattell, R. 1951. New concepts for measuring leadership in terms of group syntality. *Human Relations* 4: 161-84.

Chemers, M. M., and Skrzypek, G. J. 1972. An experimental test of the contingency model. *Journal of Personality and Social Psychology* 24:172.

Davis, R .C. 1954. *Fundamentals of top management.* Harper & Row.

Dermer, J., and Hamilton, S. 1975. Leader behavior and budget motivation. Unpublished Manuscript, University of Toronto.

———., and Siegel, J. P. 1974. A test of the path-goal theory: Disconfirming evidence and a critique. Unpublished Mimeograph.

Dessler, G. 1973. An investigation of a path-goal theory of leadership. Doctoral Dissertation, Baruch College, City University of New York.

Downey, H. K., Sheridan, J. E., and Slocum, J. W., Jr. 1975. Analysis of relationships among leader behavior, subordinate job performance, and satisfaction: A path-goal approach. *Academy of Management Journal* 18: 253–62.

Dubno, P. 1963. Decision time characteristics of leaders and group problem solving behavior. *Journal of Social Psychology* 59: 259-82.

Evans, M. G. 1970. The effects of supervisory behavior on the path-goal relationship. *Organizational Behavior and Human Performance* 55: 277-98.

Fiedler, F. E. 1967. *A theory of leadership effectiveness.* McGraw-Hill.

Filley, A. C., and House, R. J. 1969. *Managerial process and organizational behavior,* 1st ed. Scott, Foresman.

Foa, U. 1957. Relation of worker's expectation to satisfaction with supervisor. *Personnel Psychology* 10: 161-68.

French, J. R., Jr., Israel, J., and As, D. 1960. An experiment on participation in a Norwegian factory: Interpersonal dimensions of decision making. *Human Relations* 13: 3-19.

French, R. L. 1949. Morale and leadership. Human Factors in Undersea Warfare, National Research Council.

Gibb, C. 1954. Leadership. In *Handbook of social psychology,* vol. 2, ed. by G. Lindzey. Addison-Wesley.

Graen, G., Alvares, K., Orris, J., and Martella, J. 1970. Contingency model of leadership effectiveness: Antecedent and evidential results. *Psychological Bulletin* 74: 285–96.

Graham, W. K., and Gleno, T. 1970. *Perception of leader behavior and evaluation of leaders across organizational levels.* Experimental Publication System, Ms. 144A, Issue 4.

Hall, D. T., and Schneider, B. 1972. *Organizational climates and careers.* Seminar.

Heller, F. A. 1971. *Managerial decision making.* Tavistock.

Hemphill, J. K. 1950. Relations between the size of the group and the behavior of superior leaders. *Journal of Social Psychology* 32: 11-22.

House, R. J. 1971. A path-goal theory of leader effectiveness. *Administrative Science Quarterly* 16: 321-38.

———. 1974. Leader initiating structure and subordinate performance, satisfaction, and motivation: A review and a theoretical interpretation. Mimeograph.

———., and Dessler, G. 1974. The path-goal theory of leadership: Some post hoc and a priori tests. Mimeograph.

———., and Mitchell, T. R. 1974. Path-goal theory of leadership. *Journal of Contemporary Business.* (Also in *Readings in organizational and industrial psychology,* 2nd ed., ed. by G. A. Yukl and K. N. Wexley. Oxford University Press.)

Kerr S.; Schriesheim, C. A.; Murphy, C., J.; and Stogdill, R. M. 1974. Toward a contingency theory of leadership based upon the consideration and initiating structure literature. *Organizational Behavior and Human Performance* 12: 62-82.

Likert, R. 1961. *New patterns of management.* McGraw-Hill.

Lodahl, T. M., and Porter, L. W. 1961. Psychometric score patterns, social characteristics, and productivity of small industrial work groups. *Journal of Applied Psychology* 45: 73-79.

Maas, H. S. 1950. Personal and group factors in leader's social perception. *Journal of Abnormal and Social Psychology* 45: 54-63.

Maier, N. R. F. 1960. *Problem solving, discussions and conferences: Leadership methods and skills.* McGraw-Hill.

Mitchell, T. R. 1973. Motivation and participation: An integration. *Academy of Management Journal* 16: 160-79.

———., Smyser, C. R., and Weed, S. E. 1974. *Locus of control: Supervision and work satisfaction.* Unpublished, Technical Report No. 74-57, University of Washington.

Runyon, K. E. 1973. Some interactions between personality variables and management styles. *Journal of Applied Psychology* 57: 288-94.

Schuler, R. S. 1973. A path-goal theory of leadership: An empirical investigation. Doctoral Dissertation, Michigan State University.

———. 1974. Leader participation, task structure and subordinate authoritarianism. Unpublished Mimeograph, Cleveland State University.

Seeman, M. 1960. *Social status and leadership: The case of the school executive.* Bureau of Educational Research, Ohio State University.

Smetana, R. W. 1974. The relationship between managerial behavior and subordinate attitudes in motivation: A contribution to a behavioral theory of leadership. Doctoral Dissertation, Wayne State University.

Sterling, T. D., and Rosenthal, B. G. 1950. The relationship of changing leadership and followership in a group to the changing phases of group activity. *The American Psychologist* 5: 311.

Stinson, J. E., and Johnson, T. W. 1974. The path-goal theory of leadership: A partial test and suggested refinement. Proceedings of the 17th Annual Conference of the Mid-West Division of the Academy of Management; Kent, Ohio; April, 1974; 18-36.

Stogdill, R. M. 1959. *Individual behavior and group achievement.* Oxford University Press.

———., Wherry, R. J., and Jaynes, W. E. 1956. A factorial study of administrative performance. In *Patterns of administrative performance,* ed. by R. M. Stogdill and C. L. Shartle. Bureau of Business Research, Ohio State University.

Szilagyi, A. D., and Sims, H. P. 1974. An exploration of the path-goal theory of leadership in a health care environment. *Academy of Management Journal* 17: 622–34.

Tosi, H. 1970. A re-examination of personality as a determinant of the effects of participation. *Personnel Psychology* 59: 322-27.

Vroom, V. H., and Mann, F. C. 1960. Leader authoritarianism and employee attitudes. *Personnel Psychology* 13: 125-40.

———., and Yetton, P. W. 1973. *Leadership and decision making.* University of Pittsburgh Press.

Weed, S. E., Mitchell, T. R., and Smyser, C. R. 1974. A test of House's path-goal theory of leadership in an organizational setting. Paper presented at the Western Psychological Association Meeting.

Wexley, K. N., Singh, J. P., and Yukl, G. A. 1973. Subordinate personality as a moderator of the effects of participation in three types of appraisal interviews. *Journal of Applied Psychology* 58: 54–59.

Part 3

Organizational Structure and Design

The chapters in Part 3 are concerned with the systemic, or more formalized, practices in which managers are engaged. Thus, these chapters build on the topics presented in Parts 1 and 2 and show the applications of those topics to the design of organizations, establishment of objectives and policies, division of labor, formal departmentation, and the management of professionals in organizations. While Parts 1 and 2 were largely descriptive of phenomena facing managers and students of management, Part 3 is concerned with prescriptions resulting from research, applications of theories, and experiences of practicing managers.

Chapter 13 is concerned with the design of formal organizations as social systems. It reviews the classical and human relations approaches to organizational design and the functions of managers. The principles and prescriptions of both approaches are still practiced in organizations today. However, the main focus of the chapter is on current contingency theories which argue that there is no "one best way," and that organizational design must reflect both internal and external factors. Finally, two major propositions of contingency theory are empirically evaluated.

In Chapter 14 the related concepts of objectives (ends) and policies (means to those ends) are discussed. The major question addressed in the chapter, in both the presentation of theory and the empirical evaluation, is how objectives and policies should be formulated.

Chapters 15 and 16 consider division of labor from two different viewpoints. Chapter 15 deals with the design and character of individual jobs and considers how variations in job design may be expected to affect performance and satisfaction. In contrast, Chapter 16 looks at the division of labor into major organizational divisions. The chapter discusses the appropriate use of and consequences of three fundamental designs for organization structure.

Chapter 17 considers the ways in which professionals in organizations may be expected to behave and their effect on other workers. This issue is related to the classic problem of relations between line and staff employees. Of particular interest is the proper management of such professionals.

Chapter 18 considers still another design dimension, the concept of span of control—the number of subordinates a manager should supervise. The chapter reviews the classical approach to this issue and discusses recent criticisms of the concept. Various factors which influence the proper span are identified as are the effects of larger or smaller spans on employee attitudes.

Chapter **13**

Management Process and Organizational Design

The heavens themselves, the planets, and this center
Observe degree, priority, and place
Insisture, course, proportion, season, form
Office, and custom, in all line of order

WILLIAM SHAKESPEARE
Troilus and Cressida

There are, in general, two approaches to the study of management and organization. One of these, as noted in Chapter 2, is *normative* (that is, prescriptive or evaluative, stating what *ought* to be done). Classical theory, for example, is normative in that it sets forth guides for actions and activities to be performed. Krupp (1961, pp. 77–78) points out that according to classical theory the organization "is, in essence, a machine; the administrator is the engineer who can draw on a body of 'principles' to design the apparatus most suited to his ends." It asks: "How may these principles be applied to get things done?" The principles are supposedly applicable to all structures, regardless of differences in goals or environments.

The other approach is *positive* (that is, explanatory or descriptive) stating not what ought to be done, but that "such and such a state of affairs is invariably accompanied by such and such conditions" (Krupp, 1961, p. 78). This approach tells organizers what will happen if they do things in a certain way, but does not state whether the result will be "good" or "bad."

It might be noted in passing that, although organizational theories derived from behavioral science experiments do not prescribe what ought to be done, behavioral scientists themselves often do, for they have their own value systems and, like all human beings, frequently cannot refrain from considering the results of given actions normatively. In general, they are inclined to place human values above market values, and this may in some cases influence their selection of the facts from which they draw their inferences.

In this chapter we will be concerned with approaches to the design of formal organizations as social systems. We will first take an historical perspective and review two traditional schools of management thought, the classical school and the humanistic school, as they relate to organizational design. We will see that both schools pose a different "one best way" to organize. A substantial amount of research has attempted to determine which of the two schools offers the most valid prescriptions. Rather than supporting either one or the other, however, research has shown that the prescriptions of both schools have some valid applications, *in limited circumstances.* What has emerged, therefore, is a *contingency* theory of organizational design, based upon the identification of the contingent factors which determine the most effective organizing method for a particular situation. (For an explanation and an illustration of a contingency theory, see Chapter 12—especially Figure 12–1.)

This chapter will review the two traditional approaches to organizational design and then present an overview of current contingency theory. This overview will be followed by a presentation of the two most basic propositions of contingency theory and a review of pertinent research.

Classical Theory

According to classical theory, managers are most effective if they clearly define the objectives of their organizational unit, divide the work of the unit into manageable groups, establish plans, policies, procedures, and rules to govern the execution of work, delegate work to their subordinates, and then supervise and control their efforts to ensure attainment of objectives.

This set of managerial activities prescribed by the classical school is generally referred to as the "management process." The management process, if executed effectively, is expected to result in the development of a sound organizational structure and continued attainment of objectives.

The structure of an organization is a prescribed pattern of relations between (1) the various tasks necessary to meet the objectives of the enterprise, and (2) the individuals who perform the tasks. It also determines to a large extent how available physical and financial resources are allocated to various phases of the work.

In setting up an organization, several ends are sought. First, the structure is designed to provide a means by which many diverse tasks can be systematically allocated. Second, it is expected to provide a system for coördinating the efforts of all toward a common goal. Third, since no real coordination is possible without cooperation, organizational arrangements must be designed to foster rather than hinder cooperation. Fourth, since there can be no coordination or cooperation without communication, the aim is to set up a structure in which there are both recognized formal channels of communication between incumbents of the various positions, and informal exchange of information to meet the needs of unplanned events. Finally, the structure is designed to allocate decision-making powers in such a way that the decisions will be made by the persons most qualified to make them and have the best available information.

The relationships established are vertical, horizontal, and diagonal. Vertical relationships are those of superior and subordinate; horizontal relationships, those of people on the same level. Vertical relationships are established by assigning tasks, authority, and accountability, which results in a line of authority running from the chief executive to each operating employee. Horizontal relationships, on the other hand, are those between the basic building blocks of the organization, which are determined by the major functions necessary to meet organizational objectives—for example, finance, manufacturing, marketing, and research and development in a business organization.

"Principles" of Classical Theory

As mentioned, the classical theory of organization is distinctly normative; however, even its advocates do not claim that what it prescribes can always be done. Rather, they consider the principles as ideals to aim at, recognizing that modifications because of specific circumstances will probably be necessary. These principles, developed in part from observations by practicing managers over time, were designed to correct shortcomings which were hampering attainment of efficiency, profitability, and harmony.

The classical theory of organization advocates that structure be kept simple, with as few levels as possible, and with clear-cut authority and responsibility for every position. It asserts that the work of each person should, so far as possible, be confined to a single function (the principle of *specialization*), and that activities and functions are justified only if they contribute to organizational objectives (the principle of the *objective*).

All functions should be specified in writing (the principle of *functional specification*); related functions should be grouped together under a single supervisor, the various groups of functions should be grouped again at the next higher level, and so on, up to the chief executive; the result is a pyramidal hierarchy. In this hierarchy, there should be a clear chain of command and *unity of command*—each person should take orders from and be accountable to only one supervisor. To insure horizontal coordination, organizational policies, rules, and procedures should be formulated and controlled by the top management.

However, the demands of specialization make the simple chain of command inadequate by itself. For example, the straight line of authority in a production organization may run from plant manager to production manager to first-line foremen to rank-and-file workers. But there are a number of other people whose work directly affects tasks of those on the lower levels; for example, methods and production control analysts influence the ways various tasks are handled.

This duality has led to the distinction between line and staff activities, which will be considered in a later chapter. Line personnel are said to contribute directly to primary objectives (e.g., production of goods), while staff people develop plans and procedures for the line, provide advice, and sometimes monitor performance. In classical theory staff has absolutely no authority over line. Thus a production control analyst may only influence line foremen by transmitting ideas to their supervisor, the production manager, who then issues the orders. By this principle of *separation of line and staff,* unity of command is maintained.

Another of the classical principles holds that there should be *equality between authority and responsibility.* That is, incumbents of given positions should have enough authority to meet their responsibilities. This is a common-sense principle, since it is obviously unfair to hold people accountable for a given task if they do not have the authority to do what is necessary to get that task done. It is, however, a difficult principle to observe in practice, especially when staff people may prescribe work methods and sequence, thereby interfering with line managers' authority.

The most definite of classical principles is that concerning the *span of control,* which will also be examined at length in a later chapter. Span refers to the number of subordinates who report to any one supervisor; classical theorists believed that if subordinates' work was interrelated, the executive level span should be between three and eight people.

Classical Theory Criticized

Criticisms of classical theory have come primarily from behavioral scientists or from others who have considered management theory in the light of behavioral research findings. Argyris (1957) has argued, for example, that formal organizational principles make demands on relatively healthy individuals that are incongruent with their needs. Simon (1958) has characterized the principles as "proverbs" which are overly vague, sometimes contradictory, and "essentially useless." Another critic (McGregor, 1960) has stated that the principles are derived from a fallacious theory of human nature (called *Theory X*) which is based on the belief that most people dislike work and responsibility, and therefore they must be coerced, threatened with punishment, and closely directed to get them to work toward organizational objectives.

Other critics (e.g., Fisch, 1961) state that the distinction between line and staff is obsolete, in that staff must have direct authority over areas where it has expertise. This point is also considered more fully in a later chapter.

Likert (1961) characterizes the classical plan of organizations as the "job-organization plan." He argues that this structure provides for interactions between supervisors and each of their subordinates as individuals, but makes no formal provision for interactions between the group as a whole and supervisors. As a result, the classical plan allows managers to keep information to themselves. Not only can they thus obtain decisions from supervisors which are beneficial to themselves, they can use knowledge secretly to connive with peers or subordinates, or play one peer or subordinate against another. The one-to-one method of operating fosters the filtering of upward communication. Since subordinates' futures are appreciably influenced by how well they sense their supervisors' values, biases, preferences, and orientations, upward communication will be tailored to what supervisors want to hear rather than to what they should hear. Problems tend to be solved from the orientation of a particular individual rather than from the broader perspective of the entire organization. Sharply defined lines of responsibility and tight hierarchical control from the top encourage dependence upon supervisors and limit the group's capacity, and thus effectiveness, to press for decisions and action in the best interests of all members.

The Human Relations School

Following the Hawthorne studies (discussed in Chapter 1) a school of management thought emerged which emphasized the social and emotional nature of people rather than their rational and economic nature. This school, which may be referred to as the human relations school, includes among its advocates McGregor (1960), Argyris (1957), and Likert (1961). McGregor's contribution included a comparison between the Theory X assumptions, described earlier, and those stemming from what he called *Theory Y*. Theory Y assumes that people enjoy work and will exercise *self*-direction and *self*-control when pursuing objectives to which they are committed. It assumes further that most people can learn to accept and even seek responsibility, and to exercise high degrees of imagination and creativity in solving organizational problems.

These Theory Y assumptions about human nature are shared by the human relations theorists, who propose organizational designs in sharp contrast to the classical pyramidal structure. Likert (1961), for example, would substitute for classical theory a "cooperative motivation system" of group-oriented management. He would encourage group problem solving, and would design the organizational structure so that all individuals are in constant interaction with several different groups within the organization. The organization would therefore be run on a basis of mutual influence by members—a concept similar to pluralism in government.

Likert argues that under such a system there is greater motivation to accurately communicate all relevant and important information, because if one person holds back important facts, the omission will be more easily detected by others who have equal access to the same information, and each person will be subject to the influence of the group. According to Likert, groups can get across to their supervisors ideas that no single subordinate dares tell them. As a consequence there is better communication, which results in heightened awareness of problems and better decision making than in the one-to-one system. Effective group action also stimulates individual motivation, providing members an opportunity for a high level of identification with goals because of their personal involvement in decisions. Finally, Likert argues that a group-oriented organizational design can be staffed more economically: when one person is overburdened, their colleagues can temporarily pick up part of the load; in a classical design, clearly defined responsibilities inhibit collaboration.

There are many prescriptions, shared by almost all of the human relations theorists, which are in direct contrast to prescriptions of the classical school: emphasis on teamwork and development of voluntary cooperation as opposed to coordination through supervision; control reliance on voluntary assumption of responsibility as opposed to assignment of responsibility by supervisors; enriched jobs consisting of broadened and varied individual duties as opposed to narrow specialization; accountability to peers instead of to supervisors; a broadened span of control to encourage delegation of responsibility and general rather than close supervision; emphasis on group decision making rather than "top down" decision making; and the use of informal norms rather than rules and policies to guide and coordinate efforts.

The Human Relations School Criticized

The human relations school has been severely criticized. For example, Hellriegel and Slocum (1974) argue that it tries to solve organizational problems by drawing attention to the individual and work group, ignoring the formal organization as a whole. They point out that such factors as organizational power structures, technological constraints within which jobs must be designed, and market competition are ignored by the human relations school, and that it assumes that all problems can be reduced to matters of feelings, with minimal attention paid to individuals' rational problem-solving processes.

Others have criticized the human relations school for assuming that *all* people meet the assumptions of Theory Y, whereas preferences for independence (Vroom, 1959) and for enriched jobs consisting of challenging, broadened, and varied duties are preferred by some individuals only (Hulin and Blood, 1968). Furthermore, the highly informal structure advocated by the human relations school frequently results in role conflict and ambiguity for individuals, which in turn result in lower satisfaction and performance (House and Rizzo, 1972; House and Kerr, 1973).

Krupp (1961) criticized the human relations school for ignoring power and conflict, arguing for the view of an organization as a system of conflicts between different interest groups joined in various ways—by the pricing system, through voluntary association, by power and control, and by the temporary balance of collective bargaining. Krupp states that the human relations view of organizations is naive and utopian in its emphasis upon the *integrating* aspects of diverse and conflicting perspectives, and in its inattention to mechanisms for conflict resolution and reduction and to how internal relations are shaped by broader environmental forces. This last point, that human relations theory has focused on what goes on within the organization to the exclusion of external demands imposed from outside, has been made against classical theory as well. Other criticisms levied against both schools are that they assume the absence of major conflict among organizational groups and members, they take for granted that adequate resources will always be available to the organization, and they believe that adherence to their prescriptions will always result in success.

Thus it can be seen that while both the classical and human relations schools claim knowledge of a universally effective way to manage, their prescriptions often contradict each other. Furthermore, the results of research pertinent to this question have led us away from any belief in a universal approach, in favor of one characterized by contingency theories and "open system" analysis. This point will be elaborated on shortly.

Analysis of Classical and Human Relations Theories: Organizational Differentiation and Integration

Two fundamental concepts of current contingency theories of organizational design (which will be discussed in the next section) are useful in analyzing the principles of classical theory and the prescriptions of the human relations school. Before turning to those contingency theories, therefore, we will define and explain the concepts of *differentiation* and *integration,* and compare classical and human relations thought in terms of both.

Differentiation refers to the degree that social units, functions, hierarchical levels, and individuals within an organization are distinct from each other in terms of attitudes, specialization of activities, goals, and formal organizational policies, practices, or structural arrangements. Where there are wide differences in the authority, attitudes, tasks, and goals of two parties, and when their policies, practices, and structural arrangements differ sharply as well, we would say that they are highly differentiated.

We have already said that classical theory prescriptions would include such things as clear definitions and specialization of the work of each person, sharp divisions between line and staff activities, and utilization of a chain of command in which the amount of authority granted to each position decreases as one proceeds downward. Classical theory prescriptions, then, tend to result in a highly differentiated organization.

In contrast, human relations theory prescribes an undifferentiated process and structure. Power and authority between organizational levels should be equalized to the extent possible, jobs should be enriched rather than specialized, and structures which consist of committees made up of members from various functions and levels are favored. One purpose of these committees is to decrease differences in attitudes among people at different levels and in different positions. Furthermore, human relations theorists do not subscribe to the principles of chain of command and line-staff separation.

Integration refers to the degree that organizational parts cooperate with each other and are effectively coordinated. Integration is easiest when parties share common goals, attitudes, and problems, and when structural arrangements encourage interaction among members. When an organization is highly differentiated, conscious emphasis on developing common goals, attitudes, and perspectives, and provision of formal coordinative mechanisms, are required for adequate integration.

Classical theory prescribes few formal integrative mechanisms and ignores the development of informal mechanisms and processes to bring about integration. Human relations theory, in contrast, emphasizes integration through team development, group decision making and participative management, person-oriented leadership, common norms and attitudes, provision for adequate time to permit close social relationships to develop, overlapping committee membership, and multiple linkages between groups and levels.

Thus, classical theory is primarily characterized by prescriptions that result in a high degree of differentiation of the parts of the organization and a low degree of integration of these parts. Human relations theory prescribes practices that result in a low degree of differentiation and a high degree of integration throughout the organization.

In the next section we shall extend our discussion of differentiation and integration in terms of some of the more important studies that led toward the development of contingency theories of organization design.

Toward a Contingency Theory of Organizational Design

Contingency theory grew out of several studies conducted in the late 1950s and early 1960s. Notable were those by Burns and Stalker (1961), Woodward (1965), Hall (1962), and Udy (1961, 1962). Following our review of these studies, we shall present some fundamental concepts and propositions of current contingency theory of organizations and review the evidence pertinent to their validity.

The Burns and Stalker Study

Burns and Stalker (1961) made the first major attempt to determine what organization structure and management practices are appropriate for different environmental demands. They conducted interviews in 20 Scottish and English firms; 15 were in the electronics industry, 4 were heavily involved in research and development in other fields, and 1 was a rayon mill. After analyzing their interview findings and observations, they developed a conceptual scheme which describes organizations on a continuum from mechanistic to organic. A *mechanistic* management system was found to be appropriate for stable conditions. Such a system is described by:

A

(a) the specialized differentiation of functional tasks . . .
(b) the abstract nature of each individual task, which is pursued with

techniques and purposes more or less distinct from those of the concern as a whole . . .
(c) the reconciliation . . . of these distinct performances by the immediate superiors, who are also in turn responsible for seeing that each is relevant in his own special part of the main task.
(d) the precise definition of rights and obligations and technical methods attached to each functional role.
(e) the translation of rights and obligations and methods into the responsibilities of a functional position.
(f) hierarchic structure of control, authority, and communication.
(g) a reinforcement of the hierarchic structure by the location of knowledge of actualities exclusively at the top of the hierarchy, where the final reconciliation of distinct tasks and assessment of relevance is made.
(h) a tendency for interaction between members of the concern to be vertical, i.e., between superior and subordinate.
(i) a tendency for operations and working behaviour to be governed by the instructions and decisions issued by superiors.
(j) insistency on loyalty to the concern and obedience to superiors as a condition of membership.
(k) a greater importance and prestige attached to internal (local) than to general (cosmopolitan) knowledge, experience, and skill (Burns and Stalker, 1961, p. 120).

The *organic* form was said to be appropriate to changing conditions, which give rise consistently to fresh problems and unpredictable requirements for action which cannot be subdivided or distributed automatically. The organic system is characterized by:

(a) the contributive nature of special knowledge and experience to the common task of the concern . . .
(c) the adjustment and continual re-definition of individual tasks through interaction with others.
(d) the shedding of 'responsibility' as a limited field of rights, obligations and methods. (Problems may not be passed upwards, downwards or sideways as being someone else's responsibility) . . .
(f) a network structure of control, authority, and communication. The sanctions which apply to the individual's conduct in his working role derive more from presumed community of interest with the rest of the working organization in the survival and growth of the firm, and less from a contractual relationship between himself and a non-personal corporation, represented for him by an immediate superior.
(g) omniscience no longer imputed to the head of the concern; knowledge about the technical or commercial nature of the here and now task may be located anywhere in the network; this location becoming the *ad hoc* centre of control authority and communication.

(h) a lateral rather than a vertical direction of communication through the organization, communication between people of different rank, also, resembling consultation rather than command.
(i) a content of communication which consists of information and advice rather than instructions and decisions.
(j) commitment to the concern's tasks and to the 'technological ethos' of material progress and expansion more highly valued than loyalty and obedience.
(k) importance and prestige attached to affiliations and expertise valid in the industrial and technical and commercial millieux external to the firm (Burns and Stalker, 1961, p. 121).

Burns and Stalker pointed out that the two forms of systems represent extremes on a continuum with numerous intermediate stages, and that organizations frequently operate with management systems which include both types. They also pointed out that while the organic system does not feature a clear hierarchical structure, positions are nonetheless differentiated according to the amount of expertise required of the position incumbent. An essential presumption of the organic system is that the authority is taken by those who show themselves to be most informed and capable. The location of authority is settled by consensus.

Another observation made by Burns and Stalker was that individuals in an organic organization permit themselves to be used as resources far more than in mechanistic systems. Commitment, in fact, frequently approaches that of the "professional" (see Chapter 17). A further consequence of the organic system is that it is almost impossible to distinguish between "informal" and "formal" activities (p. 122). They noted that in a mechanistic organization, cooperation and coordination are insured by a hierarchical chain of command, whereas in an organic system it comes about by the development of shared beliefs about organizational values and goals.

By departing from the familiar clarity of the hierarchical structure, the organic organization often produces uneasiness and anxiety about what should be done and what is expected, and apprehensiveness about what others are doing. Burns and Stalker stated that "indeed, . . . this kind of response is necessary if the organic form of organization is to work effectively. . . . In these situations, all managers some of the time, and many managers all of the time, yearn for more definition and structure" (p. 123). The mechanistic structure has as a necessary condition of its operation that individuals work on their own in a functionally isolated manner. That is, they know their jobs and are responsible for seeing that they are done. In contrast, a distinctive feature of the organic system is the pervasiveness of the working organization as an institution. In concrete terms, this feature makes itself felt in a willingness to combine with others in serving the general goals of the organization. The individual's job ceases to be self-contained; the only way jobs can be done is by continually participating with others.

It should be apparent from these descriptions that the mechanistic system is very consistent with classical theory, resembling nothing so much as a bureaucracy (see Chapter 1). As such it provides for considerable differentiation, but not much integration. On the other hand, the organic system provides much more for integration than differentiation, and is therefore consistent with human relations theory. Burns and Stalker emphasized that neither system is superior under all circumstances. The undifferentiated, organic system was found through their interviews and observations to be better for the encouragement of innovation and for adaptation to a changing environment. On the other hand, they concluded that "nothing in our experience justifies the assumption that mechanistic systems should be superseded by organic in conditions of stability" (p. 125).

The Woodward Studies

The studies reported by Woodward (1965) provided some of the most revealing early data about organizational structures. Woodward and her associates employed a variety of research methods, including surveys, case studies, and longitudinal and historical analyses, to learn about the formal organizational structures and operating procedures of 100 British firms, employing from 100 to 8000 people; all firms were engaged in the manufacture and sale of products.

Firms were classified as "average," "below average," or "above average" in success, depending on annual reports, fluctuation of shares on the stock exchange, changes in share of market, and the state of the industry of which they were a part (this last factor was considered because some industries were expanding, some contracting, etc., and comparative success of firms in different industries could not be judged without considering their available opportunities).

After some preliminary attempts to correlate success with form and size of organization, Woodward's researchers tried classifying the firms into three groups according to complexity of technology: (1) unit and small-batch production; (2) large-batch and mass production; and (3) long-run process production of the same product, such as chemicals. Technological complexity thus ranged from the production of single articles for individual customers' requirements (the oldest and simplest form of production) to continuous-process flow plants. Twelve firms had combined systems, and in these cases there was a tendency to organize each type of production independently.

When firms were classified according to technological complexity, a strong relation between organizational structure and success appeared within each group. The successful unit-production firms had organizational characteristics in common with each other, as did the above-average large-batch production firms and process production firms.

Successful firms at the bottom of the scale of technological complexity tended toward (1) less emphasis on clear-cut, written definition of duties,

(2) greater delegation of authority, (3) more permissive management, (4) less tightly organized work forces, and (5) less organizational consciousness.

In the successful firms in the middle ranges of technological complexity line-staff organization was most highly developed. Where technology was relatively simple, the line supervisors were technically competent, and there were few specialists. In highly technical process production, it was difficult to distinguish between executive and advisory responsibility.

Successful firms in the middle-technology group also used more production administration and greater supervision of production operators. Control procedures were more elaborate, sanctions more rigorously applied, and written communications more frequent, than in firms at either of the two technological extremes.

In the successful firms of each category, spans of control of first-line supervisors tended to be close to the median for the technological category, whereas spans for unsuccessful firms were either much smaller or much greater than the median group for each category. Similar results were shown for firms in the other two technological groups. Moreover, similar trends appeared in figures on spans of the chief executives, labor costs, levels in the chain of command, and various labor ratios.

Thus successful large-batch firms tended to be organized along lines recommended by classical theory; duties and responsibilities were clearly defined, the chief executive's span of control was no greater than five or six immediate subordinates, and principles concerning unity of command and staff-line separation were adhered to. On the other hand, successful firms in the two extreme categories tended to have a less classical type of organization. As a result of these findings, Woodward suggested that the classical principles may have been drawn from observations of large-batch production industries, for many people tend to regard this type of industry as typical of modern times. Within this limited range of technology, she pointed out, the form of organization suggested by classical theory seems to be associated with success, but outside this range the most suitable form of organization is not bound by the classical principles.

Following this analysis, the investigators selected 20 firms, each employing more than 250 people, for intensive study. Among the 20 were firms of each type of technological complexity, and of each success category. Through observational methods and interviews, information was gathered about the history and structural evolution of each organization, and about the impact of individual prejudices and organizational decision preferences at various stages of each firm's development. In addition, a detailed study was made of 3 firms which employed from 2000 to 4000 people, in which manufacturing methods were mixed or changing. These were selected for study because Woodward believed they would face the most difficult organizational problems.

All of these case studies not only confirmed the link between technology and the applicability of organizational principles, but also demonstrated that this link is causal rather than coincidental. However, the studies also showed that relationships were more complex than they had seemed from the preliminary study. Specifically, the investigators found that:

1. At the extremes of the technical scale, the physical work imposed very narrow restrictions on the type of organization possible.
2. In the middle range, the physical work set limits to what could be done organizationally, but left more range for management choice.

Thus Woodward said of the extreme groups:

> . . . situational demands impose themselves more rigidly and obviously at the extremes than in the middle of the scale. Those responsible for organization planning have less room for maneuver. There are few alternative ways of organizing production in a special-order production firm, and an unsatisfactory structure seems to show itself immediately in a decline in business success (p. 155).

The Woodward studies suggested that organizations engaged in either unit and small batch or continuous process production will be most effective when organized along lines similar to those suggested by human relations prescriptions; such organizations may, in the terminology of Burns and Stalker, be called organic. They will tend to be undifferentiated, yet emphasize integrative processes. In large batch and mass production organizations, highly mechanistic groups which utilize methods of differentiation but infrequently employ methods of integration appear to be most effective. Such organizations generally make use of classical as opposed to human relations prescriptions.

The Hall Study

A study by R. H. Hall (1962) contrasted organizational structures of two fundamentally different kinds in ten organizations, focusing on task technology at the departmental level rather than at the level of an entire organization. His research was based on two hypotheses: (1) departments dealing with uniform events and traditional skills (such as assembly-line work and standard clerical and routine administrative tasks) require different organizational arrangements than do departments engaged in tasks that require nonuniform and nonroutine social and creative skills (such as research, sales, design, or advertising); (2) hierarchical organizational levels whose tasks are not uniform require different organizational arrangements than those whose tasks are uniform.

Hall further hypothesized that departments and levels characterized by routine tasks are also characterized by Weber's bureaucratic model of organizations (described in Chapter 1), including as components of effective organizations many of the characteristics of the mechanistic organization described earlier in this chapter. According to Weber (1947), the most effective organization has:

1. A well-defined hierarchy of authority.
2. A division of labor based on functional specialization.
3. A system of rules covering the rights and duties of position incumbents.
4. A system of procedures for dealing with work situations.
5. Impersonality of interpersonal relationships.
6. Selection for employment and promotion based on technical competence.

Hall examined the *degree* to which each of the above characteristics were present in different departments and at different organizational levels by conceiving of each characteristic as a *dimension*. He stated that "The concept of a dimension assumes that the phenomena under study exists in the form of a continuum along the dimension."

Hall developed a scale for each dimension, designed to measure employee perceptions of the organization. These scales were administered to a random sample of personnel in the ten organizations: five were profit-making organizations, and five were government organizations.

By comparing responses from 16 departments, Hall found that, consistent with his first hypothesis, nonroutine departments were perceived to be significantly different from routine departments in hierarchy of authority, division of labor, and specified procedure. No significant differences were found in the remaining three dimensions (specified rights and duties, impersonality, and criteria for hiring and promotion).

To test his second hypothesis, Hall administered his scale statements to 116 executives and 187 nonexecutives. Here he assumed that, because their work is less routine, executives work in a less bureaucratic setting. He found his assumption to be true for four of the six dimensions: emphasis on hierarchy, division of labor, specified procedure, and impersonality.

From the Woodward study we saw variations *among* organizations; from the Hall study we saw variations *within* organizations. Task technology within an organization appears to have an effect on organizational procedure similar to the effect of technology within an industry. Thus the findings from Hall suggested that within organizations, the more routine the task the more differentiated will be the organization structure. This differentiation occurs as a result of application of classical or Weberian practices.

Having distinguished between two different levels of analysis as they relate to technology, we will now examine additional studies to further clarify the effect of technology and other factors on the design of an organizational structure.

The Udy Studies

Two studies conducted by Udy (1958, 1962) also dealt with the relation between technology and bureaucratic elements in organizations.

Udy (1958) analyzed 25 production-oriented organizations that had three or more levels of authority. He paid specific attention to the following organizational characteristics: (1) the use of explicit mutual employment agreements; (2) emphasis on quantity or quality of work performed; (3) specialization of labor; and (4) the allocation of money or goods by members of higher authority to those of lower authority in return for their participation. By listing the 25 cases, starting with those possessing all four attributes, and proceeding downward to those possessing none of them, Udy was able to demonstrate a clear pattern of association between the variables (see Table 13–1). He stated:

> If the pattern suggested by our data is generally valid, it has some far-reaching implications. It suggests, for example, that in order for [explicit employment agreements] to be institutionalized in any bureaucratic organization, performance emphasis, specialized division of labor, and rewards [allocated from above] must also be institutionalized. It similarly suggests an order in which different characteristics must be introduced in the course of organizational development under conditions where they cannot be introduced simultaneously . . . (pp. 416–18).

In a subsequent study intended to test the above result further, Udy (1962) analyzed 34 organizations from 34 different societies and found general confirmation, with the exception of eight cases in which reward based on merit or specialization was not present. In all eight cases he found the deviations were in part a function of purely technical considerations:

> Certain kinds of tasks, as for example many involving agriculture or construction, are by nature cumulative and do not lend themselves particularly to specialization, although there is no reason why they cannot be otherwise rationally organized. [The 34 case studies] suggest that rationality (explicit limited objectives) involves specialization only where the latter is clearly relevant technologically. Similarly, . . . where activities are highly routinized with a minimum of uncertainty involved, performance seems less likely to be emphasized. . . . In sum, it appears that specialization and a performance emphasis can in effect not be a part of rational administration unless their presence clearly contributes to technical efficiency in the physical sense (pp. 303–304).

Thus, consistent with Woodward, Udy found that technology governs the need for, and effective use of, specialization of labor and also governs the formal methods by which employees are rewarded on the basis of their performance.

TABLE 13-1. Bureaucratic Elements in Twenty-five Nonindustrial Production Organizations.

Explicit Contractual Employment Agreements	Emphasis on Quantity or Quality of Work Performed	Specialization	Reward Based on Performance
Yes	Yes	Yes	Yes
Yes	Yes	Yes	Yes
Yes	Yes	Yes	Yes
Yes	Yes	Yes	Yes
Yes	Yes	Yes	Yes
No	Yes	Yes	Yes
No	No	Yes	Yes
No	No	Yes	Yes
No	No	Yes	Yes
No	No	Yes	Yes
No	No	Yes	Yes
No	No	No	Yes
No	No	No	Yes
No	No	No	Yes
No	No	No	Yes
No	No	No	Yes
No	No	No	Yes
No	No	No	Yes
No	No	No	Yes
No	No	No	Yes
No	No	No	Yes
No	No	No	No
No	No	No	No
No	No	No	No
No	No	Yes	No

Based on Udy (1958) p. 417. The Table headings have been reworded to conform with the non-technical approach taken in describing the studies reviewed in this chapter.

Conclusions from Early Studies

The first edition of this text reviewed the above studies, along with others bearing less directly on the classical-human relations controversy, and concluded from the early studies that *classical principles of organization, as a group, are not universally applicable*. Rather, the organizational structure produced by adherence to classical principles is necessary only when there are no overriding factors (such as professionalization of workers, contractual or legal restrictions, and certain types of production processes) which structure relations between members. When one of these factors does exist, formal hierarchical systems and specialization of labor are not only unnecessary, but may confuse members and interfere with their response to situational demands. Thus the early evidence against any "one best way" theory, and for a contingency theory, was already compelling.

In 1967, two books were published which were explicitly concerned with the development of a contingency theory. The books were written independently, yet had in common many fundamental concepts and propositions. Thompson set forth the most complete and formally articulated organizational theory of that time, while Lawrence and Lorsch presented a theory which was less detailed and formal, but which was accompanied by some data in support of their major propositions.

Before describing Thompson's major concepts and propositions, and reviewing the pertinent research evidence, we will discuss some basic terms and concepts used in contingency theories.

Contingency Theory: Terms and Concepts

Almost all contingency theorists agree that an organization can be conceived of as an "open system" that interacts with, is dependent on, and seeks to control and adapt to its environment. This "systems" perspective employs several well-developed and somewhat technical concepts. These include:

System. A system is a "set of objects together with relationships between the objects and between their attributes" (Hall and Fagin, 1956). The set of objects to be studied as a system is determined somewhat arbitrarily by the analyst, and depends partly on the degree that objects seem to be interrelated, and partly on which objects the analyst is interested in. Bobbitt et al. (1974) point out that the key concept in a system concerns the idea of relationships. A system behaves in a unique way because of the relations among its parts; since these parts are interdependent, the behaviors of a system are more than the sum of the behaviors of the parts.

Open System. A system is said to be open if objects in its environment influence the behavior of the system's parts and the relationships among parts. Obviously, no system is completely open or completely closed. Rather, we should think in terms of the degree of openness. Organizations are systems consisting of physical, economic, human, and intangible parts. Since human beings are not total captives of the organization, inasmuch as their behavior is partially determined by their lives apart from the organization, the organization cannot be completely closed with respect to its human components. Since availability and value of funds is largely determined by the general economy, the organization cannot be completely closed with respect to its economic parts. The same can be said with respect to physical (e.g., weather) and intangible (e.g., patents) parts of the organization.

Boundaries. When we speak of an organization's environment, we necessarily imply that the organization has a boundary, which theoretically consists of that set of parts which affect and are affected by both the organization and the environment simultaneously. From this standpoint, organizational members make up part of the boundary, since their behavior affects the organization and is affected by the outside environment. To the extent that a boundary element is under the organization's control, we call the organization closed with respect to that element. Otherwise we call the organization open with respect to that element.

This definition of a boundary element suggests that nearly all organizational parts are boundary elements, and that the analyst would require information about all environmental parts which affect organizational members. Because of the unworkability of this definition, a simplifying assumption is often made by analysts, who decide which objects within the organization are of greatest interest and place a closed line around them (Bobbitt et al., 1974). This line is then considered to be the system's boundary. As a guide to placing the line, these writers suggest including within the system objects with less intense interaction across the line, or outside the line, than among objects within the line.

System Requirements. Just like any living system, organizations must meet three requirements to survive. These requirements have been referred to by Argyris (1964) as core activities that every organization must perform: achieving objectives; maintaining itself internally; and adapting to its environment. In any short period of time the organization may concentrate upon only or two of these requirements; however, it must at least meet some minimum constraint with regard to all three if survival is to be assured.

Simon (1964) points out that the concept of a single organizational goal is unrealistic, and that "in the decision-making situations of real life, a course of action, to be acceptable, must satisfy a whole set of requirements, or constraints. Sometimes one of these requirements is singled out and referred to as the goal of the action. But the choice of one of the constraints from many, is to a large extent arbitrary. For many purposes it is more meaningful to refer to the whole set of requirements as the 'complex' goal of the action" (Simon, 1964).

Domain and Range. The domain and range of the organization define the points at which it is dependent on, or interdependent with, its environment. The domain of the organization consists of its set of inputs. The organization's range consists of (a) the products or service rendered by the organization, and (b) the populations served by the organization. Thus, the range of a business organization would be defined in terms of the markets served and the particular products sold in those markets. The domain and range of the organization are to some extent determined by the organization itself, and to some extent by the relevant influences in the environment of the organization. For example, an organization may decide to use particular sources of financial, labor, or material supplies. However, the choice will largely be determined by the availability of such sources in the environment. If few sources exist, the organization can exercise few options. If sources of supply come from a single supplier the organization may have *no* choice, at least in the short run.

Similarly, the organization may partially determine its range by deciding what products to sell, what services to render, and what populations to serve. However, such decisions will be constrained by existing and potential competitors, regulatory agencies, public opinion, etc.

Thompson's Theory of Organizational Design

As we mentioned earlier, Thompson's theory of organizational design was one of two contingency theories published in 1967 (the other being Lawrence and Lorsch's); because it is the most complete and formally articulated theory, it will be the main focus of the remainder of this chapter. Thompson's theory treats the design of organizations as a function of the *environment* in which the organizations exist and of the technology they employ. The theory deals with organizations which seek to coordinate their input, technological, and output activities such that they are economically, or at least instrumentally, efficient.[1] Organizations are *economically* efficient when they obtain results with minimal expenditure of resources; they are *instrumentally* efficient when their activities do in fact produce desired outcomes.

While there are no absolute measures of economic or instrumental efficiency, many organizations are required by clients, regulators, owners, competitors, or other elements of their environment to strive for at least a relatively high level of efficiency. Organizations therefore strive to make their technological performance as efficient as possible. Technological efficiency is greatest under closed system conditions, where all demands and requirements are predictable and controllable. However, absolute control and predictability are seldom, if ever, possible, for two reasons. First, the organization's environment is constantly changing, and the uncertainty which accompanies environmental change works against efficiency. Second, the technology is often poorly understood. That is, those who perform the activities required to produce organizational products and services frequently do so without complete knowledge about what activities can most efficiently be performed, and how. Examples of such activities include research tasks, artistic tasks, and tasks which require great judgment rather than application of known rules and principles.

Consequently, Thompson's theory asserts that the central problem of complex organizations is coping with uncertainty. Due to lack of complete knowledge about the technology, organizations operating even in relatively stable and predictable environments frequently face unsolved and unpredictable problems. These problems cause uncertainty, and prevent the organization's technological core from operating in an economically efficient manner.

The theory deals with how organizations are designed to cope with various forms (or forces) of uncertainty. It is a contingency theory because the predictions (propositions) of the theory state that the form the organi-

---

[1] Not all organizations seek such efficiency. Some family-owned businesses, for example, place higher value on family control than on economic or instrumental performance. Other organizations, such as political parties and churches, are primarily concerned with preserving and disseminating certain moral convictions.

zation will take, and the actions of the policy decision makers, will be contingent upon the kinds of forces causing uncertainty in the environment and the kinds of problems presented by the technology.

The theory is an elaborate one, and addresses many issues that will not be covered here. We take the liberty of summarizing the essential thrust of the theory into two major propositions.[2]

Propositions

1. Organizations seek to control their environments. If control of the environments is not possible, organizations seek to adapt to the demands of the environments in such a manner as to meet the economic and instrumental efficiency criteria imposed by the environments. Specifically, organizations seek to control environments by increasing their power over environmental units, and seek to adapt to environments by monitoring environmental demands and by designing structures and practices to permit effective responses to such demands.
2. Organizations seek to adjust to the demands of their technological core to permit economical and efficient coordination and scheduling of interdependent parts.

Empirical Evidence

Proposition 1

Organizations seek to control their environments. If control of the environments is not possible, organizations seek to adapt to the demands of the environments in such a manner as to meet the economic and instrumental efficiency criteria imposed by the environments. Specifically, organizations seek to control environments by increasing their power over environmental demands and by designing structures and practices to permit effective responses to such demands.

An early study (Simpson and Gulley, 1962), although not a direct test of this proposition, found that organizations facing the widest range of pressures tended to score lowest on an index of centralization of authority and highest in emphasis on member involvement in organizational activities and on attention devoted to internal communication. When environmental pressures were restricted, these tendencies were reversed.

More recently, Aiken and Hage (1968) found that among 16 social welfare organizations, highly interdependent organizations, i.e., those having

---

[2] While these propositions are consistent with the theory, they hardly do justice to the precision with which the theory deals with the specific sources of uncertainty. For a detailed appreciation of the theory, consult the original work.

many joint programs with other organizations, tended to have a greater number of occupations represented, to be more innovative, to have employees who engaged in more professional activities, to have more active internal communications channels, and to be somewhat more decentralized.

These two studies illustrate how organizations respond to diverse and complex demands from external sources. They suggest that organizations which face demanding and complex environments tend to have a more complex structure, i.e., greater numbers of occupational skills and functional specializations, more decentralized decision making, and greater emphasis on internal coordination and communication. We shall return to the conclusions from these two studies later on.

A series of studies by Pfeffer are also relevant to this proposition. Pfeffer found that the more an organization is dependent on its environment for critical resources, the more likely it is that managers report spending considerable time with external organizations and rank external factors as more important to success than internal factors (Pfeffer, 1972a). Further, organizations tend to select more outside members for their boards of directors when they are dependent on the environment for outside financing. When they are influenced by external legal regulations they tend to select a higher proportion of attorneys (Pfeffer, 1972b). Finally, organizations operating where there is high interdependence among firms in the industry tend to have higher frequencies of intra-industry mergers and exchanges of executives (Pfeffer, 1972c).

The practices identified in Pfeffer's studies illustrate some of the ways organizations seek to control and adapt to their environment. By adopting attitudes that outside factors are most important, managers are better able to deal with such factors. By having larger boards organizations are able to attract more of the skills needed to cope with environmental demands and to establish more contacts with sources of financing. By selecting attorneys, organizations faced with legal regulations are better able to both control the impact of such regulations and to adapt to changes in such regulations. Finally, the practices of intra-industry mergers and executive exchanges help to stabilize interdependencies, and thus make the environment more manageable.

The Lawrence and Lorsch Study. A classic study by Lawrence and Lorsch (1967) illustrates in some detail how organizations adapt to their environment. Stimulated primarily by the work of Burns and Stalker and of Woodward, Lawrence and Lorsch conducted a study of ten American organizations in an attempt to answer the question: What kind of organization does it take to deal with various economic and market conditions? To guide their research, they developed a theory about the differentiation and integration that organizations require. While the theory is different from Thompson's, the findings from the Lawrence and Lorsch study are consistent with Proposition 1.

Like Thompson, Lawrence and Lorsch view the organization as an open system whose internal characteristics must fit external demands from the environment. They describe the internal relationships of members of the organization as intertwined, influenced by "the nature of the task being performed, the form of relationships, rewards, and controls, and by the existing ideas within the organization about how a well-accepted member should behave." According to Lawrence and Lorsch, these internal factors must be integrated to function harmoniously if the organization is to perform effectively.

However, organizational differentiation, "the difference in cognitive and emotional orientation among members in different functional departments," also exists; that is, managers in various functional units can be expected to differ from one another in goal orientation, time orientation, and interpersonal orientation. Furthermore, formality of structure will differ between departments and between organizations. Thus, "because the members of each department develop different interests and differing points of view, they often find it difficult to reach agreement on integrated programs of action."

Lawrence and Lorsch argue that integration, which they define as "the quality of the state of collaboration," does not, as classical theorists assume, automatically follow from organizational design. For effective integration, the conflicts emerging from differing goal, time, and interpersonal differences must be resolved.

To Lawrence and Lorsch, the organization's environment determines both the character and degree of differentiation and the mode of integration. In particular, they consider two aspects of the environment as dominant: the certainty of information or knowledge about events; and the dominant competitive issue in the industry. They therefore predicted that environmental uncertainty and competitive demand would affect the organization in terms of differentiation and integration: greater innovation and environmental uncertainty would be reflected in greater differentiation of goal, time, and interpersonal orientation and of organizational structure.

Research Strategy. Lawrence and Lorsch's research was carried out in two phases. First, a series of six detailed case studies was conducted among firms in the plastics industry. This phase provided a qualitative understanding of the relations among environment, differentiation, and integration. Second, a highly effective organization and a less effective one in each of the plastics, food, and container industries were studied and compared. Lawrence and Lorsch chose the three industries because they displayed important differences among the environmental dimensions of certainty and competitive issue. Each industry had a "different rate of technological change in both product and processes," and had dominant demands which stemmed from different sectors of the environment.

Interviews and questionnaires were used to collect data. Interview data concerning internal matters were obtained from 30 to 50 upper- and middle-level managers in each organization. Information concerning the outside environment was obtained from the top executives in each organization.

Environmental uncertainty was measured with a questionnaire, expressed in terms of clarity of information, uncertainty of cause-effect relationships, and the time span of definitive feedback.

Findings on Environmental Demands. Lawrence and Lorsch found in the plastics industry that continually emerging technological developments created an environment of high uncertainty, in which the dominant competitive issue for firms was the capacity to innovate. The major competitive issue in the food industry was also innovation, but to a somewhat lesser extent. In the container industry, on the other hand, the main competitive issue was the ability to provide customer service. Lawrence and Lorsch also found that food and plastics firms worked under conditions of change and uncertainty; container companies worked under conditions of relative stability.

Findings on Differentiation. The goals of department managers in all three industries generally coincided with functional specialization. Thus manufacturing personnel were primarily concerned with cost reduction, process efficiency, and similar matters. Research and engineering personnel were oriented toward techno-economic goals and scientific matters, and marketing personnel with marketplace events. In the food industry, with its relatively greater sales orientation, all managers tended toward a market-oriented view of goals.

With respect to time orientation, Lawrence and Lorsch found (as might be expected) that the managements of plastics firms, with their separate fundamental research divisions, had a slightly higher level of total time differentiation among functional departments than did the food firms.

The interpersonal orientations of managers were measured to determine whether a particular manager was personnel-relationship or task oriented. In the most uncertain industry, plastics, it was found that sales personnel were quite relationship-oriented and production personnel quite task-oriented. On the other hand, interpersonal orientation in the container industry did not differ greatly among sales and production personnel. In the food industry interpersonal differentiation fell between the plastics and container extremes.

Differences in formal structure also reflected uncertainty and the diversity of environmental demands. The plastics industry required the greatest differentiation of interdepartmental structure: production, involving relatively routine procedures, was the most highly formalized department; sales, applied technology, and fundamental research had less formalized structures. Similarly, the environment which demanded the least diversity, that of the container industry, led to a lower level of differentiation along the structure dimension: all three departments were similar in structure. Again, the food industry fell between the plastics and container industries in this respect.

In summary, it was found that the actual amounts of goal, time, interpersonal, and structural differentiation were in line with the prediction that the environmental factors of uncertainty and innovation would be associated with increased differentiation.

Differentiation, Integration, and Performance. Lawrence and Lorsch found that "the most successful organizations tended to maintain states of differentiation and integration consistent with the diversity of the parts of the environment and the required interdependence of these parts." They judged perfomance by changes in profits and in sales volume over five years, and new products introduced as a percentage of sales over five years. In all three industries, high performing firms had fewer deviations from the theoretical amount of differentiation required by the environment. Lawrence and Lorsch conclude that "the more the parts of the environment differ in certainty and time span of feedback, and the less dominant any part was, the more differentiated were the pairs of the units in the high performing organizations."

In addition to effects on differentiation, environmental factors were found to require qualitative differences in modes of integration. The highly differentiated plastics industry used formal integrating departments; the less differentiated food industry used individual integrators; and the least differentiated container industry used direct managerial contact (interestingly, the low-performing container firm used a formal integrating unit, and the high-performing container firm used direct managerial contact).

It was also found that all effective integrators or integrating units had positional influence, sufficient knowledge and information to make decisions, and influence based on competence; furthermore, they all used confrontation to resolve conflict, as opposed to smoothing over or forcing.

Environment was found to determine the relative influence of departments in the most effective organizations. For example, in the plastics industry, with its great need for integration, the integrating departments had the greatest influence. All members of the effective plastics and food firms reported having a high degree of influence over decisions. This finding is consistent with the prediction that the demands of an uncertain environment will require more decision making at lower levels. In the container industry, where the environment is relatively predictable, influence was found to be concentrated at the top of each organization, which was consequently less "democratic."

In organizations with effective integration, the reward system emphasized the achievement of *unified effort* rather than individual achievement.

Thus, relative to performance, the effective organization must exhibit the differentiation and integration demanded by the environment. As Lawrence and Lorsch say, "we have found that the state of differentiation in the effective organization was consistent with the diversity of the parts of the environment, while the state of integration achieved was consistent with the environmental demands for interdependence."

Relation to Other Studies. The findings of the Lawrence and Lorsch study provide an excellent framework for understanding and drawing together several of the studies reviewed so far in this chapter.

In a relatively predictable environment, decisions are more effectively made at the top of the organization, and we might expect to find a classical type of formal structure. In a highly unpredictable type of situation, in which all levels of management need considerable influence to deal with environmental uncertainty, a more participative structure along the lines suggested by Likert would be advisable. Recall that Woodward found in the medium technology group (i.e., large batch and mass production firms) that successful firms were classically organized while less successful firms were not. This medium technology group corresponds to Lawrence and Lorsch's high certainty group (i.e., the container industry). Since large batch and mass production technology is relatively predictable, Woodward's findings are consistent with those of Lawrence and Lorsch, and can be explained in terms of the relatively high degree of environmental certainty that accompanies large batch and mass production technology. Hall found that departments with predictable work had more hierarchical differentiation, greater division of labor, and more specified procedures than did the nonroutine departments, again in keeping with the Lawrence and Lorsch findings.

Udy concluded that technology would govern the method by which employees were rewarded, which is in keeping with the Lawrence and Lorsch findings that the integrating unit should be rewarded in terms of the unified result.

Further, Lawrence and Lorsch's theory and the supporting evidence also explain the findings of Simpson and Gulley (1962) and Aiken and Hage (1968). If it can be assumed that widespread environmental pressures and extensive organizational interdependence with other organizations increases environmental uncertainty, then Simpson and Gulley's and Aiken and Hage's findings that environmental pressures and interdependencies are associated with decentralization can be interpreted as indicating that organizations operating under conditions of uncertainty decentralize to permit adequate differentiation. The findings from both of these studies, that such organizations also place more emphasis on internal communication and coordination, can be interpreted as an effort to achieve adequate integration of their differentiated parts.

A study by Khandwalla (1974) sheds further light on how organizations adapt to environmental demands. Khandwalla selected a number of firms from each of several industries. He made the assumption that uncertainty is in part a function of the level of competition within the industry, and in part a function of the industry's rate of technological change. He found that, for high performing companies, the correlation between competition and uncertainty-reduction efforts, differentiation, and integration, was consistently greater than for low performing companies. The same pattern held, though to a lesser extent, when technological change was substituted for competition as an indicator of uncertainty. These findings are consistent with Proposition 1, and with Lawrence and Lorsch's theory, and also provide information about some of the techniques organizations use to accomplish differentiation, integration, and uncertainty-reduction. Khandwalla reasons that, as environmental uncertainty increases, so does planning difficulty, and therefore the need to reduce uncertainty. In his study uncertainty was reduced by the use of participative management, vertical integration, and increased use of information seeking and processing methods. Such devices result in reduction of uncertainty, but are also accompanied by increased differentiation and specialization of attitudes and functions. In his study differentiation was accomplished by decentralization, divisionalization, and functional departmentation.

A study by Child (1974, 1975) extends the findings of the prior studies to show how the environment and size of an organization interact with organization design. He studied the relationship between organizational structure, economic performance, and environmental factors in 80 British companies in six industries, selected to provide contrasting environments and sizes. Organizational practices and design factors were determined through standardized interviews, and performance was measured over the five-year period prior to the study. Measures of profitability and sales growth were also obtained.

Analysis of the joint relationship between environmental uncertainty and organizational size as it interacts with organizational structure to produce growth and profit revealed several findings consistent with contingency theory. It was found that as company size increased, so did the development of formalized and specialized organization structures of successful firms. Recall that formalization and specialization are, in Burns and Stalker's terms, characteristics of a mechanistic organization. The degree of such mechanistic attributes was significantly greater for companies in the more certain environment than for companies in the less certain environment. These findings indicate that it is necessary for an organization to become more formalized and specialized as it grows. Further, the amount of formalization and specialization required with growth is greater for organizations in certain environments. This finding is consistent with the findings of prior studies, but suggests that organizational size, as well as environment, influences organization structure.

Child's findings that organizational growth was associated with a tendency to hold down formalization and specialization constitutes an important phenomenon that will be dealt with in more detail in Chapter 22. If it is assumed that rapid organizational growth causes uncertainty among the firm's employees, then it follows from the theories and findings of Burns and Stalker (1961) and Lawrence and Lorsch (1967) that internal adjustment to the uncertainties associated with rapid growth will be impeded by mechanistic organizational characteristics such as formalization and specialization of activities.

The relevant research suggests support for this proposition. Studies by Pfeffer demonstrate that organizations seek to control environments by acquiring the necessary skill and social contacts to influence environmental factors. Furthermore, organizations simultaneously adapt to heterogeneous demands from complex environments by decentralization, and by such integration efforts as internal communication and having members emphasize involvement in organizational activities and actually engage in professional activities (Simpson and Gulley, 1962; Aiken and Hage, 1968; Khandwalla, 1974). Finally, studies by Lawrence and Lorsch (1967), Khandwalla (1974) and Child (1975) demonstrate more clearly how organizations accomplish differentiation and integration in the face of complex, heterogeneous, and uncertain environmental demands.

Proposition 2

Organizations seek to adjust to the demands of their technological core to permit economic and efficient coordination and scheduling of interdependent parts.

This proposition is based on the assumption that effective and efficient performance of the technological core of the organization requires that coordination and scheduling demands imposed by the technology are accommodated and facilitated by management practices. If such demands are facilitated, then scheduling and coordination of effort are possible. Thus, at the technical level of the organization, that is, the level engaged in performing the operations which produce the goods or services consumed by the client of the organization, it is argued that management strives to facilitate technological performance by (a) sealing off or buffering out unpredictable disturbances to the technological core, or (b) providing a structure that can react to, and accommodate, demands from the technological core.

Thus, the *managerial* level is viewed as mediating between the environment and the technological level of the organization, and serves the function of "ironing out some irregularities stemming from external sources, but also pressing the technological core for modifications as conditions alter" (Thompson, 1967, p. 12).

This line of reasoning leads to the conclusion that

> . . . differences in technological functions, or technologies, cause significant differences among organizations, and since the three levels (technical, managerial and institutional) are interdependent, differences in the technical functions should make for differences at managerial and institutional levels of the organization" (Thompson, 1967, p. 12).

Thompson's reference to the *institutional* level is intended to describe the highest organizational level, responsible for the "overall articulation of the organization and the institutional structure and agencies of the community" (Thompson, p. 11).

The theory which evolves from this line of thought has been called the *technological imperative* position, since it is argued that the technology imposes an imperative on the organization's design, i.e., on the form which the formal organizational factors take. For example, it is suggested that the appropriate span of control, number of organizational levels, and degree of formalization, standardization, and specialization are all to a significant extent determined by the technology of the organization.

One controversial aspect of the technological imperative position concerns the interaction between technology and organization size. Previous theorists and researchers (e.g., Weber, 1947; Filley, 1962, 1968) have asserted that the technological imperative holds only for small organizations, or those parts of large organizations that are interdependent with, or dependent on the technological core of the organization.

A second subject of controversy surrounding the technological imperative concerns the range of variables affected by the technology. Mohr (1971) and Hrebiniak (1974) have examined the relationship between technology and social interactions among organizational members, thus implying that the influence of technology and organizations may not be restricted to formal organizational factors, but may include informal social processes as well.

A series of laboratory experiments by Mackenzie (1975) is relevant to the issue of the technological imperative. Mackenzie conducted a series of experiments with five-person groups under controlled laboratory conditions. Each group performed one of two types of tasks. One task required only the strict application of a set of rules and a correct sequence of deductions. The other task required the generation of all combinations of a set of elements, combinations which could not be deduced and had to be inferred. The processes required to perform the tasks may be viewed as the tasks' technology.

Members were permitted to write messages to one another, and from these messages it was possible to determine the kind of organizational structure that emerged within each group, as well as the effects of that structure upon performance. Detailed results of these experiments are presented in Mackenzie (1975). In general it may be said that groups performing the deductive task had a much stronger tendency to develop a centralized communication pattern than groups performing the inferential task. That is, for deductive tasks one member, whose role was differentiated from the others, functioned as the central clearing house for exchange of all messages. During the period prior to the formation of centralized information channels there was a strong tendency for message content to be concerned with how the group communication channels were to be organized. However, once a centralized organization was established this tendency disappeared. Further, groups that established a centralized communication channel significantly outperformed groups that did not. They took less time, required fewer messages, and made fewer errors during the process of solving the problem.

The inferential tasks required more participation of all members, and therefore less centralization, in order to generate all possible solutions. Consequently, the lower the centralization, the higher was the group performance as evaluated by objective data such as number of messages, time required, and errors committed, and by subjective data gathered by administering a questionnaire to the subjects.

These experiments by Mackenzie and his associates demonstrate rather clearly that under controlled conditions, where extraneous factors such as organization size or variations in organizational environment are held constant, there is a clear technological imperative at work. The kind of organization structure that emerges is in direct response to the kind of task processes required of the small groups. Further, if the kind of structure that emerges fits the task requirements, the performance of the groups is superior to groups for which the structure is inappropriate.

An experimental study by Bridge, Doyle, and Mahan (1968) concerning the effects of hierarchical differentiation of group members on group productivity, efficiency, and risk taking is also revealing. These authors asked groups of four people to solve a problem requiring logic and creativity. Ten groups were composed of three teachers and a principal, all employed at the same school. These groups were considered hierarchically differentiated, since there was one person with higher formal status than the others. Ten other groups, composed of four teachers employed at the same school, were considered to be undifferentiated. These undifferentiated groups were found to be more productive and more efficient; they initiated more ideas and exhibited more risk-taking behavior.

Mackenzie's findings show that on deductive tasks not requiring creativity, a centralized form of organization, which necessarily entails high differentiation of member roles, is more effective. Bridge, Doyle, and Mahan's findings suggest that, on tasks which *do* require creativity, differentiation impedes creativity. It should be kept in mind, however, that these were experimental conditions; under natural conditions other factors are likely to be important influences upon relationships between technology, structure, and performance.

Harvey (1968) reported findings somewhat in conflict with Woodward's, but consistent with those of Hall, Mackenzie, and Bridge, Doyle, and Mahan. Harvey examined the organizational structures of firms with various levels of technological complexity, measured by computing the average number of different products produced and introduced during the preceding ten years. He computed an index which measured the degree of technical *diffuseness* (many products and product changes) versus technical *specificity* (few products and product changes).

He found that the greater the technical specificity, the greater the tendency to be organized in a mechanistic manner. To the extent that Harvey's high specificity class is similar to Woodward's continuous process production firms, their findings vary because Woodward found a tendency for this class of firms to be organic where Harvey found a tendency for them to be mechanistic. Unfortunately, there is not enough information given to determine whether this inconsistency is due to the type of firms in the samples, or to some other factor not considered by the researchers.

Subsequent studies by Zwereman (1970) and Keller, Slocum, and Susman (1974) have examined organization structures among continuous production firms with technologies similar to those of Woodward's high technologically-complex firms. The results of both studies are consistent with those of Woodward's initial findings. However, a study by Hage and

Aiken (1969) reveals additional findings that appear to conflict with Woodward's. Specifically, Hage and Aiken found that routine tasks were associated with decentralized decision making, the presence of rules, manuals governing standard operating procedures and job descriptions, and highly specified and specialized jobs. The more routine the task, the greater efficiency and quantity were emphasized, and the less quality of service and morale were emphasized. Finally, routine tasks were found to be negatively related to the amount of professional training, and to have little association with other measures of organizational complexity.

It is possible that the discrepancy in the studies by Woodward, Zwereman, and Keller, Slocum, and Susman, as compared to those by Harvey and Hage and Aiken, is due to the differences in their measures. To the extent that continuous process production technology frees individuals from routine tasks by having routine physical tasks performed by production machinery, it is possible that most tasks performed by humans under such technological conditions are nonroutine. If this is found to be the case in future research, the apparent conflict in results could be explained in terms of the level of routineness of tasks associated with continuous process technology.

Hickson, Pugh, and Pheysey (1969) analyzed the relationship between technology and organization structure among 46 diverse organizations and found that, overall, technology had only a weak relationship with mechanistic elements of structure. They thus offered a new interpretation of the relationship between size, technology, and structure:

> . . . structural variables will be associated with operations technology only where they are centered on workflow. The smaller the organization the more its structure will be pervaded by such technological effects: the larger the organization the more these effects will be confined to variables such as job counts of employees on activities linked with the workflow itself, and will not be detectable in variables of the more remote administrative hierarchical structure (pp. 394–95).

Further, Blau and Schoenherr (1971) in a study of U.S. employment security agencies, found significant relationships between size, utilization of computers, specialization, extent of regulations, number of hierarchical levels, and decentralization.

Child and Mansfield (1972) analyzed data collected from 89 organizations in six industries in England and Scotland. They found that size, more than technology, accounted for differences in organization structure. Further, they found that for small firms (with less than approximately 200 employees) technology had a stronger relationship to several mechanistic organizational characteristics, such as formalization, standardization, and decentralization, than for larger firms. They also found technology to have a lesser association with the formalized organizational structural characteristics of staff and service functions removed from the production work flow than with functions directly associated with the manufacturing process (such as maintenance). Finally, they found that as technology became more continuous and rigid, specialization in functions directly associated with the manufacturing process increased and became more formalized for highly successful companies, but not for less successful companies.

Khandwalla (1974) reported study results relating the use of mass output technology to environment, vertical integration, internal differentiation, and integration of internal organizational activities. He asked company presidents to indicate the extent to which each of five technologies (custom, small batch, large batch, mass production, and continuous) was used in their firm's manufacturing process. From custom to continuous, these technologies represent an increasing degree of "mass output orientation." Khandwalla reasoned that the greater the use of mass output technology, the greater would be the need to insulate the technological core from the environment in order to facilitate scheduling, coordination, etc. He further reasoned that *vertical integration* would be one method to accomplish such insulation.

> For example, a firm manufacturing steel may acquire limestone quarries and coal and iron mines to secure itself against possible future fluctuation in the supplies and prices of these crucial raw materials. A firm producing automobiles may acquire retail outlets for its cars if competition with other automobile firms introduces uncertainties in the normal distribution network (Khandwalla, 1974, p. 78).

Such vertical integration naturally results in an increase in the range of organizational activities, which in turn results in internal differentiation of the activities. According to this argument, internal differentiation leads to delegation of authority by the chief executive because it is unlikely that the chief executive will be able to supervise the diverse sub-organization within the vertically integrated whole, or directly manage the highly specialized operations in such functional areas as operations, marketing, finance, and personnel. However, as Lawrence and Lorsch had reasoned, Khandwalla also argues that a differentiated organization must use integrative coordinative mechanisms, such as sophisticated controls, to perform effectively.

Based on this reasoning Khandwalla advances a theory containing a number of hypotheses, three of which are presented below:

(I) The more mass-output oriented the technology used by an organization, the more vertically integrated it is likely to be.

(II) The more vertically integrated the organization is, the more decentralized is its top level decision making likely to be.

(III) The more decentralized the top level decision making, the more the organization is likely to use sophisticated controls to coordinate the activities of the organizations.

These hypotheses were tested against data collected by means of a questionnaire sent to presidents of 79 American manufacturing firms.

Khandwalla found, consistent with the findings of Hickson, Pugh, and Pheysey (1969) and Child and Mansfield (1972) that firm size was fairly strongly related to measures of organization structure. He also found that technology and dimensions of organization structure were significantly correlated, independent of size. (The measures of organization structure involved were vertical integration, decentralization, and the use of sophisticated controls.) Khandwalla found considerable support for the three hypotheses.

To resolve questions of optimal organizational adaptation to technology, he divided his sample into sub-samples of 38 relatively profitable and 41 relatively unprofitable firms. The two sub-samples were alike in other respects, such as size and distribution of their industry membership.

When correlations between mass-output orientation and organizational characteristics were computed separately for each sub-sample, the correlations for the profitable group showed stronger support for Khandwalla's hypotheses than correlations for the other group. Therefore, this research supports the desirability, from a profitability standpoint, of having balanced and congruent technology, vertical integration, decentralization, and sophisticated controls.

Most of the research described so far has considered the effects of the technological imperative upon formal aspects of organizational design. However, Mohr (1971) and Hrebiniak (1974) have interpreted the technological imperative to include its effects on social processes and interaction patterns within the organization, as well as on formal structure. Mohr failed to support the hypothesis that technology (as measured by uniformity, complexity, and analyzability to task and materials) is a primary determinant of the extent to which supervisory styles are participative. However, he did find other aspects of technology at least moderately related to participativeness of supervision. These included such things as noise level of the job (which may interfere with the consultative process) and interdependence of tasks (which influences supervisor-subordinate interaction patterns). Even these relationships, however, were not particularly strong, probably because many other factors contribute to the determination of supervisory styles.

Hrebiniak (1974) argued that the effects of technology on work group interaction patterns may be either enhanced or hampered by the kind of controls employed by the organization. Specifically, Hrebiniak argued that the more the organization relied on fragmented and decentralized control techniques rather than integrated and centralized techniques, personal rather than impersonal directions and feedback, and personal expertise rather than impersonal role-based authority, the less impact the technology would have on organization structure. Hrebiniak's investigation took place in a hospital, where control was highly fragmented, but where supervisors were subjected to varied amounts of impersonal control.

Hrebiniak found that (a) the more impersonal control was imposed on a supervisor from the organization, the more the organization was described by supervisors as being mechanistic; and (b) the more tasks were routine, manageable, predictable, and noninterdependent with others, the more mechanistic was the work group's structure. Thus Hrebiniak demonstrated, as have most of the other studies reviewed in this section, that there exists a technological imperative. He found that organizational structure varies, as predicted, with task technology, but that other factors (such as the amount of control imposed on supervisors, and the behavior of supervisors toward subordinates) were also significantly related to work group interaction patterns which presumably reflect differences in structure.

Summary

Proposition 1: Organizations seek to control their environments. If control of the environments is not possible, organizations seek to adapt to the demands of their environments in such a manner as to meet the economic and instrumental efficiency criteria imposed by the environments. Specifically, organizations seek to control environments by increasing their power over environmental units, and seek to adapt to environments by monitoring environmental demands and by designing structures and practices to permit effective response to such demands. *Consistently supported.*

Proposition 2: Organizations seek to adjust to the demands of their technological core to permit economical and efficient coordination and scheduling of interdependent parts. *This proposition is consistently supported for small organizations, for those parts of the larger organization that have direct interaction with the technological core, and in laboratory studies; not supported at higher organization levels of large organizations.*

General Conclusions

Overall, the research concerned with relationships between technology, size, and organizational structure leads to the following conclusions:

1. Organizational structure is in large measure related to the extent to which control over the environment is possible. The greater the predictability and controllability of the dominant technology, the greater will be the tendency for the organization to be mechanistic at those levels where individuals must respond to technological demands.
2. Social processes and task structure at the lower organizational levels are significantly influenced by the kind of control systems imposed on supervisors at these levels, and by the supervisor's behavior toward subordinates at these levels.
3. With increases in size, and at higher levels removed from the technology, the organization's formal structure is weakly and inconsistently influenced by technology. It may be that at the higher levels optimal organizational structure is more a function of the environment than of technological

characteristics. However, additional research will be required to shed further light on this issue.

References

Aiken, M., and Hage, J. 1968. Organizational interdependence and intra-organizational structure. *American Sociological Review* 33: 219-30.

Argyris, C. 1964. *Integrating the individual and the organization.* Wiley.

———. 1957. *Personality and organization: The conflict between system and individual.* Harper & Row.

Blau, P. M., and Schoenherr, R. A. 1971. *The structure of organizations.* Basic Books.

Bobbitt, H. R., Jr.; Brienholt, R. H.; Doktor, R. H.; and McNaul, J. P. 1974. *Organizational behavior: Understanding and prediction.* Prentice-Hall.

Bridge, E. M., Doyle, W. J., and Mahan, D. J. 1968. Effects of hierarchical differentiation on group productivity, efficiency and risk taking. *Administrative Science Quarterly* 13: 305–19.

Burns, T., and Stalker, G. M. 1961. *The management of innovation.* Tavistock.

Child, J. 1974. Managerial and organizational factors associated with company performance, Part I: A contingency analysis. *The Journal of Management Studies* 11: 175–89.

———. 1975. Managerial and organizational factors associated with company performance, Part II: A contingency analysis. *The Journal of Management Studies* 12: 12–27.

———., and Mansfield, R. 1972. Technology, size, and organization structure. *Sociology* 6: 369-93.

Filley, A. C. 1968. A study of business growth. Unpublished Study, University of Wisconsin.

———. 1962. A theory of small business and divisional growth. Doctoral Dissertation, Ohio State University.

Fisch, G. G. 1961. Line-staff is obsolete. *The Harvard Business Review* 39: 67-69.

Hage, J., and Aiken, M. 1969. Routine technology, social structure and organization goals. *Administrative Science Quarterly* 14: 366-76.

Hall, A. D., and Fagin, R. E. 1956. Definition of a system. *General Systems* 1: 18.

Hall, R. H. 1962. Intraorganizational structural variation. *Administrative Science Quarterly* 7: 295-308.

Harvey, E. 1968. Technology and the structure of organizations. *American Sociological Review* 33: 247-58.

Hellriegel, D., and Slocum, J. W., Jr. 1974. *Management: A contingency approach.* Addison-Wesley.

Hickson, D. J., Pugh, D. S., and Pheysey, D. 1969. Operations technology and organization structure: An empirical reappraisal. *Administrative Science Quarterly* 14: 378-97.

House, R. J., and Kerr, S. 1973. Organizational independence, leader behavior, and managerial practices: A replicated study. *Journal of Applied Psychology* 58: 173-80.

———., and Rizzo, J. R. 1972. Role conflict and ambiguity as critical variables in a model of organizational behavior. *Organizational Behavior and Human Performance* 7: 467-505.

Hrebiniak, L. G. 1974. Job technology, supervision, and work group structure. *Administrative Science Quarterly* 19: 395-410.

Hulin, C. L., and Blood, M. R. 1968. Job enlargement, individual differences, and worker responses. *Psychological Bulletin* 69: 41-55.

Keller, R. T., Slocum, J. W., Jr., and Susman, G. I. 1974. Uncertainty and type of management system in continuous process organizations. *Academy of Management Journal* 17: 56-68.

Khandwalla, P. N. 1974. Mass output orientation of operations technology and organization structure. *Administrative Science Quarterly* 19: 74-97.

Krupp, S. 1961. *Pattern in organization analysis: A critical examination.* Holt, Rinehart and Winston (paperback reprint, 1964).

Lawrence, P., and Lorsch, J. 1967. *Organization and environment.* Division of Research, Graduate School of Business Administration, Harvard University.

Likert, R. 1961. *New patterns in management.* McGraw-Hill.

Mackenzie, K. D. 1975. *A theory of group structures.* Monograph, University of Kansas.

McGregor, D. 1960. *The human side of enterprise.* McGraw-Hill.

Mohr, L. B. 1971. Organization technology and organizational structure. *Administrative Science Quarterly* 16: 444-59.

Pfeffer, J. 1972a. Interorganization influence and managerial attitudes. *Academy of Management Journal* 15: 317-30.

———. 1972b. Size and composition of corporate boards of directors: The organization and its environment. *Administrative Science Quarterly* 17: 219-28.

———. 1972c. Merger as a response to organizational interdependence. *Administrative Science Quarterly* 17: 382-94.

Simon, H. A. 1958. *Administrative behavior,* rev. ed. Macmillan.

———. 1964. On the concept of organization goal. *Administrative Science Quarterly.* (Reprinted in *Studies in managerial process and organizational behavior,* ed. by J. H. Turner, A. C. Filley, and R. J. House. Scott, Foresman, 1972.)

Simpson, R. L., and Gulley, W. H. 1962. Goals, environmental pressures, and organizational characteristics. *American Sociological Review* 27: 344-51.

Thompson, J. D. 1967. *Organizations in action.* McGraw-Hill.

Udy, S. H., Jr. 1962. Administrative rationality, social setting, and organizational development. *American Journal of Sociology* 68: 299-308.

———. 1958. "Bureaucratic" elements in organizations: Some research findings. *American Sociological Review* 23: 415-18.

———. 1961. Technical and institutional factors in production organization. *American Journal of Sociology* 67: 247-54.

Vroom, V. H. 1959. Some personality determinants of participation. *Journal of Abnormal and Social Psychology* 59: 322-27.

Weber, M. 1947. *Theory of social and economic organization* (1921). Tr. and ed. by A. M. Henderson and T. Parsons. The Free Press.

Woodward, J. 1965. *Industrial organization: Theory and practice.* Oxford University Press.

Zwereman, W. 1970. *New perspectives on organization theory.* Westport.

Chapter **14**

Objectives and Policy

"Would you tell me, please, which way I ought to go from here?"
"That depends a good deal on where you want to go to," said the Cat.
"I don't much care where," said Alice.
"Then it doesn't matter which way you go," said the Cat.

LEWIS CARROLL
Alice in Wonderland

Objectives relate to the motives which underlie individual and organizational behavior, and to the values toward which action is directed as a result of these motives. *Policy* refers to the formal strategies and decision rules *by which* objectives are to be reached. Policies are guides through which organizational members are directed toward objectives.

A related distinction can be made between the *means of achieving* objectives and *ends* of objectives. For example, a policy that the organization "pay equal or greater salaries than our competition in the labor market" may be a good means of attaining the objective of a "constant state" of technology in the organization. To the extent that the strategy proves ineffective in accomplishing such a constant state, it may be abandoned. Should "equal or better pay" become an objective rather than a policy, however, to be pursued regardless of its contribution toward a steady state, the results could be disastrous.

This illustration of a case where "the means become the ends" is the most common form of *goal displacement,* defined by Etzioni (1964, p. 10) as occurring "when an organization displaces its goal—that is, substitutes for its legitimate goal some other goal for which it was not created, for which resources were not allocated to it, and which it is not known to serve."

A number of reasons for goal displacement have been proposed. Sills (1970, p. 227) relates the problem to the means-end hierarchy to be described shortly:

> . . . Members to whom authority and functions have been delegated often come to regard them as ends in themselves, rather than as means toward the achievement of organizational goals. As a result of this process, the activities of the organization become centered around the proper functioning of organizational procedures, rather than upon the achievement of the initial goals.

Clearly, this is most likely to happen in cases where the official goals of the organization have not been communicated to lower-level employees. In such cases the means-end hierarchy will, unfortunately, serve as the means whereby "the official goals of the organization are neglected in favor of goals associated with building or maintaining the organization" (Kast and Rosenzweig, 1974, p. 165). Even when communication of official goals does occur, however, some employees tend to take refuge in the rules and regulations of the enterprise, thinking that they can immunize themselves from responsibility and blame by doing so.

What conditions stimulate such self-protective and defensive tendencies in employees? Blau and Scott (1962) believe that a key factor is the relationship between an organization and its environment. They see a hostile environment as leading the organization toward goal displacement, whereas a friendly one is more likely to result in *goal succession,* which is a conscious, intentional replacement of one goal with another, either because the original goal has been met or because it seemingly cannot be met.

Objectives

The word *objective* may be taken to mean either a personal aspiration or a value to be attained through the performance of some activity. In the first sense objectives are states of motivation derived from the needs of a particular individual. Such objectives are personal, attached to individuals and not to organizations. In the second sense, as values to be attained, objectives can be sought by individuals *or* by organizations. Values defined by a group or an organization constitute *organizational* objectives. The distinction between organizational purposes and individual motives is an important one.

> It is frequently assumed in reasoning about organizations that common purpose and individual motive are or should be identical. With the exception noted below, this is never the case; and under modern conditions it rarely even appears to be the case. Individual motive is necessarily an internal, personal, subjective thing; common purpose is necessarily an external, impersonal, objective thing even though the individual interpretation of it is subjective. The only exception to this general rule, an important one, is that the accomplishment of an organization purpose becomes itself a source of personal satisfaction and a motive for many individuals in many organizations (Barnard, 1938, p. 85).

Individual Objectives

Members of organizations have long been considered by classical management theorists (see Chapter 1) to be passive agents or tools through which the work of the enterprise was accomplished; their objectives have been characterized as the satisfaction of purely material needs. The classicist, then, described the organization

> . . . as consisting of an entrepreneur (either the top of the managerial hierarchy or some external control group such as stockholders) and a staff. The goals of the organization are then defined to be the goals of the entrepreneur. Conformity to these goals is purchased by payments. . . . In return for such payments employees contract to perform whatever is required of them—at least within the range of permissible requirements. For a price, the employee adopts the "organization" goal (Cyert and March, 1963, pp. 28–29).

As Chapter 10 suggested, most modern theorists recognize that inducements other than financial rewards often motivate individuals to contribute to organizational objectives. According to behavioral theory, it is essential that managers be aware of the needs individuals expect to satisfy through organizational membership, that is, the rewards they require in return for the investment of their time and effort. These rewards are necessary to induce their continued contribution to the organization. To the extent that management is aware of what individuals want in return for their contributions, it may be possible to structure and operate the organization in such a way that it affords individuals opportunities to attain their individual objectives in a manner which contributes to major organizational objectives. Therefore, objectives may be viewed not only as a basis for designing an organization, but also as a tool for eliciting motivation and teamwork from the members of an organization.

Organizational Objectives

An interesting question concerning organizational objectives was addressed by Barnard (1938), who considered

> . . . whether the whole is more than the sum of the parts; whether a system should be considered as merely an aggregate of its components; whether a system of cooperative efforts, that is, an organization, is something more or less than or different from its constituent efforts; whether there emerge from the system properties which are not inherent in the parts (p. 79).

Barnard went on to conclude that the organization was indeed more than a mere aggregate of its components, that in fact organizations—and each of their components—have objectives which are uniquely organizational. The existence of the organization then becomes closely identified with, and dependent upon, the achievement of those objectives.

Primary Objectives. In 1951, R. C. Davis proposed a classification of organizational objectives into primary, secondary, and social. The primary objectives of the organization are defined in terms of those whom the organization serves.

The organization attains its primary objectives by providing salable values as defined by its market. Through the provision of these values the organization is able to reward its participating members. As an example of the way a primary objective is factored into parts that specific organizational units or members can accomplish, consider the case of an automobile manufacturer. Its primary goal may be said to be the provision of a line of automobiles and trucks which will be judged by the potential market to be desirable. The primary goal of a passenger-car division within the firm is the provision of automobiles desired by the potential market for that car. The primary goal of an assembly plant within the division is the assembly of autos in a manner which provides the value desired by the customer. The primary goal of a small department within the assembly plant may be to produce a particular component which will later become a part of the finished automobile. In such a fashion, it is possible to trace primary goals down to the level of the job assignment filled by individual members.

This example also serves to illustrate the operation of the *means-ends hierarchy,* mentioned earlier:

> The fact that goals may be dependent for their force on other more distant ends leads to the arrangement of these goals in a hierarchy—each level to be considered as an end relative to the levels below it and as a means relative to the levels above it. Through the hierarchical structure of ends, behavior attains integration and consistency, for each member of a set of behavior alternatives is then weighted in terms of a comprehensive scale of values—the "ultimate" ends. In actual behavior, a high degree of conscious integration is seldom attained. Instead of a single branching hierarchy, the structure of conscious motives is usually a tangled web or, more precisely, a disconnected collection of elements only weakly and incompletely tied together; and the integration of these elements becomes progressively weaker as the higher levels of the hierarchy—the more final ends—are reached (Simon, 1957, p. 63).

The "disconnected collection of elements" is only one of several problems cited by Simon and others, which leads to the conclusion that caution must be observed in applying the means-ends hierarchy to any analysis of human behavior in organizations.

Secondary Objectives. Secondary objectives are instrumental in attaining primary objectives. Like primary objectives they are impersonal in nature, and are specifically directed at accomplishing economy and efficiency in the performance of the organization's work. Traditionally, secondary objectives have been thought to be the responsibility of staff components within the organization, which perform such supportive auxiliary tasks as analysis, coordination, interpretation, facilitation, and advice. Theoretically the line organization directs its attention to meeting primary goals, while the staff helps assure that operations performed by the line are economical and efficient. In practice the distinction is far less clear, as will be evident from the discussion of line and staff in Chapter 17.

As an illustration, the personnel department in a manufacturing organization would not contribute directly to providing sales value. Rather, it would contribute indirectly by assisting managers in hiring and efficiently using employees, and by fostering harmonious relations between employees and management. The personnel department may therefore be said to contribute directly only to the secondary organizational objectives and, through achievement of these secondary objectives, to support the organization's efforts to achieve its primary objectives.

Social Objectives. Organizations also have obligations to meet objectives above and beyond those already mentioned. For example, a corporation is legally considered a person through its charter and, day by day, community expectations that it honor its social responsibilities are increasing.

Today society apparently requires from most organizations more than purely economic contributions. At a minimum the organization is obligated to perform as a law-abiding "citizen." It must not violate conditions that have been established by the community in such areas as health, safety, minimum wages, child labor, restraint of trade, labor practices, price regulation, and pollution. Social objectives must be established by the organization so that, at a minimum, they meet these community-imposed conditions.

Additionally, the organization may elect to serve as a dynamic, participating, involved citizen of its community. Its activities would then include contributions to the social, moral, and physical betterment of its environment, and might take the form of financial support as well as less tangible encouragement of community and civic activities.

Alternative Classifications

Since 1951, a number of authors have proposed alternative classifications for organizational objectives. One of these, put forth by Drucker (1954) included the following subgoals:

1. Market standing
2. Innovation
3. Productivity
4. Physical and financial resources
5. Profitability
6. Manager performance and development
7. Worker performance and attitude
8. Public responsibility

One year later, the General Electric Company attempted to classify subgoals by addressing the question: In which areas will continued failure prevent the fulfillment of management's responsibility for advancing GE as a leader in a strong, competitive economy, even if results in all other key areas are good (Lewis, 1955)? Several resulting subgoals were identical to those on Drucker's list (market standing, productivity, profitability, and public responsibility), while others were similar (product leadership, personnel development, and employee attitudes). The only subgoal appearing on the General Electric list which is clearly different from Drucker's is one pertaining to "balance between short-range and long-range goals."

More recently, Perrow (1970) has proposed a broader classification, which is not so much directed toward business firms as toward organizations in general. His classification of objectives include:

1. Societal goals—these refer more to collectivities of organizations than to any particular firm's goals, and have "little to do with functioning organizations."
2. Output goals—objectives aimed at satisfying the organization's potential market.
3. System goals—objectives having to do with the organization itself, such as high profit, large market share, growth, and economy of operation.
4. Product goals—characteristics of the goods or services produced.
5. Derived goals—a "residual category" for political aims, community service, etc.

As was true of each of the other classifications described, the distinctions among Perrow's types of objectives are not nearly as clear in practice as they might seem in theory.

Policy

When pressed for a definition of "policy," managers will often cite rules (e.g., "promote from within"), goals (e.g., "growth"), or vague statements about values (e.g., "public service"). Even academicians have difficulty in agreeing on the true nature of policy; in his analysis of policy and decision making, Nicolaidis (1960, p. 74) synthesized eleven different meanings of the term into the following definition:

> Policy is a rule for action, manifesting or clarifying specific organization goals, objectives, values or ideals and often prescribing the obligatory or most desirable ways and means for their accomplishment. Such a rule for action established for the purpose of framing, guiding, or directing organizational activities, including decision-making, intends to provide relative stability, consistency, uniformity, and continuity in the operations of the organization.

Note the characteristics that are stressed in this definition:

1. Policy is a *guide to action,* directing organizational activities toward prescribed goals.
2. Policy *limits behavior* by prescribing methods of goal accomplishment which are judged to be legitimate. Policy statements may place *positive limits* ("should"), *negative limits* ("should not"), or *value constraints* "good" or "bad") on behavior.
3. Policy is an *aid to decision making.* It establishes decision rules which can be used by a decision maker to judge the acceptability or unacceptability of alternative strategies of action or solutions to a problem.
4. Policy serves the need of a collective enterprise for behavior which is *stable, consistent, uniform, and viable* (Pfiffner, 1960).

Importance of Policy

The operation of all organizations is governed by some system of rules, guides, constraints, and procedures. This is as true of sandlot baseball teams, families, small businesses, and government agencies as it is of large-scale industrial enterprises. The specific system may vary considerably from organization to organization, but the basic principle continues to hold: If two or more people are to carry out an activity over an extended period of time, a regular pattern of relationships must be established so that all persons concerned will have some basis for predicting the consequences of their actions.

When there is no clear basis for such prediction, members often become frustrated and dissatisfied, and find membership less attractive. There will be a lack of coordination, and conflict may result. Thus one characteristic of an effective and efficient organization is the presence of a predictable pattern of interpersonal relationships (Stogdill, 1959). Such a pattern can result from precedent, custom, and tradition, as in tribal law; from the personal influence of a single individual, as in a dictatorship; from formalized agreement, as under constitutional law; or from emergent norms established by a group of people who work together.

It is perhaps ironic that the existence of policies, which seemingly serve to *restrict* freedom of action, simultaneously *provide* freedom of action. Chapter 17 discusses more fully the research which shows that too much of a "laissez-faire" attitude by top management, accompanied by a lack of policies, structure, etc., can produce as undesirable a situation as the more celebrated case where individuals are totally "boxed in" by excessive rules, procedures, and policies. One important reason for this is that, as a system of law, rational policies limit the discretion of managers in dealing with their subordinates. In part, this discretion is limited because management rules for dealing with subordinates must be legitimate, and the legitimacy of rules depends upon their relationship to formal objectives and their acceptability to subordinates. This is another way of saying that the laws of the organization must be "constitutional." As stated by Vollmer (1960, p. 31):

> . . . Once formal rules and regulations are established governing the types of offenses for which disciplinary action may be taken, management itself is constrained to obey these same rules. In other words, management is placed under a severe "burden of proof" in cases where managers administer discipline for causes other than those specifically enumerated in the regulations.

In addition to increasing the predictability of organizational members and constraining personal and arbitrary acts of discipline by managers, policy also permits a greater degree of decentralization within the organization. Inasmuch as policy deters deviations from planned courses of action by suggesting rules of action and by making clear why these rules should be followed, and since the entire organization is presumably guided by the same basic principles, policy increases the likelihood that action will be consistent and facilitates coordination and cooperation. It fosters intelligent exercises of initiative in that it helps individuals know what is expected of them. It also provides a guide to determine equitable personnel relations by defining rules that apply to all.

The effective delegation of decision making to subordinates is also greatly aided by workable policy. Decentralized decision making frees higher executives to deal primarily with exceptions to policy. Where subordinates have policy guidelines, they can better make their own decisions. Where exceptions to policy seem warranted, or where no policy exists, the matter can be referred to a higher executive. In fact, one symptom of a weak policy system is the involvement of higher-level executives with routine matters, or frequent "appeals" from subordinates for definitions of new policy.

Types of Policy

To account for the operation of a large organization and to analyze it effectively, we must understand its pattern of relationships. These patterns fall into various types: policy by tradition; policy by fiat; and regulated or rational policy.

Policy by Tradition. Traditional policy is determined by history and precedent. In its extreme form such policy is static and rigid, an end in itself beyond any rational evaluation. For example, in the feudal cultures of Medieval Europe, tradition assigned the social role of serfdom by birth, and ranked the levels of personal power within the feudal system according to age, ownership of resources, title, and inheritance. The traditional system also prescribed a policy of three-year crop rotation in agriculture; planting oats, peas, or beans the first year, wheat or barley the second year, then allowing the land to lie fallow during the third year. Today this system of crop rotation would be dismissed as unscientific, yet it remained unchallenged for a long time because it was traditional and the tradition was not questioned.

It is likely that there was, initially, some rational basis for most long-established traditional policies. However, once behavior becomes rigid and habitual, those who adhere to the policies expect and require neither explanation nor reason. Instead, traditional practices are often accepted as part of the natural order of things.

Traditional policies can probably be found to exist to some degree in all organizations, since institutions tend to establish a kind of "common law" that is accepted even by those who, if asked, would be hard pressed to give a reason for it. It may begin with a management decision which creates a precedent, which then persists long after the reason for the decision has been forgotten and after the circumstances prompting it no longer exist. When such a policy becomes merely a part of the customs of the organizational culture, and affects conduct only in minor ways, it may have little effect on efficiency; when it leads to rigid, fixed behavior in an environment which requires change, however, the consequences can be serious.

Policy by Fiat. Policy by fiat entails the arbitrary pronouncement of policy by a single individual. Such policy is illustrated by the centralized improvisation of day-to-day policies by a promoter or an entrepreneur, and tends to bind subordinates to the source of policy—the individual—since it is frequently necessary to "touch base" with the boss to obtain redefinition or clarification. Since the boss may change the rules at any moment, subordinates have difficulty in judging how they should act in any given instance; they therefore have little freedom to act in the boss' absence, which may result in the kind of frustration expressed in Walter Chrysler's description of his problems as general manager of Buick Division under G.M. President William Durant:

> A number of arguments (over policy) occurred during our three years together. I remember I went to see him once and said, "Billy, for the love of God, please, now say what your policies are for General Motors. I'll work on them; whatever they are, I'll work to make them effective. Leave the operations alone; the building, the buying, the selling and all the men—leave them alone, but say what your policies are!"
>
> Billy laughed at me. "Walt, I believe in changing the policies just as often as my office door opens and closes" (Dale, 1960, p. 76).

In many instances policy by fiat has undesirable effects, but where the situation is fluid and uncertain, it may be necessary. For example, promoters who lead mass movements or build industrial empires must often direct group efforts under rapidly changing conditions. Lacking precedent, they may play upon the resources of the organization, guided primarily by their intuition. William Durant is an example of such a person, as is Henry Ford.

In general, policy by fiat may afford great freedom and satisfaction to the individual who originates it, but may provide little freedom and satisfaction to those who must try to anticipate what is expected of them. It is quite inconsistent with decentralized decision making, since under policy by fiat organization members are most likely to be satisfied when they share a high degree of interaction and a high degree of expectation of rewards to be gained through their efforts. Such a situation is often exemplified in mass movements and revolutions.

Rational Policy: Rule of Law. To violate traditional policy is usually considered to be immoral; to violate rational policy is illegal. While traditional policy requires unquestioning obedience, rational policy may be changed as conditions change, and even allows for exceptions.

Rational policy serves the same purpose in organizations that the "rule of law" serves for nations. Law expresses the values and codes of behavior by which a society, formally and explicitly, chooses to operate. It is stable and predictable, and frees any one member of the society from the arbitrary acts of another. The rule of law may be legislated or it may be established through interpretation by a judicial body.

In an organization, rational policies are typically initiated by top management. Individual administrators can make policy, but policy making can also be effectively handled by a group. The board of directors makes policy in most companies, and nearly every large firm has a "policy committee" made up of principal corporate officers—for example, the coordinating committees in Standard Oil of New Jersey and United States Steel, and the executive committee of DuPont.

The notion that objectives and policy should be defined by a group, and that this group be separated from those who administer the policy, is found in the classic literature of public administration. For example, Pfiffner and Sherwood (1960) cite the ineffectiveness of the old Continental Congress which, faced with both legislative and administrative duties, was unable to function smoothly. Observation of this weakness by those establishing other governmental bodies led to the development of the council-manager model in which the functions of legislation and administration were separated. The National Labor Relations Board suffered from similar problems until it was reorganized by the Taft-Hartley Act in 1947, when a five-man judicial board was separated from the newly established General Counsel.

Ideally, rational policy should originate in legislative groups, leaving administrators to act within the policy limits. This pattern is seen in school districts where a school board sets policy and a superintendent administers it, and in businesses which have boards or policy committees to set policy and presidents to administer it. Practically speaking, however, much policy will continue to be made by individuals.

In the modern corporation, the rule of law is usually expressed in policies or principles of operation, and the policies are generally supplemented by procedures, job descriptions, committee minutes, standards of performance, formal planning and control techniques, organization charts, etc. These supplementary documents explain how policies should be carried out, and add consistency and continuity to organizational operations.

Group Norms. Norms which emerge from groups working together are another kind of "policy." They serve as guides to make behavior predictable, but lack the permanence of traditional policy and do not rely upon the policy-generating sources of tradition, fiat, or rational legislation. Group norms represent the need of group members for a set of ground rules governing their behavior in the group. Norms are seldom articulated in any formal sense, but are usually enforced by group members.

For example, it was mentioned in Chapter 1 that the Hawthorne studies revealed that work groups established informal production standards. These informal standards dictated that no worker should be a "rate buster" and work too fast, or a "chiseler" and work too slow. These norms were enforced by group members by striking offenders on the arm or by rejecting them socially.

Interaction of Types of Policy

All organizations contain some combination of the types of policy described above, although one type is likely to predominate at a single point in time. Policies change over time, as when rational policies become traditional. There are two reasons for this. First, the desire of many people for guides to behavior and for clues to the ways others will behave is so strong that they come to prefer fixed rules to more flexible guidelines, and eventually begin to regard rules as ends in themselves. Second, as obedience to the rules becomes habitual, there is a tendency to continue using them long after the reason for their existence is forgotten. At this point, Anshen's recounting of the classic remark "Why do we do things this way? There is no reason; it's our policy" becomes appropriate (1960, p. 72).

As previously stated, when conditions are fairly static, traditional policy may suffice. However, even when the need for change suggests that traditional policy be abandoned, the substitution of policy by rule of law is often very difficult. Sometimes, the structure of tradition may be shattered by a charismatic leader. For example, when Lawrence of Arabia planned to cross the desert to the sea, he was told by the Arabs that he could not do so. When Lawrence asked why, he was told "It is written" (a clear example of traditional policy). Lawrence replied emphatically "Nothing is written!"

Just as the necessity for change may cause change from policy by tradition to policy by fiat, the subsequent reduction of the need for change in favor of a need for stability and efficiency may cause a further change, to policy by rule of law. As Boulding (1958, p. 433) states:

> The heroes break through the crust of the established order to set great dynamic processes in motion—these are the prophets, the saints, the poets, the conquerors, the revolutionaries. Then the prudent come

> along behind them and fit the pieces together into a new establishment; these are the priests and the popes, the professors, the politicians and the businessmen. Without the heroes society soon settles down into a dull and self-perpetuating equilibrium; without the prudent society flies apart, disintegrates into chaos.

While it may appear that traditional rule is most often followed by rule of fiat and then rule by law, there are also many cases where traditional rule is appraised and revised by executives directly into rule by law. Each individual situation dictates whether policy will be revised by revolution or by evolution.

Developing Rational Policy

For rational policy to follow the ideal form described in classical literature, it should contain both a set of specific *guides*, or constraints to govern action, and a *principle* which states the justification or logical reason for the guides (Davis, 1951; Davis and Filley, 1962). For example:

> *Principle:* Chemicals used in certain stages of the production process are highly flammable. Care must be taken to avoid their contact with sparks or flames, in order to protect both our workers and our property.
> *Rule:* Smoking is prohibited in the plant, except in posted areas.

In this example the policy states the reason behind the prescribed rule. Should changing conditions render invalid the principle justifying the policy, the policy can be changed. For example, if flammable chemicals are eliminated from the production process, the rule against smoking would become obsolete and could be eliminated. The danger that originally rational policies will become traditional and fixed—while always present—is reduced considerably when the reasons, conditions, and assumptions leading to the rules are made clear. An explicit statement of the policy principle serves as a constant reminder of the rationale underlying the rule.

A policy should be flexible enough to allow for exceptions without those exceptions invalidating the policy itself. For example, the case studies of the sources of peaceful labor-management relations conducted by the National Planning Association (1953) showed that policy statements in collective bargaining contracts were most successful when both parties viewed the policies as permitting exceptions. "Literalism" in interpreting collective agreements was found to cause the parties to lose sight of the greater purpose of the contract and to become obsessed with rigid adherence to the rules.

This last point deserves emphasis: Policies are *not* meant to exclude exception. They are intended merely to alert those operating under them to the fact that exceptions must be justified. For example, a policy of "promotion from within" should not mean that hiring from outside the firm is strictly prohibited; it should merely require that hiring from outside be justifiable, and be explained. To adhere to policy prescriptions when conditions cry out for exception would be as illogical as waiting at a traffic light that is jammed on red.

Propositions

In the preceding discussion we have enumerated many statements concerning objectives and policy, drawn from both classical and modern organization theory. While many hypotheses are suggested by our discussion, the propositions listed below seem to us to be relevant and, equally important, seem testable with reference to the research literature. We emphasize this last point because little research above the first level of rigor (see Chapter 3) has been conducted on the effects of objectives and, particularly, policy. It is therefore necessary in considering the effects of policy to broaden the term to include recorded effects of formalization in general, rather than policy alone. Since we have described policy as the rules and values that guide individual behavior, we would expect that objectives, organizational structure, defined responsibility and authority, and other standards of performance would perform similar functions. That is, although objectives, structures, and job definitions each have unique properties, they all function as rational job constraints which formalize the ground rules of the organization.

In analyzing the effects of formalization we shall concentrate upon formal rather than informal role-taking behavior.

1. A clear statement of the organizational objectives to which an individual is expected to contribute directly improves individual performance and coordinated group action, by directing individual contributions and encouraging cooperative effort.
2. The existence of rational policy creates a perceived freedom of action on the part of organization participants because it reduces the degree to which higher-level members can exercise arbitrary control, and because participants are better able to predict the actions of others and to know themselves how they are expected to behave.
3. When those affected by a policy know the reason for it and can participate in its formulation, they are more likely to accept it. The same is true with regard to objectives.

Empirical Evidence

Proposition 1

A clear statement of the organizational objectives to which an individual is expected to contribute directly improves individual performance and coordinated group action, by directing individual contributions and encouraging cooperative effort.

This proposition is based upon the assumption that employee ignorance about individual and organizational objectives can result in negative consequences for both their own satisfaction and organizational performance. One such consequence is *role ambiguity,* described by Kahn et al. (1964, p. 73) to be "a direct function of the discrepancy between the information available to the person and that which is required for adequate performance of his role." Such discrepancies can result from incomplete information in a number of areas, but many of these center around incomplete knowledge of objectives.

While Kahn et al. point out that "there are almost as many kinds of emotional reaction to ambiguity as there are foci of ambiguity," they go on to state that "tension, anxiety, and fear are common concomitants of uncertainty; anger and hostility also can be aroused" (p. 84). Such reactions are clearly unlikely to result in individual satisfaction, and are also inconsistent with organizational performance.

There is considerable evidence that clear statements of organizational objectives often do not exist. For example, survey responses of 3500 research workers in 23 firms revealed that many workers didn't know what was expected of them, and didn't think that management knew either. In response to the question "Are the aims, goals, and purposes of research clearly established by your company?" more than one third of the employees said "No," or claimed to be doubtful about the objectives (Fromes, 1957).

It is possible that objectives for research workers are particularly poorly defined; however, based on in-depth interviews of 58 high-ranking managers and their subordinates from five companies, representing all major functions of an organization, Maier et al. (1961) found that 35.4 percent of responding pairs (supervisor and subordinate) agreed on *almost none* of the future changes expected in the subordinate's job; 59.7 percent of the pairs agreed on fewer than half of the expected changes.

If most managers seek to ensure that their subordinates have a clear understanding of objectives, how can we explain the widespread ignorance of objectives that is apparent from the study results cited above? For one thing, it is far from clear that most managers know how to establish and communicate objectives in a manner that contributes to the effective operation of their enterprise. This may be characterized as a failure to make objectives *operational*—that is, a failure to translate *official* goals into *operative* ones.

According to Perrow (1969, p. 66):

> Official goals are the general purposes of the organization as put forth in the charter, annual reports, public statements by key executives and other authoritative pronouncements. . . . Official goals are purposely vague and general. . . .

On the other hand (pp. 66–67):

> Operative goals designate the ends sought through the actual operating policies of the organization; they tell us what the organization actually is trying to do, regardless of what the official goals say are the aims. . . . For example, where profit-making is the announced goal, operative goals will specify whether quality or quantity is to be emphasized, whether profits are to be short run and risky or long run and stable, and will indicate the relative priority of diverse and somewhat conflicting ends of customer service, employee morale, competitive pricing, diversification, or liquidity.

The failure of many managers to translate official goals into operative ones is probably one of the major causes of employee uncertainty and ignorance about objectives.

Based upon his experiences with a large number of organizations, Drucker (1954, p. 126) set forth his position concerning the validity of Proposition 1, at least so far as managerial employees are concerned:

> Each manager, from the "big boss" down to the production foreman or the chief clerk, needs clearly spelled-out objectives. These objectives should lay out what performance the man's own managerial unit is supposed to produce. They should lay out what contribution he and his unit are expected to make to help other units obtain their objectives. Finally, they should spell out what contribution the manager can expect from other units toward the attainment of his own objectives. . . .
>
> These objectives should always derive from the goals of the business enterprise. In one company, I have found it practicable to provide even a foreman with a detailed statement of not only his own objectives but those of the company and of the manufacturing department. Even though the company is so large as to make the distance between the individual foreman's production and the company's total output all but astronomical, the result has been a significant increase in production.

In theory, there are a number of reasons why the increase in production observed by Drucker could have occurred. We have already mentioned that clearly defined objectives let organizational members know their responsibilities and the scope of their authority to initiate independent action. Clearly defined objectives may also contribute to performance by delineating a commitment to achieve those objectives, as evidenced by Kappel's remark (1963) that ". . . by the very act of stating their purposes, (more businesses) greatly encourage their own effort to achieve them. This involves what I call giving *hostages to performance.* When you commit yourself to the public plainly, for all to read or hear—well, you are committed. You are out on a limb. You have to stand or fall."

Supposedly, clearly defined objectives also aid in performance evaluation; by clearly spotlighting desired results, they make it easier to tell whether they have been achieved.

Studies Relevant to Proposition 1. Studies pertinent to this proposition have been conducted under a variety of conditions. For example, Raven and Rietsema (1957) influenced Dutch students' understanding of group task goals and the paths to those goals. By comparing reactions of students with a clear understanding to students with no such understanding, and by examining task performance and attitudes under both conditions, they found that a clear understanding of goals led to a greater interest in their individual tasks, greater feelings of group belonging, and greater individual willingness to accept influence from the group. Clear understanding also led to greater individual commitment to group goals.

A survey of telephone operators (Cohen, 1959) found that when they had received inconsistent and ambiguous direction, and when they were uncertain about what kind of performance led to a favorable evaluation, they were insecure, poorly motivated, ineffective, and had difficulty in adjusting. Questionnaire responses and production performance data from several thousand workers revealed that those who clearly perceived productivity objectives performed better and produced more than workers whose perceptions of objectives disagreed with their supervisor's perceptions (Likert, 1961). Similar findings have been obtained from widely differing populations, including managers (Rosen, 1961), nurses (Taves, Corwin, and Haas, 1963), and operative industrial employees (Harrison, 1959; Barrett, 1963).

A study by Tomekovic (1962) yielded conclusions which offer a somewhat different and possibly more sophisticated interpretation of Proposition 1 than the studies previously mentioned. Tomekovic found that the explanation of instructions for work (a statement of the purposes of the work), followed by joint supervisor-subordinate decision making concerning the work, acted as significant motivational factors. A simple explanation of the instructions for the work, however, did *not* act as a motivational factor. These conclusions, based upon a comparison of the differences in the output of experimental groups, suggest that the clarity of the objectives may have been less important than the manner in which the objectives were made known to the work group. (In other words, it may be that Proposition 3 contains a more fundamental truth than does Proposition 1.)

Another study, by Kahn et al. (1964), consisted of an analysis of questionnaire and interview responses from workers in 778 widely varied industrial positions, to determine the effects of uncertainty about their supervisors' evaluations of their work. Their data showed that "ambiguity leads to increased emotional tension and to decreased satisfaction with one's job. It also contributes significantly to a sense of futility and to a loss of self-confidence" (p. 85).

More recently, Rizzo, House, and Lirtzman (1970) developed a 30-

item questionnaire, half of which related to role conflict and the other half to role ambiguity. In two samples of managerial and technical employees, in which salesmen, clerical workers, and first-level foremen were excluded, role ambiguity in particular was found to correlate negatively and significantly with seven different measures of respondent satisfaction. The role ambiguity measure, which considered several sources of ambiguity including ignorance and uncertainty about authority, policies and guidelines, responsibilities, goals, and objectives, also related negatively and significantly to "general fatigue and discomfort" and to respondent propensity to leave the organization in both samples, and to job-induced anxiety in one sample.

In 1971, Lyons reported a study of registered nurses who worked in a large hospital; the study included measures of both "role clarity" and "need for clarity." He found that role clarity related positively and significantly to satisfaction, and negatively and significantly to voluntary turnover, tension, and propensity to leave the hospital. For the low "need for clarity" group of respondents, however, only the negative relationship between role clarity and tension was significant. Lyons therefore concluded that, consistent with Kahn et al. (1964), role ambiguity will have more adverse consequences for employees with high needs for clarity. However, the converse is not true; that is, provision of role clarity did *not* relate to dissatisfaction, tension, and propensity to leave for employees with low needs for clarity.

Still another study (Hamner and Tosi, 1974) showed that role ambiguity was negatively and significantly correlated with job satisfaction, and positively and significantly related to "job threat" and anxiety. Respondents in this case were high-level managers from a number of different industries, thus making more general the conclusion that a clear understanding of productivity objectives and instructions indicating work objectives is associated with high performance in individuals and work units (in several studies), and is related to greater satisfaction, motivation, and commitment (in many studies).

Management By Objectives (MBO). Several studies which are concerned with the MBO approach are relevant to Proposition 1. MBO has been used by many authors to refer to a wide variety of programs and procedures; lack of agreement as to its meaning and its content is one of the many difficulties related to its use as an organizational development technique (see Chapter 21 for a detailed discussion of MBO). Typically, however, MBO features joint goal-setting between those at each level of management and those at the next higher level, the expression of objectives whenever possible in quantifiable terms such as dollars, units, and percentages, and the subsequent measurement and comparison of actual performance with the agreed-upon objectives.

Raia (1965) reported the results of the introduction of a "goal setting and self control" program, a variant of MBO, in the Purex Corporation. Some eighteen months after its introduction, the effects of MBO seemed generally favorable:

> The productivity of the individual manufacturing plants had improved considerably. Before the introduction of "Goals and Controls" average productivity for all plants was decreasing at a rate of approximately 0.4 percent per month. During the first eighteen-month period, average productivity was 18 percent higher and increasing at a rate of approximately 0.3 percent per month. The increase in productivity was accompanied by improved morale and an increase in the level of motivation in most of the plants. It was also noted, however, that lower levels of management were not yet meaningfully participating in the process and that the program had imposed an additional administrative burden on the operating managers (Raia, 1974, p. 160).

One year later another study was conducted, which generally supported the conclusions drawn from the first. Productivity in all plants was still high, but had leveled off to an average increase of 0.02 percent per month. The program was still not fully implemented at the lower managerial levels, and the additional administrative burden on managers was still in evidence. Several additional problems emerged:

> There appeared to be some distortion in the managerial philosophy underlying the program. More than a dozen managers reported that it was "used as a whip" and that it "treats people like statistics." An equal number of people reported that it had become a statistics game which was based upon "unrealistic standards" and "unrealistic or unchallenging goals." There was also evidence of an overemphasis on the attainment of production goals and targets. Some managers complained that this was generally done at the expense of other goals, particularly those related to quality (Raia, 1974, p. 160).

In another study, Mendelson (1967) administered a "Goal-Setting Index" to pairs of managers and their immediate subordinates, and found no significant relationship between the extent to which each pair set goals and the supervisor's rating of the subordinate's current performance. However, a significant positive relationship was found between goal setting and the supervisor's rating of the subordinate's promotability.

In a recent book, Carroll and Tosi (1973) discussed their study of managers' reactions to the installation of an MBO program in a large tool manufacturing concern. As part of the study, managers were asked to state the advantage of the program; by far, they most often stated that under MBO one was more likely to "know what is expected of him by his boss" (pp. 24–25). Additional comments from managers which are pertinent to Proposition 1 include the following:

> While I did not have much to say in what the final determination of my goals were, at least I knew what my boss wanted and I knew what to do. I think this motivated me to work harder, or at least to work on

> those things that I knew were important to him. I also knew whether or not I achieved targets set for me.
>
> I like the fact that I sit down with my boss to set these objectives. Every time I sit down and talk with him I can't help but learn more about what he expects of me. Anything that does that is a help (p. 25).

The study also determined that as goals increased in perceived clarity and importance, subordinate managers were more positive toward the program and reported improved relations with their boss as compared to previous periods. Differences were observed, however, concerning the importance of goal clarity:

> . . . Clear goals may be more important to some managerial groups than to others. For example, to obtain higher effort levels from managers, clear goals may be especially important for those with lower job interest and for important decision-makers. Clear goals are also related to higher levels of satisfaction with the superior and to a subordinate perception that the objectives program is important (p. 40).

Costs of Clarifying and Quantifying Objectives. From the studies of MBO it is apparent that organizational objectives can usually be made specific and operational, and it is often efficient to do so. Locke (1968), for example, reviewed 11 pertinent studies and found that in all but 2 of them individuals with very specific goals significantly outperformed those with more general goals. However, it is also true that clear, explicitly delineated goals can be dysfunctional. In opposition to the classical view (described earlier in this chapter) that the organization's goals are those of the entrepreneur or of the managerial hierarchy, and that other organizational members conform (for a price) to these goals, the prevailing view today is that *all* participants set goals and organizations must meet these goals, at least minimally, or lose continued participation. Furthermore, goals set by members cannot be easily combined into a few superordinate goals; rather, they are often in conflict and organizational decision makers must "strike a balance among so many conflicting values, objectives, and criteria that it will always be suboptimal from any single viewpoint. Every decision or choice affecting the whole enterprise has negative consequences for some of the parts" (Katz, 1970, p. 13). The resulting "quasi-resolution of conflict" has been described in Chapter 7.

From this standpoint goals are "essentially the future domain intended by the decision-makers and attained through a series of policy commitments in which a dominant decision-making coalition is formed within the organization" (Perlstadt, 1972, p. 73). Then "the operative goals will be shaped by the dominant group, reflecting the imperatives of the particular task area that is most critical, their own background characteristics . . . and the unofficial uses to which they put the organization for their own ends" (Perrow, 1969, p. 68).

A number of studies (e.g., Friedlander and Pickle, 1968) support the point that the organization can only meet the goal expectations of some participants at the expense of others, and therefore "the intangibility of goals makes it possible for the organization to accommodate diverse and even inconsistent subgoals. The program can be 'all things to all people' at an abstract level, so that different people can feel satisfied that their interests are being served" (Warner and Havens, 1968, p. 543). It can thus be argued that the more clear and explicit the goals, the more members will realize that their particular wants and needs are in conflict with those of other members, perhaps even with those of the dominant coalition. Such realization could lead to goal displacement and subversion, or to resignation from the organization.

Other benefits of intangible goals cited by Warner and Havens include: facilitation of flexibility and adaptation, dramatization of objectives which may motivate individuals toward action, and perpetuation of the conviction that the organization is performing well.

Quantification of goals is an extreme form of clarification, and involves stating desired objectives in terms of sales units, dollars, percentages, etc. Most MBO theorists recommend that objectives be quantified whenever possible, and that numbers chosen reflect the objectives themselves rather than relating merely to activities which precede the objectives. An amusing example of the consequences of ignoring this recommendation, and focusing attention upon the activities rather than the objectives, is contained in a transcript of a Senate Foreign Relations Committee hearing during the Vietnam War; the hearing was held to investigate an elaborate attempt to land American soldiers behind enemy lines to free prisoners of war believed held captive there. When the soldiers landed, they found the site deserted.

> Mr. Fulbright: I don't like to say it was all a bad idea simply because it failed, but it did fail. There was something wrong with the intelligence.
>
> Mr. Laird: This was not a failure, Mr. Chairman, and I would—
>
> Mr. Fulbright: Well, it was a failure.
>
> Mr. Laird: These men knew full well the chance that there might not be POWs present.
>
> Mr. Fulbright: I'm not complaining about the men but those men responsible for it.
>
> Mr. Laird: I would like to tell you, Mr. Chairman, that we have made tremendous progress as far as intelligence is concerned—
>
> Mr. Fulbright: You mean since Friday?
>
> Mr. Laird: —but we have not been able to develop a camera that sees through the roofs of buildings. We had—the intelligence in this mission was excellent. But let me give you the intelligence rundown, as far as the location of troops were concerned, the location of buildings, the makeup of the camp, where the SAM missiles were located, where the anti-aircraft was located, where the radar blanks were in

> the radar screen, so that we could make penetration without detection.
>
> Mr. Fulbright: But, Mr. Secretary, I don't think this is relevant. There weren't any prisoners there, so what difference does it make?
>
> Mr. Laird: There were prisoners there, Mr. Chairman, and we knew full well. . . . (*New Yorker,* 1970, p. 47).

The *New Yorker,* which reported the testimony, went on to discuss the pitfalls of concentrating upon activities alone:

> In Secretary Laird's remarks there is to be found a remarkable definition of "success" and "failure" . . . Success is measured wholly in terms of the vigor and health of the war machine, without any reference to what's happening to the war itself. The world outside of the confines of the government's own organizational machinery disappears from view, and success and failure are judged by standards that are completely internal. One might compare the government to a doctor who tries to judge the health of his patient by taking his own temperature. . . (p. 47).

On the other hand, fascination with quantifiable objectives can result in underattention to important aspects of organizational performance merely because they are not susceptible to easy expression in numerical terms. Many writers (Drucker, 1954; Warner and Havens, 1968; Paine and Naumes, 1974) have commented upon this point and have provided illustrations of its occurrence. For example:

> Easy quantification leads to counting publications of university faculty rather than evaluating classroom performance, looking at output per worker rather than diligence, cooperation, punctuality, loyalty, and responsibility, and counting parishioners in a church rather than assessing the spiritual guidance of the parishioners (Hall, 1972, pp. 90–91).

> . . . Scoring baskets and hitting home runs are more readily observable than feeding teammates and advancing base runners. Similarly, the adverse consequences of pronouncing a sick person well are more visible than those sustained by labelling a well person sick. "Team-building" and "creativity" are other examples of behaviors which may not be rewarded simply because they are hard to observe (Kerr, 1975).

Not only does overemphasizing quantification lead to ignoring nonquantifiable goals, it also fosters misdirection in effort toward the goals which have been quantified. In this sense quantification leads to goal displacement; by establishing a number which is to serve as the test of goal-attainment, the objective-setter runs the risk that the number will come to be considered as the objective itself. Again, two examples may be helpful in understanding this important point:

> When a factory puts great pressure on its production people to increase their efficiency, they might well produce more items but of a lower quality. If quality control is then tightened, the production people might neglect the maintenance of their equipment to put more efforts into satisfying the increased pressure to maintain quality (Etzioni, 1964, p. 9).

> Attempting to measure and reward accuracy in paying surgical claims, the (insurance) firm systematically keeps track of the number of returned checks and letters of complaint received from policyholders. However, underpayments are likely to provide cries of outrage from the insured, while overpayments are often accepted in courteous silence. Since it is often impossible to tell from the physician's statement which of two surgical procedures, with different allowable benefits, was performed, and since writing for clarification will interfere with other standards used by the firm concerning "percentage of claims paid within two days of receipt," the new hire in more than one claims section is soon acquainted with the informal norm: "When in doubt, pay it out!" (Kerr, 1975).

The research discussed here certainly indicates that clarity of goals is often a contributing factor to both member satisfaction and organizational performance; similarly, quantification of objectives is often associated with increased efficiency. However, there are certain advantages to ill-defined and intangible goals. Furthermore, extreme quantification of objectives may lead to goal displacement and to inadequate emphasis being placed upon important but hard-to-quantify areas of organizational economy, efficiency, and growth.

Proposition 2

The existence of rational policy creates a perceived freedom of action on the part of organizational participants because it reduces the degree to which higher-level members can exercise arbitrary control, and because participants are better able to predict the actions of others and to know themselves how they are expected to behave.

Classical theory emphasizes the need for policy explanation, both by a statement of the principle supporting the rule and by communicating policy to all organizational levels. Once explained, it is assumed that policy will be accepted by subordinates and expressed in their overt behavior.

Classical theory holds also that the codification of policy establishes a rule of law regarding personal relationships within an organization. Once policy is established management is expected to show proof of policy violation before imposing penalties and is less free to dispense discipline by arbitrary decree.

The history of the labor movement in the United States offers a useful illustration of the role of codified policy (in this case, collective bargaining agreements) in limiting arbitrary action by employers. Such agreements typically bind employers with regard to seniority, handling of grievances, disciplinary action, retirement, and union representation.

A study by Vollmer (1960) further illustrates the role of policy in restricting arbitrary employer behaviors. Vollmer surveyed personnel policies in four enterprises, and found that employees typically agreed that management has the right to control job-related practices, but that personnel policies place procedural limits on the exercise of managerial power. The existence of stated policies forced management to document rule violations, and tended to result in greater equity in applying the rules. Management was expected to give adequate warning following violations, apply policies consistently, and thoroughly investigate employee intentions prior to imposing disciplinary actions. Employees also felt that, where policies had not been made clear, management had less right to discipline them for violations.

Individual differences seemed to largely account for the degree to which employees expected application of personnel policies to be uniform. For example, Vollmer's interviews led to the conclusion that career-oriented male staff specialists and skilled workers were highly involved in their work and sought recognition of their "rights" on a universal basis. Skilled workers sought uniformity in policy application because of desires for security; female unskilled and clerical workers sought uniform treatment because it enabled them to operate under explicit standards, without having to be personally involved in their work.

From other studies it has been learned that structure has positive effects on productivity and little negative effect on employee satisfaction so long as the supervisor is perceived to be considerate (Fleishman and Harris, 1962; Cummins, 1972; Dessler, 1973; and many others—see Kerr et al., 1974, for a review); that individual stress is often reduced by high formalization (Kahn et al., 1964); and that intergroup stress is lowest and cooperation highest among groups whose leaders establish structure (Oaklander and Fleishman, 1964). A more comprehensive analysis of the effects of leader-imposed structure upon satisfaction and performance of subordinates was presented in Chapters 11 and 12.

There is limited evidence that rational policy may also free participants from arbitrary power exercised by individuals within the organization other than the immediate supervisor. Kessler (1964) asked managers in 33 firms: "To how many supervisors do you directly report for any or all of your activities?" The number of supervisors named was compared under conditions of "explicit" policy and under conditions of "implicit" policy. It was found that where policies were undefined, or were ignored, significantly more supervisors were named than where policies were clearly stated and understood, and these differences could not be explained in terms of organization size. A possible explanation is that, to the extent that policy is explicit, subordinates will be comparatively free from role demands from several supervisors.

The position that rational policy serves to increase the perceived freedom of subordinates has been carefully delineated by Stogdill (1959). His review of research with respect to structure and control led him to conclude that the formal specification of desired actions creates an area of personal freedom for organizational participants. Stogdill states that productivity, individual freedom, and job satisfaction bear curvilinear relationships to structure and control or, in broader terms, formalization. This relationship is illustrated in Figure 14–1.

At Point A individuals are given no guidelines to behavior and are therefore dependent upon directions from others, or upon clues their actions provide, in order to know how to act. At the other extreme, Point C, formalization is so extensive as to become restrictive. It is at the center, Point B, that guides are provided and individuals can predict with reasonable certainty what they and others are expected to do; armed with this information individuals will often feel greater freedom and satisfaction, since it is at this point that they retain enough autonomy to have some choice of action, yet recognize that enough policy exists to give them some measure of protection against arbitrary managerial actions and unfair second-guessing.

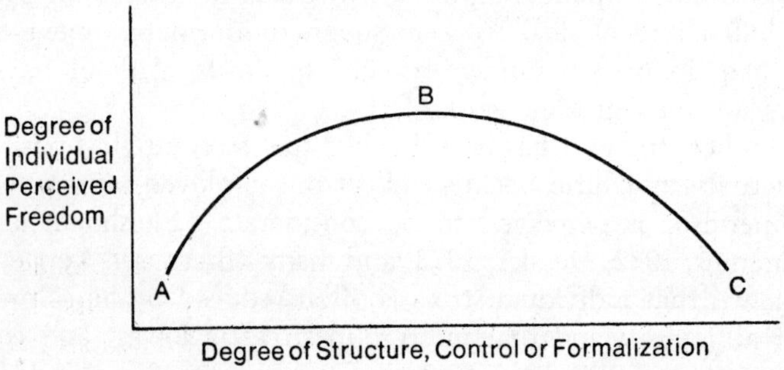

Figure 14–1. Relationship of Perceived Freedom to Formalization.

Stogdill has shown that his conclusion is consistent with a substantial amount of indirect evidence, and Lippitt and White earlier (1943) expressed much the same opinion concerning the relationship between freedom and formalization. Despite the absence of direct evidence, the curvilinear relationship shown in Figure 14–1 seems to explain much of the confusion in the literature regarding the positive and negative effects of the use of policy.

Effects of policy statements upon individual freedom when policy was previously absent was demonstrated in a study by Bakke (1950). He found that a job-training program led to the establishment of precise job procedures and descriptions, which were thoroughly explained to employees. When the effort to describe jobs was first begun, many organizational members were concerned that the job descriptions would unduly constrain their freedom of action; however, the effort actually *increased* their perceived freedom, because they felt better able to judge what was expected of them, needed less guidance and correction, and were therefore subject to less interference from their supervisors.

Explicit policies may also be an important factor in group effectiveness. A survey of workers and supervisors conducted by Comrey, Pfiffner, and High (1954) revealed that the most significant correlate of effectiveness was formalization of policy, with "formalization" defined to be the degree to which the organization operated according to plan, with specified job relationships and work assignments, and with written statements of procedure.

From these studies (and those by Cohen, 1959; Rizzo, House, and Lirtzman, 1970; and Hamner and Tosi, 1974, reviewed for Proposition 1) it seems that, where policy is absent or poorly understood, individuals perceive little freedom and are often insecure, inefficient, and poorly motivated. Policy insulates members from arbitrary actions by higher-ups, thereby lessening anxiety and tension. Where policy formalization is carried to an extreme, however, little opportunity exists for initiative, and negative consequences often result.

Proposition 3

When those affected by a policy know the reason for it and can participate in its formulation, they are more likely to accept it; the same is true with regard to objectives.

Before evaluating this proposition let us narrow our focus a bit. First, let us assume that reasons are expressed when policy is first legislated and objectives initially set. Objectives and policy may sometimes be made more acceptable subsequent to installation by explanation of intent, but no evidence exists to evaluate the effects of such delayed explanation. We are therefore primarily concerned with new policy and objectives.

Second, it should be clear that Proposition 3 is tenable only in cases where those affected are not strongly opposed for personal reasons. We are, in other words, concerned with *assimilation effects,* that is, the degree to which policy and objectives become acceptable after explanation, rather than with *contrast effects,* in which they remain unacceptable after explanation (Sherif and Hovland, 1961). To the extent that objectives and policy are inherently objectionable to employees, failure to provide underlying reasons and to make them explicit may be the best course of action, as was stated in the discussion of Proposition 1.

There are various mechanisms whereby knowledge about an objective or policy is gained. These mechanisms involve an interaction between the potential policy acceptor and the initiator, or between the individual charged with attaining the objective and the objective-setter. Much of the pertinent research on this subject has been contained under the general label of "participation." Participation has been found to have a number of consequences for those who participate and for resultant performance, and these can be expected to accrue whether the participation concerns policy, objectives, or other areas. A general discussion of the effects of participation, with emphasis upon leader-subordinate participation, was contained in Chapter 11. The overall conclusion expressed in that chapter was that participation often leads to subordinate satisfaction and productivity; however, there are important task and individual differences. For example, simple, routine, unambiguous tasks do not easily lend themselves to participative leadership. Furthermore, participation has its most positive effects upon unit performance and subordinate satisfaction when subordinate needs and expectations are of a certain kind. (For more specific descriptions of such differences, and for a comprehensive review of recent studies of the effects of participation, see Chapter 11; Chapter 20 also discusses the effects of participation in acceptance of change.)

A large number of laboratory and field experiments generally confirm the notion that acceptance of an action or a decision is enhanced by joint decision making, clarification of policy intent through discussion, and overt, public expressions of acceptance. One classic study of the effects of knowledge and participation on the acceptance of change was performed by Coch and French (1948). Machine operators in a pajama factory were introduced to changes in manufacturing procedures at several levels of involvement. A "no participation" control group was merely given an explanation of the change; a "participation through elected representatives" group received a similar explanation of the change, as well as having the opportunity to elect representatives who would participate with management in planning and initiating the change; two "full participation" groups were given an explanation of the change, then provided with full opportunities to work with management in carrying it out.

It was found that the level of productivity following the change was positively related to the degree of participation. As the chance to make suggestions and to assist in the changes increased, disruption and turnover caused by the change decreased.

Lewin (1958) was responsible for another classic study of the effects of explanation and participation. Red Cross study groups attended lectures about nutrition, run for the purpose of encouraging the use of meats not generally purchased by housewives, such as beef hearts and kidneys. In some groups only a lecture was presented; in others the lecture was followed by group discussion, following which the participants were asked to make a commitment to try these meats and to visibly indicate their commitment to each other by raising their hands. A follow-up survey revealed that only 3 percent of the lecture group attendees subsequently tried one or more of the meats, compared to 32 percent of the discussion and public commitment groups.

The study by Tomekovic (1962), cited earlier, also illustrates the effects of explanation and participation. In a laboratory situation he assigned mathematical tasks to groups of subjects, to be performed on six consecutive days. One group was given an explanation for the tasks, while a second group was given none. A third group was given an explanation similar to the first, and was encouraged also to make suggestions concerning how the tasks would be carried out. The third group proved to be the most productive, and the group with no explanation least productive.

The studies cited above and many others support the position that acceptance of a new policy is likely to increase as the level of involvement increases (from none at all, to an explanation only, to explanation and discussion, to explanation, discussion, and public display of acceptance). On the other hand, a few studies do not fully support this position. For example, Pelz (1958) used different degrees of involvement in trying to persuade undergraduate students to participate in experiments. His results indicated that discussion produced no more positive effects than did explanation alone; furthermore, public commitment was not a significant factor. However, the extent to which the group obtained consensus was significant in determining group acceptance. This suggests an advantage of policy making by groups, which not only permits participation but also facilitates opportunities for individuals who are affected by the policy to gain consensus.

Another study (Pennington, Haravey, and Bass, 1958) conducted a similar investigation of the effects of different degrees of involvement by measuring attitude changes after various combinations of discussion and decision. Results showed that effectiveness was greater after discussion by the group, or after the group's choice was announced, than when neither discussion nor announcement of the decision was permitted. Opinion change was greater in groups which permitted either discussion or announcement of the group's decision than in groups which allowed announcement of a group decision but denied discussion. This study thus supported earlier findings concerning the usefulness of both group participation and decision making, and is also consistent with the notion that group change and effectiveness result primarily from interaction among members.

The literature on management by objectives (MBO), reviewed briefly in this chapter, also stresses the importance of explanation and participation. In one of the first statements about MBO, Drucker (1954) declared:

> . . . Every manager should responsibly participate in the development of the objectives of the higher unit of which he is a part. To "give him a sense of participation" (to use a pet phrase of the "human relations" jargon) is not enough. Being a manager demands the assumption of a genuine responsibility. . . . He must know and understand the ultimate business goals, what is expected of him and why, what he will be measured against and how. There must be a "meeting of minds" within the entire management of each unit. This can be achieved only when each of the contributing managers is expected to

> think through what the unit objectives are, is led, in other words, to participate actively and responsibly in the work of defining them (pp. 128–29).

Based on his own experiences with MBO, Raia (1974, p. 47) takes a similar position, and goes on to point out some of the advantages of participation.

> To begin with, the individual develops a greater awareness of his managerial role in the organization. He becomes more conscious of overall goals and objectives. The better he understands them, the more accurately he can develop his own role and the part he plays in their attainment and the more able he is to develop meaningful objectives in his area of responsibility. . . . Vertical and horizontal work relationships are also improved. The necessity for more contact and communication tends to break down protective barriers and provides the basis for realistic, clear-cut accountability of results. Perhaps most important, the individual develops a new level of motivation and sense of accomplishment.

Similar results concerning the effects of participation in objectives-setting have been observed by Meyer, Kay, and French (1965) at General Electric, where employees who had considerable influence in setting goals achieved more of their "improvement" goals and reported more favorable attitudes than those with less influence. However, in keeping with the caveat expressed earlier in this chapter that individual differences are important, it should be noted that the chance to participate under MBO did not affect the performance of participants who had traditionally been denied opportunities to participate with their superiors.

A study by Ivancevich (1972) concluded, however, that MBO's introduction had no important effect upon managers' satisfaction at each of three levels in one firm. Furthermore, this finding was observed at each of three different time periods, from immediately after introduction to 18 months later. In another firm MBO was associated with lower-level managers' satisfaction, but only for a short while after installation.

More negative evidence was found by Carroll and Tosi (1973, p. 41):

> . . . The degree of subordinate influence in the goal-setting process does not seem to be an important factor in the perceived success of the objectives program. Subordinate participation in setting goals did not result in higher levels of perceived goal success or of effort expenditures (except in one case), nor in more favorable attitudes toward the superior.

They also found, though, that among employees who had traditionally been given opportunities to participate in the past, there was a "small positive relationship to effort expenditures, goal success, and improvements in relations with the boss" (p. 41).

In summary, we can say that the process by which knowledge of changes in policies and objectives is acquired is an important determinant of acceptance by those affected by such changes. In general, the more individuals can participate in planning and implementing changes, the greater will be their acceptance. This point is elaborated upon in Chapter 21. There are some important exceptions to this general rule, however; these are discussed in Chapter 11.

Summary

Proposition 1: A clear statement of the organizational objectives to which an individual is expected to contribute directly improves individual performance and coordinated group action, by directing individual contributions and encouraging cooperative effort. *Generally supported by the available evidence; however, there are certain advantages to ill-defined goals, and extreme quantification may lead to goal displacement.*

Proposition 2: The existence of rational policy creates a perceived freedom of action on the part of organization participants because it reduces the degree to which higher-level members can exercise arbitrary control, and because participants are better able to predict the actions of others and to know themselves how they are expected to behave. *Generally supported; however, extreme formalization can have negative consequences.*

Proposition 3: When those affected by a policy know the reason for it and can participate in its formulation, they are more likely to accept it. The same is true with regard to objectives. *Generally supported, with some important exceptions (see Chapter 11).*

A Closing Note

At the close of this chapter, two questions seem appropriate. The first concerns the extent to which participation is really possible among hierarchical unequals. While "explanation and discussion" forms of participation are clearly possible to implement even with the lowest-level employees, more extreme forms, such as the "joint goal-setting" recommended by most MBO theorists, present much greater difficulties. For example, Meyer, Kay, and French (1965), in their discussion of General Electric's MBO system, claim that meetings between bosses and subordinates are "strictly man-to-man in character. . . . In listening to the subordinate's review of performance, problems, and failings, the manager is automatically cast in the role of *counselor*. This role for the manager, in turn, results naturally in a problem-solving discussion" (p. 129).

Seemingly, this view does not take into account the evidence in the research literature that hierarchical status differences "produce some very predictable effects upon interaction patterns, subordinate defensiveness, and quantity and quality of communications, which 'stack the deck' against joint goals set by unequals" (Kerr, 1973, p. 39). A fuller discussion of this problem as it affects MBO in general is contained in Chapter 21, but with particular regard to Proposition 3, the following thoughts from Bennis (1959, p. 285–87) seem appropriate:

> Two factors seem to be involved. . . . The superior as a helper, trainer, consultant, and co-ordinator; and the superior as an instrument and arm of reality, a man with power over the subordinate. . . . For each actor in the relationships, a *double reference* is needed. . . . The double reference approach requires a degree of maturity, more precisely a commitment to maturity, on the part of both the superior and the subordinate that exceeds that of any other organizational approach. . . . It is suggestive that psychiatric patients find it most difficult to see the psychiatrist both as a human being and helper and an individual with certain perceived powers. The same difficulty exists in the superior-subordinate relationship.

The second question concerns the extent to which the first and third propositions are incompatible; specifically, to what degree must clarity of policy and objectives be sacrificed in return for opportunities for participation? So long as we view participation by subordinates as being increased by lessening the amount and explicitness of objectives and policy, that is, "reducing the specificity of role prescription by allowing employees more control of the details of their own tasks" (Hickson, 1966, p. 231), some sort of tradeoff between participation and clarity seems inevitable. However, Lyons (1971, p. 107) argues that the dilemma is not serious since with participative methods:

> . . . group members know the facts and factors that were considered in arriving at the decision, know what the goal is and know the information relevant to working on the problem. . . . Optimally the interaction process provides for the sharing of role-structuring information. This participative process may be more motivating since the role prescriptions and proscriptions are situationally legitimized and are partly influenced by the role occupants themselves rather than unilaterally presented in varying degrees of comprehensibility to the role occupants by higher authorities. In short, the degrees of specificity and the clarity of roles are *conditions* that may be attained by the *processes* of either autocratic and unilateral decree or participative interaction.

It therefore appears that clarity in objectives and policy, and participation by organizational members in their establishment and implementation, are not only desirable ends from the standpoint of the organization, but are simultaneously attainable as well.

References

Anshen, M. 1960. Price tags for business policies. *Harvard Business Review* 38: 71-78.

Bakke, E. W. 1950. *Bonds of organization.* Harper & Row.

Barnard, C. 1938. *The functions of the executive.* Harvard University Press.

Barrett, R. S. 1963. Performance suitability and role agreement: Two factors related to attitudes. *Personnel Psychology* 16: 345-57.

Bennis, W. G. 1959. Leadership theory and administrative behavior: The problem of authority. *Administrative Science Quarterly* 4: 259-301.

Blau, P. M., and Scott, W. R. 1962. *Formal organizations.* Chandler.

Boulding, K. 1958. *Principles of economic policy.* Prentice-Hall.

Carroll, S. J., Jr., and Tosi, H. L. Jr. 1973. *Management by objectives: Applications and research.* Macmillan.

Coch, L., and French, J. R. P. 1948. Overcoming resistance to change. *Human Relations* 1: 512-32.

Cohen, A. R. 1959. Situational structure, self-esteem, and threat-oriented reactions to power. In *Studies in social power,* ed. by D. Cartwright. Institute for Social Research, University of Michigan.

Comrey, A. L., Pfiffner, J. M., and High, W. S. 1954. *Factors influencing organizational effectiveness.* University of Southern California.

Cummins, R. C. 1972. Leader-member relations as a moderator of the effects of leader behavior and attitude. *Personnel Psychology* 25: 655-60.

Cyert, R. M., and March, J. G. 1963. *A behavioral theory of the firm.* Prentice-Hall.

Dale, E. 1960. *The great organizers.* McGraw-Hill.

Davis, R. C. 1951. *Fundamentals of top management.* Harper & Row.

——., and Filley, A. C. 1962. *Principles of management.* Alexander Hamilton Institute.

Dessler, G. 1973. A test of the path-goal theory of leadership. Doctoral Dissertation, City University of New York.

Drucker, P. 1954. *The practice of management.* Harper & Row.

Etzioni, A. 1964. *Modern organizations.* Prentice-Hall.

Fleishman, E. A., and Harris, E. F. 1962. Patterns of leadership behavior related to employee grievances and turnover. *Personnel Psychology* 15: 43-56.

Friedlander, F., and Pickle, H. 1968. Components of effectiveness in small organizations. *Administrative Science Quarterly* 13: 289-304.

Fromes, R. 1957. How to say what you mean. *The Nation's Business* 45: 76-84.

Hall, R. H. 1972. *Organizations: Structure and process.* Prentice-Hall.

Hamner, W. C., and Tosi, H. L. 1974. Relationship of role conflict and role ambiguity to job involvement measures. *Journal of Applied Psychology* 59: 497-99.

Harrison, R. L. 1959. Workers' perceptions and job success. *Personnel Psychology* 12: 573.

Hickson, D. J. 1966. A convergence in organization theory. *Administrative Science Quarterly* 11: 224-37.

Ivancevich, J. M. 1972. A longitudinal assessment of management by objectives. *Administrative Science Quarterly* 17: 126-38.

Kahn, R. L.; Wolfe, D. M.; Quinn, R. P.; Snoek, J. D.; and Rosenthal, R. A. 1964. *Organizational stress: Studies in role conflict and ambiguity.* Wiley.

Kappel, F. R. 1963. Speech reported in *MBW News* 4: 1.

Kast, F. E., and Rosenzweig, J. E. 1974. *Organization and management: A systems approach,* 2nd ed. McGraw-Hill.

Katz, R. L. 1970. *Management of the total enterprise.* Prentice-Hall.

Kerr, S. 1973. Some modifications in MBO as an OD strategy. *Academy of Management Proceedings,* 39-42.

———. 1975. On the folly of rewarding a, while hoping for b. *Academy of Management Journal.*

———.; Schriesheim, C. A.; Murphy, C. J.; and Stogdill, R. M. 1974. Toward a contingency theory of leadership based upon the consideration and initiating structure literature. *Organizational Behavior and Human Performance* 12: 62-82.

Kessler, W. D. 1964. The effect of business policy upon managerial behavior. Unpublished Paper.

Lewin, K. 1958. Group decision and social change. In *Readings in social psychology,* 3rd ed., ed. by E. E. Maccoby, T. M. Newcomb, and E. M. Hartley. Holt, Rinehart and Winston.

Lewis, R. L. 1955. Measurement, reporting, and appraising results of operations with reference to goals, plans, and budgets. In *Planning, managing, and measuring the business: A case study of management planning and control at General Electric Company.* Controllership Foundation.

Likert, R. 1961. *New patterns of management.* McGraw-Hill.

Lippitt, R., and White, R. K. 1943. *Child behavior and development.* McGraw-Hill.

Locke, E. A. 1968. Toward a theory of task motivation and incentives. *Organizational Behavior and Human Performance* 3: 157-89.

Lyons, T. F. 1971. Role clarity, need for clarity, satisfaction, tension, and withdrawal. *Organizational Behavior and Human Performance* 6: 99-110.

Maier, N. R. F.; Hoffman, R. L.; Hooven, J. J.; and Read, W. H. 1961. *Superior-subordinate communication in management.* Study No. 52, American Management Association.

Mendelson, J. L. 1967. Managerial goal-setting: An exploration into meaning and measurement. Doctoral Dissertation, Michigan State University.

Meyer, H. H., Kay, E., and French, J. R. P. 1965. Split roles in performance appraisal. *Harvard Business Review* 43: 123-29.

National Planning Association. 1953. *The causes of industrial peace.*

New Yorker. 1970. Dec. 5: 47-48.

Nicolaidis, N. G. 1960. *Policy decision and organization theory.* University of Southern California.

Oaklander, H., and Fleishman, E. A. 1964. Patterns of leadership related to organizational stress in hospital settings. *Administrative Science Quarterly* 8: 520-32.

Paine, F. T., and Naumes, W. 1974. *Strategy and policy formation: An integrative approach.* Saunders.

Pelz, E. B. 1958. Some factors in group decision. In *Readings in social psychology,* 3rd ed., ed. by E. E. Maccoby, T. M. Newcomb, and E. L. Hartley. Holt, Rinehart and Winston.

Pennington, D. F., Haravey, F., and Bass, B. M. 1958. Some effects of decision and discussion on coalescence, change and effectiveness. *Journal of Applied Psychology* 6: 404-8.

Perlstadt, H. 1972. Goal implementation and outcome in medical schools. *American Sociological Review* 37: 73-82.

Perrow, C. 1969. The analysis of goals in complex organizations. In *Readings on modern organizations,* ed. by A. Etzioni. Prentice-Hall.

———. 1970. *Organizational analysis: A sociological view.* Wadsworth.

Pfiffner, J. M. 1960. Administrative rationality. *Public Administration* 3: 125-32.

———., and Sherwood, F. P. 1960. *Administrative organization.* Prentice-Hall.

Raia, A. P. 1965. Goal setting and self control. *Journal of Management Studies* 2: 34-53.

———. 1974. *Managing by objectives.* Scott, Foresman.

Raven, B. H., and Rietsema, J. 1957. The effects of varied clarity of group path upon the individual and his relationship to his group. *Human Relations* 10: 29-45.

Rizzo, J., House, R. J., and Lirtzman, S. I. 1970. Role conflict and ambiguity in complex organizations. *Administrative Science Quarterly* 15: 150-63.

Rosen, H. 1961. Managerial role interaction: A study of three managerial levels. *Journal of Applied Psychology* 45: 30-34.

Sherif, M., and Hovland, C. I. 1961. *Social judgment: Assimilation and contrast effects in communication and attitude change.* Yale University Press.

Sills, D. L. 1970. Preserving organizational goals. In *The sociology of organizations,* ed. by O. Grusky and G. A. Miller. Free Press.

Simon, H. A. 1957. *Administrative behavior,* 2nd ed. Free Press.

Stogdill, R. M. 1959. *Individual behavior and group achievement.* Oxford University Press.

Taves, M. J., Corwin, R. G., and Haas, J. E. 1963. *Role conception and vocational success and satisfaction: A study of student and professional nurses.* Bureau of Business Research, Ohio State University.

Tomekovic, T. 1962. Level of knowledge of requirements as a motivational factor in the work situation. *Human Relations* 15: 197-216.

Vollmer, H. M. 1960. *Employee rights and the employment relationship.* University of California Press.

Warner, W. K., and Havens, A. E. 1968. Goal displacement and the intangibility of organizational goals. *Administrative Science Quarterly* 12: 539-55.

Chapter **15**

Division of Labor: Job Design

Division of labor has often been accused of degrading the individual by making him a machine. . . . Every day he repeats the same movements with monotonous regularity, but without being interested in them, and without understanding them. . . . Surely, no matter how one may represent the moral ideal, one cannot remain indifferent to such debasement of human nature. If morality has individual perfection as its goal, it cannot thus permit the ruin of the individual, and if it has society as its goal, it cannot let the very source of social life be drained, for the peril does not threaten only economic functions, but all social functions, as elevated as they may be.

EMILE DURKHEIM
The Division of Labor in Society

Although division of labor antedates the development of the complex organization, we shall be discussing it within the context of such organizations. As suggested in the quotation above, the problem of work division contains both economic and social issues. Viewed in the former light, division of labor permits specialization of knowledge or skill, and the problem facing an organizational specialist is selecting the design strategy that will make the organization most effective. As a social issue, division of labor may lead to degradation of individuals or groups. Is this degradation a natural consequence of division of labor? If not, what steps must be taken to avoid such "debasement of human nature"?

In its broadest outline, the formal organization divides an enterprise vertically by a ranking or hierarchy of status or authority, and horizontally by differentiating function. More specifically, the horizontal division consists of:

Span of Control. The proper number of subordinates that a supervisor should direct.

Line and staff. The grouping of people or functions into organizational units distinguished by goals and authority relationships in the larger organization.

Departmentation. The division of the organization into segments or units, i.e., divisions, departments, or sections.

Job Definition. The grouping of tasks or functions into jobs and the relationships between these jobs. Particularly important here is the determination of the proper degree of specialization.

The first two means of differentiating horizontal units focus on the *control of work* while the second two concern the *nature of the work itself.* This chapter will deal with the design and character of individual tasks, i.e., with job definition. The other topics will be dealt with in subsequent chapters.

Why Division of Labor?

The division of labor into specialized process units occurred before the development of large-scale manufacture and the factory system. In the latter part of the tenth century, for example, the textile industry in England was divided into small units for spinning, weaving, dyeing, and printing textiles. Merchant middlemen acted as intermediaries between these independent units, buying from some and perhaps contracting out to others. These middlemen sometimes loaned money to their clients, often taking a loom or other equipment as collateral. As middlemen came to own such equipment and to consolidate certain processes into a single manufacturing enterprise, the larger organization, with its division of labor, emerged (Mantoux, 1962).

Obviously work division is not necessarily a function of organizational size. What, then, are the reasons for the division of labor? Litterer (1965) suggested three. The first is the inability of one person to perform all tasks. Thus there are physical limits which require the allocation of functions among different individuals. The second is limitations of knowledge. Since the scope of a project or production system is often far beyond what an individual may be expected to grasp in detail, it becomes necessary to divide jobs in order to permit specialization of knowledge among participants. The third reason for division of labor is the assumed efficiency in such division. Where jobs can be standardized, the result is generally greater uniformity of action and greater skill in accomplishment.

Unlike the first two reasons, which focus on the strengths and weaknesses of the worker, the third reason is concerned with the requirements of the task or technology. This concern for maximum efficiency is indicative of an "organization striving for maximum interchangeability of personnel . . . to reduce dependence" on the individual workers (Davis, 1966).

For example, the classic studies by Adam Smith (1776) and Charles Babbage (1832) on the manufacture of pins described how production is broken down into a series of steps divided among several workers. Smith, who is given credit for originating the phrase "division of labor," [1] described a small shop employing ten men. Some of these men performed two or three steps each, but the group could produce as many as 4800 pins in a day. If each man had performed all steps himself, Smith claimed that "they certainly could not each of them have made twenty, perhaps not one pin in a day."

Adam Smith mentioned three reasons why the division of labor increases the quantity of work. First, the skill of the workman increases; second, no time is lost in passing from one type of work to another; third, it encourages the invention and use of special machinery which, in turn, increases productivity. As we shall see, there is empirical evidence contradicting his first two claims for division of labor, and observations which place the third in a questionable light. It may be noted that writers from Smith's time until the end of the nineteenth century emphasized the economic virtues of the division of labor, virtues which benefited the individual as well as the institution, and paid little attention to the possible effects of such division on individual satisfaction or emotional well-being.

Such concern has led employers whose organizations manifest extreme division of labor, called fragmentation, to various attempts to reintegrate different aspects of the job. This may be seen in Figure 15–1.

As indicated, the first step in the division of labor involved the role specialization required for craftsmanship. This means that some workers continued to till the soil while others became tailors, carpenters, potters, or metal workers. This degree of work division was sufficient for tribal societies, but with the advent of modern cities, based on a market economy, such craftsmanship quickly became inefficient.

The solution was to divide the work involved in each craft into smaller, specialized units, which facilitated cottage industries; these were, in turn, displaced by the development of the power loom and other early machines. While this arrangement was more efficient than the general craft system, it still required skilled labor, which meant that absenteeism and turnover were serious problems for the maintenance of production. In addition, since the manufacture of each item was dependent upon the pace of the slowest worker, much time was wasted when work-in-progress stacked up at that point. This balance-delay time cost was improved through the introduction of further division of the task, combined with line-balanced assembly, which attempted to make all jobs of equal duration or utilize additional workers for the more complex operations in order to smooth out the flow of work.

By this time, the division of labor had resulted in fragmentation as the task cycle became shorter and more repetitive. The worker no longer controlled the job. Instead, the work system controlled the worker, as is still the case of assembly-line workers. The problem of fragmentation is that

---

[1] "The greatest improvement in the productive powers of labor, and the greater part of the skill, dexterity, and judgment with which it is any where directed, or applied, seem to have been the effects of the division of labor" (Adam Smith, 1776).

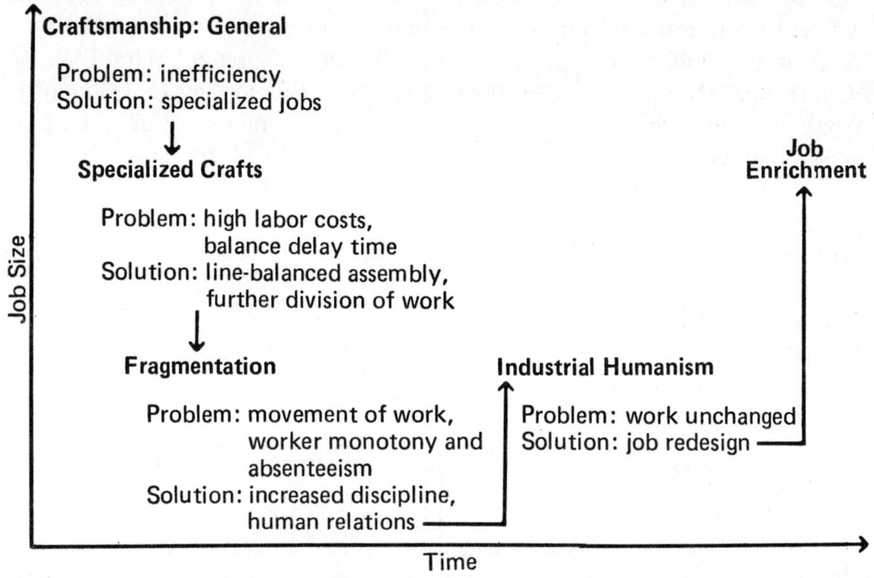

Figure 15-1. Evolution of Job Design.

some workers perceived such routine work to be monotonous, leading to boredom, absenteeism, and increased turnover. In addition, there is some evidence indicating that fragmentation can produce more time lost in moving the work-in-process from one worker to the next than is saved by simplifying the workers' movements (Kilbridge, 1960a).

Employers, reacting only to the workers' response of boredom and absenteeism, tried to solve the problem by "adding-on" features to the work. These attempts have been labeled Industrial Humanism and include activities designed to create a more pleasant work environment and instill a greater sense of belonging in the organization.

Many workers, however, continued to view the work as tedious and unchallenging. Since their perceptions had not changed, neither did their behavior. It is at this point that some employers began to experiment with redesign of the work itself.

Job Design

In order to deal with the issue of the division of labor in terms of a specific job, it is necessary to identify two dimensions of a job: depth and scope. The depth of a job refers to the degree to which job occupants are able to influence their work environment and can plan and execute their work without control or supervision from others. Both the same type of job and different jobs can vary in depth. One foreman may have greater job depth than another foreman, and we would expect a foreman's job to have greater depth than an assembly-line worker under his direction.

A second job dimension is its scope. Where job scope is limited, the incumbent performs few operations, repeating the job cycle frequently. Where scope is wider, a greater number of different operations are performed and the job cycle is repeated less frequently (Litterer, 1965). The relation between these dimensions is illustrated in Figure 15–2.

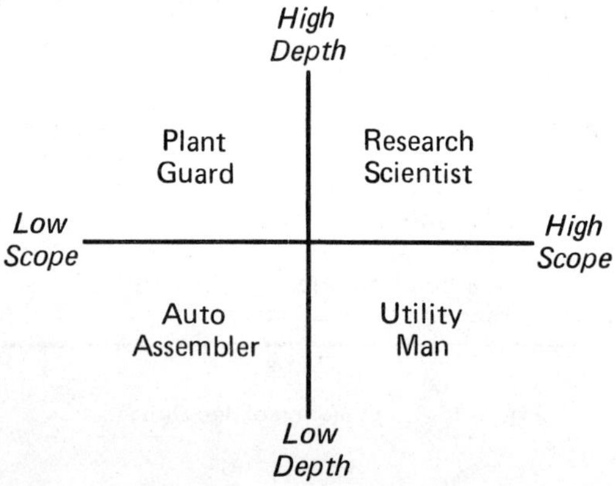

Figure 15–2. Job Dimensions.

As indicated, research scientists probably exemplify broad scope and depth. They receive relatively little supervision and control and perform a wide variety of tasks. By contrast, auto assembly-line workers have relatively low scope and depth. Their work is paced by the mechanical line, offering them little discretion and independence in their work, and they repeat their job cycles many times.

One may also find mixed types. A utility man on the assembly line has broader scope to his job than an assembly-line worker since he moves from job to job as needed, but he has little control over the way in which the operations are performed and the speed with which they must be accomplished. The plant guard, on the other hand, may have little scope to his job but he operates with greater freedom to plan and execute his duties.

The distinction between scope and depth takes on greater significance when related to the notion of job enrichment. Modern writers have placed much less emphasis upon the organizational and individual economic rewards of division of labor, emphasizing instead the presumed negative effects of such division upon the individual's emotional well-being and satisfaction (Argyris, 1957, 1964; McGregor, 1960). They believe that the worker in a highly specific, repetitive, and routine job is alienated from work, dependent, immature, and perhaps less productive. They argue that these negative effects occur because modern organizations have moved beyond specialization, to which Smith and Babbage refer, to fragmentation.

As one solution to this problem, they suggest that the job be enlarged in some way.

Proponents of job enlargement seldom bother to distinguish between enlargement in scope and enlargement in depth.[2] While we do not propose that scope and depth are completely separable, we do believe that various jobs can be compared on these dimensions, and altered to increase or decrease the scope or depth as needed. For instance, it seems clear that the depth of a job may be increased by giving incumbents greater freedom to control their own work, greater influence over their environment, and greater opportunity to plan for the future. Job depth may also be increased by reducing the closeness of supervision and by permitting greater participation by incumbents in planning matters that affect their jobs. We will investigate the general effects of job enlargement and the differential effects of changing scope and depth when we review research on the topic in the next section.

In trying to determine worker attitudes toward job design it is helpful to classify employees according to the degree of their attachment to their jobs. That is, some workers gain intrinsic satisfaction from their work and identify with the company. Others gain minimal need satisfaction from their jobs and have little identification with their employing firms. The former are described by some writers as "nonalienated," while the latter are classified as "alienated." We shall not bother to identify the possible reasons for alienation or the degrees to which people are alienated or nonalienated at this point in our discussion. We merely wish to suggest that alienated workers have less interest in job advancement, increased responsibility, or interesting work than their nonalienated counterparts. In addition, they make fewer social contacts through their jobs and are more concerned with work as a source of income.

Given the crude classification of employees into alienated and nonalienated categories, it is logical to propose that nonalienated workers would respond more positively to increases in job depth than alienated workers. If the job is a source of pride and satisfaction, increasing responsibility and personal control might be expected to improve employee attitudes and performance. We shall investigate these notions in detail in the next section.

Propositions

The preceding discussion has focused upon theory pertaining to the effect of the division of labor on the productivity and satisfaction of those

[2] One exception is Herzberg (1968), who discusses horizontal and vertical job loading. Horizontal job loading includes: expecting increased production from a worker, adding tasks, rotating job assignments, and removing difficult tasks from the job. Vertical job loading includes: removal of job controls, increasing personal accountability, giving the worker a complete natural work unit, giving him direct responsibility for reports, assigning tasks of greater difficulty, and increasing task specialization to increase expertise. Herzberg reports that an experiment with vertical job loading in a group of stockholder correspondents of a large company improved their work attitudes and service measures.

in positions with limited scope and depth. The following propositions are important to the theory:

1. Division of labor leads to decreased job satisfaction and increased productivity.
2. Performance and satisfaction are positively related to job depth for non-alienated workers and negatively related to job depth for alienated workers.

Empirical Evidence

Proposition 1

Division of labor leads to decreased job satisfaction and increased productivity.

Although some writers who discuss division of labor argue that social and psychological as well as monetary values should be considered in measuring its effects, we shall see that the relevant studies have tended to ignore the complexities of such multidimensional measures of utility. Instead, they generally employ simpler criteria, such as (1) attitudes toward simple or enlarged jobs, (2) measures of work quality, (3) labor turnover and absenteeism, (4) individual or group productivity, and (5) cost saving.

Study designs generally follow rather well-defined themes. One form is to contrast attitudes held by members of different status groups or organization levels. The argument is that if satisfaction is related to status, dissatisfaction must somehow be related to restrictive job design at lower status levels, since higher status jobs have greater scope and depth. Another approach is to study the attitudes of people in simple, repetitive work to determine sources of dissatisfaction. It is assumed that if these sources of dissatisfaction are reversed or eliminated, workers will be more satisfied and perhaps more productive. The third popular basis for evaluating the effects of division of labor is to vary the degree of scope or depth in the same type of work to determine the relation of value criteria to job design.

Much of the literature on division of labor is heavily value-laden, and proponents of job enlargement schemes support their contentions with studies at a low level of rigor, permitting themselves a great deal of interpretative freedom. Job enlargement schemes are frequently part of larger programs of change: thus if positive results are demonstrated, they may well be the result of factors not identified or not directly associated with job enlargement.

In the research summary which follows, we shall look first at studies which support the proposition directly or which show positive values associated with job enlargement. Then we shall summarize studies which show negative, mixed, or inconclusive results.

Supporting Studies. The principle thrust for modern interest in job enlargement came from a reorganization of the parts manufacturing department in the Endicott plant of IBM in 1944. In an effort to improve job design and worker morale, four distinct jobs were combined: machine operator, setup man, tool sharpener, and inspector. Following the reorganization, machine operators not only worked the machine, but also sharpened their own tools, set up their own equipment, and inspected their own finished parts.

The results attributed to this job enlargement program were increased worker satisfaction, lower production costs, and better quality. Costs increased by the program were for additional inspection equipment and higher wages. The change increased both the scope and the depth of jobs affected. One entire level of supervision was eliminated, giving workers greater responsibility and authority.

Conclusions regarding the IBM study are stated in general terms with no published empirical data from which independent judgments can be drawn. Yet there is little reason to doubt the interpretation of the researchers.

IBM later apparently reversed its job-enlargement philosophy by introducing a program of engineered work standards. However, the negative effects of such controls were demonstrated by the IBM personnel research group (Dunnington, Sirota, and Klein, 1963). Since the early 1960s, steps have been taken to expand the depth of worker's jobs and restore control to local line managers.

Positive results from job enlargement programs are reported for clerical jobs in the Detroit Edison Company (Elliott, 1953), the Colonial Insurance Company (Guest, 1957), the Social Security Administration and the U.S. Civil Service (Goode, 1964; Pelissier, 1965), and AT&T (Ford, 1969).

One of the more persuasive (certainly more rigorous) studies of job enlargement was conducted at the Maytag Company (Kilbridge, 1960a). The study involved a conveyor assembly line on which a washing-machine water pump with 27 parts was assembled by six operators. After this system was used for about a year, it was changed to a four-man operation. Finally, the work previously done on a conveyor line was done at four one-man work stations.

The differences between the conveyor and bench assembly arrangements serve to illustrate several facets of a job enlargement program. First, the variety of tasks was increased. Second, the shift from a continuous to a batch assembly operation permitted the operator to control the work pace. Third, operators performed inspection duties and stamped the product with their own mark. Finally, operators could vary their work methods and motion patterns instead of following prescribed techniques.

Pump assembly time dropped with each change, from 1.77 minutes per pump, to 1.76 minutes, to 1.49 minutes, chiefly because assembly-line "balance-delay" time was reduced by two-thirds. Here we see the first refutation of Adam Smith's arguments for the division of labor. Where he claimed that time was lost in passing from one type of work to another, it now appears that time is also lost in passing the work from one station to another. At least in those instances in which the job has been greatly fragmented, it appears that the number of man-hours required for the task may decrease when the job is enlarged. Even allowing for increased learning time, increased space requirements, and the additional cost of duplicate equipment, the reported saving was about $2000 per year.

Biggane and Stewart (1963) report in detail two other job enlargement programs at Maytag. In one, a top cover assembly involving 46 component parts, a conveyor, and separate inspection operation was changed to total assembly and inspection at six work benches. In the other, a complete assembly line of 100 workers was reorganized to provide seven assembly stations through which work passed progressively. Line pacing was eliminated. In both cases, costs were reduced and quality increased.

Given the opportunity to compare the effects and attitudes associated with line versus bench production at Maytag, Conant and Kilbridge (1965) administered an opinion questionnaire to 61 workers who had worked for at least three months on both line and bench jobs at Maytag. The results indicated that the workers had a strong preference for the bench (enlarged) jobs, and that preference for either type of work could not be associated with personal data. Apparently, there was not an "assembly line type."

Table 15–1 presents a summary of the questionnaire responses. It is interesting to note that, although 47 of the 61 workers indicated that they liked the variety of the bench jobs, a slight majority also favored line task specialization. The authors point out that work simplification on the line was one of the least disliked characteristics of line assembly work. Thus, there does not appear to be a simple positive correlation of attitudes with task complexity. It is also interesting to note that social interaction was apparently greater in line jobs than in bench jobs.

The Maytag studies are particularly useful for demonstrating that job enlargement or similar job design programs are not panaceas. It is worthwhile to note some of the advantages and limitations of enlargement mentioned by Biggane and Stewart. Job enlargement is useful in making jobs more meaningful and satisfying; workers can complete a total work unit or a large segment of it. It also has a marked effect on quality, since workers check their own work and apparently respond favorably to such an opportunity. Further, production standards can be maintained even though production rates are flexible; work benches may be operated or not as production levels vary. In addition, the work pace is not controlled by others. Finally, operators can exercise a variety of skills.

There are limits to the degree of job enlargement that is desirable or possible. It would appear that the policy at Maytag was to enlarge jobs to a semiskilled level rather than to move to a skilled craft orientation. Enlarged jobs, at least of the bench variety, require more space and duplicate equipment. There are also some processes that must retain balanced assembly or continuous production characteristics. Finally, since retraining takes longer as skill levels are increased, absenteeism and turnover are costly. Workers cannot be replaced as easily as they can be for routine assembly-line jobs.

TABLE 15–1. Worker Responses to Bench and Line Attributes.

Attribute	Like	Dislike
Bench		
Self pacing	48	13
Tie to work	55	6
Subassembly completion	50	11
Quality responsibility	53	8
Quality opportunity	52	9
Amount and variety of tasks	47	14
Social interaction	33	28
Individual incentive	53	8
Learning time	38	23
Line		
Mechanized pacing	24	37
Tie to work	19	42
Absence of completion	29	32
Quality anonymity	14	47
Task specialization	32	29
Social interaction	45	16
Group incentive	18	43
Learning time	44	17
Overall Attitudes	*Bench*	*Line*
Like extremely well	20	4
Like very much	12	8
Like fairly well	14	18
Neutral feelings	11	16
Dislike	4	13
Extreme dislike	0	2

Conant and Kilbridge (1965)

Although the Maytag studies do suggest some cost advantages in job enlargement programs, the main advantages seem to be increased job satisfaction and improved quality. As we shall see in other research reported in this chapter, these latter two factors are perhaps the most defensible results of job enlargement.

The effect of job enlargement on productivity is less clear. Some of the best work relating job change to productivity is that of L. E. Davis and his associates. In one of the first controlled field experiments on job design carried out in an industrial plant, A. R. N. Marks (1954) measured the effects of four different types of job design. The first, line-job design, was a regular conveyor-paced assembly line. The second, group-job design, eliminated the conveyor, allowing workers to set their own pace, but maintained the line assembly operation. The third, individual job design 1, allowed workers to perform all nine assembly operations at their own stations, where they controlled the sequence of assembly, procured their own supplies, and inspected their own products. The fourth method, individual job design 2, was the same as design 1, but the workers were located in the main production area instead of in an adjacent room.

The results are illustrated in Figures 15–3 and 15–4. Figure 15–3 shows the average daily productivity indexes under each condition. As indicated, productivity averages never reached the level of the first condition. In commenting on Marks' study, Davis suggests that the averages were affected by the fact that workers were assigned to experimental groups on an overlapping basis; that is, the memberships in the groups were not fully distinct from each other. Other data showed that the trend of productivity for each successive day of individual work was consistently upward, but the argument that enlarged jobs would eventually be more productive is not conclusive here.

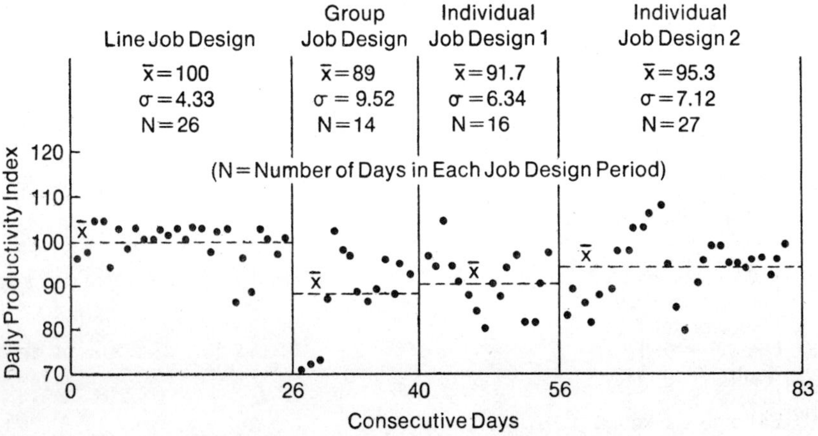

Figure 15-3. Average Daily Productivity Indexes.

Quality data, shown in Figure 15–4, present a clearer picture. The quality measure used here was the number of "kinked assemblies." The individual job designs provided much better product quality than did the first two conditions. In fact, the results indicated that the moving conveyor maintained output at the expense of quality. However, the comparative cost advantage of productivity versus quality is not identified.

In another study, Davis and his associates (1964, 1965) enlarged the responsibility and authority of the work group rather than of the individual. Their general hypothesis was that giving line supervision control over all operations and inspection related to a product would lead to lower total costs and greater satisfaction for group members. Using eleven shops in one operating division of an industrial facility, they matched experimental and control groups and used two experimental treatments. The first treatment, called "product responsibility," involved a change from functional organization (State I) to product organization, excepting quality control (State II). The second treatment, called "quality responsibility," involved a change from State II to product organization with responsibility for final quality control (State III).

The *product* responsibility change resulted in improved quality, but no change in direct costs of production, productivity, or personnel. The

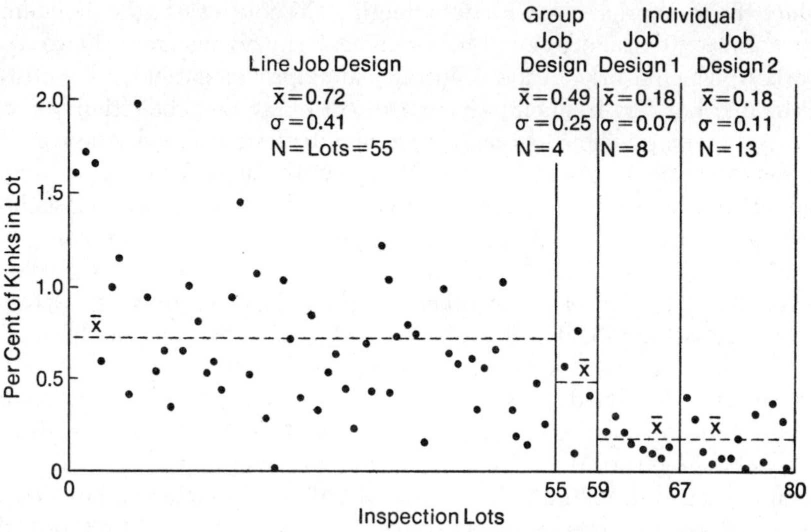

Figure 15-4. Percentage of Kinked Assemblies in Consecutive Lots.

quality responsibility change resulted in improved direct costs of production and quality, but no change in productivity or personnel costs. Both treatments had positive effects on the need satisfaction of foremen.

A study by Folloni (1971) is a case of enlargement in job depth. In this study, the workers continued to perform the same tasks under the same conditions and with the same degree of control over the operation; the only change was the provision of a "self-certification" program by which nearly all of the workers were able to certify their work as defect-free. The results of the program, which included some 2000 employees measured over a four-year period, include: over a 40 percent decline in defects, a 50 percent decrease in "rework" costs, and a 58 percent decline in defects per order.

In contrast with the change in job depth described above, a study by Miller, Dhaliwal, and Magas (1973) involved an empirical examination of the effects of job rotation—an enlargement of job scope. In this study a group of workers involved in assembly-line production of part of a vacuum pump were rotated among four different stations on the line. The order and duration of job assignments were manipulated by the experimenters. For the fragmented assembly-line jobs under observation, the researchers were able to demonstrate that efficiency decreased steadily from the moment a worker began work at each station. This appears to contradict the first of Adam Smith's principles of specialization since workers appear to become less efficient with the passage of time in a specialized job. Again, it should be noted that this apparent contradiction is, in all likelihood, related to the increase in fragmentation—the use of workers to serve machines rather than of machines to serve workers.

Finally, one of the better summaries about the kinds of experiences which firms are having with job depth (O'Toole et al., 1973) identifies more than 40 instances of job enrichment, involving from 10 to 20,000 workers, which nearly always resulted in an improvement in worker attitudes or morale but less frequently have a direct effect on productivity or costs.

Another approach to the subject of job design and division of labor is the assessment of attitudes held by individuals working in routine, repetitive jobs, or a comparison between attitudes of people in such jobs with attitudes held by individuals in jobs with greater depth or scope. One such study was conducted by Walker and Marriott (1954), who surveyed the attitudes of 976 workers in three large factories to determine what factors they liked and disliked about their jobs. Two of the factories mass produced motor vehicles, involving simple, repetitive work on a short time cycle. The third consisted of six metal mills, with fewer repetitive jobs. The results showed that more than one third of the men in the mass production enterprises complained of boredom; only 8 percent made similar complaints in the rolling mills. In the motor vehicle factories, boredom was indicated as more intense among conveyor workers than among those whose work was not controlled by a conveyor. Similarly, satisfaction with work in the motor vehicle factories was lower than satisfaction in the rolling mill —but only among men on conveyor work. In still another survey of more than 1500 workers, Sheppard and Herrick (1972) found that the four aspects of work considered most important (and six of the top eight) were intrinsic factors of the job itself—factors which are lost or destroyed when division of labor takes place.

More detailed insights into job depth and scope were found by Walker and Guest (1952), who interviewed a sample of 180 workers from an automobile assembly line at home, to obtain information regarding jobs, working conditions, pay, promotions, and social relations with other workers, supervisors, and unions. In general, the results indicated that a majority disliked the mass production characteristics of their jobs; only 10 percent preferred or were indifferent to jobs with such characteristics. Mechanical pacing was disliked the most. When the number of operations performed was compared with work interest, a positive relationship between the two was clearly indicated (see Table 15–2). Thus, it would appear from this study that increased job scope is accompanied by increased work interest or satisfaction.

TABLE 15-2. Correlation of Job Scope with Worker Interest.

Operations Performed	Very or Fairly Interesting	Not Very or Not at All Interesting
1	19	38
2-5	28	36
5 or more	41	18

Walker and Guest (1952).

In addition, when a "job factor score"—which might well be interpreted as a measure of depth—was compared with absenteeism rates, a negative relationship was indicated (see Table 15-3).

TABLE 15-3. Absenteeism Related to Job Factors.

	Below Median Job-Factor Score (0-5 points)	Above Median Job-Factor Score (6-12 points)	Totals
Lower than median absentee record (0-6 points)	35	54	89
Higher than median absentee record (7 or more points)	54	32	86
Totals	89	86	175

Walker and Guest (1952).

Disinterest in work and low job satisfaction in limited, repetitive jobs were consistently reported in other studies as well (Argyris, 1957; Guest, 1955). Individual differences are generally ignored, however, leaving the impression that restricted work is *invariably* associated with disinterest in work, apathy, monotony, disinterest in quality, and minimal production.

A third strategy of research on the effect of division of labor compares attitudes and behavior among employees at different occupational levels to examine the hypotheses that satisfaction, mental health, concern for production, etc., are positively related to skill, occupational, or organizational level, and that higher level characteristics can be transferred to lower levels to reduce dysfunctions.

An early study of this type by Super (1939) of 273 men in managerial, professional, commercial, skilled, and semiskilled positions reported a significant, though not linear, relationship between job satisfaction and occupational level. Among white-collar jobs, professionals had the highest job satisfaction, commercial workers the least. In blue-collar jobs skill and satisfaction were also related. An interview study (Centers, 1952) of 1100 men representing a cross section of the adult male population found distinct differences in job satisfaction among occupational groups. Similarly consistent findings are reported in other studies (Ash, 1954; Crisera, 1966; Kornhauser, 1962). The notion that satisfaction is related to occupational or organizational level is well supported, although the idea that higher-level conditions can be transferred to lower levels is still open to question.

More recently, researchers have begun to relate workers' job satisfaction to other conditions in addition to, or in place of, job level or job depth and scope. For instance, Turner and Lawrence (1965) questioned 470 workers in 47 different jobs which they had rated on six criteria of depth and scope (variety, autonomy, required and optional interactions with others, knowledge or skill required, and responsibility). Although they discovered the expected positive relationship between enriched jobs and improved attendance, and between such jobs and worker satisfaction, upon further examination of the data it was learned that the relationships were stronger for those workers who were employed by firms located in small towns. They concluded that workers' reactions to enriched jobs were significantly mediated by the nature of their socio-cultural backgrounds.

This finding touched off a series of surveys which have yielded sometimes contradictory results. Hulin and Blood (1968), in a survey of 1900 male workers in 21 plants in the East, confirmed the Turner and Lawrence findings and explained the differential response to enlarged jobs by means of an index which measures alienation from middle-class norms supportive of the work ethic. Shepard (1969, 1970, 1971), while confirming the negative relationship between alienation and satisfaction, associates the occurrence of alienation not with *place* of employment, but rather with the *type* of employment. In a survey of over 300 workers he found that alienation (as measured by powerlessness, meaninglessness, and autonomy) and satisfaction were strongly correlated with the degree of "functional specialization" inherent in the job. His subjects were auto assemblers, oil refinery control room monitors, and maintenance craftsmen in the same auto plant. The assembly-line workers, whose jobs were most highly specialized, were the most alienated and the least satisfied. The findings for the less specialized refinery workers, and for the least specialized craftsmen, were equally strong and in the predicted direction.

Finally, Hackman and Lawler (1971) attempted to integrate several of these factors into a model which has as its independent variables both measures of job enrichment and the degree to which individual employees desire the fulfillment of higher order needs (see Chapter 10). They found that

> when jobs are high on [measures of job enrichment], employees who are desirous of variety, autonomy, task completeness, and feedback tend to have high motivation, have high job satisfaction, be absent from work infrequently, and be rated by supervisors as doing high quality work (p. 259).

Nonsupporting Studies. The positive results attributed to job enlargement programs create the impression that specialized division of labor must invariably have a strong negative effect on job satisfaction and, perhaps, even on productivity. This being the case, we would expect to find consistently negative effects reported in studies focusing on attitude toward routine work. But there are several studies which report satisfaction with routine work, or no difference in satisfaction between different types of work.

One such study (Smith, 1959) was a questionnaire survey of 72 female workers performing light repetitive work in a knitwear mill. Boredom in the job was found to be associated with youth, restlessness in daily habits and leisure-time activities, and dissatisfaction with plant, home, and personal circumstances. It was not related to personal ambition, tendency to daydream, extroversion, or intelligence. In general, the study found that job boredom is related to individual characteristics rather than to the task.

Another study of female workers in routine assembly was conducted by Turner and Miclette (1962), who interviewed 115 operators over a two-year period. They report that "monotony or boredom did not emerge as an important source of dissatisfaction or frustration among . . . operators, in spite of the highly repetitive nature of the work." In response to a specific question concerning interest in their work, fewer than 20 percent of the interviewees felt that their work was monotonous or boring. Nor did interest in work correlate with intelligence. The apparent interest in work and job satisfaction was derived from pride in the skill necessary to perform the job, and perceived autonomy with respect to work pace and methods. The authors of the study emphasize that repetitive work need not be dissatisfying when there is adequate "traction" (an absence of "distraction"); when the smooth pull of the process is not interrupted by excessive pressure for quantity, by interruptions from outsiders, or by problems with materials or equipment.

One of the most persuasive arguments against the automatic supposition of unalloyed virtue in nonroutine jobs appears in a study by Kennedy and O'Neill (1958). They surveyed the attitudes of workers in four departments of an automobile assembly plant in terms of 14 job dimensions. Survey responses were compared for assembly operators and utility men. Since the latter had broader job scope, it would be expected that their attitudes would be significantly more favorable than the attitudes of assembly workers. There were no statistically significant differences among the scores in the two departments where utility and assembly jobs varied only in scope. In the two other departments, where the utility jobs were upgraded in responsibility to include training and method functions, there were significant differences. From this we might infer that job enlargement in depth has a more positive effect on worker attitudes than job enlargement in scope.

Some further evidence regarding the effect of sex and job scope on satisfaction with routine assembly jobs is provided in an interview study (Kilbridge, 1960b) of 202 assembly line workers employed in a radio and television set factory. Two types of production lines were studied: chassis assembly lines operated by women seated side by side; and cabinet assembly lines operated by men standing several feet apart. To determine whether the operators preferred to do a smaller or a larger amount of work on each unit or product, they were asked whether they preferred a line which turned out 400 sets a day or a line which turned out 200 sets a day. Approximately half the sample (104 workers) indicated a preference for the smaller task; 37 percent (74 workers) appeared indifferent to the size of the task; and 12 percent (24 workers) preferred the larger tasks. Nearly all workers who chose the smaller task said that it seemed like less work or seemed less complicated. Those who preferred the larger task gave a variety of reasons for doing so. Significantly, not a single operator mentioned monotony or boredom, nor did an analysis of responses by sex show any significant relationships.

Kilbridge also wanted to determine whether the workers found mechanical pacing unpleasant. The workers were asked whether they would prefer a push line (stationary rollers along which workers slide the product) or a belt line (motor-driven conveyor belts which move the product at a set speed). One hundred seventy operators preferred the belt line, 12 had no preference, and only 20 preferred the push line. Again there was no difference between responses of men or women.

In a more detailed later study, Kilbridge (1961) compared turnover, absenteeism, and transfer rates with repetitive line work, repetitive batch work, and nonrepetitive work in two different manufacturing concerns. The details of the study are too complicated to be reported here, but the general results are indicative:

> The study shows no consistent relationship between . . . turnover, absence, and transfer rates, which are frequently used indices of job satisfaction and the nature of the work itself. In the situations studied, stronger factors seem to influence job satisfaction, making it impossible to sort out the effect of repetitiveness. . . . In general, [the study] shows that: (1) In the companies studied, there is no discernible correlation between the repetitiveness of work and job satisfaction, if job satisfaction is assumed to be measured by turnover, absence, and transfer rates. A multitude of other factors seems to influence turnover and absenteeism more strongly than the repetitiveness of work, and it is virtually impossible to sort these out from the factor of repetitiveness. (2) Turnover and absence rates, considered as indicators, may move in different directions under the same set of changes in the nature of the work; that is, as indicators they may be inconsistent with each other (p. 22).

For a final look at the question of the effect of simple, repetitive work on job satisfaction, we will refer to an early study (Hall and Locke, 1938) of workers in an English cocoa factory. The principal method of inquiry was an unguided interview of approximately 1000 women and 300 men, which took place at the work bench or machine while work was in progress. The authors reported that 95 percent of the women interviewed felt that they were assigned to jobs suited to their powers and temperaments and only 5 percent were dissatisfied with their jobs. No figures were reported for the men.

Many factors were felt by Hall and Locke to determine job satisfaction, the foremost being the suitability of the worker for the job. They found no simple or direct relationship between the type of work and satisfaction with it:

> The degree of satisfaction experienced was not constant: it varied greatly from day to day and from week to week; indeed in some cases even hourly changes could be detected. . . . Few workers were completely satisfied with all aspects of their work: but they learned to balance its disagreeable features against its attractions. In no case did one group of factors operate alone in creating satisfaction. For each worker there was a whole network of factors, two or three of which stood out prominently; but even the latter did not remain supreme throughout a year, or indeed a week. . . . Few men and women could completely dissociate their attitudes toward a particular task regarded simply as such, from their view concerning the wages derived from it or their feelings towards the actual environment; hence the task was sometimes blamed when the real trouble was an uncongenial foreman, or perhaps unsympathetic work-mates (pp. 54–55).

Considering these studies of attitudes toward routine, repetitive work, it seems rather clear that there is no simple, direct relationship between such work and job satisfaction. Women workers in particular are frequently shown to be generally satisfied doing such work, and there is some evidence that the same applies to men. Given a choice of wide versus narrow job scope, workers often state a preference for the latter. It does not seem unreasonable to conclude that division of labor can be carried to a relatively high degree without destroying satisfaction or creating monotony—provided other job factors are satisfactory (these other factors were discussed in Chapter 10, Motivation).

From the evidence reported in this section it seems clear that the proposition regarding division of labor and performance or job satisfaction is not generally supported. It would appear also that where positive results occur, increasing the depth of a job will have more positive effects than merely increasing its scope. This notion is in harmony with the evidence regarding positive effects from delegation, democratic supervision, participation in decision making, and studies of occupational or organizational level.

Proposition 2

Performance and satisfaction are positively related to job depth for nonalienated workers and negatively related to job depth for alienated workers.

The preceding discussion indicated that while division of labor is related to performance and attitudes for some workers, it is by no means true that this is always the case. Apparently, there is a difference among workers which affects their degree of satisfaction with routine, repetitive jobs. Some writers have suggested a systematic difference, called "alienation," which they indicate is associated with the way job depth is related to performance.

One of the first studies to identify such employee differences was reported by Katzell, Barrett, and Parker (1961). This survey of 72 wholesale warehouse divisions of a large drug manufacturer found that both satisfaction and performance of employees were related to the "rurality" of the community in which the warehouses were located. Measures used were the site of the firm, population, and the proportion of male workers.

This study was followed by the Turner and Lawrence survey discussed earlier (1965), in which workers in urban settings reported less satisfaction with jobs which ranked high on six criteria of job size. Turner and Lawrence concluded that the systematic differences observed were due to the cultural backgrounds of the workers surveyed.

The relationship between alienation, attitudes, behavior, and job design was clarified considerably in a review article by Hulin and Blood (1968) summarizing research on job design. They pointed out that earlier work had posited a simple relationship between division of labor and worker attitudes and behavior. They suggested further that the conclusion that organizations cause workers to be alienated was not necessarily true. Some workers displayed little or no interest in having their jobs enlarged, little interest in advancing in their work, and relatively more interest in monetary rewards, but these attitudes were not necessarily caused by the company or the job design. In fact, they reported evidence (Hulin, 1966) that worker attitudes seemed to vary according to their location. That is, blue collar workers in small towns seemed to display a middle class work ethic in which greater responsibility, loyalty to the employer, and job interest were valued; blue collar workers in large industrialized environments, on the other hand, did not respond to such values. Instead, they seemed to display an ethic of responding to the job as a place to work in order to gain extrinsic rewards. White collar workers, both rural and urban, expressed middle class values.

Summarizing their findings, Hulin and Blood proposed that:

—At a high level of alienation (e.g., urban blue collar workers), increases in job level (e.g., job depth) are associated with decreases in satisfaction with work.

—At a low level of alienation (e.g., rural blue collar workers), increases in job level (e.g., job depth) are associated with increased satisfaction with work.

—For high skill levels (e.g., high depth), as alienation increases satisfaction of work will decrease.

—For low skill levels (e.g., low depth), as alienation increases satisfaction with work will increase.

Consistent with these statements, Hulin and Blood report a negative relationship between job depth and satisfaction for alienated workers ($r = -.52$) and state that "the argument for larger jobs as a means of motivating workers . . . is valid only when applied to certain segments of the work force—white collar and supervisory workers and nonalienated blue collar workers" (p. 50). Similarly, they report a positive relationship (r = .39) between job depth and satisfaction for nonalienated workers.

Later research has reported consistent findings. Hackman and Lawler (1971), reporting a survey of 208 telephone company employees in 13 different jobs, found a positive relationship between measures of satisfaction, performance, and job depth:

> The higher jobs are on Variety, Autonomy, Task Completeness, and Feedback, the more employees tend to report feeling internal pressures to take responsibility for their work and to do higher quality work. [And such employees are rated as] among the most effective performers on the job . . .
>
> . . . The core dimensions [indicated above], as expected, . . . were strongly and positively related to overall job satisfaction, to the degree that employees feel personally involved in their work, and to low absenteeism (p. 271).

In addition, Hackman and Lawler report that the desire for these characteristics of job depth were related in the expected direction to residence in urban or rural settings. Finally, Susman (1973) found the expected relationship between worker attitudes and satisfaction with depth in rural workers, although, contrary to our expectations, "urbans and transitionals . . . instead of responding unfavorably to job discretion, responded with greater job interest" (p. 12).

In general, it appears that Proposition 2 is supported with respect to satisfaction with work, but the relationship of job design to performance is not. Clearly, there is no necessary relationship between satisfaction and performance, except that turnover and absenteeism rates are generally more favorable for satisfied than for dissatisfied workers (Lawler, 1970). In addition, caution should be exercised in equating alienation and rurality of the work setting. Alienation may be derived from socialization, from individual experiences, or from some other source, and need not necessarily occur in urban or rural environments.

Summary

Proposition 1: Division of labor leads to decreased job satisfaction and increased productivity. *Conflicting evidence; not supported.*

Proposition 2: Performance and satisfaction are positively related to job depth for nonalienated workers and negatively related to job depth for alienated workers. *Generally supported with respect to satisfaction, evidence too limited to generalize with respect to performance.*

Discussion

From the preceding review of research it is clear that there is no necessary relationship between job satisfaction, performance, and the division of labor. The issue is far too complex to permit such a simple generalization. With the addition of moderating effects from worker alienation, however, the issue does begin to gain some clarity. It would appear—and this must be taken tentatively—that alienated workers will be most satisfied, and perhaps most productive, where the job design is clear and relatively simple, where the rewards are essentially extrinsic (e.g., money), and where rewards are clearly associated with performance. Attempts at job enlargement or increases in depth may have no effect under these conditions.

In contrast, there is some suggestion that nonalienated workers will be more satisfied, and perhaps more productive, where the job depth is relatively great, where rewards are partially intrinsic, and where rewards are associated with performance. In other words, for such workers, attempts at job enlargement or increases in depth may be expected to have positive effects on satisfaction and performance.

If the foregoing speculation is true, then employers should base their job design upon the characteristics of their employees or should change the employees to fit the jobs as they are designed. This match of worker and job might be accomplished in several ways:

1. The job may be changed by giving it more or less depth, and by making it more or less explicit in nature. For example, if urban workers with a high level of alienation are employed, then employers may wish to make the job requirements simple and explicit, invest resources in training, and emphasize money payments as rewards for effective performance.
2. Employers may control worker input to match the type of job designs which are present. This may be done by selection or transfer activities. For example, employers may select workers who are likely to be nonalienated for high depth jobs.
3. Employers may attempt to adjust attitudes toward work so that they are congruent with the job designs available. For example, where jobs display relatively high degrees of depth, the employer may attempt to develop a work ethic and a company identification in a group of workers who would otherwise be alienated from work.
4. Finally, employers may choose to move their organizations to a location where the labor supply is likely to contain workers whose attitudes are consistent with the job requirements.

Doubtless there are other possibilities as well. We wish only to suggest that strategies such as job enlargement or increased worker autonomy are not, in themselves, automatically effective. To decide how to design the job, one must consider: For what organization purpose? And, for what worker need?

References

Argyris, C. 1964. *Integrating the individual and the organization.* Wiley.

———. 1957. *Personality and organization.* Harper.

Ash, P. 1954. The SRA employee inventory—a statistical analysis. *Personnel Psychology* 7: 337-64.

Babbage, C. 1832. *On the economy of machinery and manufactures.* Knight.

Biggane, J. F., and Stewart, P. A. 1963. *Job enlargement: A case study.* Research Series No. 25, Bureau of Labor and Management, State University of Iowa.

Centers, R. 1952. Motivational aspects of occupational stratification. *Journal of Social Psychology* 28: 187-217.

Conant, E. H., and Kilbridge, M. D. 1965. An interdisciplinary analysis of job enlargement: Technology, costs, and behavioral implications. *Industrial and Labor Relations Review* 18: 377-95.

Crisera, R. H. 1966. A study of job satisfaction and its relationship to performance in the job situation. *Dissertation Abstracts* 26: 4793-94.

Davis, L. E. 1966. *The design of jobs.* Institute of Industrial Relations, Reprint No. 163, University of California.

———., and Valfer, E. S. 1965. Intervening responses to changes in supervisor job designs. *Occupational Psychology* 39: 171-90.

——— et al. 1964. *Supervisory job design.* Report No. 1E-64-5, Institute of Industrial Engineering, University of California.

Dunnington, R. A., Sirota, D., and Klein, S. 1963. Research for organization theory and management action. *Proceedings of the Sixteenth Annual Meeting* (Part V), Industrial Relations Research Association, pp. 150-79.

Durkheim, E. 1933. *The division of labor in society.* Free Press.

Elliott, J. D. 1953. Increasing office productivity through job enlargement. In *The human side of the office manager's job,* AMA Office Management Series, No. 134, pp. 5-15.

Folloni, J. R. 1971. Production certifies quality of its work. *Industrial Engineering* 3: 10-17.

Ford, R. N. 1969. *Motivation through the work itself.* American Management Association.

Goode, C. E. 1964. Greater productivity through the organization of work. *Personnel Administration* 27: 34-49.

Guest, R. H. 1957. Job enlargement: A revolution in job design. *Personnel Administration* 2: 13-15.

———. 1955. A neglected factor in labor turnover. *Occupational Psychology* 29: 217-31.

Hackman, J. R., and Lawler, E. E. 1971. Employee reactions to job characteristics. *Journal of Applied Psychology Monograph* 55: 259-86.

Hall, P., and Locke, H. W. 1938. *Incentives and contentment.* Pitman.

Herzberg, F. 1968. One more time: How do you motivate employees. *Harvard Business Review* 46: 59.

Hulin, C. L. 1966. Job satisfaction and turnover in a clerical population. *Journal of Applied Psychology* 50: 280-85.

———., and Blood, M. R. 1968. Job enlargement, individual differences, and worker responses. *Psychological Bulletin* 69: 41-55.

Katzell, R. A., Barrett, R. S., and Parker, T. C. 1961. Job satisfaction, job performance, and situational characteristics. *Journal of Applied Psychology* 45: 65-72.

Kennedy, J. E., and O'Neill, H. E. 1958. Job content and workers' opinions. *Journal of Applied Psychology* 42: 372-75.

Kilbridge, M. D. 1960a. Reduced costs through job enlargement: A case. *The Journal of Business* 357-62.

———. 1960b. Do workers prefer larger jobs? *Personnel* 37: 45-48.

———. 1961. Turnover, absence, and transfer rates as indicators of employee dissatisfaction with repetitive work. *Industrial and Labor Relations Review* 15: 21-32.

Kornhauser, A. 1962. Toward an assessment of the mental health of factory workers. *Human Organization* 21: 43-47.

Lawler, E. E. 1970. Job attitude and employee motivation: Theory, research and practice. *Personnel Psychology* 23: 223-37.

———., and Hall, D. T. 1970. The relationship of job characteristics to job involvement, satisfaction, and intrinsic motivation. *Journal of Applied Psychology* 54: 305-12.

Litterer, J. 1965. *The analysis of organizations.* Wiley.

Mantoux, P. 1962. *The industrial revolution in the eighteenth century.* Harper & Row.

Marks, A. R. N. 1954. An investigation of modifications of job design in an industrial setting and their effects on some measures of economic productivity. Doctoral Dissertation, University of California.

McGregor, D. 1960. *The human side of enterprise.* McGraw-Hill.

Miller, F. G., Dhaliwal, T. S., and Magas, L. J. 1973. Job rotation raises productivity. *Industrial Engineering* 5: 24-26.

O'Toole, J. et al. 1973. *Work in America.* MIT Press.

Pelissier, R. F. 1965. Successful experiences in job design. *Personnel Administration* 28: 12-16.

Shepard, J. M. 1971. *Automation and alienation.* MIT Press.

———. 1970. Functional specialization, alienation, and job satisfaction. *Industrial and Labor Relations Review* 23: 207-19.

———. 1969. Functional specialization and work attitudes. *Industrial Relations* 8: 185-94.

Sheppard, H. L., and Herrick, N. Q. 1972. *Where have all the robots gone? Worker dissatisfaction in the 70's.* W. E. Upjohn Institute for Employment Research. Free Press.

Smith, A. 1776. *The wealth of nations.* Random House (1937).

Smith, P. C. 1959. The prediction of individual differences in susceptibility to industrial monotony. *Journal of Applied Psychology* 43: 322-29.

Super, D. E. 1939. Occupational level and job satisfaction. *Journal of Applied Psychology* 23: 547-64.

Susman, G. I. 1973. Job enlargement: Defects of culture on worker responses. *Industrial Relations* 12: 1-15.

Turner, A. N., and Lawrence, P. R. 1965. *Industrial jobs and the worker.* Harvard University Graduate School of Business Administration.

———, and Miclette, A. L. 1962. Sources of satisfaction in repetitive work. *Occupational Psychology* 36: 215-31.

Walker, C. R., and Guest, R. H. 1952. *The man on the assembly line.* Harvard University Press.

Walker, J., and Marriott, R. 1954. A study of some attitudes to factory work. *Occupational Psychology* 25: 181-91.

Chapter **16**

Division of Labor: Departmentation

There are two kinds of unity, natural and artificial, the blood ties of family and the enterprise bond of authority. To unite men one must first become collected within oneself. . . . Those who congregate around a leader are encouraged by his own spirit. When people move toward unity they must give some of their wealth and talent, and surrender some of their biases and conceits.

I Ching: Taoist Book of Days

In the previous chapter we indicated the ways jobs may be designed to meet organizational or individual needs. This chapter deals with the organization of work content on a broader scale: We shall consider the question of how jobs may be grouped together into work units in order to meet individual or organizational goals. These work units may be labeled departments or divisions; whatever their identification, they represent groupings of jobs for some purpose.

Classical writers approached the subject by identifying the various groupings to be found. The more common types of departmentation which they discussed were by *product* (e.g., the Chevrolet Division, Buick Division, Oldsmobile Division), *customer* (e.g., institutional sales department, direct sales department, wholesale sales department), *geographic area* (e.g., east coast division, west coast division), *process or machine type* (e.g., punch press department, casting department, painting department), *simple numbers* (grouping by spans of supervision; e.g., infantry squad A, infantry squad B), and *time* (e.g., day shift, night shift).

When one looks at the various departments in an organization it is obvious that such a list is descriptively accurate. Organizations do use these bases for departmentation. The difficulty in using such distinctions, however, is that they offer little information about which one to use when. That is, when organizing or reorganizing, we need to know which form of departmentation is best to meet specific purposes.

The answer to this problem has been at least partially provided by classifying departmentation into two general forms and by studying the relative costs and benefits of each type. The two general types which we shall discuss may be identified as *goal-oriented* departmentation and *functional* or *process-oriented* departmentation. Goal-oriented departmentation is usually based on division of the organization according to different products, different geographic areas, different customer types, or different projects. The units or divisions are relatively self-contained and they have a variety of skills or specialties within them. Thus, two goal-oriented product divisions might each have the necessary people, skills, and equipment to design, produce, and sell a product. Similarly, as shown in Figure 16–1a, the goal-oriented public utility commission has two divisions, one for utilities and the other for transportation. The utilities division might be expected to have personnel within it dealing with legal services, engineering, finance, rate making, and the like. The transportation division would also have its own personnel dealing with such matters.

In contrast, functional or process-oriented departmentation will organize around specialized skills, processes, or machine types. A manufacturing company which has a sales department, an engineering department, a manufacturing department, a finance department, and the like is organized by specialized functions. Similarly, as indicated in Figure 16–1b, the public utility commission with departments for legal services, engineering, accounting, etc., has a process-oriented form. All of the specialties are grouped into individual departments rather than according to the type of customer served. We shall be discussing the relative advantages or purposes of goal versus functional departmentation shortly.

Since World War II a third form of departmentation has been developed, matrix organization, which is actually a special combination of the goal and functional types. In the typical matrix organization, individuals are members of functional departments but they are also assigned on a full- or part-time basis to projects. Such individuals have two bosses, one in a functional department and the other the leader of the project.

This arrangement is illustrated in Figure 16–2, which is a simplified version of the structure used by NASA in its Weather Satellite Program.[1] As indicated, the organization is divided into technical groups (such as propulsion, tracking, camera construction, and satellite design). The structure is also divided into projects which are devoted to the design, development, and construction of individual satellites. A member of Technical Group A may be assigned to Project 1 and retain membership and responsibility in both departments for the period of the project. This form of organization is well suited to structures which need to combine specialties on a temporary basis in the form of projects. It may be seen in publishing houses, road construction businesses, research and development divisions, and other organizations requiring a team of different specialists for the completion of a project. It should be noted, however, that the existence of projects does not automatically mean that a matrix structure exists. The matrix organization is a planned combination of goal and functional units.

[1] See A. Delbecq and A. C. Filley (1974).

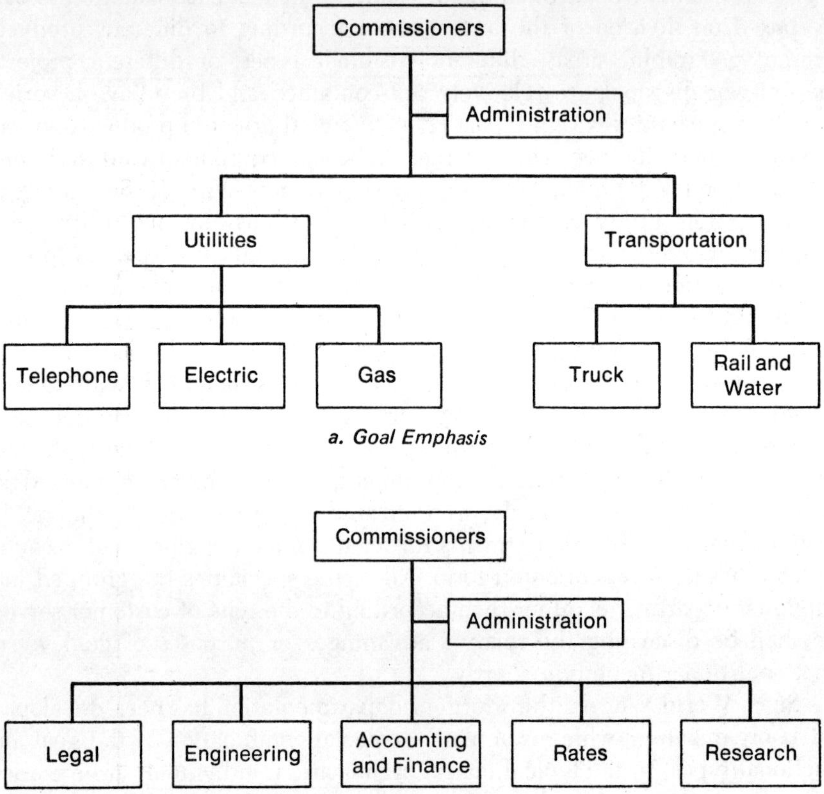

a. Goal Emphasis

b. Process Emphasis

Figure 16-1. Public Utility Commission Organization.

Departmentation and Organizational Requirements

Whatever the structure of an organization there will be some essential requirements which it must achieve in order to exist. Such requirements are determined by those who exchange resources for the goods or services provided, and the structure of the organization will facilitate or interfere with the achievement of such goals. For some organizations, the primary requirement for survival will be the ability to compete with other organizations providing a similar product or service. In such cases, the most important needs of the organization may be efficiency and economic operation. For other organizations, the most important factor to ensure survival may be the satisfactory accomplishment of a project or task. If the objective is to place a man on the moon, for example, the need for economy and efficiency may be far less than the rather clear-cut accomplishment of manned space flight

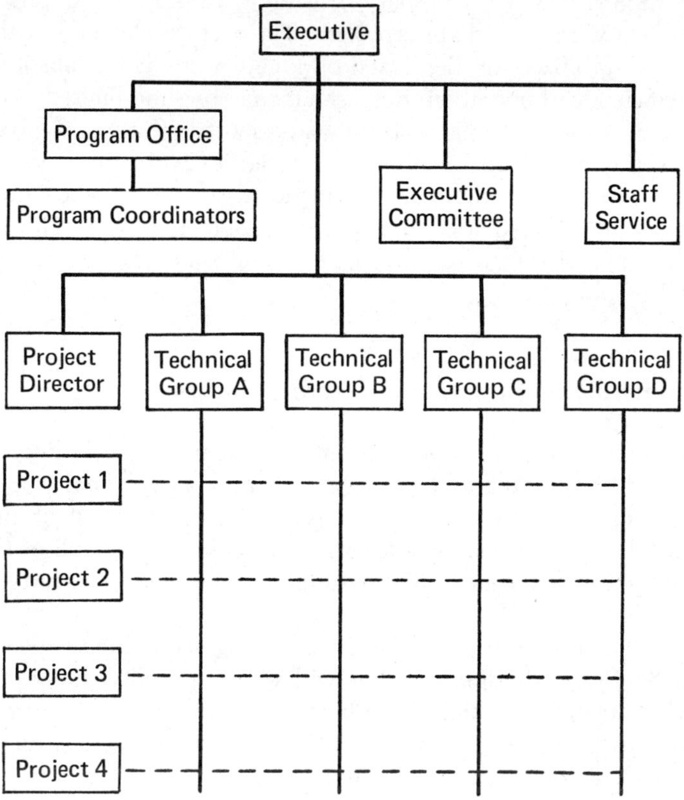

Figure 16-2. Matrix Structure. Source: Delbecq and Filley, 1974, p. 16.

to the moon and back again. Finally, the primary determinant of survival may be the ability of the organization to provide the product or service desired by the customer. A company making fashion clothing would succeed on the basis of pleasing the customer much more than on the basis of product cost.

The exact needs of the organization will help determine the most suitable kind of departmentation. As we shall see in the following discussion, where an organization must make maximum use of resources the functional form of departmentation is usually most appropriate. On the other hand, where client service or project needs are emphasized, the goal-oriented structure is preferred.

This difference may be illustrated in the structure of large universities in this country in the 1960s and 1970s. In the earlier period enrollments were increasing, monetary resources were readily available, and universities were concerned with solving social and environmental problems. As a result, project groups, special programs, and interdisciplinary research groups proliferated. Money was not a primary constraint; rather, the concern was the ability to deal with immediate problems. The picture changed in the 1970s. Enrollments stabilized or decreased. Budgets were cut. Constituents demanded efficiency of operation. Research money became limited. As a result, the universities shifted emphasis from goal-oriented efforts to the basic functional structure in which members of specialties were grouped into their regular teaching departments. Such functional structures made greater use of resources and placed less emphasis on problem solving. The following discussion may suggest why universities made such changes from goal to functional emphasis.

Characteristics of Functional Departmentation

In functional structures departments are organized according to similar activity, process, or machine type. In a university all economists are located in a Department of Economics; in a production facility all of the punch presses will be in the same department; in a book publisher all of the artists will be in the art department. Such groupings will have some rather distinct characteristics.

Development of Subspecialties. By grouping according to specialty, it is easier to develop a division of labor within the specialty. For example, an engineering department might have both an electromechanical engineer and an electronics engineer (Galbraith, 1971). A goal-oriented structure with two departments, each having a single engineer, would require duplicate skills from each engineer working alone.

Advancement in the Specialty. Where specialists are grouped together it is easier to provide advancement opportunities within the specialty. A company typing pool, in contrast with assignment of typists to individual managers, provides an opportunity for job progression within the typing pool according to skill level, tenure, status, etc.

Supervision by a Specialist. Since all of the members of a single functional department have related skills it is likely that the supervisor of the department will have such technical skills as well. Such an arrangement facilitates the supervisor's evaluation of departmental members according to technical or professional requirements as well as organizational requirements.

Professional Contagion. By grouping in specialties, the functional structure provides opportunities for specialists to gain professional knowledge from each other. Members will focus their attention on advancement and recognition in the specialty. The danger, however, is concentration by the functional department on its own professional role in the organization or upon recognition by similar specialists outside the organization, and not upon the goals of the organization of which it is a part.

Maximum Use of Resources. The addition of personnel or equipment in a functional department is often based on a demonstration of full-time utilization of the resource. For example, a new typist will be added to the typing pool when it can be demonstrated that the new person would be kept busy full time. Similarly, a new lathe would be added to the milling department when the full utilization of the equipment could be demonstrated. Such is not the case with goal-oriented units, where it is more likely that the new personnel and equipment would be used sometimes, but not all the time.

Satisfaction with Work. There is some evidence that, in contrast with goal-oriented structures, members of functional departments are more satisfied with their work (Walker and Lorsch, 1968). The reason for this phenomenon, if generally true, is not entirely clear. Perhaps it has to do with the stability of work or the lack of pressure in meeting deadlines. Perhaps it has to do with professional status as perceived by departmental members. Further investigation on this point would be useful.

Difficulty in Coordinating and Scheduling. Functional departments are not likely to be self-contained units. Instead, they have mutual dependencies with other departments. In manufacturing, for example, functional departmentation is accompanied by a great emphasis on production control so that goods in process may be moved for processing from department to department, while at the same time keeping the specialists or machines busy full time. As Galbraith (1971) points out: "The problem of simultaneously completing all tasks on time, with appropriate quality and while fully utilizing all special resources, is all but impossible in the functional structure." For this reason, functional structures typically have difficulty in meeting scheduled dates.

Conflict and Competition Between Departments. Mutual dependency (Filley, 1975), professional emphasis, and differences in personnel cause the functional structure to experience more interdepartmental conflict than is typical in a goal-oriented structure. Functional structures will often have special personnel and procedures to deal with these disagreements.

Formal Organization. Functional structures are more formal than goal-oriented structures. Goal-oriented units are smaller and self-contained, permitting informal contact by members within units and less need to refer questions up the hierarchy. On the other hand, functional organizations are highly differentiated by task and level and are more likely to be characterized by formal rules, reporting relationships, and goals.

Short Time Perspective. It appears that functional structures induce a focus on the immediate activities to be performed. Rather than mobilizing efforts to complete a project or to meet some client goal, the functional organization emphasizes the routines necessary to complete the daily task.

Inflexible Structure. The functional structure tends to be less flexible and less adaptable than the goal-oriented structure. By grouping specialists in the same department, the goals of the profession or specialty rather than the goals of the customer or project are emphasized. Formal relations between departments and between levels in the hierarchy also bring rigidity. When new activities are added to the structure they are likely to be added as separate departments reporting to a top administrator in the organization, since specialists will claim that the new function is not part of their profession.

These characteristics suggest that when efficient use of resources is essential, the functional structure will be appropriate. Thus, a company making a standardized product with stable demand might well benefit by the professionalism, the division of labor, and the satisfaction with work associated with functional structures, and relatively little difficulty may be caused by problems of scheduling and coordination because of the stable demand. In functional structures, management will exert its energies to develop formalized processes and to deal with conflict and competition between departments.

Characteristics of Goal-Oriented Departmentation

In goal-oriented structures, departments are organized by geographic areas, projects, products, or types of customer served. Each department is relatively self-contained, with all of the specialties and devices necessary to meet departmental goals. In a university, an environmental research institute and an industrial relations institute might each have its own economist on the staff. Likewise, each product division in a company might have its own production, sales, engineering, and personnel people. Such structures also have some rather distinct characteristics.

Perhaps the greatest difficulty in the goal-oriented structure is the tendency to duplicate skills and equipment in the various units of the organization. When a product division needs a piece of equipment it is justified on the basis of usefulness rather than on the basis of full time utilization. Similarly, when executives need the services of a secretary, the request is made on the basis of required service rather than on the basis that they will be kept busy full time. While this assignment by "sometimes need" may be tempered by shared facilities or part-time assignment of personnel, the logic of the goal structure encourages the assembly of people and equipment necessary to make the unit self-contained. Where economies of scale are a factor, the goal structure may reduce efficiency by duplication of smaller, less efficient devices as well.

Nor does the goal structure permit the division of labor within a specialty or advancement in the specialty as is possible where a number of specialists work in the same department. Specialists in goal-oriented units will be required to display a wider variety of professional skills than in the functional structure. On the other hand, specialists in goal structures will not have the opportunities provided by professional contagion. They represent their specialty in the department and neither comparison with other professionals nor evaluation by a supervisor on professional qualifications is as likely. The heads of goal-oriented units must, of necessity, be generalists.

They will be responsible for a wide variety of specialties and must rely upon criteria other than professional standards for their evaluations.

The limit on the number of any particular kind of specialist in any department and the supervision of the goal-oriented unit by a professional manager rather than by a specialist create still further difficulties. The professional in a goal-oriented unit who wishes to advance must do so either by moving out of the department and into a better job elsewhere or by moving from a specialist job into a managerial job.

Goal-oriented units tend to focus attention on customer, environmental, or project requirements. That is, the energies of the people and the evaluation of their performance depend more upon the solution of problems or the accomplishment of organizational goals than the day-to-day routines of a functional structure. There is more stress and involvement in the work to be done and more attention to future requirements. For example, if the department is involved in developing an integrated advertising campaign for the client of an advertising agency, the artists, editors, copywriters, and sales personnel will have a specific target of meeting specific client needs. Scheduling and coordination will be easier than in functional departments, the atmosphere more informal, and jobs more flexible. Departmental members will be mutually dependent on each other and minimally dependent upon resources in other departments.

These characteristics suggest that when it is essential to meet target dates, to provide client service, or to solve a unique problem, the goal-oriented structure is favored. Thus, a research organization providing service to a limited number of clients and relatively unconstrained by needs for efficiency and economy might profitably organize into project groups. Managers of such units would exert energy to provide resources, maintain teamwork, and coordinate effort.

Modifying Factors in Goal or Functional Departmentation

Several conditions will affect the characteristics which we have been describing:

Size of Unit. Our discussion of goal and functional departmentation must be tempered with the consideration of size. For example, a small business with six or seven employees led by an owner-manager may be expected to exhibit the characteristics associated with the goal-oriented structure. The organization will adapt readily, jobs will be flexible, relationships between employees will be informal. Yet as the organization grows, and more personnel are added in each functional area, the characteristics associated with a functional structure may be expected to emerge. Having arrived at a point in which there are, say, fifteen engineers in one department, and with the continued need to adapt to client requirements, the company may wish to reorganize into product departments. The engineers would be distributed into each of the departments with goal-oriented characteristics.

The organizational analyst must thus consider the size of the unit as well as the organizational imperatives. What appears to be a goal-oriented unit, like the Chevrolet Division of General Motors, may by its size have all of the characteristics of a functional structure.

Client Emphasis. Another factor which tempers the effects of goal or functional departmentation is the extent to which the unit is free from direct influence or control by the client. As Etzioni (1964) points out, an organization is less likely to attend to client needs to the extent that it is independently financed by other than the client directly or is a monopolistic source of client service. Such conditions enhance professionalization or bureaucratization, or both. Thus a public utility might be expected to be more calloused toward its clients than a washing machine manufacturer, however organized by unit.

Technology and Work Flow. The characteristics of goal-oriented units described previously assume that the people involved have control over the work process and interact with each other in the performance of the task. Where the jobs become fragmented, as described in the previous chapter, then people are subservient to the work system and are easily replaceable. Thus a line-balanced production process or a fragmented assembly line may be organized to produce a single product but such a goal-oriented unit will not have the characteristics mentioned. There will be little attention to end product objectives, little identification with the job or company, and little satisfaction of social needs. Technology and work flow can thus ameliorate the usual characteristics of goal-oriented units.

Matrix Organization

In the past decade a new form of organization has been developed, known as matrix organization (Shull, 1965). The matrix structure is actually a combination of functional and goal-oriented units which attempts to minimize the inherent disadvantages in each and maximize their advantages. The matrix structure may be permanent in nature or it may contain temporary projects which exist until project goals are completed (Galbraith, 1973). In both cases, however, individuals are assigned to two or more units in the organization and experience supervision from several sources.

The permanent matrix may be illustrated by one form of regional health services structure. In such a structure the various health services of a state are organized at the county level: each county has its own physicians, dentists, social workers, and mental health services. Thus, each county is a goal-oriented unit with personnel reporting to the county director. Relations between the specialists are informal, services are adjusted to client needs in the area, and county staffs work together on a team basis. At the same time members of county organization are also assigned to appropriate program offices, or functional units, for purposes of professional development and evaluation of professional skills. Thus, the physicians from all counties would be assigned to a program office for physicians, the dentists to a dental program office, and so on. The program offices facilitate assignment of specialists to counties according to special abilities, the sharing of special services, and the movement between counties as a form of job progression. The permanent matrix is used less often than the more flexible project matrix structure.

Project Matrix Organization. It must be emphasized at the outset of this discussion that "a project doeth not a matrix make." That is, projects are, in themselves, goal-oriented units. They may be established in functional structures in cases where special committees, task forces, or work groups are brought together for some purpose. Projects may also be used as one basis for developing a goal-oriented structure. For example, in the construction industry it has been customary to establish a project to construct a dam, an air base, or a building. In the project matrix organization, members are assigned on a permanent basis to functional departments and *also* to projects for as long as their services are required.

Let us first consider the characteristics of a project itself. First, it has a definite operational objective, such as placing a satellite containing specified instrumentation in a specified orbit at a particular date within certain budgetary constraints. Second, a project generally has a time priority; that is, the emphasis in a project is on time more than money. Where money constraints predominate, the work effort is more likely to be scheduled through functional departments with less attention given to completion time (Delbecq and Filley, 1974). Third, a project is generally supported by one or more interest groups within or outside the organization. In NASA, for example, the projects connected with manned space flight, earth observation, and weather surveillance were initiated by President Kennedy and congressional mandates. Fourth, a project is characterized by its cumulative expenditures over time. Thus, the farther the project moves into its time cycle, the greater the investment and the greater the cost of failure or abandonment. Fifth, the project requires interdependence among several organizational units or several distinct specialties. Finally, a project typically deals with issues that are new or different from the prior experience of the organization.

When these requirements are present, the appropriate organizational strategy may be the development of a project group. For example, a plastics manufacturer may determine that a scientific breakthrough has provided a new form of plastic which can make the company's present products obsolete. Survival needs rather than efficiency take priority and a task force may be formed containing members of several functional departments and charged with preparing a feasibility study of application of the new material.

The usefulness of this approach is suggested by natural alternatives to it (Galbraith, 1971). One alternative is for chief executives to take the responsibility for the activity. Since unusual issues tend to move to higher levels in an organization the executives may drop their normal duties and deal with the immediate problem. By so doing, they reduce their administrative capability. On the other hand, the executives may try to "decentralize" the issue by asking functional units to investigate their specific interests as they relate to the problem. This strategy has the advantage of moving the problem into the hands of those closest to technical details, but necessarily limits the range of attention to the vested interests or professional limits of the technical people. Nor is there any coordination of plans generated by various departments.

Galbraith (1973, pp. 54–65) has suggested characteristics which should be present if project groups are to be effective:

1. Induce perceptions of reward and importance in members serving on the project. Participation must be rewarded intrinsically or extrinsically; otherwise, members will devote attention to functional departments from which they gain their rewards.
2. Include in the project group representation by line managers who will subsequently be accountable for the implementation of joint decisions and plans.
3. Include technical specialists from all departments significantly affected by the work of the project group. Lower level personnel are closer to the technical details than top management.
4. Project participants should have the authority to commit their departments to decisions by the project group.
5. Influence in the group should be based on knowledge and information rather than upon hierarchical position. Members will frequently come from different levels of the organization and such status differences should not interfere with necessary teamwork.
6. Build project activities into the regular processes of the organization. Project requirements are less likely to disrupt the organization if project group members keep their regular superiors informed about progress and needs.
7. Construct project groups with a small staff of full time people and a majority of part time individuals. Full time assignment of non-administrative people severs ties with other technical members and may reduce performance.
8. Insure use of conflict resolution methods based on group problem solving rather than on force or compromise.
9. Attend to conditions necessary for development of teamwork and joint effort. Participants should have the necessary skills for dealing with interpersonal and group decision issues which may arise.
10. Provide leadership by an integrator. Such individuals will manage the *process* of the group activities rather than making his own decisions and imposing them on the project group.[2]

The suggestions for effective project operation stated above apply whether the project is a temporary unit in a regular functional organization

---

[2] Reprinted by special permission from *Designing Complex Organizations* by Jay Galbraith, Addison-Wesley Publishing Co., Inc. Copyright © 1973.

or whether the organization has a matrix form with multiple projects containing members of functional departments. In the matrix organization, such as was shown in Figure 16–2, the basic design of the structure balances a multiple project activity with a functional structure.

The actual titles of project managers will vary between organizations. In manufacturing firms they may be called materials managers, integrating the work flow in a common system. In some cases, they are called product managers. In aerospace, they may be called program managers, while in hospitals they are designated as unit managers (Galbraith, 1973). Whatever the title, project managers are basically involved in scheduling, coordinating effort, assembling resources, and maintaining time and budget constraints. Unlike the typical line manager, project managers have little or no formal authority over the group for which they are responsible. Indeed, they may not even select the technical members assigned to their projects. Project managers merely evaluate project members on the basis of their contribution to the project.

It is the head of the functional or technical department who typicallly determines the professional competence, level of financial reward, and job assignment or progression of a unit's members. As might be supposed, then, a basic prerequisite for effective performance of matrix organization is a balance of power and influence between those responsible for projects and those responsible for functional departments. One way to maintain such balance is to provide project funding directly to project or program administrators, with functional departments dependent upon project assignments by their members for maintenance of their own existence. In such cases the project managers have the power derived from ownership of money, and the functional managers have the power derived from their expertise and services. Without some sort of power balance, matrix organizations tend to disintegrate.

From the foregoing discussion it may be seen that matrix organizations will be used where the organization is large enough to support functional departments containing relatively large groups of technical personnel and where the organizational requirements suggest the need for multiple projects. The primary requirements will be those of task accomplishment within essential time constraints rather than upon maximization of efficiency and economy.

Propositions

The previous discussion suggests several propositions which are central to the division of labor through departmentation:

1. Goal-oriented structures are more adaptable than functional structures.
2. Goal-oriented structures are less efficient than functional structures.
3. Matrix structures combine goal-oriented units and functional units.

Empirical Evidence

Proposition 1

Goal-oriented structures are more adaptable than functional structures.

A review of the research literature reveals little analysis of the behavioral consequences of organizing around goal or function. Yet this issue is important and, for that reason, we shall discuss a few illustrative examples in order to add clarity and insight to this issue.

The first proposition suggests that goal-oriented structures are more adaptable than functional structures. The theory discussed earlier suggested that the informality, the team effort, and the relative independence of a goal-oriented unit provide ease of change and adjustment to meet changing customer or environmental requirements.

A revealing case study related to this issue is reported by Kover (1963). A large advertising agency which had been organized primarily along functional lines, with coordination between departments handled by account executives, was reorganized into teams of specialists to deal with different products. While previously all specialists of a particular type had been grouped into the same department, now different specialists worked together in teams to serve a few clients each. Kover states

> . . . the existing services were disbanded and their personnel were formed into heterogeneous marketing or creative groups to help fulfill the goal of more tightly integrated client service. Service was now provided by formal, permanent, client-oriented groups in place of less structured, shifting client assignments (1963, p. 255).

Kover found that client-agency communication was greatly simplified by the change and limited to fewer channels. However, communication among specialists was severely reduced. They were spread among various client groups, creating a spatial separation which had not previously existed, and were now judged by nonprofessionals. This change in departmentation resulted in a marked shift from evaluation of work in terms of both professional and client requirements toward a single client satisfaction criterion. As a result, client service reportedly increased. The change also facilitated "coordinated manipulation and transmission of work" with fewer delays, mistakes, and omissions. Apparently, both the focusing of client contact with a single departmental group and the unified efforts of the specialists grouped to serve the client made the structure more adaptable.

The study also raises another point. How willing are the members of an organization to remain in or work for the goal or functional structure? Kover found that with specialists scattered throughout the structure under the new arrangement, they could not be compared with each other in terms of performance and had less in common with their fellow workers. As one researcher said: ". . . What do these people know about research? I can't talk to them about what I do. So what *do* I talk about—sales figures?" (p. 257). With the new emphasis on client service and reduced attention to professionalism there was a tendency for the "craftsman" to become alienated and for the "careerist" to become better adapted to the new structure.

In a second study comparing goal versus functional organization, Walker and Lorsch (1968) compared two manufacturing organizations which were essentially alike except for their method of departmentation. One plant was organized around product divisions, the other around functional divisions. In the functional plant, professional goals were emphasized, while the product division plant displayed dual concern for both professional and organizational goals. Comparing time horizons in each, there was a general concern for short-run goals and daily problems in the functional structure and a variety of time horizons in the goal-oriented structure. Apparently, employees in a functional structure are more concerned with today's job. Where the goal is a specific event in the future, like completion of a project, attention is directed to that future event (Delbecq and Filley, 1974).

The relative flexibility and adaptability of the goal structure is suggested by Walker and Lorsch in comparing the formality of the two plants. The product division plant had less explicit definition of jobs, less division between jobs, and less reliance on rules and processes, compared with the functional plant. Similarly, communications were more frequent, informal, and face-to-face. In the more formal functional structure, boundaries between specialized departments blocked communication. Finally, they observed that the product division plant changed more easily to improve capabilities and contained people who were more involved in their work, though feeling more stress and pressure in their jobs. In the functional structure, employees displayed more job satisfaction and less work involvement.

Both this and the previous study (Kover, 1963) suggest that a goal-oriented structure enhances the integration or teamwork of employees working jointly to meet some future set of goals. Where the survival and success of the organization depends upon problem solving, creativity, or adapting to customer or environmental needs, the goal-oriented rather than the functional structure seems advisable. Such evidence is too limited to support the initial proposition about relative adaptability, but it is clearly consistent with that notion.

Proposition 2

Goal-oriented structures are less efficient than functional structures.

In assessing the relative efficiency of the two structures, we shall focus on two bases of comparison. The first is the utilization of people and equipment. Here we are concerned with the extent to which people and equipment are likely to be used to their fullest and the extent to which the structure facilitates effective division of labor. The second basis for comparison has to do with the economics of scale associated with using one big piece of equipment or a single office containing specialists versus duplicated skills or equipment in several divisions. The empirical evidence is limited and at a low level of rigor, but it does permit an examination of an important managerial issue.

In the study by Walker and Lorsch (1968) reported earlier, the researchers found that the functional structure was better at maximizing the use of present people and equipment. Apparently, the formality of planning and operations in the functional plant was effective and provided for efficient operations so long as conditions were stable, requiring little change or problem solving. The functional structure contained a clear statement of responsibility for each person, an explicit set of rules and procedures, and a primary focus upon meeting immediate goals.

Finally, Galbraith (1969, 1971, 1973) has described the characteristics of functional, goal, and matrix organizations after considering the development of several organizations. He points out that the functional structure makes maximum use of resources for several reasons. For one thing, by grouping machines or people together on the basis of their specialty the work may be divided into subspecialties. The goal structure, on the other hand, requires that specialists or equipment be able to handle a much broader range of tasks. In addition, the functional structure permits time sharing of people or equipment. Further, the functional structure permits individuals to advance in the specialty as they gain greater skill. The goal structure permits no such career path for specialists simply because each goal unit contains fewer of each type with no resulting avenue for advancement. The functional structure also provides greater advantage of scale and efficient use of machines or people since they serve the entire organization, while in the goal organization people and machines, perhaps in smaller, less efficient numbers and sizes, must be duplicated in each of the goal divisions of the organization.

In general, the limited evidence is quite consistent. It appears that where the environment is stable (Morse, 1970) and efficient use of resources is required the functional structure is to be preferred.[3]

Proposition 3

Matrix structures contain a planned, joint relationship between goal and functional units.

The third proposition is based upon a need to determine whether or

---

[3] It should be noted that we are discussing the design of the total structure in this section, not the design of an individual functional department. In production operations, for example, the availability of stable, high volume production, with single purpose machines, lends itself to a straight line production layout. Such line balanced production is often organized around product groupings but otherwise has all of the formalization characteristics which have been attributed to functional structures.

not there is a deliberate organization design through which members of goal and functional departments have joint accountability to both a goal and a functional department. Unlike goal or functional structures, which may evolve through no conscious organization planning, the matrix organization is a hybrid structure which is intentionally created to meet specific purposes. While the information regarding matrix designs is limited, a discussion of empirical evidence will suggest how it is formed and the proper use of such a structure.

The operation of the matrix structure in NASA's Weather Satellite Program has been described in detail by Delbecq and Filley (1974). That structure was developed under rather distinct conditions. First, the NASA structure was influenced by the space race with the Russians in the late 1950s, culminating in President Kennedy's State of the Union Message in 1961 in which he proposed the "development of meteorological satellites." Second, it was characterized by the influence of NASA Administrator James Webb, a professional manager with experience at Sperry Gyroscope, in the Bureau of the Budget, and as under secretary of state, who developed an organization planning staff to design a proactive organization necessary to meet the tight schedule of project completion. Finally, it was characterized by a situation in which economy was far less important than the problem solving demands thrust upon NASA.

The resulting structure is abstracted in Figure 16–3. The NASA headquarters operation contains staff services and program offices, including an associate administrator who is responsible for the Office of Space Science and Applications. Contained within that office are the Earth Observation Programs including an experimental satellite program, an operational satellite program, an atmospheric research program, and others. The program offices are concerned mainly with developing and designing a program, planning and coordination of projects, and, importantly, gaining the necessary money and support from outside agencies. It is this level which deals with the external environment of NASA.

In contrast, the centers which report to headquarters are primarily concerned with internal, technical matters. The Goddard Space Flight Center, which does much of the work on the weather satellite projects, contains the combination of functional and project units which we have described as a matrix structure. Prior to 1965, it was organized around a few projects with full-time assignment of specialists. At that time it was reorganized to contain technical departments which furnished personnel to projects as needed. The rationale for the change is described by J. Clark, Director of Goddard:

> In 1965 the Goddard Space Flight Center was reorganized. The reorganization was based on the recognition that the center now had many more projects. This was the end of the maximum growth period of individual projects which had been permitted to develop according to the preferences of the project managers. Several projects, e.g., NIMBUS, had 100% assignments of functional and specialist personnel to

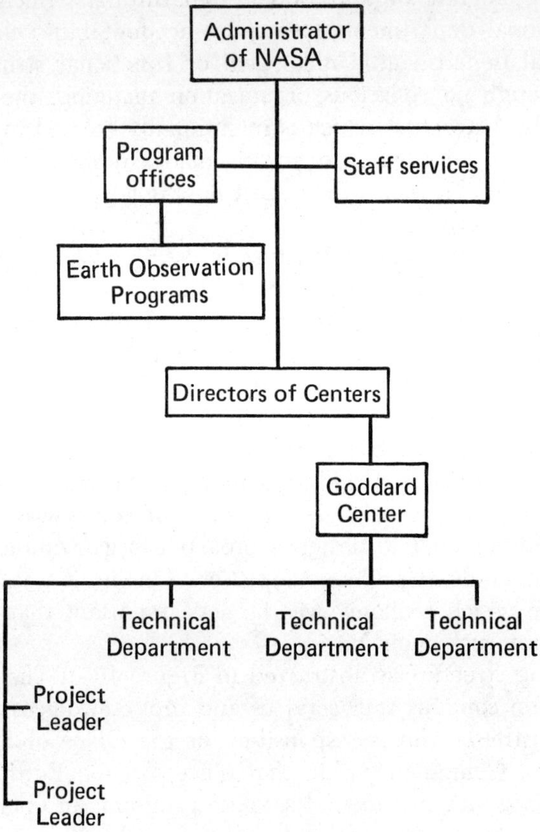

Figure 16-3. NASA's Matrix Structure.

the project. This meant that they could command in a line sense all the skills they needed.

As funding became tighter and more projects emerged, it was obvious that we could not afford such an arrangement. Projects tied up functional specialists full time, even though the functional specialists were underutilized.

The result of not assigning personnel full time to projects has resulted in more realistic early estimates of personnel needs by the project, an honest commitment of released resources from functional groups.

This has resulted in the need for firm negotiation and realistic manpower estimates in planning. Our norm is to sharply fix the situation by manpower estimates due to the limitations in total manpower resources at the center.

Without this manpower estimate, the functional and specialist groups tend to take on more work than they can handle and individual projects tend not to ask for what they will really need for fear the project will seem too expensive.

The program office is not concerned with Goddard as an institution.

It thinks in terms of the Office of Space Science and Applications Programs.

On the other hand, headquarters cannot adjust manpower unilaterally. Thus, Goddard, in practice, budgets people and headquarters budgets dollars. Headquarters tries to persuade us they need more people in their program on individual projects. We try to persuade them we need more dollars for manpower resources. Each program is sure to do a better job with just a little larger manpower pool.

Each of us has a veto. I can indicate we have too much work already. The program can reply they will take their work to another center. Thus, we are faced with the need to negotiate honestly. (J. Clark, Director, Goddard Space Flight Center; quoted in Delbecq and Filley, 1974, p. 80.)

This quote indicates the movement away from goal-oriented projects where manpower was assigned full-time and was underutilized to a matrix form which could maintain the requirements of project work while increasing the efficiency of personnel assignment. At the peak of activity in satellite development and financial support, it is estimated that 80 percent of the members of technical departments were assigned to project groups. Thus, the technical departments depended upon the project groups for dollar support and the project groups depended upon the functional departments for technical services. This balance of power helped to maintain cooperation between the two halves of the matrix structure.

By 1971, the picture had changed. NASA's budgetary support was restricted and the need for economy and efficiency became important. As a result, the balance of power shifted to the functional departments. Fewer personnel were assigned to projects, projects themselves were curtailed, and schedules for completion of projects were extended. The effects of this shift in power balance may be illustrated by an anecdote. It will be recalled from the earlier discussion that members of functional departments may become interested in professional stature rather than organizational requirements. In this case a project manager at Goddard went to a functional department requesting several copies of a device to be used on a series of satellites. The representative of the technical (functional) unit replied: "We'll make one for you because it has never been done before. But not the whole series. What do you think we are, a production line?"

Galbraith (1973) has described the reorganization of a commercial airplane division from a functional to a matrix form. The product branch employed about 10,000 people and produced about ten aircraft a month. The functional structure existed for the division as a whole and for its branches, which specialized in the construction of different planes. This structure was sufficient until the period 1963–66 when there was an enormous increase in the demand for commercial jet aircraft. This pressure for production and economy was accompanied by task uncertainty and interdependence caused by compressed schedules.

To cope with this situation, task forces were created to coordinate work and set priorities for each major segment of a plane. Personnel were assigned to task forces full-time until the first six to ten aircraft were completed. Once the routine was established there was no further need for the groups.

Other case studies provide the same basic logic of matrix organization (Shull, 1965, 1973; Shin, 1974). It seems likely that the general proposition stated for this section is correct, though reliance on case examples is insufficient proof.

Summary

Proposition 1: Goal-oriented structures are more adaptable than functional structures. *Consistent but limited evidence. Insufficient for judgment.*

Proposition 2: Goal-oriented structures are less efficient than functional structures. *Consistent but limited evidence. Insufficient for judgment.*

Proposition 3: Matrix structures contain a planned, joint relationship between goal and functional units. *Consistent but limited evidence. Insufficient for judgment.*

Discussion

The paucity of evidence on the subject matter of this chapter makes generalizing difficult and tentative. While the moderating effects of organization, size, client emphasis, and technology are important, as indicated, there is evidence that if an organization wants to maximize dollar efficiency and use of resources in a stable environment then the functional organization is better. On the other hand, if the organization wants to maximize problem solving potential or customer service, and the environment is fragmented or unstable, then the goal-oriented structure is favored.

This same logic and the same organization alternatives may be carried down to the job assignment level as well, and may be used to answer the question: "Should I have a secretarial pool in my company or should the executives have their own secretaries?" If what we have said is accurate, then the functional typing pool should be used where economy is favored, and the individual secretary (goal-oriented structure) should be used where service, adaptability, and creativity are favored.

The development of a matrix organization offers the organization designer some alternative structures which may be useful. For example, a simple project management structure has sometimes been accompanied by low job satisfaction simply because of anxiety about continued employment when the project ends (Galbraith, 1973). The matrix organization provides a way to give employees a home base to which they may return after project completion. On the other hand, if a functional structure has a number of time pressures and uncertainties thrust upon it suddenly, then the use of task forces or special committees may facilitate coordination between functions. Finally, a growing organization whose technology is not routine and programmable and which relies heavily for its success on customer service might well plan for the development of a matrix or a goal-oriented structure once the functional structure becomes unwieldy and customer service starts to decay.

References

Delbecq, A., and Filley, A. C. 1974. *Program and project management in a matrix organization: A case study*. Monograph No. 9, Graduate School of Business, Bureau of Business Research and Service, University of Wisconsin.

Etzioni, A. 1964. *Modern organizations*. Prentice-Hall.

Filley, A. C. 1975. *Interpersonal conflict resolution*. Scott, Foresman.

Galbraith, J. R. 1973. *Designing complex organizations*. Addison-Wesley.

———. 1971. Matrix organization designs. *Business Horizons* 14: 29-40.

———. 1969. *Organization design: An information processing view*. Working Paper No. 425-69, Alfred P. Sloan School of Management, MIT; Mimeograph.

Kover, A. J. 1963. Reorganizing in an advertising agency: A case study of a decrease in integration. *Human Organization* 22: 252-59.

Morse, J. J. 1970. Organizational characteristics and individual motivation. In *Studies in organization design*, ed. by P. R. Lawrence and J. W. Lorsch. Irwin.

Shin, B. P. 1974. Extension of matrix organization theory: Particular emphasis on planning function. Dissertation submitted to the Graduate Faculty of the University of Georgia in partial fulfillment of the requirement for the Degree of Doctor of Philosophy, Athens, Georgia.

Shull, F. A., Jr. 1965. *Matrix structure and project authority for optimizing organizational capacity*. Business Monograph No. 1, Business Research Bureau, Southern Illinois University.

———. 1973. Three generations of matrix design: Its derivations and prospects. A paper presented at the meeting of the Academy of Management, Boston, Mass.; October 1973.

Walker, A. H., and Lorsch, J. W. 1968. Organizational choice: Product vs. function. *Harvard Business Review* 46: 129-38.

Chapter **17**

Professionals in Organizations and Line-Staff Relationships

The integration of the professionals into the business organization . . . emerges as the central social problem of Twentieth Century America.

PETER DRUCKER

Modern employees are far better trained and educated than their predecessors. For this reason, among others, today's workers expect and receive much more in the way of financial rewards. In general, the more years of formal schooling and the greater their specialized skills, the more value they have to their employing organization, and the more they will consequently be offered.

Specialized skills and formal education also seem to be accompanied by expectations concerning the kind of work it is "fitting" to do. Management by Objectives, job enrichment, and participative management are but a few of the techniques which modern organizations have adopted in hopes of providing the kinds of tasks and overall environment that will prove stimulating to employees. In general, the more years of formal schooling and the greater their specialized skills, the greater will be the likelihood that the organization will provide workers with opportunities to control large segments of their work situations and to participate in the goal-setting process.

There are therefore a great many costs which the organization must be prepared to pay if it is to attract, motivate, and ultimately retain the highly educated and skilled employee. In addition to high initial salary and benefits, the firm must be willing to provide extensive training so that new workers can successfully perform their "enriched" jobs and take part in meaningful establishment of objectives. The organization must also accept the fact that it is difficult to satisfy employees whose expectations are so high.

Finally, it is necessary to remember that today's dissatisfied workers are more likely to leave the organization than their counterparts a generation or so ago. Educated employees have more of a stake in their education, and less in their firms. Having entered at a relatively high level, they were able to bypass the years of low-reward work which have customarily been the way to success for the uneducated worker.

This combination of circumstances has created an uncomfortable paradox for the organization: The firm's ability to retain employees, particularly highly skilled and educated employees, is diminishing at the very time when more of these people are needed than ever before, and when recruitment, selection, and training costs for such people have never been higher.

In this chapter we will (1) examine the concept of "professionalism" and define the essential characteristics of the organizational professional; (2) review the research pertinent to some of the problems which result from assimilating the professional employee into the bureaucratic organization; and (3) explore some suggested remedies to these problems. We will also consider one of the more knotty problems in management theory, the classic concepts of line and staff. Subject to limitations which we shall presently make clear, the primary bases for conflict between line and staff personnel closely resemble those between the professional and the bureaucrat. Furthermore, although it is true that there are staff functions which are not carried out by professionals, just as there are line functions which are, still "there is a high correlation between staff and professionals and between line and nonprofessionals" (Etzioni, 1964, p. 81).

Professions and Professionals

Not too long ago the very idea of writing about "professionals in organizations" would have seemed illogical since, by definition, professionals did not work for anyone but themselves. The original model of the professional was that of "a free agent contracting to perform a service for his client" (Daniels, 1969, p. 255). Today, however, we recognize that professionals may work in any of four settings: individual private practice; autonomous professional organizations, such as law firms and medical clinics; professional organizations which are part of larger external systems, such as public schools and social work agencies; and in professional departments which are part of nonprofessional organizations (Hall, 1968, p. 94). In fact, today it may be said that:

> More and more professions are being pursued in bureaucratic settings. Even for the physician and the lawyer, the last of the "free professionals," practice is increasingly a group enterprise, boxed in with various organizational constraints. Private practice as a style of professional work is rapidly disappearing, while many new and emergent professions have never practiced in anything except a bureaucratic setting (Haig and Sussman, 1971, p. 528).

Definitional Characteristics of Professionals

If professionals can no longer be defined in terms of self-employment, what then are their definitional characteristics? A great many attitudes and behaviors have been claimed by various authors to be associated with "professionals," but a recent review of the literature reveals that the following have been most widely used (Schriesheim, Von Glinow, and Kerr, 1975) and are probably most important.

Expertise. Professionals possess expertise, usually as a result of prolonged specialized training in a body of abstract knowledge. Their expertise is specific to their area of specialty, and they make no claims for its applicability to other areas.

Ethics. Professionals perceive an obligation to render service to the public. They have internalized a code of ethics which requires that they behave toward clients with neutrality, making decisions by applying universalistic standards, without being swayed by self-interest and without becoming emotionally involved. Professionals also feel an obligation to society to maintain quality standards within the profession.

Collegial Maintenance of Standards. Professionals believe that they can best assure quality of service through collegial maintenance of standards. Rather than through hierarchical supervision or government control, professionals feel that they alone have the technical knowledge and ethical codes necessary to police their specialty.

Autonomy. The professional claims "self-control over both his decisions and his work activities . . . " (Engel, 1969, p. 31). Demands for autonomy relate to:

1. Innovation—professionals seek responsibility for origination, claim the right to alter established methods, etc.
2. Individual responsibility—professionals seek to define their own goals, and will not subordinate themselves to those they feel are less knowledgeable.
3. Free communication—they require access to all relevant information, to be privy to all discussions impinging on their areas, and to communicate without constraint (Blau and Scott, 1962).

Commitment to Calling. Professionals feel a sense of calling to their field, a dedication to their work, and a strong commitment to their careers. They believe that their chosen profession is valuable, even essential to society, and they are proud to be a member of it.

Identification with Profession and Fellow Professionals. "Identification" may be said to occur when "an individual accepts influence because he wants to establish or maintain a satisfying self-defining relationship to another person or group" (Kelman, 1958, p. 52). Professionals feel a strong identification with their chosen profession, and use fellow professionals and professional organizations as important referents. In their high professional loyalty, their employment of external (to the employing organization) referents, and their commitment to specialized role skills, professionals are *cosmopolitan* rather than *local* (Merton, 1957; Gouldner, 1957, 1958).

Definitional Characteristics of a Profession

Many of the characteristics necessary for an occupation to be considered a profession follow logically from the description of professionals. Thus a profession requires an abstract body of knowledge, a base of systematic theory, work which is challenging, for which long training is necessary (Wilensky, 1964). A profession also contains a code of ethics and has an orientation toward service. Professional societies typically exist and have the power to restrict entry to the field, license practitioners, and maintain educational, training, and performance quality standards.

In addition, to be judged a profession an occupation must be full-time and terminal, as opposed to being merely a stepping-stone to another field. It should also offer a training school for would-be practitioners which provides, in addition to the necessary technical education, a thorough socialization of students. It is also important that clients and the general community recognize and accept the authority based on the abstract knowledge of the profession, and that the practitioner within the profession be relatively free from lay restrictions and control, with most legislation concerned with the profession being shaped by the profession (Greenwood, 1957; Goode, 1960; Blau and Scott, 1962; Wilensky, 1964; Freidson and Rhea, 1965; Perrucci and Gerstl, 1969; Moore, 1970; and Perrucci, 1971).

It is probably worth noting here that these definitions of professions and professionals should not be considered as descriptive of many occupations and individuals, but should rather be viewed as ideals against which comparisons can be made. Were these definitions taken literally, probably no person or occupation could be said to qualify. Occupations which are usually considered to fall within these definitions (e.g., law and medicine) possess these characteristics to a relatively high degree, but still fall considerably short of the ideal.

Professional Attributes

Much of what researchers have learned about professional attitudinal and behavioral patterns stems logically from their definitional characteristics. For example, it has been found that, compared to other organizational members, professionals (and cosmopolitans) tend to be less loyal to and more critical of their employing organizations and their communities. Consistent with such attitudes is their reported greater willingness to relocate. However, one study found that "more professionally-oriented nurses did not differ from others in loyalty to the hospital . . ." (Bennis et al., 1958); in another study cosmopolitanism (an attribute of professionals) and geographical mobility "did not scale together, indicating that they were not part of the same dimension" (Abrahamson, 1965, p. 100). Some possible reasons for these apparently divergent findings will be discussed shortly.

It has also been found that professionals are not as concerned with seeking and attaining influence within their employing organization and that they tend to avoid extensive social involvement with others in their firm or local community, preferring to socialize with those few who are similar to them in education, training, and field of specialization (Merton, 1957; Gouldner, 1957, 1958; Barnes, 1960; McNaul, 1969; Sheldon, 1971; and Kerr, 1972).

Areas of Professional-Bureaucratic Conflict

Conflict between professionals and the organizations which employ them may result from any of the professional's definitional characteristics.

Expertise. The professional's expertise, earlier described as being typically acquired through specialized training in a body of abstract knowledge, is seen by some authors as creating tendencies to be somewhat *too* specialized and *too* abstract for the organization's liking. For example, it is argued that the professional

> . . . takes a field which might appear to be extremely narrow to the layman and develops it to the Nth degree. General management, on the other hand, takes pride in its integrative skills and its ability to move about freely in a variety of fields. From management's standpoint, the specialist often appears to be overelaborating the obvious. . . . From the professional's standpoint . . . the ability to reach decisions on the basis of partial information and what might appear to be flimsy evidence is not held in high esteem (Moore and Renck, 1955, pp. 60–61).

In short, professionals are often seen by the organization as being rather esoteric individuals who seem to take greater pleasure in performing their narrow specialties than in addressing organizational problems. The organization in turn is seen by professionals as being too pragmatic, as too often taking a seat-of-the-pants approach to problems rather than attacking them scientifically.

Ethics. The internalized code of ethics of professionals has also proved troublesome to employing organizations and has generated considerable conflict, centering upon the requirement that professionals permit neither their means nor their ends to be influenced by any consideration other than the welfare of their clients. The professional has also "been disciplined to appraise 'many sides of a question'; his professional training inhibits the reflexive display of reassuring sentiments of loyalty to a particular company or client. . . . As a result, it may be that the expert is not easily viewed as a thoroughly 'reliable' member of the in-group" (Gouldner, 1954, pp. 226–27).

A related matter concerns the question of openness or secrecy with regard to programs, methods, inventions, and discoveries made by professionals while in the employ of the organization. The firm quite naturally considers such things to be its "property," to be secluded or revealed as it sees fit. Legal protection in the form of patents and copyrights exists to furnish such protection. Professional training, on the other hand, often includes an instillation of the value that such knowledge, however acquired, rightfully "belongs" to society in general and to the scientific community in particular. This potential source of conflict may become severe in cases where the knowledge in question could be of great general benefit, as would be true of a new method of drilling for oil, or of an influenza vaccine.

This discussion has not been intended to convey the impression that the professional is "right" in this disagreement and the organization "wrong"; the conflict is simply the result of different allegiances. "The professional is bound by a norm of service and a code of ethics to represent the welfare and interests of his clients, whereas the bureaucrat's foremost responsibility is to represent and promote the interests of his organization" (Marcson, 1960, p. 244).

Collegial Maintenance of Standards. Peer and self-control and maintenance of standards provides further grounds for conflict, in that this characteristic is usually inconsistent with the principles of bureaucratic authority and hierarchical control. The source of the authority of organizational leaders, as we saw in Chapter 6, is their formal position within the hierarchy. They have the *right* to exercise formal sanctions over subordinates, and subordinates have a *duty* to obey their directives. Bureaucratic authority may be limited to the employee's immediate supervisor, or may be extended to all who possess higher rank. In either case compliance is expected *whether or not* the leader possesses superior knowledge and competence. Bureaucratic authority permits relatively smooth changes in command, since authority vested in former leaders can formally and immediately be transferred to their successors, and subsequently to anyone who occupies the higher position.

Professionals, on the other hand, "tend to be organized in terms of a 'colleague group of equals' with ultimate control being exercised by the group itself. Hence, bureaucratic control violates the professional's traditional mandate of freedom from control by outsiders" (Miller, 1967, p. 760). "Outsiders" may seem a strange label for one's own administrative superiors but, unless leaders are also recognized professionals with competence in their professional subordinates' particular specialties, their authority may be questioned, on two grounds.

First, professionals may deny that their hierarchical superiors have the skills to determine whether performance standards are being met. From the professonal's viewpoint, only fellow professionals know enough about their work to evaluate it competently. Second, professionals may deny that their superior's performance standards are even relevant. Such attributes as knowledge of the specialty, originality of approach, and impact upon the professional community may seem reasonable criteria for performance evaluation to the professional, but may not even be a part of the organization's formal evaluation procedure. Conversely, data relating to the effects of employee efforts upon short-term sales and earnings will probably seem more pertinent a test of performance to management than to the organization's professionals.

In sum, conflict may arise concerning not only *who* is to judge performance, but *what* characteristics of performance will be considered as well.

Autonomy. Professional demands for autonomy cause conflict for several reasons, some of which have already been alluded to. Thus the organization's bureaucratic authority and hierarchical control systems described above, and its frequent willingness to "cut corners" and depart from strict application of scientific method when making decisions, may be seen by professionals as constituting an intrusion upon their freedom to work on projects they deem important, and to work on them in their own way. Furthermore, requirements of secrecy can seriously interfere with freedom to disseminate knowledge and information to those outside the organization.

Autonomy is also limited by the network of *rules* which binds the organization together. More impersonal than directives from superiors, these rules may nevertheless severely restrict the freedom of movement of professionals and their ability to make decisions and solve problems in ways consistent with their specialized training. A number of authors have commented upon this particular source of conflict. Finally, autonomy is threatened to some extent by the organization's frequent tendency to place employees, even professional employees, into work *teams* in which individual goals and methods tend to be subordinated to those of the larger group.

Commitment to Calling. We have mentioned that professionals feel a commitment to their chosen specialty, and believe it to be valuable to society. Through a combination of initial preference, socialization, and "sunk cost," professionals become committed to their specialized role skills, and are typically reluctant to abandon them even for higher-level positions offering greater pay, power, and prestige.

We have also mentioned earlier that there is likely to be considerable coolness toward employees whose allegiance and commitment is not primarily to the organization. Several researchers (Dewhirst, 1971; Kornhauser, 1962) have noted that high-level administrators may exert powerful pressures upon professionals to direct their ambitions toward administrative positions. Since such positions usually contain few or no technical, nonadministrative duties, and since specialized role skills will consequently decay over time, professionals who are committed to their technical specialty are likely to resist.

External Referents and Identification. Pressures to pursue administrative work may also conflict with the professional's external referents and identification. It has been mentioned elsewhere (Gouldner, 1957, p. 292) that loyalty to the organization implies not only "a willingness to limit or relinquish the commitment to a specialized professional task," but also "a dominant career orientation to the employing organization as a reference group." It is of course conceivable that an employee might have a "dominant" orientation to both the organization and the profession; however, the kinds of planning, budgeting, evaluation, and control activities performed by most administrative personnel are likely to compete for time with, and are unlikely to be as visible or as impressive to the external professional community, as articles, copyrights, patents, and research reports.

The external orientation of the professional will tend to conflict with some of the other organizational features discussed above. A major factor is the professionals' desire for *recognition* by those outsiders whose opinions are important to them, and whose bases for recognition may be incompatible with their internal assignments and activities. One type of professional often confronted with this dilemma is the industrial scientist.

> The traditional manager would like to have his scientists be creative —but in solving just those problems that would lead to commercial advantage. He wants to keep their ideas secret. . . . He would like the scientists to be . . . devoted to the interests of the company. . . . The scientist . . . is very much interested in publication of his research findings, for such communication is essential to building his reputation among fellow scientists. He wants to be free to attend scientific meetings and maintain and develop his association with fellow scientists . . . (Whyte, 1969, pp. 596–97).

It is easy to see that organizational preferences for secrecy can make it all but impossible for the professional to publicize and receive recognition for his work. It is also clear that organizing professionals into work groups and teams may create barriers to individual recognition, particularly when reports are written and patents and copyrights are taken out in the name of the group, the administrative director, or the organization.

The above discussion clearly suggests, and few researchers would deny, that there are some very real difficulties involved in assimilating the professional into the bureaucratic organization.

Line and Staff Relationships

The concepts of line and staff have been attended by considerable difficulties, no small part of which is semantic. The terms are frequently poorly defined; writers use the terms to refer variously to functions, organizational units, or authority patterns. Thus the terms are by no means consistently or universally applied. Furthermore, there is little empirical evidence regarding the proper use of staff. As a result of these and other problems, Browne and Golembiewski (1974, p. 406) claim that "perhaps no area in organization theory stands more in need of clarification than the line-staff concept." Some writers are ready to abandon the concepts altogether, while others invent new but similar terms for their own use.

Early theorists assumed an equality between formal authority, technical competence, and power, providing for a chain of authority emanating from the top manager and continuing downward within an orderly pyramid. Such a structure, described as a "line organization" in the contemporary literature, is illustrated in Figure 17–1. There are only a few organizations of this type. Such an organization would assume that the production manager also performed the duties of product, methods, and plant engineering; production, quality, and cost control; purchasing; personnel; and perhaps janitorial and secretarial work thrown in for good measure.

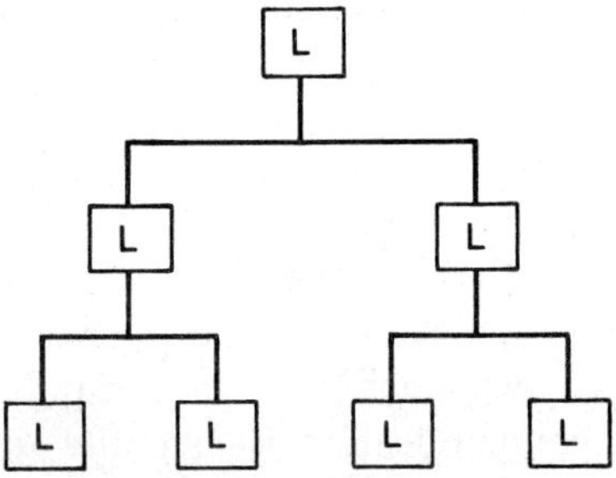

Figure 17–1. Line Organization.

Frederick Taylor was among the first to recognize that formal, hierarchical authority is not equal to technical authority. Today, the most common means for coping with the need for an unambiguous hierarchy of supervision combined with specialized technical support is the "line and staff" organization (Figure 17–2). So far as the individual employee in the line and staff organization is concerned, direct day-to-day supervision comes from one formal supervisor, although advice and specialized direction may also come from staff people.

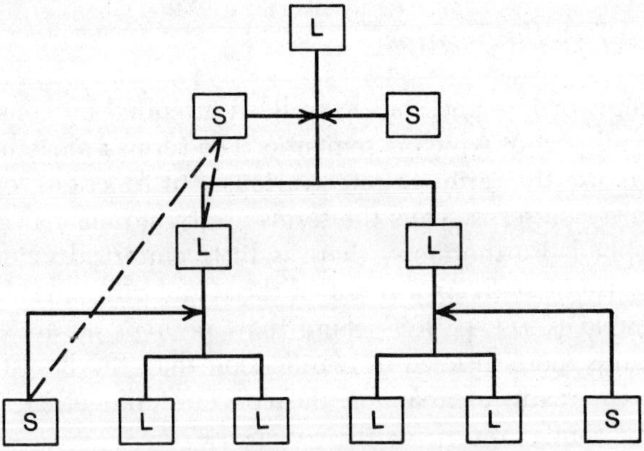

Figure 17–2. Line and Staff Organization.

As mentioned, the terms *line* and *staff* have been used to refer variously to (1) functions; (2) organizational units, including both individual and larger organizational divisions (sections, departments, etc.); and (3) authority relationships.

Line and Staff Functions. When used in the functional sense, *line* refers to work activities which contribute directly to the primary service objective (see Chapter 14). *Staff* functions, on the other hand, are supportive in nature, contributing to the efficiency and maintenance of the enterprise, and therefore serving secondary objectives. Thus the fabrication of materials in a production process or the sale of a product to the ultimate consumer are line functions. The training of personnel, the maintenance of machines, or the provision of legal advice to management are staff functions. Improper performance of line functions will quickly lessen a firm's ability to create saleable value; improper performance of staff functions might not damage an organization for some years, if at all.

The distinction between line and staff functions has been described with reference to the terms *task* and *element.* Task functions have to do with the "basic activities" of an enterprise, such as product development, finance, manufacturing, and marketing. Element functions, such as personnel management, planning, control, inspection, and maintenance, are intrinsic parts of the management process and may be performed by line management or assigned to specialized units (Woodward, 1965).

Line and Staff Units. Like the distinction between line and staff functions, the identification of line and staff units is often based upon the objectives which they serve; line units are concerned with the direct creation of saleable value, staff units with organizational support or maintenance.

Line and Staff Authority. Line authority usually refers to a direct command relationship between supervisor and subordinate, expressing the economic concept of authority described in Chapter 6. Staff authority is more complex, with at least four major types identifiable: staff advice, compulsory staff advice, concurrent line-staff authority, and functional authority.

Many staff activities are purely advisory in nature. Action is suggested, comments are given, and information is communicated, but acceptance or rejection is the clear perogative of the line advisee, who is free to seek or not to seek the advice of staff specialists.

In the case of compulsory staff advice, managers must at least listen to the advice of appropriate staff personnel, although they need not follow it. Such a policy ensures that the maximum use is made of specialized advisory services, but does not restrict the manager's decision-making freedom.[1] Explicit statements about compulsory advice policies are seldom found in business, but in practice informal understandings that particular staffs are to be consulted are not at all unusual.

Concurrent line-staff authority exists when the staff manager and the

---

[1] This principle has been described with reference to the Catholic church organization. The Pope is expected to consult with the Sacred College and the Curia on matters of church doctrine, although he is not bound to follow their advice (Mooney, 1947).

head of a line unit must agree on a decision to be made. Such an arrangement provides staff confirmation of line decisions without disrupting unity of command, but does restrict the manager's freedom to make decisions.

The strongest form of staff authority occurs when the line grants limited command (functional) authority to a staff unit, permitting a staff executive to give legitimate orders to other organizational units. Such authority most often exists when the staff executive possesses some special technical competence. An example of the use of functional authority by staff is the safety engineer's ability to stop any production operation which is being performed unsafely. Similarly, a quality control inspector may have the authority to reject products which are below standard, and a personnel officer may be able to fire employees whose absences have exceeded the maximum number allowed.

Informal Staff Authority. It is easy to see that staff authority is more limited than line authority. Staff units must frequently rely upon the willingness of others to accept their advice; except in the case of functional authority, they cannot expect automatic compliance with their suggestions. Yet observation indicates that staffs exert much greater influence than the preceding discussion would suggest.

The reason for this is that staff members often possess political authority (described in Chapter 6) and can exercise informal sanctions. Also, they are typically experts in their functional areas, and it may therefore be difficult for line officials to challenge their advice. Furthermore, staff members are frequently in a position to control information vital to a line manager's job and are often in closer proximity to top management than the line manager, who may be separated from the top by several hierarchical levels. Finally, staff members more often have the prestige which accompanies academic degrees, titles, and recognized skills to add weight to their requests and suggestions.

Difficulties in Distinguishing Line from Staff. In addition to the problems caused by the fact that the terms line and staff are often poorly defined and can be used to refer to differences in functions, units, or authority, several other difficulties arise in attempting to distinguish line from staff. For example, are managers of staff departments also staff, even though they exercise line authority over their own departments?

One major difficulty in using the concepts line and staff is that they cannot be readily applied to all types of organizations. In some types of business organizations the distinction works rather well; in others, it does not. In bureaucratic organizations where operations tend to be highly programmed or standardized, such as in many manufacturing enterprises, it is usually possible to identify one group of employees engaged in support, planning, or control activities, and another group essentially engaged in sales or production. In jobbing or continuous process firms, however, the distinction between line and staff becomes muddied. Woodward (1965) found, for example, that in "unit" and "small batch" production, relatively few specialists were employed and technical knowledge was retained in the line. At the other extreme of technology, "process production," the tendency was "for firms to move away from the line-staff type of organization towards either functional or predominantly line organization"; that is, staff functions were either retained by or returned to the line, or made more distinct in a functional organization.

As another example consider the large retail establishments, which have standardized operations and a separation of direct and indirect labor. In such organizations line and staff can generally be distinguished with little trouble. On the other hand, where operations are not routine, as in the specialty store, the concepts of line and staff are of questionable value.

The difficulty is compounded by the fact that line units commonly engage in many staff functions. For example, a production manager may advise the sales department on delays in shipment, keep accounting records, and train employees. While there is general agreement that personnel, purchasing, accounting, legal aid, and quality control are staff departments in a manufacturing operation, and sales and production are line, what about engineering and finance—are they line or staff? Management writers disagree. A reasonable criterion might be that if engineering services are contributing directly to product value they are line; if not, they are staff. Finance should definitely be considered to be line; however, the accounting function would be staff. And how would truck drivers, materials handlers, or advertising managers be classified?

In nonbusiness organizations the distinction between line and staff is often particularly difficult to establish; the roles may even be reversed. For example, it has been pointed out that "in professional organizations, administrators are in charge of secondary activities; they administer *means* to the major activity carried out by professionals. In other words, to the extent that there is a line-staff relationship at all, professionals should hold the major authority and administrators the secondary staff authority" (Etzioni, 1964, p. 81). Thus in a university the professional staff (faculty) is directed to the primary service objectives (teaching and research); line administrators handle support and auxiliary functions. In hospitals, the technical staff (physicians) seek to cure patients; line administrators concern themselves with organizational maintenance (Etzioni, 1959; Blau and Scott, 1962).

Line-Staff Conflict

Authority differences between line and staff units suggests some potential problems between the two. Line managers generally follow their legitimate formal authority in influencing the behavior of others. Staff managers, on the other hand, must frequently go beyond their legitimate authority if they are to influence others. Classical theory describes the staff manager as "selling" ideas to the line, but we have seen that informal authority can give the staff manager considerable leverage.

Another factor aggravating line-staff relationships is that line and staff personnel differ in their personal characteristics and behavior. For example, in Dalton's descriptions of observed differences in three industrial plants (1950, 1966), he noted that staff members were generally younger and came from a different social background than line personnel. Staff personnel were better educated, were more concerned with appearance and dress, and had different recreational preferences. They were specialists caught up in the politics of the organization. Given few levels to advance to, each tried to enlarge their own group of subordinates. Since they were always "on trial" to contribute to the organization, they were compelled to get their ideas accepted by the line. Yet staff members depended upon line managers to approve their promotions—line managers who, at the same time, tended to fear the staff for their undermining of line authority.

Considerable research has been done and undoubtedly will continue to be done concerning types of linkage between staff and line personnel, optimal and appropriate amounts of staff services, attitudinal and demographic differences between line and staff employees, etc. While such research unquestionably has value, it should be remembered that, as is the case with regard to research on professionalism, major differences in terminology and in the use of key measures continue to be common. Such differences impair the usefulness of any data obtained by reducing the comparability and generalizability of studies. Better agreement on definitions and standardization of terminology will therefore be necessary before research on the topics reviewed in this chapter will really pay off.

Propositions

The remainder of this chapter will deal with empirical evidence relating to three of the most important questions involving professionals in organizations. Specifically, (1) What are the primary causes of the professional's orientation and value system? (2) How inevitable is the conflict that tends to arise from the differences between the definitional characteristics of professionals and the bureaucracy that employs them? and (3) What, if anything, can organizations do to reduce or eliminate such conflict? Restated as propositions, these questions will be subject to empirical evaluation:

1. "Professional" orientation and values result from the extensive specialized training and socialization undergone by all professionals. Since such training predates the individual's organizational experience, the orientation will already be formed at the time of initial employment.
2. Due to fundamental incompatibilities between the definitional characteristics of professionals and those of the bureaucracies which employ them, conflict must inevitably ensue. By "inevitably" is meant that such conflict will arise and be maintained regardless of any actions undertaken by the employing firm.

3. Reduction of conflict between professionals and the organizations which employ them will be successful to the extent that the organizations provide adequate autonomy, individual recognition, linkages between its professional employees and the outside professional community, and collegial rather than bureaucratic authority and control systems.

Empirical Evidence

Proposition 1

"Professional" orientation and values result from the extensive specialized training and socialization undergone by all professionals. Since such training predates the individual's organizational experience, the orientation will already be formed at the time of initial employment.

This proposition, if true, could be considered grounds for pessimism by the employing organization, since it suggests that the firm is presented with a fait accompli in the form of an individual whose allegiance will always be suspect, whose major referents and social involvements will be largely external, and whose demands for autonomy will likely conflict with the standard operating procedures, organization chart depictions of authority, and job descriptions typical of the bureaucratic system.

The research evidence certainly seems to show that much of a professional's orientation, attitudes, and value system stem from experiences while in graduate school. In addition to providing the base of technical expertise required of professionals, such training has been found to cause individuals to value independence (Marcson, 1960) and autonomy, and to solve problems dispassionately without permitting company loyalties to cloud their judgment (Gouldner, 1954). Graduate training has been found by many to be a major source of professional norms and values, and of identification with the occupation. Length and type of graduate training have been found to be negatively associated with "bureaucratic" orientations (Miller and Wager, 1971), and positively related to willingness to leave the employing organization (Miller, 1967; Friedlander, 1971).

The influence of professional education is felt by the student in a number of ways. Certainly the formal coursework is itself a major factor, but in addition

> . . . The less advanced students derive both cognitive and affective cues from those farther along in training. . . . Challenging and painful experiences are shared with others, who thus have a sort of fellowship of suffering. Now if we add the probability that peers and adult role models constitute significant others . . . we are well on the way to comprehending how an occupational identity gets formed. . . . The person who successfully learns the language and skills of a trade, and

> survives the ordeals that punished him and his fellows will emerge . . . not only with an internalized occupational commitment, but also with an identification with the collectivity, the brotherhood (Moore, 1970, pp. 76–79).

Other forces are also at work during the training period, including identification with legendary figures whose lives embodied the ideal norms and identification with idealized professors (Abrahamson, 1967).

There is, however, considerable evidence that other forces subsequent to graduate training help to form and shape the professional's attitudes, norms, and values. For example, one study found that individuals with cosmopolitan values had, on the average, been in the organization two years longer than individuals who were indifferent. Such data indicate that "in time, working on professional problems, developing competence, and achieving some professional prestige results in a crystallization of professional identity, and produces commitment to professional values" (Sheldon, 1971, p. 148).

While other support exists for the position that professionalism increases as the result of *success* within the organization, other research, ironically, indicates that experiences of *failure* within the firm may increase professionalism. One study showed that individuals adopted professional values as they found themselves becoming more and more competent without being promoted (Barnes, 1964, p. 77). Another study found that inability to advance rapidly within the civil service had the effect of stimulating greater intrinsic satisfaction toward the job, as well as a more professional attitude toward it (Blau, 1963, p. 258), and a third obtained data suggesting that "professional identification sustains many in a position of blocked mobility by providing them both with a reason for their lack of mobility and an alternative chance to advance within their 'profession' " (Goldner and Ritti, 1967, p. 500).

In the same way that failure to advance within the organizational hierarchy may lead to development or strengthening of a professional identification, failure to achieve recognition and success within the profession may be responsible for development of an organizational identification, often at the expense of the individual's professionalism.

> Research suggests that . . . as the scientist gains experience in the organization . . . some scientists appear to make a realistic evaluation of themselves in relation to their peers. . . . The scientist may decide that it is not worthwhile to try to struggle to keep in the competition as a specialist, but instead to take the management route. For such individuals, the management ladder provides a resolution of conflict rather than an intensification of it (Whyte, 1969, p. 598).

Another major factor which has been found to influence the degree to which a professional orientation is maintained after entry into the organization is the opportunity or lack of opportunity for interaction with other professionals. Where such opportunity exists professionals are very likely to take advantage of it, for several reasons:

> The norms of most professions orient practitioners toward collegial relationships. There are additional forces within the organization which also push professionals into collegial associations. The first is propinquity. Professionals are apt to be located spatially close to each other, and this has been shown consistently to be related to relationship formation. Similarity of background and interest also encourage collegiality. Finally, there are pragmatic pressures toward collegiality based upon the need to share information in an environment which generally isolates the professionals from their colleague groups located outside of the organization (Abrahamson, 1967, pp. 59–60).

Other factors have been found by researchers to influence maintenance of a professional orientation, including the distribution of power within the organization and the career stages of particular individuals (Bucher and Stelling, 1969), and the kind of environment (basic, applied, developmental, etc.) provided for employees (Schein et al., 1965; Kast and Rosenzweig, 1970). Even broader are factors which consider the occupation's position within the wider social structure. For example, "if the occupation receives relatively few rewards in a material sense, the level of dedication is likely to be higher. If the occupation is allowed to be self-regulating, it will tend to believe very strongly in this. Therefore changes in the social structure may bring about corresponding attitudinal adjustments" (Hall, 1968, p. 103).

Proposition 2

Due to fundamental incompatibilities between the definitional characteristics of professionals and those of the bureaucracies which employ them, conflict must inevitably ensue. By "inevitably" is meant that such conflict will arise and be maintained regardless of any actions undertaken by the employing firm.

You may recall that we labeled "pessimistic" the view that an individual's professional orientation is totally determined by educational experiences prior to joining the firm. This view may be considered a "sunk cost" explanation of professional orientation, since its rationale is that the professional's long years of training represents an investment in a technical specialty, whereas the nonprofessional's investment is in years of experience with the firm. The professional will therefore "*expect* higher rewards from the organization in return for his services. Moreover, if these rewards are not forthcoming, professionals with advanced degrees are in a better position to market their skills and find employment in an organization that does offer such rewards" (Miller, 1967, pp. 756–57).

The "sunk cost" view, then, depicts the organization as a rather passive onlooker, perhaps able through selection techniques to screen out some of those individuals most likely to be disloyal and least likely to work toward organizational goals, but unable to counter the professional's external references and commitment to the field. Another view, which we may term the optimistic position, is that advanced formal education may instill *latent* predispositions toward such references and commitments, but that most professionals will not *manifest* such tendencies unless they perceive opportunities in the profession to be greater than those available within the organization. This position has been espoused by many theoreticians and researchers, and portrays the organization as able to actively affect the extent to which professionals come to care about and work for its goals.

It is true that some data show that formal advanced education is associated with high commitment to the profession and low commitment to the organization (Miller, 1967; Hrebiniak and Alutto, 1972), and that overcoming obstacles within the firm to achieve success is related to high commitment to the organization (Grusky, 1966). However, in general the pessimistic, "sunk cost" view seems much *too* pessimistic. Research evidence indicates that professional-bureaucratic conflict is *not* inevitable.

Table 17–1 portrays in outline form our earlier discussion of the primary areas where definitional characteristics of the professional and fundamental aspects of the bureaucratic organization are likely to come into conflict. In considering the extent to which these conflict points are inevitable, let us first take note of data showing that individuals, even professional individuals, tend to develop strong commitment to the organization when their opportunities outside the firm are not as attractive as those within (Blau and Scott, 1962), or when external opportunities seem to be absent altogether (Becker, 1960; Marscon, 1960; Shepherd, 1961; Kornhauser, 1962; Sheldon, 1971). Dissatisfaction with various aspects of the organization has been shown to be negatively associated (Hrebiniak and Alutto, 1972) and movement into management positively associated (Glaser, 1964) with organizational commitment.

Several researchers have reported that the amount of organizational prestige enjoyed by professionals affects their commitment and loyalty. Fairly high loyalty to the firm was observed even among professionals with high professional prestige, providing they had at least medium prestige within the firm. However, those low in organizational prestige were also low in loyalty (Lee, 1969; Lewis, 1967; Reissman, 1949).

Other studies have found that the more "professionally-oriented" nurses in a clinic did not differ from the others in their loyalty to the hospital (Bennis et al., 1958) and that the most "cosmopolitan" scientists in the Federal Health Service had the highest organizational identification and the lowest propensity to leave (Lee, 1970). Possible explanations for these results include the greater opportunity to demonstrate performance within the clinic than outside it, and the atypical nature of the Health Service, an organization where "professional activities of the specialists are not in conflict with organizational expectations," and where "the professional status

TABLE 17–1. Areas of Conflict Between Professional and Organization.

	Professional Characteristics					
Organizational Characteristics	*expertise*	*ethics*	*collegial maintenance of standards*	*autonomy*	*commitment to calling*	*external referents and identification*
bureaucratic authority and hierarchical control			conflict	conflict		
desire for loyalty to the organization		conflict			conflict	conflict
desire for professionals to adopt a managerial orientation					conflict	conflict
placement of employees into work groups				conflict		conflict
desire for secrecy		conflict		conflict		conflict
use of unscientific decision-making processes	conflict			conflict		
network of rules				conflict		

is an important criterion necessary for organizational prestige" (Lee, 1970, p. B708).

There is also considerable research indicating that organizational commitment tends to increase with age (Hrebiniak and Alutto, 1972), seniority (Sheldon, 1971; Hall and Schneider, 1972; Hrebiniak and Alutto, 1972), and number of years in present position (Schein et al., 1965). While these factors are not directly controllable by the organization, they nevertheless attest to the fact that conflict is *not* inevitable, that professionals can be loyal to their employing organization and committed to its goals. In fact, many writers now believe that orientation toward an organization may under many circumstances be independent of orientation toward the profession (Reissman, 1949; Pelz, 1956; Luecke, 1973; Goldberg, Baker, and Rubenstein, 1965; Friedlander, 1971; House and Kerr, 1973; McCarrey and Edwards, 1973; Berger and Grimes, 1973; Flango and Brumbaugh, 1974).

Overall, the evidence suggests that the professional's "sunk cost" in education and training will produce and maintain tendencies to be oriented externally; however, this orientation will *not* necessarily be accompanied by coolness to the employing organization. The level of organizational commitment will be influenced by factors which the organization can barely control, such as age and seniority, and also by factors which can be influenced, such as the amount of task satisfaction and positional prestige provided and the extent to which internal opportunities are competitive with those available elsewhere.

It has even become apparent that large bureaucratic organizations can help individuals to act as professionals.

> Alterations taking place within the professions themselves have made them more compatible, in certain ways, with bureaucratic employment. The knowledge explosion . . . has tended to change the internal pattern of relationships as well as the work settings of many professionals. . . . More complex problems have created the need for collective efforts or team approaches to solve them. . . . Much bulky and expensive equipment has, by necessity, been centralized. . . . The bureaucratically structured organization, then, appears to be able to serve many of the needs created by the alterations in professional practice more successfully than solo practice. It is better able to supply those professionals who work within it with the funds, various items of equipment, technical personnel and other physical facilities which have become necessities for effective practice. It can also provide a stimulating intellectual climate, wherein colleagues can both interchange information and censure poor performance (Moore, 1970, pp. 32–33).

Proposition 3

Reduction of conflict between professionals and the organizations which employ them will be successful to the extent that the organizations provide adequate autonomy, individual recognition, linkages between its professional employees and the outside professional community, and collegial rather than bureaucratic authority and control systems.

It should be apparent from the discussion to this point that although conflict between professionals and their employing organization may not be inevitable, professional workers nevertheless constitute quite a challenge to the bureaucratic firm. Many theorists and researchers have suggested that the definitional characteristics of professionals render all but useless some traditional features of most authority, supervisory, evaluation, and reward systems. For example, regarding administration of rewards:

—Such status symbols as job titles, private parking spaces, access to executive cafeterias and private, windowed, carpeted offices will probably be less attractive to professional than to nonprofessional employees. These things are more visible, and therefore more impressive, to fellow employees than to professional outsiders. Furthermore, such rewards are typically dispensed for accomplishing organizationally relevant activities (such as sales or profits), or for attendance, promptness, time in job or seniority, rather than for professionally relevant activities such as advancing knowledge, publishing papers, and attending meetings.

—The use of monetary rewards, so large a part of traditional systems, is likely to be less effective in motivating the professional. Several researchers (e.g., Strauss, 1963) have noted that, while professionals are certainly not indifferent to money and the things money can buy, they typically attribute less importance to money than do nonprofessionals.

—The "promotion," or advancement to the next higher hierarchical level, is often unattractive to professional employees, particularly when it threatens to take them into general administrative work and out of the technical specialty for which they have been trained. The increase in pay, influence, and status which accompanies a promotion will often seem scant consolation for the almost inevitable abandonment of professional skills and activities.

It therefore appears that in the future organizations will be required to consider major alterations in their procedures and practices if they are to successfully attract, motivate, and ultimately retain the professional employee. Each of the definitional characteristics of professionalism is related to some of these alterations.

With regard to professional *expertise,* suggestions for changes involve both the utilization of expertise and providing for maintenance and growth of professional skills over time. For example, quality of facilities and services (such as space, privacy, and equipment) have been found by researchers (Riegel, 1958; Hower and Orth, 1963) to be very important to professionals, and in another study of government scientists "facilitative support services" was listed as one of the most important goals (McCarrey and Edwards, 1973). This last study also reported that scientists attributed high importance to "opportunities for personal and professional self-development." Leaves of absence for industrial professionals have also been recommended as a means to permit and encourage the strengthening of technical skills and expertise (Barber, 1970).

Concerning professional *ethics,* it is perhaps most important that the organization avoid placing professional employees in positions where they will tend to experience role conflict and role tension. These maladies are a common result of instances where the professional "is confronted with conflicting demands for behavior—from himself, from his colleagues, and from his superiors" (Saxberg and Slocum, 1968, p. B-484). For example, the organization should not attempt to enforce regulations which conflict with professional norms and obligations, should permit the sharing of knowledge and information with others outside the employing firm (LaPorte, 1965; Whyte, 1969), and should provide recognition for scientific and technical contributions which add to human knowledge regardless of their direct and immediate impact on company sales and profits.

This last suggestion is important not only because of the professionals' internalized code of ethics, but also because of their belief that *maintenance of standards* be accomplished with reference to professional criteria. Many researchers (Roman, 1968; Hall, 1967) have commented upon the importance of using professional performance as a prime determinant of initial selection and advancement, and studies of professional scientists have shown the importance of a reward system where "promotions and salary increases . . . are primarily based upon . . . scientific contribution" (Lee, 1969, p. 334), and where the system "reinforces technical contribution and the values associated with commitment to professional skills" (Schein et al., 1965, p. 348). To insure that such reinforcement occurs, and that competent evaluation of technical accomplishment occurs, other authors (Thompson, 1961; Pelz and Andrews, 1966b) have suggested that peer evaluations be used to augment or to substitute for appraisals by hierarchical superiors, and that *collegial authority* rather than *executive authority* (discussed in Chapter 6) characterize the organization.

The professional's need for *autonomy* has been the basis for a number of suggested changes in organizational practices. It has been suggested that time and funds be provided to professionals to pursue personal research unrelated to organizational goals, and it has been found that provision of such time is statistically associated with low alienation from the firm (Miller, 1967), and that "funding for research of interest to me" ranked among the goals most important to a sample of government scientists (McCarrey and Edwards, 1973). Freedom to select projects to be worked on has also been found to be an important means of accommodation (Meltzer, 1956), and "freedom to carry out my own ideas" was given top priority by scientists rating the importance of various job factors (Pelz, 1956).

Autonomy is also important as it relates to the managerial style of the hierarchical supervisor. Many writers caution that professional employees should not be subjected to tight controls and close supervision, but should instead have the freedom they require to make decisions about what needs to be done, and how. In this respect one sample of scientists and engineers, including many employees who could be classified as professionals, who worked for supervisors with managerial styles which were participative or laissez-faire, reported much less alienation than others who worked for supervisors with directive styles (Miller, 1967). Many of these same writers have recommended that managers should participate and consult with professionals concerning assignments and changes, and in general display a *Theory Y* (defined in Chapter 13) rather than a *Theory X* orientation. Studies supporting this recommendation (e.g., House and Kerr, 1973) show, for example, that data from professionally oriented "organizational independents" depict much stronger relationships between leader *Consideration* (the extent to which a leader shows trust for subordinates and respect for their ideas; see Chapter 11) and various satisfaction and performance measures, than do data from less professional "dependents."

These studies have also tended to show, however, that data from independents reveal stronger and *positive* relationships between leader *Initiating Structure* (the extent to which leaders structure their own and their subordinates' roles toward goal attainment; see Chapter 11) and satisfaction and performance than do data from dependents. In fact, a seeming paradox emerges from the research literature to the effect that, as was suggested in Chapter 14, *too much* autonomy may be as undesirable as too little. Some of the major reasons for this condition include the following:

> Perhaps highly technically trained personnel prefer leadership which provides for clear definition of role relationships and clear specification of work methodology. Physical science training emphasizes the need for careful methodological specifications before engaging in engineering or research activities. Consequently, it is plausible that as a result of their previous training, (respondent professionals) preferred orderly, systematic leadership behavior that provided for clear definition of policies and ground rules in the work environment to one of relative ambiguity. (House, Filley, and Kerr, 1971, pp. 26–27)

> Too little bureaucratization may lead to too many undefined operational areas if the profession itself has not developed operational standards for these areas (Hall, 1968, p. 104).

> For the completely autonomous man, no one else helps him to chart his course. Does this mean that no one else is interested? And if no one else is interested, does he lose interest himself? . . . Full autonomy may encourage complacency rather than zest, narrow specialization rather than breadth (Pelz and Andrews, 1966b, pp. 231, 237).

Consistent with these arguments are the recommendations that, based on study results, the optimal climate for scientists in organizations is one of "controlled freedom," whereby innovative pursuits are guided by procedures and programmed problem-solving approaches (Pelz and Andrews, 1966a), and that "a moderately bureaucratic setting provides more professional autonomy for the physician than either a non-bureaucratic or a highly bureaucratic setting" (Engel, 1969, p. 34). These arguments are also consistent with data showing that research and development employees prefer democratic to laissez-faire leadership, and with results from other studies as well (Vollmer, 1972; Filley and Grimes, 1968; Wigdor, 1969).

The professional's *commitment to calling* presents a particularly thorny problem for the organization. Considerable research shows that in most organizations advancement into management is far easier than advancement within the technical specialty, and that professional employees therefore experience pressure to abandon their profession in favor of an administrative position (Marcson, 1960; Thompson, 1961; Gouldner, 1954; Hall, 1967). Since professionals are, by definition, reluctant to do this, the result has typically been a stalemate of frustration and blocked mobility for the professional, and high turnover and low morale for the organization.

The Dual Ladder (Dual Hierarchy). In recent years an innovative method for relieving this source of conflict has begun to be discussed in the literature, and to be implemented by several organizations. Known as the *dual ladder,* it refers to:

> . . . the side-by-side existence of the usual ladder of hierarchical position leading to authority over greater and greater numbers of employees and another ladder consisting of titles carrying successively higher salaries, higher status, and sometimes greater autonomy or more responsible assignments. . . . The professional ladder makes no pretense in the direction of increasing the authority of title-holders. It is based on the same assumptions that support an ideology of professionalism, . . . that upward mobility in the power hierarchy is of no importance compared to autonomy (Goldner and Ritti, 1967, pp. 489–91).

This second ladder, usually called the "professional ladder," is therefore established to provide advancement opportunities for professionals unable or unwilling to ascend the regular organizational hierarchy, and to prevent the movement of key professional personnel away from research positions where their scientific contributions are needed. It is designed to provide the incentive value and rewards associated with promotion, but without an increase in managerial duties, and to allow for compensation, recognition, and status which is equivalent to that of managers. In theory, then, the professional ladder permits employees who are "committed to their calling" to advance within the organization without being forced to abandon their professional specialty.

In practice, however, as a recent review (Schriesheim, Von Glinow, and Kerr, 1975) concludes, the dual ladder has for the most part failed to live up to its promise. A typical conclusion from one study seeking to determine the effectiveness of this approach is that "the dual ladder has failed in its aim of conferring equal prestige and equal compensation for managers and technical personnel, at least in the eyes of the two groups concerned" (Schoner and Harrell, 1965, p. 57).

The review by Schriesheim et al. (1975) cites the following as primary problems with dual ladder systems:

—Lack of power. The professional ladder is intended to "free" incumbents from budgeting, staffing, purchasing, and other "managerial" responsibilities which would interfere with their technical and professional activities (Kaplan, 1961). Yet, by removing professionals from such sources of organizational power, the ladder seems unable to provide much autonomy and independence.

—Sign of failure. The professional ladder often comes to be seen as a face-saving device for individual failures. Goldner and Ritti (1967) describe the widespread feeling, even among professionals, that if individuals possess managerial talent they will be encouraged to advance on the managerial rather than the professional ladder. In the same vein, Shepard (1958) points out that since the possession of managerial talent is highly socially desirable in our society, an individual without such talent may be considered a failure.

—Lack of equity between the two ladders. Many organizations fail to provide equal benefits for parallel positions on the managerial and professional ladders. Marcson (1960) reports, for example, that in one company studied the uppermost position on the managerial ladder provided a salary two and a half times as large as that of the highest position on the research ladder, and results of several studies show that both managers and professionals often agree that status and influence are more characteristic of the managerial than the professional ladder.

—Inadequate number of professional ladder positions. In some systems the number of positions on the professional ladder is so much fewer than for the managerial hierarchy that the professional ladder's incentive value is greatly reduced (Shepard, 1958). This may result from lower prestige and income ceilings (Raudsepp, 1963), or from an insufficient number of positions in the middle ranges of the ladder.

—Poor or inequitable evaluative criteria. If the organization uses nonprofessional personnel to perform evaluative functions for the professional ladder, or if "inappropriate" criteria (e.g., "effect on profit") are used, the professional ladder may be unable to provide recognition for professional contributions.

Schriesheim et al. (1975) point out that some studies (e.g., Hallenberg, 1970; Bralley, 1960) report successful implementations of the dual ladder system; however, they conclude that in general the dual ladder has not been effective. Instead of permitting professional employees to maintain their commitment to calling, the dual ladder "actually serves to formalize the powerlessness of the staff professional by creating a second-class management without management influence" (Ritti, 1971, p. 233).

A number of recommendations have been made to accommodate the professional's desire for *external identification and referents* within the bureaucratic organization; some of these have already been alluded to. For example, several researchers have found that providing time, money, and encouragement to write papers for and attend professional meetings may be related to lower alienation from the organization (Miller, 1967), and greater harmony within it LaPorte, 1965). Naturally for such a practice to be successful the organization must be willing to forego any desire for secrecy, and must permit professional employees to advance patents, copyrights, and publications in their own names. External recognition also depends upon the ability of professionals to obtain assignments where their individual contribution can be identified (Campfield, 1965), and where their accomplishments will satisfy professional, not just organizational, standards.

Overall, the research literature thus provides ample support for Proposition 3; there *are* at present a variety of techniques which have been found to reduce professional-organizational conflict, and these do involve a conscious attempt by the employing firm to provide greater autonomy, collegial authority, opportunities for external recognition, etc., so that professionals will not be required to make a painful choice between available organizational rewards and those professional incentives which their socialization and training have taught them to value.

Summary

Proposition 1: "Professional" orientation and values result from the extensive specialized training and socialization undergone by all professionals. Since such training predates the individual's organizational experience, the orientation will already be formed at the time of initial employment. *Only partly supported; professional orientation also appears to be partly the result of demographic characteristics which predate training, and partly the result of particular organizational experiences which occur after training.*

Proposition 2: Due to fundamental incompatibilities between the definitional characteristics of professionals and those of the bureaucracies which employ them, conflict must inevitably ensue. By "inevitably" is meant that such conflict will arise and be maintained regardless of any actions undertaken by the employing firm. *Not confirmed; although areas of conflict do exist, there is little evidence that such conflict will "inevitably" arise irrespective of organizational actions and policies.*

Proposition 3: Reduction of conflict between professionals and the organizations which employ them will be successful to the extent that organizations provide adequate autonomy, individual recognition, linkages between its professional employees and the outside professional community, and collegial rather than bureaucratic authority and control systems. *Appears to be generally true, although "cures" differ markedly in their effectiveness and some may turn out to be worse than the "disease."*

Conclusions

This chapter has attempted to examine the six fundamental characteristics of professional employees, and to view conflict with their employing organization as arising from some basic differences and inconsistencies between these characteristics and certain basic organizational features. The resultant conflict is *not* seen as inevitable, however; although it is true that the professional's "sunk cost" in formal training, coupled with typically extensive socialization, creates latent tendencies to behave independently and, to some extent, counter to any organizational bureaucracy, there still remain many options available to the organization. Techniques and incentives already exist which, though inadequate to fully resolve all of the problems discussed, are probably sufficient to reduce these problems to manageable proportions. In a sense, the existing research literature indicates that professionals do, over time and as a result of experiences, show a willingness to reconsider their professional values and standards, and in many cases to adopt an organizational orientation in place of, or at least as a supplement to, their professional orientation. Now the organizations of tomorrow are beginning to learn how to meet the professional "half-way."

It is also probably worth noting that the literature does *not* suggest that organizations should try to transform professionals into "organization men." Despite the many difficulties which professionally oriented employees create for the firm, their training, skills, and external linkages are usually badly needed. The organization's goal should therefore be to create "complex individuals" whose exceptional skills and extensive education are accompanied by a loyalty to the employing organization and a desire for it to survive and be successful.

References

Abrahamson, M. 1965. Cosmopolitanism, dependence–identification and geographical mobility. *Administrative Science Quarterly* 10: 98-106.

———. 1967. *The professional in the organization.* Rand-McNally.

Barber, B. 1970. *Science and the social order.* Collier.

Barnes, L. B. 1960. *Organizational systems and engineering groups.* Harvard University Press.

———. 1964. Organizational systems and engineering groups. In *Administering R & D*, ed. by C. D. Orth III, J. C. Bailey, and F. W. Wolek. Irwin.

Becker, H. S. 1960. Notes on the concept of commitment. *American Journal of Sociology* 66: 32-40.

Bennis, W. G.; Berkowitz, N.; Affinito, M.; and Malone, M. 1958. Reference groups and loyalties in the out-patient department. *Administrative Science Quarterly* 2: 481-500.

Berger, P. K., and Grimes, A. J. 1973. Cosmopolitan-local: A factor analysis of the construct. *Administrative Science Quarterly* 18: 223-35.

Blau. P. M. 1963. *The dynamics of bureaucracy.* University of Chicago Press.

———., and Scott, W. R. 1962. *Formal organizations.* Chandler.

Bralley, J. A. 1960. Proceedings of Industrial Research Institute study group meetings: Job status as an award for scientific and administrative accomplishment. *Research Management* 3: 227-38.

Browne, P. J., and Golembiewski, R. T. 1974. The line-staff concept revisited: An empirical study of organizational images. *Academy of Management Journal* 17: 406-17.

Bucher, R., and Stelling, J. 1969. Characteristics of professional organizations. *Journal of Health and Social Behavior* 10: 3-15.

Campfield, W. 1965. Motivating the professional employee. *Personnel Journal* 44: 425-42.

Dalton, M. 1966. Changing line-staff relations. *Personnel Administration,* 3-5.

———. 1950. Conflicts between staff and line managerial officers. *American Sociological Review* 15: 342-51.

Daniels, A. K. 1969. The captive professional: Bureaucratic limitations in the practice of military psychiatry. *Journal of Health and Social Behavior* 10: 255-65.

Dewhirst, H. D. 1971. Impact of organizational climate on the desire to manage among engineers and scientists. *Personnel Journal* 50: 196-203.

Engel, G. V. 1969. The effect of bureaucracy on the professional autonomy of physicians. *Journal of Health and Social Behavior* 10: 30-41.

Etzioni, A. 1959. Authority structure and organizational effectiveness. *Administrative Science Quarterly* 4: 43-67.

———. 1964. *Modern organizations.* Prentice-Hall.

Filley, A. C., and Grimes, A. J. 1968. The bases of power in decision processes. In *Promising research directions,* ed. by R. W. Millman and M. P. Hottenstein. Academy of Management.

Flango, V. E., and Brumbaugh, R. B. 1974. The dimensionality of the cosmopolitan-local construct. *Administrative Science Quarterly* 19: 198-210.

Freidson, E., and Rhea, B. 1965. Knowledge and judgment in professional evaluations. *Administrative Science Quarterly* 10: 107-24.

Friedlander, F. 1971. Performance and orientation structures of research scientists. *Organizational Behavior and Human Performance* 6: 169-83.

Glaser, B. 1964. *Organizational scientists.* Bobbs-Merrill.

Goldberg, L. C., Baker, F., and Rubenstein, A. H. 1965. Local-cosmopolitan: Unidimensional or multidimensional? *American Journal of Sociology* 70: 704-10.

Goldner, F. H., and Ritti, R. R. 1967. Professionalization as career immobility. *American Journal of Sociology* 72: 489-502.

Goode, W. J. 1960. Encroachment, charlatanism, and the emerging profession: Psychology, sociology, and medicine. *American Sociological Review* 25: 902-14.

Gouldner, A. W. 1957. Cosmos and locals: Toward an analysis of latent social roles, I. *Administrative Science Quarterly* 2: 281-306.

———. 1958. Cosmos and locals: Toward an analysis of latent social roles, II. *Administrative Science Quarterly* 2: 444-80.

———. 1954. *Patterns of industrial bureaucracy.* Free Press.

Greenwood, E. 1957. Attributes of a profession. *Social Work* 2: 45-55.

Grusky, O. 1966. Career mobility and organization commitment. *Administrative Science Quarterly* 10: 488-503.

Haig, M. R., and Sussman, M. B. 1971. Professionalization and unionism. *American Behavioral Scientist* 14: 525-40.

Hall, D. T., and Schneider, B. 1972. Correlates of organizational identification as a function of career pattern and organizational type. *Administrative Science Quarterly* 17: 340-50.

Hall, R. H. 1968. Professionalization and bureaucratization. *American Sociological Review* 33: 92-104.

———. 1967. Some organizational considerations in the professional-organizational relationship. *Administrative Science Quarterly* 12:461-78.

Hallenberg, E. X. 1970. Dual advancement ladder provides unique recognition for the scientist. *Research Management* 13: 221-27.

House, R. J., Filley, A. C., and Kerr, S. 1971. Relation of leader consideration and initiating structure to R & D subordinates' satisfaction. *Administrative Science Quarterly* 16: 19-30.

———., and Kerr, S. 1973. Organizational independence, leader behavior, and managerial practices: A replicated study. *Journal of Applied Psychology* 58: 173-80.

Hower, R. M., and Orth, C. D., III. 1963. *Managers and scientists.* Harvard University Press.

Hrebiniak, L. G., and Alutto, J. A. 1972. Personal and role-related factors in the development of organizational commitment. *Administrative Science Quarterly* 17: 555-73.

Kaplan, N. 1961. Research administration and the administrator: U.S.S.R. and U.S. *Administrative Science Quarterly* 6: 51-72.

Kast, F. E., and Rosenzweig, J. E. 1970. *Organization and management: A systems approach.* McGraw-Hill.

Kelman, H. C. 1958. Compliance, identification, and internalization: Three processes of attitude change. *Conflict Resolution* 2: 51-60.

Kerr, S. 1972. Cosmopolitan-local theory: A reoperationalization and some new data. In *Research in organizations,* ed. by J. W. Slocum, Jr. Proceedings of the Ninth Annual Conference, Eastern Academy of Management.

Kornhauser, W. 1962. *Scientists in industry: Conflict and accommodation.* University of California Press.

LaPorte, T. R. 1965. Conditions of strain and accommodation in industrial research organizations. *Administrative Science Quarterly* 10: 21-38.

Lee, S. M. 1969. Organizational identification of scientists. *Academy of Management Journal* 12: 327-37.

———. 1970. Professional employees in organizations. *Management Science* 16: B708-B710.

Lewis, L. S. 1967. On prestige and loyalty of university faculty. *Administrative Science Quarterly* 11: 629-42.

Luecke, D. S. 1973. The professional as organizational leader. *Administrative Science Quarterly* 18: 86-94.

Marcson, S. 1960. *The scientist in American industry.* Princeton University Press.

McCarrey, M. W., and Edwards, S. A. 1973. Organizational climate conditions for effective research scientist role performance. *Organizational Behavior and Human Performance* 9: 439-59.

McNaul, J. P. 1969. Behavioral patterns among professionals in a research and development environment. Doctoral Dissertation, Stanford University.

Meltzer, L. 1956. Scientific productivity in organizational settings. *Journal of Social Issues* 12: 32-40.

Merton, R. K. 1957. *Social theory and social structure.* Free Press.

Miller, G. A. 1967. Professionals in bureaucracy: Alienation among industrial scientists and engineers. *American Sociological Review* 32: 755-67.

———., and Wager, L. W. 1971. Adult socialization, organizational structure, and role orientations. *Administrative Science Quarterly* 16: 151-63.

Mooney, J. D. 1947. *Principles of organization.* Harper & Row.

Moore, D., and Renck, R. 1955. The professional employee in industry. *Journal of Business* 28: 58-86.

Moore, W. E. 1970. *The professions: Roles and rules.* Russel Sage Foundation.

Pelz, D. C. 1956. Some social factors related to performance in a research organization. *Administrative Science Quarterly* 1: 310-25.

———., and Andrews, F. M. 1966a. Autonomy, coordination and stimulation, in relation to scientific achievement. *Behavioral Science* 11: 89-97.

———., and ———. 1966b. *Scientists in organizations.* Wiley.

Perrucci, R. 1971. Engineering. *American Behavioral Scientist* 14: 492-506.

———., and Gerstl, J. 1969. *Profession without community: Engineers in American society.* Random House.

Raudsepp, E. 1963. *Managing creative scientists and engineers.* Macmillan.

Reissman, L. 1949. A study of role conceptions in bureaucracy. *Social Forces* 27: 305-10.

Riegel, J. 1958. *Intangible rewards for engineers and scientists.* Bureau of Industrial Relations, University of Michigan.

Ritti, R. R. 1971. The engineer in the industrial corporation. Columbia University Press.

Roman, D. D. 1968. *Research and development management.* Appleton-Century-Crofts.

Saxberg, B. O., and Slocum, J. W., Jr. 1968. The management of scientific manpower. *Management Science* 14: B473-B489.

Schein, E. H.; McKelvey, W. W.; Peters, D. R.; and Thomas, J. W. 1965. Career orientations and perceptions of rewarded activities in a research organization. *Administrative Science Quarterly* 10: 333-49.

Schoner, B., and Harrell, T. W. 1965. The questionable dual ladder. *Personnel* 42: 53-57.

Schriesheim, J., Von Glinow, M. A., and Kerr, S. 1975. The dual hierarchy: A review of the evidence and a theoretical alternative. In *Proceedings of the Twelfth Annual Conference,* Eastern Academy of Management.

Sheldon, M. E. 1971. Investments and involvements as mechanisms producing commitment to the organization. *Administrative Science Quarterly* 16: 143-50.

Shepard, H. A. 1958. The dual hierarchy in research. *Research Management* 1: 177-87.

Shepherd, C. R. 1961. Orientation of scientists and engineers. *Pacific Sociological Review* 4: 79-83.

Strauss, G. 1963. Professionalism and occupational associations. *Industrial Relations* 2: 7-31.

Thompson, V. A. 1961. Hierarchy, specialization, and organizational conflict. *Administrative Science Quarterly* 5: 485-521.

Vollmer, H. M. 1972. Basic and applied research. In *The social contexts of research,* ed. by S. Z. Nagi and R. G. Corwin. Wiley.

Whyte, W. F. 1969. *Organizational behavior.* Irwin.

Wigdor, L. A. 1969. Effectiveness of various management and organizational characteristics on employee satisfaction and performance as a function of the employee's need for job independence. Doctoral Dissertation, City University of New York.

Wilensky, H. L. 1964. The professionalization of everyone? *American Journal of Sociology* 70: 137-58.

Woodward, J. 1965. *Industrial organization.* Oxford University Press.

Chapter **18**

Span of Control

Thou shalt provide out of all the people able men . . . to be rulers of thousands, rulers of hundreds, rulers of fifties, and rulers of tens: and let them judge the people at all seasons: and it shall be, that every great matter they shall bring unto thee, but every small matter they shall judge; so shall it be easier for thyself, and they shall bear the burden with thee.

JETHRO TO MOSES
Exodus 18: 17–36

Span of control consists of the number of subordinates who report directly to a supervisor. The desired width of the span is a major determinant of organizational structure; if it is seen as becoming too wide, it may be deemed necessary to insert another level between the chief executive and the organization's lower-level members in order to narrow it. For example, if the Israelites in the Biblical example above had numbered more than one hundred thousand at the time of the Exodus, a hundred "rulers of the thousands" would have been reporting directly to Moses, and he probably would have been more than happy to have created the position "ruler of the ten thousands" to reduce the span of control to more manageable proportions.

History

Theories of the span of control were originally based upon casual observations by experienced managers and on deductive reasoning. Henri Fayol (1949), who was probably the first to propose a "science of administration," stated that "whatever his rank, a man has only to command a very small number of direct subordinates, usually less than six, except that a foreman, who is dealing with quite a simple operation, is in direct command of 20 or 30 men."

Graicunas (1937) was able to demonstrate mathematically that arithmetical increases in the number of subordinates reporting directly to a manager are accompanied by potentially geometric increases in the number of personal relationships within the manager's immediate work unit. This principle is illustrated by Urwick (1974, p. 351):

If an executive adds to subordinates, the amount of additional help he receives only increases by arithmetic proportion. If he adds one to four existing subordinates he increases his capacity to delegate responsibility by 20 percent. But the direct and cross relationships between the different members of the group, which he must bear in mind if business is to progress smoothly, increase by geometrical progression, or by close to 100 percent, if he adds a fifth subordinate to the four. Above 5, the curve rises even more steeply.

Graicunas expressed this relationship in the formula

$$C = N(2^n/2 + N - 1)$$

where C represents the total possible contacts and N represents the number of subordinates reporting directly to the manager. This relationship is shown numerically in Table 18–1, from which it can be seen that the marginal increase in complexity of the manager's job resulting from the addition of one more subordinate becomes quite large beyond spans of five. A number of other writers (for example, Bossard, 1945; Entwisle and Walton, 1961) have presented other mathematical estimations of this same basic idea.

TABLE 18-1. Possible Relationships with Variable Number of Subordinates.

Number of Subordinates	Number of Relationships
1	1
2	6
3	18
4	44
5	100
6	222
7	490
8	1,080
9	2,376
10	5,210
11	11,374
12	24,708
18	2,359,602

Source: Koontz and O'Donnell (1972).

R. C. Davis (1951) attempted to distinguish between *executive* and *operative* spans of control. He believed that executive spans, which applied at the middle and upper organizational levels, should be between 3 and 9, depending upon such conditions as the company's rate of growth and the nature of the work to be done. The operative span applied to the lowest organizational levels, and was thought to be acceptable even when as high as 30 subordinates. To these Keith Davis (1962) added the *policy* span, to apply in cases where subordinates are not supervised in the usual sense, but are subject only to general policy control. Under these circumstances, chief executives might have from 6 to 15 other executives reporting directly to them.

Controversy

The span of control has been the subject of more controversy than any other classical management principle; many theorists have argued over how many subordinates constitute an optimal span, while others contend that the very notion of a principle concerning span of control is absurd. Likert, for example, believes that the idea is fallacious because it assumes a "man-to-man" rather than a "man-to-group" form of supervision.

Suojanen (1955) asserted that the principle has become a management fable. He said that it was misappropriated from literature about military organizations in the first place, and has since been made obsolete by new decision-making processes such as team management, by advanced communication techniques, and by social science insights and research into the role of informal relationships within the formal organization. In support of this view he cited Dale's report (1952) to the effect that the number of subordinates in successful companies often exceeds the optimal spans advocated by classical theorists.

In defense of the classical position, Urwick (1956) pointed out that Dale's measure includes all subordinates having access to the supervisor, not just those reporting directly in the chain of command—in Urwick's opinion an invalid measure of what is "exclusively a principle of formal organization concerned with responsibility for the immediate supervision of subordinate activities."

While Urwick (1974, p. 350) is correct in his assertion that the original principle of the span of control attributed to Graicunas "has often been attacked by individuals on the ground of instances which do not fall within the definition," the definition itself is inadequate to prevent certain ambiguities which Ouchi and Dowling (1974, pp. 357–58) describe:

> The span of control is ordinarily regarded as a measure of the limits of hierarchical authority exercised by a single manager. That interpretation is appropriate for some research questions but not for others. Most studies seek to determine how many subordinates an individual manager can or should supervise. For such purposes, it is reasonable to define the supervisor's span in terms of the total number of subordinates over whom he has some authority, responsibility, or control. . . . For much research concerning organizational phenomena, however, the equation of the span of control as the span of authority

> or responsibility has led to an inappropriate operational measure. The concept is also of interest in much organizational research as an expression of the amount of supervisory time needed for one department. . . . The difference of interpretation has implications for the way in which the span of control is measured. If it is viewed in terms of hierarchical authority, it can be measured by the number of subordinates divided by the number of superiors. If it is thought of in terms of the closeness of contact, it should be adjusted to reflect only that portion of a supervisor's time which is devoted to supervision or contact with subordinates.

Ouchi and Dowling then demonstrate that the choice of operational definition will determine not only the mean value of span of control, but will influence various correlation coefficients between span of control and a number of structural variables.

Determinants of an Appropriate Span of Control

Extent to Which Subordinates' Work Is Interrelated. Graicunas' original principle of the span of control was that "no supervisor can supervise directly the work of more than five or, at the most six subordinates whose work interlocks" (Urwick, 1938, p. 8). The degree of interrelationship must be taken into account because, if the work of two units is so closely related that what one of them does has an immediate and important effect on the results achieved by the other, then there must be constant coordination of their activities. If, on the other hand, the relationship between the two is only intermittent, a supervisor need give coordination of activities only occasional attention. One reason, then, why Urwick (1974, p. 352) believes that "the principle of the span of control does not apply at the *lowest* level of supervision in many instances," is that often at that level "their work does not 'interlock.'"

Extent to Which Standardization Is Possible. Mackenzie (1974, p. 165) points out that:

> Standard operating procedures reduce the content and frequency of interactions, decrease the need for experience. . . . "Management by exception" schemes for only notifying higher levels when there is an exceptional case . . . reduce the frequency of interactions. . . . These factors all tend to increase the possible span of control.

Just as standardized procedures can serve as alternatives to personal attention from the leader, other substitutes for direct supervisory control have been found to exist. Udell (1967) found, for example, that spans of control tend to increase with the amount of supervision received by subordinates from others in the organization. Furthermore, professional employees' self- and peer-control and collegial maintenance of standards (discussed in Chapter 17) can make it possible for the manager to maintain a relatively large span of control. Sometimes, however, organizational units with many professional employees are characterized by *small* rather than large spans of control, for reasons to be taken up shortly.

Amount of Nonsupervisory Work Performed by Managers. Stieglitz (1962) suggests that the extent to which supervisors must carry out nonmanagerial responsibilities will greatly affect their optimal span of control. While seemingly an obvious point, some writers have apparently assumed in suggesting definite numbers for the span of control that managers do nothing but manage. In practice, however, most managers have additional responsibilities, as typified by sales managers who do some of the selling. There are even company presidents who do some selling to important customers, and a great many who engage in what is in effect public relations work, since they see many outside groups and deliver speeches in the interest of making the company's name well and favorably known.

Demands made on managers' time from nonsubordinates within the organization will also influence their optimal span of control, although the effect may be either to enlarge or to reduce it.

> The more colleagues and superordinates he has, the smaller his maximum span of control. . . . The time taken . . . depends upon how experienced he is in interacting with them . . . and the frequency of the incidence of interactions . . . and the depth of the interactions. . . . It is very possible, that, as a result of an interaction with his nonsubordinates, a person will be aided in his other duties. If these savings in time exceed the time for interaction, the greater his maximum span of control (MacKenzie, 1974, p. 162).

Supervisor and Subordinate Competence. A highly competent supervisor should certainly be able to manage more subordinates than one who is less competent, or who is less familiar with organizational details. Similarly, subordinate competence, expertise, and experience should also contribute to larger spans of control, since in such cases little direct supervision ought to be needed. However, the evidence in this regard is quite mixed, and some studies (e.g., Udell, 1967; Blau, 1968) conclude that expertise in the operating staff is likely to be accompanied by *small* managerial spans of control. A possible explanation for these findings is offered by Blau (1968):

> Expert training may be expected to make a man not only more independent in the performance of his duties but also more aware of the broader implications of his work and more capable of detecting operating problems and finding solutions for them. . . . In addition, experts can make greater contributions to the improvement of operating procedures than men without specialized training. Hence, feedback

communication from the operating staff is especially valuable for management if this staff consists of experts (p. 458).

Meyer (1968) adds:

> . . . The kind of work done by expert employees requires freer and more open channels of communication than the work of non-experts demands. Intuition tells us that where spans of control are low, supervisors and subordinates have better access to one another than where spans of control are high. Where spans of control are low, then, two-way interchange between superordinates and subordinates becomes possible. . . . Thus it is not expertness in and of itself but rather the need for frequent consultations and communication that produces low spans of control in parts of organizations that employ highly qualified personnel (p. 950).

Of course, the same narrowness of span of control which permits two-way interchanges and upward communication also tends to encourage increased flows of downward communications, and suggests at least the possibility of closer supervisory control. This point is made by Brewer (1971) among others, and will be considered briefly later in this chapter.

Dissimilarity of Activities Being Supervised. This is related to, though not the same as, the question of standardization raised earlier. Udell (1967) found spans of control to increase with similarity of functions supervised, and Stieglitz (1962) refers to this factor as an important determinant of optimal span as well. Clearly, it is more difficult to supervise a number of dissimilar activities than an identical number requiring the same background knowledge.

Incidence of New Problems Within the Manager's Unit. Another factor which will influence the extent to which standardization is possible, and will affect the optimal span of control of managers, is the extent to which they must confront problems and situations which they have not seen before. Lawrence and Lorsch (1967) found, for example, that environments which were relatively stable and predictable called for approximately equal spans of control in production, sales, and research areas, whereas changing and unpredictable environmental pressures required much larger spans of control in research than in production functions. Bell (1967) found that the more complex the tasks that subordinates perform, the smaller the administrators' spans of control tended to be. Complexity in this case was operationally defined to include aspects of variety of tasks, amount of discretion and responsibility exercised, and degree of predictability of work demands.

Extent to Which Activities Are Physically Dispersed. It would be logical to assume that geographical dispersion of activities ought to contribute to a small span of control, since it is clearly more difficult to manage such activities than to manage those concentrated in a single area; after all, the manager may lose a great deal of time in travel (R. C. Davis, 1951). However, in the Udell (1967) study, geographical separation and functional similarity were found to be positively related and to predict *broad* spans of control. It may be that functional similarity is a prerequisite for geographical separation, and we have already suggested that subordinates whose functions are similar should be easier to supervise. An alternate explanation is that geographical separation interferes with face-to-face supervision, and requires executives to delegate more freely; having delegated more authority, they can tolerate larger spans of control.

Current Practice

Several attempts have been made to determine the extent to which organizations actually apply the principle of span of control, on the assumption that if successful organizations disregard it, it is probably not valid. Surveys on the subject have dealt mainly with spans at the top level, and the findings show that spans of chief executives vary widely—from 1 to as many as 24.

Dale (1952), in a survey conducted for the American Management Association, found that the number of executives reporting to the chief executive in 100 large organizations varied from 1 to 24; in only 26 of the companies was the span as narrow as 6. The median was 9. In 46 medium-sized organizations the chief executive had from 1 to 17 immediate subordinates, and the median in this case was between 6 and 7.

Healey's survey (1956) of 620 managers revealed that 93.7 percent of the plant executives had spans of 8 or less, and that 84.2 percent of the branch managers shared a similar span. Entwisle and Walton (1961) studied colleges and small businesses, and found median presidential spans of between 5 and 6.

A National Industrial Conference Board study (Janger, 1960) of 81 large organizations disclosed a range which was the same as in Dale's study; the median span, however, was only 5.

Simonds (1969) compared data gathered from 16 organizations in 1966 to results obtained from the same firms eight years earlier. He found a mean increase in subordinates reporting to the chief executive, from 4.87 to 5.56. The range, which had been from 3 to 9 in the first study, was 3 to 11 in the later one.

Actually, the practices which are in existence at any point in time do not necessarily prove or disprove the validity of the span-of-control principle. Some organizations seem to operate successfully with very wide spans at the top. However, the tendency to increase the number of hierarchical levels as an organization grows indicates that wide spans are to some extent burdensome, and that steps to reduce them are likely to be taken sooner or later.

Research on Group Size

At this point let us turn to a substantial body of analogous research findings which throw additional light on the validity of the span of control principle, namely the research into the effects of size on work groups. The organizational unit, like any group, must be maintained through the efforts of both leaders and followers. As has been pointed out in Chapter 8, in face-to-face contact group members establish communication systems, common values, and mutual expectations. In this way the unit becomes a cohesive group capable of cooperative performance. However, when the unit becomes so large that frequent face-to-face contact among members is difficult or impossible, cohesiveness and performance often begin to deteriorate. For this reason much of the research dealing with the effects of group size upon various outcomes is pertinent to questions about span of control. Research which bears on these questions will be discussed below; for a fuller examination of this literature see Chapter 8.

Group Cohesiveness and Member Consensus. A cohesive group does not break into cliques or factions, and its members find it easier to reach a consensus on major issues. Cohesiveness and group size have been found in a number of studies to be negatively related. Hare (1952) found, for example, that groups of 12 have a greater tendency to divide into subgroups than do groups of 5. Miller (1952) discovered that, as groups increase in size beyond 10 members, the size of the group is significantly (.77) correlated with the number of cliques which emerge. Hare also found (as did Rath and Misra, 1963; and Kashida, 1956) that consensus is more readily obtained in groups which range in number from 5 to 7 individuals.

Jennings (1960) conducted a study in which people were asked about the number of close associations they preferred on the job and in leisure-time activities, and found a preference for 8 on the job and 12 in social groups. In general then, membership cohesiveness tends to lessen as group size increases beyond the 9-person upper limit prescribed by R. C. Davis (1951) for executive spans of control. Furthermore, above this number groups tend to break into cliques and subgroups, whose goals may be quite different from those of the total group.

Member Participation. Group size also influences the quality and quantity of participation among the members. In a 1962 review of research on this subject, Hare asserted that as group size increases "there is a more mechanical method of introducing information, a less sensitive exploration of the point of view of the other, and a more direct attempt to control others and reach a solution whether or not all group members indicate agreement" (p. 240). Hare also suggested that, as group size increases, members feel less directly involved in task success.

According to Delbecq (1968, p. 50), the reduction in sensitivity to other points of view in large groups "is due partly to time constraints and, even more importantly, to the fact that in larger groups careful attention to viewpoints calls for considerable computational ability, great psychological concentration, and empathy—in each case to a degree beyond the capabilities of most individuals."

Other consequences of increased group size are that members are required to talk less and listen more (Hare, 1952), and feel increasingly threatened and less willing to participate (Gibb, 1951). The number of vertical interactions between the members increases with group size, but the ratio of actual to possible relationships decreases (Castore, 1962), and many members tend to withdraw from participation (Bales et al., 1951; Stephen and Mishler, 1952; Carter et al., 1951).

There seems also to be a lower limit on group size, below which interaction and opportunities for participation again decline. Slater (1958) analyzed the interactions taking place within groups containing two to seven members, for example, and concluded that inhibiting forces in the very small groups prevented expressions of dissatisfaction and disagreement. Scores on an inhibition index were significantly higher in groups containing two, three, and four members than they were in groups of five, six, or seven.

Member Satisfaction. Research in this area is generally consistent with conclusions described above concerning participation. Many studies have shown that satisfaction of members tends to be greater in small than in large discussion groups and groups of factory workers (e.g., Hare, 1952; Slater, 1958; Hewitt and Parfit, 1953; Campbell, 1952). A review of various studies (Forehand and Gilmer, 1965) confirms the fact that smaller groups tend to generate greater member satisfaction than do larger ones, and that members' satisfaction with the group is positively related to their opportunities for participation, which we have already mentioned will be greater in small groups.

The same caveat must be expressed, however, concerning groups which are *too* small. In Slater's study (1958), members of two-, three-, and four-person groups made significantly more statements that the group was too small than did members of five-person groups; consistent findings were obtained by Hackman and Vidmar (1970).

An explanation for these findings is offered by Shull, Delbecq, and Cummings (1970, p. 151):

> In groups of less than five participants, satisfaction drops off, as a result of strains of face-to-face relationships implicit in the special characteristics of diadic and triadic interaction, odd-even effects, and overexposure—the fact that the participant cannot withdraw quietly from a position, without group attention being prominently focused upon him. . . . In groups larger in size than five, satisfaction tends to drop off, as a result of restrictions on participation caused largely by time constraints; increased aggressiveness, impulsiveness, and competitiveness on the part of more dominant members; withdrawal by more passive members; increased tendencies toward leader centralization; and the increased probability of clique formation.

Group Performance. Many studies show that smaller groups often tend to perform better than larger ones. Marriott (1949) found, for example, a significant inverse relationship between individual productivity and the size of the (10 to 50 member) work group, and Hare (1952) discovered that groups of 5 take less time to make group decisions than groups of 12. Cummings, Huber, and Arendt (1974) did not find significant differences in the speed with which 3, 4, and 5 person groups solved problems, but did note a general trend toward decreasing speed as group size increased, in two types of spatial arrangements.

Studies by Hackman and Vidmar of groups with two to seven members (1970) and Bouchard and Hare of five to nine person groups (1970) concluded that group size made no real difference so far as *quantity* of group performance was concerned. Bouchard and Hare (p. 54) considered their own and others' results in examining possible explanations for their findings:

> This was not because subjects did not have time to talk—there were long lags in the conversation. Evidence recently presented by Campbell (1968) suggests it is not because the groups were ad hoc and did not know each other before the experiment, although this must be part of the explanation. Previous work by Bouchard (1969) using feedback techniques revealed that it is probably not because subjects are too busy planning what to say and do not listen to others. . . . The same study ruled out the argument that interpersonal difficulties take up much of the groups' time. The crucial problems appear to be the lack of effective management of time in the group situation. As Horowitz and Newman (1964) have shown, and our impressions confirm, individual problem-solvers initially find it difficult to tolerate silence, even brief breaks create an uneasiness which motivates the individual to continue to produce. . . . On the other hand, subjects in the group situation do not experience this drive to any appreciable extent. The result is that some participants monopolize much of the time in a very inefficient manner, elaborating in ways that do not contribute significantly to the problem and taking the pressure to contribute off the shoulders of the other participants who might have something different and useful to say.

Other studies (e.g., Watson, 1928; Gibb, 1951; Taylor and Faust, 1952) indicate, however, that a larger group may be able to solve a greater variety of problems, because the variety of member skills is likely to increase with group size, and because someone in a larger group is more likely to have essential bits of information. In studies by Ziller (1957) and Cummings, Huber, and Arendt (1974), among others, the *quality* of group solutions was found to increase with group size. Yet Hare's review (1952) reminds us that there comes a point—which varies with the task—after which the addition of new members brings diminishing returns. As group size increases, coordination of the group becomes difficult and members cannot function easily together.

The negative effects of increased group size on coordination are most marked when the task involves no clear and objective criterion for judging the quality of performance. On the other hand, when the task is a technical one with a clear performance criterion, or if effective performance requires a specific resource such as a high level of intelligence or the ability to work rapidly, a large group is more likely to contain some member who will generate an answer which is of acceptable quality.

Support for this general conclusion comes from several sources. A classic example is the work of South (1927), who found that groups of six took longer than groups of three on a committee task which required modification of opinion with no objective criterion. However, on "abstract" tasks the groups of six were faster.

Group Leadership Behavior. Another factor related to the span of control is the type of management skills needed for spans of different sizes. Forehand and Gilmer (1965) reviewed several studies and concluded that, in coordinating larger groups, face-to-face techniques of management tend to give way in favor of dealing with subgroups. Hemphill (1950) and Maas (1950) found that as groups become larger demands on the leader become not only more numerous but also more complex and exacting, and group members become more tolerant of highly structured and directive leadership. Under such circumstances the manager "tends to become increasingly differentiated from other group members in terms of initiating and receiving the majority of verbal communications. Other members become increasingly undifferentiated in the same terms, and the tendency toward factionalism and dissatisfaction increases" (Delbecq, 1968, pp. 49–50).

General Conclusions Regarding Group Size

Let us now summarize the research findings concerning the effects of group size. In general, as group size increases the number of member relationships increases sharply, placing greater demands upon the leader in coordinating group activity, and often producing a more formal pattern of leadership. Cliques and factions begin to form. Subgroups generate their own leaders, and subgroup goals emerge which are frequently incompatible with the goals of the larger group. Member participation decreases in large groups, although very small groups may suffer from inhibition of expression.

It is also true that larger groups often have greater resources available for problem solving and decision making, and may enjoy benefits due to division of labor and specialization. These advantages may result in improved group performance, but the evidence concerning this point is inconclusive, due in part to the many criteria of performance employed in the research on this topic. In addition (and this pertains to small-group research as a whole) the great variety of tasks and measurement procedures utilized makes comparisons all but impossible. Even operational definitions of "small groups" vary widely.

In any event, such performance advantages as might accrue with larger groups will often be at the expense of decreased member satisfaction and increased time and difficulty in reaching consensus.

In their review of the literature on group size, Shull, Delbecq, and Cummings (1970, p. 151) conclude that groups of five and, to a lesser degree, seven, offer the greatest advantages. These are said to include:

1. A strict deadlock is not possible, given the odd number of members.
2. The group tends to split into a majority of three and a minority of two, so that a minority position does not isolate an individual member.
3. The group appears large enough for members to shift roles, withdraw from embarrassing positions, and shift coalitions, thus minimizing problems of smaller groups, but
4. Is small enough to allow even more reticent members to play an active role in the discussion.

Morale and the Long Chain of Command

A long chain of command necessarily results if spans of control are kept small. Since a long chain of command and its consequent formality of relationships would be detrimental to morale (because members would tend to regard themselves merely as small cogs in a complex machine) it is necessary to consider just how important this morale factor is.

One investigator whose findings argue against a long chain of command is Worthy (1950), who asserts that "flat," decentralized organizational structures with wide spans of control are superior to "tall" structures with narrow spans. His reasoning is based partly upon the fact that tall structures and small spans tend to result in extensive red tape and difficulties in communications; furthermore, managers with small spans may tend to delegate less and to supervise more closely. Worthy's assertion is based on a Sears, Roebuck survey which found employee satisfaction to be inversely related to the size and number of levels in organizational units.

However, another study suggests that a tall structure is not necessarily detrimental. Meltzer and Salter (1962) obtained questionnaire data from 75 percent of all physiologists employed in the United States in 1953, and found no relationship between organizational size and the number of organizational levels, on the one hand, and job satisfaction and productivity (number of research papers published) on the other. These findings may indicate that no general relationship exists between satisfaction and organizational structure, or they may simply reflect the fact that many respondents were not primarily engaged in scientific endeavor but were performing administrative and advisory functions which precluded the publication of research papers.

Two additional studies may help to explain the apparent contradictions. Porter and Lawler (1963) classified 1900 managers according to whether they were part of tall, intermediate, or essentially horizontal (flat) hierarchies, and then surveyed them by questionnaire. Then Porter and Siegel (1965) conducted a similar survey of 2976 managers in companies in 13 nations. Responses in both studies showed that managerial satisfaction was higher within horizontal hierarchies in organizations containing fewer than 5000 employees; however, for larger organizations the reverse was true. These findings imply that at some point in the growth of an organization it is necessary to formalize hierarchical relationships and to establish limited spans of control.

Conclusions

The implications of group-size research for span of control seem to be that (1) the optimal span is in the range five through ten; and (2) the largest spans, say eight through ten, are particularly appropriate at the highest, policy making levels of an organization, where greater resources for diversified problem solving and decision making appear to be needed.

At the level of the first-line supervisor, according to House and Miner (1969), the size of effective spans of control is very much dependent upon the organization's technology. House and Miner also caution that (pp. 461–62):

> In prescribing the span of control for specific situations consideration must be given to a host of local factors such as the desirability of high group cohesiveness, the performance demands of the task, the degree of stress in the environment, task interdependencies, the need for member satisfaction, and the leadership skills available to the organization. In particular, the degrees of stability, diversity and uncertainty in both the environment of the unit and of the organization appear to be important considerations.

Clearly, as suggested by early management theorists, there is a limit beyond which the size of a work group and the complexity of a manager's job cannot be extended without resulting in undesirable consequences for the organization, for the manager, and for the members of the work group. For managers whose subordinates' jobs interlock and require personal supervision, this limit has fairly consistently been found to be as originally stated by Henri Fayol—in the range of four to six.

For managers whose subordinates are geographically decentralized, little evidence concerning effective spans exists. However, there are some data that spans covering geographically separated subordinates can be relatively wide. Perhaps this results from greater decentralization of responsibility, increased reliance on formal reporting, and less frequent face-to-face supervision.

Also, as briefly mentioned earlier, it should not be concluded that small spans of control are necessarily related to closeness of supervision. Bell's data showed no such relationship, and his conclusions are in agreement with those of Whisler et al. (1967), Blau (1968), Perrow (1972), and others:

> Evidently, even though an administrator is keeping a close rein over his subordinates, this does not restrict the number of employees he can oversee, and/or when supervisors control only a few subordinates they will not necessarily do so in a close manner. It is also possible that this lack of association could be due to the fact that administrators who desire to closely regulate their charges might do so, to a large extent, by using rules and regulations (Bell, 1967, p. 108).

References

Bales, R. F.; Strodtbeck, F. L.; Mills, T. M.; and Roseborough, M. E. 1951. Channels of communication in small groups. *American Sociological Review* 16: 461-68.

Bell, G. D. 1967. Determinants of span of control. *American Journal of Sociology* 73: 100-109.

Blau, P. M. 1968. The hierarchy of authority in organizations. *American Journal of Sociology* 73: 453-67.

Bossard, J. 1945. The law of family interaction. *American Journal of Sociology* 50: 292-94.

Bouchard, T. J. 1969. Personality, problem-solving procedure, and performance in small groups. *Journal of Applied Psychology Monograph* 53: 1-29.

———., and Hare, M. 1970. Size, performance, and potential in brainstorming groups. *Journal of Applied Psychology* 54: 51-55.

Brewer, J. 1971. Flow of communications, expert qualifications and organizational authority structures. *American Sociological Review* 36: 475-84.

Campbell, H. 1952. Group incentive pay schemes. *Occupational Psychology* 26: 15-21.

Campbell, J. 1968. Individual versus group problem-solving in an industrial sample. *Journal of Applied Psychology* 52: 205-10.

Carter, L. F.; Haythorn, W.; Meirowitz, B.; and Lanzetta, J. 1951. The relations of categorizations and ratings in the observation of group behavior. *Human Relations* 4: 239-54.

Castore, G. F. 1962. Number of verbal interrelationships as a determinant of group size. *Journal of Abnormal and Social Psychology* 64: 456-58.

Cummings, L. L., Huber, G. P., and Arendt, E. 1974. Effects of size and spatial arrangements on group decision making. *Academy of Management Journal* 17: 460-75.

Dale, E. 1952. *Planning and developing the company organization structure.* Research Report No. 20, American Management Association.

Davis, K. 1962. *Human relations at work.* McGraw-Hill.

Davis, R. C. 1951. *Fundamentals of top management.* Harper.

Delbecq, A. L. 1968. The world within the 'span of control'. *Business Horizons* 11: 47-56.

Entwisle, D. R., and Walton, J. 1961. Observations on the span of control. *Administrative Science Quarterly* 5: 522-33.

Fayol, H. 1949. *General and industrial management.* Pitman.

Forehand, G. A., and Gilmer, B. 1965. Environmental variation in studies of organizational behavior. *Psychological Bulletin* 62: 361-82.

Gibb, J. R. 1951. The effects of group size and of threat reduction upon creativity in a problem-solving situation. *American Psychologist* 6: 324.

Graicunas, V. A. 1937. Relationship in organization. In *Papers on the science of administration,* ed. by L. Gulick and L. Urwick. New York Institute of Public Administration.

Hackman, J. R., and Vidmar, N. 1970. Effects of size and task type on group performance and member reactions. *Sociometry* 33: 37-54.

Hare, A. P. 1952. A study of interaction and consensus in different sized groups. *American Sociological Review* 17: 261-67.

———. 1962. *Handbook of small group research.* Free Press.

Healey, J. H. 1956. *Executive coordination and control.* Bureau of Business Research, Ohio State University.

Hemphill, J. K. 1950. Relations between the size of the group and the behavior of 'superior' leaders. *Journal of Social Psychology* 32: 11-22.

Hewitt, C., and Parfit, J. 1953. A note on working morale and size of group. *Occupational Psychology* 27: 38-42.

Horowitz, M. W., and Newman, J. B. 1964. Spoken and written expressions: An experimental analysis. *Journal of Abnormal and Social Psychology* 68: 640-47.

House, R. J., and Miner, J. B. 1969. Merging management and behavioral theory: The interaction between span of control and group size. *Administrative Science Quarterly* 14: 451-64.

Janger, A. 1960. Analyzing the span of control. *Management Record* 22: 7-10.

Jennings, H. 1960. Sociometric choice processes in personality and group formation. In *The sociometry reader,* ed. by J. L. Moreno. Free Press.

Kashida, M. 1956. A study of the effects of group norms upon the change of opinions. *Journal of Psychology* 27: 172-73.

Koontz, H., and O'Donnell, C. 1972. *Principles of management,* 5th ed. McGraw-Hill.

Lawrence, P. R., and Lorsch, J. W. 1967. *Organization and environment: Managing differentiation and integration.* Harvard University Press.

Maas, H. S. 1950. Personal and group factors in leaders' social perception. *Journal of Abnormal and Social Psychology* 45: 54-63.

Mackenzie, K. D. 1974. Measuring a person's capacity for interaction in a problem solving group. *Organizational Behavior and Human Performance* 12: 149-69.

Marriott, R. 1949. Size of working group and output. *Occupational Psychology* 23: 47-57.

Meltzer, L., and Salter, J. 1962. Organizational structure and performance and job satisfaction. *American Sociological Review* 27: 351-62.

Meyer, M. W. 1968. Expertness and the span of control. *American Sociological Review* 33: 944-51.

Miller, N. 1952. The effects of group size on decision-making discussions. *Dissertation Abstracts* 12: 229.

Ouchi, W. G., and Dowling, J. B. 1974. Defining the span of control. *Administrative Science Quarterly* 19: 357-65.

Perrow, C. 1972. *Complex organizations: A critical essay.* Scott, Foresman.

Porter, L. W., and Lawler, E. E. 1963. The effects of 'tall' versus 'flat' organization on managerial satisfactions. Paper delivered to the American Psychological Association, Philadelphia, September 1963.

———., and Siegel, J. 1965. Relationships of tall and flat organization structures to the satisfactions of foreign managers. *Personnel Psychology* 65: 379-92.

Rath, R., and Misra, S. K. 1963. Change of attitudes as a function of size of discussion groups. *Journal of Social Psychology* 59: 247-57.

Shull, F. A., Delbecq, A. L., and Cummings, L. L. 1970. *Organizational decision making.* McGraw-Hill.

Simonds, R. H. 1969. Is organization structure reflecting new techniques and theory? *MSU Business Topics* 17: 65-71.

Slater, P. E. 1958. Contrasting correlates of group size. *Sociometry* 21: 129-39.

South, E. B. 1927. Some psychological aspects of committee work. *Journal of Applied Psychology* 2: 348-68, 437-64.

Stephen, F. F., and Mishler, E. G. 1952. The distribution of participation in small groups: An exponential approximation. *American Sociological Review* 17: 598-608.

Stieglitz, J. 1962. Optimizing span of control. *Management Record* 24: 25-29.

Suojanen, W. W. 1955. The span of control: Fact or fable? *Advanced Management* 20: 5-13.

Taylor, D. J., and Faust, W. L. 1952. Twenty questions: Efficiency in problem solving as a function of size of group. *Journal of Experimental Psychology* 44: 360-84.

Udell, J. G. 1967. An empirical test of hypotheses relating to span of control. *Administrative Science Quarterly* 12: 420-39.

Urwick, L. F. 1938. *Scientific principles and organization.* American Management Association.

———. 1956. The span of control: Some facts about the fable. *Advanced Management* 21: 5-15.

———. 1974. V. A. Graicunas and the span of control. *Academy of Management Journal* 17: 349-54.

Watson, G. B. 1928. Do groups think more efficiently than individuals? *Journal of Abnormal and Social Psychology* 23: 328-36.

Whisler, T. L.; Meyer, H.; Baum, B. H.; and Sorenson, P. F. 1967. Centralization of organizational control: An empirical study of its meaning and measurement. *Journal of Business* 40: 10-26.

Worthy, J. 1950. Organization structures and employee morale. *American Sociological Review* 15: 169-79.

Ziller, R. C. 1957. Group size: A determinant of the quality and stability of group decisions. *Sociometry* 20: 165-73.

Part **4**

Organizational Dynamics

Implicit throughout this book has been the idea that organizations are not static entities; indeed, as we have seen, many theories are today considered outdated largely because they failed to deal with the dynamics of a particular phenomenon. Further, we have indicated that what may be proper, rewarding, and functional in one setting may be improper, unrewarding, and dysfunctional in another. In these final chapters, we are concerned with dynamic processes that occur within organizations. These processes are ongoing and constantly changing, and their characteristics and effects must be understood by practicing managers and students of management alike.

Chapter 19 focuses upon planning and control, suggesting the balancing mechanisms which move the organization to its objectives or which correct deviations from such activity. Particular emphasis is placed upon alternative methods of control: feedforward and feedback.

Chapters 20 and 21 deal with closely related topics. Chapter 20 discusses within a theoretical framework why some individuals and groups resist change and what procedures have been developed to promote change effectively. These concepts are then applied in Chapter 21 to explore a particular kind of change, one that is deliberately invited by organizations—organizational development (OD). Four popular OD techniques (Management By Objectives, T-groups, Managerial Grid, and System 4) are assessed in terms of available research into their effectiveness.

Finally, in the last chapter the rational processes and structures which have been the focus of this book are contrasted with other strategies—the craft organization and the promotion organization. In this fashion, it is possible to classify individual organizations and to know their probable strengths and weaknesses. It is also possible to make some decisions about how to improve the management and organizational strategy in use in a single organization at a particular point in time.

Chapter 19
Planning and Control

Anyone can hold the helm when the sea is calm.

PUBLILIUS SYRUS

Planning, organization, and control are considered to be important elements in the job of the manager. While classical theory offers much substantive and operational information on organizing activities, it offers much less on planning and control. In contrast, modern management theory does provide a great deal of information pertinent to the latter functions. Decision theory, systems theory, and a number of modern planning techniques found in the fields of management science and operations research offer much of value to the practicing manager. Similarly, the field of cybernetics, concerned with the study of communication and control systems, offers insight to a manager wishing to improve information flows between organization units or between people.

In discussing these topics we must, for reasons just stated, draw far more on modern than on classical theory. We will not, however, be much concerned with the many specific techniques for planning or control developed in recent years; while these approaches are useful applications, they do not sufficiently explain the processes or their effects. We will be concerned here with systems of planning and control.

Planning: The Process

Planning is the specification of means necessary to achieve a prescribed end, before action toward the end takes place. Note what this simple definition says. First, a plan specifies an end or goal. This may be a manufactured product, arrival in New York, or a completed house. Second, it includes the statement of a series of activities which will result in achievement of the goal. We have *not* said that the *best* course of action is necessarily selected, merely that the acts chosen must make goal attainment possible. Thus, according to certain criteria, it might be "better" to go from Chicago to New York through Cleveland, yet one might also have a legitimate plan which would specify going through Lexington, Kentucky. Finally, we have said that planning precedes action. Humans are unique animals in that we are able to plan because we can visualize the future.

The specification of the means to an end in the form of a plan has certain values in itself. As we shall see later, it makes the goal and the path to that goal unambiguous. Moreover, specifying the means provides measurements for control. If the prescribed means are followed, the plan is said to be in control.

In complex organizations, the steps or means in a plan often become ends or goals of other plans. Thus a plan for producing 100 engine blocks for an auto engine assembly line will include a step in which each block is milled to prescribed tolerances. This step, however, becomes the *end* of the milling department plan for milling the blocks.

An outline of the planning process is suggested in Figure 19–1 and discussed below.

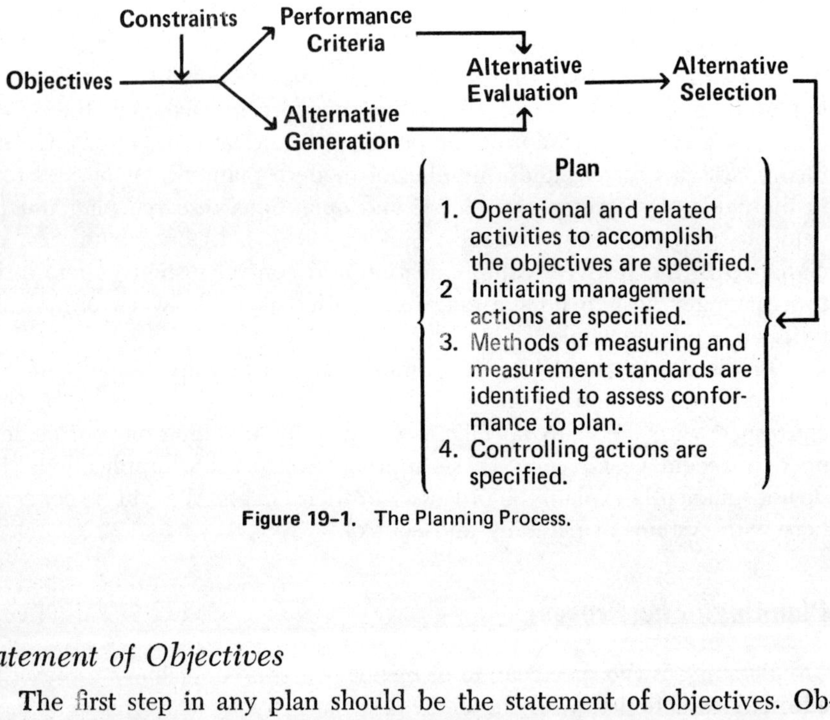

Figure 19–1. The Planning Process.

Statement of Objectives

The first step in any plan should be the statement of objectives. Objectives, as was discussed in Chapter 14, serve as the direction for both organizational and individual performance. The objectives of the organization or activity must be clearly understood first, before the basic processes of the organization or activity can be identified and appropriate strategies developed for attaining them.

Identification of Constraints

Frequently there are constraints on the plan—limits on the value criterion to be maximized. In the plan for traveling to New York, one constraint might be travel cost; that is, we might want to maximize time saved in the trip so long as a maximum cost is not exceeded. While it might be possible to travel by chartered private jet to arrive most quickly, we would not likely meet the cost constraint and would therefore choose commercial air travel instead.

Search for Alternatives and Specification of Performance Criteria

The next step in the planning process involves both the search for alternatives and the specification of value criteria. As we have seen in Chapter 7, early writers often assumed that once a goal was defined, all appropriate alternatives would be apparent. If this were true, the planner would have only to choose the best alternative according to the values judged to be important. Although "perfect knowledge" of alternatives can be approximated in some very simple planning situations, the assumption has certain dangers. Perhaps the greatest of these is the tendency to ignore the practical difficulty of developing alternatives and to place greater emphasis on goal definition and the process of weighting alternatives.

The danger of ignoring the alternative-generating process in planning is suggested by Maier (1964), who demonstrated that groups derive better solutions when they delay the evaluation process and spend relatively more time in the generation of alternatives. In his study, groups which spent more of their time in the evaluation process often ignored better alternatives and wasted energy in conflict and compromise over less suitable strategies. The danger is also demonstrated by the fact that managers often accept a plan which is merely satisfactory—that is, which works—rather than attempting to derive a variety of alternatives from which the best may be selected (March and Simon, 1958).

The generation of alternatives depends on the availability of information and upon the ability to develop strategies for the future. Except for very simple problems which can be solved under conditions where the effects of known alternatives are certain, the actual situation of the planner is more often one in which few alternatives are known and understood. Frequently, then, a problem of successful planning is one of generating alternatives. Once a number of alternatives have been established, they are evaluated in terms of the criteria of value and the constraints which have been set.

A brief example of the planning behavior of two small businessmen will illustrate the value of search behavior:

The first businessman owns a furniture store, selling middle-quality furniture on long credit terms in a suburban area. The income level in the neighborhood has dropped sharply in recent years, and losses due to bad debts have increased from 3 percent to 14 percent of his sales. Store policies on credit terms and merchandise quality have not changed. The owner wishes to regain at least his previous level of profits, but he has not explored new policies for operation in his present location, nor has he explored new locations, nor has he sought information from others for an answer to his dilemma. Consequently, because of the absence of planning his profit situation is not likely to improve.

The second businessman owns a small appliance-repair business near a downtown shopping area, which deals only with appliances delivered to the business: electric toasters, electric razors, irons, etc. His business has declined in recent years because of increased suburban shopping, a shift in traffic flow on his streets, and a decrease in the income level of people living in the neighborhood. The owner wishes to increase business and maintain an adequate level of profit. After seeking information from his trade association, from appliance dealers, from his suppliers, from the local college faculty, and from news media, he has defined the following alternatives as appropriate:

1. Establish pick-up stations in suburbs and repair in present store.
2. Establish pick-up stations with on-site repair and keep present store.
3. Establish pick-up stations with on-site repair and sell present store.
4. Expand parking facilities at present location.
5. Move to the suburbs.

There are, of course, other alternatives which might be considered, but they are either unknown or have been eliminated by explicit constraints. In defining his alternatives, the owner-manager of this business has systematically gathered information on site costs, population growth and density by district, and traffic flows. He has also considered the different effects of a varying number of pick-up stations where they are required. The likely result of his subsequent actions will be the attainment of his objectives.

The contrast between the search behavior of the two businessmen suggests the desirability of seeking alternatives. From this we can see that planning is less a simple matter of selecting the proper alternative, and much more one of searching for alternatives and information.

Concurrent with search behavior is the identification of measures by which the plan is to be evaluated. This is generally an iterative process, repeated as new information is discovered.

Maximizing the Plan. The mere fact that a plan will make goal attainment possible is usually not enough to satisfy the planner. Generally a criterion of value is associated with the goal, and the planner seeks a plan which will maximize the goal in terms of this value. The criterion of value thus becomes the measure of the "goodness" of the plan. The principal value of a trip to New York might be time saved, for example, in which case the best plan would be that which scheduled the shortest travel time. Note that the "best" plan depends entirely upon the particular value criterion chosen.

Multiple Versus Single Criteria of Value. Often there is more than one value criterion in a plan. Where this is the case, some combination is sought which optimizes two or more value criteria, that is, which is the best combination of these criteria.

A common example of this situation may be seen in the determination of the least costly lot-size in manufacturing. Suppose parts which will be used throughout the year in assembling automobiles are to be produced. The plan to produce these parts in batches or lots must optimize the cost of setting up the machines to produce these parts (value criterion 1) and the inventory cost of storing the completed parts (value criterion 2). Obviously the smaller the lots produced during the year the more often setup costs will be incurred. These costs are measured by the cost of labor to do the set-up work, plus the cost of having the machine idle during setup. However, the smaller the lots produced during the year, the smaller will be the average inventory (and inventory costs) of parts in storage during the period. Inventory costs include the cost of space to store the parts, insurance, deterioration, possible theft loss, and the manufacturing cost tied up in inventory. Figure 19–2 illustrates the relation between setup and carrying costs as lot-sizes are varied.

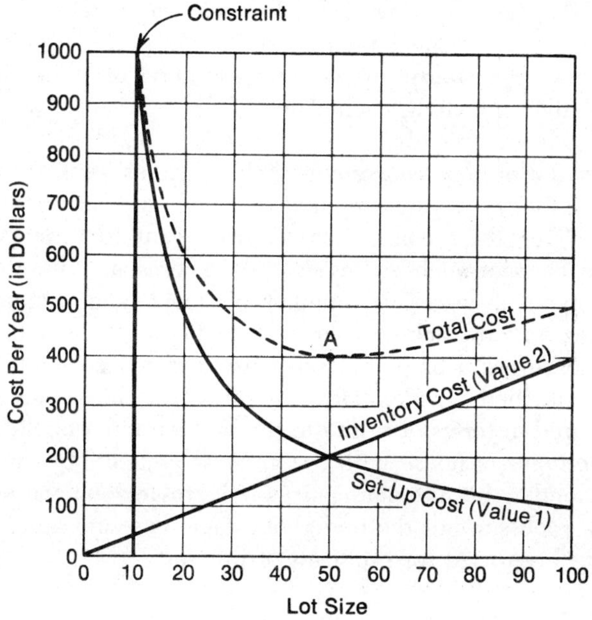

Figure 19–2. Optimizing Multiple Criteria of Value.

The best or optimum combination of these two cost curves is the minimum of the total cost curve, point A. The goal of the most economic lot-size will be met by producing lots of 50; this lot-size is the best combination of values 1 and 2, measured in terms of cost. Again, constraints on the plan may be operating. The figure shows, for example, that it is impossible to schedule lots for production of less than 10 units.

As a practical matter, it should be noted that the lot-size example deals with a situation in which costs can be calculated with some certainty. Often this is not the case. Furthermore, the plan that we are discussing is extremely simple, far more simple in fact than the usual plans and procedures which a manager must devise. It is also convenient to have dollar measures of the value criteria under consideration, as was the case in this example. It is much more difficult to find suitable and comparable measures for such values as morale, customer satisfaction, technological capability, or leadership potential.

Selection of Alternatives: The Conversion of Values

Each plan contains a goal or goals and one or more criteria of value which determine an optimum choice within specified constraints. The best or optimum plan therefore depends upon *the criteria and constraints chosen.* It is therefore important to select relevant criteria. However, having chosen them, the planner then confronts the problem of conversion of values. By conversion we mean stating the criteria of values in a common measure and then weighing each value.

Suppose, for example, that our objective is to build a house. Constraints will doubtless be present concerning such things as location of the house, the amount of money we are prepared to spend, and the time available for completion. Given these constraints, we will want to compare alternative plans on the basis of such values as style, floor space, number of rooms, quality and type of materials, number of floors, and aesthetic qualities. With no common yardstick of value, the homebuilder soon begins to say, "Well, this house has a fireplace and more floor space, but that house has more rooms and better style." However, if all of the values stated above can be measured in terms of *utility* to the builder and weighted in terms of *relative importance*, a house with the greatest total utility can be selected. This may sound a bit utopian, particularly to anyone who has actually faced such a problem, but the underlying logic is sound and the technique described has been used for problems of this sort.[1]

[1] Some writers suggest that there is only one goal in any planning situation; others refer to multiple goals. Where the single-goal thesis is present, the writer assumes that a conversion of multiple goals into comparable value criteria may be achieved; the optimum utility which incorporates these criteria thus becomes the single goal. Equally correct, however, are the empiricists who recognize that it is often impractical or impossible to establish a conversion of multiple goals into a single measure of utility. Here the planners merely try to achieve their multiple goals as best they can. The latter line of reasoning is not necessarily weak or impractical. For example, where the goal of the organization and the goal of an individual within the organization are involved, frequently a plan is sought which will meet both the individual and the organization goal—without trying to convert both to some common measure of utility.

Standardization Versus Improvement in Planning

Frederick Taylor (1919) suggested that managers have two critical responsibilities in the planning process: (1) the analysis of the work process for purposes of improvement, and (2) the standardization of the work process to reduce its variability. These two dimensions deserve attention, because they point to the concurrent obligation of the manager to change and to stabilize at the same time.

One of the important values of planning is that it reduces ambiguity in a complex organization because a plan can be used to predict the behavior of those to whom it applies. As suggested in Chapter 14, people working in complex organizations have greater perceived freedom to operate when they can predict the behavior of others and when they know how others expect them to behave.

Plans also provide standards against which behavior can be measured, and in this sense they become the basis for control. Once standards have been established, actual behavior may be compared with standards and corrective action taken where necessary. Plans also become the mechanism for coordinating the relationship between different units of the organization. They define systems of work flow which cut across the hierarchy of the formal organization structure, binding units together in a meaningful way.

It should be noted that we have not said anything about best or optimum plans. Rather, we are suggesting that even though a plan may not be the best possible, the mere fact that it exists and is acceptable provides important values to organization members. Thus, one important outcome in planning is the reduction of ambiguity.

The second important planning responsibility of the manager is to improve upon plans. Since plans are means for achieving objectives, it is important that managers continually improve these means. This observation may seem rather obvious, yet it is clear that often managers are unwilling to change plans which work and that such an attitude leads to rigidity in organization processes.

Current literature in decision theory abounds with techniques for determining optimum plans. Often, however, these planning techniques give little consideration to the values of reducing ambiguity.[2] As indicated in Figure 19–3, the manager has a dual responsibility in planning: to establish plans to reduce ambiguity *and* to improve upon these plans where possible.

An Example: Planning for Executive Selection

The planning process which we have discussed above may be illustrated by describing the plan for selecting a new president for a small in-

[2] An excellent and readable treatment of decision theory may be found in Miller and Starr (1960).

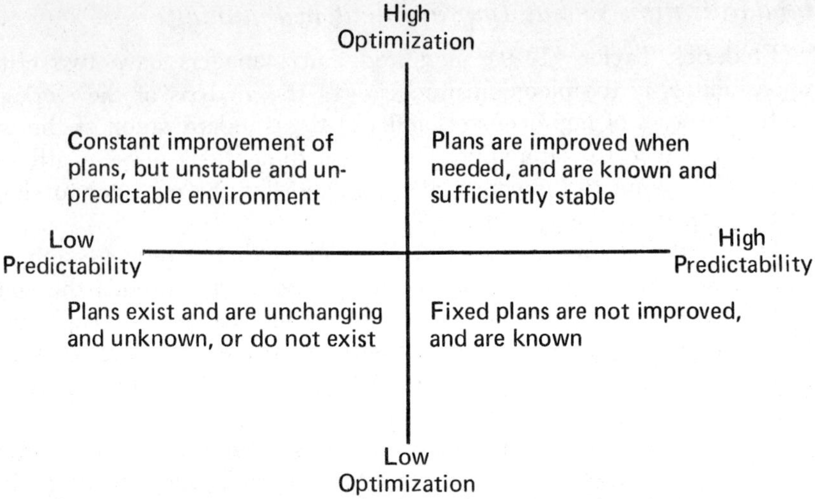

Figure 19-3. Managerial Responsibility in Planning.

surance company in northern Wisconsin. Succession activities were begun one year prior to the scheduled retirement of the current president and were initiated by him and the Board of Directors. The succession plan was developed by two members of the Board, with the assistance of a personnel consultant.

1. *Objectives.*

The purpose of the plan was to provide a qualified president for the company who would take office one year hence. Secondary objectives also included a desire to minimize hard feelings or turnover among existing managers as a result of the selection of a new president.

2. *Constraints.*

Attempts were made by the Selection Committee to determine the limits or constraining factors involved in the selection process. For example, the Board was unwilling to consider a salary of more than $35,000 a year for the new person. It was also clearly indicated that the individual should be male, experienced in the industry, and have a future productive life as president of at least five years. External candidates were limited to those known personally by company management. It was also specified that candidates for the position should express interest in the job and that no one should be considered who would be vetoed by the current president at the outset of the selection process.

3. *Standards for Decision Making.*

Criteria for selection were developed by the Selection Committee from factors they believed to be associated with effective executive performance in general or from factors which the president and Board members felt to be uniquely important in that particular company. The following factors were identified:

a. Social skills—the ability to work personally and closely with other managers and subordinates.
b. Managerial skills—the ability to plan, organize, and control operations.
c. Technical knowledge—the ability to initiate action and evaluate performance in major functional activities in the company (underwriting, investments, loss prevention).
d. Decision-making skills—the ability to use varied decision-making strategies according to appropriate requirements; and the ability to use problem solving rather than force or avoidance in areas of disagreement.
e. Futurity—the ability to articulate and realize improved or innovative company operations in the future.
f. External knowledge—demonstrated awareness of the economic, political, social, and industry environment outside the company.
g. Personal health and energy—demonstrated resources to meet the physical and emotional demands of the position.

On the basis of these standards an interview schedule was developed to assess the kind or level of competence in each. In addition, sources of information for similar assessment from personal histories were identified and used.

4. *Identification of Alternatives.*

The president, Board members, and Selection Committee met to generate a list of candidates for the position. The process yielded five internal and two external candidates. All expressed interest in being considered and the president indicated that he would not automatically veto any of the candidates at the outset. All fell within the planning constraints stated earlier.

5. *Selection of Alternative.*

Having established the alternatives to be considered and the standards for selection, the two Board members on the Selection Committee reviewed the personal histories of each candidate and interviewed each person, taping the responses. The other members of the Committee then reviewed the tapes in private and evaluated each candidate on each of the factors specified. They then met jointly to compare ratings and discuss discrepancies.

Further details of the plan included the identification of areas of relative weakness in the chosen person with suggestions for remedial development, a schedule for joint work with the retiring president, and a recommendation for company reorganization following the new appointment. This information was submitted to the Board along with the identity of the candidate for its approval. Plans were then made for the official announcement; the proposed reorganization was delayed for consideration by the new president.

Following announcement of the selection other candidates indicated their support for his selection, in part because the process itself had demonstrated in detail the high level of skills and knowledge expected. The new president subsequently exceeded expected levels of performance for himself and the company.

Planning Under Certainty, Risk, and Uncertainty

Thus far in our discussion of planning we have been concerned with situations in which the alternatives were identifiable and the measures for comparing alternatives could be established. Probably most planning takes this form.

Yet there also are situations where the evaluation of alternatives depends upon the conditions which may occur. For example, if my objective is to avoid getting wet from a rainfall and my alternatives are to carry or not to carry an umbrella, the values associated with carrying or not carrying an umbrella depend upon the conditions of the sky, whether it is cloudy or clear and blue. Similarly, a businessman planning to introduce a new product will evaluate alternatives differently depending upon a competitor's actions in introducing a similar product.

In addition, the likelihood of conditions will vary. Thus, if we know that it will rain or not rain, or know the behavior of our competitor, the planning condition is said to be *certain*. If we know the odds or probability of these things happening, the condition is said to be one of *risk*. If we don't know the odds or probabilities, the condition is said to be *uncertain*.

This kind of decision or planning situation involves selecting the appropriate plan from among several presented by comparing each plan against the alternatives of an opponent or against various possible "states of nature"—under conditions of different degrees of certainty. The results of such comparisons can be expressed in a payoff matrix (Table 19–1) which shows the costs or rewards associated with each combination of plan and "state of nature."

For example, in Table 19–1, the three plans might well represent three competitive strategies being considered for our company. The three "states of nature" might represent the three strategies which a competitor might take. Under Plan A, if the competitor takes State 1, our company will gain 15 units of value. If the competition takes State 2 we gain 3 units; if they take State 3, we gain 2 units.

We can deal with this payoff matrix under the three conditions of

TABLE 19–1. Payoff Matrix.

	State 1	State 2	State 3
Plan A	15	3	2
Plan B	12	10	30
Plan C	5	4	10

analysis discussed above. The first is a condition of *certainty.* If we are certain that the competitor will take State 1, we will obviously choose Plan A, which provides the highest payoff. Under conditions of certainty, the best alternative is determined simply by ranking the payoffs associated with each alternative.

Second, there may be conditions of *risk.*[3] A condition of risk in decision theory is one in which there is a calculable probability of gain or loss. For example, suppose we know in Table 19–1 that the probability of our competitor taking States 1 and 3 is 25 percent, and the probability that he will take State 2 is 50 percent. By averaging on the basis of these weights, we can determine the expected value (ES) of each of our plans (the W's represent the payoffs from each combined plan and competitor state, and the p's represent the probabilities that the W's will occur):

$$ES = W_1p_1 + W_2p_2 + W_3p_3$$

Multiplying payoffs for each plan by probabilities, we get

$$ES_A = 15(.25) + 3(.5) + 2(.25) = 5.75$$
$$ES_B = 12(.25) + 10(.5) + 30(.25) = 15.5$$
$$ES_C = 5(.25) + 4(.5) + 10(.25) = 5.75$$

Thus, under conditions of risk where probabilities of gain or loss are known, we would choose Plan B.

The third condition under which decisions are made is the condition of *uncertainty.* Here there is an uncalculable probability of gain or loss. Since this probability is unknown, we must establish ground rules for our logic in selecting the best plan. There are several suggested criteria for use in making decisions under uncertainty, but perhaps the most popular is the *maximin* criterion.[4] Here the planner says, "I would like to select the plan which will assure me of the highest minimum payoff, no matter what the state of nature is." Using this logic, we see in Table 19–1 that the lowest payoff in Plan A is 2, in Plan B it is 10, and in Plan C it is 4. Taking the *highest* minimum (the *maximim*) we select Plan B.

It may be noted that the special planning case illustrated in this section can yield different solutions, depending upon the degree of knowledge of the planner and the particular decision criterion selected. Once again, what is *best* depends upon the definition and measure of "best."

Management Control

As with planning, control is defined as a management function. The manager's role in planning is to identify the operational and related activities

---

[3] For a more detailed discussion, see Miller and Starr (Chapter 5, 1960).

[4] Other criteria include the *maximax* (the maximum-maximum); the *minimax regret* (the difference between the payoff received and the highest payoff in the state of nature); and the *Laplace criterion* (the assumption of an equal probability of occurrence in the various states of nature).

necessary to carry out the objectives. Measurements for those activities must be established and the management actions necessary to initiate and control the plan stated. The measurements themselves become standards or bases of control. We define a *state of control* as one in which action conforms to a plan or a measurement standard. The *process of control* is, then, the maintenance of conformity between plans and activities.

The usual concept of the control process visualizes a manager as attempting to adjust action to meet a predetermined standard, but it should be noted that there are other ways of establishing control. A manager may prefer to bring about control by changing the plan to conform to the operational activities. Such a situation might occur where a present measurement standard is no longer appropriate. Similarly, control might be established by adjusting the activity *and* the standard. We call attention to these different methods of control because systems can be established which adjust plans, which ultimately will change measurement standards, as changing conditions make old standards obsolete.

Basic Control Systems

There are two types of basic control systems: *feedforward* and *feedback.* In feedforward control, deviations from standards are predicted and compensatory action is taken before errors take place. On the other hand, in feedback control an *error* in a system becomes the basis for correction in the system. Because of the more general familiarity and identity with feedback control, we will discuss it first.

Feedback Control. This system of control deals with a single process. It is invoked after the activity occurs and therefore represents a reaction to an error situation. Figure 19–4 depicts a feedback control mechanism. Sensing or measuring functions are invoked as operational activities occur during the process. Specific measurements of those activities are taken and compared to predetermined standard measurements, the result of which determines the subsequent controlling actions to be invoked. Thus information is "fed back" to the operational activities for maintaining or adjusting the activities or measurement standard, or it calls for a revision of the plan.

An example of the feedback system is the thermostatic heat control system used in most buildings. A measure of the heat in the room is taken by a thermometer (sensor). The measure of actual temperature is compared with the standard desired for the room through the movement of a contact arm in a thermostat (controller). If the comparison shows the actual temperature to be below that prescribed, an electrical impulse to a motor switch (actuator) starts a furnace and heat is released until a deviation from standard in the other direction is observed. If the thermostat should fail for some reason and the temperature exceeds a specified limit, the furnace plenum contains a fail-safe mechanism to shut off the supply of fuel to the furnace.

Feedback control systems abound in business operations as well. In

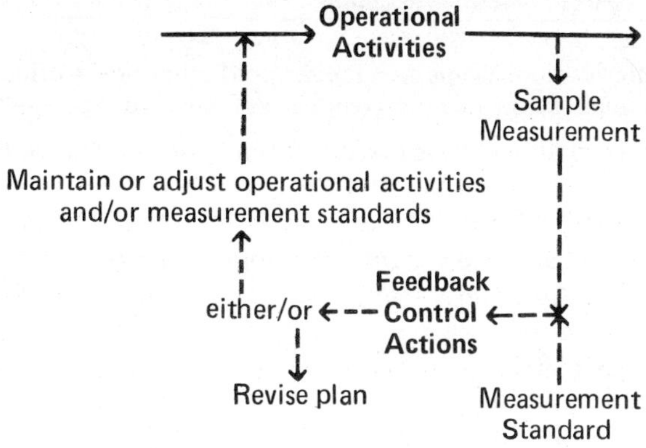

Figure 19–4. Feedback Control.

the control of production quality, for example, inspectors sample goods in process (sensor) and compare measures of these goods against predetermined standards (controller). If a deviation from standards is observed, directions are sent to the operator to adjust the method (actuator) to correct the deviation. In the event extreme situations are encountered complete new plans can be called for.

This type of control system has its weaknesses. In the first place it must rely upon *error* as the basis for correction. Thus, the control process begins only after an error has taken place. Second, because there is a time lag between a deviation from standard and the consequent corrective action, the actual performance tends to fluctuate (oscillate) around the standard. A system designer faced with an oscillation problem will try to reduce it by reducing the time lag for correction.

Feedforward Control. The essentials of feedforward control were disclosed by Harold Black in a 1925 patent filing. Unlike feedback systems, feedforward control systems do not rely upon error for correction to take place. Instead, as shown in Table 19–2, they anticipate deviations from standard and take compensatory action before error actually occurs. Anticipation of deviation from standard depends upon the correlation of two systems such that a change in one enables prediction of change in the other. A controlling activity, which we shall call the "related activity," is ahead of the primary activity and "feeds forward" information to it.

Figure 19–5 shows the operation of a feedforward control mechanism. Sensing or measuring functions are invoked as related activities occur. Specific measurements of those related activities are taken and compared to predetermined standard measurements, the result of which determines the subsequent controlling management actions to be invoked. Thus we have information from the related activities being "fed forward" by the feedforward control to maintain or adjust the operational activities or the measurement standards, or to revise the plan. The use of the feedforward control concept is not always possible. The determining factor is whether the future

TABLE 19-2. Types of Feedforward Control.

Type I - Single Predictor Type — Requires prediction of the effect which a disturbance which is now occuring will have on behavior at some future time.

A. Disturbance external to the system. A disturbance is known (or believed) to be occuring at [t-1] and the effect of this disturbance on the element X's goal seeking behavior is predicted for [t]. Compensatory action is taken.

Example: Football player learns that field upon which the game will be played is frozen. He puts on specially cleated shoes in order to achieve suitable footing.

B. Disturbance internal to the system. Knowing Y's behavior at the present time, [t-1] X predicts the effect of that behavior on X's goal seeking behavior at the succeeding time period [t]. If necessary, compensatory action is taken.

Example: With two candidates running for public office, Candidate A starts an untrue rumor regarding the accumulated wealth of Candidate B. Candidate B predicts that the rumor would hurt his chances for election. Candidate B therefore makes a public disclosure of his financial condition.

Type II - Double Predictor Type — Requires prediction of disturbances and prediction of the effects of those disturbances.

A. Disturbance external to the system. At the present [t-1] some external disturbance is predicted at a later time period [t]. The effects of such a disturbance on goal seeking behavior is predicted as well. Compensatory action is taken (A_1) or, compensatory action is planned to take place when needed (A_2).

Example (A_1): A government predicts a world wide petroleum shortage, and further predicts that the shortage would cause a curtailment of production. The government reduces tariffs on petroleum imports to create a domestic surplus.

Example (A_2): An investment group predicts that there will be a change in government economic policy and further predicts that this will have an adverse effect on the stock market. The investment group prepares contingency plans to be used when policy changes occur.

B. Disturbance internal to the system. At the present [t-1], X predicts that a given behavior of Y will occur at some later time period [t], and further predicts the effect of Y's behavior on X's goal seeking behavior. Compensatory action is taken (B_1) or, compensatory action is planned to take place when needed (B_2).

Example (B_1): Program Chairman A predicts that Speaker B will take more than his alloted time at a conference. The consequence will be a reduction in time available for the other speakers. Program Chairman A places Speaker B in the program just before the luncheon break so that the other speakers will come first and so that he will have to terminate his talk at noon.

Example (B_2): In a chess game, the first player predicts that his opponent will castle, and predicts that such a move would cripple his offensive plans. He therefore plans to put the opponent in check when such a move is apparent, forcing his opponent to move from a castling position.

Source: Adapted from Foss (undated)

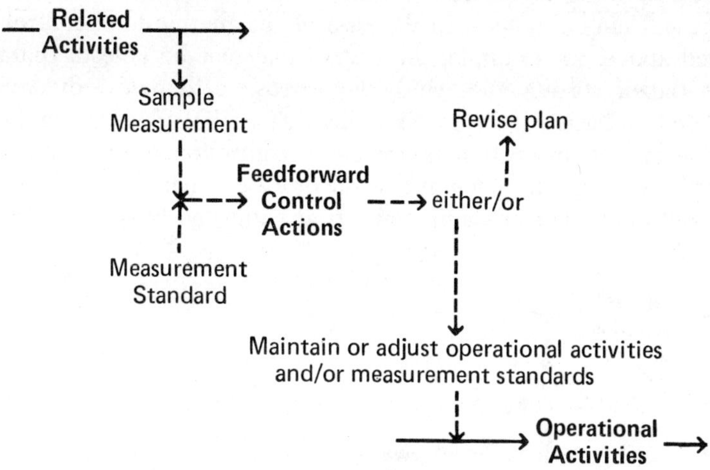

Figure 19-5. Feedforward Control.

effect of an action which is now occurring can be predicted or the effects of future actions can be predicted.

Feedforward control could be used in a thermostatic control for room temperature (Tustin, 1955): A thermometer measures outside temperature and, as the outside temperature changes, the thermometer activates a device to adjust a cam connected to a fuel valve in the furnace to release a predetermined amount of heat energy into the room. By knowing the direct relationship between outside temperature, inside temperature, and the necessary heat to maintain a constant inside temperature, it is possible to keep the room temperature constant as the outside temperature changes. In this system, the room temperature is not being controlled directly, but is being controlled by the outside temperature. In fact, our measurement standard is set on the outside temperature. The essential ingredient is the specification of a precise functional relationship between inside and outside temperature.

In a business setting, a feedforward control system might be used to adjust levels for inventories, production volume, purchase schedules, and employment as sales volume increases or decreases. A change in sales volume could automatically adjust the prescribed levels in the other factors in order to maintain a predetermined relationship of costs and activities to income. For example, in staffing for a workload in a production shop, a feedforward control can be very effective. Staff levels can be related to the level of new orders coming in. The necessary condition is a well-defined relationship between sales orders and staffing requirements to handle the workload.

The feedforward control system (Box and Jenkins, 1966, 1970) feeds information forward in the system to compensate for an activity not being directly controlled at that point. The system suffers from two primary limitations. First, it requires an accurate determination of the relationship between two or more processes or activities. Second, the system cannot deal with unusual circumstances. In the case of the thermostatic control system described above, for example, the system may not be able to differentiate between the effects of a cold, windy day versus a cold, nonwindy day.

These two basic control mechanisms may be linked, as shown in Figure 19–6. The operational activities are being controlled by both feedforward and feedback. Here the general control process is handled by feedforward control and unusual or unplanned events are adjusted by a feedback system.

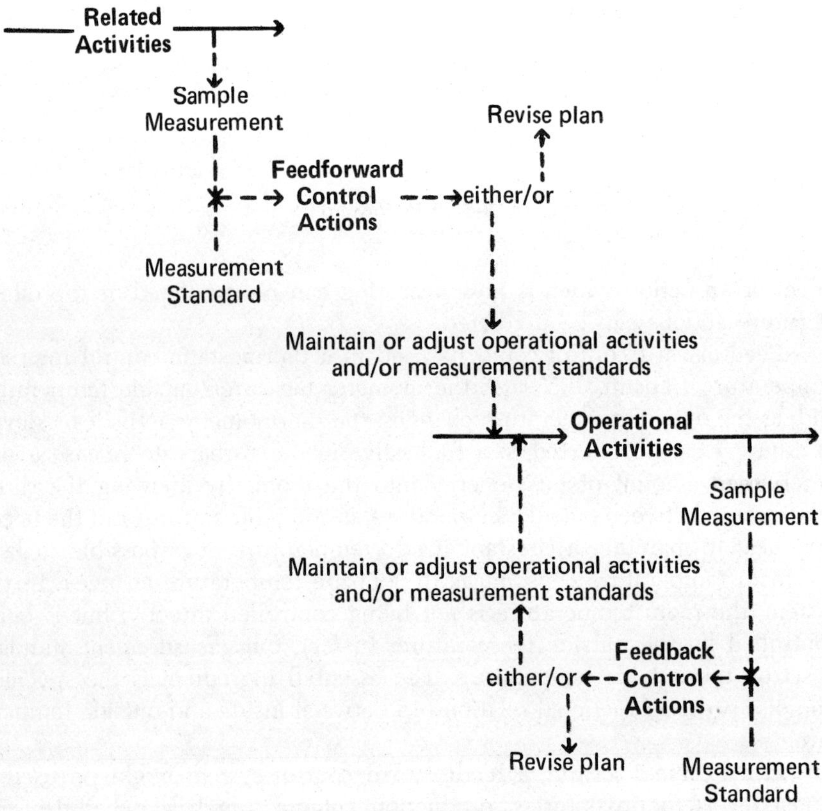

Figure 19–6. Feedforward and Feedback Control.

Implications for Application Purposes

Before proceeding further in the analysis of planning and control it may be useful to emphasize certain points in the preceding discussion and to provide additional examples for clarity.

1. In choosing between alternative plans, the "best" plan depends

upon the criteria which have been identified and the relative weighting of those criteria.

> It is reported that a major airline had difficulty in scheduling departures of its planes. In planning procedures for takeoff, the single criteria of "maximize departure on time" was used. The airline discovered that while it increased the percent of planes departing on time it also increased the number of passengers who were left behind and the incidence of passenger baggage not placed on planes. As a result, the airline replanned takeoff procedures to include the three criteria of performance.

2. Evaluation of planning performance is enhanced when the standards have been made explicit at the outset. Common bases for performance include: (a) a comparison of present performance with past performance, (b) comparison of performance with some generally accepted standard, (c) comparison of performance with standards set at the outset of planning, (d) comparison of performance with performance of similar individuals, groups, or organizations (Filley, 1975).

> Department managers in a small insurance company in northern Wisconsin reported on their planning accomplishments to the Board of Directors every six months. Their usual pattern was to specify improvement in company activities and then to report that the volume of underwriting in different lines had increased or that an underwriting profit had been achieved. The basis for evaluation was essentially a comparison of present performance with past performance.
>
> When performance was compared with that of insurance companies of the same type and size, however, it was discovered that performance was typically less than that of other such companies. That is, the department managers reported "good" performance compared with their past efforts, while a measure based on similar efforts in other companies indicated "poor" performance.
>
> The planning process was changed and department managers outlined their plans to the Directors at the start of each six-month period, and indicated the measures by which their performance could be judged as effective. These measures included stated objectives, performance of similar companies, and historical improvement. The Directors approved such measures at the outset of the planning period. As a result, arguments about whether performance had been good or bad ceased and the basis for evaluation was explicit.

3. The measurement process in planning and control includes both (a) the method for measuring and (b) the standards or levels set as the basis for evaluation. Neither is, in itself, sufficient for control of plans. For

example, a company may decide to assess employee morale by measuring rates of absenteeism and turnover. Yet without indicating the rate to be attained, the measures themselves have little meaning.

In addition, an important element in planning is that of establishing a measurement process and appropriate standards for subjective performance areas. Planners have a tendency to focus upon measures which are easily obtainable, such as profits or costs. Perhaps equally important are measures of environmental change, product quality, or customer satisfaction.

4. Managers may be able to choose between feedforward and feedback control systems for the same purpose. This point is easier to understand if we start with a mechanical example:

> Devices for drying clothes may be constructed with either feedback or feedforward control systems. Where feedback is utilized the amount of moisture in the clothes is monitored during the drying process and when the moisture reaches the desired standard of dryness, the machine is stopped. In contrast, drying systems using feedforward control will be based upon correlations between drying time with specified levels of heat, and the volume and type of clothes in the machine. In this case the drying *time* will be controlled on the assumption that calibrated relationships between time and relative dryness will result in the desired performance.

Similarly, either feedforward or feedback control may be utilized in managerial systems:

> A company wishing to maintain the proper level of staffing in one of its production departments may choose to use feedback control. In that case, the foreman will merely revise his need for people as production levels change or turnover occurs and will call the personnel department to tell them that he has too many or too few workers. Or the company may choose to utilize feedforward control. In this case, the relationship between staffing requirements, turnover, and number of workers on hand will be calibrated so that the number of workers required will be adjusted before deviations take place.

Again, it may be noted that feedforward systems depend upon a calibration of indirect operations and the direct operations to be controlled. Such systems depend upon contingency planning by management to provide for control before error takes place.

5. Control systems may be combined. One such practice is with feedforward systems changing standards and feedback systems adjusting action to meet the standards.

A company may utilize feedforward systems to set budget standards at three levels of sales volume. If sales occur at the high level, then standards of income and expenses associated with that level are maintained by managers through correction of deviations, feedback control. If sales should drop to the low estimate, then income and expense standards would similarly drop and managers would adjust actions based on those new standards.

Planning and Control Process Model

Figure 19–7 shows the complete planning and control model. The model treats planning and control as interrelated but separable processes. During the planning process, the control steps must be considered hand-in-hand with the operational and related activities as these are identified. It is not until the plan is actually initiated by management action that the control aspects come into play.

The following is an example using this model, based on an actual planning activity in a data processing center. In our example, the department has been requested to begin the periodic production of information on new employees of the company.

Step 1: Objectives and Constraints

The company has been growing rapidly and so has its number of employees. The volume of reports and inquiries related to personnel information has been increasing too fast for the current methods of the Personnel Department. The Data Processing Department has been asked to help solve this problem. The objective decided upon for this effort is to provide company personnel information to the Personnel Department on a timely, accurate, and legible basis.

The constraints identified were the number of people available to work on the project and the requirement by top management to do something about the problem by the first of the year, which was five months away.

Step 2: Alternative Generation

A team consisting of individuals from personnel, data processing, and corporate staff was assigned the responsibility of generating alternatives for meeting the objective, and the assistant manager of the personnel department was assigned as team leader. The team had a brainstorming meeting and generated twenty possible alternatives ranging from "doing away with the requirement to produce information" to an "on-line real-time computer system with a terminal on the desk of everybody in the Personnel Department."

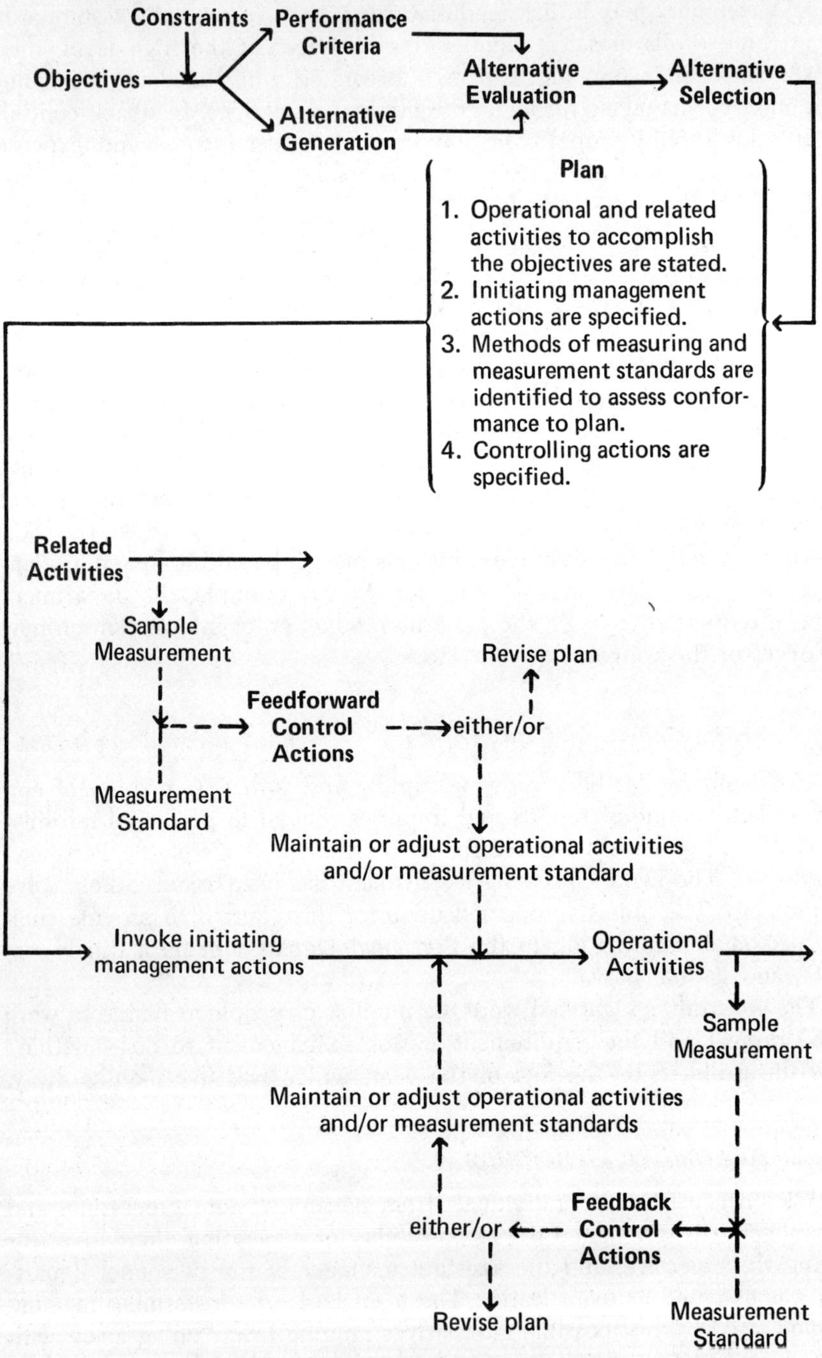

Figure 19-7. Planning and Control Process Model.

Step 3: Criteria for Performance

As a separate activity the team leader met with the heads of the Personnel and Data Processing Departments to identify the criteria against which the alternatives would be measured in the evaluation phase. Those measurements would ultimately be used during the actual selection process to choose the alternative to be used.

The group determined the following criteria:

1. long-term solution is necessary because of investment of funds and operational impact of changes
2. minimal operational impact for Personnel Department
3. utilize data presently automated from new payroll system
4. encourage modernization with new automated procedure
5. minimize corporate administrative cost growth.

Step 4: Alternative Evaluation

The team was then told to evaluate the alternatives. The team used the value criteria and constraints identified above to evaluate each of the alternatives.

Their process resulted in three alternatives remaining as viable candidates:

a. Hire additional administrative assistants in the Personnel Department to insure all information requests are honored.
b. Change the Personnel Department record keeping to a technique using the new automated manual file retrieval concept.
c. Implement a computer based Personnel information system with daily, weekly, and monthly reports going to all department heads.

The final evaluation of the alternatives was expressed as follows:

a. Short-term solution, won't keep up with the continued growth. Most expensive approach with salaries being the expansion item. It does, however, keep the Personnel Department on current procedures.
b. A somewhat longer-term solution, relatively minor cost for new equipment, and it might reduce the staff costs even in the short-run after everyone is trained on the new file procedures. Not a long-term solution however.
c. The long-term solution. It does take advantage of the personnel data already in the computer because of the new payroll data system recently implemented. It will require some procedure changes, for imput and reports will be handled differently, but everyone understands and is excited about working with the computer. There is a strong recommendation that this system be implemented in stages to ensure complete acceptance and proper utilization of resources.

The team reported its findings to the two department heads in a review meeting. The discussion included a detailing of the benefits, costs, and savings for each of the alternatives along the several measurement dimensions.

Step 5: Alternative Selection

The two department heads had an initial meeting to discuss the alternative selection. They discussed the pros and cons from their respective positions and tried to convert the benefits, costs, and savings to a common measure. They generally agreed that the computer system was best. They made a joint recommendation to their superior, the vice-president for administration, who accepted their recommendation and urged them to proceed as quickly as possible.

Step 6: Planning Specification

The team was now given the task of completing the plan. During the alternative evaluation (Step 4) the general plan for the computer alternative had been prepared. The plan had an implementation deadline of three months, with no more planning or development until some results were received. Table 19–3 is the general plan, giving operational and related activities and measurement dimensions, with the method of measurement and the measurement standard for each dimension.

Now the team had to develop the detailed planning specification showing the measurement standards and the controlling management actions for all measurement dimensions. Examples of the detailed plan, the cell containing the time dimension of design and the cell containing the quality dimension of development, are shown in Table 19–4.

The detailed planning specification contained both feedforward and feedback control aspects. Information on the status of an operational activity before its completion, e.g., at the one-half to three-fourths states of completion, was feedforward control for that operational activity and served to keep the whole project running smoothly (Table 19–4). Feedback control on those same activities, on the other hand, was provided for by the measurement standards on completion day and the two days after.

Step 7: Implementing the Plan

The initiating management actions to be invoked after the plan is successfully completed would be:

a. Project approval.
b. Personnel assignments.
c. Authorization to proceed.

Once under way the activities of Tables 19–3 and 19–4 will take place. The following scenario is a hypothetical portrayal of part of those activities as the project moves through its life cycle.

TABLE 19-3. General Planning Specification for Producing a Computer Information System.

Operational Activities and Related Activities	Measurement Dimensions: Time		Budget		Quality		Customer Satisfaction	Environment Impact
I Design	Man days of effort	20 MD	Salaries	2,000	Level of agreement in project team	80%	Design participation measure	New information awareness
	Completion date	7-1-75	Supplies & Services	500			Acceptance measure	Obsolescence of current information
			Capital	100				
			Total	$2,600				
II Development	Man days of effort	35 MD	Salaries	3,500	Level of agreement in project team	85%	Development participation measure	New information awareness
	Completion date	9-1-75	Supplies & Services	2,000			Acceptance measure	Obsolescence of current information
			Capital	400				
			Total	$4,900				
III Operate	Computer hours (CH) per week	4 CH/Wk	Salaries	20	Level of agreement in project team	90%	Information utilization	New information awareness
	Man hours to operate per week	8 MH/Wk	Supplies & Services	1,540			Feedback measure	Obsolescence of current information
			Capital	10				
			Total	$1,570				

TABLE 19–4. Detailed Planning Specification for Design Dimension of Time and Development Dimension of Quality for Producing a Computer Information System.

Operational Activities and Related Activities	Measurement			Management Controlling Action
	Dimension	*Method*	*Standard*	
I Design	A. Time	1. Man days (MD) of effort	a. 1/2 MD schedule complete and 10 MD reported	1) Full team briefing on status of Operational Activities (OA) a) If OA on schedule, eliminate standard and continue to next method. b) If OA not on schedule, replan.
			b. 3/4 MD schedule complete and 15 MD reported	2) Full team briefing on status of OA a) If OA on schedule, eliminate standard and continue to next method. b) If OA not on schedule, replan.
			c. Less than or equal to 20 MD reported and OA complete	3) Eliminate this and next standard and go to next method.
			d. 22 MD reported	4) Full team briefing on status a) If OA complete before 23 MD eliminate all standards this method when complete, go to next method. b) If OA not complete before 23 MD, replan.
		2. Completion date (CD)	a. 1/2 CD schedule complete, date is 6/15/75, and 1/2 MD schedule complete	1) Eliminate this standard and next standard and continue to next dimension.
			b. 1/2 schedule complete, date is 6/15/75, and 1/2 MD schedule not done	2) Full team briefing on status a) If OA on schedule, eliminate this and previous standard and continue to next standard. b) If OA not on schedule, replan.

			c. 3/4 CD schedule complete, date is 6/22/75, and 3/4 MD schedule complete	3) Eliminate this and next standard and continue to next dimension.
			d. 3/4 CD schedule complete, date is 6/22/75, and 3/4 MD schedule not done	4) Full team briefing on status a) If OA on schedule, eliminate this and previous standard and continue to next standard. b) If OA not on schedule, replan.
			e. Date is less than or equal to 7/1/75 and OA complete	5) Eliminate this and next standard and go to next OA
			f. Date is 7/3/75	6) Full team briefing on status a) If OA complete before 7/4/75 eliminate all standards this method when complete, go to next method. b) If OA not complete before 7/4/75, replan.
II Development	A. Quality	1. Level of agreement in project team that quality is good.	a. Greater than or equal to 85%	1) Eliminate all standards this dimension and go to next dimension.
			b. Less than 85%	2) Replan.

At the 10 man-day (MD) point the ½ MD schedule is invoked by the Project Control System (Table 19–4). The PCS receives regular input on resource use for the company. Data on personnel and equipment are received in the form of time slips for hours worked on a project by the people and machine time charged to a project.

The scenario now moves to the completion date method of measurement for the time dimension. Suppose the date is 6/25/75 and the design phase goes to completion. Step "2–e" of Design (see Table 19–4), with the measurement standard of "Date is less than or equal to 7/1/75 and OA complete," will be invoked. Since the operational activity of design is complete the controlling management action of removing this standard and the fail-safe standard of two days leeway is invoked. Then control will pass out of design stage and into development stage.

Let's now change the scenario and assume we are at 7/3/75 without completion of design. The feedback control would invoke a full briefing on project status. Status had been okay up through the three-fourths checks of man-days and completion dates. A new piece of equipment had been announced on 6/24/75 that appeared to impact the project significantly. The team leader decided to attend a demonstration in a distant city and had just returned. He briefed the team on his findings. It was apparent to all that the new device would change some of the original assumptions about cost, use, and other human factors related to the equipment originally proposed. The team may decide that the alternatives should be reconsidered and a revision of the plan initiated.

Propositions

In our discussion of planning and control, we have described the processes of planning and control, including the values of both processes. The following propositions are central to this theory, and will be evaluated empirically.

1. Managers who engage in planning activities are more effective than managers who do not.
2. Search behavior is positively related to planning success.
3. Organizational effectiveness is positively related to the amount of total control provided.
4. Organizations employing feedforward control are more effective than those not using feedforward.

Empirical Evidence

Proposition 1

Managers who engage in planning activities are more effective than managers who do not.

There are several studies reported in the literature which bear on this proposition. Laboratory experiments have been conducted which measure managerial effectiveness in terms of attitudes toward work, or in terms of productivity. Also related to the proposition are studies of company or industry performance in which criteria such as growth or profitability are related to measures of planning behavior. From these studies we shall infer that the degree of planning reported reflects a general tendency to engage or not to engage in planning activities.

A positive relationship between planning behavior and superior managerial performance is reported in a study by Hemphill (1964). In this study 232 high school principals were given "in-basket" problems to simulate administrative work. Problem-solving behavior in these tasks was compared with ratings of the subjects by superiors in their home schools, measures of work output, and other criteria of effectiveness. In general, the results showed that subjects who stressed preparation for decision in the simulated setting were also those who earned very high performance ratings from superiors in their home schools. The planners also scored higher on a test of general reasoning ability, learned presented material more quickly, were fluent, and produced more work.

Planning is also shown to be related to objective measures of organizational effectiveness. In a study by Comrey, High, and Wilson (1955) questionnaires to determine managerial behavior were administered to 213 workers, 244 supervisors, and 29 foremen at a division of the Lockheed Aircraft Corporation. Behavior patterns were then compared with four measures of organizational effectiveness: the need for rework, acceptance rates, production rates, and an executive rating of departmental effectiveness. Planning was shown to have a significant, though curvilinear, relationship to rework and acceptance-rate criteria and some relationship to production rate. None of the questionnaire dimensions, including planning, were related to executive ratings of the departments.

As might be expected, plans are shown to have a more positive effect when individuals who must use them develop their own, rather than having plans imposed on them by others. Bass and Leavitt (1963) conducted three separate experiments designed to determine how planning affects performance and attitudes among individuals engaged in several different tasks. Both morale and productivity were found to be higher when subjects followed plans which they had developed themselves rather than plans developed by others.

A field experiment at General Electric (1964) showed similar results. In this case the effects of joint work planning by a manager and a subordinate were compared with the effects of routine performance appraisal interviews. The researchers attempted to discover whether WP (joint work-planning and goal-setting) discussions between a manager and subordinate would produce greater improvement in job performance than that produced by the typical PA (performance appraisal) interview, in which the need for improvement was the main subject of discussion. In the experimental group, subjects were first given the usual appraisal interviews, then switched to the joint planning approach. The control group continued with the appraisal interview format throughout the experiment. Questionnaires designed to measure attitudes toward work were administered to all participants.

Results showed that the joint planning group had significantly greater improvement in five of the six areas measured. Respondents felt that they were receiving more help from their managers in doing their current jobs better, that there was more agreement on job goals, avenues of improvement, and development, and that they participated more in job-related decisions. Their attitude toward appraisal discussions also improved. The appraisal group showed no change in any of these areas. The measure of attitude toward salary practice showed no improvement in either group.

Although the experiment dealt primarily with attitudes, there is some evidence that the joint planning sessions did affect performance. Members of the joint planning groups reported that action had been taken on 70 percent of their improvement needs; in the routine appraisal group, 40 percent of the improvement needs were reported as met. Thus, it would seem planning in this sense did increase organizational effectiveness, and that plans whose development subordinates had an opportunity to influence had more positive results than imposed plans.

It would appear that planning is a distinct activity which is performed more effectively prior to performance. Thus not only planning, but uninterrupted planning, may be important. For example, Shure et al. (1962) established three types of planning groups in a laboratory setting. In the "separate planning" group, members were allowed a definite amount of time for planning before work was to begin. In the "contemporary planning" group, time was allowed for planning, but the periods for planning and performance were not separated. The "no planning" group members were provided no time for plânning at all. Results showed that efficiency in task performance was clearly related to planning, improving from no planning to contemporary planning to separate planning.

Positive results are also indicated for planning at the company level. Thune and House (1970) compared the financial performance of 36 firms (17 formal planners and 19 informal planners). The firms were classified as formal planners if they determined corporate strategy and set goals for at least three years in advance and, in addition, established specific programs of action for achieving those goals. Firms not meeting these criteria were classified as informal planners. Five performance measures were considered: sales, stock prices, earnings per common share, return on common equity, and return on total capital employed. The 36 firms represented six industrial classifications: drugs, food, chemicals, steel, oil, and machinery.

The comparisons indicated that formal planners outperformed informal planners on three measures—earnings per share, earnings on common equity, and earnings on total capital employed. Results on the other two criteria were substantially the same. When performance of the formal planners (other than in the steel industry) was compared with their performance for an equal time period prior to the inception of formal planning, they outperformed themselves on sales, earnings per share, and stock price appreciation. Data on the other two economic measures were not available for comparison.

An industry-by-industry comparison indicated that formal planners in the drug, chemical, machinery, and oil industries outperformed the informal planners on all five economic criteria. In the food industry formal planners did substantially better with respect to earnings per share, stock appreciation, and earnings on common equity.

A further industry-by-industry analysis compared formal and informal planners in each industry in terms of performance before and after the use of formal or informal planning. The long-range planning firms in the drug, chemical, and machinery industries consistently outperformed the informal planners on all five criteria of business success. Planners in the food industry did better with respect to earnings per share, stock price appreciation, and earnings on common equity, were about equal to informal planners on sales increases, and were slightly lower with respect to earnings on total capital. In the oil industry, planners showed a greater increase in stock prices, earnings on common equity, and earnings on total capital. They did less well on sales increases and earnings per common share. Comparisons in the steel industry were not possible because of the early date at which planning was initiated in that industry.

In general, the limited information available suggests that planning does increase effectiveness, whether considered at the level of the individual manager, a decision-making group, or a company as a whole.

Proposition 2

Search behavior is positively related to planning success.

Current theory on planning indicates positive values associated with search behavior. Put most simply, the manager is directed to "take time to plan." Explanations for the value of search are varied. Perhaps most interesting is the belief that added search contributes to a situation of *synergy*, in which the attainment of individual objectives furthers the attainment of group or organization goals. Synergy may be contrasted with situations of power or bargaining in resolving conflict (see Chapter 9). In a synergistic system, both parties in a conflict resolve the conflict to the gain of both; in a power or bargaining situation, conflict is resolved by submission of one party or by a partial loss of goal attainment by both parties.

A search for and use of facts has also been described as the basis for resolving substantive (factual) conflict. A study by Guetzkow and Gyr (1954) of business and governmental decision-making conferences found that conflict was usually reduced when facts were present and where orderly procedures for solving problems were used. Finally, search behavior probably contributes to the "idea-getting" process and to "problem-mindedness," both of which contribute to better problem-solving behavior by groups (Maier, 1964). The exact implications of these benefits from search behavior are most readily demonstrated in studies of group problem solving and in studies which relate time for search with group creativity.

N. R. F. Maier, who has contributed to a number of studies related to this subject, used as the basis for his investigations a multiple role-playing technique which he developed. Typically, a large group of students or trainees is broken down into small groups, each of which "acts out" a case situation. One such case is a change-of-work problem. Of three workers working on an assembly task, two are able to produce at a faster rate than the third, and each is superior at one task. The workers are rotating their tasks to reduce monotony on the job. However, a time-study engineer has determined that, if they work only at their most efficient task, the overall productivity of the three can be increased markedly. The foreman has the problem of changing the work pattern to increase productivity.

The obvious solutions to the problem are typically effected by fiat: either the foreman imposes the engineering method on the group, or the group imposes the rotation method on the foreman. There are, in fact, other solutions which would meet both organizational and individual goals. For example, the slowest worker, who doesn't particularly want to rotate anyway, can work on his fastest task, and the other two workers can rotate tasks. Another solution is to use different rotation arrangements which permit the workers to spend more time at their most efficient task, such as rotating the two best tasks, or spending more time on the fastest task while rotating among all three.

The implications of search in finding a synergistic (creative) solution to this problem may be seen in an experiment by Maier and Solem (1962), which used 96 four-man experimental groups and 50 four-man control groups. The experimental groups were instructed to list and discuss all of the important factors related to the problem situation. Having done this, they were to use this list in proposing a solution. The control groups, on the other hand, were told only to propose a solution.

The results showed that in the experimental groups, 20.8 percent decided to continue the present rotation method, 37.5 percent decided on the engineering suggestion, and a synergistic solution was proposed by 41.7 percent. In the control groups, 22 percent elected the present method, 66 percent decided on the engineering method, and only 12 percent arrived at a creative solution.

It would appear from these results that the search behavior of the groups increased planning success (if success is interpreted to mean attainment of production goals while meeting individual goals as well).

Maier (1963) also obtained similar results when he directed groups which had solved the change-of-work problem to solve it again, increasing their search for solutions. Only 11.1 percent of the groups derived a creative solution on the first try; 42.6 percent developed creative solutions with the added search of another attempt. Repeated attempts at problem solving also reduce the time necessary to arrive at a solution (Maier and Hoffman, 1960).

It would appear from the foregoing discussion that increasing search behavior in group problem solving increases the likelihood of obtaining a creative, high-quality decision. Some insight into the effects of search behavior is also gained through studies of "brainstorming." Brainstorming is a technique for generating ideas in which group members are told to generate as many ideas as possible, disregarding any judgment of quality.

In an experiment by Meadow, Parnes, and Reese (1959), subjects were told to produce ideas for solving two problems. Half of the group, the control, was told to produce only high-quality solutions and that there would be penalties for poor solutions. The other half was instructed to suggest as many solutions as possible and told that there would be no penalties for poor ideas. Results showed that those free to brainstorm (to suggest any ideas that occurred to them) actually produced more good ideas than those who were restricted to suggesting only good ideas. Mean scores were 7.94 good solutions for the brainstorming group, compared with 3.88 good solutions for the control group.

In another experiment, Parnes (1961) found that significantly more good ideas were produced in the second half of the time allowed for brainstorming than in the first half. He also found that when the time allowed for brainstorming was extended from five minutes to fifteen minutes, the last five minutes yielded significantly more good ideas than the first ten minutes.

The experiments reported above indicate that increased search behavior increases the chance of planning success. They also suggest that systematic gathering of alternatives, postponement of judgment concerning the quality of alternatives, and an increase in the time available for search behavior all contribute to success in planning.

Proposition 3

Organizational effectiveness is positively related to the amount of total control provided.

Inherent in the earlier discussion of control was the suggestion that controlled systems are more effective than noncontrolled systems, regardless of the type of control utilized (feedforward or feedback). One approach in evaluating this proposition is the use of a presumed measure of control developed by Tannenbaum (1968). He and his associates define control as the degree of perceived power or influence which an individual or group at one hierarchical level has over those at another level. Our evaluation must be cautious, therefore, because (1) there are other dimensions of control not considered in Tannenbaum's definition (Dessler et al., 1969), e.g., control by an individual over his environment, and (2) because control defined as influence may not be the same as control as defined in this chapter. Because of the limited substantive and empirical information on the subject, however, we shall include this work for its information value.

Using a questionnaire to measure perceived control by the respondent or others, and then averaging responses (say, by organization level), it is possible to develop a profile for the organization showing the amount of control exercised at each level of the organization. It is also possible to determine relative differences in the amount of total control exercised in different organizations. For example, Tannenbaum compared the amount of total control with the organizational effectiveness of 104 local Leagues of Women Voters. Total control was determined by totalling the amounts of control exercised by the three hierarchical levels in the League organizations. Effectiveness was measured by judgments of the League units by members. On this basis, effectiveness was significantly related to the amount of total control exercised.

Similarly, McMahon and Perritt (1973) found a direct relationship between organizational effectiveness and the amount of control exercised by 12 geographically dispersed plants in a single manufacturing organization. First-level managers in plants with greater total control reported more favorable assessments in terms of communications, performance ratings, interunit cooperation, problems with the bureaucracy, cost reduction, and work pressure.

Finally, in a study by Farris and Butterfield (1972) of 16 regional banks in Brazil, the relationship between total control and organization performance was also investigated. Respondents to the control questionnaire included presidents, directors, department chiefs, supervisors, and technical personnel. The effectiveness of the banks was rated by experts from the national bank. The two measures were significantly related.

The authors of the study also concluded that control was related to effectiveness when each level saw the hierarchical level immediately above themselves as exerting relatively more control. As indicated in Table 19–5, when three phases of decision making on loan applications were examined at each hierarchical level, a significant relationship between effectiveness and control was demonstrated.

Bank effectiveness was also shown to be related to the control exerted by the national bank. In this case national bank control was related to two other measures of regional bank effectiveness: a rating by their borrowers and by the number of loan development projects approved. The results, while weaker, were in the same direction, indicating that greater control is associated with effectiveness in inter-organizational as well as intra-organizational decision making.

In general, the findings from this study indicate that total control is related to effectiveness and that control is most effective when it is exerted by the party most responsible for a particular phase of decision making. The authors suggest that the necessary control to do a job and the competence necessary in the job are predictors of successful performance.

In general, the findings from these and other studies (Kavcic, Rus, and Tannenbaum, 1971; Bachman, Smith, and Slesinger, 1966) consistently show organizational effectiveness to be related to the degree of organizational control (as defined by Tannenbaum). They also indicate that the control exercised at one level of an organization is not determined by

TABLE 19-5. Rank-Order Correlations Between Control at Different Stages of Decision Making and Bank Effectiveness (n = 15 banks; data from technical personnel).

	Correlation between effectiveness and control in		
Measure of control	Determining methods	Evaluation	Approval
Total control	0.34	0.37	0.13
Top management	0.11	0.21	0.57*
Department heads	0.54†	0.22	0.31
Technical supervisors	-0.07	0.28	0.04
Technical personnel	0.12	0.50*	0.17
Slope (Variance from grand mean)	0.04	-0.12	0.27

*$p < 0.01$ (one-tailed test).
†$p < 0.05$ (one-tailed test).

reducing the amount of control at another level. Thus, the volume of control in parts of an organization may increase or decrease without affecting the control of other parts. The findings also emphasize that control should be exercised appropriately—by the party concerned with that particular phase of decision making—and that competence must accompany control if successful performance is to take place.

Other evidence indicates that the amount of total control does not always insure success, however. McMahon and Perritt (1971) investigated the association between total control and three organizational variables: adequacy of communication, group-oriented management, and supportive behavior. Two plants in the same corporation were studied and, because the measure of total control was equal in both plants, the authors expected that criterion variables would also be similar. Quite to the contrary, they were different.

In attempting to explain these findings, the authors proposed that it is not the amount of total control that affects the variables, but rather the degree to which the perceptions of control at each level of the organization are in agreement. As suggested, the plant which had greater agreement about the degree to which control was exercised rated higher on criterion variables than the plant where there was less agreement. These findings do not necessarily negate the earlier statement that the amount of total control is associated with effectiveness; they merely indicate that perceptions about the relative control exercised by different levels of an organization should also be in agreement.

In sum, the research on this subject consistently supports the proposition. All studies, it should again be noted, define control operationally in terms of influence exercised as measured by the Tannenbaum instrument.

Proposition 4

The use of feedforward control is positively related to organization effectiveness.

It is safe to say that this proposition is virtually untested in management research either directly or through analogous research. The articulation of feedforward control systems has been limited to specialized engineering applications and the evaluation of the effectiveness of such systems is essentially limited to its application in chemical process control situations. For example, a study by MacMullan and Shinskey (1964) dealt with the problem of separating pentane and isopentane through the use of superfractionators. Several control methods were used but only the use of feedforward control proved to be efficient. Reportedly, the use of feedforward controls resulted in a 1.5 percent increase in product recovery which provided an after-task saving of $30,000 a year.

Another study (Shinskey, 1968) concerned the application of feedforward control to maintenance of pH balance (acid or base) in a chemical process. According the Shinskey, "even if the feedforward part of the system were accurate to ± 10 percent, it would still provide a ten-fold improvement over feedback alone, in response to sudden load changes." Of perhaps greater usefulness for present purposes, the study emphasizes that the application of feedforward control is best used in conjunction with feedback as well.

Finally, a paper by Nisenfield and Miyasaki (1972) reports the relative savings of feedforward applications in distillation columns. The authors say that "Feedforward control is the intelligent use of process information to compensate for changes in an independent variable before the process is upset. Feedforward systems theoretically can achieve perfect control: that is, they can prevent any change in the controlled variable despite changes in operation" (p. 1.1). In practice, however, feedforward controls were used for major sources of deviation and the remaining upsets were left for feedback controllers.

The first of the before and after assessments of feedforward control was its application in a Fluid Catalytic Cracking Unit. Due to sensitivity problems concerning ambient conditions, quality of heating medium, and load changes affecting capacity, the two columns in the unit became a plant bottleneck. Feedback controls and equipment improvement were tried first but neither was sufficient. When relatively inexpensive feedforward controls were installed, the following results were noted: (1) the system could cope with larger and faster changes than had previously been the case; (2) energy cost decreased by $9000 per year; and (3) capacity increased 22 percent.

The second case was application to a gasoline depropanizer. Because of changes in the feedrate and composition plus changes in the quantity and temperature of the hot oil heating medium, the column was frequently upset. In addition it caused problems downstream in the process as well. In order to cope with problems the column was operated at reduced capacity and with increased utility cost, and it still produced products off-specification nearly 15 percent of the time. Before expanding the whole operation to compensate for reduced efficiency, management was persuaded to install feedforward controls at a cost of $7500. The following results occurred: (1) column capacity increased 25 percent; (2) products were in specification 99 percent of the time; (3) increased recovery of materials resulted in an estimated annual saving of $26,000 per year; (4) only one new column was eventually added, instead of the planned three; and (5) daily utility costs were reduced from $125 to $100.

The third application concerned a superfractionator. Due to the column's extreme sensitivity to changes in feedrate it was operated in a way which reduced the recovery of propylene from the required 80–90 percent to an inefficient 50–60 percent. A feedforward system was installed at a cost of $4300. According to the authors, "the system virtually paid for itself . . . before the start-up team left." By the end of the third day, the recovery rate of propylene was better than 97 percent, resulting in a yearly saving of $438,000.

While the technical details of these applications may escape the reader and while the examples are limited to chemical refining, they do suggest the relative merits of applying feedforward controls.

Discussions of technical applications emphasize that for feedforward control systems to work the process to which they are applied must be thoroughly understood. Such understanding is necessary if deviations are to be predicted and compensatory actions are to be taken. Technical discussions also emphasize that while feedforward systems are useful in dealing with events which may be anticipated, such systems are best linked with feedback mechanisms to handle events which cannot be determined in advance. The use of feedforward control in managerial systems remains to be evaluated, however.

Summary

Proposition 1: Managers who engage in planning activities are more effective than managers who do not. *Consistently supported.*

Proposition 2: Search behavior is positively related to planning success. *Consistently supported.*

Proposition 3: Organizational effectiveness is positively related to the amount of total control provided. *Support limited to Tannenbaum measure of total influence.*

Proposition 4: The use of feedforward control is positively related to organizational effectiveness. *Untested.*

Discussion

In general the research cited indicates that specifying action to be taken will have positive effects on performance. A variety of studies which define planning from the individual, group, or company point of view show consistent support for the notion that planning adds to effectiveness. Related to the issue of planning is the question of whether search behavior adds to planning or decision-making effectiveness. While not considering the costs associated with search, the clear outcome of the review is that search behavior increases the quality of planning. It increases the chance of finding a solution which benefits several parties with different needs, it increases the quality of final outcomes, and it increases the number of high-quality solutions. Planners are thus well advised to avoid premature closure in their search behavior.

Issues surrounding the subject of control are far less clear. If control is related to the total amount of influence exercised in an organization (re: Tannenbaum, 1968) then there is reason to suppose that control is related to organizational effectiveness. Perhaps most useful is the suggestion that control in this sense is not a zero-sum situation. One group may increase its influence without reducing the influence of another. Control at all organization levels may, in fact, be increased.

When one considers individual types of control systems, and in particular, feedforward control, the evaluation of such systems is not yet possible. It appears that where the organizational system is understood well enough to specify causal relationships, balance systems may be provided to maintain control without reliance on error. Contingency planning, flexible budgeting, critical path scheduling, and internal coordinating mechanisms appear to be forms of feedforward control but their role as control mechanisms requires further theoretical elaboration and testing before much more can be said definitively.

References

Bachman, J. G., Smith, C. G., and Slesinger, J. A. 1966. Control, performance, and satisfaction: An analysis of structural and individual effects. *Journal of Personality and Social Psychology* 4: 127-36.

Bass, B. M., and Leavitt, H. J. 1963. Some experiences in planning and operating. *Management Science* 10: 574-85 .

Box, G., and Jenkins, G. M. 1966. *Models for prediction and control.* Technical Report No. 72, Department of Statistics, University of Wisconsin, Mimeograph.

———., and ———. 1970. *Time series analysis: Forecasting and control.* Holden Day.

Comrey, A. L., High, W., and Wilson, R. C. 1955. Factors influencing organizational effectiveness. IV. A survey of aircraft workers. *Personnel Psychology* 8: 79-99.

Dessler, G.; Kerr, S.; Shiffman, L.; and Turner, J. 1969. A review of *Control in organizations* by A. S. Tannenbaum. *Administrative Science Quarterly* 14: 318-21.

Farris, G. F., and Butterfield, D. A. 1972. Control theory in Brazilian organizations. *Administrative Science Quarterly* 17: 574-85.

Filley, A. C. 1975. *Interpersonal conflict resolution.* Scott, Foresman.

Foss, D. C. Undated. Feedforward mechanisms in control and goal-seeking behavior systems. University of New Hampshire, Mimeograph.

General Electric Company. 1964. *A comparison of a work planning program with the annual performance appraisal interview approach.* Management Development and Employee Relations Services.

Guetzkow, H., and Gyr, J. 1954. An analysis of conflict in decision-making groups. *Human Relations* 7: 367-82.

Hemphill, J. J. 1964. Personal variables and administrative styles. In *Behavioral science and educational administration.* National Society for the Study of Education.

Kavcic, B., Rus, V., and Tannenbaum, A. S. 1971. Control, participation, and effectiveness in four Yugoslav industrial organizations. *Administrative Science Quarterly* 16: 74-86.

Kotnour, K. D., Box, G. E. D., and Altpeter, R. J. 1966. A discrete predictor-controller applied to sinusoidal pertubation adaptive optimization. *ISA Transactions* 5: 255-62.

MacMullan, E. C., and Shinskey, F. G. 1964. Feedforward analog computer control of a superfractionator. *Control Engineering* 11: 69-74.

Maier, N. R. F. 1964. Maximizing personal creativity through better problem solving. *Personnel Administration* 27: 14-18.

———. 1963. *Problem-solving groups and discussions.* McGraw-Hill.

———., and Hoffman, L. R. 1960. Quality of first and second solutions in group problem-solving. *Journal of Applied Psychology* 44: 278-82.

———., and Solem, A. R. 1962. Improving solutions by turning choice situations into problems. *Personnel Psychology* 15: 151-57.

March, J. G., and Simon, H. A. 1958. *Organizations.* Wiley.

McMahon, J. T., and Perritt, G. W. 1971. Control structure of organizations: An empirical examination. *Academy of Management Journal* 14: 327-40.

———., and ———. 1973. Toward a contingency theory of organizational control. *Academy of Management Journal* 16: 624-35.

Meadow, A., Parnes, S. J., and Reese, H. 1959. Influence of brainstorming instructions and problem sequence on a creative problem solving test. *Journal of Applied Psychology* 43: 413-16.

Miller, D. W., and Starr, M. K. 1960. *Executive decisions and operations research.* Prentice-Hall.

Mockler, R. J. 1972. *Business planning and policy formation.* Appleton-Century-Crofts.

Nisenfield, A. E., and Miyasaki. 1972. Applications of feedforward control to distillation columns. *Proceedings of the IFAC*, Paris, France, June 1972; Part 1, 1.1, p. 1-7.

Parnes, S. J. 1961. Effects of extended effort in creative problem-solving. *Journal of Educational Psychology* 52: 117-22.

Shinskey, F. G. 1968. Feedforward control of pH. *Instrumentation Technology* 15: 65-69.

Shure, G. H.; Rogers, M. S.; Larson, I.; and Tassone, J. 1962. Group planning and task effectiveness. *Sociometry* 25: 263-82.

Steiner, G. A. 1974. Comprehensive managerial planning. In *Contemporary management,* ed. by J. W. McGuire. Prentice-Hall.

Tannenbaum, A. S. 1968. *Control in organizations.* McGraw-Hill.

Taylor, F. W. 1919. *Scientific management.* Harper & Row.

Thune, S. S., and House, R. J. 1970. Where long-range planning pays off. *Business Horizons* 13: 81-87.

Tustin, A. 1955. Feedback. In *Automatic control.* Simon & Schuster.

Chapter **20**

Individual and Group Change

The British created a civil-service job in 1803 calling for a man to stand on the Cliffs of Dover with a spyglass. He was supposed to ring a bell if he saw Napoleon coming. The job was abolished in 1945.

ROBERT SOBEL

It has been stated by Toffler (1970) that "90 percent of all scientists who ever lived are now alive" (p. 27). If we could calculate an equivalent percentage that would apply to social scientists, we would probably find that an even higher proportion of all psychologists, sociologists, political scientists, etc., who ever lived are alive today. Throughout the world many millions of people are working for the express purpose of creating change, of making the future different from the present.

Toffler also points out that not only are changes taking place at an unprecedented rate, but also that the lapse of time between discovery and application is decreasing.

> It was literally centuries between the time Paracelsus discovered that ether could be used as an anasthetic and the time it began to be used for that purpose. . . . The first English patent for a typewriter was issued in 1714. But a Century and a half elapsed before typewriters became commercially available. . . . Today such delays between idea and application are almost unthinkable (Toffler, p. 27).

If continuous change is so much a part of life today, clearly it seems pointless for people to fight the inevitable. Yet resistance to change has been a part of human experience as long as change itself. This has even been true with regard to changes which might, at first glance, appear to be quite noncontroversial. One example of such a change might be the invention and mass distribution of the bicycle, about which Aronson (1968) wrote: "This is not to say that the adoption of the bicycle came spontaneously and without . . . opposition. . . . Often the horsemen and teamsters deliberately turned on the cyclists and ran them down. Fist fighting between wheelmen and draymen was frequent and fierce" (pp. 294–95).

This chapter will first consider some of the reasons why people, acting individually, as group members, and within organizations, tend to resist change. We will then consider models of change and examine various views concerning patterns of successful and unsuccessful changes. The next chapter will then review the research pertinent to some of the more important organizational development approaches in use today.

Resistance to Change [1]

Why Individuals Tend to Resist Change

While "sunk cost" is ordinarily thought of as relating to tangible assets, when considered in broader terms it can help to explain opposition to change in a great many instances. People's time, energy, and experience may all be considered to be investments, and any loss or reduction in their value may be felt as keenly as if actual money or property were involved. Considered from this standpoint the introduction of a new invention or a new procedure may threaten individuals' investments in their own experiences, and may perhaps even jeopardize their careers.

Remember that when we say that a job "requires experience," what we really mean is that it demands that its occupant has done some work of a similar nature in the past. After all, anyone who has been alive for twenty years has, by definition, twenty years' "experience." Important differences exist, however, in the *variety* of experiences possessed by various people and the *relevance* of past experience to future activities. When we reject a welder who has applied for an engineering position on grounds that the welder "lacks experience," we are really voicing our opinion that working as a welder has probably not provided the aptitudes, skills, and knowledge required of an engineer. The value of any person's "experience" therefore depends largely upon the degree of similarity between present and past duties and those which it will be necessary to perform in the future. Yet we have already mentioned that the end product of change is a future *different* from the present and the past.

Perhaps an example may be useful in further clarifying this important point. Suppose that you play golf, and Jack Nicklaus plays golf, and (speaking hypothetically, of course) he plays golf better than you do. Suppose further that the rules are changed drastically, banning the use of tees, permitting only one-handed swings, and so on. Both of you might oppose such a change, but who do you think would be more likely to go berserk altogether, denying all possible benefits of the new system, and possibly even seeking to undo the change through active resistance? Probably Nicklaus, and for reasons having nothing to do with obstinacy or close-mindedness. It is just that, having invested an extraordinary amount of time and effort into mastering the game *as it is presently played,* he is unlikely

---

1 The outline and some of the material for this section stems from Kerr and Kerr (1972).

to be very receptive to suggestions for playing it differently. Change might seem to him to impair his most important asset—his reservoir of skills—and could neutralize the competitive advantage he currently holds.

This situation is not very different from the one a carpenter faces when a new manufacturing process is introduced, or which confronts a bank auditor when control procedures are rendered obsolete by method changes. By keeping in mind the notion of sunk cost we may better be able to understand the phenomenon of resistance to change, and may also be able to shed some light on why it is that older people often seem more resistant to change than younger ones. Are "people over thirty" so rigid, so narrow, so set in their ways? Or is it that younger people can afford to be more responsive to change because, having invested relatively little time and effort in learning the old ways, they have no vested interest in the old system and therefore suffer no great loss in adapting to the new?

Another important reason for resistance to change occurs when information about the change is inadequate. In the absence of complete information, most of us tend to feel ambiguous and uncertain, feelings which are usually unpleasant. Many people will resist any change which threatens to disturb their state of equilibrium. It should also be remembered that, analogous to the old saying that "nature abhors a vacuum," the absence of explicit information about a change will seldom be accompanied by an absence of curiosity; rather, gossip and half-truths may emerge in the form of rumors, and these may well be far less flattering to the perpetrator of the change than the truth would be.

Too often, inadequate information is provided about the reasons for a change, or about the mechanics of change. Even when full explanations are supplied an important source of uncertainty—concerning the consequences of the change—will almost always remain. If everything went according to plan, then there would be no difference between reasons and consequences; in practice, however, *unanticipated consequences* inevitably emerge.

Personality factors also play a part in determining the extent to which people will tend to resist change.

> . . . There are certain types of individuals who are particularly likely to resist change, quite apart from other considerations. These are people who rely heavily on their own personal experience in making decisions, who assume that prior conditions will continue to prevail, who take the position that there is always one best way of doing things (Pym, 1966), and who have little general propensity to take risks (Nedd, 1971). They tend to be more anxious and worried about their work. In addition, they tend to be less well educated and less intelligent; and females are represented with a disproportionately high frequency (Trumbo, 1961). . . . Resistance may stem from a threat to basic assumptions, personal values, sources of security, and to friendship relationships (Miner, 1973, p. 267).

Why Groups Tend to Resist Change

Since groups are comprised of individual human beings, it is logical that the reasons discussed above for resistance to change would apply to them. However, we have suggested several times in this text that people in groups often act differently than any of them would have acted separately. Where group action is concerned it is often true that "the whole is greater than the sum of its parts."

To fully appreciate this fact it is necessary to reconsider the concept of *norms,* which we earlier implied tell people what they can do, what they must do, and what they cannot do. Such social rules are established by all groups and societies, and serve to communicate behaviors expected of members. While nonconformity to norms is often not formally punishable, the group is usually able to effectively punish violators and to reward conformers. Cooperation, prestige, and friendship frequently serve as rewards, while withholding of these things may act as punishments.

The reason that norms sometimes act as a source of both individual and group resistance to change is that, as blueprints for behavior, they often substitute for thinking. By presenting solutions to basic social problems they help us to outline our actions, but they can also impede our ability to reason when new problems and situations arise.

> By hanging out a "do not disturb" sign over established rules, customs, and procedures, the group may influence an individual to oppose changes he would rationally support. To the group members, the organization's penalty for resisting the change may seem far less severe than the group's probable penalty for opposing its norms (Kerr and Kerr, 1972, p. 6).

Occasionally, in extreme situations, resistance to any management-instigated change may itself become a group norm. In most cases, however, norms are not static, but rather change in response to a variety of pressures. Changes imposed upon the work group by management, or by outside staff people, nevertheless are likely to meet with resistance, due to the likelihood that such people are inadequately familiar with the norms operating within the group.

> Management actions leading to what we commonly label "change" are usually initiated outside the small work group by staff people. These are the changes that we notice and the ones that most frequently bring on symptoms of resistance. By the very nature of their work, most of our staff specialists in industry do not have the intimate contact with operating groups that allows them to acquire an intuitive understanding of the complex social arrangements which their ideas may affect. . . . As a result, all too often the men behave in a way that threatens and disrupts the established social relationships (Lawrence, 1954, p. 53).

A striking example of the potential effects of group norms upon performance of individuals within the group is presented by Coch and French (1948), and illustrated in Table 20-1. Coch and French explain that the

TABLE 20-1. One Employee's Production Record.

Days	*Phase*	*Efficiency Rating*
1-3	working within the group	46
4-6		52
7-9		53
10-12		56
13-16	scapegoating begins	55
17-20		48
21-24	after becoming a single worker	83
25-28		92
29-32		92
33-36		91
37-40		92

Source: Coch and French, "Overcoming Resistance to Change," 1948.

data are of an employee who worked as a presser, during the 40 days following a job change. Their description, which follows, helps explain the table:

> For the first 20 days she was working in a group of other pressers who were producing at the rate of about 50 units per hour. Starting on the 13th day, when she reached standard production and exceeded the production of the other members, she became a scapegoat of the group. During this time her production decreased toward the level of the remaining members of the group. After 20 days the group had to be broken up and all the other members were transferred to other jobs, leaving only the scapegoat operator. With the removal of the group, the group standard was no longer operative, and the production of the one remaining operator shot up from the level of about 45 to 96 units per hour in a period of four days. Her production stabilized at a level of about 92 and stayed there for the remainder of the 20 days.

This clearly appears to be a case where the norms of the group included a work rate far less than what the members were capable of had there been no norm governing production rates.

The existence of rivalries and conflicts among work groups will also tend to be a facilitator of resistance to change, since each "side" will naturally oppose innovation introduced by the other. Furthermore, third-party changes will also be viewed with suspicion, since the smallest change may cause a shift in the "balance of power." Even an innocuous change, say, in accounting procedures, may be actively opposed because of the chance that it may cause one "side" to be accountable to the other, or because the data may be usable "against" someone.

As was true in the discussion on why individuals tend to resist change, personality factors play an important part in resistance among group members. Miner (1973, p. 268) concludes from his review of the literature that "where group members feel a strong sense of belonging, evince a desire to remain in the group, and perceive their group as superior to others, resistance to change is likely to be considerable. . . . This is particularly true if the manager in charge of the group is himself predisposed to resist change and tends to be somewhat dogmatic." Management predispositions toward or against change are themselves a function of various personality and situational characteristics; one recent study (Kirton and Mulligan, 1973, p. 101) found that "older managers were more conservative than the younger managers, and the confident more radical than the unconfident. Stable introverts and emotional extraverts tended to support innovation, while emotional introverts and stable extraverts did not."

Before moving on to an examination of various change models and patterns it might be worthwhile to take note of Lawrence's reminder that:

> When resistance *does* appear, it should not be thought of as something to *overcome*. Instead, it can best be thought of as a useful red flag—a signal that something is going wrong. To use a rough analogy, signs of resistance in a social organization are useful in the same way that pain is useful to the body as a signal that some bodily functions are getting out of adjustment.
>
> The resistance, like the pain, does not tell us what is wrong but only that something *is* wrong. And it makes no more sense to try to overcome such resistance than it does to take a pain killer without diagnosing the bodily ailment (1954, p. 56).

Change as a Three-Step Procedure

Lewin's Original Model

An interesting perspective on resistance to change was advanced by Lewin (1947, p. 34):

> A change toward a higher level of group performance is frequently short-lived; after a "shot in the arm," group life soon returns to the previous level. This indicates that it does not suffice to define the objective of planned change in group performance as the reaching of a different level. Permanency of the new level, or permanency for a desired period, should be included in the objective. A successful

> change includes, therefore, three aspects: *unfreezing* (if necessary) the present level, *moving* to the new level, and *freezing* group life on the new level.

This point of view is interesting first because it suggests, and subsequent research for the most part substantiates, that many if not most individual and organizational change efforts generate changes which are, at best, short-lived. Change efforts sometimes produce a Hawthorne effect, whereby employees who are specially treated and who believe that the change agent respects them and is trying to help them, initiate morale and performance improvements which are more the result of their feelings toward the change agent than of the wisdom and appropriateness of the actual changes. Hawthorne effects may at first closely resemble changes due to improvement in methods, procedures, etc., and may be largely responsible for the continued employment of many mediocre consultants, who have the good sense to "move on to another opportunity" before the effect wears off. The Hawthorne effect is usually temporary, however, and is therefore a poor substitute for intelligently planned and executed change.

Another reason why Lewin's remarks are important is that he calls attention to the fact that no change is likely to be successful unless the change attempt is first preceded by something (unfreezing), and then followed by something else (refreezing). Therefore, dragging unwilling or uninterested individuals into a room and subjecting them to a change program is not likely to result in very much change. This is particularly true when the trainer's goal is to change attitudes, but is also likely to be the case where change in knowledge is intended.

Schein's Adaptation

Schein (1973, p. 139) has elaborated upon Lewin's model, conceiving of unfreezing, changing, and refreezing as three phases in a process of influence:

> (1) *Unfreezing:* an alteration of the forces acting on the individual, such that his stable equilibrium is disturbed sufficiently to motivate him and to make him ready to change; this can be accomplished either by increasing the pressure to change or by reducing some of the threats or resistances to change.
>
> (2) *Changing:* the presentation of a direction of change and the actual process of learning new attitudes. . . .
>
> (3) *Refreezing:* the integration of the changed attitudes into the rest of the personality and/or into ongoing significant emotional relationships.

Schein has provided a number of illustrations of the importance of these three phases to the change effort; probably the most dramatic of these illustrations concerns the attempts made by the Chinese Communists to "brainwash" American prisoners of war during the Korean conflict.

According to Schein, a very important first step was to remove the "target person" (the individual to be changed) from any social situation or relationship which might work against the Communists by reinforcing and preserving the old (to be altered) attitudes. Isolation of the target person from all family, friends, and "co-workers" was therefore required, as was denying the person access to accustomed communications media. Unfreezing was also accomplished by pleas and demands to confess to war crimes; these were backed by threats of physical punishment. After one or more prisoners had "confessed," new target people were often placed in contact with them, thus creating social support for the new (to be learned) attitudes as well as isolation from the old ones. This combination of physical and social pressures succeeded in "unfreezing" a great many American prisoners, causing them to "confess" to (and, in many cases, believe in) war crimes. Record numbers of POWs actually "reformed," apparently coming to feel great guilt about their actions as American soldiers, and to adopt communist values.

In the long run, however, when faced with the choice of returning to the United States or remaining behind the Iron Curtain, only about two dozen American prisoners chose to stay. It can be argued, then, that the "refreezing" phase was not accomplished successfully; it is possible that the majority of those who came to adopt certain communist values *still* continued to believe in "apple pie, motherhood, and the American flag," and so ultimately the new attitudes obtained while in prison were never truly integrated into the remainder of most individuals' personalities. For those who stayed behind, of course, it is more likely that refreezing took place, although other factors may also have been responsible.

Lippitt, Watson, and Westley's Adaptation

While the three-step model for change may be adequate to describe the process in some cases, as illustrated above, Lippitt, Watson, and Westley (1972) argue that other conditions are often necessary. What they propose, then, is a five-phase description of the change process. These include:

1. Development of a need for change ("unfreezing").
2. Establishment of a change relationship.
3. Working toward change ("moving").
4. Generalization and stabilization of change ("freezing").
5. Achieving a terminal relationship (p. 71).

While three of the five phases are clearly the same as those described by Lewin and Schein, they are described somewhat differently. Unfreezing, for example, depends upon a desire by the individual to change, and to seek the help of others for the purpose of changing. Confidence in the skills and knowledge of the change agent, and in the likelihood of success of the change effort, are also required.

Lippitt, Watson, and Westley subdivide the "moving" or change phase into three parts. The first of these comprises the diagnosis and clarification of the problem of the individual or system to be changed.

> . . . During this phase the client system is usually coping with a changing and broadening interpretation of the question at hand. As data are collected and analyzed, the problem, which seemed simple at first is likely to take on the appearance of an intricate, many-faceted difficulty. This is the point at which vested interests—either particular pressure blocs within social units or particular segments of the individual personality—are likely to become aware of the threat which is posed by change, and their defensive reactions may smash the whole mechanism of collaboration between the system and the change agent (p. 76).

The second of the three parts of the change phase involves the examination of alternative means and ends, and the establishment of plans of intended action. The third part of this phase then entails the transformation of these action plans into an actual change effort.

The generalization and stabilization (refreezing) phase will largely determine "whether or not the change which has been accomplished will remain a stable and permanent characteristic of the system" (pp. 78–79). Then, assuming that refreezing has been successful, the question arises as to the timing and method of extrication of the change agent from the situation.

> Some change agents emphasize the problem of dependency as the major issue of the final phase. If the client system has come to depend heavily upon the change agent for support and guidance throughout the processes of diagnosis, change, and evaluation, then naturally the end of the relationship is likely to be a somewhat painful affair (p. 80).

Unfreezing, Change, and Refreezing in Management Development

Management development can be thought of as any attempt to improve managerial effectiveness through a planned and deliberate learning process. This definition would include the organizational development techniques discussed in the next chapter, as well as such diverse approaches as on-the-job training, coaching, counseling, appraisal, job rotation, selected reading, and the use of understudy positions. There are two common elements in all of these approaches—change and planned learning.

From the standpoint of the three-step model of change:

> The essential elements of unfreezing are the removal of supports for the old attitudes, the saturation of the environment with the new attitudes to be acquired, a minimizing of threat, and a maximizing of support for any change in the right direction. In terms of this model it becomes immediately apparent that training programs or other activities which are conducted in the organization at the place of work for a certain number of hours per day or week are far less likely to unfreeze and subsequently influence the participant than those programs which remove him for varying lengths of time from his regular work situation and normal social relationships.
>
> . . . there are a variety of training activities which are used in management development which approximate . . . the conditions necessary for effective unfreezing. These would include programs offered at special training centers. . . . university-sponsored courses in management, liberal arts, and/or the social sciences; and especially, workshops or laboratories in human relations. . . . The practice of rotating a manager from one kind of assignment to another over a period of years can have some of the same unfreezing effects and thus facilitate attitude change. . . . Another example of how unfreezing can be facilitated in the organizational context is the practice of temporarily reducing the formal rank and responsibilities of the manager by making him a trainee in a special program, or an apprentice on a special project, or an assistant to a high ranking member of the company (Schein, 1973, pp. 147–48).

It is once again worth mentioning that the importance of the refreezing phase cannot be overstated. Management development is basically a social-influence process of change. The change results from information received within a context of selected reinforcement unique to the managerial environment. This reinforcement influences the degree to which learning takes place, and therefore the degree to which learning can be translated into improvement in attitudes and job performance. Since job performance takes place in a social setting, social reinforcement (or influence from others) plays an important part in determining whether changes in job performance actually occur.

When subordinates are exposed to new concepts they are likely to adopt new personal goals and values, which may then come into conflict with those of their supervisors. If coupled with ego defensiveness on the part of the supervisor, this conflict can become exaggerated, even traumatic, when it is not anticipated or understood. Change authorized by individuals who are unaware that they must *live with* and *support* it is frequently followed by confusion, frustration, bitterness, and other dysfunctional consequences (see House, 1968, for an extensive discussion of this point).

Two well-known studies show that when new attitudes and behaviors learned in a management development program are not reinforced on the job, refreezing fails to occur and change proves only temporary. In the first of these Fleishman (1953) trained International Harvester Company foremen in leadership techniques and principles. At the conclusion of training the foremen rated significantly higher in their attitudes toward "Consideration-oriented" behavior (that is, toward exhibiting warmth, interest, and egalitarianism toward subordinates—see Chapter 11 for a more precise description), and rated significantly lower in their attitudes toward planning, scheduling, organizing, and other "Structure-oriented" behaviors. These changes were in accord with the goals of the training program.

Once back on the job, however, the foremen abandoned their "new" attitudes in favor of those existing prior to training or even, in some cases, in favor of low-Consideration high-Structure attitudes which were *more extreme* than those existing prior to training. In short, the on-the-job consequences of the program seemed to be in the opposite direction of what was intended. This was borne out by questionnaires administered to the foremen's subordinates, who described their perceptions of the "trained" foremen's Consideration behavior, and questionnaires completed by subordinates whose foremen received no training. Results showed that the Consideration scores of the untrained foremen were actually higher.

The key to the puzzle lay in the attitudes and behavior of those who supervised the foremen. Questionnaire scores revealed that, as a group, these supervisors were even more Structure-oriented than were the foremen prior to training. In a climate where planning, scheduling, and organizing behaviors were approved of and exhibited extensively, and where consideration toward subordinates was viewed with suspicion, it is hardly surprising that reinforcement was not provided and permanent change failed to occur. Interestingly, even in the face of a generally high-Structure low-Consideration climate, some trained foremen did continue to exhibit Consideration behaviors back on the job which were consistent with their training. Investigation revealed that these foremen reported to supervisors who were themselves high in Consideration.

The second study involved an attempt by Sykes (1962) to run a training program for first-level supervisors which emphasized human relations, participation, and open and honest displays of opinions and feelings. Attitudes were apparently changed among those who attended. However, later efforts by Sykes to change the attitudes and behaviors of higher management, who were seen by the supervisors as privately opposing the very changes they claimed to support in the training program, were largely inadequate. The net result was that soon after the training program was completed, first-level supervisors began to leave the company; in fact, within one year 20 percent of the 97 supervisors had actually gone, and another 25 percent were actively seeking other employment. This was in sharp contrast to the quit rate in previous years.

Although there are important differences between the two studies, they both serve to illustrate the importance of post-training reinforcement for refreezing to be accomplished, and also provide information about the adverse consequences likely to occur in the absence of such reinforcement.

Patterns of Change

Today a great variety of change techniques are in use; methods of grouping and categorizing these techniques are also numerous. One such method which is potentially useful is to distinguish between efforts which seek to alter individuals' personal characteristics and others which aim to change the conditions under which they operate. This distinction is often a difficult one, however.

> The confusion between individual and organizational change is due in part to the lack of precise terminology for distinguishing between behavior determined largely by structural roles within a system and behavior determined more directly by personality needs and values. The behavior of people in organizations is still the behavior of individuals, but it has a different set of determinants than behavior outside of organizational roles (Katz and Kahn, 1966, pp. 390–91).

Despite such difficulties, we shall attempt to employ this distinction as we consider some of the more important change techniques in the next chapter.

Another useful distinction which can be made among change alternatives relates to the extent to which authority is retained by the change agent or dispensed to those individuals who will be affected by the change. According to Greiner (1967), at one extreme along the "power distribution continuum" are those approaches which rely upon *unilateral* authority, whereby change is accomplished by means of "an emphasis on the authority of a man's hierarchical position in the company. Here, the definition and solution to the problem at hand tend to be specified by the upper echelons and directed downward through formal and impersonal control mechanisms" (p. 120).

Greiner states that three forms of this approach to change are commonly employed by organizations. Most often used is the *decree* approach, which amounts to nothing more than an announcement by a highly placed individual which is directed toward lower-level members. The specific form of the announcement may vary, but is usually in the nature of a memorandum, lecture, policy statement, or verbal command.

Another unilateral approach is that of *replacement*. This tends to be more personal than are decrees, since it is normally aimed at a few individuals in particular; however, it shares with the decree approach a concern for task accomplishment. The third unilateral approach is to change the *structure*, for example, to better fit the job to the worker, or to alter formal authority to bring it more into accord with informal authority.

According to Greiner, somewhere in the middle of the power distribution continuum we find the *shared* approaches, "where authority is still present and used, yet there is also interaction and sharing of power" (p. 121). Two forms of this approach can be identified. With *group decision making,* problems still tend to be defined unilaterally by high-level individuals, but groups lower down are at least free to develop and select among alternative solutions. With *group problem solving,* lower-level groups can participate in the definition as well as the solution of the problem.

Furthest away from the unilateral approaches to change are those which involve *delegated authority,* whereby low-level members possess nearly complete responsibility for defining and solving problems. The two forms identified by Greiner are *case discussion,* whereby the persons in authority use their power only to guide the general discussion pertaining to a problem, encouraging group members to develop their own insights and solve their own problems, and the *T-group,* which downplays discussion and solution of task-related problems in favor of discussion aimed at increasing self-awareness and sensitivity by the members. T-groups will be examined in fuller detail in the next chapter.

Successful and Unsuccessful Patterns

The tremendous number and variety of change efforts in use today makes identification of commonalities difficult; however, a number of authors have attempted to distinguish between successful and unsuccessful methods and patterns of establishing and maintaining change. A number of "pointers" stem from the literature on learning, reviewed in Chapter 5. For example, Jablonsky and DeVries (1972, p. 356) state that "if organizations are to influence systematically the direction of their members' behaviors" they should avoid the use of punishment as a primary means of obtaining desired behavior, apply positive reinforcement frequently for desired behavior, and minimize the time span between individuals' desired behavior and the dispensing of reinforcement. Most of these points agree with those made by Bass and Vaughan (1966), who also emphasize the importance in any training effort of providing trainees with knowledge of results of their efforts to learn and apply the new material.

Another requirement by Jablonsky and DeVries, that desired behaviors be specified in "explicitly operational terms," is consistent with an important model for change presented by Dalton (1973), shown in Table 20–2. By examining the results of his own and a number of other studies, Dalton was able to identify four major subprocesses which tended to be associated with change efforts which had been successful. The first of these Dalton describes as a movement from generalized goals toward specific, concrete objectives; he claims that "one of the clearest signals that a new pattern of behavior will not be established and maintained is the objectives' remaining general and non-specific" (p. 164), and that "movement toward increasingly specific goals, while seeming the most obvious, is, from my observation, probably the dimension on which most change efforts flounder. General

TABLE 20-2. A Model of Induced Change.

	Phase 1	Phase 2	Phase 3	Phase 4
Overall pattern of successful change effort	*tension experienced within the system (unfreezing)*	*intervention of a prestigious influencing agent*	*individuals attempt to implement the proposed changes*	*new behavior and attitudes reinforced by achievement, social ties and internalized values—accompanied by decreasing dependence on influencing agent (refreezing)*
Subprocess 1	⟶	generalized objectives established ⟶	growing specificity of objectives—establishment of sub-goals ⟶	achievement and resetting of specific objectives
Subprocess 2	tension within existing social ties ⟶ ⟶	prior social ties interrupted or attenuated ⟶	formation of new alliances and relationships centering around new activities ⟶	new social ties reinforced—altered behavior and attitudes
Subprocess 3	lowered sense of self-esteem ⟶ ⟶	esteem-building begun on basis of agent's attention and assurance ⟶	esteem-building based on task accomplishment ⟶	heightened sense of self-esteem
Subprocess 4	⟶ ⟶	external motive for change (new schema provided) ⟶	improvisation and reality-testing ⟶	internalized motive for change

Source: Dalton, "Influence and Organizational Change," 1973.

goals, often widely and genuinely shared, too frequently die for the lack of the crucial idea as to how the first few concrete steps can be taken" (p. 180).

The second major subprocess which typifies successful change efforts concerns the movement from the old social relationships, built around behavioral patterns previously in evidence, to new ties which support the desired changes.

> Old behavior and attitudes are often deeply imbedded in the relationships which have been built up over the years, and as long as the individuals involved maintain these relationships unaltered, changes are unlikely to occur. By the same token, new behavior patterns are most readily and firmly established when they are conditions of regular membership in a new group, for group members exercise the most powerful tool for shaping behavior, selective reinforcement of responses with immediate rewards. . . . Breaking up or loosening former social ties may act to unfreeze an individual or group, but this alone provides no assurance that any resulting changes will be in a given direction or that they will have any permanency. Establishing new relationships which reward the desired behaviors and confirm the modified attitudes also seem to be essential. Otherwise, there will be an active seeking to return to former attitudes and to the relationships which supported and reinforced them (Dalton, pp. 166–67).

Moving from an initial state of self-doubt to a heightened sense of self-esteem is the third major subprocess described by Dalton. As this transition is made, individuals may experience a sense of accomplishment and a relief from the tension which normally accompanies the unfreezing phase, about which more will be said shortly. The fourth subprocess involves a movement from an external motive for change to one which has been internalized by the individual. Again, for reasons to be discussed presently, Dalton believes that the initial impetus for change will stem from someone other than the individual to be changed. However, for the new behaviors to become permanent, "the individuals involved must internalize or come to 'own' the rationale for the change" (p. 175). This is most likely to occur as the individual begins to see the usefulness of these behaviors to solve a problem, or to reduce stress.

From Table 20–2 it can be seen that Dalton sees a necessity for a state of tension or pressure as a precursor to successful change, and also that the intervention of a "prestigious influencing agent" is required. Both of these requirements are also included in a six-phase process of successful change proposed by Greiner (1967). The first of these phases Greiner labels Pressure and Arousal, which may come from either of two general sources: (1) serious environmental factors, such as lower sales or competitor breakthroughs; and (2) serious internal events, such as a strike or a blowup between departments. Most dramatic, of course, is when both sources transmit pressure simultaneously. Greiner concludes from his review of a number of change efforts that relatively unsuccessful changes tended to be characterized by the absence of severe pressures.

The second phase, Intervention and Reorientation, depends upon the intervention of an outsider. Consistent with Dalton's specification that the outsider be prestigious, Greiner says that what is important here "seems to be the combination of the fact that the newcomer enters at the top of the organization and the fact that he is respected for his skills at improving organization practices" (p. 127). Dalton (1973) points out, in fact, that confidence in the power and judgment of the influencing agent can often go a long way to ensure the success of the change, by acting as a "self-fulfilling prophecy." He illustrates the importance of this factor by describing some of Frank's work (1963):

> . . . Even healers regarded by the community as charlatans or quacks were able, in some instances, to bring about change and symptom relief among persons who regarded them as sources of authority and power. Their success appeared to rest on their ability to evoke the patient's expectancy of help. In medical treatment, the fact that relief and healing can be brought about solely by the patient's expectation of help from the physician, is demonstrated by experiments verifying the so-called "placebo effect." In these studies, the doctor administers a pharmacologically inert substance to the patient rather than an active medication. . . . There is evidence that placebos can have marked physiological effects. Studies have shown that their use has been accompanied by healing of tissue damage ranging from warts to peptic ulcers. A similar effect is the "hello-goodbye" effect in psychotherapy. Patients who merely had contact with a prestigeful (in their eyes) psychiatrist improved significantly over the individuals in a control group who were placed on a waiting list and did not see a psychiatrist. In fact, these minimal contact patients showed almost as much improvement of certain kinds as a third group who underwent prolonged treatment (Dalton, pp. 162–63).

A more recent experiment, and one which directly relates to the consequences of individual expectations that an organizational change effort will be successful, is reported by King (1974). In this experiment managers were given false information relating to previous results from job rotation and job enlargement programs. King found that after being led to believe that higher productivity would result from these changes, the managers' plant output increased during the experimental period. Furthermore, his analysis revealed that expectations of success were more important as a source of variation than were the particular innovations themselves.

Greiner labels the third phase of successful change Diagnosis and Recognition, during which information is assembled and the problem identified. Greiner reports that in successful change programs *shared* approaches were employed during this phase, while in less successful efforts this phase featured approaches which were closer to either end of the power distribution continuum (either unilateral or delegated).

During the fourth phase, Invention and Commitment, successful changes tend to feature widespread and intensive searches for new solutions. The Experimentation and Search phase follows next during which, prior to introduction of large-scale and permanent changes, many small decisions are implemented on an experimental basis for the purpose of "reality testing." The final phase of Reinforcement and Acceptance hopefully involves the obtaining of positive results by the organization, which serve to reinforce individuals for their adoption of the new behaviors, thus solidifying the change.

Several additional requirements for successful change are offered by Margulies and Wallace (1973). The first of these is that change is much more likely to succeed when initiated and supported by key management people within the organization. Second is the conclusion that change is best accomplished by bringing those who will be affected into the process at an early stage. With their reminder that "nobody appreciates the *fait accompli* except the person who manages to pull it off" (p. 156), Margulies and Wallace show a skepticism for unilateral approaches to change similar to Greiner, already discussed, and to Bass and Vaughan (1966).

A third requirement is that, whichever change technique is employed, repeated applications will normally be necessary for new behavior patterns to be learned. An isolated intervention, however massive and dramatic, is unlikely to succeed.

Margulies and Wallace also add that, however necessary the initial intervention by someone outside the organization, the ultimate responsibility for maintenance of change must fall to informed and motivated individuals within the organization. Furthermore, these internal people must be trained, developed, and given legitimacy if they are to be able to carry out this responsibility.

The Leavitt Model

In one sense this model is an elaboration of the categorization schema discussed earlier, whereby efforts aimed at changing the individual are differentiated from those aimed at changing one or more conditions relating to performance of the task. The model is, however, characterized by nearly total interdependence among variables; Leavitt points out that "change in any one will most probably result in compensatory (or retaliatory) change in others" (1973, p. 32) and that "sometimes we may aim to change one of these as an end in itself, sometimes as a mechanism for effecting some changes in one or more of the others" (p. 32).

There are four variables in the model. *Task* refers to the organization's principal reasons for existence and the subtasks which exist in service of these principal tasks. *Actors* refer primarily to the human beings within the system. *Technology* refers to the technical tools—whether drill presses, computers, or work programs. Finally, *Structure* includes the organization's systems of communications, authority, and work flow.

The pertinence of Leavitt's model to our topic is that, by considering each of the variables as a possible "entry point" for an effort to create change, it is possible to categorize a number of different change efforts. This is what Leavitt (1973) has done. For example, the "administrative organization" approach to organizational change (described in Chapter 1), with its emphasis upon improving performance by clarifying relationships and defining jobs, can be classified as a structural approach. Here the concern is often with "modifying spans of control, defining nonoverlapping areas of responsibility and authority, and logically defining necessary functions" (p. 33). Decentralization efforts are also classified as structural.

One of the most important technology approaches to change has been the effort by Taylor and others to employ "scientific management" (also described in Chapter 1). Its emphasis on work measurement and job analysis, and its creation of the technical skill of industrial engineering, have been discussed by Leavitt as clearly involving changes in technology; so have the more recent applications of operations research.

In contrast with most early efforts toward organizational change, recent attempts to create change have often been primarily concerned with the variable that Leavitt calls "actors." He writes that:

> The people approaches try to change the organizational world by changing the behavior of actors in the organization. By changing people, it is argued, one can cause the creative invention of new tools, or one can cause modifications in structure (especially power structure). By one or another of these means, changing people will cause changes in solutions to tasks and performance of tasks as well as changes in human growth and fulfillment (p. 38).

The work of Lewin (1947), Coch and French (1948), the Hawthorne experimenters (see Chapter 1), McGregor (1960), and others is cited as illustrative of attempts to change this variable, as are the advocates of T-groups and such popular practitioners as Dale Carnegie.

Conclusions

While useful as a classification device, the Leavitt model must not create the impression that its variables can, in any but the most academic sense, be considered separately. Leavitt himself, and Margulies and Wallace, underscore the importance of this reminder:

> On occasion we have tried to manipulate only one of these variables, and discovered that all the others moved in unforeseen and often costly

> directions. . . . The Scientific Management movement, for example, enamored of its measurement techniques, worked out efficient task solutions only to have many of them backfire because the same methods were also evoking human resistance and hostility. The human relations movement, I submit, is only now bumping into some of the unforeseen costs of building a theory of organization exclusively of human bricks. . . . Approaches with strong structural foci have also on occasion fallen into the one-track trap, changing structure to facilitate task solution only then to find that humans do not fit the cubbyholes or technology does not adapt to the new structure (Leavitt, 1973, pp. 43–44).

> Academics may debate the relative worth of "structure versus people," "technology versus structure," "technology versus people," "people versus structure," etc., as the basic material to be changed, but such polarization can only be called unfortunate. It fails to grasp the reality of the *system* properties of complex organizations. . . . Changes in organizations can begin anywhere—in structure, in technology, or in people. In the final analysis, however, change in the *behavior of the individuals who cause the organization to function* must occur (Margulies and Wallace, 1973, p. 155).

In this chapter we have considered some basic features of change and resistance to change, and have reviewed several authors' models and descriptions of successful and unsuccessful patterns of change. In the next chapter we shall examine the characteristics of planned organizational change, and critically review four major approaches to organizational development.

References

Aronson, S. H. 1968. The sociology of the bicycle. In *Sociology and everyday life,* ed. by M. Truzzi. Prentice-Hall.

Bass, B. M., and Vaughan, J. A. 1966. *Training in industry: The management of learning.* Wadsworth.

Coch, L., and French, J. R. P. 1948. Overcoming resistance to change. *Human Relations* 1: 512-32.

Dalton, G. W. 1973. Influence and organizational change. In *Changing organizational behavior,* ed. by A. C. Bartlett and T. A. Kayser. Prentice-Hall.

Fleishman, E. A. 1953. Leadership climate, human relations training, and supervisory behavior. *Personnel Psychology* 6: 205-22.

Frank, J. 1963. *Persuasion and healing.* Schocken Books.

Greiner, L. E. 1967. Patterns of organization change. *Harvard Business Review* 45: 119-30.

House, R. J. 1968. Leadership training: Some dysfunctional consequences. *Administrative Science Quarterly* 12: 556-71.

Jablonsky, S. F., and DeVries, D. L. 1972. Operant conditioning principles extrapolated to the theory of management. *Organizational Behavior and Human Performance* 7: 340-58.

Katz, D., and Kahn, R. 1966. *The social psychology of organizations.* Wiley.

Kerr, S., and Kerr, E. B. 1972. Why your employees resist perfectly 'rational' changes. *Hospital Financial Management* 26: 4-6.

King, A. S. 1974. Expectation effects in organizational change. *Administrative Science Quarterly* 19: 221-30.

Kirton, M. J., and Mulligan, G. 1973. Correlates of managers' attitudes toward change. *Journal of Applied Psychology* 58: 101-107.

Lawrence, P. R. 1954. How to deal with resistance to change. *Harvard Business Review* 32: 49-57.

Leavitt, H. J. 1973. Applied organization change in industry: Structural, technical, and human approaches. In *Changing organizational behavior,* ed. by A. C. Bartlett and T. A. Kayser. Prentice-Hall.

Lewin, K. 1947. Frontiers in group dynamics. *Human Relations* 1: 5-41.

Lippitt, R., Watson, J., and Westley, B. 1972. The phases of planned change. In *Organizational development: Values, process, and technology,* ed. by N. Margulies and A. P. Raia. McGraw-Hill.

Margulies, N., and Wallace, J. 1973. *Organizational change: Techniques and applications.* Scott, Foresman.

McGregor, D. 1960. *The human side of enterprise.* McGraw-Hill.

Miner, J. B. 1973. *The management process: Theory, research, and practice.* Macmillan.

Nedd, A. N. B. 1971. The simultaneous effect of several variables on attitudes toward change. *Administrative Science Quarterly* 16: 258-69.

Pym, D. 1966. Effective managerial performance in organizational change. *Journal of Management Studies* 3.

Schein, E. H. 1973. Management development as a process of influence. In *Changing organizational behavior,* ed. by A. C. Bartlett and T. A. Kayser. Prentice-Hall.

Sobel, R. Cited in R. Townsend. 1970. *Up the organization* (p. 75). Fawcett.

Sykes, A. J. M. 1962. The effects of a supervisory training course in changing supervisors' perceptions and expectations of the role of management. *Human Relations* 15: 227-43.

Toffler, A. 1970. *Future shock.* Bantam.

Trumbo, D. A. 1961. Individual and group correlates of attitudes toward work-related change. *Journal of Applied Psychology* 45: 338-44.

Chapter **21**

Organizational Development

There is nothing more difficult to carry out, nor more doubtful of success, nor more dangerous to handle, than to initiate a new order of things. For the reformer has enemies in all those who profit by the old order, and only lukewarm defenders in all those who would profit by the new order, this lukewarmness arising partly from fear of their adversaries, who have the laws in their favour, and partly from the incredulity of mankind, who do not truly believe in anything new until they have actual experience of it.

MACHIAVELLI
The Prince

Change is often the result of uncontrollable and unpredictable forces which act upon a group or individual. However, sometimes change results from a conscious and deliberate effort by powerful people within organizations to make the future systematically different from the present. This chapter will be concerned with such changes as they affect either the total organization or major subunits of the organization.

Organizational development is a very hard term to define; a great number of formal definitions have been proposed, and many authors have simply referred to organizational development without suggesting a definition at all. In general, it can be said that organizational development (OD) relates to a large and diverse body of concepts, tools, and techniques for improving an organization's effectiveness (Margulies and Raia, 1972, p. 2). Argyris (1971, p. ix) adds, "at the heart of organizational development is the concern for the vitalizing, energizing, activating, and renewing of organizations through technical and human resources." He points out that technical development is achieved through programs of marketing, finance, engineering, and manufacturing. On the other hand, "human-resource development concerns people, interpersonal relationships, small groups, intergroups, and organizational norms and values" (p. ix). This chapter will be concerned with the type of OD which focuses upon human-resource development.

Characteristics of Organizational Development

While by no means an exhaustive list, the following elements of OD have been included in definitions by many authors and are important for an understanding of the process.

Planned Change. As compared to the general process of change, which was considered in the last chapter to include anything which made the future different from the past and the present, intentional or not, the planned, systematic nature of organizational development has been described by many authors (Burke and Schmidt, 1971; Sherwood, 1971; Gibson, Ivancevich, and Donnelly, 1973). This feature distinguishes OD efforts from other kinds of changes.

Comprehensive Change. Burke and Schmidt (1971), Sherwood (1971) and others have pointed out that OD efforts typically involve a "total system," either the entire organization or an identifiable unit within the organization.

Emphasis upon Work Groups. While a few change efforts which meet most of the definitional characteristics of organizational development programs are individually oriented (for example, some management development programs), most place special emphasis upon the formal work team (French and Bell, 1972). The rationale underlying this approach is that "the basic building blocks of organizations are groups of people; therefore, the basic units of change are also groups, not simply individuals" (Sherwood, 1971, p. 3).

Long-Range Change. Nearly all theorists agree that OD efforts require sustained, continuous efforts over a period of many months or years. Although often there is "considerable pressure on OD practitioners to produce results in a hurry," for the most part "the OD technology does not respond effectively to short-term crises" (Burke, 1972, p. 174).

Participation of a Change Agent. Consistent with the earlier-cited (Chapter 20) views of Greiner (1967) and Dalton (1973) concerning the necessity for such a person, French and Bell (1972, p. 147) state:

> The notion of the use of a "change agent" or "catalyst" as one of the distinguishing characteristics of OD has a purpose in our definition. We are somewhat pessimistic about the optimal effectiveness of OD efforts which are "do-it-yourself" programs. In the early phases, at least, the services of a third person who is not a part of the prevailing organization culture are essential. This does not mean that the third party cannot be a member of the organization but that he at least be external to the particular subsystem which is initiating an OD effort.

Emphasis upon Intervention and Action Research. Sherwood (1971, pp. 1, 5) points out that:

> The major strategy of OD is to intervene in the ongoing activities of the organization to facilitate learning and to make choices about alternative ways to proceed. . . . A major characteristic of organizational development is that it relies heavily on an educational strategy emphasizing *experience-based learning* and on the skills such a procedure develops.

The basic intervention model characterizing OD efforts is that of *action research,* which normally includes the following steps (French and Bell, 1972):

1) preliminary diagnosis
2) gathering data from those to be involved in the change
3) working from the data, providing feedback to the group affected
4) use of the data by the group
5) diagnosis of the problem, with the aid of the data
6) planning of necessary action
7) taking of necessary action.

Objectives of Organizational Development

Organizational Objectives

The following objectives have been mentioned by various authors as being closely associated with most organizational development programs.

Increasing Effectiveness. This broad and self-evident objective is included here only as a reminder that OD efforts ultimately "must be justified in terms of the organization's objectives" (Gibson, Ivancevich, and Donnelly, 1973, p. 341).

Improving Problem Solving. This objective has a "technical" component (for example, relocating problem-solving responsibilities closer to relevant resources), but is primarily concerned with programs aimed at conflict reduction and conflict resolution within and between organizational units. Sub-goals in this area could include building trust among groups, creating an open climate throughout the organization, and achieving greater collaboration among groups (Sherwood, 1971).

Increasing Adaptability. OD efforts are often concerned with increasing flexibility so that the organization "can adapt better to the accelerated rate of change in technology, in our industrial environment and society in general" (Winn, 1968, p. 367).

Substitution of Systematic Concepts for Outmoded Precedents. A common barrier to commitment, creativity, and involvement is the existence of outmoded traditions and precedents. Many OD efforts seek to replace these with systematic management concepts and up-to-date standards and values (Blake and Mouton, 1964).

Individual Objectives

The preceding objectives have in common a primary focus upon *organizational* outcomes; those that follow, while still ultimately aiming at organizational change, are particularly concerned with change in attitudes, beliefs, and behaviors of individuals.

Providing Opportunities to be "Human." Stated most broadly, this includes "providing opportunities for people to function as human beings rather than as resources in the productive process" (Margulies and Raia, 1972, p. 3). Subgoals within this area could include such things as allowing organization members to develop to their full potentials, treating them as people with complex sets of needs which are important to their work, and attempting to create an environment where they can find exciting and challenging work (Margulies and Raia, 1972, p. 3).

Increasing Awareness. Many OD efforts have as a major objective the development of self-awareness among participants, as well as awareness of the mechanics and consequences of various group processes.

Increasing Participation and Influence. There is widespread agreement that "providing opportunities for people in organizations to influence the way in which they relate to work, the organization, and the environment" (Margulies and Raia, 1972, p. 3) is a critically important component of many organization development programs, and that successful attainment of this objective can ease the path toward attainment of most of the others.

Integration of Individual and Organizational Objectives. This "composite" objective focuses upon both the organization and its members, and is viewed by many authors (Burke and Schmidt, 1971; Sherwood, 1971; Gibson, Ivancevich, and Donnelly, 1973; Argyris, 1964) as a particularly important concern of organization development.

Underlying Assumptions of Organizational Development

Sherwood (1971) has described a number of assumptions which underlie the concept of organization development. Among these are the following:

1. Work which is organized to meet individual needs as well as organizational requirements will tend to result in the highest productivity.

2. Most organizational members are motivated more by work which offers challenge and responsibility than by tight controls and threats of punishment.

3. Most organizational cultures tend to suppress the open expression of feelings by people about each other, and about where they and the organization are going. This suppression adversely affects personal growth and problem solving, and also impairs commitment to a decision or a task.

4. Groups which can work in an open way, providing constructive feedback to members, learn more from experience and can more fully apply their resources to the task at hand. Personal growth is also facilitated by open, supportive, and trusting relationships.

5. Change is most effectively introduced, and commitment most likely to be attained, when all groups and individuals involved come to have a sense of ownership in the process. This is most likely to follow from an opportunity for members to become actively involved in the planning and implementation of the change.

Propositions

Throughout this and the preceding chapter, the work of Greiner (1967), Margulies and Wallace (1973), Sherwood (1971), Margulies and Raia (1972), and others has placed heavy emphasis on the strategy of *involvement,* of bringing individuals who will be affected by a change into the process of change at an early stage and permitting and encouraging them to participate in and influence the program. One of the most timely and important questions related to organizational development therefore concerns the extent to which opportunities for individual involvement will affect resistance to change.

1. Providing opportunities for individuals to have influence over and participate in the change process will significantly lessen individual resistance to change.

While the first proposition deals with participation and influence prior to and during the change effort itself, another question arises concerning the effectiveness of efforts to provide continuing involvement after the initial change effort.

2. Organizational development efforts which include as an objective the continuing involvement of employees will produce significant increases in motivation, satisfaction, and performance.

Empirical Evidence

Proposition 1

Providing opportunities for individuals to have influence over and participate in the change process will significantly lessen individual resistance to change.

In reviewing the evidence we should probably start by pointing out that several studies reviewed earlier in this book, concerned with participative leadership (discussed in Chapters 11 and 12) and with participation in setting policy and establishing objectives (see Chapter 14), are also pertinent to this proposition. We can look, for example, to the study by Coch and French (1948), in which employee groups who were permitted to participate fully in the planning and implementation stages of the change effort subsequently performed significantly better than workers who were offered no chance to participate. Other workers, allowed limited participation through an election of representatives, performed better than the "no participation" group, but less well than the "full participation" groups. Coch and French concluded that involvement of employees was an important factor in reducing resistance to change.

An alternate explanation for the findings is offered by Lawrence (1954), who refers to Coch and French's statement that the firm was unusually progressive, with employees being encouraged to deal fairly and openly with management, and to come to management with grievances and problems. In such an atmosphere, Lawrence contends, the "new" full participation group condition may have seemed less new than the "customary" no participation one. If this is true, then the data may be better understood in terms of threatened changes in established working relationships, rather than in the participation differences per se.

Another study reviewed in Chapter 14 which is relevant to the proposition under discussion is that by Lewin (1958), in which Red Cross study groups who heard lectures *and* participated in group discussions changed considerably more than groups where no post-lecture group discussion followed. Similar results were obtained by several researchers, including Radke and Klisurich (1947), Pelz (1958), and Tomekovic (1962). Pelz's study was designed, however, to provide information about the relative contributions of several variables to the overall pattern of results; it concluded (as Chapter 14 indicated) that group discussion and public commitment to the decision were unimportant as determinants of change. Most important were that the group arrived at a decision, and that consensus was obtained and perceived by group members. These last two variables were able to produce differences as great as those observed by Lewin.

Other studies reviewed in Chapter 14 (for example, those on MBO by Raia, 1974, and Meyer, Kay, and French 1965) provide support for Proposition 1, while others provide little (Ivancevich, 1972) or mixed (Carroll and Tosi, 1973) support for the proposition. A study by French, Israel, and As (1960), attempting to replicate Coch and French's results in a Norwegian factory, showed that participation by workers who neither seek nor expect to participate will not have much of an effect upon resistance to change.

The effort to "brainwash" American prisoners of war during the Korean conflict, described briefly in the previous chapter, provides another view of the importance of participation and involvement to successful change. Schein (1958, p. 325) writes, for example, that "it was never enough for the prisoner to listen and absorb; some kind of verbal or written response was always demanded. Thus, if a man would not give original material in question-and-answer sessions, he was asked to copy something. Likewise, group discussions, autobiographical statements, self-criticisms, and public confessions all demanded an active participation by the prisoner."

Some interesting work involving role-playing (Janis and King, 1954; King and Janis, 1956) provides further support that change is abetted and resistance decreased through active participation. Both studies found that individuals who played a role in which they actively advocated various positions and attitudes were more influenced in favor of these attitudes than individuals who were exposed to the identical materials in a more passive way. In their 1956 study, reading a statement aloud generated more change than studying it silently, and play-acting a part which approved the statement caused even more change; in short, the greater the involvement, the more the change. The authors (1954) also attempted to isolate the factors which might be responsible for the results obtained. As a result of their analysis they tentatively concluded that two factors might be at work:

> The first factor suggests that the gain from role playing may occur primarily because the active participant tends to be impressed by his own cogent arguments, clarifying illustrations, and convincing appeals which he is stimulated to think up in order to do a good job of "selling" the idea to others. The second factor suggests an alternative explanation in terms of the rewarding effects of the individual's sense of achievement or feelings of satisfaction with his performance in the role of active participant (p. 218).

More recent support for the proposition comes from two studies which examined the effects of participation upon the installation of pay incentive plans to reward attendance. In the first of these Lawler and Hackman (1969) found that significant increases in attendance followed installation in three groups who had actively participated in the development of the plan. No such increase resulted from the plan in groups where it had been installed without worker participation. In the follow-up study (Scheflen, Lawler, and Hackman, 1971) data were collected after company management had discontinued the plan in two of the three participative groups. By this time the plans had been in effect for six months in one plant, and for eleven months in the other.

In the weeks just before discontinuation of the pay incentive plan, average attendance in the two groups was 92 percent. Since the original (1969) study showed a 94 percent average within the participative groups, this indicates that the effects observed at that time did not wear off in the ensuing months. In the weeks following discontinuation, however, attendance dropped to 82 percent, a reduction which is not only statistically significant, but which brought attendance levels below what they had been prior to the initiation of the original experiment.

While these studies certainly show support for Proposition 1, it should be noted that, by the time of the follow-up study, only 40 percent of the employees who had originally participated in the establishment of the pay incentive plan were still with the company. Therefore, while participation may have initially contributed to acceptance of the plan, other factors were clearly at work at making it acceptable to the many new employees who joined the organization after it was already installed.

Not all recent studies have found unequivocal support for the proposition, however. Powell and Schlacter (1971) found that involvement of workers in the establishment of work schedules resulted in higher morale, but productivity showed insignificant change, and absence actually increased. Veen (1972) found that performance and two responses concerning satisfaction changed significantly after respondents were permitted to participate in the establishment of training content; however, items related to other aspects of satisfaction, and to sympathy and identification toward the trainer, showed no such change. Ivancevich (1974a) found that a structured, directive trainer style was more effective in attaining cohesiveness, communication, and productivity, and that groups subjected to such a style had less participant conflict and more favorable attitudes toward the trainer than groups where the trainer lectured minimally and where free discussion was encouraged. And Lundgren (1971) found that cohesion, openness, and productivity eventually were higher in T-groups with inactive, nondirective trainers than in groups whose trainers were directive; however, this only occurred after a period of time during which the reverse was generally true.

Overall, the weight of evidence indicates that involvement of individuals in the change process does tend to lessen resistance to change and to facilitate the change process. However, there appear to be a number of exceptions to this general rule; these will be considered later in this chapter.

Proposition 2

Organizational development efforts which include as an objective the continuing involvement of employees will produce significant increases in motivation, satisfaction, and performance.

The preceding section was concerned with employee participation and influence *during* and immediately *prior to* the change effort itself, as a means of lessening resistance to change. In most of the studies cited there were no *continuing* efforts to involve those affected by the change in subsequent activities. Our discussion of Proposition 2, however, will consider the mechanics and consequences of several organizational development programs which feature permanent, ongoing involvement by members in organizational affairs. The programs selected for study include MBO, T-group, Managerial Grid®, and System 4. While other OD programs could have been selected for study, these were chosen because they are among the most important and popular methods. Furthermore, amidst the overall poor state of the art concerning OD effectiveness, these programs have at least been subjected to some studies, however rigorous, of their effectiveness. (Other approaches to OD, such as job enrichment and management development, have been discussed in previous chapters.)

Management By Objectives

Perhaps the most widely employed OD effort is Management By Objectives (MBO), which has already been mentioned briefly above and in Chapter 14. There it was defined as encompassing joint goal-setting between those at each level of management and those at the next higher level, the expression of objectives whenever possible in quantifiable terms, and subsequent measurement and comparison of actual performance with agreed-upon objectives.

Some research results discussed in Chapter 14 are also pertinent to our evaluation of MBO. The original study and follow-up by Raia (1974), for example, brought out some of the advantages of the Management By Objectives approach in raising morale, motivation, and productivity, at least in the short-run (18 months). Even after two and a half years productivity remained high, but undesired consequences of the system were more obvious. These included inadequate usage of MBO at the lower managerial levels, overemphasis on the attainment of production goals and targets, the occasional use of the program as a "whip," and a heavy burden on administrative personnel with consequent large amounts of paper work.

Research by Carroll and Tosi (1973), also described in Chapter 14, concluded, as had Raia, that the introduction of MBO apparently caused a number of improvements within the organization, concerning in particular a reduction in role ambiguity through provision of information about performance expectations. Increases in planning, communications, and feedback were also reported in the Carroll and Tosi study, just as they had been by Raia. The "administrative burden-paper work" problem cited by Raia was listed as the major difficulty by Carroll and Tosi's respondents.

Another similarity between the Raia and the Carroll and Tosi findings is the failure of MBO to become fully implemented at the lower managerial levels. For example, as can be seen from Figure 21–1, there was a noticeable decline in influence over performance goals by low-level managers, as compared to influence over goals reported by vice-presidents and directors. Those at the highest organizational level indicated that they had great influence over their own performance goals; however, perceived influence declined sharply for the next two levels, only to rise very slightly for those at the lowest level.

As was also mentioned in Chapter 14, however, the degree of subordinate influence over their performance goals was an unimportant factor in the perceived success of the program. Participation in goal-setting did not generally result in higher levels of perceived goal success, nor in more favorable attitudes toward the respondent's supervisor (Carroll and Tosi, p. 41). A small positive relationship to goal success and favorable attitudes did exist, however, among employees who had traditionally been given opportunities to participate in the past.

Generally opposite conclusions concerning the consequences of MBO were reached in separate studies by Meyer, Kay, and French (1965) and Ivancevich (1972). Meyer, Kay, and French observed that General Electric employees who had high influence in goal-setting achieved a higher percentage of their goals, and displayed more favorable attitudes, than other employees who had less influence. Managers operating under MBO regarded it as an aid to planning, and claimed that it enabled their supervisors to be more helpful to them.

Ivancevich investigated MBO's effects in two medium-sized industrial goods manufacturers, and found that the system had no important effect on the job satisfaction of managers at each of three levels studied. This

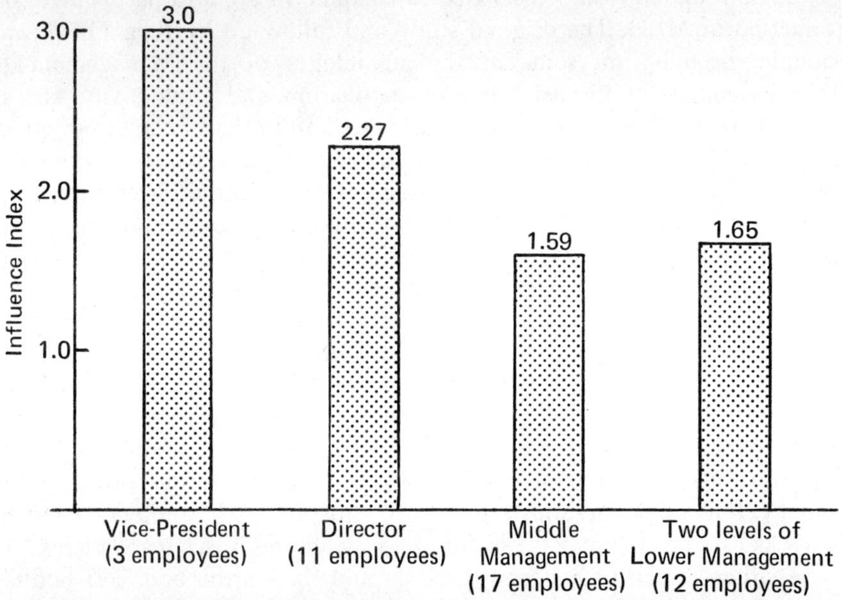

Each manager was asked: "Who had the most influence over the performance goals that finally ended up on your Work-Planning and Review form?" Responses were grouped into one of three categories. A "1" indicated that the boss had the most influence; a "2" reflected mutual influence of boss and subordinate; and a "3" indicated that the subordinate had the most influence. These responses were used to construct an "influence index" within each analytical class.

Source: Carroll and Tosi, 1973, p. 28.

Figure 21-1. Perceived Influence Index as Reported by Managers at Each Organizational Level.

finding held true at three different time periods, ranging from immediately after introduction to eighteen months later. In the other firm MBO was associated with lower-level managers' satisfaction, but only for a relatively brief period after installation. By the eighteenth month, results were as discouraging as in the first firm. From these findings, and from his review of the literature, Ivancevich strongly urges (1972, p. 135) that "before a particular MBO intervention strategy is deemed a success, it should be examined over an extended period of time."

More recent data from production and marketing departments in three large plants of one of the two organizations studied in the earlier research suggest that the converse is also true; that is, time may be necessary before an intervention can be deemed a failure. In this study (Ivancevich, 1974b) both production and marketing departments in one plant showed improvement on several performance indices six months after full implementation; however, after two years the only lasting change of statistical significance was an *increase* in the grievance rate. In the other plant, although a number of improvements remained after two years, these changes were generally not apparent until about six months after full implementation. Had data been taken right after implementation, therefore, and had no follow-up been conducted, this plant too would have been considered as evidence of an MBO failure.

One problem with MBO which is pertinent to Proposition 2, and which has been frequently noted by researchers, concerns the inability of MBO to reach the lower managerial levels. In part this reflects the difficulty of establishing "joint" goal-setting among hierarchical unequals, as discussed in Chapter 14. Another contributing factor to this dilemma is described by Kerr (1973, p. 39):

> . . . even if we assume democratic goal-setting at the top, their meetings must still produce some hard goals for the months ahead. The most collegial of atmospheres cannot then keep these goals from serving as lower limits, as monkeys on the back of any lower-level manager who seeks to establish democratic goal-setting with his own subordinates. Having agreed with the President that 8% growth is a fair objective, the Vice President is unlikely to accept his subordinate's carefully-worded argument that 6% is better. Low-level managers may set objectives even more challenging than those agreed to higher-up, but will seldom be permitted to set objectives which are less challenging. They may thus enjoy the illusion of participation, but will probably soon realize that their objectives are pretty much predetermined by meetings already held higher up.

Based on this and other problems, Kerr (1973, p. 42) concludes that "MBO is usually offered as a high-cost long-run package whose success is by no means guaranteed (or even likely), which generates many side effects impossible to predict or to control." Others have expressed more positive conclusions, but even advocates of MBO speak of it as a "complex organizational change process which may be painful and time-consuming" (Tosi and Carroll, 1969, p. 50), and caution that "it will take four to five years to achieve a fully effective management by objectives system" (Howell, 1970, p. 45).

The contributions of MBO to planning, communications, and emphasis upon goal-setting have been noted by many researchers, and these seem to be associated with several positive outcomes for both the individual and the organization. On the other hand, the risks and challenges of the system are underscored by Carvalho (1972), who claims that "successful implementation of MBO requires, even demands, that all managers have . . . an attitude which accepts collaboration, cooperation, and joint sharing of responsibilities as the norm rather than the exception," and that to develop such attitudes a "mini-cultural revolution" will probably be needed. And we have already noted in Chapter 14 Bennis' opinion (1959, p. 286) that the double-reference (supervisor as helper and as boss) necessary for MBO to work "requires a degree of maturity, more precisely a commitment to maturity, on the part of both the superior and subordinate that exceeds that of any other organizational approach."

Considered from the standpoint of Proposition 2, it should be clear from our review of the MBO research that neither acceptance nor rejection of the proposition is justified. On the one hand, benefits are reported in most (though by no means all) studies of MBO; on the other hand, major costs seem to be associated with even the most successful installations.

Sensitivity Training (T-Groups)

An approach to organizational development which, although controversial, is rapidly increasing in popularity, is that of sensitivity training or T- (for training) groups. Participants in such training efforts may be strangers to one another, organizational "cousins" (that is, from different work groups within the same organization), or members of an organizational "family" (that is, from the same work group). Being temporary structures, T-groups have no existing rules and norms, except as informally established by participants during the training experience. Unlike programs whose aims are to expand skills and knowledge of some task or procedure, sensitivity training seeks to accomplish just what its name implies—an increase in sensitivity toward the needs and attitudes of others, and an increase in individual self-awareness. Of course, when utilized by organizations, a major goal is the improvement of organizational effectiveness.

More specifically, Campbell and Dunnette (1968) have listed six objectives which are common to most T-group efforts. These include:

1. Increased self-insight concerning one's own behavior and its meaning in a social context. This includes learning how others interpret one's behavior, and gaining insight into why one acts in certain ways in particular situations.
2. Increased sensitivity to the behavior of others.
3. Increased awareness of the types of processes which facilitate or inhibit group functioning.
4. Increased diagnostic skills in social situations, to provide individuals with explanatory concepts for diagnosing conflict situations, reasons for faulty communications, etc.
5. Increased ability to intervene in interpersonal situations so as to increase satisfaction and performance.
6. Learning how to learn, by increasing abilities to analyze the individual's own interpersonal behaviors.

The actual process by which these objectives are, hopefully, attained is often similar to the following description of a T-group experience by Delbecq (1972, p. 411):

1. There is an initial lack of directive leadership and formal agenda, and participants fill the behavioral vacuum by engaging in traditional behaviors such as status cue sending, power plays, etc.

2. Feedback, based on member behavior within the anxiety-laden environment, is provided to confirm or disconfirm individual impressions of role effectiveness and personality impact.
3. Interpersonal relationships begin to develop, and members serve as resources to one another; previously untried personal and interpersonal behaviors, particularly collaborative behaviors, are attempted.
4. Relevance of the T-group experience to "back home" situations is explored, and problems are introduced to maximize transferability of what has been learned beyond the training laboratory.

Trainers are normally present throughout the T-group process, but their roles are considerably different from what might be expected. They will tend to refuse any continuing leadership role, and may reject all pleas and demands from members that they provide advice or guidance. It is said by Gibson, Ivancevich, and Donnelly (1973, p. 355) that "the artistry and style of the trainer are critical variables in determining the direction of the T-group's sessions. He must walk the uneasy path of unobtrusive leadership. He must be able to interpret the role of participants and encourage them to analyze their contributions without being perceived as a threat himself."

From the standpoint of the three-step procedure of change described in the previous chapter, it is apparent that a number of features of T-group training are intended to "unfreeze" participants so as to prepare them for change. Bass (1970, p. 173) points out that unfreezing is provided in part "by removing the familiar props and customary social mechanisms, by violating the expectations of trainees, and by creating an ambiguous, unstructured situation for them of unclear goals and minimum cues." Later, "refreezing" may or may not occur, depending "primarily on the opportunity for the participants to try out the values and behaviors that emerge from the laboratory, and on the ability of the participants to generalize from the laboratory situation to the everyday situation" (Bobbitt et al., 1974, p. 173).

Assumptions about T-groups. Campbell and Dunnette (1968) believe that, in order for the T-group process to be successful in attaining the objectives listed above, a number of assumptions must in fact be correct. These include:

1. Many group members, when confronted with the feelings and behavior of others in a psychologically "safe" atmosphere, can give articulate and constructive feedback.
2. Enough members must agree on the information to be fed back to each individual so that the feedback is useful.
3. The feedback must be complete, and deal with important aspects of the individual.
4. People must behave within the group essentially as they do "back home"; otherwise learning points will not be generalizable.

5. A psychologically safe atmosphere can be achieved within the group.
6. Almost all people have sufficient difficulties with their perceptions, self-images, and communication styles so that T-group training will be beneficial.
7. Anxiety facilitates new learning.
8. Transfer of learning will occur between the training laboratory and the situation "back home."

These assumptions, as well as most of the discussion which has preceded them, have been primarily concerned with effects of the training experience upon the individual, either within the laboratory or back on the job. However, we have mentioned earlier in the chapter that one of the major goals of many T-groups is to generate a change in *organizational* effectiveness. It may be necessary, then, to add one more assumption to the above list:

9. To the extent that the individual is changed in accord with the objectives of T-group (enumerated above), the organization will be more effective.

This assumption may be as questionable as most of the others. Consider, for example, some results reported by Bass (1970, p. 171):

> Nine quasi-T-Groups (T-Groups without trainers) met for 15 weeks. . . . After another 15 weeks had passed, three of the nine groups were each splintered into three parts and the parts reassembled into three new teams. Three other groups were divided in half and reassembled as three new teams. Three groups were left intact. Then the teams competed with one another in the Carnegie Tech Management Game. Interpersonal comfort, openness, familiarity, communication ease, and cohesiveness were greatest in the three intact groups, according to member ratings. . . . Nevertheless, it was these three intact groups that lost an average of $5.37 million in the competition with the remaining splintered groups. The splintered groups broke even or made a good profit, on the average. Yet these splintered groups were less successful interpersonally. . . .

Consistent results are reported by Powell and Stinson (1971). In their study "family" T-groups showed a greater increase in group cohesiveness than did "stranger" groups and control groups, but performed least effectively.

Bass (1970, p. 171) reached the conclusion that:

> T-Group theorists often imply that what is good for an individual's mental health and maturity is good for the organization's well being. . . . But this position may be as wrong as assuming that what is good for the organization is good for its members. Sensitivity training may

be necessary for organizational development, but it is not sufficient. By itself, T-Grouping is not enough.

Studies of T-group Effectiveness. Between 1967 and 1971 a fairly large number of reviews were conducted of T-group approaches to organizational development (House, 1967, 1969; Friedlander, 1967; Campbell and Dunnette, 1968; Dunnette and Campbell, 1968; Buchanan, 1969; Mosvick, 1971). In general, these reviews may be said to agree with respect to several major points:

1. T-group training is likely (though by no means certain) to cause important changes in the participating individual. Improvements in such things as listening ability, supportive behaviors, consideration, openness, and individual growth and development have been reported in many studies.

2. Due to the generally low level of rigor of T-group research (in the terminology of Chapter 3, nearly all studies are of rigor level 1), many of the investigations reporting changes such as in (1) above must be considered with caution. Dunnette and Campbell (1968) point out that when *objective* measures of attitudes, values, interpersonal perceptions, self-awareness, and sensitivity are used, sensitivity training has usually not been shown to cause meaningful changes in participants.

3. In general, the changes which individuals experience as a result of T-group training are likely (though by no means certain) to result in changes "back home" in the work environment. The lasting effects of such changes are questionable, however, and depend in large part upon the receptiveness of others in the organization to encourage and support the changes. (The importance of such receptiveness to change efforts generally has been underscored in the previous chapter.)

4. So far as "back home" changes are concerned, it is very hard to predict in advance what specific effects upon organizational behaviors will result from sensitivity training. T-groups are capable of bringing about positive changes, but may also create feelings of role conflict and may bring on other undesirable consequences as well. Of nine studies reviewed which dealt with T-group effects on managerial behavior in the posttraining job situation, House (1969) found four which reported positive effects, four which claimed both positive and undesirable effects, and one reporting no measurable change. Concerning such important organizational activities as analyzing problems, synthesizing information, resolving interpersonal conflict, and solving organizational problems, Dunnette and Campbell (1968) concluded that "we have practically no evidence."

5. When the broader question of changes in overall organizational effectiveness as a result of sensitivity training is considered, no answer based on research evidence is possible. Almost no studies bear directly on this point.

6. Sensitivity training also involves several ethical considerations, and these have been illuminated by most of the reviews cited, but have not

been resolved. For example, T-group training depends in large part upon the creation of an atmosphere of anxiety for participants. Researchers differ as to the actual number of individuals who have been badly harmed by T-group experiences, but few deny that the possibility exists and is probably more likely in sensitivity than in conventional kinds of training. Dangers are increased when participation is involuntary (as sometimes appears to be the case, particularly when organizational "families" are involved) and when the trainer is of questionable experience and competence, which also appears to be the case in too many training efforts.

7. It is far from evident that T-group training is superior to lower-risk "conventional" human relations training. Campbell and Dunnette have pointed out in this regard that "it still cannot be said with any certainty whether T-groups lead to greater or lesser changes in self-perceptions than other types of group experience, the simple passage of time, or the mere act of filling out a self-description questionnaire" (1968). More recently Mosvick (1969, 1971) concluded that six of twelve T-group efforts involving nontechnical personnel were generally successful (50 percent), compared to only six of eighteen (33 percent) "standard human relations" programs. On the other hand, when "technically oriented professionals" were involved all four conventional programs reviewed showed generally positive results, whereas three of the four T-group programs obtained generally negative outcomes.

Recent investigations of T-group results have fairly well followed the patterns observed by previous reviewers. Favorable effects have been noted by some researchers (e.g., Golembiewski and Carrigan, 1970a, 1970b; Golembiewski et al., 1971), mixed or generally negative results by others (e.g., Powell and Stinson, 1971; DeMichele, 1973). In a recent survey of personnel directors from 225 responding firms employing 1000 or more employees, asked whether they would personally recommend to other firms that sensitivity training be emphasized in their management development programs, 59 respondents (26.2 percent) said "yes," 110 (48.9 percent) said "no," and 45 did not respond (Kearney and Martin, 1974). In an earlier survey of 117 responding training directors (Carroll, Paine, and Ivancevich, 1972) sensitivity training was rated significantly more effective than eight other training methods for causing attitude change and, along with role-playing (another participative method), most effective for developing interpersonal skills; it was, however, relatively ineffective for knowledge acquistion according to the training directors, and was judged to be less well accepted by participants than were a number of alternatives.

Still, there are some encouraging signs. The research by Golembiewski and his associates has generated some optimistic conclusions about the durability of changes produced by sensitivity training. Furthermore, researchers have begun to turn their attention to some of the questions which critically need to be answered. While it is far too soon to speak of a "weight of evidence," at least data have begun to be accumulated concerning such things as the effects of different trainer styles (e.g., Lundgren, 1971), the consequences of varying degrees of participant choice of attending for training outcomes (e.g., Steele, Zand, and Zalkind, 1970), and the moderating influence of participant characteristics (e.g., McConnell, 1971; Anderson and Slocum, 1973). Until considerably more research has been conducted, however, it can only be said that so far as T-group training is concerned, Proposition 2 is neither confirmed nor disconfirmed. Such training often does generate changes which result in more active participation and involvement by participants once back on the job; however, it is not clear that such changes have any consistent effect upon subsequent motivation, satisfaction, and performance.

The Managerial Grid

This approach to organizational development depends in part upon the values and techniques of sensitivity training; however, there are many important differences. One is that the Grid approach is structured, while the T-group is unstructured. Another is that Grid seminars focus upon managerial styles and behaviors which are directly relevant to the organizational setting,[1] rather than dealing with participant personality characteristics which may or may not be relevant. A third difference is that Grid's emphasis is upon *organizational* rather than individual development, and individual training is merely the initial phase of a six-phase program. During this first phase group members study the Managerial Grid, engage in face-to-face feedback concerning each other's managerial styles, and participate in structured experiments relating to the effects of interpersonal relations upon task accomplishment. Participation in any seminar is on the "cousin" or "diagonal slice" basis; this permits many organizational levels to be represented, while assuring that no one interacts directly with their bosses or immediate co-workers (Blake and Mouton, 1964). Subsequent phases emphasize team and intergroup integration and development, development of long-range organizational goals, implementing changes by attaining these goals, and accomplishing stabilization. The total program may take several years to complete.

The Grid itself, for which the approach is named, is shown in Figure 21–2 and described by Blake and Mouton (1974, p. 174) as follows:

> The Grid is an 81-squared framework on which styles of behavior can be plotted. A manager has to think about two things—how to get the work done and the people who are going to do the work. Some managers have production on their minds more than people; others, people more than production. On the horizontal axis of the Grid, which goes from 1 to 9, the 9 represents high concern for output, the 1 low concern for output. On the vertical axis, the 9 represents high concern for people and the 1 low concern for people.

[1] See Chapter 8 for a discussion of the Managerial Grid as a model of managerial styles.

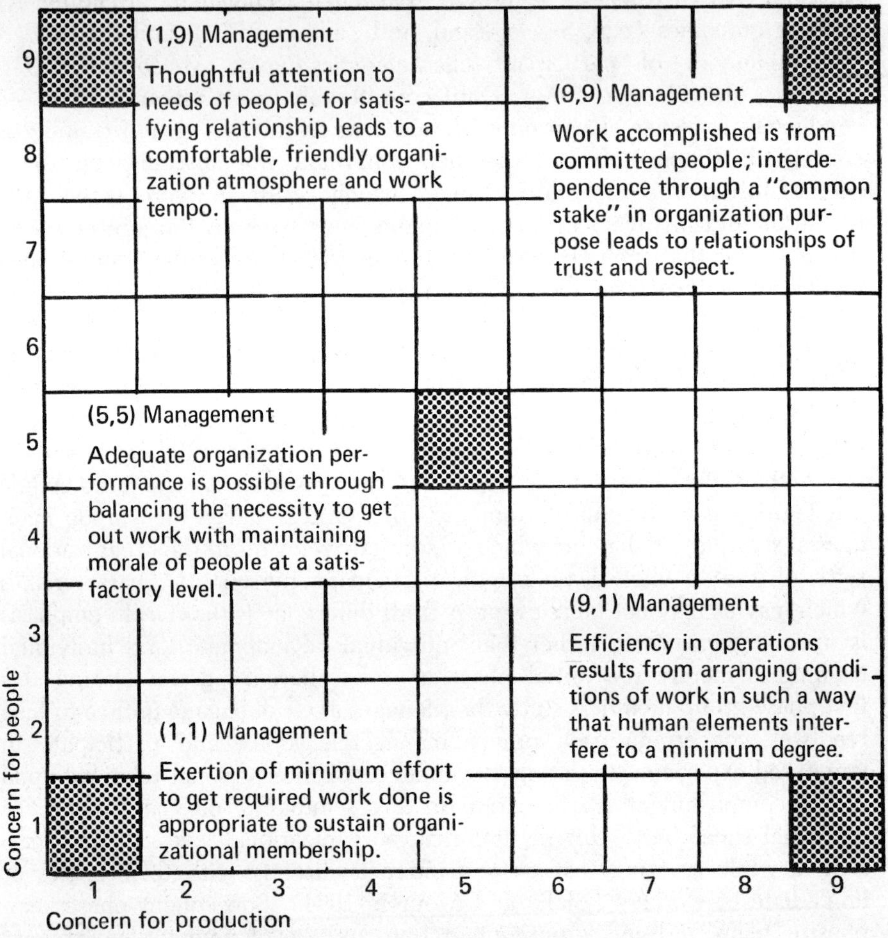

Source: Blake and Mouton, 1964, p. 10.

Figure 21–2. Managerial Grid.

In the lower right-hand corner, "9,1" represents a great deal of concern for output but very little for the people who are expected to produce. At the opposite corner of the Grid is "1,9" representing much concern for people and little for the output needed in a healthy business.

Another Grid corner is 1,1. . . . These are the ones in an organization who go through the motions of being a part of it but are invisible though present. . . . Still another possibility is in dead center of the Grid. This is the 5,5 style. A manager with this approach . . . tells himself not to push too much or he will be seen as hardnosed, and not to let people off too easy or he will be seen as soft. . . .

The upper right-hand corner, 9,9 position, denotes a high concern for both production and people. . . . The 9,9 position is characterized

> by commitment of organization members to accomplishment of work which contributes to organization goals.

Not very many research studies of the effectiveness of the Managerial Grid approach have been conducted, and those which do exist suffer from a number of difficulties. The best-known investigation of a Grid program followed its installation at "Sigma Corporation" (Blake et al., 1964; Blake et al., 1968). It was reported that Grid "was responsible for at least several million dollars of controllable cost savings and profit increase. In addition, the program seems to have been responsible for a sizable increase in employee productivity during its first year" (Blake et al., 1964). A number of individual attitudinal and behavioral changes consistent with 9,9 concepts were also observed. Later the Grid program was applied to the lowest levels in the firm and it was reported that:

> . . . specific advantages have been shown in the gain in dollar savings. Plant-wide practical application of cooperative effort toward greater effectiveness is shown by: decreased time of plant units' tasks, such as unit shutdowns; increased use of capacities and energies of plant personnel through union-management agreed-upon arrangements . . . ; and a greater personal interest and involvement in the work (Blake et al., 1968, p. 78).

Many authors have suggested that results such as these be treated with caution. They have pointed out that much of the information obtained is anecdotal and subjective (in the language of Chapter 3, level of rigor 1), that individuals were asked to describe changes which had occurred more than one year earlier, and that Grid programs have typically been carried out without control groups. Among the questions Dunnette and Campbell (1968, p. 21) have asked about the conclusions to be drawn from the "Sigma Corporation" research are these:

> Would *any* total push emphasis pointing up organizational problems, emphasizing the need for more cost consciousness, and calling for greater team effort among the 800 supervisors and managers have worked as well? Or was the specific technology of the T group-like early phases of the grid program specifically responsible for the changes in organizational outcomes? Might the changes in profits not have occurred without any training at all—merely as a consequence of widespread cost emphasis and extensive manpower reductions? Unfortunately, it is impossible to answer these important questions from the data of this particular investigation.

A more recent review of the research evidence pertaining to the Managerial Grid as an OD technique (Huse, 1975) reaffirms the conclusion that most Grid programs are either not evaluated at all, or are evaluated by low-rigor methods. What few relatively rigorous studies there are have generated mixed and often contradictory conclusions.

The System 4 Approach

Another criticism of the Managerial Grid, that its values and conceptual underpinnings are strongly in favor of the 9,9 managerial style as a "one best way" almost regardless of the situation, is contested by its proponents. No such argument exists with respect to the System 4 approach to organizational development. Likert, who originated the concept of System 4, believes strongly that it is universally applicable to all organizations, all situations, and all cultures. He has summarized existing research on this approach to organizational development as follows:

> Whenever persons in an organization are asked to . . . describe their organization as it is *now* and then to answer . . . what they would *like* their organization to be, a consistent pattern emerges. This pattern has been found to occur . . . in the United States, Europe, and Asia. Irrespective of where people see their organizations at present, whether System 1, 2, or 3, they invariably would like it to be closer to System 4. . . . Substantial research shows that if a moderate shift toward System 4 occurs, the persons affected respond favorably both in attitude and behavior, such as performance (Likert, 1974).

Seashore and Bowers (1970) amusingly differentiate between System 1 and System 4 by remarking that "the bad guys are thought to have and to prefer System 1 organizations while good guys aspire to and approach the System 4 state." A more complete differentiation is offered in Table 21–1, assembled by Gibson, Ivancevich, and Donnelly (1973) from Likert (1967, pp. 197–211). From this table it can be seen that System 4 organizations are characterized by continuing involvement of employees in organizational affairs. Participation is strongly encouraged, upward communications flow freely, and members at all levels have opportunities to influence managerial attitudes and impact upon organizational goals. Certainly the System 4 concept seems based on the assumption stated in Proposition 2.

Unlike the carefully structured approach which typifies the Managerial Grid, there is no single way that organizations should travel to move closer to the System 4 profile. For example, the previously cited work by Golembiewski and his associates (Golembiewski and Carrigan, 1970a, 1970b; Golembiewski et al., 1971) utilized a developmental approach based upon sensitivity training, and produced sizable shifts in the unit's profile in the direction of System 4. Perhaps the best-known example of a "System 4" approach to OD occurred at the Weldon Company in 1962, after its purchase by the Harwood Manufacturing Company. In this organization rather massive changes were instituted, including "some modernization of the plant, improved layout and flow of work, improvement in records and production control methods, and product simplification, as well as changes in the human

TABLE 21-1. Classical Design and System 4 Organization.

Classical Design Organization	System 4 Organization
1. *Leadership process* includes no perceived confidence and trust. Subordinates do not feel free to discuss job problems with their superiors, who in turn do not solicit their ideas and opinions.	1. *Leadership process* includes perceived confidence and trust between superiors and subordinates in all matters. Subordinates feel free to discuss job problems with their superiors, who in turn solicit their ideas and opinions.
2. *Motivational process* taps only physical, security, and economic motives through the use of fear and sanctions. Unfavorable attitudes toward the organization prevail among employees.	2. *Motivational process* taps a full range of motives through participatory methods. Attitudes are favorable toward the organization and its goals.
3. *Communication process* is such that information flows downward and tends to be distorted, inaccurate, and viewed with suspicion by subordinated.	3. *Communication process* is such that information flows freely throughout the organization—upward, downward, and laterally. The information is accurate and undistorted.
4. *Interaction process* is closed and restricted; subordinates have little effect on departmental goals, methods, and activities.	4. *Interaction process* is open and extensive; both superiors and subordinates are able to affect departmental goals, methods, and activities.
5. *Decision process* occurs only at the top of the organization; it is relatively centralized.	5. *Decision process* occurs at all levels through group processes; it is relatively decentralized.
6. *Goal-setting process* located at the top of the organization, discourages group participation.	6. *Goal-setting process* encourages group participation in setting high, realistic objectives.
7. *Control process* is centralized and emphasizes fixing of blame for mistakes.	7. *Control process* is dispersed throughout the organization and emphasizes self-control and problem solving.
8. *Performance goals* are low and passively sought by managers who make no commitment to developing the human resources of the organization.	8. *Performance goals* are high and actively sought by superiors, who recognize the necessity for making full commitment to developing, through training, the human resources of the organization.

Source: J. L. Gibson, J. M. Ivancevich, and J. H. Donnelly, Jr., 1973, p. 80.

organization" (Seashore and Bowers, 1970; see Marrow, Bowers, and Seashore, 1967, for a full account). The effort produced substantial improvements in many attitudinal, behavioral, and performance indices, and these were found to persist even after eight years. For example, by 1969 "Weldon had improved return on investment by one-third, cut absenteeism in half, reduced manpower turnover by 60 percent, and increased employee productivity by nearly 40 percent. Union management relationships also improved greatly" (Likert, 1974).

Administration of the Likert profile at various times during the interval revealed that the organization moved from a low System 2 profile in 1962 to one quite close to System 4 by 1969. The Weldon Company experiment thus provides convincing evidence that OD efforts can result in sizable shifts in employee perceptions toward System 4, and that these perceptions persist over time. The extent of the changes, however, in both the "human organization" and in numerous technical areas, makes it impossible to determine to what degree the improvements described by Likert were the result of those human-relations changes which led the firm toward System 4. Nevertheless, Likert (1974) presents other data from the United States (e.g., from General Motors Corporation) and from many foreign nations, and concludes from these that in each nation:

1. The higher producing, more successful enterprises, departments, or offices tend to fall more toward the System 4 end of the range for that nation;
2. The low producing, less successful organizations have management systems more toward the System 1 end of the range.

To the extent that future research continues to show that OD efforts can systematically lead an organization toward System 4, and that such movement results in individual satisfaction and organizational effectiveness, this approach may be considered to be supportive of Proposition 2. However, it will be necessary for future research to be carried out in a more rigorous manner than has been true of much of the System 4 research to date.

As matters stand now, studies of the effectiveness of System 4 are subject to many of the criticisms which have been levied against the other OD techniques reviewed in this chapter. In particular, most System 4 research has been carried out without the presence of control groups; furthermore, some researchers and consultants attempt to move a firm toward System 4 through the introduction of so many simultaneous changes that, even to the extent that specific effects can be identified, their assignment to any one cause is impossible. In general, many OD efforts are as methodologically suspect as would be the treatment of a patient with drugs, deep heat, surgical procedures, and physical therapy, all administered simultaneously. The point is that some portions of the "cure" will be likely to further progress, some to inhibit progress, and some to have no effect. When OD is conducted in such a fashion, coherent research is all but impossible.

Summary

Proposition 1: Providing opportunities for individuals to have influence over and participate in the change process will significantly lessen individual resistance to change. *Supported, but only weakly, due in part to the virtual absence of rigorous research.*

Proposition 2: Organizational development efforts which include as an objective the continuing involvement of employees will produce significant increases in motivation, satisfaction, and performance. *Neither confirmed nor disconfirmed, again largely due to the virtual absence of rigorous and controlled studies.*

Conclusions

Despite the virtual absence of rigorous research surrounding most OD efforts, existing research is adequate to highlight a few exceptions to the benefits of participation. The following list (adapted from work by Lawrence, 1954; Blake and Mouton, 1969; Powell and Schlacter, 1971; Chaney and Leel, 1972; Gibson, Ivancevich, and Donnelly, 1973; and Ivancevich, 1974a) describes situations where participation in change efforts would *not* be likely to prove advantageous:

1. When higher management (or the change agent) are clearly insecure in terms of their positions in the group, or when the leader-trainer possesses personality characteristics which definitely interfere with adoption of a participative style, participation is unlikely to be successful.
2. When knowledge, skills, and abilities of participants are lacking, participation may result simply in a "pooling of ignorance" leading to inefficient solutions.
3. When subordinates (or trainees) expect and are prepared for authoritarian approaches, and when they have relatively high needs for structure and low needs for autonomy, participation may be seen as a "managerial gimmick," or may make them uncomfortable.
4. When knowledge change rather than attitude change is the goal of a developmental effort, directive training styles may be more fruitful than participative approaches.
5. When subordinates (or trainees) are concerned with fostering friendly relationships to the point that task accomplishment is unimportant, participative approaches will be unlikely to result in critical remarks, and may cause acceptance of unsound proposals.
6. When subordinates (or trainees) are concerned with task accomplishment to the point that people's feelings become inconsequential, participative approaches may lead to fixed position-taking, polarization, and unhealthy conflict.

It is clear from the research reviewed in this chapter that a great variety of approaches to organizational development are available; obviously, some of these will tend to be more effective than others, both at creating change in the participating individual and at providing linkage between such individual changes and various organizational outcomes.

There is not a single approach to organizational development, however, which has been consistently evaluated by the rigorous methods and test designs described in Chapter 3. On the contrary, the great majority of OD efforts are not evaluated at all, or are evaluated in the most anecdotal, subjective manner imaginable. In part this is due to the manner in which OD is typically introduced into the organization. When massive and simultaneous changes are made to the organization's authority, control, evaluation, and reward systems, as is the case with many MBO, System 4, and other approaches, isolation of the effects of various components of the OD process upon organizational criteria is virtually impossible.

The lack of rigorous evaluation of most OD efforts is also due in part to what Margulies (1972) labels the "myth of nonresearchable variables," whereby it may be claimed by apologists for the current state of affairs that the evaluation methods and test designs normally required of those who would boast of a new "cure" are somehow irrelevant, unimportant, or even dysfunctional when organizational development is involved. Such statements may reflect honest differences of opinion, or may result from the partial incompatibility of goals and motives between those who promote OD and those who would benefit from knowing whether it works. It has been observed that:

> Interestingly, the same individuals (whether in Personnel, Manpower Planning, or wherever) who would normally be responsible for conducting such evaluations are the ones often charged with introducing the change effort in the first place. Having convinced top management to spend all that money, they are usually quite animated afterwards in collecting arigorous vignettes and anecdotes about how successful the program was. The *last* thing they desire is a formal, systematic, and revealing evaluation. . . . And if Personnel abdicates its responsibility who is to step into the breach? The change agent himself? Hardly! He is likely to be too busy collecting anecdotal "evidence" of his own, for use on his next client (Kerr, 1975).

Another problem which is evident from the research reviewed for this chapter is that most OD alternatives currently available require not only considerable effort and expense, but a great deal of time as well. Burke (1972, p. 173) points out that few OD interventions are useful in short-term crises, and that therefore "much of the current technology of OD is irrelevant to many of the issues of importance to managers and their organizations. Needless to say, there is a great need for more 'short-term' technology."

On the encouraging side is that, at long last, theory-building and conceptualization are beginning (though *just* beginning) to catch up with OD practice. Perhaps fewer developmental efforts in the future will resemble "gimmicks in search of some underlying rationale." Also, researchers are starting to concern themselves with those individual, task, and situational variables which are likely to moderate OD effects; however, this line of research too is still in its infancy.

References

Anderson, C., and Slocum, J. 1973. Personality traits and their impact on the success of T-group training. *Training and Development Journal* 27.

Argyris, C. 1964. *Integrating the individual and the organization.* Wiley.

———. 1971. *Management and organizational development.* McGraw-Hill.

Bass, B. M. 1970. The anarchist movement and the T-group: Some possible lessons for organizational development. In *Current perspectives for managing organizations,* ed. by B. M. Bass and S. D. Deep. Prentice-Hall.

Bennis, W. G. 1959. Leadership theory and administrative behavior: The problem of authority. *Administrative Science Quarterly* 4: 259-301.

Blake, R. R., and Mouton, J. S. 1969. *Building a dynamic corporation through grid.* Addison-Wesley.

———., and ———. 1964. *The managerial grid.* Gulf.

———., and ———. 1974. Organization excellence through effective management behavior. In *Organizational behavior: A book of readings,* 4th ed., ed. by K. Davis. McGraw-Hill.

———.; ———.; Barnes, L. B.; and Greiner, L. E. 1964. Breakthrough in organizational development. *Harvard Business Review* 42: 37-59.

———.; ———.; Sloma, R. L.; and Loftin, B. P. 1968. A second breakthrough in organization development. *California Management Review* 11: 73-78.

Bobbitt, H. R.; Breinholt, R. H.; Doktor, R. H.; and McNaul, J. P. 1974. *Organizational behavior: Understanding and prediction.* Prentice-Hall.

Buchanan, P. C. 1969. Laboratory training and organization development. *Administrative Science Quarterly* 14: 466-80.

Burke, W. W. 1972. Organizational development: Here to stay? *Academy of Management Proceedings,* 170-77.

———., and Schmidt, W. H. 1971. Management and organizational development. *Personnel Administration* 34.

Campbell, J. P., and Dunnette, M. D. 1968. Effectiveness of T-group experiences in managerial training and development. *Psychological Bulletin* 70: 73-104.

Carroll, S. J., Paine, F. T., and Ivancevich, J. J. 1972. The relative effectiveness of training methods—expert opinion and research. *Personnel Psychology* 25: 495-509.

———., and Tosi, H. L. 1973. *Management by objectives: Applications and research.* Macmillan.

Carvalho, G. F. 1972. Installing MBO: A new perspective on organizational change. *Human Resources Management* 8-19.

Chaney, F. B., and Leel, K. S. 1972. Participative management—a practical experience. *Personnel* 49: 8-19.

Coch, L., and French, J. R. P. 1948. Overcoming resistance to change. *Human Relations* 1: 512-32.

Dalton, G. W. 1973. Influence and organizational change. In *Changing organizational behavior,* ed. by A. C. Bartlett and T. A. Kayser. Prentice-Hall.

Delbecq, A. L. 1972. Sensitivity training. In *Contemporary readings in organizational behavior,* ed. by F. Luthans. McGraw-Hill.

DeMichele, J. H. 1973. Measuring the effectiveness of laboratory training in organizational development. *Academy of Management Proceedings,* 47-48.

Dunnette, M. D., and Campbell, J. P. 1968. Laboratory training: Impact on people and organizations. *Industrial Relations* 8: 1-24.

French, J. R. P., Israel, J., and As, D. 1960. An experiment on participation in a Norwegian factory. *Human Relations* 13: 3-20.

French, W. L., and Bell, C. H. 1972. A definition and history of organization development: Some comments. *Academy of Management Proceedings,* 146-53.

Friedlander, F. 1967. The impact of organizational training laboratories upon the effectiveness and interaction of ongoing work groups. *Personnel Psychology* 20: 289-307.

Gibson, J. L., Ivancevich, J. M., and Donnelly, J. H. 1973. *Organizations: Structure, processes, behavior.* Business Publications.

Golembiewski, R. T., and Carrigan, S. B. 1970a. Planned change in organization style based on the laboratory approach. *Administrative Science Quarterly* 15: 79-93.

———., and ———. 1970b. The persistence of laboratory-induced changes in organization styles. *Administrative Science Quarterly* 15: 330-40.

———., Munzenrider, R.; Blumberg, A.; Carrigan, S. B.; and Mead, W. R. 1971. Changing climate in a complex organization: Interactions between a learning design and an environment. *Academy of Management Journal* 14: 465-81.

Greiner, L. E. 1967. Patterns of organizational change. *Harvard Business Review* 45: 119-30.

House, R. J. 1967. T-group education and leadership effectiveness: A review of the empiric literature and a critical evaluation. *Personnel Psychology* 20: 1-32.

———. 1969. T-group training: Good or bad? *Business Horizons* 6: 69-77.

Howell, R. A. 1970. Managing by objectives: A three stage system. *Business Horizons* 7.

Huse, E. A. 1975. *Organization development and change.* West.

Ivancevich, J. M. 1972. A longitudinal assessment of management by objectives. *Administrative Science Quarterly* 17: 126-38.

———. 1974a. A study of a cognitive training program: Trainer styles and group development. *Academy of Management Journal* 17: 428-39.

———. 1974b. Changes in performance in a management by objectives program. *Administrative Science Quarterly* 19: 563-74.

Janis, I. L., and King, B. T. 1954. The influence of role playing on opinion change. *Journal of Abnormal and Social Psychology* 49: 211-18.

Kearney, W. J., and Martin, D. D. 1974. Sensitivity training: An established management development tool? *Academy of Management Journal* 17: 755-60.

Kerr, S. 1975. On the folly of rewarding a, while hoping for b. *Academy of Management Journal* 18.

———. 1973. Some modifications in MBO as an OD strategy. *Academy of Management Proceedings,* 39-42.

King, B. T., and Janis, I. L. 1956. Comparison of the effectiveness of improvised vs. non-improvised role playing in producing opinion change. *Human Relations* 9: 177-86.

Lawler, E. E., and Hackman, J. R. 1969. Impact of employee participation on the development of pay incentive plans. *Journal of Applied Psychology* 53: 467-71.

Lawrence, P. R. 1954. How to deal with resistance to change. *Harvard Business Review* 32: 49-57.

Lewin, K. 1958. Group decision and social change. In *Readings in social psychology*, 3rd ed., ed. by E. E. Maccoby, T. M. Newcomb, and E. L. Hartley. Holt, Rinehart and Winston.

Likert, R. 1967. *The human organization*. McGraw-Hill.

———. 1974. *New ways of managing conflict*. McGraw-Hill.

Lundgren, D. C. 1971. Trainer style and patterns of group development. *Journal of Applied Behavioral Science* 7: 689-709.

Machiavelli, N. 1953. *The prince*. Tr. by L. Ricci. New American Library.

Margulies, N. 1972. The myth and magic of OD. *Business Horizons* 15: 77-82.

———., and Raia, A. P. 1972. *Organizational development: Values, process, and technology*. McGraw-Hill.

———., and Wallace, J. 1973. *Organizational change: Techniques and applications*. Scott, Foresman.

Marrow, A. J., Bowers, D. G., and Seashore, S. E. 1967. *Management by participation*. Harper & Row.

McConnell, H. K. 1971. Individual differences as mediators of participant behavior and self-descriptive change in two human relations training programs. *Organizational Behavior and Human Performance* 6: 550-72.

Meyer, H. H., Kay, E., and French, J. R. P. 1965. Split roles in performance appraisal. *Harvard Business Review* 43.

Mosvick, R. K. 1969. Twenty years of experimental evaluation of human relations training in the United States and Great Britain, 1949-1969. Mimeograph, Macalaster College (cited in Mosvick, 1971).

———. 1971. Human relations training for scientists, technicians, and engineers: A review of relevant experimental evaluations of human relations training. *Personnel Psychology* 24: 275-92.

Pelz, E. B. 1958. Some factors in 'group decision.' In *Readings in social psychology*, 3rd ed., ed. by E. E. Maccoby, T. M. Newcomb, and E. L. Hartley. Holt, Rinehart and Winston.

Powell, R. M., and Schlacter, J. L. 1971. Participative management: A panacea? *Academy of Management Journal* 14: 165-73.

———., and Stinson, J. E. 1971. The worth of laboratory training. *Business Horizons* 14: 87-95.

Radke, M., and Klisurich, D. 1947. Experiments in changing food habits. *Journal of the American Dietetic Association* 24: 403-409.

Raia, A. P. 1974. *Managing by objectives*. Scott, Foresman.

Scheflen, K. C., Lawler, E. E., and Hackman, J. R. 1971. Long-term impact of employee participation in the development of pay incentive plans: A field experiment revisited. *Journal of Applied Psychology* 55: 182-86.

Schein, E. H. 1958. The Chinese indoctrination program for prisoners of war: A study of attempted 'brainwashing.' In *Readings in social psychology*, 3rd ed., ed. by E. E. Maccoby, T. M. Newcomb, and E. L. Hartley. Holt, Rinehart and Winston.

Seashore, S. E., and Bowers, D. G. 1970. Durability of organizational change. *American Psychologist* 25: 227-33.

Sherwood, J. J. 1971. *An introduction to organization development.* Ms. No. 396-1, 11, Experimental Publication System.

Steele, F. I., Zand, D. E., and Zalkind, S. S. 1970. Managerial behavior and participation in a laboratory training process. *Personnel Psychology* 23: 77-90.

Tomekovic, T. 1962. Level of knowledge of requirements as a motivational factor in the work situation. *Human Relations* 15: 197-216.

Tosi, H. L., and Carroll, S. J. 1969. Some structural factors related to goal influence in the management by objectives process. *Business Topics* 17: 45-50.

Veen, P. 1972. Effects of participative decision-making in field hockey training: A field experiment. *Organizational Behavior and Human Performance* 7: 288-307.

Winn, A. 1968. The laboratory approach to organizational development: A tentative model of planned change. Paper read at the British Psychological Society, 1968. (Cited in R. T. Golembiewski. 1969. Organization development in public agencies: Perspectives on theory and practice. *Public Administration Review* 29.)

Chapter **22**

Organizational Types and Growth

The legendary Phoenix, a beautiful female bird, was said to dwell in the Arabian desert; whereupon, every five hundred years, she built for herself a funeral pyre of fragrant gumwood, and fanning the flames with her wings, burnt to ashes; arising in youthful freshness from these ashes to begin her life cycle anew.

In this chapter we are primarily concerned with the classification of organizations into three types, and with the characteristics associated with each type. We shall also make some tentative statements about the performance of organizations so classified. In such an analysis, there is no concern with a possible ordering of types nor with the change of a single organization from one type to another. The types simply provide identification in much the same way that classification of organizations as retail or manufacturing, or as public or private, does.

In contrast, we shall also deal with the question, "How do organizations change or develop as they grow or evolve?" This approach deals with the changes in *kind* which occur as an organization evolves or is consciously moved from one organization type to another. When taking such an approach when dealing with organisms, a specific ordering of types is identified; thus a tadpole becomes a frog, a caterpillar becomes a moth, and an adolescent becomes an adult. Clearly, however, organizations are not organisms, and can move from Type I (as we shall identify it) into Type III or vice versa. In either organismic change or organizational change, we are concerned with conditions which cause the change and with the characteristics associated with such change.

This chapter is much more concerned with the former approach than with the latter. It will identify the ways in which organizational growth has been described and studied and common classification methods used to categorize organizations. Then it will describe three organizational types—these are labeled craft, promotion, and administrative. The actual growth experience of firms is discussed and, finally, the chapter reviews research related to the three types and to their leadership.

It will be seen that this text has been concerned with only one of the three types, the administrative organization. It will also be evident that judged in terms of performance and survival, the administrative type is to be preferred.

Organizational Growth and Change

In his rather heroic review of the literature on this subject, Starbuck (1965) identified four approaches to the subject of growth and development. The first is the *cell-division model.* In this model the organization is often considered to be analogous to an organism and its growth is viewed as occurring in the same way as an organism expands—through cell division. For example, Haire (1959) drew on the work by Thompson (1952) on biological growth to postulate a similar relationship between size, shape, and function as an organization grows. He stated, for example, that "the rate of increase (in organization size) can be determined from the first few generations" (pp. 277–79), which in practice is the first three years. This growth is limited at the upper end by environmental constraints. Cell-division models emphasize the prediction of total size over time and pay little attention to adaptation or internal change processes.

The second approach to growth and development is through the use of *metamorphosis models.* These models focus on the different patterns of structure and function that appear as an organization grows. That is, where the cell-division model emphasizes changes in degree, the metamorphosis model emphasizes changes in kind. For example, Lester (1958) identified several stages in the growth of the United States labor movement. The first was a pregrowth period prior to 1932, the second was a period of rapid growth and development from 1933 to 1946, and the third was a period of institutional middle age which occurred after 1946. Although in the thirties and the forties nearly every national union was militantly organized and was led by a visible, charismatic leader, the later period was characterized by corporatelike operations with staffs of experts and professional managers. Similar metamorphosis models have been presented for the growth of nations (Rostow, 1960; Bennett and McKnight, 1956); political and economic institutions (Weber, 1947); mass social movements (Hoffer, 1958); and business organizations (Lippitt and Schmidt, 1967). Such models are poorly suited to identify cause and effect but they do facilitate the classification and comparison of organizations.

The third model for growth is the *will-o'-the-wisp.* Here growth is viewed as the process of pursuing some kind of resource or advantage. For example, Penrose (1959) suggests that in planning growth a firm considers its inherited resources—that is, its available factors of production, including management—and the resources that must be obtained from the market. Growth or expansion will draw on the services of present management, and such services constitute the limit on the rate of growth. Unlike those economists who have assumed management to be a fixed factor, Penrose argues that, additions to management aside, present management becomes an increasing resource through experience and improvements in its own ability. Will-o'-the-wisp models try to explain causal relations related to growth in a limited number of processes.

The fourth type of model is the *decision-process model.* Here the model builder attempts to reproduce the basic characteristics of a single decision process in enough detail to permit actual prediction of decisions made. Once an accurate simulation is demonstrated, it then becomes possible to test the outcome of possible alternate decision strategies. For example, as we saw in Chapter 7, Clarkson (1963) constructed a model of a trust investment process employed by trust officers of a bank that rather closely approximated decisions actually made on portfolio selection. Decision-process models tend to be limited in scope but they do set forth causal factors in the process of change.

Organizational Typologies

Partitioning or classifying a population into categories has advantages for describing behavior and for predicting future behavior. As already demonstrated in this book many times, while one cannot generalize about all organizations, some rather specific positive or normative statements can be made once the population of all organizations is broken down into categories of different technologies, different environments, or even different sizes.

Hall (1972) describes the present lack of a generally accepted typology and the utility of such approaches:

> The fact is that there is not a generally accepted typology of organizations, in spite of the general agreement that a good typology or set of typologies is desperately needed. While simple typologies can be used for limited analyses, such as comparing organizations on the basis of their turnover rates, growth rates, or rates of investment in research and development, classifications of this sort have only limited usefulness. We end up knowing only one thing about organizations, not understanding them in their rich complexity.
>
> The essence of the typological effort really lies in the determination of the critical variables for differentiating the phenomena under investigation. Since organizations are highly complex entities, classificatory schemes must represent this complexity. An adequate overall classification would have to take into account *the array of external conditions, the total spectrum of actions and interactions within an organization, and the outcome of organization behaviors* (p. 41).

Hall then offers an empirically derived taxonomy of organizations. Other popular conceptions include the following:

Technology. Thompson (1967) classifies organizations into those with *long-linked, mediating,* or *intensive technology.* Long-linked technology involves a serial interdependence of work as it flows in one direction through a series of steps. Mass production is an example of long-linked technology. Mediating technology links clients who wish to be interdependent. Examples are banks, insurance companies, and the post office. Finally, intensive technology involves processes in which a change in an object requires feedback from the object itself. Examples are job shops or therapeutic processes. Based upon these classes Thompson is able to describe, explain, and predict organizational behavior.

Control Systems. Etzioni (1964) classifies organizations according to the type of control systems involved. These are *coercive, utilitarian,* and *normative.* Coercive control involves physical control of participants with the use of threat and punishments. Utilitarian control provides material rewards or tokens which may be exchanged for needed items. Normative control involves the manipulation of symbolic or social values; it is control of beliefs.

In this system, organizations are classified according to the usual control exercised over lower participants. For example, correctional institutions are examples of coercive organizations, businesses are utilitarian, and religious organizations are normative. In addition, the control systems may be used to classify organizations of the *same* type. For example, one can identify relatively coercive, utilitarian, or normative political organizations. On this basis, Etzioni predicts the manner in which participants will comply with controlling behavior.

Prime Beneficiary. A third example of organizational classification, developed by Blau and Scott (1962), uses as its basis the group which receives the greatest benefit from its existence. The four basic types are the *mutual benefit association,* which benefits the members themselves; the *business concern,* which benefits the owners; the *service organization,* which benefits the clients; and the *commonweal organization,* which serves the public at large. Examples of the four might be, respectively, a labor union, an automobile company, a school, and a law enforcement agency. With this classification Blau and Scott are able to explain and predict the central problems faced by each type.

An Organizational Strategy Typology

Filley and his associates (1962, 1974, 1975) have developed a typology based upon three different strategies for organizing and dealing with the environment. The types—craft, promotion, and administrative organizations—are identified by a syndrome of structural and leadership characteristics which are observed to exist together. It is not known which characteristics are cause and which are effect, only that they seem to be present when the other characteristics are also present. The types are identified by their characteristics, not by any absolute level of size. The types, summarized in Table 22-1, may be described as follows.

TABLE 22-1. Characteristics in Three Organization Types.

Continua of Growth	Craft	Promotion	Administrative
1. Objectives	comfort-survival	personal achievement	market adaptation
2. Policy	traditional	personal	rational
3. Leadership	craftsman	entrepreneur	professional
4. Structure	power levels	field of force	rational hierarchy
5. Staff	housekeeping	technical-personal	technical-coordinative
6. Functional development	single	successive emphasis	full development
7. Work-group bonds	fixed roles	interaction-expectation	homogeneity
8. Innovation	no creativity	innovation	development
9. Uncertainty-risk	nonrisk	uncertainty	risk
10. Basis for success	benevolent environment	innovation exploitation	planned adaptation to environment
11. Pattern of growth	stable	S-curve	linear

Type I—The Craft Organization

The objectives of the craft firm are essentially those of organizational survival, the comfort of the owner, and the well-being of the participants. Success is measured in terms of continued profitable existence of the organization. Rules, policies, and paper work are avoided in favor of traditional methods of operation. The owner believes that operating methods are best learned by experience and that little relevant information is to be gained from outside sources or educational processes.

Owner-managers of craft firms operate more within the arena of technical knowledge than as professional managers. They are likely to spend much time in manufacturing or sales activities and are involved in day-to-day operations. Their preference is for security rather than risk or uncertainty and they express little or no interest in organizational growth.

The organization is arranged or structured into levels of power rather than into an impersonal hierarchy of offices; each level defers to those of higher rank. A social elite exists at the top, containing close friends and relatives of the craftsman. The next level contains long-service, trusted employees who are given nominal supervisory responsibility as a reward for their loyal contributions to the organization and its owners. The lowest level is a transient group. Those transients who remain may expect to move to the second level as seniority and loyalty warrant.

The craft firm will utilize relatively few staff and supervisory personnel. Staff services typically engage in extensive planning and control activities; since craft firms may well buy from the same suppliers in the same amounts, sell to the same customers, and produce in the same way, there is little felt need for planning and control. So long as the environment in which the firm operates remains benevolent, the minimal use of indirect labor may create operating economies which are expressed as profits.

Craft firms are essentially single function operations. Employment and effort will be concentrated in either sales or manufacturing. As was generally common in this country before 1840, craft businesses may be characterized as peddlers or makers. Peddlers simply obtain merchandise from others or engage in minimal assembly, processing, or packaging; for makers, the customers come to them and ask for the product, or selling is handled through a related factor or representative.

Morale in the craft firm may be expected to be good. In terms of relative deprivation, the members of the craft enterprise have minimal expectations about being promoted, having their jobs change significantly, or seeing the enterprise grow larger. In addition, for those who remain in the craft firm from their entry jobs, the availability of other employment becomes limited, as does knowledge about the relative advantages of working in other companies.

The technology of the craft firm is the familiar conventional wisdom of the trade, however skillfully it may be applied. In that sense the craft firm is not innovative. It does not adopt new methods. The reasons seem clear: The craft firm is insulated and its personnel are not cosmopolitan. They do not believe that information may be gained from books or outside sources. Craftsmen operate as if they had certainty about the world in which they make decisions.

In describing the craft firm we assume that it is not characterized by growth and we further assume that size alone does not predict whether a firm is craft. Both growth and size have some impact on profitability, since both create opportunities for profit. Size permits division of labor, specialized management, economies of scale, and other elements which may add to efficiency and profitability. In some industries, however, very small firms are also profitable, possibly because they are staffed with low-cost family labor. In contrast with issues of size, it may also be shown that economies of growth, such as costs which lag income and the spreading of fixed costs, will provide a growing company with opportunities for profit which are not present in the stable firm.

We expect any craft firm to profit by the relative advantages associated with its size, according to its particular industry and region. Where growth takes place, it occurs as an unplanned event. Its reputation may cause increased sales or the environment may become better for business, but the craft firm remains a passive participant in its environment.

Type II—The Promotion Organization

The objectives of the promotion firm are exaggerated and appealing, e.g., "we'll all be rich," "we'll all have our own piece of land," "we'll all drive white Corvette convertibles." As is true in any mass movement, including those at the level of the single organization, it is possible to generate active and enthusiastic member participation by establishing high expectations and providing some evidence that they will be achieved.

Formalizing mechanisms such as rules, policies, and structure are minimal in the promotion organization. Actions are improvised and subject to the whims of the leader. Moreover, since leaders have personal contact or influence with a large segment of the organization, such tactics are not inappropriate. Since the promotion organization exists to exploit an innovative advantage, the use of efficiency-gaining formalizing mechanisms is quite unnecessary. With high margins the firm can afford to have expensive operating methods.

The leadership role in the promotion type of firm is filled by a charismatic entrepreneur, who is viewed as a hero by the employees. They believe the leader can perform in an exceptional manner to obtain the goals which have been established. The entrepreneur is characterized as having a high need for achievement, as having difficulty in dealing with authority, and as being able to make effective decisions under conditions of uncertainty.

The personal influence role of the entrepreneur necessitates the establishment of a congruent structure. In the promotion firm this is a minimal hierarchy with the entrepreneur having contact, visibility, and direct influence with everyone in the organization. The entrepreneur functions as the central communications center and a major source of decision making in the organization. As a result, the structure tends to be quite flat with, insofar as possible, everyone partially reporting to the entrepreneur.

Given such structures, leaders of promotion organizations must extend their capacities through more extensive efforts, through attention only to immediate issues, or through the use of personal staff. Like Jesus and the twelve disciples, promoters often extend their capacities through the use of assistants or other personal staff positions. In addition to personal support, entrepreneurs will also employ technical staffs. Where scientists and engineers operate outside the knowledge of the entrepreneur, such staff personnel are evaluated on the basis of completion criteria rather than efficiency criteria. They are also valued to the extent that they create no visible problems. Other indirect labor, such as middle management and supervision, receives scant attention or support and is bypassed freely by the leader.

The functional development during the growth of the promotion firm, for manufacturers, will generally start with the expansion of production facilities and personnel. As will be discussed shortly, the promotion firms develop to exploit some kind of innovation, and if the innovation is desired by consumers their main problem is that of supplying their needs. The next function to receive attention is sales and marketing. Issues about channels of distribution, sales compensation, or whether to open sales offices are not uncommon. Following this is concern with budgeting and cost control.

At this point the firm may have stopped having progressively larger yearly increases in sales and may begin to experience yearly increases of decreasing size. In addition, the firm may begin to experience competition for the first time. Pressures on finance will generate greater attention to money problems. Finally, the firm may begin to add indirect labor and to separate administration from operations. Staff personnel will begin to develop planning and control systems and consequent efficiency, middle managers will be used and supported by top management, and the top personnel may cease to get involved in day-to-day matters. With such changes, the promotion firm may develop into the administrative type.

Morale in the promotion firm tends to be very high in the early years but may deteriorate rapidly in later years. At first people are enthusiastic in moving toward the highly desirable goals which have been established. In this period there is little attention to extrinsic rewards in the job and the high expectations can unify a very heterogeneous group. However, there seems to be a crucifixion syndrome in promotion firms with the entrepreneur going from hero to antihero. A number of factors seem to contribute to this. For one thing the exaggerated promises made early can seldom be realized, creating disenchantment and disappointment. Further, when authority channels begin to be used, perhaps staffed by personnel brought in from outside the enterprise, the strong emotional bond with the charismatic leader is strained. Finally, charismatic leaders seem to attract people who want to be changed, saved, or enriched in some way and who will continue to attach themselves to presumed charismatic figures, only to move on in disappointment when the leader turns out to be fallible. In any case, the high-to-low morale pattern is common, creating loss of long-service personnel, bad feelings, and attempts at unionization when it happens.

The promotion firm is developed to exploit some kind of innovative advantage. It has something to offer which is believed to be new or unique. This innovation may be a new market, a new product, a new method of distribution, a new source of supply, a new method of production—anything which gives the firm a distinct innovative, competitive advantage for a few years. If the innovation is desired by the market the firm can operate inefficiently and with minimal attention to customer service and yet prosper. Promotion firms are always temporary in nature, however. They must end their lives or else take on different characteristics.

Since the promotion firm is based upon exploitation of an innovative advantage by an entrepreneur, the atmosphere is one of uncertainty. In the beginning, anyway, there is no way to calculate the odds of gain or loss as decisions are made. There is no experience in dealing with the innovation, there may be no comparable experiences to draw from, and there are no plans, records, and reports to accumulate facts and learning. Once it becomes possible to shift from dealing with uncertainty, which is the talent of the entrepreneur, to dealing with risk, which is the substance of staff work, the successful promotion company will do so.

The basis for success in the promotion firm is clearly the exploitation of its innovative opportunity. The pattern of innovation, entrepreneur, tactical structure, and optimistic employees is uniquely suited for such a situation. As a result, if the innovation is desired, the promotion firm grows with a characteristic S-shaped pattern. The rapid initial growth is explained easily enough by the demand for the innovation. The slowing seems to occur because of several reasons. For one thing, the firm becomes large and visible enough that competitors enter the market. Further, the firm may be reaching the saturation point in the market. Finally, the effectiveness of the promoter as a prime motivator and center for information processing may decline through loss of charisma, loss of energy, or some other reason.

Type III—The Administrative Organization

The administrative organization is institutionalized. That is, it exists apart from the individuals within it. Ideally, the administrative type has no indispensable people. Its objectives are those of adapting to the needs of its chosen market, and these objectives are separate from the objectives of the people within it. In addition to norms of efficiency and rationality, the goals of the institution are shaped by the various contributing and claiming groups related to it.

The policies of the administrative type are legislated and in writing. They are the "rule of law" at the organizational level. Through them organizational participants can more easily judge the legitimacy of their own actions and more easily anticipate behavior on the part of others. Although much policy probably arises from formal recognition of official acts or practices, another part is purposive, initiated by various policy-making groups. Where they describe desired acts or practices in the form of written procedures, policies act to identify a system of action into which employees can move.

The leadership in the administrative type of firm is that of professional managers. As described elsewhere in this book, while the exact behavior required is contingent upon the circumstances involved, the behavior of the professional manager includes the display of social skills, the utilization of instrumental behaviors, the ability to properly utilize an array of decision-making strategies, technical knowledge, and a sense of futurity. Through impersonal records and reports professional managers monitor preplanned behavior and take corrective action where required.

The structure of the administrative firm is that of a rational hierarchy of defined positions. With the definitions of legitimate job behavior individuals in the system are free from discretionary power of superordinates and are limited in their own exercise of power as well. Officeholders are selected on the basis of their presumed ability to perform the specified tasks and are rewarded according to their approximate contribution to enterprise goals and marketplace demands for their services. Structural arrangements will vary according to the information-processing requirements of the firm, as described in earlier chapters, and are consistent with the rational, adaptive posture of the organization.

Administrative firms contain an array of staff specialists engaged in planning and control. These specialists support the production and sales activities and perform the actions necessary to calculate relative probabilities of gain or loss from actions by organization members. In short, they translate uncertainty into risk. Supervisory personnel coordinate actions between units and offices through successive levels of organization. The organization contains full functional development, dictated by competitive and adaptive imperatives.

Morale in the administrative firm is a complex phenomenon depending upon a variety of factors. In part, it depends upon the satisfaction of individual needs through rewards for job-related performance. In part it also depends upon equitable ratios of investments and rewards among personnel, vertically and laterally. In varying degrees, it depends upon intrinsic satisfaction gained through job performance. Administrative organizations anticipate needs and preferences of their members and provide desired rewards by an implicit definition of the climate to be maintained. The administrative firm has a relatively high level of homogeneity of values among its members, established in part by indoctrination and in part by selection standards.

Administrative firms are not characterized by innovation so much as by development and improvement. With sunk costs in equipment, technical experience, and an established clientele, the administrative firm evolves in its product base protected from uncertainty by calculated decisions and contingency plans. It is not uncommon for products to be added by imitation once the market shows their potential. Administrative firms are expected to grow at a rate which reflects the condition of the industry in which they operate and the relative efficiency of individual firms in attracting business. The basis for its success is planned action in adapting to the needs of the marketplace.

Patterns of Growth

The organizational strategy typology may be viewed in terms of the metamorphosis model of organizational development discussed earlier, provided it is understood that the characteristics of each type are merely associated with and not necessarily the causes or effects of each type. In addition, there is no necessary order in which the types must appear and, except for the following, no imperatives which cause a firm to change from one type to another.

The imperatives of change from one type of organization to another seem to be two. First, the promotion stage is a period of transition, a temporary form (Weber, 1947; Hoffer, 1958). It must turn into something else or end its life. If a firm starts as a promotion organization it must become a more permanent craft or administrative type once its relative advantages come to an end, or it must perish.

The second imperative, collective rationality, occurs when it is seen that an alternative form of organization will aid in organizational survival or in achieving desirable objectives. In this sense, it is reasonable for a firm to move out of the craft type when growth, greater profits, or protection against external crises are desired. For example, since craft firms are expected to have relatively little growth, and yet growth is a frequently held objective, one would expect pressures to build in craft firms to move into something else. In these limited senses, then, the stages of growth may be ordered in various ways to provide something on the order of a metamorphosis model of organizational growth.

We suggested earlier that the growth of each organizational type is probably best characterized as nongrowth in craft firms, an S-shaped curve in promotion firms, and a more linear growth trend in administrative firms. This does not mean that other patterns are not possible. For example, a craft firm in a particularly benevolent environment might experience growth through no particular efforts of its own.

One of the questions which arises regarding growth patterns is whether there are any regularities which may be anticipated so that organizations may be more meaningfully compared. It will be recalled from our earlier discussion that writers utilizing a cell-division model of growth are primarily interested in this question. Cell-division models see the organization as an organism with properties much the same as those of living organisms (Dunn, 1971). Such models naturally propose that the organization, like other organisms, will grow at an increasing and then a decreasing rate. For example, Boulding (1953) has claimed that due to the requirements of organization maintenance all growth must eventually proceed at a declining rate and thus exhibit an S-shaped pattern. Such a pattern has been observed in nations (Kuznets, 1956, 1959; Dewey and Dakin, 1947) and industries (Gaston, 1961).

A difficulty with the organismic or cell-division model view is that it seems to point to decline and death, even though simple observation demonstrates the contrary. Given the assumptions of such models one would expect organizations to stabilize at their upper limits, or else to grow to some upper level and then to decline. This difficulty is overcome when one recognizes that organizations are similar to organisms only in limited ways and that it is possible to redesign an organization according to its requirements. Thus, there is no particular reason why a cell-division model might not predict growth with some accuracy within a single structure and a single set of environmental constraints, followed by a deliberate reorganization of the enterprise and a distinctly new pattern of growth.

At least three studies have investigated the historical growth pattern of business organizations. The first study (Haire, 1959) analyzed the growth of employment in four firms, as shown in Figure 22–1. A logistic curve was fit to the employment data with no upper limit in Company A and with an upper limit assigned in Companies B, C, and D. We do not know the internal conditions of these firms during growth. The firms do approximate an S-shaped biological growth curve but other curves approximate the growth data equally well (Strother and Draper, 1963). Haire also observed that the rate of growth in later years may be determined remarkably well by the rate established in the first three years. He felt that the rate of growth may be related to the technological character of the work and the ratio of investment per worker. According to Haire, the upper limit on growth is related to the state of competition in the industry and to product demand.

A second analysis of growth is an unpublished study by Filley. Figure 22–2 shows sales of six promotional firms and the approximate beginning and ending points of their promotion stage (standardized between −2 and +2 standard units; this period actually varies between ten and eighteen years for the six firms). Transition periods were marked by changes in top management, major company reorganization, the appearance of competition, and shifts in company goals. No statistical analysis is provided because of limits of the data.

As indicated in Figure 22–2, all six firms followed a hypothetical S-shaped curve rather closely in the promotion phase of the business. Companies A, C, E, and F developed the characteristics of the administrative type. In both B and D, the entrepreneurs turned their attention to new, unrelated enterprises while their original businesses drifted into decline. The data show that the reorganized firms grew at varying rates, some quite rapidly, in the administrative type.

Finally, Starbuck (1968) conducted a time series analysis of the histories of ten firms in an effort to assess the efficacy of metamorphosis models of development. As we have seen, such models focus on the structural changes which occur between hypothesized stages of development. Using data collected for the ten manufacturing firms, Starbuck developed a hypothetical production function which relates the number of employees in each of six categories to the firms' output. As stated in his "tentative conclusion":

> A significant portion of the variation in structural-functional relationships cannot be explained in terms of smooth evolution, and the deviations of actual from evolutionary are clearly nonrandom in nine of the ten firms studied. (Hence) it appears that metamorphic theories are both meaningful and useful (p. 297).

These studies suggest that there are regularities in the growth of organizations. It seems likely that with no attention to type, the pattern of growth can be predicted fairly well with a cell-division model, providing the firm makes no departure from its regular organization and product base. The chief difficulty in such efforts is determining the upper limits on growth. It

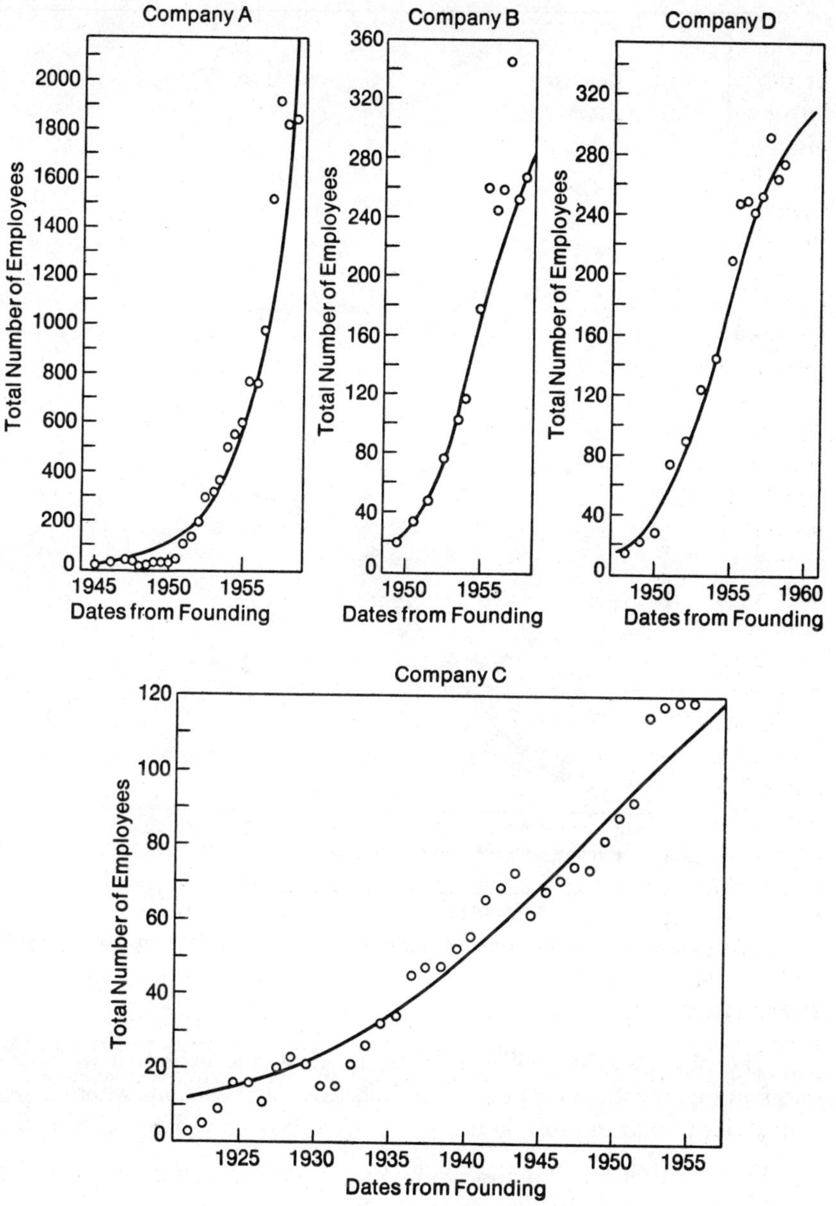

Figure 22-1. Actual Growth in Four Companies. (Haire, 1959)

also appears likely that the natural course of growth can be altered through intervention in its structure and management processes. By taking a firm out of one type and placing it in another, natural limits on growth may be overcome. This change may occur through metamorphosis, as Starbuck suggests, or through deliberate reorganization.

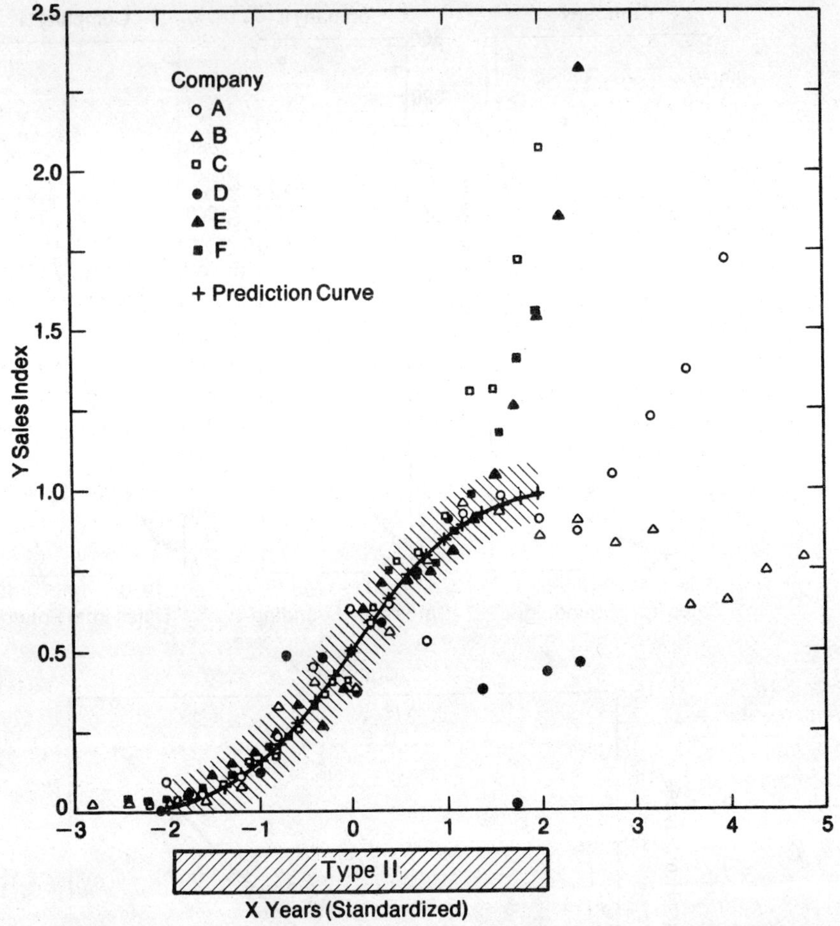

Figure 22-2. Actual Growth of Promotion Type Compared with Theoretical Curve.

Propositions

The two issues we will deal with are, first, the extent to which differences in organizational types do, in fact, exist, and second, whether leadership styles similar to those indicated for each type have been observed.

1. Characteristics may be observed which are associated with types of firms classified as craft, promotion, and administrative.
2. Characteristics may be observed which are associated with leaders identified as craftsmen, entrepreneurs, or administrators.

Empirical Evidence

Proposition 1

Characteristics may be observed which are associated with types of firms classified as craft, promotion, and administrative.

The first proposition may be analyzed by considering work in progress by Filley and Aldag (1975). Three studies are reported. In the first, 379 top executives in small or medium-sized manufacturing firms were asked to check two of six possible responses to nine questions dealing with goals, operating policies, managerial beliefs, structure, functional emphasis, future expectations, preferences regarding employee types, and attitudes about change. The first two responses for each question were related to Type I (craft), the second two to Type II (promotion), and the final two to Type III (administrative). Analysis showed that responses to individual questions were more similar to other "same-type" responses than to responses related to the other two types of firms.

In the second study, five of the original questions were used to develop a questionnaire with randomized item ordering; this questionnaire was completed by a different group of 28 executives. Again, the "same-type" items related more than between-type items.

Finally, a new questionnaire with 63 scaled-response items based on the three types of firms was prepared; this questionnaire was completed by 85 top executives from different companies. A factor analysis yielded 40 items which loaded above .30 for one factor and which were not duplicated in the same direction above that level in more than one factor (except for one item which loaded heavily on Factors II and III). These results are shown in Table 22–2. Comparing performance data with the factor items shown, Type I (craft) firms are negatively related to size and growth measures; Type II (promotion) firms are positively related to growth in employment but not to size; and Type III (administrative) firms are not related to size or growth measures.

These studies seem to support the proposition regarding the types of firms identified as craft, promotion, and administrative. They also show that while craft firms, contrary to expectation, do appear to be related to size, one cannot predict promotion or administrative characteristics on the basis of size.

Proposition 2

Characteristics may be observed which are associated with leaders identified as craftsmen, entrepreneurs, or administrators.

Theoretical treatments frequently distinguish between leadership roles based on tradition, innovation and promotion, and executive leadership (Rostow, 1960; Lester, 1958; Weber, 1947; Hoffer, 1958). In addition, the analysis reported for the previous proposition suggests that craft and promotion types are strongly influenced by the personalities and preferences of their leaders while the administrative type exists as a system apart from the roles played by its professional leaders. It is the contrast between the entrepreneur and the professional executive which has received attention however, and the following discussion will attempt to identify the entrepreneurial role as contrasted with that of the professional managerial role which has been discussed through this book.

TABLE 22-2. Factor Analysis of Company Characteristics.

Factor I (Craft)

Item	*Factor Loading*
We are doing things pretty much the way they have always been done in this type of business.	.365
The fact that I make a comfortable living is enough success for me.	.305
We are selling to the same customers this year that we did last year.	.309
I practice the open door policy—I am always available to people in the company when they want to see me.	.387
Next year we will continue to operate pretty much as we always have.	.647
I prefer a safe income to a gamble.	.558
I don't want to shoot for the moon in my business, just make a good living and see the business survive.	.442
In evaluating employees I place great emphasis in their loyalty to me.	.444
One has to learn this business by experience.	.413
I'd have to say that business survival is my main goal at present.	.479
I am more effective in handling technical or production problems than I am with management issues.	.327
I am worried about what to do with some loyal supervisors who expect to be promoted but just don't have the ability.	.359
I have daily contact with the workers in the plant.	.476
My employees are good workers or craftsmen who appreciate the security of the job.	.547

Factor II (Promotion)

Item	*Factor Loading*
I'm afraid to leave the office for a few days for fear of what I'll find when I get back.	.475
We avoid the use of job titles in our company.	.326
When I am away from the business I call in at least once a day to make sure that everything is all right.	.416
Key personnel have left the company in the last two years because of conflicts with me or others.	.340
We are successful because we have a unique product, source of supply, or method of distribution.	.599

Factor II (Promotion), continued

Right now our firm is growing so fast that it's almost impossible to plan and control the way I'd like to.	.607
We are gamblers—it is impossible to plan for the future.	.425
I am a promoter at heart.	.565
My business policies change daily as conditions change.	.487
I hire people who will sacrifice pay and fancy titles now for the tremendous opportunity the job offers.	.542
I have been self-supporting since high school age.	.408
We can afford some internal confusion in this company because profit margins are high.	.499
An organization chart would be outdated before we could get it on paper.	.386
Things are changing so fast in my business that I have to take complete control to avoid confusion.*	.545*

*Also loaded on Factor III at .329.

Factor III (Administration)

Item	*Factor Loading*
I prefer an employee who will do his present job well and continue to develop for future advancement.	.409
In our company, specialized employees handle planning and control.	.321
Things are a lot more predictable in my firm than they used to be.	.345
In our business there are no indispensable people, including me.	.413
We estimate our sales for each year and prepare budgets for internal financial control.	.594
We have sales forecasted for at least the next three years and are planning facilities and operations on the basis of that forecast.	.470
I am able to take a two-week vacation with the assurance that business operations will continue effectively in my absence.	.434
We have a company policy manual.	.536
In my business, controls and operating methods are in writing.	.568
I employ good workers who believe in the goals and values of the company.	.312
We have a working board of directors in our company that meets at least four times a year.	.368
When we hire new people, we compare their characteristics with written job descriptions.	.428

Schumpeter (1935) has provided the classic description of the entrepreneur—egocentric, against tradition, and personally ambitious:

> . . . the typical entrepreneur is more self-centered than other types of (leader) because he relies less than they do on tradition and connection and because his characteristic task—theoretically as well as historically—consists precisely in breaking up old, and creating new, tradition. Although this applies primarily to his economic action, it also extends to the moral, cultural, and social consequences of it. It is, of course, no mere coincidence that the period of the rise of the entrepreneur also gave birth to Utilitarianism. . . .
>
> First of all, there is the dream and the will to found a private kingdom, usually, though not necessarily, also a dynasty. The modern world really does not know any such positions, but what may be attained by industrial or commercial success is still the nearest approach to medieval lordship possible to modern man. . . .
>
> Then there is the will to conquer: the impulse to fight, to prove oneself superior to others, to succeed for the sake, not of the fruits of success, but of success itself. From this aspect, economic action becomes akin to sport—there are financial races, or rather boxing matches. . . .
>
> Finally there is the joy of creating, of getting things done, or simply of exercising one's energy and ingenuity (pp. 91, 93).

Entrepreneurs are also perceived by subordinates as possessing exceptional qualities which set them apart from ordinary people (Weber, 1947). This charismatic image is effective so long as their efforts are successful and their presence is immediate. Thus entrepreneurs must spend a good deal of time in direct contact with the members of the organization. When face-to-face contact becomes impractical, substitute measures may be taken in the form of propaganda, television contact, mass assembly, or the transfer of charisma through assistants. The result is a form of emotional, communal relationship with all employees, who view themselves as members of the enterprise "movement," rather than as holding an office or position in an impersonal organization.

Entrepreneurs attract a heterogeneous group to the organization. Employees are drawn to them by the promise of future opportunities, either to throw off a past which they view as distasteful or to gain future rewards which they view as exceptional (Hoffer, 1947). Organizational participants regard the rapid growth of the enterprise as confirming the possibility of great reward.

Entrepreneurial leadership is transitory. Once rate of growth begins to slow, an organization should begin to develop rational executive leadership. As Weber has stated (1947): "Indeed, in its pure form charismatic authority may be said to exist only in the process of originating. It cannot remain stable, but becomes either traditionalized or rationalized, or a combination of both."

Perhaps the broadest empirical study of entrepreneurship is found in Collins, Moore, and Unwalla (1964). The authors interviewed entrepreneurs who had started new manufacturing enterprises between 1945 and 1958. The sample included 110 firms; 150 in-depth interviews were conducted, and the Thematic Apperception Test (TAT) was administered to 40 selected entrepreneurs. Because of the uniqueness and importance of the Collins study, its results are summarized below.

The Entrepreneur as a Child. Interview data indicated that entrepreneurs literally or figuratively left home at an early age. Frequently mentioned were statements of escape from poverty and insecurity in the home, and the absence of parental figures removed by death, by physical or emotional factors, or by the child's own rejection of the parent.

A separate TAT analysis indicated that entrepreneurs typically lack social mobility drives; that is, they do not seek to get ahead in the social hierarchy, or to achieve positions of authority or rewards associated with power or status. They consider themselves to be hard-working, yet evidence no love for their work. In problem solving they seem to panic at the idea of success but can tolerate failure. When dealing with subordinate figures, entrepreneurs' relations are satisfactory if they are on a patriarchal or patronly basis. If such relationships can be established, employee relations are warm and friendly. They have difficulty in establishing satisfactory relationships with superior authorities, however. They are unwilling to submit to authority, cannot work within it, and therefore must escape from it.

From the TAT analysis, the authors suggest that entrepreneurs view the business as a female figure, representing a "bad" mother. Possession of the business thus allows them to demonstrate their maleness and to prove their masculinity; at the same time, this relationship appears wrong and entrepreneurs experience a subconscious need to punish themselves for their wrongdoing—perhaps by bringing about their own failure in the enterprise. Should failure occur, however, they feel relieved and are able to respond by renewed effort on new projects.

Formal Education of the Entrepreneur. Entrepreneurial education is divided conceptually into two parts: a period of formal education, and a period of schooling in the work environment.

Formal education is continued to varying levels, but entrepreneurial experience with such education suggests that it is more suited to a future in large bureaucracies or professions than for starting new enterprises. Some left school at an early age, often because work opportunity arose. Others stayed through high school because nothing suitable came along or because they felt the diploma to be useful. Some completed college. Yet, as the authors of the Collins study suggest, no school seems to give formal training for entrepreneurship; academic inquiry is specialized, dealing with the rational resolution of problems rather than the challenges of handling uncertainty.

Many entrepreneurs spend a considerable amount of time in what the authors call the "school for entrepreneurs." This is a period of job training prior to the time that conditions for the entrepreneur's major enterprise have jelled. Some entrepreneurs seem to drift from job to job while gaining technical skills. Others learn "basic dealing" as they experience various unsuccessful attempts at enterprise promotion. A third group seems to rely heavily on being the protégé of an established executive.

Projecting the Enterprise. The first step into entrepreneurship is described by the authors as "the act of projecting." This means setting in motion events that lead to the creation of a firm. For nearly every entrepreneur the role of projector begins with deterioration of their previous roles. They come to realize that they can never adequately measure up to the demands placed on them in organizations belonging to other people. Although role deterioration is not an uncommon phenomenon among people in general, what sets entrepreneurs apart is their ability to convert their dilemma into the projection of a new business. Faced with crises, they do not seek a situation of security, but rather go deeper into insecurity by initiating a new enterprise. Most entrepreneurs responded that an idea or innovation of some kind was a determining factor in causing them to initiate their enterprise. The authors of the Collins study believe that, although the idea or innovation is a precipitative incident, it is seldom of major importance. That is, the idea is merely a part of a larger configuration of projection.

One explanation of this ability to project an entirely new enterprise may be found in the concept of "marginal individuals." According to this view there are individuals in each society or culture who are only marginally integrated into that group. These persons hold views or beliefs different from those accepted by the dominant culture. These same persons, if they are also in a position of authority or leadership, are then in a position to affect a permanent change in the way of life (Fathi, 1968).

Initiating the Enterprise. Having projected the enterprise, entrepreneurs must then create it and make it viable. This process involves three general steps: first, setting up the firm; second, passing through a crisis period; and third, establishing some kind of rational organization.

The process of establishing the enterprise generally involves getting money, often from marginal sources. Financing is difficult because, for one thing, the entrepreneurs' track records probably identify them as poor risks. Moreover, they must turn for financing to institutions which abhor uncertainty, lending instead for relatively risk-free situations. Entrepreneurs may eventually borrow from "shady" sources at high interest rates, bring in undesirable partners, or rely on trade credit.

Once the firm is started, entrepreneurs generally face a period of crisis which the authors describe as getting "through the knothole." They may be unable to meet short-term loans, a discouraged partner may wish to leave, backers may wish to withdraw, or they may find a number of unexpected costs eating into profits or creating losses.

If they make it "through the knothole," entrepreneurs begin to think more in terms of formal organization. For one thing, their finances are put on a more regular basis. For another, they establish an organization to deal with the technical problems of business administration. Where before they had a highly personal and immediate relationship with the firm and its employees, now they must establish one that is less personal and less direct in order to deal with long-run problems. Furthermore, once a crisis is past, entrepreneurs typically act to eliminate partners or unwanted backers in order to gain control of the enterprise.

Now the firm is on its way. As the authors state:

> The new phase of the firm will have set up new role demands and these the entrepreneur as leader may find increasing difficulty in playing. Either gladly or reluctantly he will pass on the power to the younger generation, a generation not of entrepreneurs but of administrators (p. 201).

The Collins, Moore, and Unwalla study suggests sharp differences between entrepreneurs and managers of a going enterprise. In contrast with the entrepreneurs, executive managers seek social mobility in an established hierarchy. They have a positive view of their supervisors in the hierarchy, probably because they are dependent on their bosses for job success and advancement. They have strong needs for accomplishment in their work, the ability to organize unstructured situations, and facility in rational decision making.

These characteristics were also suggested in studies made of leader behavior in established military and business organizations, discussed in Chapters 8, 11, and 12. It will be recalled that two factors of leader behavior examined in those chapters were "consideration" and "initiating structure." Consideration relates to the interpersonal relations between leaders and subordinates; for example, considerate leaders explain their actions, listen to subordinates, consult with them, treat everyone equally, and are friendly. Initiating structure relates to their task-centered roles as organizer and planner; for example, they make their attitudes clear, maintain standards of performance, use standard procedures, make sure that members work to capacity, and coordinate work activities (Stogdill and Shartle, 1955; Stogdill, 1956; Stogdill and Coons, 1957).

While not necessarily the case, it is often suggested that owner-operated firms are directed by entrepreneurs and that manager-run firms are run by professional executives. In this connection several authors have looked at the performance of owner-operated firms compared with manager-operated firms in an attempt to test the theory that owners sacrifice growth for profit while managers sacrifice profit for growth. The results, while not entirely clear, seem to indicate that in most instances owners (or possible entrepreneurs) have better records in terms of both growth and profit (Monsen, Chin, and Cooley, 1968; Mueller, 1972; Radice, 1971). This is consistent with the idea of a unique competitive advantage in the promotion type, and with the economies of rapid growth in that type of firm.

Once the firm begins to compete directly with others, necessitating efficiency, for one thing, it is likely that entrepreneurship as a role is less important and administrative leadership as a role is more important for enterprise success.

Summary

Proposition 1: Characteristics may be observed which are associated with types of firms classified as craft, promotion, and administrative. *Proposition supported with limited evidence.*

Proposition 2: Characteristics may be observed which are associated with leaders identified as craftsmen, entrepreneurs, or administrators. *Insufficient data for evaluation.*

Conclusions

The evidence discussed regarding the first proposition indicates that there is a clustering of characteristics which is similar to those discussed as the craft, promotion, and administrative types. In addition, associated with each type is a different leadership role. When viewed consensually in terms of theory, there is much support for the existence of these roles. However, when considered empirically, the clearest difference exists between the entrepreneur and the professional manager. Research on this difference is somewhat confounded by the use of owner-managers as proxies for entrepreneurs and paid-managers for administrators. The evidence is still too sparse to generalize at this point.

References

Alexander, S. S. 1949. The effect of size of manufacturing corporations on the distribution of the rate of return. *Review of Economics and Statistics* 31.

Baumol, W. J. 1967. Entrepreneurship in economic theory. *American Economic Review* 58.

Bennett, J. W., and McKnight, R. W. 1956. Approaches of a Japanese innovator to cultural and technical change. *Annals of the American Academy of Political and Social Science* 305.

Blau, P. M. 1970. A formal theory of differentiation in organizations. *American Sociological Review* 35.

———. 1972. Interdependence and hierarchy in organizations. *Social Science Research* 1.

———., and Schoenherr, R. 1971. *The structure of organizations*. Basic Books.

———., and Scott, W. R. 1962. *Formal organizations*. Chandler.

Boulding, K. E. 1953. Toward a general theory of growth. *Canadian Journal of Economics and Political Science* 19.

Christensen, C. 1953. *Management succession in small and growing enterprises.* Harvard University Press.

Churchill, B. B. 1955. Age and life expectancy of business firms. *Survey of Current Business* 35.

Clarkson, G. E. 1963. A model of trust investment behavior. In *Behavioral theory of the firm,* ed. by R. M. Cyert and J. G. March. Prentice-Hall.

Collins, O. F.; Moore, D. G.; and Unwalla, D. B. 1964. *The enterprising man.* Michigan State University.

Crum, W. L. 1939. *Corporate size and earning power.* Harvard University Press.

Dale, E. 1960. *The great organizers.* McGraw-Hill.

Dewey, E. R., and Dakin, E. F. 1947. *Cycles: The science and theory of prediction.* Holt, Rinehart and Winston.

Dunn, E. S., Jr. 1971. *Economic and social development: A process of social learning.* The Johns Hopkins Press.

Edwards, E. O. 1951. Studies on the growth of the individual firm with applications to firms in the chemical industry. Ph.D. Dissertation, Johns Hopkins University.

Esser, N., and Strother, G. 1962. Rule interpretation as an indicator of style of management. *Personnel Psychology* 15.

Etzioni, A. 1964. *Modern organizations.* Prentice-Hall.

Fathi, A. 1968. Marginality, leadership, and directed change. *Human Organization* 27.

Feld, M. D. 1959. Information and authority, a structure of military organization. *American Sociological Review* 24: 15-22.

Filley, A. C. 1962. A theory of small business and divisional growth. Ph.D. Dissertation, The Ohio State University.

———. 1974. Alternative approaches to organizational change. In *Contemporary management,* ed. by J. W. McGuire. Prentice-Hall.

———., and Aldag, R. 1975. *An organization typology.* Unpublished Research Report.

Gaston, J. F. 1961. *Growth patterns in industry: A reexamination.* Studies in Business Economics, No. 75, National Industrial Conference Board.

Hage, J. 1965. An axiomatic theory of organizations. *Administrative Science Quarterly* 19.

Haire, M. (ed.) 1959. *Modern organization theory.* Wiley.

Hall, R. H. 1972. *Organizations.* Prentice-Hall.

———.; Hass, J. E.; and Johnson, N. J. 1967. Organizational size, complexity and formalization. *American Sociological Review* 32.

Hoffer, E. 1958. *The true believer.* New American Library.

Hutchins, J. G. B. 1958. Business history, entrepreneur history and business administration. *Journal of Economic History* 18.

———. 1959. Recent contributions to business history. *Journal of Business History* 19.

Indik, B. P. 1963. Some effects of organization size on member attitudes and behavior. *Human Relations* 16.

Ingham, G. 1970. *Size of industrial organization and worker behavior.* Cambridge University Press.

Jones, F. W. 1952. *Growth patterns and industry.* Studies in Business Economics, No. 32, National Industrial Conference Board.

Kuznets, S. 1959. *Economic growth.* Free Press.

———. 1956. Quantitative aspects of the economic growth of nations. *Economic Development and Cultural Change* 5.

Leavitt, H. J. 1957. Some effects of certain communication patterns on group performance. *Journal of Abnormal and Social Psychology* 46.

Lester, R. A. 1958. *As unions mature.* Princeton University Press.

Lippitt, G. L., and Schmidt, W. H. 1967. Crises in a developing organization. *Harvard Business Review* 45: 102-112.

Litwin, G. L., and Ciarlo, J. A. Undated. *Achievement motivation and risk taking in a business setting.* General Electric Company Behavioral Research Service.

Mahoney, T. A.; Frost, P.; Crandall, N.; and Weitzel, W. 1972. The conditioning influence of organization size upon managerial practice. *Organizational Behavior and Human Performance* 3.

McGuire, J. W. 1963. *Factors affecting the growth of manufacturing firms.* Bureau of Business Research, University of Washington.

Monsen, R. J.; Chin, J. S.; and Cooley, D. E. 1968. The effect of separation of ownership and control on the performance of the large firm. *Quarterly Journal of Economics* 82.

Morgenstern, O. 1951. Prolegomena to a theory of the firm. *The Journal of Industrial Economics* 20.

Mueller, D. C. 1972. A life cycle theory of the firm. *The Journal of Industrial Economics* 20.

Osburn, R. C. 1950. *The effect of corporate size on efficiency and profitability.* Bulletin 72, University of Illinois.

Penrose, E. 1959. *The theory of the growth of the firm.* Wiley.

Radice, H. K. 1971. Control type, profitability and growth in large firms: An empirical study. *The Economic Journal* 81.

Rindt, K. 1965. *Characteristics of growing and non-growing firms in northern Wisconsin.* Unpublished Study.

Rostow, W. W. 1960. *The stages of economic growth.* Cambridge University Press.

Rowthorn, R. 1971. *International big business 1957–1967: A study of comparative growth.* Cambridge University Press.

Rushing, W. A. 1966. Organizational size, rules and surveillance. *Journal of Experimental Social Psychology* 2.

Samuels, J. M., and Smyth, D. J. 1968. Profits, variability of profits and firm size. *Economica* 35.

Schroeder, G. 1953. *The growth of major steel companies.* Johns Hopkins University Press.

Schumpeter, J. A. 1935. Analysis of economic change. *Review of Economics and Statistics* 17.

Starbuck, W. H. 1965. Organizational growth and development. In *Handbook of organizations,* ed. by J. G. March. Rand-McNally.

———. 1968. Organizational metamorphosis. In *Promising research directions,* ed. by R. W. Millman and M. P. Hottenstein. Academy of Management.

Stecker, H. O. 1963. *Profitability and size of firm.* Institute of Business and Economic Research, University of California.

Steinmetz, L. L. 1969. Critical stages of small business growth. *Business Horizons* 12.

Stieglitz, H. 1962. Optimizing span of control. *Management Record* 24.

Stogdill, R. M. 1959. *Individual behavior and group achievement.* Oxford University Press.

———. 1956. *Patterns of administrative performance.* Monograph No. 81, Bureau of Business Research, The Ohio State University.

———., and Coons, A. E. 1957. *Leader behavior: Its description and measurement.* Monograph No. 88, Bureau of Business Research, The Ohio State University.

———., and Shartle, C. L. 1955. *Methods in the study of administrative leadership.* Monograph No. 80, Bureau of Business Research, The Ohio State University.

Strother, G., and Draper, J. 1963. Testing a model for organizational growth. *Human Organizations* 22: 180-94.

Tansik, D. A., and Radnor, M. 1971. An organization theory perspective on the development of new organization functions. *Public Administration Review* 31.

Thompson, J. D. 1967. *Organizations in action.* McGraw-Hill.

Udy, S., Jr. 1959. Bureaucratic elements in organizations. *American Sociological Review* 23.

United Nations. 1958. *Management of industrial enterprise in underdeveloped countries.* Department of Economic and Social Affairs.

Viano, E., and Wildeman, J. 1972. Organizational size and managerial attitudes of probation administrators. *Sociology and Social Research* 56.

Villard, H. H. 1961. Some comments on growth. *The American Economic Review* 51.

Weber, M. 1947. *The theory of social and economic organization* (1921), tr. and ed. by A. M. Henderson and T. Parsons. Oxford University Press.

Weiss, L., and Hall, M. 1967. Firm size and profitability. *Review of Economics and Statistics* 49: 319-31.

Wickesberg, A. K. 1961. *Organizational relationships in the growing small manufacturing firm.* University of Minnesota.

Name Index

Subject Index